C0-DWL-521

Urbanization and Economic Growth

Vibhooti Shukla

Urbanization and Economic Growth

VIBHOOTI SHUKLA

DELHI
OXFORD UNIVERSITY PRESS
BOMBAY CALCUTTA MADRAS
1996

Oxford University Press, Walton Street, Oxford OX2 6DP
Oxford New York
Athens Auckland Bangkok Bombay
Calcutta Cape Town Dar es Salaam Delhi
Florence Hong Kong Istanbul Karachi
Kuala Lumpur Madras Madrid Melbourne
Mexico City Nairobi Paris Singapore
Taipei Tokyo Toronto
and associates in
Berlin Ibadan

ISBN 0 19 563725 9

Typeset by EPW, Bombay 400001
printed at Rekha Printers Pvt. Ltd., New Delhi 110020
and published by Neil O'Brien, Oxford University Press
YMCA Library Building, Jai Singh Road, New Delhi 110001

Foreword

Vibhooti Shukla died when the hot-air balloon she was riding in exploded on contact with a live wire in the US on 8 August 1992. She died too young; not only because she was only 33 years old at that time but because she was in the prime of her professional career as an economist, bristling with energy and research ideas, and with so much still to offer. At the same time one cannot but be impressed by how much she *had* achieved in those 33 years. Her research contributions ranged over urban studies, human geography and development economics. Having published one book and numerous papers, she had made a mark in the area; and the agenda for research that she laid out has scope for much work and hopefully this will be taken up by researchers in the future.

All this is evident in the present book, which brings together Vibhooti's main writings on urbanization and economic development. It is a surprisingly well-knit collection which begins by addressing the problem of city size and rural–urban migration; goes on to discuss the spatial dimensions of rural non-farm employment and infrastructural investment and government's role in these; and ends with a set of essays on the problem of environmental degradation and pollution in megacities. While she discusses the theoretical problem of urbanization, these are always rooted in reality, and examples from three continents—America, Asia, and Africa—are scattered throughout the book. Thus, in this book we encounter the Dallas–Fort Worth 'metroplex', Maharashtra's non-farm labourers (work, which her mother, Tara Shukla, prompted her to do) and the cities of Sub-Saharan Africa (work undertaken during her tenure as consultant to the World Bank).

Much of the book's theoretical apparatus is provided by the idea of 'agglomeration effect', which Vibhooti had worked on as a Ph.D. student at Princeton University, under the supervision of Edwin Mills. The essential idea is easy to convey. Clearly, for firms, producers and even consumers, there are advantages in being close to other firms, producers and consumers. Thus, it is usually more profitable for a firm to be located in a city with a large population (and therefore many firms and consumers) than in a sparsely populated area. The additional productivity or profitability of a firm that occurs by virtue of there being a larger population around is called the 'agglomeration effect'. Of course, when a city becomes too large, an even larger population can have a *negative* effect on each firm's productivity, which we may describe as a 'negative agglomeration effect'.

The presence of negative or positive agglomeration effects can have important implications for city size. Consider first a country with uniform low population density everywhere. Because of agglomeration advantages individuals and firms will begin to move close to one another and, in the same way that candy forms from sugar syrup, little clusters of dense population will begin to emerge providing a possible rationale for the existence of cities.

Further, one may assume (and Vibhooti does) that when a new firm considers setting itself up in a city it bases its decision on the profits that accrue to the firm and ignores the agglomeration benefit that the firm, in turn, confers on the incumbent firms by virtue of its coming into existence. Hence, the *social* benefit of a new firm being opened in a city will tend to exceed the benefit that accrues to the new firm. It follows that the city size that emerges naturally, based on the calculation of individual firms and potential migrants will not be *socially* optimal. If agglomeration effects are present, cities will turn out to be too small.

Vibhooti backs this up with some very interesting empirical work. She finds that if the population of an average Indian city is doubled, the productivity of each firm would rise by 9 per cent. That is, each firm, while using the same amount of labour and capital, will end up producing 9 per cent more output, as a result of the benefits of agglomeration. This is larger than what other studies have revealed for US cities, where the comparable figure is 5 or 6 per cent.

Of course, there can be other arguments as to why cities may be considered too large. Agglomeration effects, as already noted, can be negative and this would reverse the above argument. In addition, megacities can have disproportionately large pollution problems, as Vibhooti Shukla shows in the two chapters written with Kirit Parikh and Jyoti Parikh, respectively.

It is important, however, to note here that the relation between city size and pollution is neither monotonic nor immutable. If the right mix of policies is pursued in a large city, it could be less polluted than a smaller one. Hence there may be a case for having large cities, in order to internalize the benefits of agglomeration, while pursuing complementary measures to keep the cities' air clean.

This divergence between what would happen to a city if it were left to individual profitability calculation and the social ideal implies scope for meaningful policy intervention by government. Vibhooti addresses this at length in papers she wrote alone, with Oded Stark and with Paul Waddell.

It is her concern with policy which takes her to the subject of infrastructural investment, especially its spatial dimensions. In the paper on 'Urban Infrastructure and Regional Productivity', Vibhooti Shukla addresses the role of infrastructure in development. This is of particular interest to Indians because in the context of the current economic reforms attention has been increasingly drawn to the state of our infrastructure. Vibhooti's empirical study shows the great impact on productivity that can come from better water supply, asphalt roads and increased drainage capacity. Moreover, she urges us to recognize that *economic* infrastructure is not enough. *Social* infrastructure, that is, *inter alia*, investments in health and education, not only creates a healthier and more enlightened population but can result in higher industrial productivity.

These are important areas for public action and policy-makers in government would do well to pay heed to these recommendations.

I met Vibhooti in the summer of 1991 when we were both visiting the Indira Gandhi Institute of Development Research in Bombay. I was struck by her warm and caring nature, and her optimism. These traits combined together to give a sense of purpose to what she did. She did research because she believed it would contribute to the betterment of life; and that comes out very clearly from this collection.

Delhi School of Economics KAUSHIK BASU
May 1995

Preface

We could never have imagined that we would one day be preparing a compilation of writings of Dr Vibhooti Shukla without her by our side.

As Vibhooti says in her unfinished statement, she was a product of the development era of the sixties and seventies in India, and this foundation has been ingrained in all of her work. Her graduate education at Princeton strongly influenced her thinking, and this optimism and analytic thinking is evident in her work that ranges from urbanization to environmental studies.

We have divided her work into six sections, viz., (1) City size, Productivity and Policy Implications, (2) Agglomeration and Migration, (3) Sectoral Versus Spatial Considerations, (4) Urban Structure and Employment Dynamics, (5) Consequences of Urban Growth, and (6) Research Agenda.

A substantial number of these articles were written solely by Vibhooti; others in collaboration. Most of these articles have been published in US and Indian journals. The chapter entitled 'Sources of Urban Productivity and City Sizes: An Empirical Exercise' has been excerpted from her first book *Urban Development and Regional Policy in India: An Econometric Analysis*, published in 1988. Unpublished articles are in final form, except two, which remained unedited. We have, however, included these unedited papers for obvious reasons.

We make special reference to the inclusion of the statement that Vibhooti was writing as part of her tenure requirements at the University of Texas just prior to her death. This statement, while evaluating her work, spells out her short-term and long-term goals, along with her research agenda. It provides a perspective on the relationships between the various subjects addressed by Vibhooti, and also on the endogenization of the agglomeration variable, her main contribution to the profession, with various implications in migration, labour markets, employment, etc. We have titled this 'The Unfinished Statement'.

We have many to thank for support and encouragement, and in particular, Vibhooti's collaborators and publishers of the journals and the books for permitting inclusion of her work in this present compilation. We are also very grateful to Dr Kaushik Basu, Professor at the

Delhi School of Economics and Director, Center for Development Economics, for writing the very thoughtful and sensitive foreword to this book. Professor Basu has also taken keen interest at every stage of finalization of this manuscript, offering us valuable suggestions and guidance. We also thank Dr D.M. Nachane, Director, Department of Economics, University of Bombay, for his editorial contribution to the chapter on 'Sources of Urban Productivity and City Sizes'. Dr J.C. Sandesara, the former Director of Department of Economics, University of Bombay and now University Grants Commission Emeritus Fellow, who took keen interest in Vibhooti's development and whom Vibhooti met every time she was in India was eminently suited to write the biographical sketch. We are indeed very grateful to him. The personal interest taken by Professors Royce Hansen, Brian J.L. Berry, Paul Waddell, Irving Hoch, James Murdoch, and Kurt Beron at the University of Texas at Dallas, Professor Oded Stark of Harvard University, Professor M.L. Dantwala, former Director of Department of Economics, University of Bombay, and presently National Professor, Professor Kirit Parikh, and Jyoti Parikh, Director and Senior Professor, respectively, at the Indira Gandhi Institute of Development Research, Bombay is greatly appreciated. We are thankful to Shri T.R. Sundaram for meticulously going through the proofs. And finally, but for the enthusiastic co-operation of Oxford University Press, this book would not be available in print.

We remain responsible for any flaws in this compilation.

August 1995

TARA SHUKLA (Bombay)
SATCHIT SRINIVASAN (Dallas, USA)

Vibhooti Shukla: A Biographical Sketch

Vibhooti Shukla was born on 5 February 1959 in Bombay. She passed away on 8 August 1992 at Dallas, Texas, United States. The cruel hands of death snatched her away when the hot-air balloon she was riding in exploded in an accident at Mesquite near Dallas. In her death, her parents have lost their only child, her husband a caring wife, her circle an affectionate friend, and the profession a competent economist.

Vibhooti had natural talents for the fine arts and logical thinking, not a frequent combination in a person. In these natural inclinations, nurture helped greatly. She was guided and encouraged by knowledgeable parents and supported by her teachers, colleagues and friends. It was this combination of nature and nurture that moulded Vibhooti into a refined person and a respected professional.

Her father, Chandravadan Shukla, a novelist and journalist and her mother, Tara Shukla, an economist, earlier an academic and later a banker, encouraged Vibhooti in all her pursuits. Her love for the Sanskrit language and her appreciation of music was strongly influenced by her father. There was a unique relationship of friendship between the daughter and her parents, which enhanced the development of Vibhooti's versatile personality, but her choice of career was entirely her own. Vibhooti married Satchit Srinivasan, a polymer scientist, on 6 January 1986. Both were sources of inspiration and support to each other. In fact, they were as much best friends as they were wife and husband.

Vibhooti had her early education at a number of schools in Bombay and in the US. Whichever the school, she was a front ranker, academically and in extra-curricular activities like music, dance, poetry, debates and painting. She joined Elphinstone College, Bombay, and passed her B.A. examination in 1979 with a first class. Here also, she continued to be active in extra-curricular activities. Vibhooti proceeded to the US to qualify for her Ph.D. in economics at Princeton University. In 1984, she received her doctorate for her dissertation on 'The Productivity of Indian Cities and Some Implications for Development Policy'.

Her professional career, mostly in the US, was, alas, too short, eight years between receiving her Ph.D. and her death in 1992. It was indeed a hectic period, and her energy and ambition drove her fast. During this period, she taught, did consultancy and research, published, and developed and maintained personal and professional contacts. As a teacher, she taught almost all major branches of economics, and as a consultant and researcher also she spread herself fairly widely, in the areas of urban, labour, development, environmental and institutional economics. Some of the problems which Vibhooti tackled in these areas demanded interdisciplinary skills, and she learnt and used the same in her work.

Vibhooti worked at a number of reputed universities. She was a teaching assistant at Princeton (1982–84), post-doctoral fellow at Harvard (1984–85), lecturer at California State University, Fullerton (1986–87), and assistant professor at University of Texas, Dallas from 1987 till her death in 1992. She was a visiting fellow at the University of Michigan, Ann Arbor (1988) and a visiting associate professor at the Indira Gandhi Institute of Development Research, Bombay (1991). She also worked as a consultant to the World Bank (1985–86). She presented papers at a number of seminars and conferences, chaired sessions at some, and was a member of several professional associations in the US and India.

Vibhooti has to her credit twelve published papers, seven of which appeared jointly with others and five individually authored. This volume puts together these papers in one compilation. It also includes six other papers which she had completed but which have not been published earlier, and a Statement which outlines Vibhooti's tentative thoughts on the work which she had done and planned to do. Besides this volume, she has to her credit a book titled *Urban Development and Regional Policy in India: An Econometric Analysis*.

The future in large part is strongly influenced by the past. This account of Vibhooti's work provides substantial evidence of her wide range of interests in economics and her competence as an economist. It is also an indicator of her great potential which remained untapped due to her untimely death. With this, the reader of this book will, hopefully, concur.

Bombay
April 1995

J.C. SANDESARA

Contents

List of Other Contributors

ODED STARK	Formerly, Director of Migration and Development Program, Harvard University, presently Professor of Economics, Harvard University.
BRIAN J. L. BERRY	Former Chairman, Department of Geography at University of Chicago, Williams Professor of City and Regional Planning and Chairman Ph.D. Program in Urban Planning, Harvard University. Dean, School of Urban and Public Affairs Carnegie-Mellon University. Presently, Lloyd Veil Berkner University, Professor of Political Economy, School of Social Sciences and Director, The Burton Center for Development Studies, University of Texas at Dallas.
PAUL WADDELL	Executive Director, The Burton Center for Development Studies, University of Texas at Dallas.
KIRIT PARIKH	Director, Indira Gandhi Institute of Development Research, Bombay.
KURT J. BERON	Associate Professor of Economics and Political Economy, School of Social Sciences, University of Texas at Dallas
JAMES C. MURDOCH	Associate Professor of Economics and Political Economy, School of Social Sciences, University of Texas at Dallas
JYOTI PARIKH	Professor, Indira Gandhi Institute of Development Research, Bombay.

I / City Size, Productivity and Policy Instruments

1 / Urban Productivity Implications for Regional Policies in LDCs

VIBHOOTI SHUKLA

I. Introduction

It is widely recognized that certain types of economic activities are more productively undertaken in an urban environment. The term 'agglomeration economies' is often used to describe the risk-spreading opportunities of denser markets and the informational benefits that accrue to a firm located in close spatial proximity with a large number of its customers, suppliers and, in some respects, its competitors. The concept is generally used to encompass considerations both of absolute size and of concentration.

Economists have found it analytically convenient to characterize this urban productive advantage as a technological one; furthermore, it has been modelled as entering the set of firms' production possibilities in a neutral manner. This characterization is in keeping with the idea that, ultimately, it is scale economies in production, together with transportation costs, that are responsible for the existence of urban areas.

A strand of the urban economics literature that seeks to explain city formation and city growth with exclusive focus on the role of scale, abstracting from all other considerations, utilizes the notion of equilibrium urban size. Models in this genre[1] visualize the economy as a flat, featureless plain, wherein location decisions are made solely with regard to agglomeration considerations, as fully represented by city size. The city economy produces a good or set of goods for export to the rest of the world at a parametric price, and with residence tied to workplace, its employed labour is also its population. External scale economies in traded good manufacturing provide the impetus for city growth; diseconomies in the production of a non-traded good and/or consumption diseconomies experienced by city residents create pressures to arrest it. The balance of the two forces yields an equilibrium size of industrial and consumption activity and hence of city population.

Such an aggregative formulation satisfactorily captures, without being explicitly spatial, what are considered to be salient features of spatially contiguous production through its agglomeration specification, and without being dynamic, collapses the urban evolution process into a static equilibrium framework.

The hypothesized agglomeration economies that are pivotal to such models have been empirically verified.[2] For US cities, Sveikauskas (1975) and Segal (1976) estimated a 5–6 per cent increase in industrial productivity with every doubling of urban size. In the developing country context, Henderson (1983) ascertained their presence for the case of Brazil. Shukla (1984), working with Indian data, measured an average 9 per cent increase in factor productivity achievable upon a 100 per cent increase in city size, corroborating the presumption that these economies are likely to be even more important in situations where markets are thin and institutions for the transmission of market information inadequately developed. Shukla's results imply that resources in a city with a population of 100,000 can be, on an average, 23 per cent more efficient than in one of 10,000. They can be as much as 51 per cent more efficient in a city of one million than in a city of 10,000.

Developing countries, for a number of reasons, institute policies to influence the location of economic activity. Some of these are coercive, and take the form of denying metropolitan access to firms in certain categories through licensing and other means. That such denial by itself entails significant efficiency losses translatable into forgone output that these countries can ill afford is immediately apparent from the discussion above, but the problem is more properly viewed in the context of other locational alternatives that are made available. Our particular interest here is in examining government programmes for fostering the growth of manufacturing industry in some regions or region-types within a country. Such measures are sometimes termed 'industrial dispersal policies', in recognition of their intended effect of increasing these regions' share of national output and employment.[3] Three sets of issues are of relevance here — the targets to which dispersal is sought to be directed, the objectives of dispersal and the instruments for effecting it. The aim of the analysis that follows is to evaluate choices in these regards using a framework explicitly incorporating agglomeration effects.

The paper plan is as follows: Section II outlines a theoretical formulation for an urban area in the equilibrium size tradition. Section III develops the regional model, defines within its context industrial backwardness as perceived by policy-makers along with their perceptions of the gains to be had from dispersal, and ends by spelling out preconditions for a successful regional development strategy premised on considerations inherent in the model. Section IV is concerned with comparing alternative instruments that might be used in implementing such a strategy. This is done with a version of the basic model of Section II that is specified for easy solvability, yet equipped with the structure to pose some of the relevant questions that arise in this regard.

II. Theoretical Design for a Single Region

The model we work with features one good, or set of interrelated non-primary goods, constituting the whole of a region's 'urban' output, which is produced under conditions of significant external agglomeration economies[4] by identical firms employing the two factors, labour and capital, with decreasing returns to internal scale. Initially, firms are randomly distributed across a topographically featureless plain; subsequent decisions are made purely in response to urban size. The aggregative representation of the region's productive possibilities is:

$$Q = G(N)\, F(N, K) \tag{1}$$

where the functions $G(\,)$ and $F(\,)$ are the technology's external and internal components respectively, N and K being total labour and capital employed. $G' > 0$, indicating that agglomeration economies are present; $F(\,)$ exhibits decreasing returns to scale.[5]

The economy of the urban area is an open one, its output, Q, traded on national (or international) markets at a price that is given. Firms in the city make their employment decisions taking into account the special production benefits — agglomeration and others — of their location; however, they do not see themselves as influencing city size, which is simply the aggregation of their profit-maximizing labour demands.

The decision problem leading to the determination of equilibrium urban size in the region is collapsed into the following:

Max. $G\,F(N, K) - wN - rK$,

since the individual decision-maker treats G as a constant. The exogenous output price is normalized at one. It is assumed that the region faces an infinitely elastic supply of private capital at the going interest rate, r. The city region also faces an unlimited supply of labour at a parametric real wage, w. This can be given the interpretation, as the situation warrants, of being either an economy-wide equilibrium wage at which labour supply, to any small region, is perfectly elastic, or a subsistence wage that makes available to the city an unlimited supply of labour from a surrounding agricultural hinterland.

Alternatively, one might model the labour supplied to any particular region as upward-sloping with respect to the going money wage. Money wages varying positively with city size can be viewed as reflecting positive money — e.g., transportation or moving — costs of drawing migrants from further and further afar as the size of the region's urban sector expands; or as reflecting higher costs of living in bigger cities due to, for instance, diseconomies of urban scale associated with the production of an essential regionally non-traded good, such as housing.

If, on the other hand, real wages rise with city size, this may be indicative of preferences implying a utility formulation of the type $V = U(N, w)$, wherein N, capturing the consumption effects of urban living, directly enters resident welfare calculations as a separate argument. If it does so negatively, this forces the wage to rise as city size increases, in order that the given level of utility be maintained. One reason to presume it may do so is an increasing psychic cost to migrants of movement from farther afield. Likewise, it might be assumed that large city disamenity effects — crowding, pollution, crime — are evaluated negatively by prospective residents. Both presumptions are capturable in a condition such as $w'(N) > 0$.

Irrespective of which of the above assumptions is made, the following points must be clear with respect to the supply side formulation imbedded in this theoretical design. First, all the behavioural assumptions on the consumption side are subsumed under the postulated properties of the wage function rather than expressed through an explicit utility representation. Second, a region faces a supply of residents which is perfectly elastic at a national or 'system' utility level. This places the formulation in the tradition of the 'open city' models which have been thought more relevant to urban processes in developing economies. Third, the formulation corresponds to a situation of long-run spatial equilibrium in labour markets; utility is equalized at all points across space. Lastly, in equating city employment with city population, one assumes that full employment prevails in the urban region, and abstracts from non-working dependants. Even the surplus labour interpretation is seen as being reconcilable with full employment in the industrial sector in a manner similar to that of Lewis-type dual economy models. This is in contradiction, it may be noted, to the Harris–Todaro tradition of models of urban unemployment.[6] Ultimately, of course, the choice of assumption, interpretation and perspective is a function of reality, purpose, and time frame of the analysis.

Private actions by profit-maximizing firms yield values of equilibrium labour and capital employed,[7] N^e and K^e, satisfying the following first-order conditions:

$$G(N^e)\, F_N(N^e, K^e) - w = 0 \tag{2}$$

$$G(N^e)\, F_K(N^e, K^e) - r = 0 \tag{3}$$

and the second-order conditions:

$$GF_{NN} < 0 \tag{4}$$

$$[GF_{KK}]\,[GF_{NN}] - [GF_{NK}]^2 > 0 \tag{5}$$

which are satisfied under the assumptions we have made (see note 5) regarding the firms' internal technology.

Private equilibrium in such a model is not optimal. There is an externality in the firms' failure to perceive and incorporate in their decision-making the agglomeration effect of their cumulative employment decisions.

A social optimum, N^*, that does take these into account must satisfy the first-order conditions:

$$G(N^*)\, F_N(N^*, K^*) + G'(N^*)\, F(N^*, K^*) - w = 0 \tag{6}$$

$$G(N^*)\, F_K(N^*, K^*) - r = 0 \tag{7}$$

and the second-order conditions:

$$GF_{NN} + 2G' F_N + G'' F < 0 \tag{8}$$

$$[GF_{KK}]\,[GF_{NN} + 2G' F_N + G''\; F] - [GF_{NK}]^2 > 0 \tag{9}$$

which require that output be increasing at a decreasing rate with employment at the optimal level, N^*.

We are now in a position to compare the magnitudes of N^e and N^*. Diagrammatically, the first-order condition for labour, viz., (2), under private maximization yields the equilibrium size, N^e, as marked on Figure 1, since $G(N)\, F_N(N, K)$ must be downward-sloping with respect to N.[8] But the corresponding first-order condition under the social maximization problem, viz., (6), implies, since $G'(N)\, F(N, K) > 0$, that

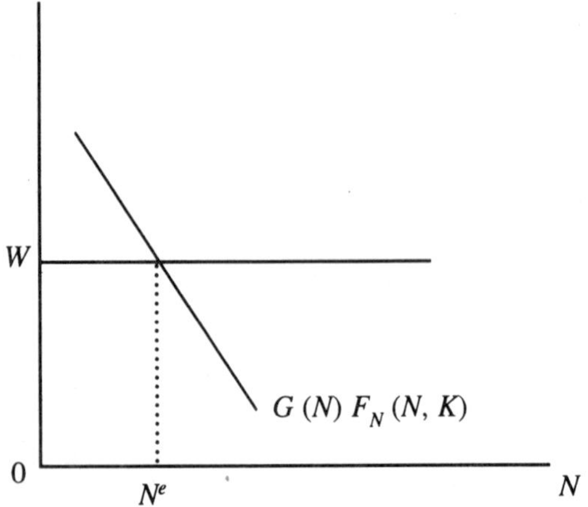

Figure 1: Equilibrium City Size

$$G(N^*)\,F_N(N^*, K^*) < w \qquad (10)$$

That is, $G(N)\,F_N(N, K)$ must be below w at N^*. Therefore, N^*, the optimal size, must lie to the right of N^e, the equilibrium size of the urban sector, implying that the latter is suboptimal[9] in any given region.

It follows from the analysis above that the urban productive environment can sustain a larger employed population than is brought about by private actions alone, if appropriate public measures are taken to internalize this externality. The externality feature of the formulation thus not only provides a role for government action, but, in addition, suggests a picture of regional industrial development that appears quite realistic. While it suggests a course of action counter to the usual policy of restricting firm location in large cities while scale economics are present, it conforms to policy-makers' notions about the dynamics of regional development. Each firm induced to locate or expand employment in a city region contributes to the productivity of that region through agglomeration effects that make subsequent expansions in industrial employment there more attractive.

Simultaneously, the analysis carries implications for migration policy. Suboptimality of size of urban area translates into suboptimal migration. The same conditions that identify socially efficient levels of employment in the model define optimal levels of spatial labour transfer, again suggesting directions contrary to those popularly prescribed.

The implications of the externality result for the regional policy problem will be taken up shortly, before which we attempt to cast this issue in compatible analytical terms to facilitate that analysis.

III. The Case for Dispersal as a Development Strategy

Specification of the Regional Issue

To permit meaningful discussion of inter-regional considerations, we must extend the model beyond a single region. We structure our framework as admitting two region types: one designated 'backward', and one, 'advanced'. Any one region is small relative to the rest of the economy.

We can set out in fairly general terms the requirements of such a model. At the outset, it is clear that there must be a dissimilarity between region types, and this dissimilarity must be spatial or site-specific to warrant intervention along regional lines. Furthermore, to warrant any intervention at all, it must be one that is not reconcilable by private market forces. In other words, a region may be advanced or backward at the time of designation owing to the presence or absence of attributes that are exogenous to the equilibrium urban growth paradigm. Without inter-regional immobilities of some kind, it must be stressed, the problem simply does not exist.

Typically, the earlier or faster growth of a region or a city in relation to others has its origin in historical, locational, topographical or endowment characteristics specific to it, and not quite generalizable. In our single region formulation, such particular sources of high productivity were abstracted from in favour of size, which was highlighted as the most significant tractable influence of interest. At this juncture, we must put back this spatial or geographical content, and moreover, do so in a manner sensitive to the perception of policy-makers regarding the more general or pervasive sources of regional backwardness.

This regional dissimilarity or immobility that gives rise to the problem can be of various kinds. For instance, one might want to model that region as advanced which is topographically or otherwise placed such that it has superior access to markets for its output compared to its backward counterpart. This might be expressed through producers in the region being able to command a higher price for its exports, due to savings in the transportation or marketing component of production costs. Likewise, in a model with more structure, one might identify a region as having a productive advantage and specializing in a specific industry as deriving this advantage from, say, access to a natural resource important to this industry. Or, one might, as the situation warrants, want to identify labour as the resource with imperfect inter-regional mobility. This would be the case if non-wage-related region-specific locational preferences[10] rendered inter-regional migration slow or limited, so as to create persistent inter-regional wage differentials in an environment where industry also was not regionally foot-loose.

The present model, of course, does not admit long-run labour immobility, and our justification for governmental intervention is on efficiency and developmental grounds (to be explained shortly). We model that region as backward which has a relatively deficient stock of productive infrastructure. Note that this represents a spatial immobility inasmuch as the economic contribution of infrastructure is predominantly site-specific. Lack of infrastructure is seen as a sort of general institutional barrier to the development of the region, preventing its natural resources from being tapped, its investment opportunities from being availed of by private capital, and its agglomerative potential from being exploited.

Finally, having defined regional backwardness in terms of the developmental concerns of the government, it remains to define how policy-makers measure and value the benefits of its removal. In a word, an indicator must be developed that adequately reflects the implicit social objectives of the policy measures we are considering. We model the developmental objectives of the planners to be served by securing the maximum possible increase in industrial employment. The desirability of the transfer of labour resources to the non-primary sector, as an assumption, is defensible on two grounds from the viewpoint of economic development. First, it is a natural concomitant of the development process, one that has historically characterized the maturing of economies. It is the 'structural change' that is supposed to be the harbinger of attitudinal and institutional revolution, the emergence of smoothly functioning markets where none or imperfect ones existed before, and the flowering of entrepreneurial talent. Second, and more concretely, under conditions of disguised unemployment in the agricultural sector, the productive employment of surplus labour in industry must result in a net increase in aggregate output and welfare.[11]

Below, we bring together these ideas with the results of Section 2 to examine the rationality of the industrial dispersal strategy.

Application of the Model

We have abstracted thus far a positive externality, a spatial institutional barrier and a success criterion in this problem. Government's role arises in the context of the correction of the externality, and of the manipulation of the institutional barrier, which is, in this case, also within the range of feasible public actions. Wherever agglomeration economies persist, urban size is suboptimal, and externality correction desirable. Likewise, infrastructure investment in any region has unambiguous rewards. But while there are a number of areas where fruitful intervention is possible, and a variety of actions which are feasible, a non-trivial choice problem arises because government works with scarce resources. In this part of the analysis, we take up the question of where scarce government resources can be most fruitfully applied in realization of the benefits incorporated in the social objectives. Particularly, we shall ask whether the policy of industrial dispersal — the concentration of governmental remedial efforts in the backward regions — is defensible in the face of both the overall developmental objective and the regional production conditions characterizing manufacturing industry in LDCs. The next section will address the question of the choice of policy instrument.

Let us start by modelling the contribution of economic infrastructure, represented by $H(I)$, to the productive process in the fashion implied by

$$Q = H(I)\, G(N)\, F(N, K)\; H' > 0 \tag{11}$$

for any particular region.[12] To the extent that the direct removal of the cause of regional backwardness is seen as securing its cure, we note this implies that there are direct employment-augmenting effects in a region of additional infrastructure investment. Our main interest here, however, is in exploring the implications of the interaction between inter-regional disparity in infrastructure stock and externality correction efforts for the validity of the industrial dispersal approach. To do this, we specify the general function $H(I)$ as its projection, I. We consider two regions, A, the 'advanced' and B, the 'backward'. I_A and I_B are the existing stocks of productive infrastructure in the two regions respectively. It is assumed that $I_A > I_B$. Labour is supplied to each region at the same constant wage, w.

Equilibrium industrial employment (and urban size) is given in the two cases by N_A^e and N_B^e with private equilibrium entailing under the assumptions of our model, the satisfaction of :

$$G\,(N_A^e)\,F_N\,(N_A^e, K_A^e) = w/I_A \tag{12}$$

$$G\,(N_B^e)\,F_N(N_B^e, K_B^e) = w/I_B \tag{13}$$

the respective first-order conditions for labour. As $w/I_A < w/I_B$

$$G\,(N_A^e)\,F_N(N_A^e, K_A^e) < G(N_B^e)\,F_N(N_B^e, K_B^e) \tag{14}$$

implying, since $G\,(N)\,F_N(N,\,K)$ has been shown to decrease with N, $N_A^e > N_B^e$. Thus, not surprisingly, the advanced region is the one that is more urbanized than the backward region.

Now, drawing upon the earlier result of Section II, N_A^e and N_B^e are both smaller than they might be under government intervention. The question, of course, is where should government concentrate its remedial efforts so as to secure most in terms of its objectives with the limited resources at its disposal. Comparing the expressions from the private and social optimization problems, viz.,

$$IG\,(N^e)\,F_N\,(N^e,\,K^e) = w \tag{15}$$

$$IG\,(N^*)\,F_N\,(N^*,\,K^*) + IG'\,(N^*)\,F(N^*,\,K^*) = w \tag{16}$$

we see that, as $G'\,(N)$ tends to zero, N^e approaches N^*, so that the employment-augmenting scope of government action diminishes. On the other hand, if $G'(N)$ is positive and large, more stands to be gained in terms of employment. If success is measured in terms of employment gain, then it is obvious that the value of G' in backward regions (representing the employment cost, so to speak, of reallocating resources away from them and toward the more urbanized areas) must be relatively large to make these regions the most favoured candidates for receiving government assistance. Intuitively, therefore, to support the case for the backward or less urbanized regions, we appear to need the presumption that agglomeration economies rise at a diminishing rate, becoming less important, and finally petering out at large enough city sizes, rendering minimal the employment gains to be had from dispersal.[13]

We stipulate that, under our specification of the problem, a prerequisite for justifying the diversion of regional assistance to the backward areas is

$$N_B^* - N_B^e > N_A^* - N_A^e \tag{17}$$

A necessary condition for this can be understood with the help of Figure 2. N_A^e and N_B^e represent the private optima; N_A^* and N_B^* those of the planners.

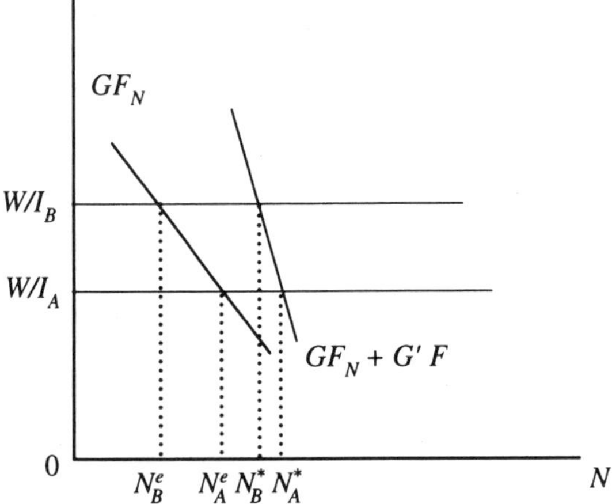

Figure 2: Condition for Successful Dispersal

For $N_B^* - N_B^e$ to be greater than $N_A^* - N_A^e$, it is required that the curve representing the social demand for labour be falling more steeply with city size at the optima than the one representing private labour demand. The horizontal distance between the two curves represents the net employment contribution of taking into account the agglomeration influence. It is seen that for employment gain in the backward region to dominate that in the advanced, this gap must narrow with increasing N.

More formally, to vindicate industrial dispersal as a regional strategy consistent with its goals and with implications arising out of the agglomeration feature, we need, from equations (4) and (8):

$$GF_{NN} + 2G'F_N + G''F < GF_{NN} \tag{18}$$

This reduces to the condition:

$$2F_N/F < G''/G' \tag{19}$$

at the point of the optimum. Since the left-hand side of this expression is always positive, it is easy to see that this condition is never satisfied under the possibility that increments to productivity in large cities are infinitely sustained, i.e., if $G'' > 0$ or $G'' = 0$. On the other hand, if $G'' < 0$, and its absolute value is very high, indicating a very rapid exhaustion of the added agglomerative benefits of increasing city size, there is greater likelihood of its satisfaction.

The condition given by (19) may be tested against the data, with estimates obtained using relevant functional forms. In general, it will reduce to a condition involving the parameters of the agglomeration and production specifications, labour supply functions, and the numerical equilibrium and optimal sizes calculated therefrom. Operationalizing this condition, should this be desired, can be made to take account of industry-wise differences in propensity to benefit from agglomeration, and could, conceivably, result in the identification not only of a range of city sizes to which dispersal might be fruitful, but also of industries in respect of which it entails the least cost.

A widely held presumption about the behaviour of agglomeration effects with respect to urban scale may be used to demonstrate that dispersal over all ranges of city size is not implied by the foregoing. The proposition is that urban productive benefits act as depicted in Figure 3, viz., increasing rapidly at small city sizes, but eventually slowing down as larger sizes are reached.

Taking as indicative (but not exact) the hypothetical mark-off points of the *X*-axis of the curve, it is plausible that at city sizes below some threshold level, which might lie anywhere between the 500,000 and (for some industries) the 1,000,000 mark, condition (19) does not hold. In respect of this urban size class, then, dispersal to smaller cities will almost certainly not meet the aforementioned success criterion.

Operational recommendations can come only out of country- and industry-specific studies on the viability of dispersal to permissible size

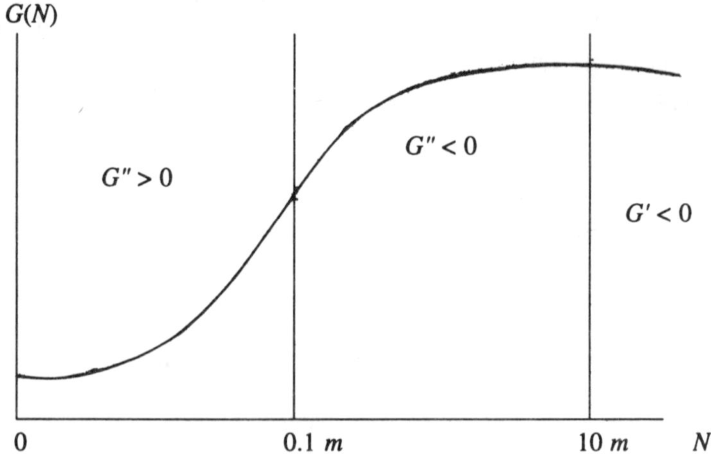

Figure 3: Urban Productivity Thresholds

classes. Also, it must be constantly borne in mind, this analysis represents one out of many possible ways of looking at the problem. On the other hand, further support may be found for a policy of industrial dispersion as a regional strategy if, in addition, the social welfare function disfavours 'oversized' urban agglomerations for political or administrative reasons, or if it weighs backward region employment more highly than advanced region employment out of equity considerations.

IV. Evaluating Instruments for the Dispersion of Industry

Context and Scope of the Problem

Recapitulating a bit, we may say that the nature of the problem we are faced with is as follows: in any region, the marginal social product of labour diverges from its private product, due to an agglomeration externality characterizing the production technology. Efficiency may be achieved by equating the marginal social product of employment (or city formation) with its marginal social cost, viz., real wage. Restoration of efficiency requires that size of the urban area be increased, more fully, so to speak, to utilize the production possibilities that the region has to offer. The situation is portrayed by the bold lines in Figure 4, where labour supply to the city is assumed to rise with real wage.

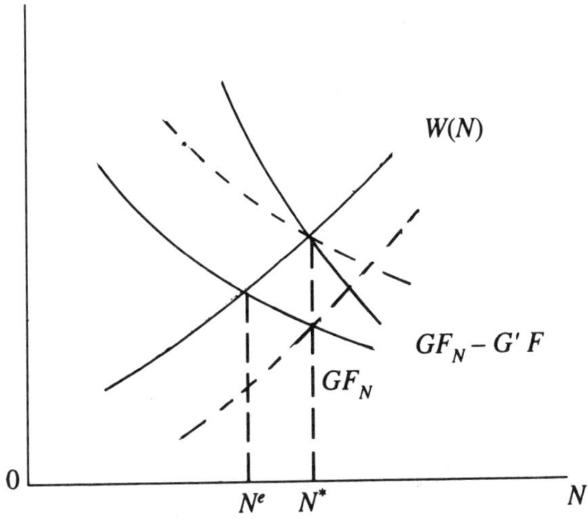

Figure 4: Externality and Subsidization

In the abstract, we can see that the social optimum is sustainable as a private equilibrium by means of one of two possible actions — that of moving out the private demand schedule for labour, or that of moving out the supply schedule of residents. Both possibilities are depicted by the broken lines in Figure 4. The former action may be implemented through, say, an output or a capital subsidy to producers. The latter action, on the other hand, is implementable through a labour subsidy paid to employers.

More concretely, it is government-financed intervention that must bring about this externality correction. In the context of our problem, this necessitates two kinds of policy choices. One is that of the optimal target; i.e., selection of a region or region-type where assistance will be concentrated. The other is choice of optimal instrument. In the last section, we identified a condition that must hold if the backward regions are to be selected as the favoured recipients of intensified assistance. In this section, we address the question of the comparative merits of some of the commonly used instruments for implementing a regional strategy.

The analysis that follows in a sense complements, but in another way is independent of, the target identification problem of the previous section. The implications for the optimal instrument that will be developed here of course apply to the class of city sizes or region-types selected under the aforementioned criteria. But, in the view of the suboptimality of all (except perhaps the very large) urban areas under the assumptions of our model, they apply more generally to cases where the regional problem is premised on justifications other than those we have been considering, or even to situations where there is no perceived conflict of interests between one region class and another. The analysis will therefore be conducted in terms of a single region — a region towards which, for some reason or other, employment dispersal has been thought worthwhile.

Before beginning our analysis, we may mention some of the previous work that has gone into this area. The bulk of the writing[14] on this subject has its origin in Great Britian, where it has largely taken the direction of statistical measurement of the employment effects of one or more of the many dispersal programmes that have been in effect there for some time. The main debate featured in the more analytical strand[15] of this literature has been in connection with the use of capital subsidies for the purpose of relocating industry to depressed regions in order to raise employment therein. The difficulty with these is their tendeny to divert resources toward raising capital intensity rather than toward augmenting employment. Since this is especially acute in respect of those industries with a high degree of substitutability between capital and labour, principal policy recommendations have been to prescribe capital subsidies only for industries with low elasticities of substitution.

Our purpose here is slightly different. We are interested in guidelines for the optimal choice of dispersal instrument, for the specific purpose of externality correction in the context of a particular urban growth (and regional development) formulation. In the following part we specify this further to facilitate the explicit evaluations we hope to perform subsequently.

A Specified Model for the Evaluations

Below, we set forth a regional model featuring specific functional forms for the agglomeration influence, internal technology and labour supply relationship. The purpose is to assess the comparative efficacy of three dispersal instruments — output, capital and labour subsidies — in securing the restoration of efficiency in the wake of the agglomerative externality characterizing regional production technology.

In evolving this particular specification of the relationships, it may be mentioned at the outset, three aims have been at the forefront of consideration. One, it has been desired to render the formulation easily solvable (closed-form expressions are secured here by essentially making the model log-linear throughout); secondly, it has been desired to do so while retaining the key features, particularly, agglomeration, that are, so to speak, the motivation and focus of the entire exercise; and, finally, it has been necessary to equip it with the capability of answering the instrument choice question in a reasonably direct way. The model below presents the best balance that, in our judgement, could be arrived at in view of these diverse requirements.

In general terms, a region's output is given by the relationship, resembling (1) of Section 2,

$$Q = G(N)\ F(N, K) \qquad (20)$$

N being both total urban employment and residence, and K being the quantity of productive capital in the region. As before, this represents an aggregation of the technologies of many small firms in the urban or industrial sector of the region, each producing a single, homogeneous traded good, Q. Specifically,

$$G(N) = BN^{\gamma} \tag{21}$$

is the agglomeration formulation featuring the positive agglomeration elasticity, γ, which is assumed to lie between zero and one, incorporating the assumption that the amount of output 'shift' due to the external economies increases at a declining rate with city size. The internal technology specification is

$$F(N, K) = AN^{\alpha} K^{\beta} \tag{22}$$

This is assumed to display constant returns to scale, i.e., $\alpha + \beta$ is assumed to equal unity.[16] Finally, the supply of labour to urban industry in the region is specified as

$$w(N) = bN \qquad b > 0 \tag{23}$$

Under this unitary elasticity labour supply function is subsumed the assumption of real wages increasing with city size.[17]

Our procedure will be as follows: first, we compute equilibrium regional employment that is brought about by private market forces alone.[18] Next, we calculate the social optimum, and compare its magnitude with the former quantity. In the third stage, we recompute the private equilibrium as a function of the various subsidy rates, which are then solved for by equating equilibrium to optimum. Finally, we compare the financial burden imposed on government by the choice of each of the alternative subsidies. In effect, we can summarize the strategy as one of calculating imputed or shadow prices that will sustain the optimum as a competitive equilibrium. The first two operations will be performed in this section, and the remaining two in the next.

The private problem, then, is given by:

$$\text{Max. } ABN^{\gamma} N^{\alpha} K^{\beta} - (bN)N - rK$$

where, as before, the exogenous output price is set at unity, and r is the exogenous real capital cost to firms in the region. Treating the effect of employment decisions on city size as parametric yields the following first-order conditions:

$$Q^{e} = [\ b/\alpha\ ]\ N^{e2} \tag{24}$$

$$K^{e} = (\beta Q^{e})/\ r \tag{25}$$

Substituting (25) in the expression for total regional output, Q^{e}, we arrive at:

$$Q^e = [AB\beta^\beta r^{-\beta}]^{1/(1-\beta)} N^{e(\alpha+\beta)/(1-\beta)} \tag{26}$$

Equating this with (24) above, we are able to solve for N in terms of the exogenous prices and parameters, yielding equilibrium employment in the region as given by

$$N^e = [\alpha/b]^{(1-\beta)/(2-2\beta-\alpha-\gamma)} [AB\beta^\beta r^{-\beta}]^{1/(2-2\beta-\alpha-\gamma)} \tag{27}$$

The social optimum, on the other hand, is obtained by recognizing the variability of city size in the agglomeration component of the production specification. The maximization calculus then yields a different first-order condition for labour, viz.,

$$Q^* = [b/(\alpha+\gamma)]\, N^{*2} \tag{28}$$

Repeating the solution steps of the private problem, we are able to arrive at the following expression for optimal employment or city size:

$$N^* = [(\alpha+\gamma)/b]^{(1-\beta)/(2-2\beta-\alpha-\gamma)} [AB\beta^\beta r^{-\beta}]^{1/(2-2\beta-\alpha-\gamma)} \tag{29}$$

From the expressions for equilibrium and optimal regional employment given by equations (27) and (29) respectively, we can compute the difference in magnitude between the two. If we write $(1-\beta)/(2-2\beta-\alpha-\gamma) = c$, then this is given by

$$N^* - N^e = [AB\beta^\beta r^{-\beta}]^{1/(2-2\beta-\alpha-\gamma)} [(\alpha+\gamma)^c - \alpha^c]/b^c \tag{30}$$

It is seen that this difference is positive, implying the suboptimality of private equilibrium, provided that the expression c, as defined above, is positive. This requirement, in turn, reduces to the condition that

$$2-2\beta-\alpha-\gamma > 0 \tag{31}$$

which, given $\alpha+\beta = 1$, necessitates that γ be less than α. In other words, under our model, the optimum level of industrial employment in the region exceeds the equilibrium level provided that the external labour efficiency, i.e., the agglomeration parameter, is lower than the internal one. This analytical feature of our model is intuitively as well as empirically explainable. Since production is constant returns to scale internally, and labour is the only paid input for which costs rise more than proportionately with city size, its share must ultimately be the limiting factor to infinite expansion. Also, an externality is, by definition, an incidental by-product of a purposeful activity, and it is only natural to expect that employed resources are more productive in the purposeful one than in the incidental one; in a sense, it is this which must explain why the former is undertaken by the private market and the latter is not.

In the part below, we shall use the expression for optimal employment derived above to solve for the optimal subsidy levels that will make private firms behave in a socially efficient manner. Finally, we shall choose between different kinds of subsidy in accordance with certain criteria that we will shortly spell out.

Comparisons

We now introduce the three subsidies we are concerned with comparing, viz., the labour, capital and output, into hypothetical private maximization problems. In order to do so and still be able to maintain the convenient logarithmic linearity of the problem, we will model each of them as proportions of prevailing input and output prices. As it happens, this is also a realistic representation of actual subsidization under most programmes.

We first consider the employment subsidy. Government is assumed to pay a proportion, S_L, of the total wage bill of employers. In such an event, their private decision problem is:

$$\text{Max. } ABN^{\gamma} N^{\alpha} K^{\beta} - (1 - S_L)(bN) N - rK$$

This yields equilibrium employment level as a function of the subsidy:

$$N^e = [\alpha/b\,(1-S_L)]^{(1-\beta)/(2-2\beta-\alpha-\gamma)}\,[AB\beta^{\beta}\, r^{-\beta}\,]^{1/(2-2\beta-\alpha-\gamma)} \qquad (32)$$

To derive the subsidy level that will sustain the social optimum as the equilibrium under these circumstances, we equate this expression with the one for the optimum, viz., (29), obtained in the previous part. This yields an optimum employment subsidy, as we have defined it, of

$$S_L = \gamma / (\alpha+\gamma) \qquad (33)$$

We repeat the exercise with a capital subsidy, S_K. The problem in this case is:

$$\text{Max. } ABN^{\gamma} N^{\alpha} K^{\beta} - (bN)N - (1 - S_K)\, rK$$

yielding the equilibrium employment level

$$N^e = [\alpha /b]^{(1-\beta)/(2-2\beta-\alpha-\gamma)}\,[AB\beta^{\beta}\, r^{-\beta}\,(1-S_K)^{-\beta}]^{1/(2-2\beta-\alpha-\gamma)} \qquad (34)$$

Again, equating this with the amount N^* produces the following expression for the optimal capital subsidy:

$$S_K = 1 - [\alpha /(\alpha+\gamma)]^{(1-\beta)/\beta} \qquad (35)$$

Finally, we take up the case of an output subsidy paying firms some factor (not necessarily less than one) of their total revenue in order to encourage dispersal. In the problem below, S_P can also be looked upon as a sales-tax concession, granted to products originating in the favoured regions:

$$\text{Max. } (1 + S_p)\, ABN^{\gamma} N^{\alpha} K^{\beta} - (bN)\, N - rK$$

yielding an equilibrium regional employment of

$$N^e = [\alpha / b]^{(1-\beta)/(2-2\beta-\alpha-\gamma)}\, [AB\beta^{\beta}\, (1+S_p)^{\beta}\, r^{-\beta}\,]^{1/(2-2\beta-\alpha-\gamma)} \qquad (36)$$

The corresponding subsidy comes out to be

$$S_p = [(\alpha+\gamma)/\alpha]^{(1-\beta)/\beta} - 1 \qquad (37)$$

We are now ready to evaluate the case for adopting either one or a combination of these three to achieve the goal of externality correction as part of a regional development strategy. In the light of the partialness of the formulation, which makes difficult the application of any general theorems on optimal taxation in externality situations, it becomes necessary to develop an evaluation criterion which can serve as a decision rule for choice of optimal instrument. We stipulate that instrument to be optimal, which entails the minimum burden to the government budget in securing the socially optimal level of employment. Thus, we are interested in comparing the total costs of the subsidies we have been considering.

The subsidy amounts payable in each case are:

Total Labour Subsidy: $S_L\, [bN^*]N^*$

Total Capital Subsidy: $S_K\, rK^*$

Total Output Subsidy: $S_p Q^*$

An obvious difficulty in doing this directly, since we have defined our subsidy rates in *ad valorem* terms, is that total subsidy amounts will be sensitive to choice of both price and quantity units. To devise a comparison methodology that is admissible within the limitations of this model, we recall that, from the first-order conditions of the social maximization problem:

$$(N^*)^2 = [\ (\alpha+\gamma)/b]\ Q^* \qquad (38)$$

$$K^* = [\beta/r]Q^* \qquad (39)$$

These enable us to reduce the various subsidy amounts to multiples of a single quantity, Q^*. Making these susbstitutions together with the expressions for S_L, S_K and S_P from (33), (35) and (37) respectively gives us:

Total Labour Subsidy: γQ^* (40)

Total Capital Subsidy: $\beta[1 - (\alpha\, /(\alpha+\gamma))^{(1-\beta)/\beta}]Q^*$ (41)

Total Output Subsidy: $[((\alpha+\gamma)/\alpha)^{(1-\beta)/\beta} - 1]Q^*$ (42)

It can be analytically shown[19] that the total subsidy coefficient is always higher in the case of output than in the case of capital, establishing the capital subsidy as a more economical device. The difference between the coefficients of the output and labour subsidies, and between those of the capital and labour subsidies cannot, in general, be signed. However, numerical solutions for each of the coefficients in expressions (40), (41) and (42) indicate that for all permissible parameter values in respect of which this exercise is meaningful, i.e., for all $\alpha > \gamma$, a labour subsidy works out to be cheaper than an output subsidy.[20] Most strikingly, the results show the capital subsidy consistently dominating labour and output subsidies as a minimum cost instrument. For plausible ranges of the parameters γ and α, say, 0.10–0.20 for the former and 0.60–0.70 for the latter, it appears to be 20–35 per cent cheaper than the labour subsidy in reaching optimal employment levels. Moreover, this cost advantage is seen[21] to increase with values of the agglomeration elasticity.

This result is noteworthy. It presents an instance of optimal intervention not directly in the externality-generating market but through a related one. The inferior cost-effectiveness of the labour subsidy is at least partly due to the relatively inelastic supply to the region of that input. For equal levels of subsidization, equilibrium employment is likely to be lower with the labour subsidy than with the capital subsidy. The former thus entails a larger discrepancy between private and socially optimal sizes, and is consequently more expensive to finance.

Clearly, the result is contingent upon the nature of substitution possibilities between capital and labour. Our use of the Cobb–Douglas functional specification ensured the feature of a unitary elasticity of substitution. It is likely that with a production technology permitting higher substitutability between the two inputs, the capital subsidy could lose its dominance, as effecting the requisite increase in labour employed comes to entail higher opportunity costs for the firm.

The case for advisability of the use of one kind of subsidy over another thus ultimately rests with the degree of applicability in any particular context of the assumptions discussed. The foregoing analysis is merely indicative of what policy rankings different presumptions might produce. Of course, any decision that appeals to realism must also take into account alternative costs of administering these various instruments.[22] Finally, implicit throughout the comparisons is the assumption that the collection of revenue necessary to finance subsidization entails no distortions.

NOTES

The author would like to acknowledge the guidance of Edwin S. Mills, Princeton University, in the research underlying this work, and the many helpful comments of Oded Stark, Harvard University, in the preparation of this paper.

1 See, for example, the model in Henderson (1982).

2 All studies cited below adopt a measurement methodology involving the cross-sectional estimation of Hicks-neutral shift factors on production functions for manufacturing industry. The hypothesis tested is that these factors vary systematically and significantly with city size or some appropriate measure of regional economic activity.

3 Programmes to this end are currently in effect in Brazil, India and a number of other developing nations. They have long been in operation for economically depressed regions within quite a few industrially advanced countries, particularly in Europe.

4 It is implicit throughout the analysis that either all such regional production takes place in a single urban area, or that the benefits of agglomeration impinge on traded good production through the total volume of manufacturing employment within the region.

5 The matrix $\begin{bmatrix} F_{NN} & F_{NK} \\ F_{KN} & F_{KK} \end{bmatrix}$ is negative definite.

6 It may be remarked that the Harris–Todaro tradition is not inconsistent with spatial (expected) utility equalization. Indeed, the introduction of a two-tier urban labour market structure into the analysis might yield interesting results. It is proposed to proceed along such lines in a forthcoming paper.

7 These quantities are aggregations over identical firms' profit-maximizing factor demands. Note that N^e, on total urban employment (which is also city size), in its role as an argument of the G ( ) function, is parametric to individual firms.

8 Since $w' = 0$, stability requires that all equilibria take place in the downward-sloping segment of this curve.

It is obvious that, were $w' > 0$, equilibrium city size would be smaller than in the present instance. In fact, such a specification will generally have the effect of rendering all the equilibrium (and optimum) employment magnitudes with which we are dealing, smaller.

9 Note that this result is not guaranteed if disamenity effects of city size impinge on residents' welfare, and there is an element of congestion inherent in them which migrants, in taking the wage function as parametric, fail to see themselves as contributing to. This makes equilibrium city size superoptimal from their point of view. There is, then, in addition to the positive

externality of private production, a corresponding negative externality on the consumption side, and one cannot *a priori* ensure that internalization will cause the two effects to net out so as to produce $N^* > N^e$.

10 Note that what is needed is not just a general psychic aversion to moving, but an aproportional distribution of region-specific location preference across the various regions of a country. In our two-region formulation, we find it inappropriate to posit such a preference structure, carrying as it does the unrealistic implication of a distribution of people with tastes for 'backward' or advanced areas. [See, however, Serck-Hanssen (1975) for a probabilistic model that does this.]

11 In a model of this type, we can justify the desirability of employment generation only under rural underemployment considerations, since utility levels remain the same upon the sectoral and spatial shifts. A study of the distribution of the total utility gain consequent upon the externality-correction measures that we will be discussing can be undertaken only in the context of a more general formulation than this.

12 We note that the neutral representation of the contribution of infrastructure somewhat restricts the kinds of productive interactions it may be permitted to have with other inputs. In particular, it does not enable us to go into the interesting question of the extent of substitutability between private and public capital.

13 This presumption is reasonable, in that it seems unlikely that gains in urban productive advantage will be sustained indefinitely without eventually running into constraints dictated, among other things, by shortage of actual space. This does not, of course, necessarily imply that technological diseconomies have set in at that stage—G' may be positive and falling.

14 See Ashcroft and Taylor (1977), Buck and Atkins (1976a), or Moore and Rhodes (1976), op. cit.

15 See Buck and Atkins (1976b), McDermott (1977), and Swales (1981), op. cit., in this context.

16 The purpose behind the constant returns formulation is to establish a conceptual equivalence between the new location of a firm in the region and expansion in an existing one. In pure terms, this is a correct way to handle regional development through employment dispersal, there being no theoretical reason to discriminate between the two cases for the nature of the problem that we are studying.

17 The various possible justifications for this presumption have been mentioned earlier. To these we may add the caveat that in modelling potential migrants as having utility to depend solely on wage, we abstract from other considerations, such as risk preferences, relative deprivation avoidance, etc., that have been documented as entering the migration decision.

We might point out, also, that the upward-sloping property of the wage relationship serves to make urban/industrial employment within the region finite, even in the face of the indefinitely increasing external economies that we have posited in the agglomeration specification.

18 The compatibility of perfect competition with increasing returns to scale

when the latter are due to external economies that are parametric was demonstrated by Chipman (1970).

19 Output Coefficient — Capital Coefficient

$= [((\alpha+\gamma)/\alpha)^{(1-\beta)/\beta} - 1] - \beta[1-(\alpha/(\alpha+\gamma))^{(1-\beta)/\beta}]$

$= [d^e-1] - \beta[1-(1/d)^e]$, where $d = (\alpha+\gamma)/\alpha > 1$,

and $e = (1-\beta)/\beta > 0$,

$= [d^e - 1]\,[d^e - \beta]/d^e$

> 0, since $d^e > 1 > \beta$

20 Full results of the simulations are presented in Shukla (1988), Appendix C.

21 We differentiate the difference, D, with respect to γ:

$D = \gamma - \beta[1-(\alpha/(\alpha+\gamma))^{(1-\beta)/\beta}]$

Therefore, $dD/d\gamma = 1 - [(\alpha/(\alpha+\gamma))^{1/\beta}] > 0$,

since the expression in brackets is less than one.

22 Significantly, some factual corroboration for the efficacy of the capital subsidy over the labour subsidy in securing dispersal is found in a survey undertaken by Redwood (1982) in the course of a World Bank study investigating the characteristics of industrial establishments receiving fiscal incentives in Brazil. Of the entrepreneurs availing themselves of the incentives, only 8 per cent reported that they would have adopted more labour-intensive technologies had a labour subsidy been instituted, and only 4 per cent said they would have selected other, more labour-intensive sectors.

REFERENCES

Ashcroft, Brian and Jim Taylor (1977), 'The Movement of Manufacturing Industry and the Effect of Regional Policy', *Oxford Economic Papers*.

Buck, T. W. and M. H. Atkins (1976), 'The Impact of British Regional Policies on Employment Growth', *Oxford Economic Papers*.

——— (1976), 'Capital Subsidies and Unemployed Labour: A Regional Production Function Approach', *Regional Studies*, Vol. 10.

Chipman, John S. (1970), 'External Economies of Scale and Competitive Equilibrium', *Quarterly Journal of Economics*, Vol. LXXXIV, No. 3.

Henderson, J. Vernon (1982), 'The Impact of Government Policies on Urban Concentration', *Journal of Urban Economics*, Vol. 12, No. 3.

——— (1983), 'Efficiency of Resource Usage and City Size', Brown University Working Paper.

McDermott, Phillip J. (1977), 'Capital Subsidies and Unemployed Labour: A Comment on the Regional Production Function Approach', *Regional Studies*, Vol. 11.

Moore, Barry and John Rhodes (1976), 'Regional Economic Policy and the Movement of Manufacturing Firms to Development Areas', *Economica*.

Redwood, John (1982), 'Industrialization Policy, Fiscal Incentives and Extra-regional Establishments in Northeast Brazil: A Characterization Based on the SUDENE/BNB Survey', World Bank WUD Discussion Paper No. 16.

Segal, David (1976), 'Are There Returns to Scale in City Size?' *The Review of Economics and Statistics*, Vol. LVIII.

Serck-Hanssen, Jan (1975), 'Optimal Labour Subsidies in Backward Regions with Surplus Supply of Labour', *Swedish Journal of Economics.*

Shukla, Vibhooti (1988), *Urban Development and Regional Policy in India: An Econometric Analysis*, Himalaya Publications, Bombay.

Sveikauskas, Leo (1975), 'The Productivity of Cities', *Quarterly Journal of Economics*, Vol. LXXXIX.

Swales, J. K. (1981), 'The Employment Effects of a Regional Spatial Subsidy', *Regional Studies*, Vol. 15, No. 4.

2 / Sources of Urban Productivity and City Sizes: An Empirical Exercise

VIBHOOTI SHUKLA

Our empirical work is divided into three parts. In the first, we attempt direct estimation of firm production functions augmented by an urban size-shift factor intended to capture the agglomeration influence. The second part examines some microfoundational issues, as well as evidence for the existence of a wage–size relationship reflecting possible cost of living and disamenity effects of large city size. In the third part, we attempt to test the 'localization hypothesis', and to arrive at some idea of the sources of the urban productivity advantage in the Indian context, as suggested by our estimations.

I. The Evidence for Agglomeration Economies

Data and Estimation Issues

In this section, we conduct estimations, on the Indian data, of specific variants of the general form

$$Q = G(N)\,F(L, K) \tag{1}$$

where $F(L, K)$ is a constant returns to scale production function with Q, L, K, denoting respectively output, labour and capital, and $G(N)$ being a general shift function with N standing for city size (usually proxied by total city employment, but occasionally also proxied by total city population, the context usually making clear which concept is being used). The aim is to ascertain the existence, strength and incidence of the economies of agglomeration hypothesized to characterize the urban productive environment in a developing country such as India. While the precise estimating forms and methodology will be spelled out in detail in the next few sections, it is perhaps in order here to briefly reiterate the basic postulates that underlie this endeavour. In the tradition of the received literature (see Ahmad 1965; FICCI 1977; Kashyap 1979; Carlino 1979; Stanford Research Institute 1983; Mohan and Acharya 1983); the present article also places a *technological* interpretation on the urban agglomerative advantage. This interpretation ties in neatly with the manner in which the theory has been formulated. It is a logical implication of this presumption that the estimation of some sort of production function constitutes an appropriate econometric approach to the problem. Further, and again consistent with theory, we have stipulated that this productive influence is neutral or external, representable through the parameters of the function, $G(\cdot)$. Lastly, we assume that it is capturable by a summary measure of total urban activity, the empirical counterpart to the scale variable, N.

The agglomeration estimations of this section and the wage analysis of the next are carried out on an industry-wise basis with firm-level production data drawn from financial statements of (single-plant, single-product) companies all over India with sales exceeding Rs 50 million, compiled by the Centre for Monitoring Indian Economy (CMIE).[1] These data are over the period 1975–80. They are used in conjunction with the corresponding regional data of comparable vintage on demographic variables assumed to summarize the agglomerative benefits of the firms' locations. The variables chosen for this purpose are total population of the urban area of a firm's location, information on which is obtained from the 1981 Census;[2] and, as an alternate measure, the 1976 figure for the number of factory workers for every 100,000 of the population of its district.[3] The ranges, means and deviations of the urban and regional variables for this dataset are presented, industry-wise, in Table I of Appendix A.

There are three major advantages to working with firm-level data in any empirical study of agglomeration economies. One, these are superior to aggregate data for recovering parameters of production technology. Secondly, one important concern may be uncovering sources of the economies a producing unit enjoys at its location. A firm may be subject to urbanization economies, i.e., economies of pure urban scale, industry-size-in-city, i.e., localization economies, or the conventional internal scale economies. A high level of regional disaggregation in the production data chosen to work with opens up the possibility of making inferences about the relative importance of each of these. Clearly, production functions of entire urban economies cannot separately measure agglomeration economies 'below' the level of urbanization. Disaggregating to industry groups within cities makes possible the sorting of the influences of industry size at a location, as well as that of overall city size — in addition to urbanization, localization effects can be studied. *Industrial* disaggregation is desirable even for the study of overall agglomeration influences; to attempt to gauge, as we shall, how far different productive activities

Table 1: Digit NIC Industry Codes

Industry Code	*Description*
20	Manufacture of food products
22	Manufacture of beverages, tobacco and tobacco products
23	Manufacture of cotton textiles
24	Manufacture of wool, silk and synthetic fibre textiles
27	Manufacture of wood and wood products, furniture and fixtures
28	Manufacture of paper and paper products; printing; publishing and allied industries
30	Manufacture of rubber, plastic, petroleum and coal products
31	Manufacture of chemicals and chemical products (except products of petroleum and coal)
32	Manufacture of non-metallic mineral products
33	Basic metals and alloys industries
34	Manufacture of metal products and parts, except machinery and transport equipment
35	Manufacture of machinery, machine tools and parts, except electrical machinery
36	Manufacture of electrical machinery, apparatus, appliances, supplies and parts
37	Manufacture of transport equipment and parts
40	Electricity
97	Repair

Sources: Central Statistical Organisation (1982), *Annual Survey of Industries 1978-79, Summary Results for the Factory Sector*, Ministry of Planning, New Delhi.

Table 2: Agglomeration Elasticity Estimates—I

Industry	*Form*	*Obs*	*b*		R^2
Industry 23:	C-D	286	0.0497*	(3.38)	0.7334
Cotton	CES	286	0.0554*	(3.78)	0.5108
Textiles	Flex	285	0.0382*	(2.63)	0.4764
Industry 31:	C-D	80	0.0896‡	(1.73)	0.3956
Chemicals	CES	80	0.0887‡	(1.71)	0.4891
	Flex	76	0.1291‡	(2.77)	0.3348
Industry 33:	C-D	12	0.1508	(1.61)	0.8105
Metals and	CES	12	0.1889†	(2.54)	0.8409
Alloys	Flex	12	0.1040	(1.29)	0.7071
Industry 35:	C-D	53	0.0500	(0.88)	0.5908
Non-Electrical	CES	53	0.0993	(1.61)	0.5972
Machinery	Flex	53	0.0730	(0.86)	0.2085
Industry 36:	C-D	31	0.1006*	(3.08)	0.9241
Electrical	CES	31	0.0767‡	(1.75)	0.7328
Machinery	Flex	30	0.0685	(1.56)	0.7229

* Estimate significant at 1 per cent level. † Estimate significant at 5 per cent level. ‡ Estimate significant at 10 per cent level.

Note: Figures in brackets represent *t*-statistics of associated estimates.

might avail these benefits to differing degrees. Finally, working with firm data affords the maximal opportunities for sorting — not only permitting classification between the two categories of source just mentioned, but also enabling one to ascertain the extent to which measured economies are those of internal scale.

Thirdly, firm-specific analysis also represents the best choice of the level of disaggregation in respect of ensuring econometric exogeneity. It becomes more plausible in this case to consider all locational characteristic variables — city size or industry size in a region — as parametric from the point of view of the firm. This avoids the problem of simultaneity in estimation that might arise from using regionally aggregated data, raising a causal ambiguity in interpretation of the chicken-and-egg type: Is a city productive because the firms located there are productive, or do firms locate there because the city is productive? Although the aggregative model that serves as our paradigm does not posit the explicit choice of city size or any other locational characteristic by firms, its microfoundations must recognize at least implicitly the choice by individual firms, if not of city size *per se*, then of the factors contributing to productivity of economic resources that go with a large urban location.[4]

Constant Elasticity Estimates (CES)

The Agglomeration and Production Specifications

Our initial specification for the agglomeration factor is

$$G(N) = BN^b \tag{2}$$

the parameter of interest being b, defined as the *agglomeration elasticity*. Written in natural logarithmic terms, the relationship becomes

$$\ln G(N) = \ln B + b \ln N \tag{3}$$

whence it becomes apparent that $d \ln G(N)/d \ln N = b$

Thus, in this specification, the expression for the elasticity of output with respect to city size is assumed to be independent of N, and equal to the constant b over all ranges of city size.

An estimate of b significantly different from zero is construed as evidence of the presence of agglomeration economies in the conduct of the relevant economic activity, and its magnitude as an index of the strength of that influence. We expect our empirical work to yield sizeable and significant values of the agglomeration elasticity for each of the industry groups for which estimation is performed.

$F(L, K)$ represents the general internal production function that is postulated to be common to all firms within an industry, regardless of location. Q represents total firm output; L and K are its employment of its labour and capital inputs respectively. Q is approximated in the data by value added, L by total employment in workers, and K by the net value of the firms' fixed assets. For the firms' internal technology, we experiment with three different production specifications in this section. While each one, admittedly, entails a particular restrictiveness,[5] it is believed that relative insensitivity of results to functional form, if demonstrable, might constitute a more convincing argument in favour of the persistence and strength of the agglomeration relationship.

As our first form, we use a Cobb–Douglas (C-D)[6] production function:

$$F(L, K) = AL^{\alpha}K^{\beta} \tag{4}$$

which, augmented with the agglomeration specification (equation 2) above, is estimated in its log-linear form as:

$$\ln Q = \ln(AB) + b\ln N + \alpha \ln L + \beta \ln K \tag{5}$$

Our second form is a function of the CES form,

$$F(L, K) = A[\delta L^{-\rho} + (1 - \delta)\, K^{-\rho}]^{-\mu/\rho} \tag{6}$$

linearized in logarithms via an approximation method due to Kmenta (1967)[7] to yield the following estimating equation:

$$\ln (Q/L) = \ln (AB) + b\ln N + (\mu - 1) \ln L + \mu\,(1 - \delta) \ln (K/L) - [\rho\mu\delta\,(1 - \delta)/2]\,[\ln (K/L]^2 \tag{7}$$

Finally, we estimate a trans-log flexible function linearized about $k = K/L = 1$, of the form:[8]

$$\ln Q = \ln A + \ln \beta + b\ln N + \alpha \ln(K/L) + \beta/2\,[\ln(K/L)]^2 \tag{8}$$

with A, b, α and β as parameters.

We now proceed to describe the results of the foregoing sets of estimations.

Results

Direct estimations under each of the three production functional forms were carried out by the linear least squares procedure for five industrial groups at the two-digit level for which sample size was sufficiently large. Table 1 provides a key to a description of activities corresponding to the codes for which results will be reported in this article. Table 2 reports regression estimates[9] obtained for the agglomeration elasticity parameter that is the principal focus of our interest. Also presented are values of R^2

for each estimating equation. In general, the results are seen to display strikingly high and often statistically significant values for estimated b. Estimates under each industry head prove sufficiently robust with respect to functional form, further testifying to the widespread prevalence of agglomeration economies in the Indian urban productive environment.

The estimates range from approximately 0.04 for Cotton Textiles to approximately 0.19 for Basic Metals and Alloys. This gives an average elasticity estimate over the industries for which regressions were run in the vicinity of 0.09. It must be remarked that these estimates are considerably higher than those obtained in the US urban context— Sveikauskas (1975) reported estimated agglomeration elasticities of about 0.06, and Segal (1976), the slightly higher figure of 0.08. It may also be recalled that this was expected, for in developing countries, proximity serves as a substitute for communication by more sophisticated means and as a risk and informational buffer in the face of imperfect markets.

One way to grasp the full import of these findings is as follows: They suggest that, roughly speaking, an increase of about 9 per cent in factor

Table 3: Agglomeration Elasticity Estimates—II

Industry	*Form*	*Obs*	*b*		R^2
Industry 23:	C-D	286	0.0847*	(3.98)	0.7374
Cotton	CES	286	0.0987*	(4.64)	0.5225
Textiles	Flex	285	0.0828*	(3.83)	0.4903
Industry 31:	C-D	80	0.2276†	(2.12)	0.4072
Chemicals	CES	80	0.2357†	(2.19)	0.5012
	Flex	76	0.3653*	(4.15)	0.4066
Industry 33:	C-D	12	0.2936	(1.24)	0.7872
Metals and	CES	12	0.4717†	(2.54)	0.8413
Alloys	Flex	12	0.1783	(0.95)	0.6786
Industry 35:	C-D	53	0.2607‡	(1.76)	0.6095
Non-Electrical	CES	53	0.2420	(1.62)	0.5975
Machinery	Flex	53	0.5305*	(2.94)	0.3189
Industry 36:	C-D	31	0.2060*	(3.94)	0.9352
Electrical	CES	31	0.1898*	(2.68)	0.7667
Machinery	Flex	30	0.1921*	(2.73)	0.7656

*Estimate significant at 1 per cent level. † Estimate significant at 5 per cent level. ‡ Estimate significant at 10 per cent level.

Note: Figures in brackets represent *t*-statistics of associated estimates.

productivity is achievable with every doubling of city size. Put another way, resources in a Class I city of population 100,000 can be, on an average, 23 per cent more productive than in a Class IV city of population 10,000. They can be as much as 51 per cent more productive in a city of one million than in a city of 10,000.[10]

A set of estimations identical to the foregoing (which used total city population as the urban scale variable) was performed with factory employment per 100,000 district population representing the empirical counterpart to the *N* of the estimating equations. The results are presented in Table 3. We note that the earlier ranking, across industries, of parameter magnitudes is preserved, as is evidence of consistency between estimates from the three equation types. Also observed is the fact that these elasticity estimates are almost uniformly higher than those from estimations with city population as the external scale parameter. We shall return to this point in our discussion of the results of the localization investigations in Section III of this article.

Variable-Elasticity Estimates

An Alternative Agglomeration Specification

Though the specification of the function $G(N)$ we have been using, viz., $G(N) = BN^b$ (2), has proved successful, it is unduly restrictive. In its most common empirically validated case, viz., that of $b < 1$, it represents the agglomeration effect as increasing with city size, albeit at a decreasing rate, but never actually declining to display production diseconomies at some range of city sizes. Figure 1(A) illustrates this point.

Yet, often enough, the allegation is made, both in policy-making and in popular cirlces, of 'excessive' city size, with the insinuation that certain urban areas have reached proportions which render economic activity there counterproductive. This kind of argument tends to appeal to the notion that there is an 'optimal' size of urban area, dictated by purely technological considerations. One such hypothesized relationship is depicted in Figure 1(B).

While commonsense suggests that there must be some size beyond which an urban area manifestly becomes unviable, the appropriate question to ask is whether existing metropolitan areas, especially those that are allegedly 'too big', or urban size classes which prompt similar concern can be empirically demonstrated to fall within the range where city productivity is visibly declining. Thus, if such is indeed the case in the Indian context, we need a specification that will permit indication by the data

Figure 1: Productivity Gains From Urban Size

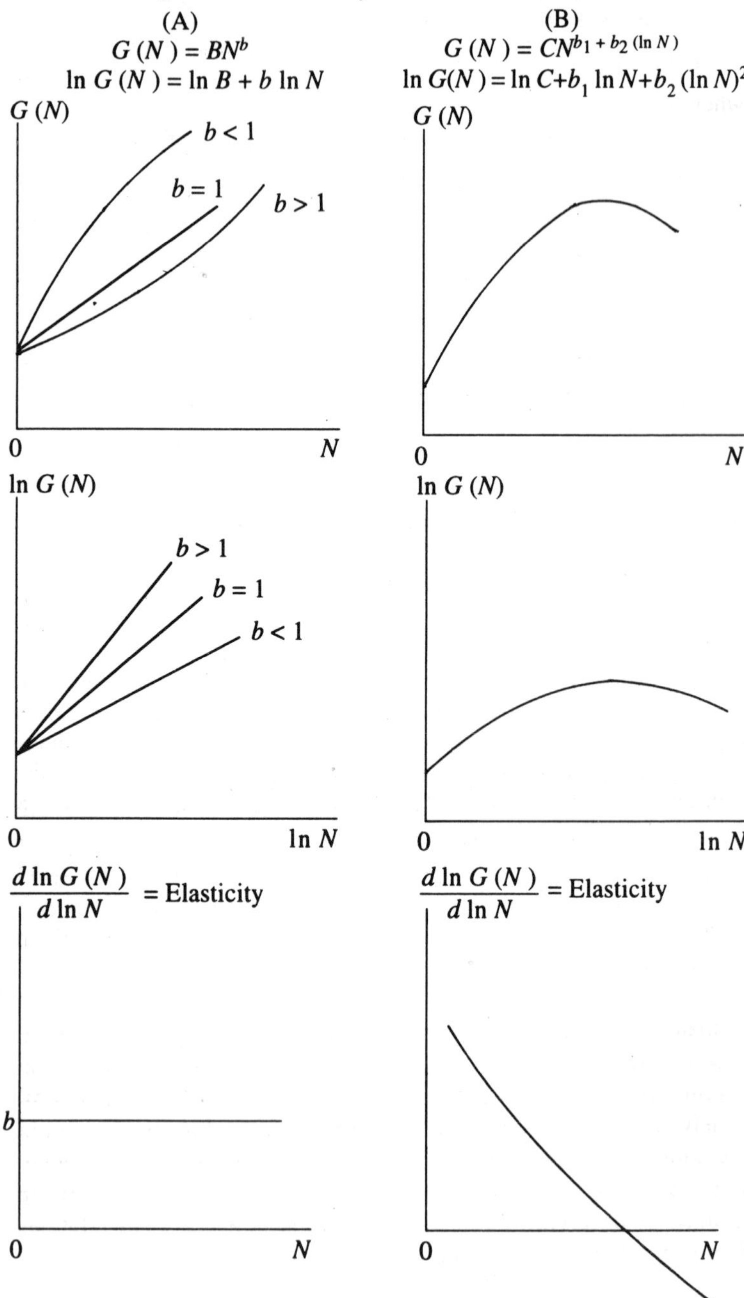

to that effect. Accordingly, in this section, we repeat our previous exercises with an estimating agglomeration specification of the form:

$$\ln G(N) = \ln C + b_1 \ln N + b_2(\ln N)^2 \tag{9}$$

where C, b_1 and b_2 are parameters.

Compatible with an expression for the function $G(N)$ of the form

$$G(N) = CN^{b_1 + b_2(\ln N)} \text{ (with } C \text{ as constant)} \tag{10}$$

the specification implies an agglomeration elasticity, $b_1 + 2b_2(\ln N)$, that varies with city size.

'Optimality' can be interpreted in terms of its parameters by differentiating $\ln G(N)$ with respect to city size to yield:[11]

$$\ln N = -b_1 / 2b_2 \tag{11}$$

or, equivalently,

$$N = e^{b_1/2b_2} \tag{12}$$

This expression represents the technologically optimal size of city. We shall, as an experiment, evaluate equation (12) for estimated parameter values. We turn next to the results of the new estimations.

Results

Estimated parameters and associated values of R^2 for each of the three production specifications and five industries when N represents total city population are presented in Table 4. Although registering high levels of R^2, the coefficients conform to the cannonical inverted-U shape for only two of five industries. Thus, it is possible to carry out the 'optimal' size calculations only for industries 33 and 36, for which maxima are defined. In respect of the former, the figure for this varies over the range of city size 4 million to one of 25 million, and in respect of the latter, from 1.5 million to 239 million, depending on which set of estimates is employed. By such a reckoning, either many of India's bigger cities are oversized, or all of them are suboptimal!

The fact of the matter is that the high element of randomness in the estimates, coupled with the extreme sensitivity of the specification to these variations renders computations of the above kind unreliable to an extreme degree. For our purpose in conducting this empirical test, namely, that of ascertaining whether or not existing Indian cities fall in size ranges associated with a reversal of the urban agglomerative advantage, a more comprehensive and meaningful picture may be obtained by observing where exactly they lie in terms of the relationships suggested by the estimations.

To do this, we graph the estimated ln$G(N)$ function against city size, $N \times 10^5$, for each of the five industries.[12] The estimates of b_1 and b_2 that parameterize the curves in Figure 2 are taken from the Cobb–Douglas estimations (equation 5) in each industry case. The solid vertical line delimits the largest sample value of N, and the broken one, the sample mean for city size. Crosses indicate the means characterizing the sample for the various industry-classes.

It is observed that firms in four of the five industries are located in cities of sample average size below the estimated 'optimum' for that industry. Likewise, the overall sample mean occurs in the rising portion of all but one of the curves. The exception is Industry 36, the Manufacturer of Electrical Machinery. (Yet, recall, estimates using the flexible-form production specification for this industry imply an optimum as high as 239 million.) Thus, the dominant message seems to be that Indian cities have yet to grow to sizes where manufacturing diseconomies are discernible. In this light, it is unlikely that arguments for the restriction of economic activity there on grounds of technological disadvantage are substantiable.

Table 4: Variable-Elasticity Agglomeration Estimates

Industry	*Form*	*Obs*	b_1		b_2		R^2
Industry 23:	C-D	285	0.0062	(0.16)	0.0109	(1.27)	0.7342
Cotton	CES	285	0.0036	(0.10)	0.0130	(1.53)	0.5134
Textiles	Flex	285	–0.0014	(–0.04)	0.0098	(1.12)	0.4788
Industry 31:	C-D	76	–0.0086	(–0.17)	0.0246†	(2.04)	0.6596
Chemicals	CES	76	–0.0018	(–0.04)	0.0223‡	(1.73)	0.6783
	Flex	76	–0.0270	(–0.39)	0.0490*	(2.94)	0.4079
Industry 33:	C-D	12	0.3961	(1.21)	–0.0537	(–0.82)	0.8297
Metals and	CES	12	0.1522	(0.53)	0.0084	(0.13)	0.8415
Alloys	Flex	12	0.1764	(0.50)	–0.0160	(–0.21)	0.7092
Industry 35:	C-D	53	0.0479	(0.51)	0.0009	(0.03)	0.5908
Non-Electrical	CES	53	–0.0003	(0.00)	0.0575	(1.45)	0.6149
Machinery	Flex	53	–0.1117	(–0.91)	0.1079†	(2.05)	0.2732
Industry 36:	C-D	30	0.2067*	(3.00)	–0.0347‡	(–1.73)	0.9402
Electrical	CES	30	0.3179†	(2.36)	–0.0578‡	(–1.85)	0.7986
Machinery	Flex	30	0.0918	(0.73)	–0.0059	(–0.20)	0.7233

* Estimate significant at 1 per cent level. † Estimate significant at 5 per cent level. ‡ Estimate significant at 10 per cent level.

Note: Figures in brackets represent *t*-statistics of associated estimates.

Figure 2: Variable-Elasticity Results

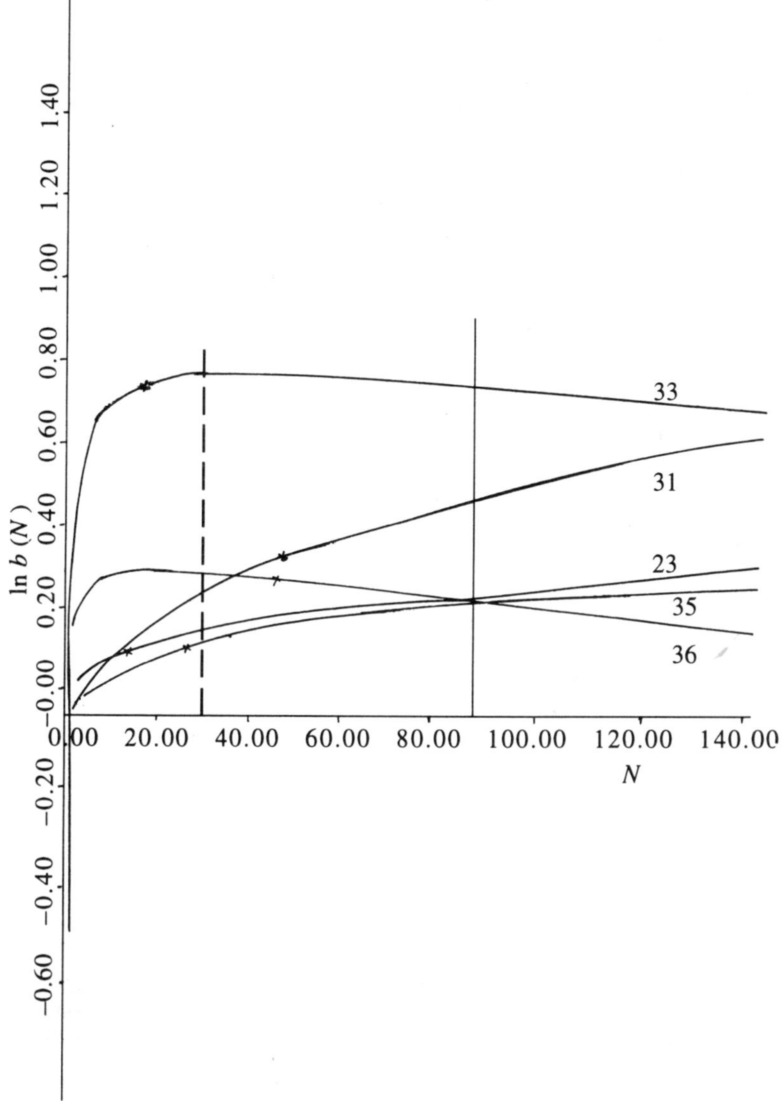

II. Indirect Estimation and the City Size–Wage Relationship

Some Econometric and Microeconomic Issues

In this section, we highlight some of the issues in the indirect estimation, i.e., estimation through first-order conditions, of the agglomeration elasticity. In so doing, we hope to gain insights into the nature of the private maximization problem underlying the aggregative formulation of urban growth (see Shukla 1988, Chapter 2). As always, such estimation carries with it, in the form of maintained hypotheses, the postulates of profit maximization and perfect competition. But, in addition to these routine assumptions about firm behaviour and the institutional environment it operates in, the problem here is seen to involve critical issues regarding the microfoundations of urban growth theory.

First, we consider a difficulty in the estimation of the parameters of the agglomeration, and indeed, the production specifications through what we have termed indirect methods. Sveikauskas (1974) initially drew attention to the problem, which he characterized in general as that of the correlation in regionally aggregated data between Hicks-neutral productivity and wages, in the cross-sectional estimation of a CES production function through the first-order labour condition for profit maximization. In general, profit maximization with a function of the type:

$$Q = G(\cdot)\,[\delta K^{-\rho} + (1-\delta)\,L^{-\rho}]^{-1/\rho} \text{ [with } G(\cdot) \text{ as in equation (2)]} \quad (13)$$

yields the following first-order condition (FOC) for labour as an estimating equation:

$$\ln(Q/L) = -\sigma\ln(1-\delta) + (1-\sigma)\ln G(\cdot) + \sigma\ln W \quad (14)$$

where $\sigma = 1/(1-\rho)$, and the empirical counterpart of W is the observed regional wage. Then, any correlation of $G(\cdot)$, or Hicks-neutral productivity, with wage will bias the estimate of σ. Correlation in regional data between productivity and wages can arise from many sources, such as greater literacy rate or higher incidence of skilled jobs in the high-wage areas. Since the primary interest here is in city size as the major determinant of regional productivity, our concern must be with the correlation between wage and city size that might potentially bias estimates from cross-sectional regressions.

The nature of the bias may be demonstrated as follows:[13] If $G(N) = BN^b$ (see equation 2) as before, and

$$W = wN^{j}; \quad j > 0 \quad (15)$$

(where W is the wage rate and w and j are parameters) then, instead of

$$\ln(Q/L) = -\sigma(1-\sigma) + (1-\sigma)\ln B + (1-\sigma)b\ln N + \sigma\ln W \quad (16)$$

where the wage relationship (see equation 15) is disregarded and the 'true' estimating equation becomes:

$$\ln(Q/L) = -\sigma(1-\delta) + (1-\sigma)\ln B + [(1-\sigma)b+\sigma+j]\ln N + \sigma \ln w \quad (17)$$

It is easily seen that using equation (16) to estimate parameter b biases the regression estimate upwards.

Yet another issue that comes up even in the context of firm-level estimation was posed in the following way by Moomaw (1981). He contends that a simultaneity problem in the estimation of the agglomeration parameter through the first-order condition for labour arises in the light of the nature of optimizing behaviour by the individual firm, which he postulates as explicitly choosing city size.

The essence of Moomaw's hypothesis is that, in a decision problem such as:

$$\text{Max. } G(N)F(L, K) - W(N)L - rK \quad (18)$$

(with the same notations as earlier)

the entrepreneur selects L, K and N to yield the following first-order conditions

$$G(N)F_L - W(N) = 0 \quad (19)$$

$$G(N)F_K - \text{r} = 0 \quad (20)$$

$$G'(N)F(L, K) - W'(N)L = 0 \quad (21)$$

A point he makes is that then, under the standard CES formulation coupled with the original agglomeration specification and wage relation of the form

$$W = CN^j \quad (22)$$

the first-order conditions for labour and city size, equations (19) and (21), both respectively reduce to the same estimating equation in $\ln N$:

$$\ln(Q/L) = \text{constant} + [(1-\sigma)b+\sigma j]\ln N \quad (23)$$

$$\ln(Q/L) = \text{constant} + j\ln N \quad (24)$$

making the two indistinguishable, and consequently, the unscrambling of the parameters impossible.

However, Moomaw's hypothesis itself is testable. As he demonstrates, conditions (19) and (21) above can be combined and written as:

$$G'(N)/G(N) = [W'(N)/(W)(N)]\,[W(N)L/Q] \quad (25)$$

which, for the specified forms, is further shown to reduce to

$$b = j\,[\text{labour's share}]. \quad (26)$$

In the next section, we conduct a few exercises to determine which of these considerations are of importance in the Indian context.

The Estimation Plan

Since the data we work with are at the level of individual firms, it seems reasonable to expect that estimating a first-order condition such as:

$\ln(Q/L) = -\sigma(1-\delta) + (1-\sigma)\ln B + (1-\sigma)b\ln N + \sigma\ln W$ (see equation 16)

can yield unbiased estimates of the true agglomeration parameter *unless* the Moomaw hypothesis regarding explicit city size choice holds in the Indian context. Provided the hypothesis is false, and the maintained hypotheses of profit maximization and perfect competition hold to a reasonable approximation, we should expect to recover parameter estimates for b that more or less tally with the direct agglomeration elasticity estimates of Table 2.

If, on the other hand, the hypothesis is true, then an estimation of the 'Moomaw' first-order equation,

$$\ln(Q/L) = \text{constant} + [(1-\sigma)b + \sigma j]\ln N \qquad (23)$$

should yield estimates for the coefficient of $\ln N$ that are no different from those of the earlier 'ordinary', first-order condition for labour given by equation (16).

Finally, recall, we have one more direct means of testing the applicability of the Moomaw hypothesis to India, viz., the condition,

$$b = j. \text{ [labour's share].} \qquad (26)$$

This implies that the true agglomeration elasticity estimates must equal those of the elasticity of *wage* with respect to city size, i.e., j times the share of labour. As a preliminary to performing this 'test', we require estimates of the parameter j. Accordingly, it becomes necessary to estimate a relationship such as (see equation 22):

$W = CN^j$ (with c and j parameters)

estimable as

$$\ln W = \ln C + j\ln N \qquad (27)$$

It is in order here to spend some time discussing the theoretical justification behind the possible existence of such a wage relationship. The most common interpretation is that the observed wage, W, depends positively on city size due to cost of living or disamenity considerations. We have shown in an earlier work that long-run spatial equilibrium implied a regionally equalized utility level that could, nevertheless, be consistent with a wage variable with city size (Shukla 1988, Chapter 2). In that model, the supply side relationships are collapsible in equilibrium to yield a general formulation of the form:

$$V_0 = V(W, P, N) \qquad (28)$$

where V_0 represents the spatially constant utility level, W the wage (entering positively), P particularly, the price of urban housing, but more generally, an index of the cost of living (entering negatively), and N, city size, entering negatively as an urban disamenity influence. From this, it is clear that if cost of living increases with size of city, as is eminently plausible, then, with increasing N, money wage must rise to maintain V_0. In addition, if disamenity is an important consideration, then real wage must likewise rise with N.

A number of studies[14] have sought to infer evidence regarding urban cost of living and disamenity effects by estimating a relationship between wages and city sizes. Often, the presumption that wages in fact decrease at an increasing rate with size of city is also put to test. The above are capturable in an estimating specification of the form:

$$\ln W = \ln C + j_1 N + j_2 N^2 \qquad (29)$$

with the coefficients expected to show positive signs. This specification also yields the following expression for the elasticity of wage with respect to city size:

$$d\ln W/d\ln N = j_1 N + 2j_2 N^2 \qquad (30)$$

In the light of the discussion above, we estimate, in turn, the first-order condition for labour in the absence of the Moomaw considerations, the Moomaw condition, and the two specifications of the wage relationship. All estimations are performed on the same data set as in the previous section, through ordinary least squares, and for each of the five industries 23, 31, 33, 35 and 36. The results are described in what follows.

Results

The results of the estimations are presented in Table 5. Comparing the coefficients of the variable $\ln N$ from the standard first-order condition for labour, equation (16), with those from condition (23) implied by Moomaw's hypothesis, we observe that they differ considerably, except, notably, in the one case (Industry 36) for which wage does not vary appreciably with city size. This fact seems to indicate lack of support for the Moomaw hypothesis, which implies that this coefficient should absorb most of the intercity variation in wages. The estimates of the agglomeration elasticity calculated from the labour condition do, however, display values that are higher than the ones obtained from the direct CES estimation of the previous section in three of the five cases.[15] No upward bias attributable to the contribution of the wage parameter, though, is evident.

Figure 3: The Estimated Wage Relationship

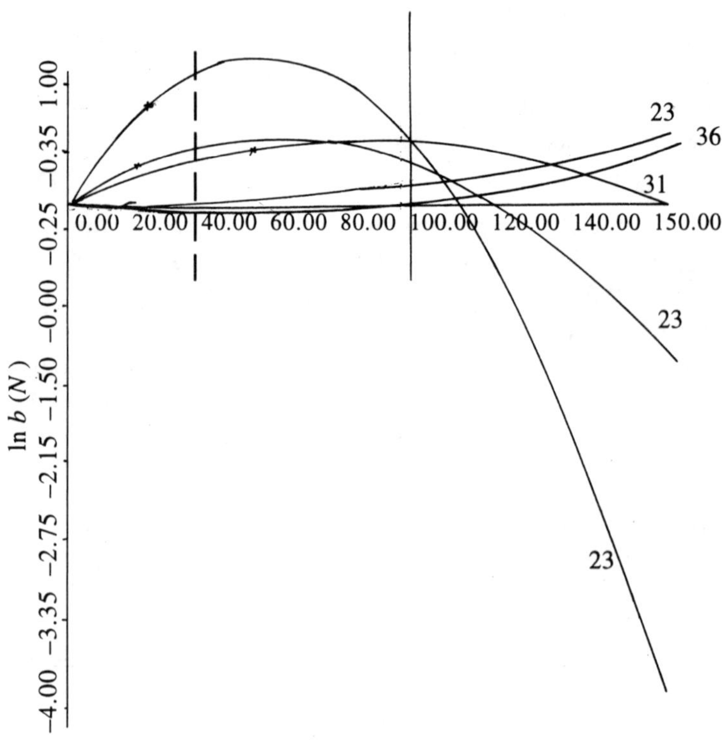

Estimates for wage elasticity, *j*, in equation (27) are statistically significant in most cases, and appear plausible. Estimated elasticity for the overall sample was found to be about 0.08, a figure fairly consistent with the results of similar estimations with US data. If this estimate is taken as reflecting a cost of living or disamenity premium that workers demand to be induced to live in a larger city, and the estimated agglomeration elasticity as the marginal productivity premium firms are willing to pay them if they work there, then the relative magnitudes of these are interpretable as making a statement about equilibrium or disequilibrium in urban labour markets. If it were so, then, in our estimations, the departure of the latter (0.09) from the former (0.08) would rationalize continued labour in-migration to the big cities.

The results of the more elaborate variable-elasticity wage specification (29) are reported in Table 6. Once again, the postulated relationship with parameter values obtained from the estimates is graphed (Figure 3) for each industry.[16] The solid vertical bar represents the maximum sample value, and the broken one, the mean for all observations, regardless of industry. All cases display wages rising with city size at the sample means, which are marked by crosses. In two of the five, wages rise at an increasing rate, and the remaining three feature a decline in the rate of the increase. This set of estimations, too, therefore, seems to indicate general support for the notion that workers supply their labour to larger cities at higher rates to compensate, presumably, for the high money or disutility costs of living in them.[17]

Lastly, the estimated values of *j* enable a more rigorous evaluation of Moomaw's hypothesis, through the testing of condition (26) implied by it, viz., that of the equality of the agglomeration elasticity with the product of the wage elasticity and labour's share. Returning to Table 5, we compare values of *j* estimated from (27) multiplied by the share of labour with those of the agglomeration elasticity, *b*, from equation (7) and note that this condition does not hold for any of the industries for which estimations were performed.[18] Thus, Moomaw's behavioural postulate in respect of the explicit choice of city size by firms does not seem validated in the Indian context.

While the above is, in many ways, a weak test of Moomaw's behavioural hypothesis — testing is in the presence of untested maintained hypotheses such as profit maximization and perfect competition — the rough picture that emerges from the foregoing exercises does not seem to support the view that entrepreneurs in India consider city size per se as a choice variable. Rather, the findings are more in line with the

Table 5: Results of the Indirect Estimates

Industry	*Obs*	*Coefficient of Labour FOC*	*Moomaw Coefficient*	*b – FOC Estimate*	*b – Direct Estimate*
23	286	–0.0536*	–0.0174	0.3478*	0.0554*
		(–5.13)	(–1.07)		
31	82	–0.0785	0.0963‡	0.0705	0.0887‡
		(–1.55)	(1.79)		
33	12	–0.0595	0.0910	0.3655	0.1889†
		(–0.71)	(1.07)		
35	53	–0.0088	0.0697	–0.0239	0.0993
		(–0.12)	(1.03)		
36	31	–0.0789†	–0.0744‡	0.0951†	0.0767‡
		(–2.53)	(–1.89)		

Industry	*Obs*	*j*	*Labour's Share*	*j (Labour's Share)*
23	286	0.0312*	0.76	0.0237
		(2.86)		
31	82	0.0936*	0.39	0.0365
		(5.62)		
33	12	0.1294†	0.59	0.0764
		(2.53)		
35	53	0.1244*	0.62	0.0771
		(4.07)		
36	31	0.0042	0.68	0.0029
		(0.30)		

* Estimate significant at 1 per cent level. † Estimate significant at 5 per cent level. ‡ Estimate significant at 10 per cent level.
Note: Figures in brackets represent *t*-statistics of associated estimates.

Table 6: The City-Size–Wage Relationship

Industry	*Obs*	j_1	j_2	R^2
23	286	0.000048	0.000021	0.0698
		(0.02)	(0.81)	
31	82	0.012570†	–0.000078	0.4535
		(2.27)	(–1.33)	
33	12	0.044760	–0.000435	0.3446
		(1.31)	(–1.20)	
35	53	0.017859†	–0.000157	0.1278
		(2.05)	(–1.62)	
36	31	–0.002452	0.000033	0.1642
		(–0.81)	(1.10)	

† Estimate significant at 5 per cent level.
Note: Figures in brackets represent *t*-statistics of associated estimates.

assumptions that the firm is modelled as choosing only its level of employment, and that city size is parametric to the decision. In a strict sense, this may actually be the case with the small set of firms in any city that sell only in the local market, locating there without considering alternative locations. Yet there can be little doubt that non-trivial location decisions are made by individual entrepreneurs in what must be, by and large, a rational and consistent way. The questions raised by the results of this section should serve to underscore the need for a microeconomic formulation of the firm's optimizing problem in respect of location decisions in a manner compatible with macro formulations such as the equilibrium city size one. The aforementioned issues expose a theoretical lacuna in the development of the microfoundations of aggregative urban growth models that it is very important to fill.

III. The Localization Investigations

Significance and Data Requirements of Study

Among the objectives of our empirical work is that of shedding light on the issue of whether it is 'localization' economies or 'urbanization' economies that predominate in a developing country. Important consequences, both positive and policy, turn on which of these competing hypotheses is closer to the truth. Elaborations on this controversy in Shukla (1988, Chapter 2) set forth the nature of the issues that turn on the possibility of the measured agglomeration advantage being that of localization. Among the presumptions of such a hypothesis is the notion that firms derive benefit principally from spatial proximity to other firms in the same industry (either narrowly or broadly[19] defined), and among its implications is the idea of a specialized system of cities exhibiting a size-hierarchy dictated, in principle, by certain simple technological conditions. Of course, the latter is a prediction of the localization hypothesis that can, and, in a limited way, has been put to test by observing the functional composition of Indian cities.[20] Here, our aim is to utilize the production function approach we have been working with to attempt to evaluate the validity of its basic premise.

To be able to do so, we must have some means of distinguishing the influence of pure urban scale, as it were, from that of industry size in a region built into the external scale specification. Our earlier specifications of the function $G(N)$ did not explicitly permit this, the 'urbanization' and 'localization' effects both being subsumed under the measured 'agglomeration' effect. In general, the arguments of this function may take the form of a vector of attributes thought to be relevant to comparative areal productivity advantages for various industries. However, for the present purpose, it is sufficient that the specification be one that will allow the data to discriminate between the two influences by including variables at the regional or city level for extent or intensity of urbanization, as well as for total industry size.

Once again, the estimation methodology involves interfacing production data with data on urban and regional characteristics. For the level of industrial disaggregation desired, Indian data on the industry size measure were not available at the city level. Thus, it was not possible to use the firm-level production dataset of the earlier sections. The localization investigations are with data aggregated up to the industry-in-district level, collected under the Annual Survey of Industries (ASI). This dataset is for the year 1977, and covers all establishments employing 20 or more persons (when using power) and 100 or more persons (when not using power) in the state of Maharashtra. The measure of regional industry size that shall serve as our 'localization' variable is total employment in the industry in a district. For our 'urbanization' variable, we experiment with a number of district-level demographic and occupational measures: total urban population, per cent urban, population density, population of the largest urban area, total population of cities in and above Class III, percentage of employment that is non-agricultural, and lastly, factory employment for every 100,000 of district population, an alternative measure employed in our earlier investigations. The success of some of these measures relative to others will hopefully convey information regarding the likely sources of regional productivity. Again, summary statistics on the industry-wise sample distributions of key urbanization variables are presented in Table II of Appendix A.

The Estimation Methodology

As the agglomeration specification, we employ the one introduced by Henderson (1983) in his similar investigation with Brazilian data. It is

$$G(L, N) = e^{-(a/L)}N^{b} \tag{31}$$

equipped with a constant urbanization elasticity, b, but a localization elasticity that is assumed to be variable. N is the urbanization measure, while L is the localization variable, represented in the estimations below by total district industry employment, which also enters the aggregate production function, $F(L, K)$. That the function $G(\,)$ is increasing in L, while its elasticity with respect to the localization variable declines (but remains positive) is apparent in rewriting the above specification as:

$$\ln G(L, N) = -(a/L) + b \ln N \tag{32}$$

whence, differentiating with respect to ln L, we get

$$d \ln G(L, N)/d \ln L = (a/L)$$

As the specification $F(L, K)$, we select the flexible form of equation (5) which avoids the restrictiveness of the more specific functional forms. The resulting estimating equation is

$$\ln Q = \ln A + \ln B - a/L + b\ln N + \alpha\ln(K/L) + \beta/2[\ln(K/L)]^2 \tag{33}$$

The results of these estimations appear in the section below.

Results

We first conducted least squares regressions for the case of the agglomeration specification without the localization component, both for comparability with the earlier results of Tables 2 and 3, as well as to observe which of the urbanization variables performed more successfully. The results for this set of estimations, for those variables, and those industries in respect of which sample size was deemed sufficiently large, are reported in Table 7. In nearly all of the industries, significant values for the agglomeration elasticity are evident. For the industries that the earlier investigations and this one have in common, the present estimates are, in fact, found to be higher. One explanation for this may be found by contrasting the two different samples that give rise to the two sets of estimates. The data descriptions of Appendix A clearly show the present (ASI) sample as being characterized by smaller urban sizes than the earlier (CMIE) one. This observation is a significant one. Of the seven variables that were experimented with as proxies for the urbanization influence, the four that proved most successful bear close affiliation with the urban and urbanization concepts actually employed in the Census.

The results of the full-fledged specification of equation (33), which we will interpret toward attempting an empirical resolution of the localization question, appear in Table 8. Overwhelmingly, estimates for the localization elasticity, a/L (evaluated at the sample industry employment means) register considerably lower values than corresponding urbanization elasticity estimates. Also, the former are significant in respect of only two industries, 33 and 37. Where positive, the estimates of a/L tend to reduce the values of estimated b only slightly from the levels of the foregoing agglomeration elasticity estimates. Further (not reported here), the increase in values of R^2 from the set of estimations in Table 7 was found to be marginal. All in all, it appears that the localization influence, at least as captured by the narrow localization variable used (following Henderson 1983), viz., industry size, is very small in Indian cities compared with the more dominant urbanization influence.

This evidence is in marked contrast to that of Henderson (1983), who finds that localization economies overwhelm those of urbanization in respect of all industries for which his results are reported. Carlino (1978)

Table 7: The Localization Investigations—I

Industry	*Obs*	*(N=UPOP)*	*(N=URBP)*	*(N=EFL)*	*(N=NAGP)*
20	23	0.30†	0.47†	0.28*	0.70†
		(2.16)	(2.52)	(2.80)	(2.50)
22	13	0.12	0.09	0.07	0.31
		(0.80)	(0.38)	(0.47)	(0.98)
23	22	0.43*	0.77*	0.32†	0.93*
		(2.72)	(3.43)	(2.48)	(3.26)
27	9	0.05	0.07	0.05	–0.06
		(0.11)	(0.11)	(0.16)	(–0.08)
28	17	0.24	0.45	0.21	0.68
		(1.37)	(1.74)	(1.16)	(1.70)
31	19	0.31†	0.34	0.28	0.32
		(2.09)	(1.42)	(1.71)	(0.81)
32	21	0.30	0.54‡	0.37†	0.62
		(1.52)	(1.98)	(2.33)	(1.53)
33	13	0.18	0.21	0.08	0.48
		(1.33)	(1.06)	(0.65)	(1.77)
34	15	0.32†	0.39‡	0.24‡	0.67†
		(2.49)	(1.87)	(2.01)	(2.34)
35	13	0.18	0.19	0.37†	0.78‡
		(0.90)	(0.65)	(2.38)	(2.09)
36	8	0.13	0.09	0.43‡	0.84
		(0.56)	(0.22)	(2.26)	(1.21)
37	8	1.53‡	1.74	0.77	2.14
		(2.57)	(1.52)	(1.33)	(1.41)
40	17	0.01	0.00	0.06	0.20
		(0.23)	(0.03)	(1.17)	(1.52)
97	20	0.09†	0.11†	0.07†	0.19†
		(2.62)	(2.10)	(2.38)	(2.30)

* Estimate significant at 1 per cent level. † Estimate significant at 5 per cent level. ‡ Estimate significant at 10 per cent level.

Note: Figures in brackets represent *t*-statistics of associated estimates.

Variable Name	Description
UPOP	Urban population of district
URBP	Urban population as percentage of total population of district
EFL	Number of workers employed in factories per 100,000 of total district population
NAGP	Non-agricultural workers as percentage of total district population

has found the localization influence dominating for a few industries in the context of US data, including industries 23, 35 and 36.

Our results do not mean, in our opinion, that the localization concept is inappropriate in the Indian context. Rather than disclaim the importance of localization economies altogether, the message from our empirical work seems to be that they operate on a somewhat wider level than one of strict specific industry employment. A general observation from the above results is that, in many industries, the localization estimates, when UPOP and URBP are the urbanization variables used, tend to be frequently

Table 8: The Localization Investigations—II

Industry	*(N=UPOP)*		*(N=URBP)*		*(N=EFL)*		*(N=NAGP)*	
	a/L	*b*	*a/L*	*b*	*a/L*	*b*	*a/L*	*b*
20	–0.0074	0.32†	–0.0054	0.48†	–0.0026	0.28*	–0.0078	0.74†
	(–0.58)	(2.20)	(–0.44)	(2.51)	(–0.22)	(2.74)	(–0.63)	(2.54)
22	0.0180	0.07	0.0227	0.02	0.0217	0.03	0.0135	0.21
	(0.62)	(0.45)	(0.79)	(0.07)	(0.77)	(0.18)	(0.41)	(0.51)
23	0.0015	0.43†	–0.0025	0.79*	–0.0019	0.33†	0.0060	0.94*
	(0.18)	(2.59)	(–0.31)	(3.31)	(–0.21)	(2.36)	(0.77)	(3.27)
27	–0.0451	0.48	–0.0429	0.72	–0.0367	0.28	–0.0562	0.95
	(–1.02)	(0.80)	(–0.98)	(0.76)	(–0.92)	(0.69)	(–1.02)	(0.79)
28	0.0151	0.16	0.0137	0.35	0.0169	0.14	0.0132	0.51
	(1.01)	(0.83)	(0.97)	(1.26)	(1.17)	(0.75)	(0.90)	(1.15)
31	0.0230	0.24	0.0262	0.18	0.0245	0.19	0.0304	0.18
	(1.33)	(1.55)	(1.37)	(0.71)	(1.35)	(1.11)	(1.70)	(0.47)
32	–0.0329	0.35	–0.0395	0.63†	–0.0828	0.53*	–0.0575	0.89‡
	(–0.60)	(1.60)	(–0.77)	(2.10)	(–1.58)	(2.89)	(–0.97)	(1.81)
33	0.0129†	0.11	0.0133†	0.11	0.0141†	0.01	0.0118~	0.23
	(2.39)	(0.97)	(2.40)	(0.65)	(2.46)	(0.10)	(1.97)	(0.86)
34	0.0027	0.30‡	0.0040	0.37	0.0023	0.22	0.0009	0.64‡
	(0.72)	(2.21)	(1.03)	(1.78)	(0.54)	(1.65)	(0.21)	(1.90)
35	0.0028	0.12	0.0033	0.11	0.0007	0.36‡	0.0013	0.73
	(0.58)	(0.50)	(0.72)	(0.32)	(0.18)	(1.97)	(0.34)	(1.71)
36	0.0066	–0.12	0.0110	–0.65	–0.0034	0.59	0.0015	0.66
	(0.77)	(–0.30)	(1.42)	(–1.02)	(–0.59)	(1.75)	(0.20)	(0.55)
37	0.0497	0.53	0.0800‡	–0.70	0.0652‡	0.01	0.0692‡	–0.26
	(1.60)	(0.66)	(2.44)	(–0.55)	(2.43)	(0.02)	(2.88)	(–0.18)
40	0.0588	–0.02	0.0614	–0.04	0.0286	0.04	0.0235	0.16
	(1.10)	(–0.32)	(1.19)	(–0.48)	(0.46)	(0.55)	(0.45)	(1.06)
97	0.0069	0.07	0.0088	0.08	0.0062	0.05	0.0073	0.13
	(0.96)	(1.71)	(1.18)	(1.20)	(0.72)	(1.23)	(0.90)	(1.25)

* Estimate significant at 1 per cent level. † Estimate significant at 5 per cent level. ‡ Estimate significant at 10 per cent level.

Note: Figures in brackets represent *t*-statistics of associated estimates.

higher than the corresponding estimates when NAGP is used, and almost uniformly higher than those regressed with EFL. One might consider UPOP and URBP the 'purer' measures of the urbanization influence than EFL, which comprises employment in large-scale manufacturing only, and could be interpreted as harbouring a localization component. NAGP, which includes household or small sector and service employment in addition, may be looked upon as an intermediate measure, more restrictive than total urban population but more broad-based than empolyment in the factory sector. This observation, in conjunction with the fact that the Constant Elasticity Estimates of Section I of this article revealed substantially higher parameter values when EFL — a variable essentially denoting the proportion of factory employment to total population — was used as the proxy for the productive advantages of urban scale, suggests that a localization-like influence may indeed be at work in Indian cities.

Such an influence is more likely to operate on the level of total manufacturing employment rather than on the volume of employment that is industry-specific. An accordingly revised definition of localization effects may not be at all inappropriate in a developing country, where the bulk of the labour force is not so skilled as to be specific to one industry or a narrowly defined industry class. Such 'broader' localization effects may well capture the salient features of the actual production economies arising from proximity in location. A possibility such as this opens up interesting avenues for the study of urban labour markets and migration policy in less developed countries (LDCs).

Appendix A: Summary Characteristics of Sample Data

Variable Name	*Description*
POP	Population of urban area
UPOP	Urban population of district
URBP	Urban population as percentage of total population of district
EFL	Number of workers employed in factories per 100,000 of total district population
NAGP	Non-agricultural workers as percentage of total district population

Characteristic	*Description*
OBS	Number of observations in the sample
MEAN	Sample mean
STD DEV	Standard deviation of observations from sample mean
MIN VAL	Minimum value in sample observations
MAX VAL	Maximum value in sample observations

Appendix Table I: Regional Variables used with CMIE Data Set

Industry/Variable	*OBS*	*MEAN*	*STD DEV*	*MIN VAL*	*MAX VAL*
All Industries					
POP	560	3,124,198	3,405,547	4,000	9,166,000
URBP	560	60	30	10	100
EFL	552	4,743	3,496	88	10,191
NAGP	560	65	26	19	100
Industry 23					
POP	286	2,603,955	3,002,541	17,000	9,166,000
URBP	286	58	27	10	100
EFL	286	4,794	3,294	88	10,191
NAGP	286	62	23	19	100
Industry 31					
POP	82	4,708,927	3,955,834	4,000	8,767,000
URBP	82	70	32	14	100
EFL	82	6,068	3,936	626	10,191
NAGP	82	75	28	29	100
Industry 33					
POP	12	1,877,000	3,329,768	55,000	9,166,000
URBP	12	43	20	22	100
EFL	12	3,243	2,442	713	10,191
NAGP	12	48	20	36	100
Industry 35					
POP	53	1,303,962	1,965,502	32,000	8,767,000
URBP	53	43	26	20	100
EFL	53	2,634	2,113	646	10,191
NAGP	53	50	23	24	100
Industry 36					
POP	31	4,505,258	3,238,425	28,000	9,166,000
URBP	31	82	24	40	100
EFL	31	4,232	3,258	605	10,191
NAGP	31	87	15	67	100

Appendix Table II: Regional Variables used with ASI Data Set

Industry/Variable	*OBS*	*MEAN*	*STD DEV*	*MIN VAL*	*MAX VAL*
All Industries					
UPOP	252	1,054,409	1,669,905	149,000	5,971,000
URBP	252	32	26	8	100
EFL	252	2,134	2,985	72	10,191
NAGP	252	40	23	16	100
Industry 20					
UPOP	23	658,609	1,197,315	153,000	5,971,000
URBP	23	25	20	8	100
EFL	23	1,344	2,243	88	10,191
NAGP	23	33	18	19	100
Industry 22					
UPOP	13	922,385	1,557,516	153,000	5,971,000
URBP	13	29	25	11	100
EFL	13	1,627	2,668	152	10,191
NAGP	13	37	22	16	100
Industry 23					
UPOP	22	680,000	1,220,924	149,000	5,971,000
URBP	22	26	20	10	100
EFL	22	1,370	2,292	72	10,191
NAGP	22	32	19	16	100
Industry 27					
UPOP	9	1,195,222	1,838,669	167,000	5,971,000
URBP	9	36	28	10	100
EFL	9	2,499	3,349	152	10,191
NAGP	9	42	27	16	100
Industry 28					
UPOP	17	807,000	1,370,587	153,000	5,971,000
URBP	17	28	22	11	100
EFL	17	1,682	2,533	152	10,191
NAGP	17	37	20	20	100
Industry 31					
UPOP	19	734,790	1,309,058	153,000	5,971,000
URBP	19	27	21	10	100
EFL	19	1,550	2,424	152	10,191
NAGP	19	34	20	16	100
Industry 32					
UPOP	21	689,714	1,250,743	153,000	5,971,000
URBP	21	25	21	8	100
EFL	21	1,411	2,337	88	10,191
NAGP	21	34	19	16	100
Industry 33					
UPOP	13	963,154	1,546,500	153,000	5,971,000
URBP	13	31	25	11	100
EFL	13	2,046	2,819	152	10,191
NAGP	13	41	21	24	100

(Contd.)

Appendix Table II: *(Contd.)*

Industry 34					
UPOP	15	885,000	1,446,673	153,000	5,971,000
URBP	15	30	23	11	100
EFL	15	1,834	2,668	152	10,191
NAGP	15	39	21	23	100
Industry 35					
UPOP	13	968,615	1,542,911	153,000	5,971,000
URBP	13	32	24	11	100
EFL	13	2,051	2,813	447	10,191
NAGP	13	41	21	23	100
Industry 36					
UPOP	8	1,328,875	1,918,574	153,000	5,971,000
URBP	8	39	29	12	100
EFL	8	2,889	3,381	476	10,191
NAGP	8	48	25	24	100
Industry 37					
UPOP	8	1,360,375	1,898,876	252,000	5,971,000
URBP	8	39	28	11	100
EFL	8	2,879	3,391	455	10,191
NAGP	8	47	26	24	100
Industry 40					
UPOP	17	802,529	1,372,969	153,000	5,971,000
URBP	17	28	22	8	100
EFL	17	1,643	2,554	152	10,191
NAGP	17	37	20	21	100
Industry 97					
UPOP	20	699,950	1,283,266	149,000	5,971,000
URBP	20	25	21	8	100
EFL	20	1,425	2404	72	10,191
NAGP	20	35	19	19	100

NOTES

This article constitutes Chapter III of the author's work *Urban Development and Regional Policy in India: An Econometric Analysis*, Himalaya Publishing House, Bombay 1988. The study, undertaken as a Ph.D. dissertation at Princeton University in 1984, marks one of the first empirical attempts at the rigorous measurement of city productivity with Indian data within a specified urban economic framework. It has been edited for this volume by Dr. D. M. Nachane to make it self-sufficient for presentation as an independent article.

1 Centre for Monitoring Indian Economy (CMIE 1982a), 'Key Financial Data on Larger Business Units', Bombay.

2 Government of India (1981), *Census of India 1981, Provisional Population Totals, Series -I, Paper 2*, Census Commissioner for India, New Delhi.

3 CMIE (1982b), 'District Level Data for Key Economic Indicators', Bombay.

4 The next section touches upon some analytical and empirical issues pertaining to the microbehavioural underpinnings compatible with the macro-urban growth formulation.

5 See Melvyn Fuss, Daniel McFadden, and Yair Mundlak, 'A Survey of Functional Forms in the Economic Analysis of Production' in Melvyn Fuss and Danieal McFadden (eds), *Production Economics: A Dual Approach to Theory and Applications*, North-Holland Publishing Company, 1978, for a discussion of analytical relationships between these alternative functional forms, and their appropriateness as estimating equations in specific applications.

6 To ascertain the extent of internal scale economies, we did not restrict $\alpha + \beta = 1$. The parameter sums we obtained were below unity, suggesting no presence of such economies for our set of industries. This result was later corroborated by our estimates of the scale parameter, μ from the CES form to be described below.

7 Used in Z. Grilliches and V. Ringstad (1971), 'Economics of Scale and the Form of the Production Function', in *Contributions to Economic Analysis* Series, North-Holland Publishing Company.

8 If $h(\ln k) = \ln f(k)$, where $F(K, L) = Lf(k)$ is any arbitrary CRS function, then $\ln A = h(\ln k = 0)$, $\alpha = h'(\ln k = 0)$, and $\beta = h''(\ln k = 0)$.

9 Empirical results presented are excerpted from the more detailed statements available with the author.

10 These calculations are done as follows:
Elasticity $= d \ln G / d \ln N = 0.09$,
where G and N are total productivity and population respectively. Then, in discrete terms, if N_1 and N_0 are two alternate city sizes, and G_1 and G_0 the respective productivities associated with them.

$$[\ln G_1 - \ln G_0] / [\ln N_1 - \ln N_0] = 0.09$$

hence

$$\ln(G_1/G_0 = 0.09 [\ln (N_1/N_0),$$

implying

$$G_1 = G_0 (N_1/N_0)^{0.09}$$

11 The second-order condition that the expressions below represent the maximum is $b_2 < 0$.

12 Relative heights of curves in the graph do not reflect actual industry-wise comparative productivities, since the y-intercept has been normalized at zero (constant = 1).

13 It is equally well demonstrable with $N = N(W)$ instead of $W = W(N)$.

14 See, for example, Fuchs Victor R (1967), 'Differentials in Hourly Earnings by Region and City Size, 1959', National Bureau of Economic Research, USA, Occasional Paper 101 and Goldfarb and Yezer, Anthony M. J. (1976), 'Evaluating Alternative Theories of Intercity and Interregional Wage Differentials', *Journal of Regional Science*, Vol. 16, No. 3.

15 Our general experience has been that indirect estimations are less stable and less consistent with each other than the direct ones. Whether this unreliability is due to failure of the maintained hypotheses, or to something

else, is not certain; the subject certainly bears further investigation.

16 Again, estimated interindustry wages are not comparable, since the *y*-intercept has been normalized at zero (constant = 1).

17 The two effects can be separated only if data on real urban wages are available, for which, typically, cross-city price indices are needed.

18 The null hypothesis that the two estimated coefficients come from populations with the same mean was rejected (with probability 0.01 that they do) in respect of all of the industries considered.

19 Studies of spatial clustering can identify interlinked industries that can be grouped together.

20 We have mentioned one such effort, that of Asok Mitra (1978), *India's Population*, Vols. I and II, Abhinav Publications, New Delhi. However, more work needs to be done using finer industrial disaggregation.

REFERENCES

Ahmad, Qazi (1965), 'Indian Cities: Characteristics and Correlates', University of Chicago, Department of Geography, Research Paper No. 102. (Study using field theoretic techniques in the tradition of geographers brings out the strong regionalization of urban activity in India.)

Carlino, Gerald A. (1978), 'Economies of Scale in Manufacturing Location', *Studies in Applied Regional Science*, Vol. XXII, Martinus Nijhoff, Leiden/Boston.

Federation of Indian Chambers of Commerce and Industry (FICCI) (1977), *Industrial Development Potential: Survey of Selected Towns of India*, New Delhi.

Henderson, J. Vernon (1983), 'Efficiency of Resource Usage and City Size', Brown University Working Paper.

Kashyap, S.P. (1979), 'Regional Planning in a Consistency Framework', Monograph Series 6, Sardar Patel Institute of Economic and Social Research, Ahmedabad. (Estimates a Leontief type interindustry model for the State of Gujarat and uses it for structural analysis and simulation.)

Mohan, Rakesh and Shankar Acharya (1983) 'Projections of Investment Requirements in Urban Infrastructure', Planning Commission, Government of India, mimeo.

Moomaw, Ronald L. (1981), 'Productivity and City Size: A Critique of the Evidence', *Quarterly Journal of Economics,* Vol. L and Vol. LXXXXV.

Segal, David (1976), 'Are There Returns to Scale in City Size?', *The Review of Economics and Statistics*, Vol. LVIII.

Shukla, Vibhooti (1988), *Urban Development and Regional Policy in India — An Econometric Analysis*, Himalaya Publishing House, Bombay.

Stanford Research Institute (1983), 'Cost of Urban Infrastructure for Industry as Related to City Size in Developing Countries: India Case Study', mimeo.

Sveikauskas, Leo (1974), 'Bias in Cross-Section Estimates of the Elasticity of Substitution', *International Economic Review*, Vol. 15, No. 2.

——— (1975), 'The Productivity of Cities', *Quarterly Journal of Economics*, Vol. LXXXIX.

3 / Population Redistribution Reconsidered: Spatial Policy Imperatives of African Development Strategies

VIBHOOTI SHUKLA

I. Introduction

The possible suboptimality of existing patterns of population distribution in Sub-Saharan Africa is once again the subject of much debate. Fuelled by concerns that the recent spate of famines is a manifestation of an endemic downward trend in the per capita availability of food in many countries, coupled with alarm at a perceptible acceleration in rates of population growth, the discussion has centred now on the concept of long-run carrying capacities of various regions. Carrying capacity calculations (on the bases of a constant state of technology and a given resource endowment) project the absolute population any region can support at a minimum standard of subsistence, and for an exogenous rate of population increase, they can specify a time horizon beyond which this sustenance capability can be said to be exceeded. A regional redistribution of population to avoid such an occurrence would then be indicated in order that this areal ecological imbalance may be redressed and catastrophic shortfalls thereby averted.[1]

All of this brings to mind prior debates on population redistribution that have taken place in the African context, and recalls the rather dismal record of resettlement programmes undertaken there earlier. Many of these attempts were coercive and, no doubt, involved heavy welfare losses on the part of those forcibly relocated. Voluntary schemes also had a high rate of failure, with numerous instances of return migration and resettlement reversal being observed.[2] Such experiences have prompted somewhat of a hands-off attitude towards the issue, primarily on the ground that policy-makers were ill-advised to tamper with the location decisions of multitudes of economically rational agents, particularly so in the absence of clear-cut alternative notions as to optimality in this context. Implicit in this judgement are two premises: one, that private actions are the most reliable guide to individual well-being in the matter of spatial choice; and second, that even if actual distributions were inoptimal, not enough is known about the desired (ideal) state to warrant intervention in the existing (non-ideal) one.

Scholarly caution, unfortunately, does not mean that local policy-makers will not continue to intervene arbitrarily in spatial decisions if rational guidelines are not provided.[3] In a 1981 article, S. I. Abeumere set forth a more comprehensive list of population-distribution related issues in the African context — to include, in addition to concerns about regional population and resource mismatches, rural poverty, high urban growth rates, population to area ratios too low to support development infrastructure, and migration — and attempted a typology of population distribution policies affecting them. He concluded, however, that '...currently there is no objective way to determine optimal population distribution ...'[4] This paper argues that current economic development imperatives have certain spatial implications which can in fact serve as more meaningful arbiters of policy than determinations made purely on 'carrying capacity' grounds.

First, it is important to point out that there need not necessarily be any superiority attached to a 'spontaneously' arrived-at distribution of people over space; very often, as will be documented in the following sections, such distributions are merely the result of past interferences with the economic environment. Neoclassical economic theory holds that a temporarily disequilibrating shock in any region is eventually accommodated through adjusting inter-regional labour flows. However, a persistent spatial mismatch between people and resources, even under conditions of privately optimizing behaviour, may come about through immobilities arising out of market imperfections or incompleteness, ethnicity-driven regional preferences, other impediments to movement due to politically erected barriers, or from historical misallocations of infrastructure. Moreover, as even the somewhat mechanical ecological concept of carrying capacities recognizes, any notion of 'optimal' is premised upon the state of technology available or in use, upon factor endowments, including population, and on chosen development norms. Were one to grant that the present regional dispersion of people under current techniques and institutions could not be substantially bettered, that is still no guarantee of such being the case in the dynamic context of rapid population growth, purposeful development and political intervention. All of the above conditions are present, in large or small measure, within the African situation and discussion of distributive issues remains highly relevant. Indeed, it is felt, these issues command the same urgency and attention the wider development problem in the region now claims from scholars and policy-makers.

Redistribution policies, to be acceptable agents of economic growth and welfare, must not only be motivated by considerations of efficiency in production, but, further, must be attainable and sustainable through incentive mechanisms rather than by force, so as to avoid both the waste and the human hardship of the earlier attempts. One useful characterization of the inefficiencies of existing population distributions is in terms of the beneficial externalities to be reaped from a greater spatial concentration of people. These may stem from the agglomeration advantages that accrue to economic activity conducted under conditions of physical proximity and significant threshold settlement size, from positive scale economies in the productive utilization of industrial infrastructure, or from the efficient provision and use of agricultural services. Such advantages of concentration also obtain with regard to consumption activities as, for instance, in the effective targeting of poverty-reducing welfare programmes and in the implementation of disease control, health, nutrition, education and family-planning programmes. Many of these, important in themselves, hold immediate consumption gains that translate, directly or indirectly, into long-term productivity gains through the creation of human capital and the opening up of economic opportunities leading to income augmentation. Moreover, investment in the infrastructure that provides these services can be viewed as an optimal spatial policy instrument for many African economic environments. The poverty of existing infrastructural bases in these countries, the low levels of economic development, the concurrent lack of development of markets, and the inadequacy of political and administrative capacity make such 'public good' type of non-price instruments much more likely to have a significant influence on economic behaviour than pure price policies, which might prove premature and ineffectual where markets are thin, non-competitive, or fragmented.

This analysis focuses especially on desirable spatial–developmental interactions in agriculture, urbanization and transportation. Migration, as the *process* wherby redistribution is brought about, including its relation to demographic phenomena, will be specifically addressed. A crucial set of questions to be asked refers to the identification of the nature, composition and spatial allocation of infrastructure, both social and productive, that will achieve the population distribution that best promotes the chosen development strategy. Since many very basic, 'up-stream' investments remain to be made in the region, the effects of which are expected to be long-lived, it is felt that this search for an appropriate spatial strategy should be an essential ingredient of the overall development effort.

Our proposed treatment legitimately begs the important question: Are situations in the countries we are studying sufficiently similar so as to admit common modes of analysis, yielding general prescriptions? Our position on this must be that, although diverse in agro-climatic type, political set-up, and in many other ways, the shared economic goals and development levels of the various countries *do* warrant similar methods of approach, facilitating, hopefully, considerable economies in analysis, policy formulation and application. Nevertheless, it is important to remain attuned to crucial structural differences between countries, and to design approaches amenable to modification as specific situations demand.

II. Implications of Sectoral Objectives

Agriculture and Population Distribution

The current consensus on African development strategy, one conditioned in part by the perceived secular decline in food production, places agriculture as the sectoral centrepiece of planned efforts, and smallholder farming as the special areas of focus within that sector.[5] Emphasis on modernization and productivity increases in this predominantly food-crop-producing sector commands greater attention than the concentration of scarce resources on the large-scale, capital intensive subsector responsible for the bulk of cash crop exports.[6] Aside from providing a measure of food security, such prioritization addresses poverty in the immediate term, and stresses the creation of a broad enough income base to support the eventual indigenous industrialization that must be a long-run mainstay of sustained economic growth for most of the countries in question.

A small-agriculturist approach in the context of the general structure of Sub-Saharan farming systems has three direct implications. Firstly, it involves the technological transformation of an overwhelmingly traditional sector.[7] Secondly, while there is evidence of spontaneous ongoing innovation, both technical and institutional, the brunt of the responsibility for effecting this transformation must of necessity fall in the public domain. Thirdly, the process must be accompanied by the conversion to commercial enterprises of what are now essentially subsistence units. We are interested in explicating the joint spatial imperatives of these propositions.

The majority of the envisaged target group practices rain-fed, hand-hoe cultivation on land alternatively farmed and kept in fallow for varying lengths of time. Intensification is the process associated with a shortening of the fallow interval. If not accompanied by the adoption of manuring practices and better land preparation, it results in soil degradation, with a rapid falling off of yields (leading to desertification, at the extreme, as in the case of the Sahel). Population pressure on land can cause it to be more intensively cultivated, and although the relative increase in the application of the labour input to land is not necessarily attended by an intensification of other complementary inputs in a traditional setting, a few writers have noted the potential for and, occasionally, even the realization of institutional change and technical innovation induced under such circumstances. Cases of development of more explicit property rights and the emergence of land markets where none existed before have frequently been observed in the African context.[8] Elsewhere, population growth has been noted to have sometimes prompted increased savings, even at near-subsistence levels, so that such capital investments as are feasible might be made to maintain per capita levels of output.[9] And, given that many new investments technologically relevant to the present structure of African agriculture are rudimentary ones, requiring no more than allocating labour time away from immediately productive pursuits toward land preparation or the mastering of simple animal traction methods, population growth may even actually provide conditions for the release of family labour to participate in such capital formation activities.[10]

Two points are, however, noteworthy here. One, such improvements cannot always be regarded as automatically following a rise in population levels; rather, they must only be viewed as being facilitated in special situations.[11] Secondly, they can occur even in the absence of population pressure. To argue that productivity adjusts spontaneously to population density and, therefore, that the most populated areas are also those most capable of sustaining large numbers is a fallacy, as evidenced by Binswanger and Pingali (1984).[12] They cite the example of the East African highlands, which have historically been farmed more intensively than, for instance, the low-lying 'bas fronds'. Although these lowlands boast heavy, high clay-content soils far superior to the light, loamy soil of the highlands, their exploitation has been slow due to the large effort that must first go into drainage and reclamation before they can be readily worked. The study also reveals that proximity to urbanized areas, reflecting an ease of access to markets, has generally led to rising land values, accelerated intensification and higher rates of technological innovation for surrounding farms. These illustrations point up to the large scope for a public role in developing Sub-Saharan agriculture, particularly in fields such as land reclamation and transportation, where the potential for private actions is necessarily small.

Indeed, within various components of the agricultural modernization and growth strategies proposed in the African context (there appears to be a consensus on ingredients, though a debate on priorities)[13] — land drainage, tractorization, irrigation and flood control, research and application of new crop varieties, and, importantly, incentives — there is a naturally embodied public bias and, correspondingly, a bias in favour of some degree of spatial concentration, both because of the nature of many of these essential activities and as well, of course, due to the general constraints on available resources. Large-scale land reclamation, a perceived urgent step for increasing the supply of arable land, as well as major irrigation projects (viewed by many as an expensive measure, but an ultimately inevitable one for making possible more frequent cropping), involve high set-up costs, spatially well-defined command areas, and hence considerable economies of spatially intensive resource use. Tractorization strategy envisages an initial shift from hand hoes to animal traction as an intermediate technological choice, to better reap the productivity benefits of intensification,[14] contributed to in part by the availability of natural manuring under this type of farming system. The transition to use of animals in agricultural tasks, and the development of farm-related livestocking enterprises in vast tracts of Sub-Saharan Africa has been impeded by the continued presence of pockets of infestation of human and cattle trypanosomiasis. It is well known that density of human habitat both justifies and facilitates attempts at control and eradication of such disease-bearing viruses and their vectors.[15] In its subsequent phase, agricultural growth is widely expected to require the mechanization of selected operations,[16] and here again, under relative capital scarcity, markets for equipment rental and maintenance are far more likely to emerge where many users can be served within reachable physical distances.[17]

Much hope for African self-sufficiency in foodgrains rides upon the anticipated steady flow of crop improvement technologies accruing from careful research in plant breeding and farm management.[18] Not only is such an approach credited with being less costly than more conventional input-augmenting alternatives, but it is also considered more potentially effective in overcoming barriers to innovation by small peasants, by promising manifold increase in crop yields. Adaptive research in fairly locale-specific, as experience around the world has shown, and its maximum cost-efficacy can be ensured if the largest possible cropland and the greatest possible numbers share its fruits.[19] In this context, another strong argument, perhaps the most important of all in the face of the acute administrative and technical manpower scarcity that is recognized to characterize most of Sub-Saharan Africa,[20] can be made to support a case for the spatial concentration of people towards productive ends. The public management of rural development in general, and the organization of extension in particular, are services the production and the utilization of which are especially space-bound, requiring as they do continuous face-to-face interaction between, say, the development administrator and the extension agent, or the extension worker and the farmer. The maximum payoff from the application and demonstration of new techniques occurs when the frequency of this interaction between limited numbers of services personnel and the many decentralized small farmholders is intensified.

Lastly, spatial intensification confers advantages in the area of providing incentives to agricultural production, thereby speeding the transition from subsistence to commercial farming. Market participation and remunerative prices, coupled with clear-cut rights to farm income, are credited, as in vent-for-surplus theories of trade expansion, with spurring efficiency and effort, and, perhaps more importantly, with inducing the use of high-yield purchase inputs. Yet, in African contexts, costs of transporting output to markets erode, in many cases, a sizeable chunk of obtainable profit margins, and sometimes discourage altogether any production for sale.[21] The development of transportation networks is seen by many as a crucial need, indeed as a prerequisite, to major agricultural breakthroughs in the region. Both to spread the cost of the investments they involve, as well as to enlarge the effective number of trades and exchanges within spatial markets defined by available transport technologies, denser concentration of people may be optimal. Again, efficient agricultural marketing demands modern physical infrastructure that may call for the role of rural towns. Issues of a real orientation in linkages between the discussed agricultural strategies and those for urbanization, transportation and social service provision will be more fully explored in succeeding sections.

Spacial Requirements of Urban Development

Sub-Saharan Africa is one of the world's least urbanized regions.[22] Despite this, the high growth rates of many of its cities have been associated in popular perception with rapidly accelerating migration flows from an impoverished countryside, emptying themselves into large pools of unemployed or underemployed at the relatively better serviced urban destinations. Governments, alarmed at the erosion of already inadequate bases of urban infrastructure, have, both through exhortations and statutory measures, tried to discourage an accentuation of what they believe to be unsatisfactory spatial trends,[23] and economists and others have alleged 'urban bias' in national policies, voicing concerns about the primate and the 'non-generative' or even parasitic character of African city systems.[24]

While some of these observations and the conclusions they prompt are well founded, many suffer from an incomplete understanding of regional urbanization processes and patterns in the African context. For example, there is evidence that growth of many urban areas may now be as much attritutable to natural increase as to net migration. The latter, as a later section will show, is a more complex and multi-faceted phenomenon in Sub-Saharan Africa than a simple response to rural 'push'. The informal sector in urban areas productively absorbs a sizeable proportion of urban residents, and cities in many parts of Africa have performed a wide range of changing functions. Lately, the recognition of this lack of knowledge, coupled with a reluctance, in its absence, to interfere with private mobility decisions, has engendered a good deal of caution among domestic policy-makers and international assistance agencies in the matter of pursuing more than a defensive urban development strategy in the area.[25] Yet, we shall argue, informed intervention perhaps nowhere else holds as much promise. Infrastructure, as a determinant of urban growth, can be used to actively promote desired spatial objectives, rather than to reactively accommodate spontaneous population changes. Development strategy can define these objectives by aggressively translating a 'development bias' into conscious urban choices.

Urban traditions in West Africa go back to pre-colonial times, when, for example, the Yoruba city states and the towns of the civilization of Benin flourished as powerful centres of political and cultural authority.[26] In the interior, many towns thrived on long-distance trade along the overland cross-Sahara caravan and pilgrimage routes,[27] while coastal centres serviced the trans-Atlantic slave trade.[28] East and South African urban settlement began with the colonial needs for administrative convenience and security. Urban centres during this phase were developed, due to Europeans' largely outward trade and communications orientation, along the continental coastline in both east and west, with many of the latter's older generation land-locked towns yielding in importance to newer, littoral settlements.[29] In the south and south-east, often large concentrations of people grew around key areas of mining interest, with discernible patterns of occupation in evidence along rail transportation lines between centres of extraction and nodes of shipment.[30] Upon independence, the agglomerative and infrastructural pull of former colonial enclaves persisted, with the major ports and erstwhile capitals continuing to attract predominant shares of both public and private capital,[31] and, consequently, of employment and job-seekers. However, partly due to the carving up of the imperial lands into independent nation-states, and partially in deference to pressures from their ethnic and regional constituencies, this phase has also seen the establishment of a few new capitals, regional and national, some even in very sparsely populated interior areas.[32]

Two issues concern us at this point, viz., what are the urban requirements of present conceptions of the design of African economic development, and what aspects of the existing urban structure are conducive or deterrent to their spatial articulation. Below we discuss a few functional generalizations that might point to some meaningful answers. A move to an overall transitional developmental emphasis on agriculture necessitates a shift to an urban strategy that induces increases in agricultural production. Urban areas may in general bear a reciprocal symbiotic relationship with the agricultural sector: They can supply vital inputs to it, and they can furnish demand for its output. In Sub-Saharan Africa, the potential of the larger urban agglomerations to serve effectively in either of these capacities seems to be severely restricted. In the case of the former function, the requirements of African agriculture, quite mismatched with the present structure of African city-based industry, preclude any significant contribution.[33] As for the latter, the smallness of the urban demand base, its relative orientation towards items of high-income consumption with large capital and import components, and the typically adverse rural–urban terms of trade[34] have historically reduced this sector's role in stimulating rural development. Clearly towns in Sub-Saharan Africa, to sustain an agriculture development strategy, need to be designed to play a more supportive role than they are currently equipped to do.

It follows as a corollary to this strategy that the towns best qualified to serve vital rural functions are, by and large, in the interior rather than the 'primate' coastal capitals. Their hinterland location is crucial to the functions they must perform. In the previous sub-section, we advocated spatial concentration for developing rural areas on the ground that, within traditional farming systems, intensification fosters innovation, leading to gains in factor productivity. Inasmuch as the successful consequent adoption of new agricultural practices also requires producer incentives and assured supplies of modern inputs, the widespread availability of marketing services is an indispensable complement to this package.[35] The availability and efficiency of agricultural marketing services is spatially circumscribed both by the number of agents participating in the trades, as well as by the level of marketing technology, encompassing both transport and communication means, that an economy has at its disposal. Small towns, their locations appropriately defined by the agricultural hinterlands they command, are ideally suited to perform marketing functions that leave the African cultivator with adequate price incentives and guaranteed market access, taking into account local resource availability, the requisite efficient market sizes, and actual or projected rural densities. Indeed, such towns can ideally reconcile distributional economies with scale economies in production of all agricultural services requiring farmers' physical presence. Most agricultural services of importance in Africa, e.g., marketing, warehousing or storage, credit, etc., fall in this category. Moreover, the larger the population coverage within the limits delineated by feasible transportation or commuting distances, the greater the scope for specialization in these various activities, resulting again in lower costs than when two or more functions are combined, as is often the case with the traditional itinerant trader or the rural moneylender.

These towns can also serve as headquarters for the administrators of rural development and as bases for farm extension or regional experiment stations. They could provide a permanent base for artisans and craftsmen who can, through effecting locally adaptive innovations in agricultural implements, augment on-farm productivity.[36] Further, such towns might become centres for production of non-agricultural commodities most popular among rural farm people. Studies of rural consumer expenditure patterns show that income elasticities of rural households are highest in respect of rurally produced, labour-intensive goods and services.[37] The forward and backward linkages of agriculture, whether arising from production or consumption, can be used to advantage in providing off-farm 'market'-town employment in times of slack or drought seasons. All in all, the locational linkages and the potential regional income and employment multiplier effects of agriculturally supported intermediate town development are considerable.[38]

In a future when the rising incomes of the rural population eventually come to express significant economy-wide final demand linkages, 'balanced' urban patterns may be expected to naturally follow. Much as the proximity to urban incomes and consumers today determines (together with the importance of capital goods imported via ports) the setting up of the more sophisticated 'enclave-type' manufacturing and specialized service industries in the larger cities, so will the future pull of rural purchasing power rationally direct indigenous African industrialization to today's medium-sized towns. As extractive and processing activities develop, rural raw material bases and the forward linkages of agricultural growth will also dictate semi-urban locations of industrial plants. In the course of balanced spatial development of this nature, agglomeration processes will be set in motion at many formerly small urban centres, with some of them gradually achieving the dimensions and character of first-ranking national centres. The evolution of such a functionally integrated urban hierarchy provides perhaps the most developmentally productive framework for the spread of urbanization that must, ultimately, accompany the long-run African structural transformation.[39]

III. Instruments of Spatial Change

Production Infrastructure: Optimal Transportation Investments

As the component of productive infrastructure with the most explicit and pervasive spatial impact, transportation merits special consideration in any region's development strategy. This is especially true in the Sub-Saharan context, where it is widely recognized that major investments in this sector are yet to be made, and constitute perhaps the single most catalytic factor that can release the forces of economic development.[40] The need for transportation investments appears very early in the sequencing of agricultural infrastructure, preceding as they must public developmental interventions in the areas of land reclamation, irrigation, drainage and rural electrification. They are a prerequisite to the performance of basic administrative functions and to the widespread delivery of social services. In addition, such investments govern many aspects of urban growth and development.

Perhaps the most important developmental role that transportation networks play is that of the physical articulation of economic markets. Notwithstanding the early origins of a market as a geographical 'place', the importance of the locational distribution of a group of transacting agents has come to be downplayed in modern connotations of the term. Nowhere is the spatial dimension of markets more operationally relevant than in Africa, where distances between settlements, their small sizes and the primitiveness of travel, communication and information transfer methods have often served to limit the emergence of efficiently functioning markets. Spatial fragmentation constrains the realization of potential gains from trade and exchange, and warps incentives to break out of self-sufficient subsistence. Indeed, the principal detriment to agricultural marketing efficiency in African situations has been documented[41] to be the high and sometimes prohibitive transport cost of selling output, which often leaves the cultivator with insufficient profit margins to expand production. Insofar as commercialization is thought to increase the productivity of resources in agriculture, and specialization makes for more efficiency in rural nonfarm activities, the opening up of spatial markets through appropriate transportation investments confers beneficial spillover effects far surpassing their direct cost-reducing role.

As with any contemplated investment strategy, and especially in view of the potentially massive amounts of resources involved, certain questions arise in connection with the formulation of optimal transportation policy for the countries of Sub-Saharan Africa. In particular, decisions about the magnitudes, locations, sources of financing and types of expenditures must be made. The existence of positive externalities in the productive contribution of transportation service provision argue for a greater quantum of transport infrastructure than dictated by explicit cost savings alone, which are presumably exceeded by wider social benefits. This factor must be taken into consideration when evaluating proposed transportation projects; not doing so would result in socially suboptimal investment levels.[42] Furthermore, this has bearing upon the mix between private financing and public subsidy contemplated for funding such ventures: insistence on full cost recovery commensurate with private benefits might substantially undercut the vital developmental role envisaged for this sector, yet total absence of cost accountability will lead to wastage and disuse.

Given that public resources to finance such investments are necessarily limited, their allocation between regions or locations is a legitimate concern. What locational characteristics would maximize social gains obtainable, for instance, through alternative road network patterns? Specifically, does economic rationality warrant concentration on building rural roads or on the construction of inter-urban or trans-regional highways? The answer must be jointly contingent, among other factors, upon resource-dictated transportation technology choice, development strategy, and current and projected spatial population densities. Public investment in a system of high-speed expressways linking big metropolitan centres and export nodes may well be justified in economies dominated by a lucrative export sector (e.g., large-scale plantation-type cash crop operations) or those launching a major industrialization effort. In such cases, often, the high values of the volumes to be transported, or the large economic sizes of the transacting agents will prompt the requisite private investments in complementary sophisticated conveyance technologies and even high enough payments in road-user charges to render the road-building investments economically viable.

But, in situations featuring a large number of relatively scattered smallholding farm producers, with their inability to bear the typically high set-up costs of such investments and in the absence of private intermediaries who can operate on a combined scale to make it efficient, this strategy is obviously inappropriate. Instances abound,[43] both within and outside Africa, where the construction of national highways linking large urban centres or regional capitals have left vast rural tracts through which they pass virtually untouched from an economic point of view, with few instances of productive use by villagers. Rural development priorities in Sub-Saharan Africa, together with the structure of the agricultural sector, imply that the most socially cost-effective productivity-increasing pay-offs are likely to accrue from following a policy initially of concentrating public resources on rural access roads from village settlements to one or more semi-urban or small urban agriculturally oriented centre. Such networks can not only spread the costs of construction and maintenance over many users and freight-loads, but also induce increases in the latter, as maximal advantage can be taken to articulate potential rural linkages. As the volumes transacted rise, market-town based private agents can increasingly take on the task of competitively providing spatial marketing services in more and more efficient ways.[44] The degree of efficiency achievable can be expected to grow with rural farm densities, which further supports the argument for spatial concentration.

Finally, what do population redistribution objectives imply for rational choices of passenger transport vehicles and travel modes? To the extent that the spatial development strategy places a premium on rural population interactions, or on movements between villages and small towns, again, a rural network is deemed more socially useful than investment patterns subsidizing rural–metropolitan migration flows.[45] Spontaneous and induced migration flows in the African context will be dealt with in a later section. Suffice it to observe here, however, that judicious transportation investments can redirect both people as well as commodity flows in desired directions implied by developmental choices for Sub-Saharan Africa.

Location of Social Infrastructure

The opportunity to reap the substantial economies of scale in social service provision[46] was, we have seen, one of the primary motivations behind the early attempts at population redistribution carried out by some African governments. These efforts, justified as they were in seeking to extend to as many as possible institutionalized basic needs coverage in the face of the scarcity of resources available for investment in location-tied social infrastructure,[47] and sometimes with the hope of achieving less strictly economic objectives (e.g., 'villagization' serving to engender a spirit of community action among the rural population),[48] generally met with failure as we have mentioned earlier. They were indicted principally on three grounds: one, the frequent recourse to coercive means to relocated people; two, because of the low retention rates in new settlements, the non-realization of the social benefits; and three, the absence of significant positive productivity-augmenting effects of the redistributions.[49] In fact, in some instances, the spatial reshuffling actually resulted in production losses, as optimal farm management practices were interfered with by physically separating residence from the field.[50]

This sub-section argues that the location of such investments be oriented towards sustaining population densities that not only permit maximization of direct welfare benefits for every public dollar spent, but which *are also deemed desirable on productivity grounds*. Where it can be demonstrated, for example, that the spillover effects of rural intensification or small town growth are sizeable from the point of view of production strategy, the spatial pull of various kinds of social infrastructure may be brought to act upon the realization of induced optimal in-migration. People value the consumption of social services, and their availability and quality serve to guide spontaneous location decisions.[51] While only under special circumstances will such considerations be the sole motivation for migration behaviour,[52] they do, in conjunction with work and income opportunities, lead a person or household to prefer over others those regions with superior endowments of social facilities. Judiciously combined with the appropriate spatial distribution of productive infrastructure, then, an optimal social investment strategy can usefully support patterns of African population distribution that best secure regional development objectives.

This highlights the importance of systematically incorporating that potentially productive aspect of social service provision into the evaluation of proposed investments in the relevant infrastructure. It is essential for the social benefits calculus to take cognizance of service consumption by the existing population in the vicinity of the investment, of the in-movement of additional population in response to the investment, and the cumulative effects of population accretion leading to a rise in the regional level of economic activity, higher per capita incomes and purchases of local and traded goods, as well as higher aggregate consumption of the site-specific services. At the same time, the expanded production of the latter in the presence of internal scale economies results in lower per unit costs, so that, under the revised evaluation, increased benefits and lowered costs might often combine to recommend going ahead with a social investment when conventional procedures would not.[53]

Health care, family planning, and education are, beyond dispute, three of the services of primary importance in the Sub-Saharan context.[54] Aside from considerations based on directly productive reasons, justifications for the adequate provision of these to large sections of the African population remain as valid as ever on grounds not only of equity, but those that invoke the social externality-bearing nature of most of these activities.

Regardless of shifting developmental priorities and the sometimes hard choices forced by the scarcity of resources, no domestic policy-maker can afford to ignore the political necessity and the humanitarian imperative of striving to ensure at least a modicum of each of these services as part of a minimum social package for his constituency. What is wished to be stressed here, however, is the remarkable degree to which the operation of the salutary externalities deriving from these activities is really spatial. In being so, their acknowledged importance strengthens the argument that a spatially concentrated population permits better articulation of these location-dependent benefits.

Nowhere is this location dependency more evident than in the case of health care. With many kinds of preventive public health measures, including sanitation and disease control, the consumption of services by those in proximity to an individual compounds his or her own health safety. In the fields of family planning and nutrition, socially optimal behaviour is encouraged through a kind of demonstration effect if those in the immediate vicinity also practise it.[55] Internalization of the beneficial externalities of population control is easier under such circumstances, since it is regionally that the adverse effects of uncontrolled expansion are initially and most directly felt. In the field of education (and especially literacy), again, there are gains to having one's neighbours similarly educated, so that the amount of learning can be greater than it would be in isolation. Also, the benefits of learning are likely to be first manifest locally, giving the community a greater perceived stake in supporting these activities, and even initiating and paying for them. For this reason, cost recovery may be more probable with a clustered rather than dispersed population, apart from the more obvious concentration argument arising from the fact that if such services are to be fully paid for by their intended beneficiaries, their pro-vision must be on a large enough scale to lower unit costs sufficiently to render them affordable to the vast majority of the African people.[56]

IV. Redistribution and Population Policy

Population Migration in Sub-Saharan Africa

Indispensable to the study of settlement patterns is an understanding of how changes in these patterns spontaneously come about. If spatial restructuring is to be a vehicle of economic change, migration is the process that must effect it. Various typologies of African migration flows have been drawn,[57] identifying forced migrations, as were those relocations prompted by slave trading, tribal warfare or natural disasters, mostly in pre-colonial times; the 'regulated' migrations of the colonial era, through discouragement of land ownership outside designated reserved areas, the levying of 'head' or 'hut' taxes to secure labour supplies for population or mining operations (East and Southern Africa) or sometimes active recruitment (West Africa) for public works programmes; more recently, planned resettlement and political refugee movements are cited.

Attesting as they all do to a tradition of a remarkable degree of mobility among elements of the African population, certain types of migration phenomena interest us particularly for the purpose of engaging population distribution as a development tool. Examination of spontaneous migrant streams reveals valuable information, both regarding the nature of people's locational responses and concerning the economic, geographic and institutional structure within which they are expressed. Several recognizable forms of systematic human mobility are in evidence in Sub-Saharan Africa. For instance, the urban–rural movements between West African market-towns illuminate the trading functions historically important to that region's economy.[58] Nomadic transhumance or circulatory flows reflect a subsistence technology under certain environmental constraints (or inhospitable land tenure). Rural-to-urban flows, gathering post-independence momentum, may manifest either changes in employment structure or attraction to a superior level of public services. Liberian step-wise migration portrays migration as dependent upon a resource information network and skill acquisition process.[59] Remittance behaviour of mining migrants from Botswana illustrates migration's role as an important avenue to inter-sectoral resource transfer.[60] Temporary[61] or seasonal rural-to-rural migration, as from Upper Volta to Cote d'Ivoire, or of Senegalese 'stranger farmers' to the Gambia,[62] suggests equilibrating responses to regional labour shortages at certain periods or for particular farming operations.

Optimal migration is implied by an optimal spatial population distribution, and starting from any position of inoptimality, it is possible to define the direction and approximate magnitude of desired movement. Under these circumstances, the constructive role of voluntary migration as an *instrument* to secure developmentally desirable patterns lies in harnessing migrant spatial responses to optimally sited productive and social infrastructure investments.

The last few examples of inter-country migration raise, incidentally, another issue relevant to the domain of optimization for migrant destination choice. Arbitrarily imposed colonial and post-colonial national boundaries restrict free movement across ecologically or culturally contiguous zones. Thus inter-state politics, often resulting in evictions of immigrant foreigners (as under Ghana's Alien Compliance Order)[63] might militate against a global optimality. This situation may, however, be potentially relieved through regional co-operation agreements permitting regulated international mobility (e. g., under the sponsorship of organizations such as the West African ECOWAS).

Demography-distribution Interactions

While examining the structure of African migration patterns, one might justifiably ask: What are the connections, if any, between the 'population problem' in Sub-Saharan Africa and the optimal population distribution problem? Notwithstanding the current spurt in scholarly and donor attention[64] given to the high rates of increase of many African populations, the concerned governments have, by and large, preferred to adopt a rather passive stance in the field of population policy,[65] partly out of the belief that a demographic transition will automatically follow once an economic or structural transition takes place. Whether such a posture is a defensible substitute for more activist measures in the area of population control has to do with perceptions of the relationships between rural-to-urban migration and population growth rates. A few of the relevant considerations that the resolution of the issue hinges upon are increasingly being studied, and merit discussion here.

Study of the fertility consequences of urbanward internal migration provides insight into some interesting interactions between the distribution of population, on the one hand, and on the other, its growth. Such migration, in Africa is often age, education, sex and marital-status selective,[66] so the urban transition may possibly have a dampening effect upon fertility. On the other hand, once female migration begins, better health care facilities in cities may immediately increase the numbers of live births, whereas the salutary effect of lowered child mortality registers upon fertility decisions only with a time lag.[67] Female migration to the city, however, has been significantly associated with education and urban workforce participation in Tanzania,[68] and this argues that low-fertility-preference selectivity among women who migrate to urban areas, which are characterized by high explicit as well as opportunity costs of child-rearing to these workers, may well be at work to slow natural increase at these locations in the long run. The effect of such rural-to-urban population flows upon birth rates in rural areas is also certain, although, again, its direction is moot. Rural households may choose to have more children once it is likely that some of these children will move away to the city, or, conversely, may curtail family size if urban incomes and tastes are transmitted back through their emigrant members.[69]

But while fertility decreases as a result of rural-to-urban migration may have to wait upon rising incomes, women's education and increasing female urban labour-force participation, hope is held out that even in rural Africa, settlement intensification phenomena might trigger processes serving to reduce family size. It is the contention of some authors that many African long-fallow farming systems with customary tenure, where menfolk traditionally limit their tasks to land-clearing, the cultivation of export crops or migrate to work as hired labour in plantations or mines, where tribal lands are assigned in proportion to the size of family and where the burden of food crop and vegetable production for subsistence falls heavily on the women, who stay behind, the motivation to reduce family size is all but absent — women appreciate the extra juvenile working hands, and men derive all their status and wealth from marrying as many wives and siring as many children as is possible.[70] The frequency of polygamy, low female marriage ages, sizeable age gaps between spouses, and the prevalence of a system of bride-prices all militate against any significant lowering of fertility in rural areas, and combine to keep women's status depressed in most of rural Africa.[71] The transition to intensification and modernized farming works in the direction of reversing these tendencies, as under emerging private property rights, land replaces children as a store of wealth (disposable at will) and security against old age, ushers in values whereby status is defined by ownership of land, and reduces the incentive to expand family size which now actually becomes a detriment to individual net worth.[72] Following this line of argument, it appears that inasmuch as any move towards intensification favours both fertility decline and a rise in the status of women,[73] it is desirable. Since spatially concentrating the rural population arguably expedites the process of modernization of farming practices, as noted in earlier sections, it can be construed as an additional desirability on the above grounds.

Finally, what relationship does aggregate population growth bear in this analysis with its optimal distribution among regions? Although overall expansion in African populations may sometimes simulate the desirable processes so far considered, current rates of population growth are not sustainable over long periods of time, and certainly not in respect of all regions. The prescriptions made on spatial productivity grounds do not advocate rising population densities in all areas; rather, it is the redistribution from some to others that is seen as potentially important. Therefore, it is necessary to affirm that there is no inconsistency between the policy of population restriction now increasingly espoused in the African context and the one favouring the promotion of regional population growth and density on the productivity and other grounds.

V. Conclusions

This paper has attempted to bring together arguments for the constructive pursuit of population redistribution policies in the light of the broad development strategies and economic structures of the countries of Sub-Saharan Africa. Hopefully, the foregoing discussion might usefully guide general policy responses to questions such as this: In view of inevitable trade-offs forced by the paucity of resources, both internal and external, what spatial choices can best secure these economies' developmental objectives? We have sought to appeal to the socially beneficial externalities of regional growth in agriculture and other activities in formulating our response. By focusing upon a 'secondary town' urban development strategy, we have hoped to illustrate the important idea that the greatest social gains, as defined by set development priorities, can be reaped by committing resources to areas where there exist significant linkage possibilities and multiplier effects. The appropriate domain of public actions, we have argued, in most of the countries of this region, lies in spatially tied productive and social infrastructure that supports the creation of environments conducive to private growth and welfare. The role of voluntary migration in effecting optimally desirable spatial redistribution through incentives, not coercion, has been highlighted. The broad themes motivating our observations are, of course, not new ones in development — but they have often been neglected or forgotten, and deserve reinterpretation in the light of new strategic developmental thrusts.

A theoretical optimality characterization and its operationalization in directing regional infrastructural expenditures towards uses that maximize social returns in the presence of developmental externalities such as those we have described are beyond the scope of this paper and are pursued elsewhere.[74] Such formal frameworks and empirical methodologies are indispensable to determining which population patterns are consistent with the norms of a chosen development path, and in planning for their attainment.

Additional structural insights obtained within the purview of various sectoral concerns are equally crucial to the proper design of spatial policy. For instance, the understanding of farming systems, the intensification and sequencing of technological improvements in African agriculture need to be improved. Urbanization phenomena in the countries of Sub-Saharan Africa can likewise be studied in depth to gain insights about the potential for and desirability of efficient inter-urban population redistributions.[75] Important in this regard is to explore the structure of African commercial enterprise and manufacturing and the possibly related productive roles of the large informal segments of urban labour markets there.[76] Transportation studies can shed light on the comparative cost structures of alternative travel options, while systematic study of current patterns of African migration and human settlement will yield insights useful for attempts to modify them.

Specific regional insights are indispensable to the realism of the above assessments. For instance, the topography of terrain will condition both the market area for a region's produce and its resident supply hinterland, ultimately limiting the size of settlement in any particular case. Similarly, intensity of regional attachments will constrain the volume of migration across cultural or ethnic borders, and must also be understood when planning spatially for a given region.[77] Geographical and anthropological input is called for in this context.[78]

The study of existing institutions in the African context can also be expected to bring forth important insights about topics ranging from producer behaviour and peasant rationality to the design of traditional marketing practices and other indigenous methods of coping with spatially fragmented settlement systems to intra-familial division of productive tasks and long-term implications thereof for regional population demographics.

Political analysis of the potential for regional co-operation within and across national borders in the contemporary African climate might help determine how restricted or unrestricted the feasible spatial policy domain in fact is. African spatial phenomena are some of the most under-researched anywhere; it is hoped that current development opportunities stimulate policy-relevant study in the area.

NOTES

The author would like to thank Brian J.L. Berry for useful suggestions on the structure of the paper, and James L. Dietz for his comments on an earlier version.

The research culminating in this paper was undertaken while the author was Consultant to the Population, Health and Nutrition Department (Policy and Research Division) of the World Bank. While the author benefited greatly from discussions with various people at the Bank, responsibility for the views and opinions expressed in the paper is strictly hers.

1 See Mahar (1985).
2 See Adepoju in Clarke and Kosinski (1982) for a review of government-sponsored population redistribution policies in the African context. Two countries with such experiences as development measures are Tanzania and Botswana. See Maro and Mlay, Thomas, and also Silikshena, in Clarke and Kosinski (1982).
3 See Kosinski and Clarke in Clarke and Kosinski (1982) for results of a UN survey which showed that 80 per cent of African governments regarded current distributions as 'Extremely Unacceptable' in 1976.
4 See Abeumere (1981).
5 See The World Bank (1981) for an affirmation of the view that a 'turn-around' in agriculture is a precondition for the continent's economic development, and The World Bank (1982) for a detailing of the sources of African agricultural growth.
6 Eicher and Baker (1982) provides a comprehensive description of the structure of African agriculture.
7 See Acharya and Johnston (1978) for the role of smallholders in traditional agriculture.
8 Noronha (1985) for the role of smallholders in traditional agriculture.
9 Shukla (1965) documents the near-consistency of the capital–labour ratio in Indian agriculture during 1920–60, a period of continual population increase.

10 This theme runs through the writings of Boserup (1981), for example.
11 See Noronha (1985) or Eicher and Baker (1982) for a critique of a strictly 'deterministic' interpretation of Boserup's views.
12 Op. cit. The authors stress that population growth and market access are the main determinates of intensification.
13 See, e.g., Lele (1984) for a donor view of African agriculture development strategy. Lele (1975) synthesizes lessons from experiences with World Bank rural projects in Africa.
14 See Pingali, Bigot and Binswanger (1985) for views on the optimal sequencing of tractorization modes.
15 See, e.g., Lee and Maurice (1983).
16 Mechanization may be warranted at advanced stages of intensification of farming operations to, say, multiple-cropping, in view of possible labour shortages; also called for by the long-run needs of structural transformation.
17 Pingali, Bigot and Binswanger (1985) cite, however, difficulties with the emergence of tractor rental markets under conditions requiring certain farm operations to be extremely time–bound.
18 See Eicher and Baker (1982) for a review of efforts, colonial and modern, at African research on agronomic practices and improved varieties.
19 Even inter-regional cooperation for more basic research in plant breeding is being carried out on the principle of organizing research stations according to ecological zone.
20 The World Bank (1983) progress report stresses this as perhaps the most important bottleneck to agricultural development in Sub-Saharan Africa.
21 See Eicher and Baker (1982) for a good discussion of agricultural marketing problems in Africa; market inefficiencies are largely attributed by them to deficiencies in transport.
22 The World Bank (1984) cites 19.2 as the percentage of people living in urban areas in low-income Africa. Rosser (1973), using standard UN definitions of urban centres as localities with not less than 20,000 persons, arrived at a figure of 11 per cent for 1970.
23 Often, independence has brought urban influxes due to relaxation of colonial laws that restricted urban residence for Africans; making countervailing measures run afoul of nationalistic sentiments.
24 Primacy is measure of the dominance of higher urban size classes or a few top-ranking cities in a country's city-size distribution. 'Parasitic' in the context may often refer to urban economies founded upon 'exploitative' rural surpluses; 'non-generative', as the product perhaps of urban government bias in government expenditure. See Cohen (1979) for an argument that the latter has occurred in the cities of the Sahel.
25 This has confined itself lately to emphasis on researching institutional innovations in financing that make urban investment pay for themselves, a stance that is neutral towards urban expansion.
26 Towns such as Abeokuta, Ife, Ogbomosho and Ibadan in Yorubaland and Kumasi, Abomey and Ketou in Benin. See Rosser (1973) and Mondjannagni in Clarke and Kosinski (1982).
27 e.g., Kano, Timbuktu, etc. See Udo (1982).

28 Towns on the West African 'slave coast', such as Badagry, Accra, Cotonou.
29 e.g., Porto Novo, Abidjan, Lagos, etc.
30 Most Zambian and Congolese towns, for instance, were located along rail lines straddling the rich copper-producing regions.
31 Dar es Salaam, Mombasa, Kampala, for example.
32 Small urban centres have often been upgraded to regional capitals, as in the Nigerian case. Federal capital shifts also occurred, as moving Tanzania's capital city from Dar es Salaam to Dodoma, and the building of the new Nigerian capital at Abuja to replace Lagos.
33 These towns are widely characterized as featuring outward-looking, 'enclave'-type development.
34 Often blamed on the sometimes corrupt and inefficient parastatal marketing board organizations.
35 Experiences in many Asian countries have shown that promises held out by new technology may stand to collapse under fragmented markets and inadequate incentives.
36 Acharya and Johnston (1978) cite the instance of the burgeoning bicycle industry in the agriculturally prosperous Indian Punjab, that arose essentially out of implement service and repair workshops.
37 King and Byerlee (1978) demonstrate the scope for locational linkages of rural consumption patterns in Sierra Leone, arguing particularly that the latter may promote non-farm rural employment.
38 See Binswanger, et al. (1983) for a demonstration of the strength of agricultural growth linkages for rural employment in the case of Thailand.
39 For a general discussion of integrated spatial policy for development, see Rondinelli and Ruddle (1976).
40 The World Bank (1981) highlights the critical role of road networks in supporting agricultural production strategies.
41 See Eicher and Baker (1982).
42 Current methods of rural transportation evaluation have begun, to some extent, to take into account some of the dynamic interdependencies between developing agriculture and such infrastructure. See, e.g., Beenhakker (1979) and Beenhakker and Lago (1983).
43 Bhooshan (1980) documents the minimal impact the construction in 1974 of the modern Lagos/Badagry expressway linking metropolitan areas in West Africa had on still-inaccessible settlements fronting the highway. Katzman (1975) attempts to measure the effects of the Belem–Brasilia inter-regional developmental highway on rural settlement in the state of Goias in Brazil.
44 The structure and operation of the traditional rural periodic markets with itinerant traders that were a characteristic feature of West Africa no doubt reflected the sparseness of settlement and were probably quite spatially efficient under low trading volumes and labour-intensive transport technology. Obviously, with envisaged growth in agricultural production and the intensity of exchange, alternative arrangements will be optimal.
45 Choices between rail and road transport would also have to be made. Low passenger travel densities do not, in general, justify railroad construction,

but might in certain cases be rendered viable by offering combined freight and passenger services.

46 This is not always evident. Sometimes, scale itself involves a choice of technology; low density technologies for, say, sanitation, able to rely on the absorptive capacities of the environment, may take a vastly different form than high-density urban sewage systems.

47 Mostly in the form of schools, access roads, electricity, piped water, medical dispensaries, etc. For some of the practical spatial considerations in the provision of primary schools in the African context, see Gould in Clarke and Kosinski (1982).

48 As in 'Ujamaa' or Nyerere's conception of rural socialism for Tanzania.

49 See Khogali in Clarke and Kosinski (1982) for highlighting some of the successful features of Sudanese resettlement projects centred on well-chosen economic enterprises in the Nile Region.

50 See Silikshena in Clarke and Kosinski (1982) for an account of land regrouping policy in north-eastern Botswana which disregarded the productivity-restoring traditional practice of putting land into rotation between fallow, residence, garden plot and farming uses.

51 Also recognized here is the notion of selectivity — that different kinds of infrastructure will attract individual and household goods of differing age, sex, family composition, income, educational and preference characteristics.

52 Such extreme instances were documented, for example, during famine periods in Sahelian regions when *en masse* migrations took place to centres for the distribution of food aid.

53 Here, again, the need is to broaden social evaluation procedures to take cognizance of the full growth implications of project benefits.

54 The World Bank (1981) stresses, especially, access to health care as an urgent need in the African context.

55 On the supply side, The World Bank (1984 b) states that the logistical obstacles to expansion of family-planning programmes parallel administrative constraints faced by other programmes in Sub-Saharan Africa, viz., weak distributional and communications networks.

56 For an example of an operational cost-recovery procedure dealing with matters of scale and pricing in balancing demand for and supply of education in Malawi, in a context of inadequate public resources, to fully subsidize recurrent expenditures, see Thobani(1983). For general issues in paying for health services in LDCs, see de Ferranti (1985).

57 For a discussion of African migration in historical perspective, see Standing (1984).

58 See Udo (1982) for a discussion of hypotheses explaining the formation of such towns.

59 For numerical estimates of West African migration, see Zachariah, Conde and Nair, Vols. 1 and 2 (1980), and Zachariah and Conde (1981).

60 In this connection, see Byerlee (1977), Wikan (1981) and Lucas (1983) for analyses of migration-induced changes in agriculture.

61 See Zachariah, Conde, et al. (1980); Upper Voltans, e.g., have traditionally

performed certain operations on coffee plantations in Ghana that natives would not do.

62 An interesting form of seasonal migration that has taken on an almost ritualistic character. See Swindell, in Clarke and Kosinski (1982).

63 Under this order, issued in 1969, all foreign workers without a valid residence permit were required to obtain one, or leave the country in two weeks.

64 The World Bank (1984a,b) highlights the population problem as a long-run constraint on African economic development, but one of increasing urgency. Bernard (1982) discusses the redistribution effects of regional population pressure in Kenya, one of the countries singled out for special concern. See also Faruqee and Gulhati (1983) for a policy-oriented discussion of population issues.

65 Highest crude birth rates in the world and declining mortality notwithstanding, population growth has remained rather low on the list of concerns of African governments. See Udo (1982). In some countries, religious preferences render child-spacing the strongest acceptable method of population control.

66 See Barnum and Sabot (1976) for a discussion of the role of education in rural–urban migration in Tanzania, and Ekanem in Clarke and Kosinski (1982) for implications of migrant selectivity for the growth of Nigerian towns.

67 See Zachariah and Conde (1981) for a discussion of health care effects on fertility and child mortality rates in Africa.

68 See Shields (1980).

69 This will, of course, depend on various institutional considerations such as the presence or absence of old-age security for parents, cohesiveness of the extended family unit, and the regularity of remittance behaviour on the part of the emigrating scions.

70 Boserup (1985) pursues this theme.

71 It is remarked that countries where women's status is low are also those that feature high fertility rates.

72 Boserup (1985) cites evidence that in Rwanda and Burundi, high population densities induced lower fertility rates.

73 Again, this process is not claimed to be automatic and infallible. It may happen that men pre-empt good land for export crops, relegating women to inferior lands. Boserup suggests a lasting improvement in status can come if these predominantly food-producing women workers are given rights to the fruit of their labour.

74 See Shukla (1989) for a rigorous model, based on the positive economic externalities from agglomeration, to characterize and evaluate optimal investment choices.

75 See O'Connor (1981) for an annotated bibliography of writings on urbanization in Africa.

76 The topic of informal markets and their productive relationship to the formal, institutional wage sector merits careful research in the African context, especially in view of African governments' alarm at swelling city populations.

77 We have, in addition, mentioned the political barriers to mobility.
78 For a numerical extrapolation model that projects current geographical population distribution trends into the future on the basis of a few macro variables for the 47 countries of Sub-Saharan Africa, see OECD (1984).

REFERENCES

Abeumere, S.I. (1981), 'Population Distribution Policies and Measures in Africa South of the Sahara: A Review', *Population and Development Review* , Vol. 7, No. 3.

Acharya, S. and B. Johnston (1978), 'Two Studies of Development in Sub-Saharan Africa', World Bank Staff Working Paper No. 300, The World Bank, Washington, D.C.

Adepoju, Aderanti, 'Population Redistribution: A Review of Governmental Policies', in Clarke and Kosinski, op. cit.

Barnum, H.N. and R.H. Sabot (1976), 'Migration, Education and Urban Surplus Labour: The Case of Tanzania', Development Centre of the OECD, Paris.

Beenhakker, Henri (1979), 'Identification and Appraisal of Rural Roads Projects', World Bank Staff Working Paper No. 362, The World Bank, Washington, D.C.

Beenhakker, H.L. and A.M. Lago (1983), 'Economic Appraisal of Rural Roads — Simplified Operational Procedures for Screening and Appraisal', World Bank Staff Working Paper No. 610, The World Bank, Washington, D.C.

Bernard, Frank E., 'Rural Population Pressure and Redistribution in Kenya', in Clarke and Kosinski, op. cit.

Bhooshan, B.S., ed. (1980), *Towards Alternative Settlement Strategies: The Role of Small and Intermediate Centres in the Development Process*, Heritage Publishers.

Binswanger, Hans, et al. (1983), 'Growth and Employment in Rural Thailand', Country Programs Department, East Asia and Pacific Regional Office Report No. 3906-TH, The World Bank, Washington, D.C.

Binswanger, Hans and Prabhu Pingali (1984), 'The Evolution of Farming Systems and Agricultural Technology in Sub-Saharan Africa', The World Bank Report, No. ARU23, Agriculture and Rural Development Operational Policy Staff Research Unit, The World Bank, Washington, D.C.

Boserup, Ester (1981), *The Conditions of Agricultural Growth*, University of Chicago Press, Chicago.

————(1985), 'Research Priorities for Population Policies in Sub-Saharan Africa', Presented at Bellagio Conference, Bellagio, Italy.

Byerlee, Derek, et al. (1977), 'Rural Employment in Tropical Africa: Summary of Findings', USAID Working Paper No. 20, Washington, D.C.

Clarke, John and Leszek Kosinski, eds (1982), *Redistribution of Population in Africa*, Heinemann-London, Nairobi, Ibadan.

Cohen, Michael A., et al. (1979), 'Urban Growth and Economic Development in the Sahel', World Bank Staff Working Paper No. 315, The World Bank, Washington, D.C.

de Ferranti, David (1985), 'Paying for Health Services in Developing Countries', World Bank Staff Working Paper No. 721, The World Bank, Washington, D.C.

Eicher, Carl K. and Doyle C. Baker (1982), 'Research on Agricultural Development in Sub-Saharan Africa: A Critical Survey', International Development Paper, No. 1, Department of Agricultural Economics, Michigan State University, East Lansing, Mi.

Ekanem, Ita I., 'The Dynamics of Urban Growth: A Case Study of Medium Sized Towns in Nigeria', in Clarke and Kosinski, op. cit.

Faruqee, Rashid and Ravi Gulhati (1983), 'Rapid Population Growth in Sub-Saharan Africa: Issues and Policies', World Bank Staff Working Paper No. 559, The World Bank, Washington, D.C.

Gould, William T.S., 'Provision of Primary Schools and Population Redistribution', in Clarke and Kosinski, op. cit.

Katzman, Martin T. (1975), 'Regional Development Policy in Brazil: The Role of Growth Poles and Development Highways in Goias', *Economic Development and Cultural Change*, Vol. 24, No. 1.

Khogali, Mustafi Muhammed, 'Western Sudanese Migrants to Khashm el-Girba Agricultural Region', in Clarke and Kosinski, op. cit.

King, Robert P. and Derek Byerlee (1978), 'Factor Intensities and Locational Linkages of Rural Consumption Patterns in Sierra Leone', *American Journal of Agricultural Economics*, Vol. 60.

Lee, C.W. and J.M. Maurice (1983), 'The African Trypanosomiases', World Bank Technical Paper No. 4, The World Bank, Washington, D.C.

Lele, Uma (1975), *The Design of Rural Development — Lessons from Africa*, The Johns Hopkins University Press (for The World Bank), Baltimore.

———(1984), 'Rural Africa: Modernization, Equity and Long Term Development', in Eicher, Carl and John Staatz, eds, *Agricultural Development in the Third World*, The Johns Hopkins University Press, Baltimore.

Lucas, R.E.B. (1983), 'Emigration, Employment and Accumulation: The Miners of Southern Africa', Migration and Development Program, Discussion Paper No. 4, Harvard University, Cambridge, Ma.

Mahar, Dennis J., ed. (1985), 'Rapid Population Growth and Human Carrying Capacity: Two Perspectives', World Bank Staff Working Paper No. 690, Population and Development Series No. 15, The World Bank, Washington, D.C.

Maro, P.S. and W.F.I. Mlay, 'Population Redistribution in Tanzania', in Clarke and Kosinski, op. cit.

Mondjannagni, Alfred C., 'Rural–Urban Migration in the South of the People's Republic of Benin', in Clarke and Kosinski, op. cit.

Noronha, Raymond (1985), 'A Review of the Literature on Land Tenure Systems in Sub-Saharan Africa', Research Unit, Agriculture and Rural Development Department, Operational Policy Staff, The World Bank, Washington, D.C.

O'Connor, Anthony (1981), *Urbanization in Tropical Africa: An Annotated Bibliography*, G. K. Hall and Co., Boston, Ma.

Organization for Economic Co-operation and Development (OECD) (1984), *A Long Term Image of Sub-Saharan Africa*, Commission of the European Communities Deposits and Consignments Office Report.

Pingali, Prabhu, Yves Bigot and Hans Binswanger (1985), 'Agricultural Mechanization and the Evolution of Farming Systems in Sub-Saharan Africa', Agriculture and Rural Development Department, The World Bank, Washington, D.C.

Rondinelli, Dennis A. and Kenneth Ruddle (1976), *Urban Functions in Rural Development: An Analysis of Integrated Spatial Development Policy*, Office of Urban Development, Technical Assistance Bureau, USAID, Washington, D.C.

Rosser, Colin (1973), 'Urbanization in Tropical Africa: A Demographic Introduction', International Urbanization Survey, The Ford Foundation, New York.

Shields, Nwanganga (1980), 'Women in the Urban Labour Markets of Africa: The Case of Tanzania', World Bank Staff Working Paper No. 380, The World Bank, Washington, D.C.

Shukla, Tara (1965), *Capital Formation in Indian Agriculture*, Vora and Co., Publishers, Bombay.

Shukla, Vibhooti (1989), 'An Optimality Framework for Setting Infrastructure Investment Criteria in Regional Economic Development', University of Texas at Dallas, Tx. mimeo.

Silikshena, Robson M.K., 'The Regrouping Policy in the North-East District of Botswana', in Clarke and Kosinski, op. cit.

Standing, Guy (1984), 'Population Mobility and Productive Relations', World Bank Staff Working Paper No. 695, Population and Development Series No. 20, The World Bank, Washington, D.C.

Swindell, Kenneth, 'From Migrant Farmer to Permanent Settler: The Strange Farmers of the Gambia', in Clarke and Kosinski, op. cit.

Thobani, Mateen (1983), 'Charging User Fees for Social Services: The Case of Education in Malawi', World Bank Staff Working Paper No. 572, The World Bank, Washington, D.C.

Thomas, Ian, 'Villagization in Tanzania: Planning Potential and Practical Problems', in Clarke and Kosinski, op. cit.

Udo, Reuben K. (1982), *The Human Geography of Tropical Africa*, Heinemann Educational Books (Nigeria) Ltd., Ibadan.

Wikan, Gerd (1981), 'Absent Workers and Changes in Subsistence Crop Production: A Study in Letlhakeng and Tutume', *National Migration Study*, Central Statistics Office, Gaborone, Botswana.

World Bank, The (1981), *Accelerated Development in Sub-Saharan Africa — An Agenda for Action*, Washington, D.C.

———(1982), *World Development Report 1982*, Washington, D.C.

———(1983), *Sub-Saharan Africa: Progress Report on Development Prospects and Programs*, Washington, D.C.

———(1984a), *Toward Sustained Development in Sub-Saharan Africa — A*

Joint Program of Action, Washington, D.C.

World Bank, The (1984b), *World Development Report 1984*, Washington, D.C.

Zachariah, K.C., Julien Conde, et al. (1980), 'Demographic Aspects of Migration in West Africa — Volume 1', World Bank Staff Working Paper No. 414, The World Bank, Washington, D.C.

———(1980), 'Demographic Aspects of Migration in West Africa — Volume 2', World Bank Staff Working Paper No. 415, The World Bank, Washington, D.C.

———(1981), 'Migration in West Africa — Demographic Aspects', World Bank–OECD Study, Washington, D.C.

4 / Urban Infrastructure and Regional Productivity

VIBHOOTI SHUKLA

I. Introduction

Investment in infrastructure represents one of the most potent instruments available to governments at all levels for promoting economic growth, especially so in the developing country context. Further, the relative spatial specificity of infrastructure dictates that it be an essential ingredient of any regional development strategy. As with most public goods, the market does not ensure that the appropriate kind and quantity of urban services will be forthcoming, while overall resource constraints, of course, make it imperative that infrastructure investment be performed in as productive and efficient manner as possible. These factors necessitate systematic study of the productive role of urban infrastructure.

This paper aims at empirically exploring the contribution of urban infrastructure to regional economic efficiency within a regional production framework, through functional forms admitting the inclusion of urban infrastructure as an explicit input. The effects of several financial as well as physical indices of infrastructure — representing both stock and flow, capacity and utilization — of urban public services on various manufacturing industries are thus measured. In particular, we are interested in the output elasticities of various components of infrastructure, to identify those categories that are most likely to impact productivity in various economic activities, and in substitution elasticities between pairs of factors, to ascertain the extent of complementarity or substitutability between private and public capital. The results have implications for the optimal allocation of infrastructure for regional development, for the choice of industrial location policy instruments and for cost–benefit analyses of urban projects in developing countries.

II. Data

Cross-sectional implementation is with urban district-level 1976-77 production data (value added, employment and net value of fixed assets) for Maharashtra, a state comprising 26 districts, in India. The data are disaggregated at the level of five two-digit industry groups, as described in Table 1. This is complemented by information from municipal yearbooks on the financial (see Table 1) and physical (Table 2) aspects of various categories of urban infrastructure present in these districts.

III. Methodology and Results

In general, infrastructure may be modelled as entering the production specification as:

$$Q_i = J_i\,(K_i, L_i, I_i) \cdot u_i$$

where Q is output, and K represents private capital, L labour, u an error term, and I an index of the infrastructure input in question for region i. When separability is assumed, this may be specialized to:

$$Q_i = J_i\,(I_i) \cdot F\,(K_i, L_i)$$

Further restricting the $J_i\,(\cdot)$ functions to the form $J\,(\cdot) = I_i^{\theta}$, and taking logarithms on both sides, we obtain

$$\ln Q_i = \theta \ln I_i + \ln F(K_i, L_i) + e_i$$

where $e_i = \ln\,(u_i)$ is assumed to be the usual error term. Alternative specifications of the production function $F\,(\cdot)$ yield variants of the above estimating equation, of which we employ the Cobb–Douglas form, viz. (dropping the i subscript),

$$\ln Q = \ln A + \theta \ln I + \alpha \ln L + \beta \ln K + e$$

and experiment with an intensive version of this specification, defining regional production and infrastructure variables in spatial density (D = area in sq. km) or per capita (C) form:

$$\ln\,(Q/D) = \ln A + \theta \ln(I/D) + \alpha \ln\,(L/D) + \beta \ln\,(K/D) + e$$

and Kmenta's linearized version of the C.E.S., also interpretable as the linear-in-parameters parsimonious flexible form:

$$\ln\,(Q/L) = \ln B + \theta \ln I + \delta \ln\,(K/L) - (^1/_2)\,\rho\,\delta\,(1-\delta)\,[\ln(K/L)]^2 + e$$

Ordinary Least Squares (OLS) estimates of the elasticity of output, θ, in each of five industries with respect to alternative *financial* infrastructure indicators are presented in Table 3, assuming the flexible form production function, our preferred specification. (Appendix Table I presents parameter estimates from alternative specifications in respect of a single industry, 20, for comparison.) Analogous estimates when *physical* quantity infrastructure measures are used are to be found in

Table 1: Industry Code Descriptions and Definitions of Financial Infrastructure Variables

A: Industry Code	Description of Activity
20	Manufacture of Food Products
23	Manufacture of Cotton Textiles
31	Manufacture of Chemicals and Chemical Products
34	Manufacture of of Metal Products and Parts
97	Repair

B: Urban Infrastructure — Financial Indicators

I. *Revenue Items*

H1	Municipal rates — total rates and taxes (Rs '000)
H2	Total rates and taxes — I (Rs '000)
H3	Total revenues from municipal property and powers apart from taxation (Rs '000)
H4	Miscellaneous recoveries on account of services rendered to individuals (Rs '000)
H5	Income of commercial enterprises (Rs '000)

II. *Expenditure*

H6	General administration and collection charges — total (Rs '000)
H7	Public safety — total (Rs '000)
H8	Public health and convenience expenditure (Rs '000)
H9	Public instructions expenditure (Rs '000)
H10	Contribution for general purposes (Rs '000)
H11	Total expenditure (Rs '000)
H12	Extraordinary debt and investments (Rs '000)
H13	Expenditure of commercial enterprises (Rs '000)
H14	Total disbursement — H11+H12+H13 (Rs '000)
H15	Grand total of municipal expenditures — H14+Deposits+ Balance (Rs '000)

Table 2: Definitions of Physical Infrastructure Variables

A.	*District-wide Networks*	C.	*Water Supply*
11	– Number of towns and villages electrified	19	– Total length of pipeline in operation ('00 metres)
12	– Total operating rail length (km)	110	– Av. daily conspn. of water for domestic uses ('000 litres)
13	– National highway length (km)	111	– Av. daily conspn. of water for industrial purposes ('000 litres)
14	– State highway length (km)	112	– Av. daily conspn. of water for other uses ('000 litres)
15	– Total road length (km)	113	– Av. daily conspn. of water for all uses ('000 litres)
B.	*Sanitation*		
16	– Length of open drainage ('00 metres)		
17	– Length of underground drainage ('00 metres)		
18	– Total length of drainage ('00 metres)		

(Contd.)

Table 2: *(Contd.)*

D. *Power*
114 – Electricity consumption—Domestic ('000 kWh)
115 – Electricity consumption—Commercial ('000 kWh)
116 – Electricity consumption—Industrial ('000 kWh)
117 – Electricity consumption—Street Lighting ('000 kWh)
118 – Electricity consumption—Other ('000 kWh)
119 – Total electricity consumption ('000 kWh)
E. *Roads*
120 – Length of urban roads—Cement (km)
121 – Length of urban roads—Asphalt (km)
122 – Length of urban roads—Metalled (km)
123 – Length of urban roads—Other (km)
124 – Total length of urban roads—(km)
F. *Transport*
125 – Public transport service routes (km)
G. *Markets*
126 – Number of market-places—Open
127 – Number of market-places—Constructed
128 – Total number of urban market-places
H. *Communications*
129 – Number of post offices
130 – Number of telegraph offices
131 – Number of letter boxes
132 – Number of telephone connections
133 – Sum of communication components
I. *Information*
134 – Number of radio licenses—New
135 – Number of radio licenses—Renewed
136 – Number of newspapers and periodicals
137 – Number of printing presses
138 – Number of public libraries
139 – Sum of information components
J. *Administrative Services*
140 – Number of local government (tax-exempt) properties
141 – Capital value of government properties (Rs '000)
142 – Annual rental value of government properties (Rs '000)
K. *Health*
143 – Number of public hospitals
144 – Total number of hospitals
145 – Number of beds in public hospitals
146 – Total number of hospital beds
147 – Number of patients in public hospitals
148 – Total number of hospital patients
149 – Number of doctors in public hospitals
150 – Total number of hospital doctors
151 – Number of public dispensaries
152 – Total number of medical dispensaries
L. *Education*
153 – Number of secondary schools
154 – Number of students in secondary schools
155 – Number of institutions of higher education
156 – Number of students in institutions of higher education
157 – Total number of schools
158 – Total number of students
159 – Number of secondary professional institutes
160 – Number of students in secondary professional institutes
161 – Number of college-level professional institutes
162 – Number of students in college-level professional institutes

Table 4. (Again, Appendix Table II compares estimates for Industry 20 across functional forms.) Table 5 is an attempt to compare two-factor substitution elasticities between capital and labour using the Constant Elasticity of Substitution (CES) specification when infrastructure is not included as a productive input (*w/o H* case), and the elasticities of substitution that result when values of various financial infrastructure indicators are added to net value of fixed assets, the private capital measure (i.e., substituting *K+H* for *K* above).

Finally, to remove the restrictive assumption of input separability and permit calculation of distinct three-factor elasticities of substitution involving the physical infrastructure measures, a translog relationship between regional output and the three-factor categories is postulated, specifying

$$\ln Q = C + a_i \ln K + a_2 \ln L + a_3 \ln I + b_i (\ln K)^2 + b_2 (\ln L)^2 + b_3 (\ln I)^2 + C_1 (\ln K)(\ln L) + C_2 (\ln K)(\ln I) + C_3 (\ln L)(\ln I) + e$$

Table 3: Total Factor Productivity Contributions of Financial Infrastructure Variables Using Flexible Form Specification[1]

$\ln(Q/L) = \ln B + \theta \ln H + \delta \ln(K/L) - (\ ) \rho\ \delta(1-\delta)\ [\ln(K/L)]^2 + e$

Infra Variable[2]	*Industry 20*	*Industry 23*	*Industry 31*	*Industry 34*	*Industry 97*
I. *Revenue Items*					
H1	0.23†	0.33*	0.25†	0.34†	0.07*
H2	0.23†	0.34*	0.24†	0.24†	0.07*
H3	0.13	0.26*	0.19‡	0.20†	0.06†
H4	0.00	0.02	0.10	0.19*	0.01
H5	–0.07	0.13	0.11	0.74†	0.02
II. *Expenditure Items*					
H6	0.34†	0.44*	0.33‡	0.38†	0.09†
H7	0.29†	0.31†	0.28†	0.31*	0.08†
H8	0.22†	0.30*	0.23†	0.23†	0.06†
H9	0.13†	0.12‡	0.17‡	0.22‡	0.03‡
H10	0.08	0.18*	0.08	0.06	0.03‡
H11	0.21†	0.30*	0.25†	0.24†	0.07*
H12	0.13‡	0.20*	0.17†	0.14‡	0.05*
H13	0.17	0.12	0.08	0.52†	0.01
H14	0.17†	0.25*	0.20†	0.19†	0.06*
H15	0.18†	0.26*	0.20†	0.17‡	0.06*

1 Reported coefficients represent estimates of θ = Elasticity of Output w.r.t. corresponding *H*.

2 See Table 1 for industry code descriptions and financial infrastructure variable definitions.

*; †; ‡ = significant at 1 per cent, 5 per cent and 10 per cent level respectively.

Estimation is performed for the pooled data set to gain degrees of freedom, and the results permit the presentation, in Table 6, of output and substitution elasticities (evaluated at sample means) for all industries by alternative infrastructure measures.

IV. Discussion and Conclusions

Coefficients of variables H1, H2 and H11, H14 and H15 in Table 3 generally measure the contribution of overall municipal revenue and expenditure, respectively, to regional industrial productivity. Elasticities for current budgetary variables (H1, H2 and H11) are found to be quite high, lying in the range between 21 per cent and 34 per cent for various industries with the exception of Industry 97 (Repairs). Decomposition by broad categories reveals surprisingly high returns to general administrative expenditures (H6), and reasonably high elasticities for public safety, public health and public instruction, in that order. The almost uniformly lower elasticities for Industry 97 suggest that firms in manufacturing may benefit to a greater extent (being subject to more government involvement?) than those in repairs and ancillary activities from various public expenditures.

Since the process of production and distribution of public services may be subject to economies of scale or density, it was thought worthwhile to examine if deflating the expenditure variables to cast them in terms of density or per capita intensity would change our findings substantially. Appendix Table I presents the results of this experiment using both Cobb–Douglas and Flexible form functional specifications for Industry 20. Coefficients when the expenditure or production variables are normalized per square unit area [(2), (3) and (7)] are very close to uninflated versions [(1) and (6)], whereas, by contrast, financial proxies in per capita intensive forms [(4), (5) and (8)] result in much higher coefficients for both specifications. This suggests that large population size may make infrastructure expenditure more efficient, but this needs further confirmation.

Measured returns to budgetary expenditures of local governments, since they include emoluments to staff — which can be relatively significant in the Indian context — will capture some of the region-wide indirect multiplier effects that cannot be attributed to any specific public investment, taken separately. Hence we can expect somewhat higher coefficients on these variables than on narrowly defined physical

Table 4: Total Factor Productivity Contributions of Physical Infrastructure Variables Using Flexible Form Specification[1]
$\ln(Q/L) = \ln B + \theta \ln I + \delta \ln(K/L) - (\ ) \rho\, \delta(1-\delta)\, [\ln(K/L)]^2 + e$

Infra Variable[2]	*Industry 20*	*Industry 23*	*Industry 31*	*Industry 34*	*Industry 97*
A. *District-wide Networks*					
11	–0.10	–0.18†	–0.07	–0.09	–0.06†
12	0.11	–0.13	–0.04	-1.06	–0.12‡
13	0.04	–0.11	0.15	0.41†	–0.02
14	–0.19‡	–0.28†	–0.06	–0.15	–0.06‡
15	–0.21‡	–0.27†	–0.03	–0.14	–0.06
B. *Sanitation*					
16	0.08	0.17	0.11	–0.02	0.07‡
17	0.05	0.20	0.04	0.03	0.04‡
18	0.17	0.31‡	0.06	–0.05	0.07†
C. *Water Supply*					
19	0.07	0.09	0.11	0.25	0.07
110	0.20‡	0.16	0.10	0.21†	0.07†
111	0.16†	0.20†	0.08	0.03	0.05*
112	0.17*	0.12	0.11	0.21‡	0.06†
113	0.21†	0.18	0.10	0.21‡	0.07†
D. *Power*					
114	0.34†	0.20	0.23	0.17	0.07‡
115	0.39*	0.22	0.17	0.21	0.09‡
116	0.26*	0.16	0.13	–0.06	0.05‡
117	0.36†	0.36	0.41‡	0.41†	0.08‡
118	0.09	0.05	0.05	–0.06	0.04
119	0.34*	0.23	0.25	0.04	0.06*
E. *Roads*					
120	–0.01	0.04	0.11	0.15‡	0.04
121	0.32†	0.35†	0.29†	0.23	0.09*
122	–0.01	–0.45†	–0.26	0.03	–0.05
123	–0.25	–0.42‡	–0.03	–0.05	–0.06
124	0.34	0.39	0.33	0.40‡	0.13†
F. *Transport*					
125	0.06	0.13†	0.05	0.11‡	0.04*
G. *Markets*					
126	–0.06	–0.17	0.41‡	0.17	0.02
127	0.28‡	0.28‡	0.40*	0.19	0.10*
128	0.33	0.37	0.63*	0.36	0.14†
H. *Communications*					
129	0.28‡	0.38†	0.19	0.21	0.12*
130	0.32	0.32	0.09	0.03	0.08‡
131	0.30‡	0.35‡	0.24	0.23	0.13*
132	0.20‡	0.26†	0.18	0.25†	0.08*
133	0.20‡	0.26†	0.18	0.25†	0.09*

(Contd.)

Table 4: (*Contd.*)

Infra Variable[2]	*Industry 20*	*Industry 23*	*Industry 31*	*Industry 34*	*Industry 97*
I. *Information*					
134	0.05	0.07	0.20	0.13	0.08*
135	0.16	0.18	0.28†	0.17	0.10*
136	0.10	0.11	0.07	0.18	0.09*
137	0.23†	0.31†	0.17	0.16	0.09*
138	0.06	–0.08	0.01	–0.10	0.04
139	0.14	0.17	0.28†	0.17	0.10*
J. *Administrative Services*					
140	0.15	0.22	0.21	0.24†	0.02
141	0.27	0.41‡	0.20‡	–0.04	0.11
142	0.10‡	0.11‡	0.04	0.11†	0.03
K. *Health*					
143	0.41†	0.63*	0.57*	0.40‡	0.14‡
144	0.22	0.33	0.45*	0.11	0.12*
145	0.23‡	0.33†	0.17	0.23‡	0.10*
146	0.25‡	0.34†	0.23	0.24‡	0.11*
147	0.00	0.12	0.25‡	0.31†	0.07‡
148	–0.03	0.11	0.31†	0.32†	0.08‡
149	0.17	0.30‡	0.22	0.26‡	0.12*
150	0.04	0.25	0.30†	0.19	0.12*
151	0.27*	0.23†	0.21†	0.10	0.05†
152	0.30	–0.17	0.41‡	0.53*	–0.02
L. *Education*					
153	0.32†	0.32	0.28‡	0.22	0.12*
154	0.32†	0.31‡	0.27‡	0.21	0.09†
155	0.12	0.19	0.24	0.18	0.12*
156	0.12	0.15	0.21	0.10	0.10†
157	0.20	0.31‡	0.15	0.08	0.10*
158	0.20	0.28‡	0.18	0.11	0.10*
159	–0.02	0.32	–0.33	–0.14	–0.02
160	–0.20	0.07	–0.03	–0.11	0.02
161	0.00	0.34†	0.06	0.15	0.03
162	0.00	0.21‡	0.03	0.08	0.01

1 Reported coefficients represent estimates of θ = Elasticity of Output w.r.t. corresponding *I*.

2 See Table 1 for industry code descriptions and physical infrastructure variable definitions.

*; †; ‡ = significant at 1 per cent, 5 per cent and 10 per cent level respectively.

indexes. However, because expenditures essentially represent a product of cost and quantity, they will not always accurately reflect levels of public service provision, affected as they are by systematic cost differences (due to differential labour costs, for instance) across regions. Cost differences may likewise result from the technology of infrastructure provision, as hinted at above.

Further, if it is desired to obtain more accurate measures of the relative contributions of various specific infrastructural components, it is advisable to use physical rather than financial infrastructure proxies. This enables a purer formulation of public infrastructure as an input, and can provide a more explicit guide to regional policy-making. Table 4 presents the results of estimations carried out using

Table 5: Substitution Elasticities Between Infrastructure-Augmented Capital and Labour Using CES Production Specification[1]

Infra Variable[2]	*Industry 20*	*Industry 23*	*Industry 31*	*Industry 34*	*Industry 97*
W/O *H*	$\ln(Q/L) = \ln B + (\upsilon-1)\ln L + \upsilon\delta \ln(K/L) - (1/2)\,\rho\upsilon\delta(1-\delta)\,[\ln(K/L)]^2 + e$				
	0.4278	0.2583	4.0561	0.2220	0.6667
W/H	$\ln(Q/L) = \ln B + (\upsilon-1)\ln L + \upsilon\delta \ln((K+H)/L) - (1/2)\,\rho\upsilon\delta(1-\delta)\,[\ln((K+H)/L)]^2 + e$				
I. *Revenue Items*					
H1	1.0854	0.4854	0.7450	0.7137	0.9129
H2	1.0862	0.4709	0.7641	0.7089	0.9103
H3	1.4264	0.3741	3.3963	–0.3341	0.7469
H4	0.4335	0.2573	3.8966	–0.1525	0.6680
H5	–0.0361	0.3909	0.8335	80.5637	0.7132
II. *Expenditure Items*					
H6	1.3954	0.5752	0.5365	0.7734	0.8141
H7	1.8024	0.5550	2.2553	0.6048	0.7316
H8	1.0966	0.5683	0.8610	0.7123	0.8978
H9	0.2485	8.4843	1.0774	0.7515	0.7726
H10	0.7606	–0.3112	1.3223	–0.6432	0.7135
H11	1.0844	–2.3168	0.6862	0.7738	0.9297
H12	0.1141	0.7186	0.1783	0.4876	0.7596
H13	0.1940	0.3847	0.8239	0.0516	0.7271
H14	1.1839	0.4703	0.6651	0.7456	0.7976
H15	1.1482	0.5469	0.7821	0.7038	0.7759

1 Reported coefficients represent estimates of $\sigma = 1/(1+\rho)$ = Elasticity of Substitution between Labour and Capital augmented by corresponding *H*.

2 See Table 1 for industry code descriptions and financial infrastructure variable definitions.

a far richer assortment of direct infrastructure variables. Grouped under 12 (*A* – *L*) categories are a mix of various capacity and utilization indexes.

A much more diverse picture now emerges. It is instructive to discuss items of maximum impact on productivity by industry. For Industry 20 (Food) — a consumer-oriented, resource-based activity — water supply, power, asphalt roads, and urban market-places appear to significantly enhance efficiency. For Industry 23 (Cotton Textiles) — an established consumer-goods industry — drainage capacity, industrial water consumption, asphalt roads, public transport (to facilitate worker commutes?), and, again, market places have maximum impact. For each of the above, general communications infrastructure and, from the information category, printing presses, augment total factor productivity. Industries 31 (Chemicals) and 34 (Metal Products and Parts) are, by contrast, more producer oriented. Chemicals, presumably the more capital intensive of the two, respond to asphalt roads, markets and, importantly, to information components. Metal Products and Parts manufacturing firms gain efficiency from power consumption, roads and public transport, telephone connections and administrative services. Lastly, producer-service Industry 97 (Repairs), is seen benefiting modestly from a wide variety of specific items, including water, sanitation, power, roads, public transport, markets, communications, and information, although, significantly, not administrative services.

Two sets of categories deserve closer attention. Firstly, we note the anomalous performance of the district-wide network category, *A*. This includes rural regional roads, highways, rail and power networks in addition to urban, but one would have expected the regional economy to benefit from hinterland connections. Insufficient spatio-economic articulation between town and country as prevails in many LDCs may explain the lack of significance of these indexes. It does not, however, explain why they should be negative in almost all instances, unless one is prepared to believe that long-distance links dissipate regional advantage through competition or adverse migration. Appendix Table II, which presents results analogous to Table 4 in intensive form also fails to alter this anomaly. The table does, however, establish, for Industry 20, that when physical infrastructure variables are entered in per capita form (compare specifications [1 and 2] with [5 and 6], respectively), higher magnitudes of coefficients, unlike with the financial proxies, do not result.

Table 6: Output and Substitution Elasticities (All Industries) Using Translog Specification[1]

$$\ln Q = C + a_1 \ln K + a_2 \ln L + a_3 \ln I + b_1 (\ln K)^2 + b_2 (\ln L)^2 + b_3 (\ln I)^2 + c_1 (\ln K)(\ln L) + c_2 (\ln K)(\ln I) + c_3 (\ln L)(\ln I) + e$$

Infra Variable[2]	*MK*	*ML*	*MI*	*SKL*	*SKI*	*SLI*
A. *District-wide Networks*						
11	0.53	0.68	0.01	0.81	–1.34	–0.37
12	0.52	0.70	–0.14	0.82	0.17	–1.50
13	0.50	0.74	0.05	2.91	31.21	–10.32
14	0.53	0.67	–0.05	0.82	0.03	0.85
15	0.52	0.68	0.13	0.48	7.84	1.76
B. *Sanitation*						
16	0.51	0.67	0.16	0.64	2.70	0.89
17	0.49	0.70	0.08	0.66	4.01	1.05
18	0.51	0.67	0.12	0.26	14.06	2.82
C. *Water Supply*						
19	0.52	0.64	0.17	0.95	–2.27	–0.56
110	0.46	0.62	0.31	0.61	2.30	0.61
111	0.51	0.63	0.12	0.76	1.15	0.67
112	0.49	0.64	0.14	0.80	1.37	0.28
113	0.46	0.61	0.30	0.63	2.29	0.57
D. *Power*						
114	0.49	0.66	0.17	–0.18	17.75	3.74
115	0.52	0.61	0.19	0.47	2.70	2.02
116	0.48	0.70	0.08	0.86	0.89	–0.02
117	0.47	0.70	0.30	0.90	2.17	–0.10
118	0.52	0.68	–0.00	–0.03	–11.36	8.97
119	0.48	0.67	0.22	0.80	1.04	0.21
E. *Roads*						
120	0.52	0.66	0.10	0.69	1.69	0.87
121	0.47	0.64	0.25	0.76	3.11	0.28
122	0.51	0.65	0.21	0.93	–0.55	–0.34
123	0.52	0.69	–0.03	0.77	–0.08	0.25
124	0.50	0.60	0.40	1.22	–3.17	–0.53
F. *Transport*						
125	0.48	0.62	0.09	0.76	1.13	0.85
G. *Markets*						
126	0.52	0.71	–0.03	0.45	–2.30	2.63
127	0.50	0.63	0.23	4.93	–58.70	–11.03
128	0.52	0.63	0.19	–0.74	–0.63	0.07

1 Reported coefficients defined in note at end of table.

2 See Table 2 for physical infrastructure variable definitions.

(Contd.)

Table 6: *(Contd.)*

Infra Variable	*MK*	*ML*	*MI*	*SKL*	*SKI*	*SLI*
H. *Communications*						
129	0.48	0.64	0.15	0.81	−1.89	0.02
130	0.54	0.65	0.12	2.26	13.78	−4.13
131	0.49	0.64	0.14	0.85	−3.01	−0.10
132	0.46	0.64	0.15	0.75	1.86	0.52
133	0.46	0.64	0.15	0.75	1.88	0.51
I. *Information*						
134	0.52	0.60	0.16	0.71	1.07	0.99
135	0.48	0.64	0.17	0.76	1.73	0.34
136	0.46	0.64	0.14	0.70	2.40	1.27
137	0.46	0.66	0.14	0.66	6.97	0.67
138	0.47	0.79	0.00	0.56	−1.35	0.80
139	0.48	0.63	0.17	0.75	1.73	0.41
J. *Administrative Services*						
140	0.52	0.64	0.14	0.72	0.89	1.04
141	0.56	0.62	0.17	0.70	0.71	0.69
142	0.50	0.53	0.12	0.91	0.96	0.96
K. *Health*						
143	0.49	0.60	0.30	0.55	12.82	0.48
144	0.46	0.67	0.32	0.92	1.36	−0.06
145	0.48	0.65	0.14	1.20	−9.73	−1.47
146	0.49	0.64	0.17	0.61	6.43	0.77
147	0.49	0.61	0.19	1.06	−1.03	−0.75
148	0.48	0.62	0.19	1.04	−1.09	−0.64
149	0.46	0.65	0.14	1.19	−9.28	−1.25
150	0.46	0.67	0.11	0.77	−2.61	0.27
151	0.46	0.66	0.18	0.69	2.86	0.62
152	0.51	0.69	0.17	0.67	1.58	0.84
L. *Education*						
153	0.48	0.61	0.14	0.98	−2.05	−0.31
154	0.48	0.61	0.16	1.54	−8.91	−2.53
155	0.48	0.62	0.13	0.95	−1.02	−0.22
156	0.47	0.63	0.13	0.98	−1.69	−0.41
157	0.47	0.63	0.15	0.92	−1.53	−0.16
158	0.46	0.64	0.15	0.94	−2.25	−0.32
159	0.59	0.55	0.00	0.24	−2.40	2.47
160	0.56	0.58	−0.04	0.45	−1.03	1.36
161	0.50	0.58	0.16	1.82	−7.95	−4.84
162	0.50	0.57	0.19	0.58	2.22	1.59

Note: MK = $d\ln Q/d\ln K$ = Elasticity of Output w.r.t. Capital.
ML = $d\ln Q/d\ln L$ = Elasticity of Output w.r.t. Labour.
MI = $d\ln Q/d\ln I$ = Elasticity of Output w.r.t. corresponding *I*.
SKL = Elasticity of Substitution between Capital and Labour.
SKI = Elasticity of Substitution between Capital and corresponding *I*.
SLI = Elasticity of Substitution between Labour and corresponding *I*.
All of the above are calculated at variable means for the entire sample.

The other set of categories we wish to highlight for comment is 'social' (as opposed to 'economic') infrastructure. Items under the Health and Education categories perform surprisingly well, even relative to more conventional infrastructure components. The coefficients observed suggest substantial returns to the industrial sector from such investments, presumably through higher worker productivity, lower absenteeism and the like. Under Health the higher returns to public hospitals and dispensaries, over totals incorporating private facilities as well, bear testimony to the potential social benefit of public involvement in health at the urban level in a developing country. The returns to education, though not as broadly evident, reveal clear gains from secondary schooling.

As noted above, the sub-components of several infrastructure categories contain both capacity as well as utilization variables. Some useful insights about congestion or under utilization may be obtained by examining the relative success of each kind of index. We observe, by and large, with economic infrastructure, that coefficients on utilization indexes fare better than those on capacity measures. For example, 'water consumption' performs better than 'length of pipeline', 'public transport service routes' better than 'length of urban roads', and 'annual rental value of government property' does better than its 'capital value'. This superiority of utilization variables is reversed in the social infrastructure categories, with 'number of public hospitals' performing better than 'patients in public hospitals' and 'number of secondary schools' doing slightly better than 'number of students in secondary schools'. We can likewise compare effects of variables suggesting different infrastructure technologies for the provision of basically the same type of service at different levels of quality. For instance, asphalt roads contribute more to regional productivity than total urban roads, constructed marketplaces more so than open ones, and for some industries, telephone facilities more than telegraph offices. Of course, costs as well as benefits need to be factored into technology selection in an LDC context.

Finally, we consider the issue of the substitutability of public infrastructure with private internal inputs used in regional production. Table 5 attempts to explore the effect of augmenting the private capital measure, net value of fixed assets, with various budgetary infrastructure components in turn. H1, H2, H14 and H15 all show a heightened substitution elasticity with labour compared to that measured in their absence, but this formulation unrealistically assumes public and private

Appendix Table I: Industry 20 – Productivity Contributions of Financial Infrastructure Variables Using Alternative Specifications[1]

Industry 20

A. *Cobb–Douglas Specifications*

Infra Variable[2]	(1) H–CD	(2) H/D–CD	(3) H/D–CD/D	(4) H/C–CD	(5) H/C–CD/D
I. Revenue					
H1	0.32*	0.26‡	0.31†	0.95*	0.90*
H2	0.31*	0.25‡	0.31†	0.92*	0.89*
H3	0.23‡	0.17	0.23‡	0.27	0.28
H4	–0.00	–0.02	–0.01	–0.03	–0.03
H5	0.01	–0.03	–0.01	–0.07	–0.06
II. Expenditure					
H6	0.43*	0.25	0.34‡	0.61	0.58
H7	0.38*	0.28‡	0.36†	0.96*	1.01*
H8	0.30*	0.27†	0.31†	0.91*	0.83*
H9	0.14†	0.11‡	0.12†	0.16†	0.17†
H10	0.09	0.07	0.08	0.08	0.09
H11	0.29*	0.23‡	0.28†	0.96*	0.94*
H12	0.17†	0.13	0.16†	0.22‡	0.24†
H13	0.24‡	0.22	0.22‡	0.23	0.22
H14	0.24†	0.19‡	0.23†	0.50†	0.50*
H15	0.24†	0.20‡	0.24†	0.52†	0.51*

B. *Flexible Form Specifications*

Infra Variable	(6) H–FLX	(7) H/D–FLX	(8) H/C–FLX
I. Revenue			
H1	0.23†	0.21‡	0.78*
H2	0.23†	0.21‡	0.77*
H3	0.13	0.12	0.14
H4	0.00	–0.02	–0.05
H5	–0.07	–0.09	–0.12
II. Expenditure			
H6	0.34†	0.24	0.57
H7	0.29†	0.25‡	1.01*
H8	0.22†	0.22†	0.74*
H9	0.13†	0.11‡	0.16†
H10	0.08	0.07	0.08
H11	0.21†	0.20‡	0.77*
H12	0.13‡	0.11	0.19
H13	0.17	0.18	0.21
H14	0.17†	0.16‡	0.40†
H15	0.18†	0.16‡	0.40†

1 See Table 1 for financial infrastructure variable definitions.

2 Estimating equations: (1) Cobb–Douglas; (2) and (3), (4) and (5) are intensive forms as specified in text; (6) Flexible form; (7) and (8) use infrastructure variables normalized for area (D) and population (C) respectively.

*, †, ‡ = Significant at 1 per cent, 5 per cent and 10 per cent level respectively.

Appendix Table II: Productivity Contributions of Physical Infrastructure Variables with Alternative Specifications[1]

Infra Variable[2]	Industry 20 (1) I–CD	(2) I–FLX	(3) I/D–CD	(4) I/D–FLX	(5) I/C–CD	(6) I/C–FLX
A. *District-wide Networks*						
11	–0.12	–0.10	–0.12	–0.10	–0.11‡	–0.09
12	0.15	0.11	–0.11	–0.10	–0.18	–0.14
13	0.08	0.04	–0.10	–0.13	–0.11	–0.12
14	–0.22‡	–0.19‡	–0.20†	–0.16‡	–0.16†	–0.13*
15	–0.22‡	–0.21‡	-0.19†	–0.18‡	–0.16†	–0.14*
B. *Sanitation*						
16	0.05	0.08	–0.06	–0.04	–0.15	–0.15
17	0.03	0.05	–0.02	0.00	–0.07	–0.06
18	0.16	0.17	0.03	0.07	–0.09	–0.07
C. *Water Supply*						
19	0.10	0.07	–0.15	–0.20	–0.36‡	–0.31‡
110	0.21‡	0.20‡	0.16	0.16	0.14	0.12
111	0.20†	0.16†	0.14‡	0.14†	0.15‡	0.17‡
112	0.17†	0.17*	0.15†	0.18‡	0.17†	0.22*
113	0.22†	0.21†	0.17	0.17	0.17	0.15
D. *Power*						
114	0.38†	0.34†	0.19	0.19	0.15	0.13
115	0.42*	0.39*	0.26‡	0.26‡	0.27	0.22
116	0.27*	0.26*	0.21†	0.21†	0.21†	0.19‡
117	0.44†	0.36†	0.17	0.17	–0.07	–0.07
118	0.08	0.09	0.03	0.05	–0.00	0.02
119	0.35*	0.34*	0.25†	0.25†	0.23	0.21
E. *Roads*						
120	–0.02	–0.01	–0.12	–0.09	–0.18	–0.17
121	0.39*	0.32†	0.23	0.22	0.25	0.24
122	0.02	–0.01	–0.15	–0.13	–0.22	–0.14
123	–0.26	–0.25	–0.35†	–0.30†	–0.30*	–0.23†
124	0.36	0.34	0.04	0.05	–0.41	–0.29
F. *Transport*						
125	0.05	0.06	0.04	0.05	0.03	0.04
G. *Markets*						
126	–0.06	–0.06	–0.28	–0.27	–0.41†	–0.35†
127	0.50†	0.28‡	0.15	0.14	–0.05	–0.04
128	0.45	0.33	–0.07	–0.06	–0.43‡	–0.38
H. *Communications*						
129	0.33‡	0.28‡	0.19	0.21	–0.10	–0.08
130	0.33	0.32	0.13	0.15	0.03	0.07
131	0.36†	0.30‡	0.23	0.25	–0.03	–0.01
132	0.25†	0.20	0.18	0.17	0.25	0.24
133	0.26†	0.20‡	0.19	0.17	0.27	0.26

(Contd.)

Appendix Table II: *(Contd.)*

Infra Variable[2]	(1) I–CD	(2) I–FLX	(3) I/D–CD	(4) I/D–FLX	(5) I/C–CD	(6) I/C–FLX
			Industry 20			
I. *Informaton*						
134	0.06	0.05	–0.01	–0.01	-0.08	–0.09
135	0.23‡	0.16	0.12	0.11	0.03	0.04
136	0.12	0.10	0.08	0.07	–0.00	0.00
137	0.28†	0.23†	0.20	0.20	0.30	0.34
138	0.05	0.06	–0.07	–0.06	–0.15	–0.12
139	0.20	0.14	0.09	0.08	–0.01	–0.00
J. *Administrative Services*						
140	0.17	0.15	0.05	0.06	–0.06	–0.05
141	0.25	0.27	0.12	0.13	0.33	0.29
142	0.10†	0.10‡	0.11†	0.11†	0.10‡	0.11‡
K. *Health*						
143	0.59†	0.41†	0.15	0.16	–0.27	–0.15
144	0.29	0.22	–0.02	0.00	–0.22	–0.21
145	0.26‡	0.23‡	0.15	0.14	0.07	0.05
146	0.30†	0.25‡	0.15	0.15	0.06	0.05
147	0.01	0.00	–0.13	–0.14	–0.39†	–0.35†
148	–0.02	–0.03	–0.16	–0.16	–0.43†	–0.39†
149	0.20	0.17	0.04	0.05	–0.19	–0.18
150	0.04	0.04	–0.11	–0.09	–0.45†	–0.45†
151	0.30*	0.27*	0.24†	0.23†	0.30†	0.30†
152	0.29	0.30	–0.00	–0.02	–0.15	–0.13
L. *Education*						
153	0.40†	0.32†	0.24	0.23	0.05	0.06
154	0.38*	0.32†	0.28	0.27	0.51	0.48
155	0.15	0.12	–0.07	–0.07	–0.38‡	–0.32
156	0.16	0.12	–0.01	–0.01	–0.21	–0.20
157	0.23	0.20	0.08	0.09	–0.20	–0.18
158	0.23	0.20	0.12	0.13	–0.13	–0.11
159	–0.03	–0.02	–0.05	–0.03	–0.12	–0.06
160	–0.25	–0.20	–0.38†	–0.34*	–0.30†	–0.27†
161	0.03	0.00	–0.06	–0.06	–0.27	–0.27
162	0.01	0.00	–0.04	–0.04	–0.14	–0.14

1 See Table 2 for physical infrastructure variable definitions.

2 Estimating equations (1), (3), (5) and (2), (4), (6) use regular and intensive versions of Cobb–Douglas and Flexible forms respectively.

*, †, ‡ = Significant at 1 per cent, 5 per cent and 10 per cent level respectively.

capital to be perfect substitutes. Estimation with the translog production specification for all industries combined indicates an average overall output elasticity to infrastructure, (*MI*), of about 16 per cent. Separate infrastructure substitution possibilities with capital (*SKI*) as well as labour (*SLI*) are presented in Table 6 for each of the physical indexes. The results are very revealing. The positive signs of many of the elasticities of substitution indicate that infrastructure and private inputs are, by and large, substitutes. Moreover, in general, the elasticities of substitution between infrastructure and capital are higher than those between infrastructure and labour. Thus, public investment in infrastructure may be able to alleviate entrepreneurs' capital constraints without the severe labour displacing effects associated with outright capital subsidies. Moreover, there are certain infrastructure components that display complementarity with both labour and capital. In particular, strong complementarities are indicated with respect to capacity variables such as length of pipeline for water supply, district electrification, urban road and highway lengths, rail lines, markets, post and telegraph offices, public libraries, and most health and educational facilities. These represent basic infrastructure investments, the absence or underprovision of which constitute potential bottlenecks to regional economic activity.

Prepared for presentation at the 64th Annual Conference of Western Economic Association International, Lake Tahoe, 18–22 June 1989.

II / Agglomeration and Migration

5 / On Agglomeration Economies and Optimal Migration

VIBHOOTI SHUKLA
ODED STARK

I. Introduction

Hitherto, urban economics does not seem to have significantly contributed to migration economics, although there are reasons to believe that such a contribution can be made. As we demonstrate in this paper, it is possible to utilize urban economics to identify socially optimal levels of urbanization and, by implication, optimal levels of rural-to-urban migration. Our analysis addresses the case where there is one urban centre (region) in the economy.[1]

After identifying the reason that private actions do not add up to the social optimum, we offer an analysis of instruments which could confer efficiency gains by closing the gap(s) between the privately efficient and socially optimal urban concentrations. On the basis of theoretical considerations and permissible parameter values, for the log-linear case, we are able to rank these instruments and thereby suggest policy implications. The private decisions identified in this paper are responsible for a smaller city size, or a smaller urban sector, than is socially optimal. We compare this outcome with another policy-related observation. A 1983 United Nations survey of 126 governments of less developed countries (LDCs) found that all but three small island nations did not consider the distribution of their populations 'appropriate': more than three-quarters stated that they were pursuing policies to slow down or reverse internal migration, almost always rural-to-urban migration. These policies do not have a remarkable success record. Might this lack of success be due to the fact that, alongside the problems of congestion and pollution usually associated with rapid urban growth, there are, over a significant range, powerful agglomeration economies conferred by urban concentration? This may help to explain why policies aimed at stemming rural-to-urban migration have a dismal success record (Stark 1980).

II. External Agglomeration Economies and Optimal Migration

We start by focusing on the role of external agglomeration economies.[2] Urban output Q, which is homogeneous and internationally traded at a given unit price, is produced by many small identical firms employing labour N and capital K with decreasing returns to internal scale and increasing returns to external scale:

$$Q = G(N)F(N, K) \tag{1}$$

where $G' > 0$ and

$$\begin{bmatrix} F_{NN} & F_{NK} \\ F_{KN} & F_{KK} \end{bmatrix}$$

is negative definite. Firms do not see themselves as influencing city size which is given by the aggregation of their profit-maximizing labour demands. With perfectly elastic supply of private capital and labour at the going interest and wage rates r and w respectively, the firm's maximization problem is

$$\text{Max.}\,[G(N)F(N, K) - wN - rK]$$

which renders the first-order conditions

$$G(N^e)F_N(N^e, K^e) - w = 0 \tag{2}$$

$$G(N^e)F_K(N^e, K^e) - r = 0 \tag{3}$$

and the second-order conditions

$$GF_{NN} < 0 \tag{4}$$

$$(GF_{KK})(GF_{NN}) - (GF_{NK})^2 > 0 \tag{5}$$

where N^e and K^e are the equilibrium levels of the employed labour and capital, respectively.[3]

Since firms do not incorporate the agglomeration effect in their employment decisions, the pair (N^e, K^e) differs from the social optima (N^*, K^*) which fulfil the first-order conditions

$$G(N^*)F_N(N^*, K^*) + G'(N^*)F(N^*, K^*) - w = 0 \tag{6}$$

$$G(N^*)F_K(N^*, K^*) - r = 0 \tag{7}$$

and the second-order conditions

$$GF_{NN} + 2G' F_N + G'' F < 0 \tag{8}$$

$$(GF_{KK}) (GF_{NN} + 2G' F_N + G'' F) - (GF_{NK})^2 > 0 \tag{9}$$

requiring that, at the optimal level N^*, output increases with employment at a decreasing rate.

In order for (2) to entail a stable equilibrium, $G(N)F_N(N, K)$ must cut w from above, and likewise for (6). Hence, over the relevant range, $\mathrm{d}[G(N)F_N(N, K)]/\mathrm{d}N < 0$. Therefore, a comparison of (6) with (2) implies $N^e < N^*$. Thus, if the externality were to be internalized, urban employment and urban size would be larger and more rural-to-urban migration would be called for. The level of this socially optimal migration is $N^* - N^e > 0$.

III. Ranking Policy Instruments

Having pointed out that the size of an urban area ought to be increased in order to enhance productive efficiency, we need to rank the instruments which a government may use for the purpose of externality correction. We shall address an economy of the type described in section 2 with one single urban region for which $N^* - N^e > 0$. In order to induce socially optimal urban growth and creation of additional employment we assume that the government considers recourse to output, capital, or labour subsidies.

Assume that (1) takes the form

$$Q = G(N)F(N, K) = BN^{\gamma} AN^{\alpha} K^{\beta} \qquad 0 < \gamma < 1,\ \alpha + \beta = 1 \tag{10}$$

and that

$$w = w(N) = bN \quad b > 0 \tag{11}$$

That is, assume a positive agglomeration elasticity with the amount of output 'shift' due to external economies increasing at a declining rate, a constant returns to scale internal technology, and a unitary elastic labour supply. The private problem is then given by

$$\text{Max.}\ [ABN^{\gamma} N^{\alpha} K^{\beta} - (bN)N - rK]$$

However, if the government were to award a wage subsidy, the firm's decision problem would be

$$\text{Max.}\ [ABN^{\gamma} N^{\alpha} K^{\beta} - (1 - S_L)(bN) N - rK]$$

where S_L is the proportion of the wage bill paid by the government. Solving the last problem gives

$$N^e = \left[\frac{\alpha}{[b(1-S_L]}\right]^{(1-\beta)/(2-2\beta-\alpha-\gamma)} (AB\beta^{\beta}r^{-\beta})^{1/(2-2\beta-\alpha-\gamma)} \tag{12}$$

This can be compared with the socially optimal city size N^* given by incorporating the variability of city size in the agglomeration component of the production specification, where

$$N^* = \left(\frac{\alpha+\gamma}{b}\right)^{(1-\beta)/(2-2\beta-\alpha-\gamma)} (AB\beta^{\beta}r^{-\beta})^{1/(2-2\beta-\alpha-\gamma)} \tag{13}$$

By equating (12) and (13), that is, by capturing that amount of subsidy that will sustain the social optimum, we obtain

$$S_L = \frac{\gamma}{\alpha+\gamma} \tag{14}$$

We employ a similar procedure in order to derive the optimal capital subsidy, that is, we solve

$$\text{Max.}[ABN^{\gamma}N^{\alpha}K^{\beta} - (bN)N - (1-S_K)\,rK]$$

and obtain

$$S_K = 1 - \left(\frac{\alpha}{\alpha+\gamma}\right)^{(1-\beta)/\beta} \tag{15}$$

and derive the optimal output subsidy (for example, a sales tax concession) by solving

$$\text{Max.}[(1+S_P)ABN^{\gamma}N^{\alpha}K^{\beta} - (bN)N - rK]$$

and obtaining

$$S_P = \left(\frac{\alpha+\gamma}{\alpha}\right)^{(1-\beta)/\beta} - 1 \tag{16}$$

From the first-order conditions of social maximization, that is, from the equivalents of (6) and (7) under (10) and (11), we obtain

$$(N^*)^2 = \frac{\alpha+\gamma}{b}\,Q^* \tag{17}$$

$$K^* = \frac{\beta}{r} Q^* \tag{18}$$

Drawing on (14), (15), and (16) we can write the total labour, capital, and output subsidies, namely, $\bar{S}_L$, $\bar{S}_K$, $\bar{S}_P$, respectively as

$$\bar{S}_L = \gamma Q^* \tag{19}$$

$$\bar{S}_K = \beta\left[1 - \left(\frac{\alpha}{\alpha+\gamma}\right)^{(1-\beta)/\beta}\right] Q^* \tag{20}$$

$$\bar{S}_P = \left[\left(\frac{\alpha+\gamma}{\alpha}\right)^{(1-\beta)/\beta} - 1\right] Q^* \tag{21}$$

Although the capital subsidy is cheaper than the output subsidy,[4] the difference between the capital subsidy and the labour subsidy cannot be signed analytically. Fortunately, simulation experimentation (Shukla, 1984) subject to $\gamma < \alpha$ (the external condition that the labour efficiency or agglomeration parameter is lower than the internal parameter) reveals that the capital subsidy is consistently cheaper than the labour subsidy; for plausible ranges of the parameters γ and α, say 0.10 – 0.20 for γ and 0.60 – 0.70 for α, the capital subsidy is 20 – 35 per cent cheaper than the labour subsidy.

Our conclusion that subsidizing capital utilization might be a more efficient means of bringing about socially optimal levels of industrial production, urban concentration, and rural-to-urban migration relates to earlier research (for example, Stark and Levhari, 1982) where it is pointed out that, although migration is a labour market phenomenon, modifying its patterns could optimally assume the form of intervention in capital markets. It was argued that it is imperfections in the latter which are manifested through, and corrected by, migratory behaviour. Interestingly, while it approaches migration from the production end, this paper also suggests that intervention in the capital market could be the appropriate tool for bringing about the desirable level of migration.

NOTES

Reprinted from Economics Letters 18, 1985, published by Elsevier Science Publishers B.V. (North-Holland), incorporating changes from the revised version printed in Oded Stark (1991), *Migration of Labor*, Blackwell Publishers, USA and UK.

1 The case where there are two urban centres is taken up in an appendix available from the authors upon request. What makes such a case particularly interesting is that the possibility of additional, namely inter-urban, migration flows opens up. Hence we critically examine in the appendix the rationale underlying dispersal from the larger to the smaller urban centre.

2 External agglomeration economies have been empirically confirmed in the United States by a number of studies (for example, Sveikauskas 1975; Segal 1976) and in India by Shukla (1984).

3 In fact, the maximization problem renders an optimal employment level for the individual firm which we should have designated by a symbol different from N^e, say n^e (likewise, for K^e). If there are m identical firms, then $N^e = mn^e$. Since N^e differs from n^e merely by a constant factor, we adopt a short-cut and refer to N^e from the start of the maximization process.

4 $\overline{S}_P/Q^* - \overline{S}_K/Q^* = (d^e - 1) - \beta[1 - (1/d)^e] = (d^e - 1)(d^e - \beta)/d^e > 0$, since $d^e > 1 > \beta$ where $d = (\alpha + \gamma)/\alpha > 1$ and $e = (1 - \beta)/\beta > 0$.

REFERENCES

Segal, David (1976), 'Are There Returns to Scale in City Size?', *Review of Economics and Statistics,* Vol. 58, No. 3, pp. 339–50.

Shukla, Vibhooti (1984), 'The Productivity of Indian Cities and Some Implications for Development Policy', Ph. D. Dissertation, Princeton University, now published (1988) as *Urban Development and Regional Policy in India: An Econometric Analysis*, Himalaya Publishing House, Bombay.

Stark, Oded (1980), 'On Slowing Metropolitan City Growth', *Population and Development Review,* Vol. 6, No. 1, pp. 95–102 (reprinted as Ch. 20 in Oded Stark (1991) *Migration of Labor*).

Stark, Oded and David Levhari (1982), 'On Migration and Risk in LDCs', *Economic Development and Cultural Change,* Vol. 31, No. 1, pp. 191–6 (reprinted as Ch. 4 in Stark (1991) *Migration of Labor*).

Sveikauskas, Leo (1975), 'The Productivity of Cities', *Quarterly Journal of Economics,* Vol. 89, No. 3, pp. 393–413.

6 / Policy Comparisons with an Agglomeration Effects-Augmented Dual Economy Model

VIBHOOTI SHUKLA
ODED STARK

I. Introduction

Urbanization processes and the impetus for city growth in less developed countries (LDCs) continue to attract much interest. Underlying this interest are the recognition of the empirical association and concomitancy between urbanization and economic development as well as policy concerns with the 'problems' of 'excessive' cityward migration and urban unemployment. Yet an important class of urban growth models, based on considerations of external scale economies in urban production, fails to acknowledge the presence of the rural economy or of less than full employment in the urban sector. The many variants of the dual economy model of development spawned by Harris and Todaro (1970), however, which have addressed the issue of the nature of migratory responses in the face of sector-specific institutional rigidities and of the inefficiencies that might arise therefrom, do not appreciate the tremendous 'pull' exercised by the economies of urban agglomeration. Yet these economies, together with infrastructure investments, appear to be the most significant factors impinging upon the expansion of the urban sector.

In this paper we incorporate agglomeration economies in a dualistic analysis of the developing economy.[1] An effort to synthesize the two approaches is important because the normative conclusions prompted by each appear contradictory. The former argues for the productive potential of cities to be harnessed aggressively in the service of economic development (see, for example, Shukla 1984). The latter advocates combining a programme of migration containment with a strong emphasis on rural development.[2] Our interest here is in examining whether the standard prescriptions associated with policy rankings under sector-specific sticky wages are sustained, strengthened, or weakened.

Accordingly, in Sections II and III we combine elements of the two modelling traditions to present an integrated analysis in which several questions can be posed. In Sections IV and V a policy-ranking exercise of the Bhagwati and Srinivasan (1974) type[3] is performed in the context of a version of the general structural model presented in Sections II and III. This allows us to make comparisons with previous prescriptions. Alternative 'first-best' interventions are evaluated with reference not only to benefits, but also to the costs of fiscal implementation. In Section VI we present and interpret the results of the simulations performed. Section VII concludes with some implications of the analysis and with suggestions for future research.

II. The Components of the Analysis

Agglomeration-based Models of City Size

The idea that firms in certain industries benefit by locating in areas of large size and high concentration is hardly new in either the popular or the scientific literature on urbanization. The advantage of such location is attributed to increased opportunities for specialization and trade, better prospects for diffusing risk afforded by large numbers, better information and communication possibilities that come with spatial proximity, and various other factors stemming from larger and denser markets.

Whatever the source of the urban productivity edge, many economists have found it analytically meaningful to characterize it as technological, typically formulated as entering the set of firms' production possibilities in the form of a scale shift factor. This characterization has been matched with considerable empirical success. Suitable parameterization has usually permitted measurement of the relative gain in efficiency associated with larger city size.[4]

Invoking the fundamental idea that scale economies of some sort account for the existence of the observed uneven spatial distribution of economic activity and, consequently, of population, a respectable class of equilibrium city size models has utilized the notion of agglomeration to explain city formation and urban growth.[5] In these models, external scale economies in the manufacture of inter-regionally traded goods generate employment expansion and continuing accretion of population, whereas diseconomies in consumption and in the production of certain non-tradeables create counter-pressures.

The foregoing ideas can be demonstrated in a one-factor one-good framework. Assume that identical firms in an urban area facing a fixed wage w in the aggregate produce output X under the technological conditions

$$X = g(N) f(N) \qquad g', f' > 0, g'', f'' < 0 \tag{1}$$

with the exogenously determined output price normalized to unity. N, as an argument of f(·), is total urban area employment of labour and, as it enters g (·), is total urban population. By definition (assuming universal labour force participation and abstracting from dependence considerations), the two are identical, but behaviourally they are not. Firms realize that they choose employment. But they do not perceive that this choice alters city size and confers a positive externality in their manufacturing activity that leads to suboptimality of employment and consequently of city size.[6] For although private decisions lead to equilibrium size N^e satisfying

$$g(N) f'(N) = \overline{w} \tag{2}$$

a social optimization that maximizes manufacturing sector output would yield N^*, which must satisfy

$$g(N) f'(N) + g'(N) f(N) = \overline{w} \tag{3}$$

Figure 1 illustrates the divergence of equilibrium from optimum that arises under our simple assumptions.

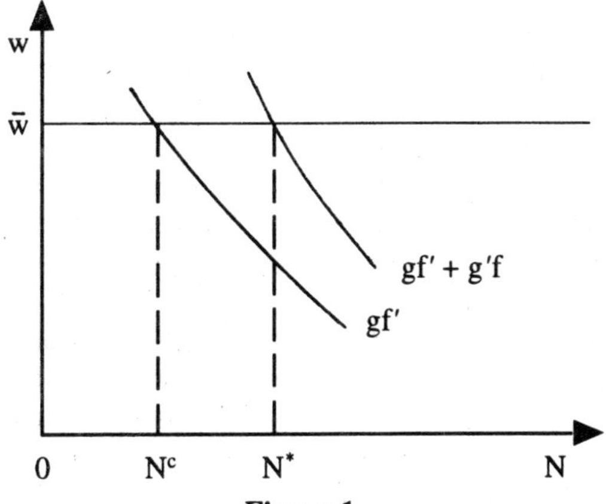

Figure 1

Naturally, the suboptimality of urban size[7] implies a suboptimality of rural-to-urban migration. We have addressed elsewhere the choice of instruments for correcting the externality that gives rise to this inefficiency (see Shukla and Stark 1985). The issue of optimal city size, however, has mainly been addressed under assumptions of complete information and full employment spatial adjustments. In reality, rural-to-urban migration in LDCs does not often take place in response to concrete job offers, and growth in the urban workforce outpaces employment growth, prompting the concern mentioned at the outset. The dualistic expected income model captures this concern and highlights an additional efficiency probelm.

The Basic Expected-Income Framework

A basic version of the model features two sectors — manufacturing, which is wholly urban, and agriculture, which is wholly rural — each employing labour as the only variable factor. The sectors mutually exhaust the total population $\bar{N}$ so that

$$\bar{N} = N_U + N_A \tag{4}$$

where N_U is the total labour supplied to the urban area. The price of manufacturing output and the price of farm output are given in this small open economy.[8] The former is assumed to be the numeraire; the latter is q. Production in the urban sector is assumed to take place under

$$X_M = \bar{f}(N_M) \quad \bar{f}' > 0, \ \bar{f}'' < 0 \tag{5}$$

which, in the light of our earlier discussion, we amend to

$$X_M = g(N_M)\ f(N_M) \quad g', f' > 0, f'', g'' < 0 \tag{6}$$

Agricultural production is

$$X_A = h(N_A) \qquad h' > 0, h'' < 0 \tag{7}$$

X_M and X_A are urban manufacturing output and rural agricultural output respectively; N_M and N_A are the corresponding levels of employment.

There is an institutional difference between wage formation in the two sectors: the rural labour market clears perfectly but the urban labour market is characterized by a relatively high fixed wage, conventionally attributed to minimum wage legislation, the bargaining power of unions, and so forth. Migration by risk-neutral labour to the high-wage urban sector takes place in response to a positive expected wage differential to equilibrate

$$w_0 = \bar{w}p \tag{8}$$

where w_0 is the rural agricultural wage. The probability p of securing an urban job is represented by N_M/N_U.

Profit-maximizing behaviour by firms and farms leads to

$$g(N_M)f'(N_M) = \bar{w} \tag{9}$$

and

$$qh'(\bar{N} - N_U) = \bar{w}_0 = \frac{wN_M}{N_U} \tag{10}$$

respectively. Equations (4), (6), (7), (9), and (10) can be solved for X_A, N_A, X_M, N_M, and N_U to yield the inter-sectoral equilibrium labour force allocations depicted in Figure 2. The broken curve is the rectangular hyperbola on which equilibrium occurs.[9] The level of urban unemployment U is given by $N_U - N_M$, and its rate by $1 - N_M/N_U$. This equilibrium is a combined consequence of urban wage fixity and the nature of the

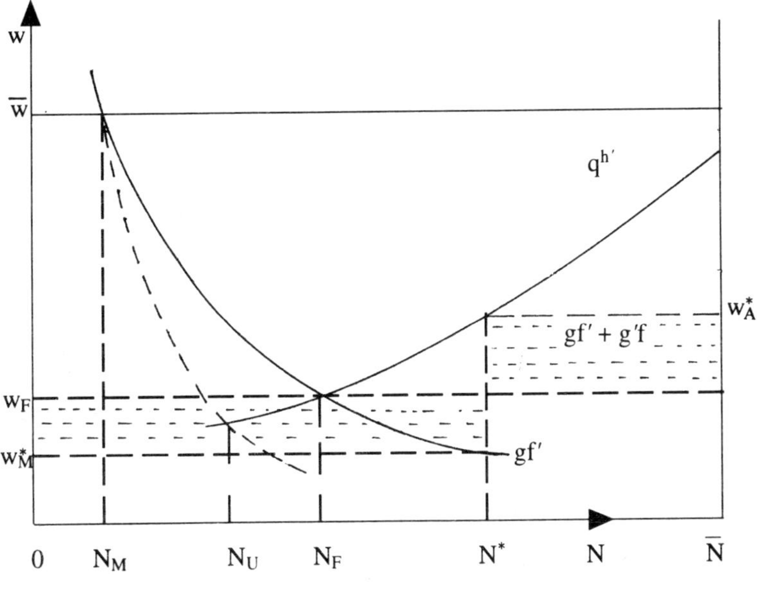

Figure 2

behavioural response of migrants, and it leads to market inefficiencies that invite the policy interventions we now consider.

III. Developmental Policy Implications

In terms of the economy's potential, the *laissez-faire* equilibrium is off the efficiency frontier. A wide range of sectoral and economy-wide[10] policies might be instituted to nudge it closer, resulting in welfare improvements. By way of a 'first-best' optimal policy in the conventional Harris–Todaro context, entailing maximum welfare and no by-product distortions, Bhagwati and Srinivasan (1974) demonstrate that a wage subsidy uniform in both sectors will take the economy to full employment equilibrium, represented in Figure 2 by the allocation N_F. A situation characterized by two *hypothetically* different subsidy rates S_M^F and S_A^F, specific to the manufacturing and agricultural sectors,

$$g(N_M)\,f'(N_M) = w - S_M^F \tag{11}$$

and

$$qh'(\bar{N} - N_U) = \frac{\bar{w}N_M}{N_U} - S_A^F \tag{12}$$

respectively, under the full employment identity $N_U = N_M$ and the efficiency condition

$$g(\bar{N})f'(N) = qh'(\bar{N} - N) \tag{13}$$

is reconcilable with $S_F = S_M^F = S_M^F$ at N_M ($= N_U$) $= N_F$, yielding a total cost of subsidization equal to $\bar{N}S_F$ or $\bar{N}\,[\bar{w} - g(N_F)\,f'(N_F)]$.

In the light of agglomeration effects, however, this intervention is no longer optimal: although one source of distortion has been addressed, the economy is still off the utility frontier because of the externality in urban production. Hence the possibility of further welfare improvement remains. The appropriate efficiency condition in this context is

$$g(N)f'(N) + g'(N)\,f(N) = qh'(\bar{N} - N) \tag{14}$$

which is seen to be satisfied at the 'true' optimum N^* rather than at N_F.

Let us now consider anew the problem of the optimal subsidy that will sustain *this* allocation in private markets. Denote by w_A^* the optimum agricultural wage and by w_M^* the optimal wage in manufacturing. An employment subsidy in agriculture must be at the level

$$S_A^* = \bar{w} - w_A^* = \bar{w} - [g(N^*)f'(N^*) + g'(N^*)f(N^*)]$$

to support socially optimal agricultural employment in equilibrium. A glance at Figure 2 reveals that this is *lower* than the previously construed 'first-best' rate S_F. Contrary to the case of no agglomeration effects, an identical subsidy in urban manufacturing will fail to elicit the required optimal employment response in that sector because firms' productivity perceptions lie along the $g(N)f'(N)$ curve, whereas real social benefits are represented by the curve $g(N)f'(N) + g'(N)f(N)$. A subsidy *higher* than before is now optimal for the urban sector, and is given by $S_M^* = \bar{w} - w_M^* = \bar{w}\ g(N^*)f'(N^*)$.

The total cost of this new subsidization package is therefore

$$N^*[\bar{w}-g(N^*)f'(N^*)] + (\bar{N}-N^*)[\bar{w}-g(N^*)f'(N^*)-g'(N^*)f(N^*)]$$
$$= \bar{N}[\bar{w} - g(N^*)f'(N^*)] - (\bar{N} - N^*)[g'(N^*)f(N^*)] \qquad (15)$$

It is analytically ambiguous whether this package is more or less expensive than subsidization prescribed under the assumption that no agglomeration economies prevail. The difference between subsidization costs C^* with agglomeration economies and subsidization costs C^F without agglomeration economies

$$C^* - C^F = \bar{N}[g(N_F)f'(N_F) - g(N^*)f'(N^*)] - (\bar{N} - N^*)[g'(N^*)f(N^*)] \qquad (16)$$

cannot be signed generally. This difference can be expressed in Figure 2 by the excess of the area of the rectangle representing the saving in agricultural subsidization costs over the area of the rectangle representing additional costs of subsidizing the manufacturing sector under the new package. A comparison of the two shaded rectangles suggests that a steeper qh' curve and a relatively flat gf' curve create a predisposition for the new subsidization package to be cheaper. With the aid of a specified model and under plausible ranges of the relevant parameter values, we shall now attempt to quantify the costs and benefits associated with alternative policy measures.

IV. A Specified Model for Policy Evaluation

In this section we specify a model geared for a numerical policy-ranking exercise of the type undertaken by Bhagwati and Srinivasan (1974),[11] but with the explicit incorporation of agglomeration factors. The aim is to trace the welfare effects of alternative policy responses to the problem of achieving a more efficient inter-sectoral allocation in the context of the general structure outlined in Sections II and III.

The policy options we consider are an optimal set of employment subsidies to each sector, a full employment uniform subsidy calculated under the presumption that no agglomeration economies exist, and, last, the *laissez-faire* situation. To facilitate comparison with results under the Bhagwati–Srinivasan scenario, where there are no agglomeration effects, we adopt functional specifications akin to theirs. Our innovation is to take cognizance of costs associated with alternative types of subsidization as part of a somewhat more comprehensive ranking scheme.

The model features production relationships $g(\cdot)$, $f(\cdot)$, and $h(\cdot)$ for manufacturing and agriculture, corresponding to (6) and (7), given by

$$X_M = (N_M)^{\gamma} (N_M)^{\alpha} \tag{17}$$

where $g(N_M) = (N_M)^{\gamma}$, γ represents what is referred to as the agglomeration elasticity, and

$$X_A = (N_A)^{\beta} \tag{18}$$

where $0 < \alpha, \beta, \gamma < 1$. It is assumed that $N_U + N_A = N_M + N_A + U = 1$, where $U = N_U - N_M$ is urban unemployment. Under full employment $U = 0$, so that $N_M + N_A = 1$. The urban wage rate $\bar{w}$ is set exogenously and can be presented as some multiple of the prevailing rural wage $w_0 = qh'$. The price of the agricultural commodity in units of output q of the manufacturing sector can be interpreted as reflecting the terms of trade given to a small open economy, or as a weight in the social welfare function $SWF(X_M, X_A) = X_M + qX_A$ of a closed economy. In the latter case, a larger q reflects a heightened societal preference for the product of agriculture.

V. Effects of Alternative Interventions

Laissez-faire

Given $\bar{w}$, equilibrium urban employment N_M is determined by

$$\alpha N_M^{\alpha + \gamma - 1} = \bar{w} \tag{19}$$

whence employment N_A in agriculture or the rural workforce can be solved for by substituting N_M into the migration condition

$$q\beta N_A^{\beta-1} = \frac{\bar{w}N_M}{1 - N_A} \tag{20}$$

$N_U = 1 - N_A$ represents total urban workforce, and equilibrium unemployment $U = N_U - N_M$ emerges.

Uniform Wage Subsidy without Attention to Agglomeration Effects

The standard policy, if we ignore the need to correct for the agglomeration externality, involves uniform subsidization at the level of

$$S_F = \bar{w} - \alpha N_F^{\alpha+\gamma-1} \tag{21}$$

where N_F is the value of N_M that solves the equality corresponding to (13):

$$\alpha N_M^{\alpha+\gamma-1} = q\beta\,(1 - N_M)^{\beta-1} \tag{22}$$

The total cost of financing this policy is given by $C^F = \bar{N}S_F$ or, under normalization, $C^F = S_F$.

The Optimal Solution and First-best Package of Employment Subsidies

The optimal allocation $(N^*, 1 - N^*)$ is obtained using $N_A = 1 - N_M$ and the optimizing condition corresponding to (14):

$$\alpha N_M^{\alpha+\gamma-1} + \gamma N_M^{\alpha+\gamma-1} = q\beta(1 - N_M)^{\beta-1} \tag{23}$$

thus it satisfies

$$(N^*)^{\alpha+\gamma-1} = q\,\frac{\beta}{\alpha+\gamma}\,(1 - N^*)^{\beta-1} \tag{24}$$

The manufacturing sector subsidy per worker S_M^* that will sustain the optimal urban employment in private equilibrium is obtained as

$$S_M^* = \bar{w} - \alpha(N^*)^{\alpha+\gamma-1} \tag{25}$$

Similarly, the corresponding subsidy rate in agriculture S_A^* is given by

$$S_A^* = \bar{w} - q\beta(1 - N^*)^{\beta-1} \tag{26}$$

Both subsidy rates are completely specified with the optimal employment N^* from above, as is the total cost of subsidization

$$C^* = N^*S_M^* + (1 - N^*)\,S_A^*$$

Table 1: Effects of Subsidization under Agglomeration

Case 1	$\alpha = 0.7, \beta = 0.2, q = 1.0, \bar{w} = 1.0$								
Laissez-faire									
		X_M	N_A	N_M	U	S_M	S_A	C	qX_A+X_M
X_A	0.873935	0.240100	0.509795	0.168070	0.322134	0.0	0.0	0.0	1.114035
Uniform wage subsidy									
		X^F_M	N^F_A	N^F_M	U^F	S^F_M	S^F_A	C^F	$qX^F_A + X^F_M$
X^F_A	0.723102	0.838438	0.197696	0.802304	0.0	0.268473	0.268473	0.268473	1.561540
Optimal subsidization									
		X^*_M	N^*_A	N^*_M	U^*	S^*_M	S^*_A	C^*	$qX^*_A + X^*_M$
X^*_A	0.700600	0.862517	0.168792	0.831208	0.0	0.273633	0.169866	0.256118	1.563117
Case 2	$\alpha = 0.5, \beta = 0.5, q = 1.0, \bar{w} = 1.0$								
Laissez-faire									
		X_M	N_A	N_M	U	S_M	S_A	C	qX_A+X_M
X_A	0.838728	0.353554	0.703464	0.176777	0.119759	0.0	0.0	0.0	1.192281
Uniform wage subsidy									
		X^F_M	N^F_A	N^F_M	U^F	S^F_M	S^F_A	C^F	$qX^F_A + X^F_M$
X^F_A	0.733892	0.628707	0.538597	0.461403	0.0	0.318701	0.318701	0.318701	1.362598
Optimal subsidization									
		X^*_M	N^*_A	N^*_M	U^*	S^*_M	S^*_A	C^*	$qX^*_A + X^*_M$
X^*_A	0.661793	0.707710	0.437970	0.562030	0.0	0.370397	0.244477	0.315248	1.369503

Case 3 $\alpha = 0.5, \beta = 0.6, q = 1.0, \bar{w} = 1.0$

Laissez-faire									
		X_M	N_A	N_M	U	S_M	S_A	C	qX_A+X_M
X_A	0.834007	0.353554	0.738952	0.176777	0.084271	0.0	0.0	0.0	1.87560
Uniform wage subsidy									
		X^F_M	N^F_A	N^F_M	U^F	S^F_M	S^F_A	C^F	$qX^F_A+X^F_M$
X^F_A	0.744832	0.566613	0.612018	0.387982	0.0	0.269794	0.269794	0.269794	1.311445
Optimal subsidization									
		X^*_M	N^*_A	N^*_M	U^*	S^*_M	S^*_A	C^*	$qX^*_A+X^*_M$
X^*_A	0.659754	0.659754	0.500000	0.500000	0.0	0.340246	0.208295	0.274271	1.319508

Case 4 $\alpha = 0.7, \beta = 0.2, q = 1.5, \bar{w} = 1.0$

Laissez-faire									
		X_M	N_A	N_M	U	S_M	S_A	C	qX_A+X_M
X_A	0.908390	0.240100	0.618532	0.168070	0.213398	0.0	0.0	0.0	1.602685
Uniform wage subsidy									
		X^F_M	N^F_A	N^F_M	U^F	S^F_M	S^F_A	C^F	$qX^F_A+X^F_M$
X_A	0.793921	0.738484	0.315417	0.684583	0.0	0.244885	0.244885	0.244885	1.929364
Optimal subsidization									
		X^*_M	N^*_A	N^*_M	U^*	S^*_M	S^*_A	C^*	$qX^*_A+X^*_M$
X^*_A	0.770264	0.776451	0.271143	0.728857	0.0	0.254291	0.147760	0.225405	1.931846

(Contd.)

Table 1: *(Contd.)*

Case 5	$\alpha = 0.5, \beta = 0.5, q = 0.5, \overline{w} = 1.0$								
Laissez-faire									
		X_M	N_A	N_M	U	S_M	S_A	C	qX_A+X_M
X_A	0.707106	0.353554	0.500000	0.176777	0.323223	0.0	0.0	0.0	0.707107
Uniform wage subsidy									
		X^F_M	N^F_A	N^F_M	U^F	S^F_M	S^F_A	C^F	$qX^F_A+X^F_M$
X^F_A	0.455574	0.869729	0.207548	0.792452	0.0	0.451242	0.451242	0.451242	1.097515
Optimal subsidization									
		X^*_M	N^*_A	N^*_M	U^*	S^*_M	S^*_A	C^*	$qX^*_A+X^*_M$
X^*_A	0.390049	0.905723	0.152138	0.847862	0.0	0.465878	0.359054	0.449626	1.100746
Case 6	$\alpha = 0.7, \beta = 0.2, q = 1.0, \overline{w} = 1.5$								
Laissez-faire									
		X_M	N_A	N_M	U	S_M	S_A	C	qX_A+X_M
X_A	0.968867	0.047427	0.853731	0.022133	0.124136	0.0	0.0	0.0	1.016294
Uniform wage subsidy									
		X^F_M	N^F_A	N^F_M	U^F	S^F_M	S^F_A	C^F	$qX^F_A+X^F_M$
X^F_A	0.723102	0.838438	0.197696	0.802304	0.0	0.768473	0.768473	0.768473	1.561540
Optimal subsidization									
		X^*_M	N^*_A	N^*_M	U^*	S^*_M	S^*_A	C^*	$qX^*_A+X^*_M$
X^*_A	0.700600	0.862517	0.168792	0.831208	0.0	0.773633	0.669866	0.756118	1.563117

VI. Simulation Results

We performed a numerical simulation exercise to rank the three options of uniform wage subsidization, optimal subsidization, and *laissez-faire* (or non-intervention). The model solution was over a fairly comprehensive range of permissible values for the principal parameters α, β, q, and $\bar{w}$. The objective was to trace the relative costs and benefits associated with each of the compared options. Allowing for agglomeration effects, we were particularly interested in ascertaining whether a cost advantage existed, in addition to unambiguous output and productivity increases resulting from subsidization. Clearly, in such a case a welfare improvement is gained *a fortiori*. Computations were performed under the assumption of an agglomeration elasticity in urban manufacturing of $\gamma = 0.10$, following magnitudes estimated by Shukla (1984).

Six appropriately illustrative cases are chosen for presentation in Table 1. As expected, utility levels, as measured by the social welfare index, are consistently higher under optimal subsidization. Our results on the cost side appear to confirm the case for the relative cheapness of optimal subsidization when conditions $\alpha \geq \beta$ or $\alpha + \gamma > \beta$ are met. To see this point, consult Table 1. With q and $\bar{w}$ held at constant levels (cases 1, 2, and 3) optimal subsidization is seen to be cheaper ($C^* < C^F$) than uniform wage subsidization in cases 1 and 2. For case 1, where $\alpha = 0.7$ and $\beta = 0.2$, the former is about 5 per cent less expensive; however, this advantage is eroded to 1 per cent as we move to case 2, with $\alpha = \beta = 0.5$, and is reversed when we come to case 3, where $\alpha > \beta$ is no longer satisfied.

Recall that α and β represent output elasticities with respect to the labour inputs in manufacturing and agriculture respectively. Since common sense and econometric estimates concur in leading us to believe that the inequalities $\alpha \geq \beta$ and $\alpha + \gamma > \beta$ do indeed hold, the dominance of the socially optimal policy package seems to be supported. An intuitive explanation of the significance of the conditions is best captured graphically. A high value for α coupled with a low value for β corresponds to a relatively flat marginal product curve in industry and a steep curve in agriculture. As noted in Section III, a flat industry curve, allowing for the agglomeration effect, mandates only a minor increase in subsidization costs, whereas a steep agriculture curve would tend to make the *saving* relative to the case of uniform subsidization much more substantial. Indeed, cases 1 and 2 show the agriculture subsidy rates falling sharply (from S_A^F to S_A^*) relative to those in case 3, which also registers the greatest *rise* in the rate of subsidy to the manufacturing sector (S_M^F to S_M^*).

Note that, provided that the condition $\alpha \geq \beta$ is met, although the ranking of costs is invariant to q and $\overline{w}$ their absolute magnitudes do vary with these parameter values, as evidenced in cases 4, 5, and 6. Comparison of 4 with 1, as well as of 5 with 2, shows that the greater the price q of agricultural goods in units of the output of the manufacturing sector, the lower the costs. This happens because, for given $\overline{w}$, raising q raises marginal value productivity in optimum and hence, in general, reduces the discrepancy that subsidization has to close. By the same token, raising $\overline{w}$ widens this discrepancy and raises the unit cost associated with both kinds of subsidization. That relative cost comparisons are neutral to the level of $\overline{w}$ can be seen by contrasting case 1 with case 6; raising $\overline{w}$ from 1.0 to 1.5 increases costs, both C^F and C^*, by precisely 0.5.[12]

VII. Conclusions

Having considered two intervention options, uniform wage subsidization and differential optimal subsidization, we have established, under plausible conditions, a case for the welfare superiority of subsidization with attention to agglomeration effects, over subsidization without them, on the grounds of both cost and benefit. For cases where cost superiority is not demonstrated, it may still be that the additional benefits outweigh the extra costs associated with subsidization under agglomeration.[13]

Analytically, the presence of agglomeration economies breaks down a previously construed optimal prescription involving the equal subsidization of labour in both sectors of an economy characterized by expected-income-led migration, and calls for a higher rate of assistance to urban than to rural productive activities. This might restore some balance to thinking about the relative developmental roles of the two sectors and may challenge extremist views that urban expansion is largely parasitic. To the extent that manufacturing is a predominantly urban activity, welfare effects arising from the agglomeration externality in LDCs' manufacturing generate one of the few legitimate bases of a protectionist argument for that sector (Corden 1974).

Three important research issues need to be pursued further. First, the microfoundations of urban agglomeration economies require empirical investigation. The more clearly we understand the nature of such economies, the more policy measures can be 'fine tuned' to address their internalization. Second, the financing sources and administrative costs of various subsidy options need to be explored systematically. Last, in the literature on expected-income migration-cum-institutionally fixed urban wage rate, explanations of the origins and functions of the high urban wage need to be reconciled with the economic behaviour of the agents involved. As a step in this direction we offer elsewhere (Shukla and Stark 1989) an 'agglomeration economies rationale for formal sector wage rigidity and for the existence of the urban informal sector in LDCs.

NOTES

Reprinted from *Journal of Urban Economics* 27, 1990, published by Academic Press Inc. (with copyright permission), incorporating changes from the revised version included in Oded Stark (1991), *Migration of Labor*, Blackwell Publishers, Oxford. Helpful suggestions and comments of an anonymous referee are gratefully acknowledged by the authors.

1 Since preparing the first draft of this paper—Discussion Paper 30, Harvard University Migration and Development—we have become aware of a paper by Panagariya and Succar (1986) who do incorporate scale economies in manufacturing within a Harris–Todaro type of framework. Panagariya and Succar model scale economies as external to the firm but internal to the industry and focus on the comparative statics properties of their approach.

2 Consider, for example, the conclusions of Harris and Todaro (1970) and Todaro (1976).

3 An approach that has also engendered a vigorous welfare-theoretic literature in the field of international trade.

4 See, for example, Shukla (1984), where estimates based on Indian data confirm presumptions that this gain is especially significant under LDC conditions. Earlier estimates with US data can be found in Sveikauskas (1975) and Segal (1976).

5 Models using external scale economies in urban production to determine equilibrium or optimal city size have had currency in the mainstream of urban economics since the work of Dixit (1973), and more recently (for example, Henderson, 1986) have been applied to address questions of urban growth in LDCs. The present model is in the tradition of the 'open city' models of this literature.

6 That this is not incompatible with perfect competition between firms is demonstrated by Chipman (1970).

7 The urban economies are assumed to be sustained positively over the entire range of city sizes. This is consistent with findings in Shukla (1984), which fail to show a significant decline in urban productivity benefits

even in the upper reaches of the Indian size distribution, and reflects the presumption that, on the pure production side, there is no *a priori* reason for assuming that diseconomies should occur. More elaborate models of urban growth with production economies often render city size finite by postulating consumption side diseconomies, or the limitedness of a site-specific factor, most commonly land, that impinges through input prices, *not* through the technology (for example, see Henderson 1982). Of course, to the extent that external diseconomies are present on the urban scene, the sign of the difference between optimal and equilibrium city size will be moot. See Shukla (1984) for indirect evidence that consumption diseconomies may not be important in an LDC context. Further, the suboptimality of each individual urban area is viewed as being sufficient for yielding suboptimality of the aggregate urbanization level, although it is obviously not necessary. See Shukla and Stark (1986) for a discussion of comparative departures from optimality with respect to small and large urban areas.

8 Inter-industry terms of trade in the Harris–Todaro model are variously treated in the literature as endogenously determined for a closed economy through specific utility or demand functions (Harris and Todaro 1970), as given exogenously for a small open economy (Corden and Findlay 1975), or as obtained through a pre-specified relationship between exportables and importables in a large open economy (Srinivasan and Bhagwati 1975). In general, the choice of treatment has hinged upon the orientation of the model and the purpose it was set up to serve. Following Bhagwati and Srinivasan (1974) we choose to have q (see below) perform double duty in representing exogenous terms of trade (a formulation we consider appropriate for most LDCs) as well as a parameter in a linear social welfare index (see sections 4 and 5) to facilitate comparability with their results. Such a restriction on social preferences does not materially alter the characteristics of the equilibrium, and the likelihood that a concave utility function might imply preferences that will yield an optimal allocation featuring a higher than *laissez-faire* agricultural product is small because of considerations of the Engel's law type.

9 The assumption implicit in Figure 2 that $g'f$ is downsloping in the $[0, \bar{N}]$ interval is sufficient to guarantee that equilibrium exists. We do not, however, address issues of stability. See Day et al. (1987) for a statement of conditions under which unstable oscillations in a Harris–Todaro model are possible.

10 In contrast with economy-wide measures, we might mention in passing the implications of agglomeration effects for cost–benefit analyses of small interventions. The urban shadow wage in the context of expected-income migration has been variously characterized as being as high as the *laissez-faire* wage rate (Harberger 1971) or, with declining marginal propensity to consume and migrant risk aversion, lower than this rate (Katz and Stark 1986). The presence of agglomeration economies in urban production in either case strengthens the argument for marginal investments in urban job creation, since benefits outweigh opportunity costs,

even if the latter are as high as the private sector wage. This follows from the result that, at *laissez-faire* urban employment levels,

$$g(N_M)f'(N_M) + g'(N_M)f(N_M) > w.$$

11 Unlike them, however, we do not attempt to rank the various second-best options; nor do we concern ourselves with the informational problems of implementability, as does Basu (1980).

12 Note that the choice of $\bar{w}$, although extraneous here, must be in conformity with plausible values of α and β and consistent with realistic ranges of sectoral employment shares, the urban unemployment rate, and the factor of proportionality between urban and rural wages. The cases presented in Table 1 feature existing agricultural employment shares ranging from about 50 per cent to 85 per cent of the total labour force, and an urban unemployment rate $[U/(1 - N_A)] \times 100$ ranging from about 32 per cent to 85 per cent. (Note, however, that the formulation does not admit the possibility of partial employment or underemployment in the urban sector.) The urban institutional wage $\bar{w} = [(1-N_A)/N_M]\, w_0$ is between 1.5 and 6.6 times as high as the rural wage in *laissez-faire*.

13 The model is not closed in the costs of subsidization. There are two principal difficulties with incorporating costs into a social utility function. First, there is the standard difficulty associated with a possibly distortionary financing of the subsidy. Regrettably, much of the literature on trade distortions also stops short of explicitly characterizing the welfare effects of financing the collection costs associated with corrective measures. Second, the exogeneity of the level of the urban institutional wage in the model poses a problem for our simulation analysis. Comparison of cases 1 and 6 in Table 1, for example, reveals that while the benefits of intervention, which are independent of w, are equal in these two cases, the costs are not. Since our primary concern is with comparing costs between alternative subsidization packages that prove sensitive to arbitrary choice of the exogenous urban wage, we pursue a separate treatment of the costs of subsidization instead of burdening the utility index with the consequences of this sensitivity.

REFERENCES

Basu, K.C. (1980), 'Optimal Policies in Dual Economies', *Quarterly Journal of Economics,* Vol. 95, No. 1, pp. 187–96.

Bhagwati, J.N. and T.N. Srinivasan (1974), 'On Reanalysing the Harris–Todaro Model: Policy Rankings in the Case of Sector-Specific Sticky Wages', *American Economic Review,* Vol. 64, No. 3, pp. 502–8.

Chipman, J.S. (1970), 'External Economies of Scale and Competitive Equilibrium', *Quarterly Journal of Economics*, Vol. 84, No. 3, pp. 347–85.

Corden, W.M. (1974), *Trade Policy and Economic Welfare,* Oxford: Oxford University Press.

Corden, W.M. and R. Findlay (1975), 'Urban Unemployment, Intersectoral Capital Mobility and Development Policy', *Economica,* Vol. 42, No. 165, pp. 59–78.

Day, R.H., S. Dasgupta, S.K. Datta and J.B. Nugent (1987), 'Instability in Rural–Urban Migration', *Economic Journal,* Vol. 97, No. 388, pp. 940–50.

Dixit, A. (1973), 'The Optimum Factory Town', *Bell Journal of Economics and Management Science,* Vol. 4, No. 2, pp. 637–51.

Harberger, A.C. (1971), 'On Measuring the Social Opportunity Cost of Labour', *International Labour Review,* Vol. 103, No. 6, pp. 559–79.

Harris, J.R. and M.P. Todaro (1970), 'Migration, Unemployment and Development: A Two-Sector Analysis', *American Economic Review,* Vol. 60, No. 1, pp. 126–42.

Henderson, J.V. (1982), 'The Impact of Government Policies on Urban Concentration', *Journal of Urban Economics,* Vol. 12, No. 3, pp. 280–303.

———(1986), 'Efficiency of Resource Usage and City Size', *Journal of Urban Economics,* Vol. 19, No. 1, pp. 47–70.

Katz, E. and O. Stark (1986), 'On the Shadow Wage of Urban Jobs in Less-developed Countries', *Journal of Urban Economics,* Vol. 20, No. 2, pp. 121–7 (reprinted as Ch. 25 in Stark (1991) *Migration of Labor*).

Panagariya, A. and P. Succar (1986), 'The Harris–Todaro Model and Economies of Scale', *Southern Economic Journal,* Vol. 52, No. 4, pp. 984–98.

Segal, D. (1976), 'Are There Returns to Scale in City Size?' *Review of Economics and Statistics,* Vol. 58, No. 3, pp. 339–50.

Shukla, V. (1984), 'The Productivity of Indian Cities and Some Implications for Development Policy', Ph. D. Dissertation, Princeton University, now published (1988), *Urban Development and Regional Policy in India: An Econometric Analysis*, Himalaya Publishing House, Bombay.

Shukla, V. and O. Stark (1985), 'On Agglomeration Economies and Optimal Migration', *Economics Letters,* Vol. 18, pp. 297–300 (reprinted as Ch. 23 in Stark (1991) *Migration of Labor*).

———(1986), 'Urban External Economies and Optimal Migration', in Oded Stark (ed.) *Research in Human Capital and Development*, Vol. 4: Migration, Human Capital and Development, Greenwich, CT: JAI Press.

———(1989), 'Why Are Urban Formal Sector Wages in LDCs Above the Market-Clearing Level?' Discussion Paper 44, Harvard University Migration and Development Program.

Srinivasan, T.N. and J.N. Bhagwati (1975), 'Alternative Policy Rankings in a Large, Open Economy with Sector-Specific, Minimum Wages', *Journal of Economic Theory,* Vol. 11, No. 3, pp. 356–71.

Sveikauskas, L. (1975), 'The Productivity of Cities', *Quarterly Journal of Economics,* Vol. 89, No. 3, pp. 393–413.

Todaro, M.P. (1976), 'Urban Job Expansion, Induced Migration and Rising Unemployment', *Journal of Development Economics,* Vol. 3, No. 3, pp. 211–25.

7 / High Wages and Unemployment in the Urban Labour Markets of LDCs

VIBHOOTI SHUKLA

I

Why is it in many urban labour markets in LDCs (less developed countries) high wages coincide with considerable unemployment? Suppose labour is perfectly homogeneous and that the urban economy needs to attract workers from rural areas to fill industrial and other positions. If workers are standard income maximizers, then, other things being equal (and ignoring transfer costs), why would not an urban wage larger than the rural wage by a mere $\varepsilon > 0$, i.e. $W_U = W_R + \varepsilon$ suffice to induce all the requisite rural-to-urban migration? Why do we so often observe $W_U = kW_R$ with $k \geq 1$?

By and large, these simple questions have not been satisfactorily answered in the development literature in general and in the urban and migration literature in particular. The standard approach, adopted and replicated in numerous writings, has been to attribute the high (often very high) urban wages relative to rural wages to exogenous, institutional factors, in particular labour and wage legislation. But this 'explanation' is far from satisfactory.[1] Suppose legislators are familiar with the expected income model of migration and believe that workers act as the model prescribes. They must then realize that the imposed high wage will entail high unemployment, and it ought to concern them that the latter could (should) undermine adherence to, or compliance with, the former. For one thing, in a bid to reduce costs, firms could 'cross-over' — switch operations away from the protected (regulated) domain (for example, sub-contract). And the unemployed would surely attempt to replace the high-paid workers by bidding-down the wage rate. What reasons would there be for the legislators and their economic advisers to believe that these reactions will not arise? The easiest explanation may have to do with the fact that productivity is dependent upon wages — the so-called efficiency wage hypothesis: When productivity is raised by increased wages, it is quite plausible for efficiency to mandate equilibrium wages at above market-clearing levels. The unemployed who may offer to work for less than the controlled wage will be turned down since productivity will be adversely affected by more than the fall in the wage rate. Notice that implicitly this assumes that the prevailing productivity-wage combination is at an optimum, which raises the possibility that causality will run in the reverse direction: Firms identify that wage rate which through its functional link with productivity maximizes their profits. They 'go to the government', letting it know which wage it should announce as the institutional wage. It should also be noted that pressure from the unemployed to obtain the high-paying jobs through means other than wage-cutting (viz., rent-seeking behaviour) must also be recognized and addressed. Yet, could it be that in general the unemployed are willing accomplices in the institutional wage fixation, thereby contributing to its stability? Consider the following argument: workers (who, to simplify, we shall assume are risk-neutral) value and evaluate alternative combinations of pay *and* leisure. Suppose $W_U = kW_R$ with the jobs paying institutional wage being periodically shuffled and randomly reallocated among all labour market participants. This means that whereas in the rural economy a worker needs, say, one unit of work per period to earn W_R, in the urban economy the expected number of work units per period necessary to earn W_R is $1/k$; to each unit of work time, $1 - 1/k$ units of valuable leisure are added — a notable improvement indeed. Firms can also be seen to favour this regime. Suppose firms can either employ given workers several periods in a row paying each W_R per period, or alternatively have a worker work for a period, be paid W_U, rest k-1 periods and then again be employed for a period and be paid the W_U wage. If there are k workers available, the firm can still have work schedule uninterrupted and yet reap significant efficiency gains if rest in periods $t-(k\text{-}1)$, $t\text{-}(k\text{-}2)$, ..., $t - [k\text{-}(k\text{-}1)]$ is strongly complementary to effort exertion in period t — as is quite likely to be the case in occupations and tasks requiring considerable physical strength (e.g., construction, assembly lines, etc.). Hence, a rationale arising from both sides of the market, leading to the 'peaceful coexistence' of unemployment and above-clearing-level wages, appears to exist.

Notice that this argument contrasts sharply with the conventional turnover argument which hypothesizes that wages are maintained at a high level in order to reduce *costly* turnover. Here high wages facilitate *beneficial* turnover. Note also that the assumed turnover does not entail a complete skill depreciation and loss in productivity. Indeed, given a rest–effort-enhancing functional relationship, firms may trade-off the effort gains against the proficiency losses to solve for the optimal k from which the ('invited', not imposed) institutional urban wage is derived as kW_R.

The mechanism through which an urban labour force significantly larger than the pool of the employed confers productive efficiency gains may, however, arise from considerations *external* to the individual firms. These considerations relate to agglomeration economies — economies of external scale which confer efficiency advantages to factors of production employed in activities carried out in locations characterized by populations of large absolute size and high density. There are several reasons for these economies of scale. One reason which is of particular interest to us can be explained as follows. Unless output demand is known to be perfectly stable or is anticipated with perfect foresight, costly inventories and slacks — lost profit opportunities — are bound to arise. Retaining our assumption of labour homogeneity, the immediate presence of a readily available (i.e., low-cost) labour pool from which extra workers can be drawn and into which redundant workers can be laid off is costless to the individual firm and, hence, constitutes a superior alternative to costly inventories and slacks. Note that since there will always be k-1 times more productive workers in the urban economy than the number of workers actually employed, the reserve ratio to allow for sudden upsurges in demand will remain, throughout, exactly the same. (The adjustment in absolute numbers will, of course, arise from rural-to-urban in-migration or from urban-to-rural out-migration.) The regulated (protected wage) sector of the urban economy thus benefits from having a large labour force at its access or disposal, at no direct cost to itself.

For nearly two decades now, a vastly popular paradigm for rural-to-urban migration in LDCs within a two-sector framework has been a model closely associated with Harris and Todaro.[2] The conclusions of this model and its variants critically depend upon the assumption of a rigid urban institutional wage which, in combination with the postulated expected income migration response, produces urban unemployment in the intersectoral labour market equilibrium. Extensions and refinements of the model (e.g., the introduction of the informal sector) have tempered its prediction of substantial urban unemployment; they all, however, retain the distinguishing high-wage feature and continue to yield the comparative static outcome of the unemployment-augmenting consequences of additional urban job expansion, and the welfare implications of the economy-wide inefficiency arising from the apparent wage fixity.[3]

Allowing a functional link between the institutional wage and urban scale economies makes it possible to model the urban economy such that firms indeed *select* a wage rate which brings their profits to a maximum by conferring upon them the associated productivity-enhancing scale economies. If scale economies cannot arise unless the urban labour force is larger than the protected labour force (that is, the labour force earning the institutional wage) then, the wage rate *must* be above the clearing level. Seen in this light, an urban institutional wage is not an impediment to productive efficiency but rather a means to bring it about.

In the literature pertaining to urban growth and equilibrium city size, agglomeration or external scale economies are hypothesized to encompass large-city advantages of low input prices, better input availability, and several informational, communication and amenity advantages — including benefits of public good availability — that positively impinge on productive efficiency. These economies contribute to the 'pull' that attracts and retains many migrants in the cities of developing countries. Recently their direct impact upon total factor productivity in developed and developing countries alike has been documented with considerable success.[4] Further, there is reason to believe that many of the stipulated advantages may occur in the form of firms' access to large site-specific urban labour markets where a large labour pool serves to perform an insurance, inventory or, when the labour force is less than perfectly homogeneous, a 'matching' function. In line with the arguments offered above, the high institutional wage, irrespective of how it comes about, seems to operate so as to foster more efficient urban production. To formalize our ideas we shall develop a model for determining the size of the urban workforce and employment in the context of rural labour flows to an urban area characterized by an institutional rigid wage and agglomeration economies.

The plan of the rest of this paper is as follows. Section II sets out an equilibrium urban size formulation with a standard expected income migration model; a noteworthy feature of this formulation is that the urban production function has as arguments two types of labour — production-enhancing employed labour and scale economies — enhancing total urban labour. Section II also adds a layer of realism to the model by accommodating the possibility of an informal sector. With the aid of a simple model a possible agglomeration-efficiency rationale for this sector is offered in Section III. Section IV sets out a choice framework wherein the high urban wage is determined as an equilibrium response. Section V provides illustrative simulations of factors influencing the urban wage premium and presents our conclusions.

II

Assume that a city's 'basic' output is produced in the formal sector under an aggregate relationship given by:

$$Q = G(N)F(N), \text{ where } G', F' > 0; F'', G'' < 0 \tag{1}$$

N enters the aggregate production function $F(\cdot)$ as total *urban employment* in the formal sector activity, and the $G(\cdot)$ function as the total *urban area workforce*. If formal sector employment is the only urban productive employment then, under full employment, urban employment is equal to the total urban workforce. The external scale shifter $G(\cdot)$ incorporates the agglomeration influence. Urban wage level in this production activity is the equilibrium economy-wide wage, W, parametric to individual firms.

In conventional formulations, with the urban export good price normalized to unity, firms' private employment decisions, derived in the aggregate from

$$\text{Max. } [GF(N) - WN] \tag{2}$$

will lead to *equilibrium* (formal) sector employment N^e given by:

$$G(N^e)F'(N^e) = W, \tag{3}$$

where the external $G(\cdot)$ factor is viewed as parametric. By contrast, the socially optimal solution which recognizes the productivity shifts associated with each employment decision, will lead to urban employment at the level N^* arising from a first-order condition incorporating the variability of $G(N)$:

$$G(N^*)F'(N^*) + G'(N^*)F(N^*) = W \tag{4}$$

Under our assumptions regarding the sign of $G'(\cdot)$, we conclude that the private urban labour force and employment are suboptimal in size, i.e., $N^e < N^*$. Also, the policy implication is that optimal migration to cities should be greater than it is.[5]

This result does not intuitively tally with the popular perception that rural-to-urban migration is excessive since migrants cannot be gainfully absorbed at LDCs' prevailing rates of industrial expansion.

The expected income model of intersectoral labour supply implies that urban employment, N_M, is determined through

$$G(N_M)F'(N_M) = \bar{W} \quad (5)$$

where $\bar{W}$ is the 'institutionally' set high urban wage (and the $G(\cdot)$ function reflects, as before, the presence of agglomeration economies). However, in this model, urban *workforce*, N_U, is determined through a distinct process wherein, given the rural wage W_R, cityward migration is in response to an N_M/N_U probability of receiving a $\bar{W}$-paying urban job, i.e.,

$$W_R = \bar{W}(N_M/N_U) \quad (6)$$

In other words, migration takes place so as to equalize the rural wage with the expected urban wage, the latter being given by $\bar{W}$ times the urban employment rate. The employment rate — the probability of obtaining urban formal sector employment — will subsequently be referred to as p_1.

The wedge introduced between formal sector urban employment and the total urban workforce (which, in the context of the formulation above, implies that $N^e \neq N_M \neq N_U$ — the first inequality arises from $W_R \neq \bar{W}$) is reflected in $p_1 < 1$, characterizing non-clearance of the urban labour market. The discrepancy between urban workforce and urban employment, $U = N_U - N_M$, represents *equilibrium unemployment.*

Given our hypothesis about the operation of the labour agglomeration advantage, might it not be that N_U in fact approaches N^* whereas N_M falls short of N^*, and the urban workforce as a whole, not just formal sector employment, enters the agglomeration specification $G(\cdot)$? An appealing possibility is that in developing countries, where fairly uniform low skill levels make labour highly substitutable, N_U is the appropriate argument[6] of the external productivity function $G(\cdot)$. The private urban employment decision then implies

$$G(N_U)F'(N_M) = \bar{W} \quad (7)$$

Following this line of thinking, there might be a need for a mechanism to sustain an N_U sufficiently larger than N_M while not actually employing the N_U–N_M workers within the formal sector. Put differently, if the desired N_U is relatively so large as to entail prohibitively high labour costs for firms, could the desired N_U be sustained through alternative means?

Assume that urban production takes place with two factors, labour and capital, the latter being available at a nationally determined equilibrium price common to all sectors and regions. As before, the urban product is sold at a parametric 'world' price, normalized in our model to unity. Formal sector production takes place under

$$Q = G(N_U)F(N_M, K), \text{ where } G' > 0 \tag{8}$$

and $F(\cdot)$ is characterized by decreasing returns to scale. Suppose first, as before, that labour supplied to the urban economy is determined through the migration equilibrium condition:

$$W_R = p_1 \ \overline{\mathrm{W}} \tag{9}$$

where, with unemployment the only alternative to absorption in the formal sector, $p_1 = N_M/N_U < 1$, and $\overline{W}_R$ is the prevailing rural wage. Private maximization by firms takes the form

$$\text{Max. } [G\ (p_1^{-1}\ N_M)\ F\ (N_M, K) - \ \overline{W}N_M - rK] \tag{10}$$

leading to the first-order conditions that yield N_M^e and K^e:

$$G(p_1^{-1}\ N_M^e)\ F_N\ (N_M^e, K^e) = \ \overline{W} \tag{11}$$

and

$$G(p_1^{-1}N_M^e)\ F_K\ (N_M^e, K^e) = r \tag{12}$$

However, a formulation incorporating the 'external' productivity factor leads to an alternative first-order condition for labour as follows:

$$G(p_1^{-1}N_M^*)\ F_N(N_M^*, K^*) + p_1^{-1}\ G'\ (N_M^*)\ F\ (N_M^*, K^*)\ \ \overline{W} \tag{13}$$

generating optimal urban sector employment N^*_M along with K^* which arises from a condition analogous to (12).

We are now ready to incorporate the urban informal sector. Predictions of urban unemployment rates based on a relationship such as (6) have consistently yielded overestimates. In addition, many urban labour market studies have documented a formal–informal dichotomy along with a residual unemployment-mitigating subsector. The combined effect of a high wage, rural workers' migration response and the presence of a low-wage informal sector to 'hold' these urban labour market entrants presents a situation conducive to reaping agglomerative benefits by formal sector firms.

We model the informal sector through a simple postulated multiplier relationship between it and the formal sector, so that the number of jobs it offers is θN_M where θ is a linkage coefficient. Such linkages are conceptualized as occurring, for example, when a modern large-scale capital-intensive sector is serviced by small-scale labour-intensive enterprises using traditional methods.[7] The employment structure which results affects the behaviour of migrants who now respond to the equilibrium condition:

$$\bar{W}_R = \bar{W}(N_M/N_U) + W_I(\theta N_M/N_U) \tag{14}$$

where W_I is at- or near-subsistence informal sector wage. Hence

$$N_U = [(\bar{W} + W_I\theta)/W_R]\, N_M \tag{15}$$

We designate $[W_R/(\bar{W} + W_I\theta)]$ as p_2. Note that $p_2 < p_1$. It is important to note that unlike p_1, p_2 does not represent the probability of finding an urban job under the new situation. Rather, it is the proportion of formal employment in total urban employment. With a positive linkage coefficient, it is obvious that the formal sector's share in urban employment is lowered. It also follows that allowing for the presence of an informal sector implies a higher overall employment probability than that which prevails in its absence. This probability, given by $(1+\theta)\,[W_R/(\bar{W}+W_I\theta)]$, increases in θ. In the special cases where there is no linkage with the informal sector ($\theta = 0$), this probability reduces to $W_R/\bar{W}$, i.e., to p_1 as per the original formulation given by (6).

In the presence of the informal sector, then, private maximization takes the form:

$$\text{Max.}\ [G(p_2^{-1}N_M)\, F(N_M, K) - \bar{W}N_M - rK] \tag{16}$$

which, through a condition similar to (11), yields the optimal private formal sector employment level N_M^{Ie}, with p_2 replacing p_1. Finally, for completeness, we characterize social optimization in the presence of the informal sector. It involves a condition analogous to (13) with p_2 replacing p_1, and where optimal formal sector employment N_M^{I*} is defined.

Our aim would now be to investigate the implications of factoring in the informal sector as a determinant of urban agglomeration. To this end we shall move in stages. We shall compare first the 'private' employment level under full employment to the 'private' employment level under migration-induced unemployment and likewise with regard to the 'social' employment levels. We shall then compare the 'private' employment level to the 'social' employment level, first under a scenario of full employment and then under a scenario of unemployment arising from expected income-induced migration. With the insights generated by these comparisons we shall turn to comparisons admitting the presence of the informal sector. Table 1 clarifies the full range of possibilities.

Table 1: Alternative Formal Sector Employment Levels

Scenario	*Private*	*Social*
Formal Sector Alone		
Full Employment	[1] $N^e_M \;\vert\; (p_1 = 1)$	[2] $N^*_M \;\vert\; (p_1 = 1)$
Migration-induced Unemployment	[3] $N^e_M \;\vert\; (p_1 < 1)$	[4] $N^*_M \;\vert\; (p_1 < 1)$
Formal and Informal Sector		
Full Employment	[5] $N^{Ie}_M \;\vert\; (p_2 = 1)$	[6] $N^{I*}_M \;\vert\; (p_2 = 1)$
Migration-induced Unemployment	[7] $N^{Ie}_M \;\vert\; (p_2 < 1)$	[8] $N^{I*}_M \;\vert\; (p_2 < 1)$

To facilitate pair-wise comparisons, in the next section we shall utilize a specific version of the model.

III

We specify the model[8] as follows: $G(\cdot) = (N_U)^\tau$, and $F(\cdot) = (N_M)^\alpha (K)^\beta$, where $0 < \alpha, \beta, \tau < 1$, and $h = \alpha + \beta + \tau < 1$, to ensure finite city size. The ratio of formal sector urban employment to the urban workforce is p_1, implying the $N_U = p_1^{-1} N_M$. Formal sector urban production is then given by:

$$Q = (N_U)^\tau (N_M)^\alpha (K)^\beta \tag{17}$$

Equilibrium formal sector employment will be determined through a private decision-making calculus that yields the following first-order conditions for maximum profit corresponding, respectively, to (11) and (12):

$$(\alpha/N_M)(p_1^{-1} N_M)^\tau N_M^\alpha K^\beta = \overline{W} \tag{18}$$

and

$$(\beta/K)(p_1^{-1} N_M)^\tau N_M^\alpha K^\beta = r \tag{19}$$

Substituting (17) in (18) and (19), we get

$$Q = (\overline{W}/\alpha) N_M \tag{20}$$

and

$$K = (\beta/r)Q \tag{21}$$

By resubstituting (21) in (17), we obtain

$$Q = (p_1^{-1} N_M{}^{[\tau/(1-\beta)]} N_M{}^{[\alpha/(1-\beta)]} (\beta/r)^{[\beta/(1-\beta)]} \tag{22}$$

and finally, by substituting (22) in (20), the equilibrium formal sector employment, $N^e{}_M$ is derived, for the general (urban unemployment admitting) case where $p_1 < 1$,

$$N_M^e = (\alpha/\bar{W})^{[1-\beta)/(1-h)]} p_1^{[-\tau/(1-h)]} (\beta/r)^{[\beta/(1-h)]} \quad (23)$$

and, for the special full employment ($N_M = N_U$) case of $p_1 = 1$,

$$N^e{}_M = (\alpha/\bar{W})^{[(1-\beta)/(1-h)]} \ (\beta/r)^{[\beta/(1-h)]} \quad (24)$$

A solution satisfying the altered first-order condition for labour likewise emerges from an expression corresponding to (13). The conditions for social optimization and subsequent derivations are similar, with the exception that (20) is now replaced by the expression below

$$Q = [W/(\alpha + \tau)] N_M \quad (25)$$

The procedure now yields N_M^*, which, for the general case wherein a hypothetical planner addresses just the externality but not the unemployment problem, is given by

$$N_M^* = [(\alpha + \tau)/\bar{W}]^{[1-\beta)/(1-h)]} p_1^{[-\tau/(1-h)]} (\beta/r)^{[\beta/(1-h)} \quad (26)$$

and for the special case where the planner's objective is also to secure full urban employment would be:

$$N_M^* = [(\alpha + \tau)/\bar{W}]^{[(1-\beta)/(1-h)]} (\beta/r)^{[\beta/(1-h)]} \quad (27)$$

Likewise, equilibrium formal sector employment in the presence of the informal sector will be

$$N_M^{Ie} = (\alpha/\bar{W})^{[1-\beta)/(1-h)]} p_2^{[-\tau/(1-h)]} (\beta/r)^{[(\beta/(1-h)]} \quad (28)$$

which is similar to (23) above, except that p_2 replaces p_1. Finally, the social planner's optimum in the presence of the informal sector is the appropriate modification of (26):

$$N_M^{I*} = [(\alpha + \tau)/\bar{W})]^{[(1-\beta)/(1-h)]} p_2^{[-\tau/(1-h)]} (\beta/r)^{[\beta/(1-h)]} \quad (29)$$

Each of these two expressions will reduce to their 'formal-sector-only' counterparts (24) and (27) under full employment.

We now have all the expressions necessary to perform the appropriate comparisons. From expressions (24) and (23) above, entailing comparisons between entires [1] and [3] in Table 1, we note that

$$\text{(A)}\ [N_M^e \mid (p_1 = 1)] / [N_M^e \mid (p_1 < 1)]$$
$$= p_1^{[r(1-h)]}$$
$$<1, \text{ since } h < 1$$

Again, from equations (27) and (26), we can compare entries [2] and [4] in Table 1:

$$\text{(B)}\ [N_M^* \mid (p_1 = 1)] / [N_M^* \mid (p_1 < 1)]$$
$$= p_1^{[\tau(1-h)]}$$
$$< 1, \text{ since } h < 1$$

From equations (27) and (24), a comparison of [2] and [1] in Table 1 gives:

$$\text{(C)}\ [N_M^* \mid (p_1 = 1)] \,/\, [N_M^e \mid (p_1 = 1)$$
$$= [\alpha + \tau) \,/\, \alpha]^{[(1-\beta)/(1-h)]}$$
$$> 1, \text{ since } h < 1$$

And similarly, from evaluating entries [4] and [3] in Table 1,

$$\text{(D)}\ [N_M^* \mid (p_1 < 1)] \,/\, [N_M^e \mid (p_1 < 1)$$
$$= [\ (\alpha + \tau) \,/\, \alpha]\ ^{[(1-\beta)/\ (1-h)]}$$
$$> 1, \text{ since } h < 1$$

Whereas results (C) and (D) nicely square with intuition, (A) and (B) are counterintuitive: they suggest that in a state of unemployment arising from an expected income-induced migration *more* workers are actually employed in the formal sector than in a state of full employment. In the full employment neoclassical scenario, when the wage rate is allowed to adjust, urban formal sector employment is expected to increase. But here, in the absence of the expected income mechanism including the institutional wage (i.e., with $p_1 = 1$), not as many workers migrate as in its presence, and the $G(\cdot)$ function is denied the productivity-enhancing effects of a larger urban workforce. Hence, *less* employment can be privately sustained. In other words, if agglomeration benefits that enter through the external productivity specification arise from the size of the total workforce, then the *expected income migration mechanism, in conjunction with a high institutional wage, makes for a more productive urban environment, facilitating higher levels of employment.*

In fact, it would be quite instructive to observe the effects of equating entries [2] and [3] in Table 1. These bear values given by (27) and (23) respectively. Suppose we assume:

$$\text{(E)}\ N_M^* \mid (p_1 = 1) = N_M^e \mid (p_1 < 1)$$

This implies $p_1 = [\alpha / (\alpha + \tau)]^{[(1-\beta)/\tau]}$ since $\alpha / (\alpha + \tau) < 1$ and $(1-\beta) / \tau > 0$, it follows that $p_1 < 1$, which is a necessary condition for the existence of urban unemployment due to the fixed institutional wage!

What we have just observed is that equivalence of the effects of private maximization with social optimization is consistent with a necessary condition for the existence of urban unemployment due to the high 'institutional' urban wage, under the assumption that agglomeration benefits stem from the presence of the overall regional workforce. Within the informal sector scenario, we can perform an analogous exercise and will similarly find that a departure from full employment, viz., $p_2 < 1$, will be necessary so that the benefits from unaided private decisions in the presence of the institutional wage approach the benefits of full employment social optimization by an omniscient planner.

We can now ask whether any useful consistency relationships obtain between the 'formal sector alone' and 'formal and informal sector' scenario. That is, can it now be demonstrated that the private informal sector serves as a repository of labour that achieves the same productivity results as social optimization internalizing agglomeration economies do in the absence of this sector? Two relevant expressions that may be chosen for comparison in order to isolate the effect of the informal sector are those from entries [4] and [7] in Table 1. Naturally, the case $p_2 < 1$ rather than the case $p_1 = 1$ is selected for the exercise of comparison because the latter case precludes the existence of any unemployment outside the formal sector at all, making the informal sector, as it were, redundant. Equating the relevant expressions,

$$\text{(F)}\ N_M \mid (p_1 < 1) = N_M^I \mid (p_2 < 1)$$

we obtain equality of expression (26) with (28):

$$(\alpha / \bar{W})^{[(1-\beta)/(1-h)]}\, p_2^{[-\tau/(1-h)]} = [(\alpha + \tau) / \bar{W}]^{[(1-\beta)/(1-h)]}\, p_1^{[-\tau/(1-h)]}$$

implying

$$(p_1/p_2)^{\tau} = [(\alpha + \tau) / \alpha]^{1-\beta} \tag{30}$$

Since $\tau > 0$, the right hand side, and hence the left hand side of (30) are greater than unity, implying $p_1 > p_2$, which, under our assumptions, *is a necessary condition for the informal sector to exist*. Thus we derive a rationalization for the informal sector emerging from comparison of the respective expressions for what we have designated 'optimum' employment, and equilibrium formal sector employment in the presence of the informal sector. What the implication confirms is that the presence of a complementary informal sector allows proportionally fewer employees to be sustained in informal sector employment as a fraction of the total urban workforce. The rationalization demonstrates that the urban informal sector serves to restore efficiency to a situation which otherwise, under conditions of agglomeration economies and expected income-induced migration, would have yielded a suboptimal urban workforce.

IV

While the foregoing analysis serves to establish the consistency of the dualistic urban wage structure postulated in the expected income migration model with an agglomeration economies explanation, it stops short of fully explaining the *formation* of the institutional wage. To model the determination of the institutional wage it is necessary to cast the problem in terms of a rational firms' choice framework. Here the distinction between private outcome and social optimum vanishes as the urban wage is sustained as an efficient *equilibrium* wage. In the present section we develop an argument along these lines, utilizing the general model of Section II.

Assume the urban wage is defined as $W_U = kW_R$, where W_R is the given rural wage level. $k \neq 0$ is a factor of proportionality that can now be regarded as a choice variable from the viewpoint of profit-maximizing urban formal sector firms. Since this maximization takes place in the context of an expected income migration framework, the migration condition is

$$W_R = (N_M / N_U) \cdot W_U \qquad (31)$$

implying, in light of $W_U = kW_R$

$$N_M / N_U = W_R / W_U = 1/k \qquad (32)$$

Hence it follows that

$$N_U = kN_M \qquad (33)$$

Note that the migration condition (31), which posits an intersectoral equilibrium labour allocation, represents the rural labour supply faced by urban producers in the formal sector. Firms now maximize the following objective function:

$$\text{Max.}\ [G(kN_M)\,\text{F}\,(N_M, K) - (kW_R)N_M - rK\,] \qquad (34)$$

where it is apparent that they choose both employment, N, and the wage factor, k, as well as the desired capital stock, K. It is evident that substituting (31) and (33) in (34), an equivalent characterization of this problem can cast the decision in terms of choosing N_M, N_U and K:

$$\text{Max.}\ [G(N_U)F(N_M, K) - W_R(N_U / N_M)N_M - rK\,] \qquad (35)$$

Recognizing that they operate under the economies of urban agglomeration, and recognizing their control over city size — the size of the total urban resident workforce that can be commanded through manipulation of the urban wage, given the rural labour supply response, formal sector firms will act as if they can choose the magnitudes both of internal employment, N_M, as well as the overall labour pool, N_U, from which this N_M is drawn. Of the three ensuing necessary first-order conditions implicitly defining the equilibrium values of N_M, N_U and K, (36) is with respect to N_M—with urban wage (and city size) treated as parametric,

(37) explicitly chooses N_U, or total urban workforce, while (38) is with respect to capital employed:

$$G(N_U)F_{N_M}(N_M, K) = W_U = KW_R \quad (36)$$

$$G'(N_U)F(N_M, K) = W_R \quad (37)$$

$$G(N_U)F_K(N_M, K) = r \quad (38)$$

Dividing condition (36) by (37), it becomes apparent that the optimal k emerging in this high-wage–high-productivity trade-off must satisfy

$$\frac{G(N_U)F_{N_M}(N_M, K)}{G'(N_U)\,F(N_M, K)} = N_U/N_M = k \quad (39)$$

Essentially, k represents the formal sector wage premium — the relative price of internally employed to 'external' urban labour. In profit-maximizing producer equilibrium, k is equated with the marginal rate of substitution between the two types of workers. That is to say, if the premium to formal sector employment is high, the marginal product of 'internal' relative to 'external' labour is high, and fewer persons will be hired formally while more are utilized in an indirect manner.

Admitting the informal sector, the ensuing migration equilibrium condition is

$$W_R = W_U(N_M/N_U) + W_I(\theta N_M/N_U) \quad (40)$$

This implies

$$W_U = W_R(N_U/N_M) - W_I\theta \quad (41)$$

The formal sector firms' problem analogous to (35) now becomes

$$\text{Max.}\ [G(N_U^I)F_{N_M}(N_M^I, K^I) - [W_R(N_U^I/N_M^I) - W_I\theta]\,N_M^I - (rK^I)] \quad (42)$$

from which it follows that the expression analogous to (39) is

$$\frac{G(N_U^I)F_{N_M}(N_M^I, K^I) + W_I\theta}{G'(N_U^I)\,F(N_M^I, K^I)} = N_U^I/N_M^I = k^I \quad (43)$$

where k^I is the analogous formal sector wage premium over migrant rural wage in the presence of an urban informal sector.

V

The magnitude of the wage premium depends in general on features of the productive environment — relative factor prices, technology and linkages, and will differ, as such, from context to context. The examples presented in Table 2 simulate the roles of agglomeration economies, urban subsectoral linkages, factor substitution possibilities and rural labour availability in the determination of the urban formal sector wage, given the behavioural model of Section IV. Functional specification enables illustration of the directional effects of selected parametric characterizations of these influences upon k.

The production function of Section III, $Q = N_U^{\tau} N_M^{\alpha} K^{\beta}$ is employed in Part (A) of Table 2 to examine, in particular, the effects of the agglomeration elasticity, τ, given plausible parameter values.[9] As expected, the magnitude of k increases with the strength of the external economy, reflecting the greater return to assembling a large urban labour pool. Part (B) uses the same specification augmented with the formal–informal employment linkage mechanism[10] to simulate effects of the latter's intensity on the wage premium. It is noted that, *ceteris paribus*, the premium is higher in the presence of an informal sector than in its absence, due to the superior productive efficiency of firms under the circumstances. Moreover, k increases with θ as these productivity benefits are multiplied. Finally, Part (C) employs the constant elasticity specification $Q = [\tau N_U^{-\delta} + \alpha N_M^{-\delta}]^{-1/\delta}$ to explicitly explore the effects of substitution possibilities between internal and external labour in urban production.[11] Not surprisingly, the greater the opportunity of substituting 'costless' external workers without having to employ them formally to maintain production, the higher is an optimal k. Through simulation under alternative scenarios, we find much that mirrors developing country phenomena. In particular, we note the association between lower rural wage rates and steeper urban wage premia. Similarly, the less remunerative the informal sector, the higher the formal sector premium and the sharper the urban wage disparities. Developing regions feature, too, the higher degree of agglomeration benefits, significant informal sector presence and technological levels permitting easy substitutability between slightly differentiated labour that entail the higher wage premia demonstrated by our examples. On these grounds, our hypothesis merits inspection as an alternative to conventional explanations of LDC urban labour market structures.

The relationships suggested above relating the urban wage premia to the internal production or agglomeration efficiency parameters of the urban production structure constitute testable propositions. Their examination for a cross-section of regional economies for which production parameters and the wage structure are known should be possible. In addition, if the behavioural hypothesis underlying the above model

Table 2: Parametric Simulation of Influences on the Urban Wage Premium

(A) Agglomeration and Output Elasticities

A.1 $\alpha = 0.5$; $\beta = 0.5$; $r = 0.5$; $Q = 1$

γ	$k\ (W_R = 0.05)$	$k\ (W_R = 0.10)$	$k\ (W_R = 0.25)$
0.1	11.49	5.00	1.66
0.2	17.41	6.60	1.83
0.3	29.30	9.67	2.23

A.2 $\alpha = 0.6$; $\beta = 0.4$; $r = 0.5$; $Q = 1$

γ	$k\ (W_R = 0.05)$	$k\ (W_R = 0.10)$	$k\ (W_R = 0.25)$
0.1	11.61	5.17	1.78
0.2	16.42	6.51	1.92
0.3	25.33	8.96	2.27

A.3 $\alpha = 0.4$; $\beta = 0.6$; $r = 0.5$; $Q = 1$

γ	$k\ (W_R = 0.05)$	$k\ (W_R = 0.10)$	$k\ (W_R = 0.25)$
0.1	12.51	5.26	1.67
0.2	21.03	7.44	1.88
0.3	40.32	11.99	2.41

(B) Formal–Informal Sector Linkages

$\gamma = 0.1$; $\alpha = 0.5$; $\beta = 0.5$; $W_R = 0.10$; $r = 0.5$; $Q = 1$

θ	$k(W_I = 0.05)$	kW_R / W_I	$k(W_I = 0.10)$	kW_O / W_I	$k(W_I = 0.25)$	kW_R / W_I
0.1	5.05	10.1	5.10	5.1	5.25	2.1
0.2	5.10	10.2	5.20	5.2	5.50	2.2
0.3	5.15	10.3	5.30	5.3	5.75	2.3
0.4	5.20	10.4	5.40	5.4	6.00	2.4
0.5	5.25	10.5	5.50	5.5	6.25	2.5
0.6	5.30	10.6	5.60	5.6	6.50	2.6
0.7	5.35	10.7	5.70	5.7	6.75	2.7
0.8	5.40	10.8	5.80	5.8	7.00	2.8
0.9	5.45	10.9	5.90	5.9	7.25	2.9

(C) Internal vs External Labour Substitution Possibilities

$\gamma = 0.1$; $\alpha = 0.5$; $Q = 1$

σ	$k\ (W_R = 0.10)$	$k\ (W_R = 0.25)$	$k\ (W_R = 0.50)$
0.1	9.61	3.24	1.17
0.2	10.42	3.55	1.36
0.3	11.59	3.98	1.59
0.4	13.32	4.62	1.91
0.5	16.20	5.67	2.41
0.6	21.73	7.66	3.34
0.7	35.47	12.59	5.59
0.8	94.48	33.75	15.23
0.9	1785.23	641.51	293.52

holds, these conditions may be used to recover unknown production and linkage parameters in any given city over time.

Several related empirical questions also arise at the microeconomic level. One set of questions involves ascertaining the quantitative importance of the relevance of the urban agglomeration advantages to the operation of urban labour markets in a variety of productive contexts. A related task consists of establishing the dominance of urbanization (total workforce) over localization (own-industry employment) economies in agglomeration effects.[12] Another important set of issues relates to the empirical verification of various facets of the informal sector's role within an integrated labour demand-and-supply framework. A study of differential migration propensities in response to alternative compositions of the urban employment structure is likewise warranted.

In conclusion, our current paper provides a synthesis and an 'explanation' of stylized LDC urban labour market phenomena such as dualism and institutional wage rigidity. It implies new directions for further research in these areas which we plan to undertake and report on in future papers. Ultimately, such research should facilitate more enlightened policies towards cityward migration, urban growth, the informal sector and urban labour markets in developing countries.

This paper was prepared in June 1984 when the author was Post-Doctoral Fellow with the Migration and Development Program, Harvard University, Cambridge, Massachusetts, USA. Helpful comments from Professor Oded Stark and Lloyd J. Dumas on an earlier draft were gratefully acknowledged by the author. The author was working on revision of the paper but the editors have not been able to retrieve it. It is hoped that scholars interested in the subject would attempt further research and sophistication. The editors of the volume thank Dr Vibhas Saha and Dr M.H. Suryanarayana for going through the paper and making some editorial suggestions.

NOTES

1 The notion that in LDCs, government and 'big industry' are sufficiently divorced, so that the former unilaterally imposes wage restrictions on the latter, appears quite far-fetched. It seems to be much more realistic for wage legislation to reflect and serve the interests of those whose support a typical LDC government may find crucial, or who even constitute part of the government.

2 The best known model appears in Harris and Todaro (1970).

3 See Shukla (1988b).

4 Early US empirical studies include Segal (1976) and Sveikauskas (1975); in the developing countries' context, one such exercise for Brazil is reported in Henderson (1986); the findings of a study using Indian data, viz., Shukla (1988), are illustrative. Estimates obtained therein imply average

total factor productivity increase of 10 per cent with each doubling of city size within a realistic range of city sizes. This contrasts with the typically lower values — 0.04 to 0.06 — for 'agglomeration elasticities' reported for developed countries.

5 See Shukla and Stark (1986).

6 In production function-based estimations of agglomeration economies it is necessary to use an aggregate proxy for the hypothesized agglomeration effect. If such economies are those of 'urbanization', the relevant variable is city population; if 'localization' economies are assumed, this proxy is industry-specific employment. The Shukla study for India cited in [4] found urbanization economies to dominate. This would support specifying N_U as an argument of $G(\cdot)$.

7 Stark (1982) develops arguments emphasizing this linkage aspect of the role of the informal sector.

8 The specification follows that used in Shukla and Stark (1990).

9 Setting $Q = 1$ as numeraire, profit maximization with this specification leads to $K = (\alpha/W_R)\,[(\tau/W_R)^{\tau/\alpha}\,(\beta/r)^{\beta/\alpha}]$.

10 Amending firms' profit maximizing calculus to substitute $[k^I W_R - \theta W_I]$ as formal sector wage in the informal sector's presence yields $k^I = (\alpha/W_R)\,[\tau/(W_R)^{\tau/\alpha}\,(\beta/r)^{\beta/\alpha} + (\theta/\alpha)W_I]$.

11 Here, $k = (\alpha/W_R)\,[\{1-\tau(W_R/\tau)^{1-\sigma}\}/\alpha]^{1/(1-\sigma)}$, where $\sigma = 1/(1+\delta)$ represents the two-factor elasticity of substitution between the labour types.

12 See Shukla (1989a) for empirical evidence that agglomeration effects may be labour-augmenting and Shukla (1989b) for a discussion of the urbanization-localization debate.

REFERENCES

Harris, John and Michael P. Todaro (1970), 'Migration, Unemployment and Development: A Two-Sector Analysis', *American Economic Review*, Vol. 60.

Henderson, J. Vernon (1986), 'The Efficiency of Resource Usage and City Size', *Journal of Urban Economics*, Vol. 19.

Segal, David (1976), 'Are There Returns to Scale in City Size?', *The Review of Economics and Statistics*, Vol. 58.

Shukla, Vibhooti (1988a), *Urban Development and Regional Policy in India: An Econometric Analysis*, Himalaya Publishing House, Bombay.

———(1988b), 'Rural Migration to an Indian Metropolis–Examining the Microfoundations of the Harris–Todaro Paradigm', *Indian Journal of Agricultural Economics*, Vol. 43, No. 4.

———(1989a), 'An Inquiry into the Nature and Sources of LDC Urban Productivity', mimeo.

———(1989b), 'Urbanization vs. Localization Economies and Economic Development', mimeo.

Shukla, Vibhooti and Oded Stark (1986), 'Urban External Economies and Optimal Migration', in O. Stark, ed., *Research in Human Capital and*

Development, Vol. 4: Migration, Human Capital and Development, Greenwich, Conn: JAI Press.

———(1991), 'Policy Comparisons with an Agglomeration Effects-Augmented Dual Economy Model', *Journal of Urban Economics*, 27, 1–15 (1990), Academic Press Inc. USA. This paper incorporating changes from the revised version published in Oded Stark (1991), *Migration of Labor* (Blackwell Publishers, USA and UK) is published in this volume.

Stark, Oded (1982), 'On Modelling the Informal Sector', *World Development*, Vol. 10.

Sveikauskas, Leo (1975), 'The Productivity of Cities', *Quarterly Journal of Economics*, Vol. 89.

8 / Rural Migration to an Indian Metropolis: Examining the Microfoundations of the Harris–Todaro Paradigm

VIBHOOTI SHUKLA

Book Review of *Rural to Urban Migration and the Urban Labour Market (A Case Study of Delhi)*, Biswajit Banerjee (1986), Himalaya Publishing House, Bombay, 1986, pp. xviii + 285.

I

Theoretical development of the migration model due to Harris and Todaro (1970) has come a long way. Attractive as a dual-economy model that took into account many salient and obvious facets of urbanization and structural change in developing countries, the model gained rapid popularity as an alternative to Lewis's model based on unlimited supplies of rural labour in the characterization of economic relationships between the urban and rural sectors.

The model views inter-sectoral labour migration behaviour as a personal equalizing response to rural–urban differences in expected incomes, and thereby seeks to explain the sort of persistent underemployment that is said to be featured in developing country cities. In doing so, it resorts to a formulation characterized by the assumption that people migrate with imperfect specific knowledge regarding prospective job opportunities available in their urban destinations, but nevertheless have a generalized idea of employment probabilities evaluated from city-wide unemployment ratios. The implicitly incorporated premise that urban job search can be conducted only in cities drives the equilibrium unemployment characteristic of such models. The rather ad hoc but allegedly empirically consistent assumption of a rigid, institutionally determined urban wage seems equally essential to the comparative static results of the model.

The model's solution features an economy in underemployment equilibrium, off its efficient production frontier, as a result of harbouring a serious inter-sectoral labour resource misallocation, wherein part of the rural labour force removes itself from productive agricultural activity to migrate to the urban areas where it is largely condemned to idle unemployment. In addition, it yields the prediction that urban job creation, far from alleviating the problem of urban unemployment, will further exacerbate it in absolute and often in ratio terms by attracting even more migrants to the city through the model's expectational mechanism. The implication, therefore, was that rural migrant influxes contributed to an urban growth in developing countries that was efficiency-reducing and inherently parasitic — one that added relatively little to the economy's product while imposing significant costs in social and infrastructural terms.

Not surprisingly, on the normative side, a series of theoretical developments in prescriptions for restoring efficiency followed in the wake of the initial formulation. With cost–benefit analysis increasingly being applied in practical solutions to the problems of underdevelopment, a burgeoning literature on shadow wage rates[1] was brought to bear on the issue. It was noted, invoking the model, that the use of a shadow wage rate lower than the prevailing urban wage (as would have been appropriate in the presence of full urban employment and a Lewisian rural labour surplus) for appraising urban projects was not warranted. In seeking economy-wide government interventions, it was proposed that an employment subsidy to urban employers to absorb the unemployed excess would work only in conjunction with a strict programme of migration restriction[2] to prevent rural-to-urban labour flows, a recommendation later tempered by a recognition of first-best policy responses entailing a broader range of sectoral subsidy options which obviated the need for coercive labour allocation mechanisms in order to achieve optimality (see Bhagwati and Srinivasan 1974). While most of these measures saw no direct implementation, the literature went a long way towards fostering a policy climate of discouraging city growth and garnering additional support for employment-generating activities in agriculture or rural industry as a strategy for deterring out-migration in many countries, including India.

Meanwhile, the empirical developments[3] that followed from the model, although initially aggregative, helped to veer away estimation formulations from specifications of migration flows as disequilibrium adjustment mechanisms, and towards more behaviourally motivated specifications.

Migration functions yielded estimates of employment elasticities, upon which hinged important quantitative predictions (e.g., Todaro 1976) of what was likely to happen to urban unemployment levels and rates should exogenous urban job creation occur. An increasing number of less developed country applications led to the realization that estimates using the original Harris–Todaro formulation that were based on simple calculations of urban–rural wage differentials systematically overstated urban unemployment rates, contradicting both actual measurements of visible joblessness featured in third world cities, as well as the commonsense observation that unemployment of such magnitudes had to be a luxury most ill-affordable in the prevailing context of poverty.

Gradually, disguised unemployment or underemployment in the urban areas came to be taken account of in the theoretical formulation. It was noticed that urban employment, far from being a homogeneous-characteristic sector, had itself a two-tiered structure, with the formal sector, featuring the high fixed wage, distinguished from the informal sector, variously designated the urban traditional, subsistence or 'murky' sector (see Fields 1975), by virtue of certain distinct occupational, organizational and wage characteristics. For the latter, these were, typically, lower capital requirements, relative ease of entry, small-scale and family ownership. The informal sector was viewed as a low-productivity, low-wage repository of underemployed rural migrants *en route* to the more desirable, high-wage formal sector jobs they ultimately sought. While these extensions were an incremental accommodation to reality, they largely kept intact the spirit of the model, and preserved the validity of its conclusions.

As data become available at the individual level, more and more studies are able to perform micro-level estimations of specified behavioural relationships subsumed in the model (e.g., Da Vanzo 1978). The most recent developments on the empirical front take the form of challenging the validity of basic hypothesized features of the paradigm and critically testing its preconceptions regarding the informal sector. Such microfoundational examination assumes much importance in the light of its weighty policy ramifications.

II

Banerjee's book very systematically addresses this re-evaluation of the conventional paradigm in the context of rural migration to an Indian metropolis, bringing to bear upon the examination the kind of close empirical observation and careful statistical work that must ultimately pass judgement on the relevance of the model. Among the credentials of the study is the use of data at the individual level, collected at destination for the purposes of the study by a survey team led by the author during 1976.

In general, four important sub-hypotheses of the Harris–Todaro paradigm are on trial: (1) Migration is in response to rural–urban differences in expected income. (2) The would-be migrant experiences job uncertainty in particularistic terms while enjoying generalized information regarding destination employment probabilities; as a consequence, he is precluded from rural-based job search but enabled to seek an urban job exclusively upon moving. (3) To the extent the informal sector is admitted into the paradigm, it is a residual sector, a temporary reservoir for migrants unable to find a formal-sector job immediately upon arrival, acceptable for a time as a lower-(real)income alternative even to rural employment, in anticipation, however, of ultimate formal employment as a culmination of successful urban search. (4) There exists an institutionally determined high wage in the formal sector, which fails to equalize formal–informal wages through the standard neoclassical market-clearing process, and thus underlies an enduring structural dualism, in less developed countries' (LDC) urban labour markets.

It is toward the micro examination of these assumptions that Banerjee's effort is largely directed. Starting with an informative description of his sample selection and data-gathering procedures, Banerjee proceeds chronologically in the path of an individual migrating from rural areas in various northern states of India to the Delhi metropolitan region.

Both macro and micro data have been used in various contexts to test the income-responsiveness of the decision to migrate,[4] whether as part of a behavioural investigation into the determinants of migration or as a general test of spatial labour market efficiency. Micro studies have, of course, the advantage of focusing upon individual characteristics in addition to regional aggregates. Banerjee's main point in Chapter I is that the issues of 'who' migrates and 'why' are often confounded in survey-type studies of the latter sort — migration propensities and motivations must in fact be carefully distinguished, and misperceptions from the erroneous inference of 'who' from 'why' avoided. Accordingly, he examines respondents both for information on 'motivations to migrate' and 'migrant selectivity', focusing largely upon their economic attributes.

He finds that the dominant reason advanced for migration is the absence or inadequacy of economic opportunities at origin, or insufficiency of income at the rural end. To infer from this, however, that rural development efforts or investment in rural income-augmenting activities — a classical Harris–Todaro prescription — focused on the disadvantaged will effectively stem the tide of cityward migration is fallacious. This would only be so if the poorest migrate, which, as Banerjee attempts to demonstrate, is often not the case. Using tabulated evidence on rural landholdings and occupations to proxy pre-migration income characteristics to investigate economic selectivity, he adduces support for a non-monotonic, inverted U-shaped relationship of migration propensity with respect to income.

In Chapter II, the author specifically explores the information transmission process in rural-to-urban migration, and investigates the nature of the job search strategy adopted by migrants. He introduces a model of job search modified to cast the decision variable as the anticipated length of search rather than in terms of subjective employment probabilities, including an explicit consideration of search costs. He formulates two versions of the choice, pitting rural-based search against migration options, incorporating in turn the assumptions that (1) urban work and search are incompatible and (2) that urban employment and city-based search are not necessarily mutually exclusive, and recognizing formal–informal sector dualism, obtains the appropriate equilibrium conditions. His model is general, not just in terms of admitting rural-based search, but also in allowing the probability of obtaining a formal-sector job from the rural area to exceed that of obtaining one in the city, an innovation that lets, under certain conditions, the equilibrium informal sector wage to exceed the rural wage. In fact, the model implies that informal-sector income for a migrant will be higher in equilibrium than rural income if his costs of searching from the transitory job exceed the costs of rural-based search by the greater margin than the difference between the two incomes. Such a compensating differential is most likely to arise when urban living costs are substantial for the migrant due to absence of village networks in the city, or when the divergence of the available from the desired job confers relatively high psychic dissatisfaction.

Evidence presented in support of the foregoing structure points up the importance of specific information in migration, and of significant incidence of rural-based search for urban jobs. A tabulation of responses as to sources and nature of migrant information confirms the importance of friends and relatives, and downplays that of more formal channels of information transfer such as the government employment exchanges. Although only about 15.7 per cent of sample migrants said they came to the urban centre with a specific pre-arranged job, the author suspects favourable assurances of jobs in the majority of other cases. However, in general, urban contacts transferred information only about entry-level jobs. Banerjee concludes on balance that the Harris–Todaro model's implicit assumption that individuals migrate to the city with generalized information and search for specific openings only upon arrival in the urban centre does not generally hold for rural migrants in Delhi.

In Chapter III, Banerjee seeks to examine the validity of the scenario of migrant transition envisioned in the Harris–Todaro model. Here, the author questions the prevailing myths that look upon migration as a two-stage process — that the informal sector is largely a point of entry for rural migrants, that participation in informal sector activities is consistent with, and indeed, frequently accompanied by search for a formal-sector job, that employment in the informal sector is only temporary and the income obtained thereby helps to finance this search, and that since the typical wage paid in informal activities is lower than the rural wage, all migrants, unless they give up search and return to their rural origin, will be observed to eventually find and end up in formal sector employment. He contrasts this rather probabilistic perception (in the original Harris–Todaro framework, the process of formal-sector job acquisition takes on the character of a random lottery) with the more extreme view of structural dualism which asserts that there is little or no worker mobility between the formal and informal sectors.

Specifically, his thesis in the light of his job search model (which, it is recalled, does not restrict informal sector wage to being dominated by the rural wage commanded by the migrant) is that migrants do settle for a lifetime career in the informal sector, and indeed, that it might be the target sector for some of them, particularly those not qualified for the formal sector, without information about jobs and contacts in that sector, or with no access to interim rural financing.

The temporal labour market progression of a typical migrant may be investigated (as attempted, for example, in migrant achievement studies comparing their economic mobility with that of the local population) by regressing current occupational attainment upon duration of urban residence, but such estimations are subject to pitfalls inherent in the inference of temporal processes from cross-sectional data (e.g., the disregard for return migration, and vintage or period-specific effects accompanying successive migration cohorts) which need to be recognized and econometrically dealt with. Alternatively, a dichotomy of the incidence of those searching and not searching in the informal sector may be attempted, but is less than ideal because those in the informal sector not seeking formal sector jobs may either be satisfied in their present employment, or may have been discouraged enough in their quest for formal sector employment to effect downward adjustments in their expectations.

Banerjee opts for an approach that explicitly relates expectations to experience, one he is able to implement by direct questioning. To determine whether informal-sector entrants consider themselves to be in the queue for formal sector jobs — whether they consciously target the informal sector as a job destination or whether, once they are in the urban area, expectational adjustments take place that cause the informal sector worker to discontinue further search — he plumbs information on migrant attitudes towards the informal sector at the time of entry.

The Delhi migrant sample showed a very close affinity between realized and expected first employment experiences, with the highest success rate (80–94 per cent) recorded among those who expected to enter professional and managerial jobs, or production workers either within specific trades or in general unskilled categories, and the lowest (31 per cent) among bottom-level white-collar job (e.g., clerks and peons) aspirants. Of the ten per cent who became self-employed in the informal sector upon arrival, 71 per cent expected to do so in the first instance. It was also found that location of first job for migrants to Delhi was through urban-based contact rather than by personal job search in more than two-thirds of the cases. Banerjee concluded that the migrants' average waiting period for the first job — 17 days — was surprisingly low, even considering the possible operation of selectivity in the sample due to the return migration of unsuccessful aspirants.

A reduced-form estimation of the determinants of the length of unemployment (the realized length of job search) was performed by ordinary least squares regression methods and, expectedly, showed that the presence of pre-migration information shortened the search, as did marital status; while educational attainment and non-manual job status created a tendency to lengthen it. Surprisingly, the expected urban income variable showed an unexpected though statistically not significant shortening of the period of search, a counter-intuitive result. The strategy of dependence upon a single source of job information (as against a personal search) was again associated with a shorter wait, interpreted by the author as being attributable to the quality or reliability of the source.

Banerjee concludes that migrant expectations, conditioned by educational attainment and specific information received prior to migration, are more or less borne out. Moreover, his findings regarding the distribution of first employment of migrants do not support the case that migrants *en masse*, unable to realize their expectations, necessarily take up self-employment. He characterizes the analysis as lending credence to the position that, contrary to popular conception, the migration process in developing countries is 'well-organised, self-regulating, and minimises disruption and unforeseen hardship for new arrivals'.[5]

Chapter IV, in the reviewer's view one of the most important of the sections of this book, aims at studying the structural features of employment and the pattern of labour absorption in an Indian metropolis. Urban labour markets in developing countries have been viewed as not fully yielding to conventional human capital-based explanations of the wage determination process. Structural dualism in such markets describes a situation wherein 'people with the same supply characteristics may have different earnings if they are located in different parts of the labour market, due to the existence of certain barriers to entry to high-paying jobs'.

In particular, the LDC urban labour market is commonly characterized as featuring a high institutionally determined formal sector wage, resistant to downward movement through market-clearing forces even in the face of severe unemployment pressures. While the reasons advanced for this wage fixity are various, the implications are that formal sector jobs are somehow rationed among their aspirants. The original Harris–Todaro model envisions a random probabilistic rationing of these desirable but scarce positions, while the alternative hypothesis proposed is that more systematic exclusionary allocation factors are responsible for any observed market segmentation. By contrast, the informal sector is not subject to this 'institutional' rigidity and thus relatively much more easy to enter — this low-equilibrium income repository of surplus labour is characterized as requiring little skill or capital and tends to be associated with self-employment activities of a highly labour-intensive, low productivity service nature. Banerjee proceeds to examine the validity of this dichotomous labour market characterization in the case of Delhi.

Analysis of the sample data on sector affiliation turns up many surprises: 56.6 per cent of the sample began their employment experience in the informal sector, the predominant majority of whom were absorbed in wage employment. Only ten per cent of the migrant sample took up non-wage employment in Delhi upon arrival, 71 per cent of whom had expected to do so in the first instance. Contrary to the impression of the informal sector as overwhelmingly featuring service activities, one-third of its employees were classified as production workers.

In bringing the survey evidence on trans-sectoral movement to bear upon the resolution of the opposing claims of the two labour market explanations, namely, the segmented labour market hypothesis that denies the possibility of much intersectoral mobility, and the 'probabilistic migration' hypothesis where such movement is the norm, Banerjee found that (1) movement out of non-wage informal sector employment is low; (2) there is, by contrast, high mobility from wage to non-wage employment within the informal sector; and that (3) four-fifths of those in the formal sector at the time of survey had in fact started there. Of those who entered the informal wage sector, 47.7 per cent had arrived with a certain job, although this, the author does point out, does not preclude their having harboured expectations of subsequently taking up formal-sector employment. Only 23.6 per cent of those who had entered the informal wage sector and 6.4 per cent of initially non-wage migrants had found their way from the informal into the formal sector within the time-frame covered by the study. Incidence of the continuation of job search efforts after the taking up of initial employment was highest among those entering the informal sector, with 41 per cent continuing job search, but upward mobility among these job searchers was far from automatic — 41 per cent of those who continued search were found to have made the transition, compared with 12 per cent of those who had discontinued it. Banerjee reasons that, at the very least, to be able to discount the segmented labour market hypothesis, one should expect to observe that, given the proportion of formal sector entries among new migrant arrivals, the proportion of those that subsequently make the transition to the formal sector from the informal one must equal to this, or, if any type of migrant awareness/orientation, information-gathering or capital accumulation process is in operation, in fact, greater.

He finds this is not the case. This suggests the operation of a prior selection process in sorting rural job aspirants between the two sectors of the urban labour market. Allocative selection may, in general, be by characteristics that are acquired (such as education, skill accretion, etc.), or by those that are ascriptive (such as caste or social contacts) and cannot be realistically altered by any action on the migrant's part. Banerjee further finds the cross-sectional summary relation between human capital levels and intersectoral mobility to be weak, suggesting that education or experience does not necessarily facilitate the transition, although it would need longitudinal data to more properly capture the influence of a dynamic learning process, if, indeed, one is at work.

It is recalled that more than half (59 per cent) of the total migrants either came with the informal sector as their target, or scaled down their expectations to settle for permanent employment in that sector. It is safe to presume that this was either the outcome of voluntary choice by the migrants themselves, or the result of denial, for whatever reasons, of formal-sector employment to them. In seeking to explain the low amount of observed mobility between the two sectors of the labour market, Banerjee hypothesized that one of the following two must hold: (*a*) either that intersectoral wage differentials may not be high enough to induce mobility, or (*b*) that 'there are constraints on obtaining specific information on, and gaining access to, formal sector employment'.

Examining earnings differentials between the informal and formal sector migrants in the sample, Banerjee presents evidence that the monthly earnings of non-wage workers in the informal sector were 47 per cent higher on the average (albeit with high dispersion around the mean) than those of workers in the formal sector. He finds that the distribution of earnings in the non-wage sector overlaps that in the formal sector, and lies to its right. The proportion of formal sector workers in lower earnings groups is higher, and that in the upper earnings groups lower than that of non-wage workers (although it is pointed out that higher non-wage earnings in the informal sector compared to findings of other researchers might be attributable partly to the non-inclusion of typically low-wage-earning secondary workers in this sample). Thus the evidence belies the belief that low earners are to be found in the non-wage employment category.

Predictably, and significantly, it was found that mean wage earnings in the informal sector were only 62 per cent of those earned by employees in the formal sector — corroborating the notion of significant earning differentials between the two subsectors, a differential, moreover, likely, if anything, to be understated due to the exclusion of non-salary benefits that typically form generous portions of the formal sector compensation packages.

To systematically explore determinants of wage, Banerjee estimates an earnings function, regressing migrant earnings on the human capital variables (age and experience), on family background characteristics of migrants (specifically, caste), and a set of demand-side or structural dummies for sectoral affiliation (formal/informal, public/private), employment status (salaried/casual) and occupational level (non-manual/manual) as explanatory variables. The coefficient of a sectoral dummy would indicate, if statistically significant, the difference in earnings between sectors of workers with the same personal characteristics, and point to a difference in the process of wage determination between the two sectors. Further, the hypothesis of alternative processes of wage determination is tested by estimating separate earnings functions for the formal and informal sectors, and then statistically testing for structural equality between the two sets of coefficients obtained.

The results indicate that the explanatory power of the earnings function substantially improves with the addition of the so-called 'structural' (or demand) variables, all of which prove significant at the 1 per cent level. Affiliation with the formal sector is seen to be associated with 9.1 per cent higher earnings than the informal sector affiliation. Non-manual occupations earn 18.1 per cent over manual, *ceteris paribus*, and salaried jobs 12.5 per cent over jobs paying daily wages. Age (reflecting rural work experience), and length of urban residence (reflecting urban experience) are both shown to have a positive effect on earnings, and are the dominant explanatory variables. To uncover the sources of the formal–informal earnings differential, separate estimations of the functions were performed for each sector. Although they show the explanatory power of the earnings relationship to be substantially smaller for the informal sector than for the formal, the coefficients on the experience and education variables in the informal sector are observed not to be significantly different from comparable coefficients for the formal sector. Thus contrary to the presumption that the observed differential arises because human capital is not rewarded as highly in the informal sector as it is in the formal, returns to these variables are not found much different between the two sectors. A Chow test for structural similarity overall, however, indicates that the two relationships do differ statistically. The difference is attributed to the systematically negative effect of manual and casual work and scheduled caste status within the formal sector, versus the negligible disadvantage to these factors in the informal sector.

Banerjee concludes on this basis that while the data are not consistent with the assumptions of the probabilistic model, they do lend partial support to the hypothesis of dual labour markets. Particularly, the divisions of the labour market into two sectors is supported by the data on earnings. Allowing for human capital differences, earnings are lower (by an estimated 9 per cent) in the informal sector, and the process of wage determination different. While it appears that returns to education and experience are similar between the sectors, there is evidence of caste discrimination in access to formal sector jobs; by comparison, the informal sector seems more competitive. This sectoral difference seems attached mainly to job status and classification. The author thus summarizes that 'a meaningful distinction can be made between the formal and the informal sector'. Banerjee speculates that, because of imperfect information flow, informal-sector workers were simply not aware of formal sector jobs filled by new arrivals in greater proportions, and that prevalent practices of recruitment through social contacts make the formal sector labour market, echoing the phrase of another Indian researcher, a 'de facto closed shop system'.

In contrast to the urban destination focus of the bulk of the study, Banerjee ends with a further elaboration of supply-side factors in the migration decision, particularly focusing on a recognition of the migrant's rural household's role in the decision-making, with a necessary consideration of some rural-end factors. There is a burgeoning literature that views the migrant-family relationship as an inter-temporal, implicitly contractual one (see Lucas and Stark 1985; Stark and Lucas 1988), with endurance of the economic integrity of the multi-centred unit expressed in the form of return visits and remittance behaviour. This discussion is meaningful in the context of the debate concerning the validity of the Harris-Todaro scenarios because of supply-side differences in reservation wage that have been hypothesized between those entering the formal versus those that choose the informal sector — in particular, the observed sectoral earnings differential is attributed by some to the possibility that informal urban workers migrate *sans* family i.e., their household supply price is greater than migrant urban income), while formal-sector entrants seek sufficient compensation from urban employment to allow for the higher cost of moving with at least their nuclear families.

The survey data indicate that even upon migration, rural ties remain sufficiently strong. The author constructs a useful typology of such linkages based upon family composition and spatial distribution and land ownership patterns. On the basis of this typology, the author concludes that while only 14 per cent of sample migrants to Delhi were accompanied by family members, family integration was, by and large, not disrupted by migration. Eighty to ninety per cent of those migrating alone, and as many as two-thirds of those migrating with their family units were observed to have maintained economic links with rural areas through remittances. He concludes that the evidence supports the hypothesis that migration is undertaken for the benefit of the family as a whole, and not for purely individual advantage.

Given that as many as 36 per cent of married migrants in the sample had left their wives behind in the rural area, and, surprisingly, 30 per cent of those who had been living in Delhi for more than 5 years did not have their wives with them, the author conducts a rigorous analysis of conjugal separation. Adduced reasons for having done so — most typically cited were low income, high cost of living in the urban areas, especially the need to meet higher housing standards and social mores — were at variance with the results of the estimation of the determinants of conjugal separation through binomial logit methods. In the course of the latter it was found that while duration of urban residence and education increase the probability of bringing the wife to the city, as rural land ownership or migration to fulfil a specific purpose reduces it, urban earnings do not have any statistically significant influence on this decision. This contradiction with articulated reasons is interesting, and casts doubt on the applicability of the supply-price dominated explanations of observed sectoral wage differentials.

Migrant remittances constitute a potential developmental link between urbanization and rural welfare. A 'Tobit' analysis of remittance behaviour (which adjusts determinants of amount remitted for the decision to remit at all) confirms that they increase with urban income at an increasing rate, but fall, *ceteris paribus*, for migrants who plan to settle in the city permanently. Tabulation of responses regarding rural uses of remittances indicates priority for household expenses, with agriculture coming a distant second. Land ownership, which may be hypothesized to affect remittances positively if construed as an index of rural investment opportunities, does not show up as statistically significant in the Tobit estimation, possibly because of its alternative role as a proxy for reduced income needs that captures a conflicting negative effect. Thus while the enduring nature of the migrants' rural ties suggests the existence of strong reciprocal advantages, the measurement of indirect benefits to the countryside remains empirically unresolved.

III

The state of migration study, both within and outside the rubric of the Harris–Todaro framework, has for some time been in the phase where the stock of existing theory was ample, and empirical testing presented the binding constraint to further advancement of knowledge in the field. Elsewhere, sophisticated survey efforts and refinements in statistical techniques have now substantially begun to fill this lacuna. Banerjee begins to address this task for movements to Indian cities admirably in the book under review. Of course, what applies to Delhi migrants need not necessarily apply to Bombay migrants in terms of characteristics with regard to occupation, incomes, mobility, etc., to the extent that the features of economic activities both at the urban and rural (hinterland) ends differ widely.[6] Hence, while one should be cautious in deriving generalizations from the exercise, the author's perspective and methodology deserve close attention. That he has drawn on a self-collected sample attests to the degree of work he has committed to the exercise, and adds credibility to his understanding of it. He has a good feel for the data and is scrupulous in interpreting it comprehensively. His is an example of the kind of careful empirical work that must take migration research in developing countries to a new threshold preceding further theory modification.

The choice of units of observation at the micro level is commendable. In general, using individual migration data lifts estimation and testing from mechanistic, reduced-form analysis of grouped aggregates to a behaviourally based investigation of primary structural relationships. The use of the micro approach is also relatively novel for the study of Indian migration, which has hitherto largely featured econometric treatment at the aggregate level (e.g., Greenwood 1971a, b), partially due to constraints of the Census migration data, which occurs at levels of regional disaggregation no finer than urban/rural state strata. The absence of any nationally institutionalized data collection effort in this field at the micro level has generally left these costly ventures to the uncoordinated efforts of individual researchers who perforce must sample for strictly specific cases and purposes.

Often, the exigencies of private collection of migration data at the individual or household level, alluded to above, force trade-offs that may sometimes restrict the full scope of any research design. Here, some aspects of the study of rural-to-urban migrant streams are handicapped by absence of information on several rural-end factors of relevance. For example, in Chapter I, one wishes Banerjee could have directly tested for the role of individuals' rural wages or pre-migration incomes (and thus the exact rural–urban economic differential facing them in their decision to migrate) to explain observed rural-to-urban flows, instead of inferring migrant income selectivity indirectly, through the use of occupational or landholding proxies. Likewise, in Chapter III, detailed information on rural variables more accurately reflecting individuals' relative rural and urban search costs or their differential ability to finance urban job search would have proved very useful in predicting search behaviour, and might possibly have raised substantially the rather poor explanatory power of the estimated relationship implied by the model of Chapter II. The incomplete specification of village-end variables is a shortcoming characterizing even the self-standing and rigorously performed inquiry of Chapter V, one that otherwise has special familial supply-side insights to add to the understanding of the rural worker's decision to migrate.

By the author's own reckoning, the worth of a micro analysis is in providing an idea of the relative importance of explanatory variables worthy of inclusion in any characterization of the migration decision. But because of data constraints of the kind that have been mentioned, the analysis is not sufficient to characterize beyond doubt how the critical relationships depend upon personal and regional characteristics. Methodologically, such deficiencies sometimes leave us reconciled with descriptive or indicative tabulations in support of, rather than systematic econometric implementation of, several interesting sub-hypotheses, e.g., the effect of remittances on agricultural investment or new technology adoption. In addition, the omission of information on rural income structure, agricultural production technologies, rural cost of living or non-pecuniary incomes exclude almost altogether from consideration several important investigations (albeit outside the immediate scope of the present study) into the rural welfare, distributional or developmental consequences of individuals'/households' urban-destined migration patterns.

Retrospective information such as the author elicits — by asking the respondents, for instance, to recall and report on pre-migration circumstances like job expectations held prior to arrival — may (notwithstanding difficulties of objectivity or accuracy of memory) ameliorate some of the problems raised by single-place migration micro data surveys, but a more fundamental methodological problem remains. Generally, urban-based surveys of city immigrants (including only destination-specific characteristics) or rural surveys based on village out-migration (incorporating only origin-specific features) each permit only imperfect inferences about migration propensities. Especially, in the case of micro data, if unobserved — or unspecified — personal characteristics interact with location-specific features that make for systematic differences in migration propensities or sectoral rewards to labour, sampling at either end may lead to misleading conclusions about origin (or destination) populations. Fortunately, methods involving logit specification and estimation now exist for the correction of the sample selection bias this entails, and are beginning to feature in some migration studies. Even better, using longitudinal data avoids the problem completely by observationally controlling for the phenomenon. In effect, panel data fully trace the individual's movement from the place of origin to the place of destination, taking account of features and circumstances not just both of origin and destination, but also of prospective destinations not selected, over which the chosen one was revealed as dominant. While admittedly a non-trivial task, given its demands of expense and logistics on a developing country, in a long view, the design and implementation of such a longitudinal survey would be ideally beneficial to the micro economic study of migration determinants in India.

The foregoing remarks notwithstanding, the basic premise of the present study is highly praiseworthy. In the concluding section of the book, the author apologises for an 'urban bias' to his study. He need not do so. In fact, it is precisely such a sectoral 'tilt' in the study of Indian migration that sets the present work apart from and elevates its marginal contribution above that of many previous treatments of the subject matter. Inherent in it is a serious recognition of the fact that migration is as much of a 'pull' as it is of a 'push' process and that one must consequently accord explicit consideration to the urban-end of the migrant stream. Given the choice, then, to document the migration phenomenon from the perspective of either the (urban) destination or the (rural) origin, it was natural for the author to have selected the former place as the point of reference for conducting his interviews. Strategically, this was where much of the information relevant to his substantive concern — namely, that of studying migrants in metropolitan labour markets — was to be found. It is noteworthy, moreover, that this course of action attempts to redress what this reviewer feels has been somewhat of an imbalance in the general context of Indian research: specialized study of the urban sector has suffered relative neglect until recently — several more micro level studies exist (e.g., of household consumption or savings or credit), which, owing to historical reasons of policy emphasis, have been able to draw upon the much better articulated Indian rural data sampling and collection systems.

Banerjee's chosen topic, and its sectoral emphasis, we have seen, are timely and important for potentially wide-ranging policy implications that hang upon investigations designed to probe the microfoundations of developing country cityward migration. Most prior studies of city economies in India[7] have rarely been directly concerned with the problem of rural-to-urban migration. In particular, the author's own criticism of earlier empirical studies may be cited with some justification: 'These exercises provide considerable insight into the structure and operation of the urban labour market, but they do not constitute conclusive tests of the predictions of the probabilistic migration model.' Those studies explicitly concerned with migration, on the other hand, have not particularly dealt with the urban ramifications thereof.

Of the countably few empirically rigorous investigations of the Harris–Todaro paradigm in the Indian urban context,[8] none (to the reviewer's knowledge) have attempted to work with a job search model until the present endeavour.[9] Some, however, have tried to characterize the processes of wage determination in Indian cities, and, like Banerjee, appealed to labour economic insights to illuminate any recognizable differences between the alleged urban subsectors. Specification of supply-side determinants of urban earnings generally predominates in these discussions — for instance, issues of measurement of workers' returns to personal human capital (education/age/experience) attributes or the migrants' subjective reservation wages — while the role of demand-side factors is relegated to the specification of a formal/informal dummy or to grouping data into corresponding ad hoc sectoral categories. In the reviewer's opinion, the major inadequacy of this approach is twofold: (*a*) even if the 'structural' dummy proves significant in distinguishing wages paid to otherwise observationally equivalent labour, specific differences subsumed within the segmented categories of urban employers are ignored rather than explained, and (*b*) in the absence of specific understanding regarding what these differences are, ad hoc or conventionally applied employer classification schemes may lead to misleading or biased estimates of the coefficient on the 'structural' variable.

From a testing point of view, the reason for inclusion of employment sector characteristics in a wage or earnings equation is that individual rates of pay differentials not fully explained by job-related personal characteristics and attributable to sector or firm affiliation often invite diagnoses of labour market imperfection. For, in a perfectly competitive market, regardless of labour demand-side differences in technology, scale, location, profitability or ownership, workers with standardized supply characteristics should equalize their wage rates through inter-sectoral mobility. If this does not happen, and pay differences persist, labour market segmentation is indicated. These may arise in general either as compensating wage differentials due to systematic variations in supply-side preferences among job classes (so there operates a supply-driven 'immobility'), or as a result of strong employer preferences between workers on bases other than their specified productivity characteristics.

In terms of the postulated formal–informal dichotomy, speculations about reasons why affiliation might significantly affect wages range from pressure on the formal sector's higher ability to pay more through intimidation or coercion on the part of unions, to the completely voluntary willingness on the part of firms therein to do so. If the latter is the case, the formal sector firm might be responding either to personal non-economic characteristics of workers, or to unseen productivity premia associated with them in its hiring and remuneration decisions.

To investigate, Banerjee estimates, in Chapter IV, a conventional human capital-type wage determination model, augmented by one ascriptive productivity-unrelated supply-side attribute, viz., caste and by as many as six demand-side or 'structural' explanatory variables: one, the usual sector-specifying (formal/informal) dummy, and a further set of dummies characterizing the worker's company or position. On the basis of the results of his estimations, Banerjee attributes the bulk of earning differences not explained by human capital variables to the non-access of workers of scheduled castes to higher paying formal-sector jobs — whether due to these workers' lack of contacts or such firms' discrimination in hiring (or nepotism towards upper castes).[10] Given the Indian social milieu, this hypothesis might well be plausible. However, several alternative hypotheses are equally plausible: a positive effect of high wages on productivity may be perceived by these firms for efficiency wage or turnover reduction-type reasons, or due to the prospect of creating a large labour inventory or queue for greater flexibility and precision of position-to-worker 'matching'. Such a productivity effect may be behind the significant premium found attached to salaried versus casual employment status.

The problem is that competing hypotheses such as those above can neither be directly tested nor convincingly eliminated due to the two broad sets of difficulties associated with the earnings-function approach that were cited earlier. Most data for fitting such functions are obtained from household-based surveys and typically tend to be heavily weighted toward the individuals' supply attributes, with only a perfunctory degree of detail articulation about characteristics of workers' places of employment. The wage equation is necessarily a reduced form engaging both sides of a labour market. Clearly, an inference about the existence of a fundamental structural difference in wage determination between the sectors in question can be made only when the list of explanatory variables has exhausted consideration of factors operating from the labour demand as well as supply sides.

One acknowledges that having to trace places of employment of migrants surveyed at home must impose additional burdens in the logistics of data collection. But a strategy of gathering data exclusively at the home (as migration studies do) or at the workplace (as do studies of informal sector production) will always necessitate some restrictions on questions that may be asked, and may entail unavoidable trade-offs in research design[11] or raise a problem of identification. Thus while admitting Banerjee's qualification that 'the choice of background and structural variables is largely governed by data availability and the objective of the study', it may be wise to interface data sets dedicated to each approach (i.e., earnings function and firm structure) for the purposes of more direct investigation and testing of certain aspects of the dualism hypothesis.

For example, migrant-reported evidence in Chapter III reveals an interesting variety in the method of worker recruitment — by jobbers in textile and construction industries operating in tight market conditions of labour shortage, by employee referrals, which provide screening among competing surplus applicants in slack labour conditions, the incidence at times of the at-gate hiring of casual labour and, in rare circumstances, recourse to formal channels such as government employment exchanges. Data enabling the systematic exploration of connections between processes of recruitment and different industrial categories (e.g., those subject to product demand fluctuations and those not), firm types and job characteristics would have complemented the analysis on strategies of employee or migrant search and shed considerably more light than a purely one-sided view.

The validity of the characterization of labour market segmentation along formal/informal lines rests critically, we have seen, on the tenability of the high formal sector 'institutional' wage concept. True explanations of the determination and sustenance of this wage need to transcend structural 'black-box' kind of approaches to spell out firm-specific behavioural and efficiency rationalizations that undoubtedly lie behind the 'institutional' label. Empirical investigation of the issue cannot be complete without explicit formulations of behavioural hypotheses about the desirability or acceptance on the employers' part of such a wage strategy, along with related issues regarding hiring practices, labour quality perceptions and measurements, and productivity specifications for jobs within various organizations. Such testable hypotheses include, for instance, propositions that high wages might perhaps result from regulation by government as a kind of minimum wage negotiated with private sector employers in exchange for other concessions such as output protection or cheap access to capital and other inputs, or may be voluntarily arrived at by wage-setting employers themselves to cut costs of recruitment by creating labour queues or inventories, or to retain human capital created through firm-specific training by promoting stability of their workforce to thus or otherwise raise profit. All this calls for greater data elaboration on the firm/industry/sectoral side of labour market transactions.

Moreover, in the light of the less than clear-cut nature of sectoral delineation, inferring structural differences by sector may be fraught with dangers of sensitivity of the estimated coefficients to firm classification. This makes it all the more imperative that characteristics at the firm level be well represented in any investigation of this sort.

For example, Banerjee assigns migrant-reported establishments to the formal or the informal sector for the purpose of their empirical identification utilizing a size criterion, classifying those with the number of employees less than 20 as being in the informal, while those with more than 20 employees as being in the formal sectors. While this cut-off demarcates government regulation under the Factories Act, such a categorization need not conform to conceptual stereotypes about the low capital requirements or relative labour intensity of small enterprises. The omission of information regarding use of power at migrants' places of employment is symptomatic of a lacuna in possibly relevant indicators of technology which are thought to distinguish the modern from the traditional sector. Likewise, organizational differences are identified in the data only in terms of private/public sector ownership, and, while there is information regarding migrant occupation upon arrival in Delhi, any detailed indication of his industry of employment at the time of survey is absent. The danger is that using employment size class as the sole criterion for distinguishing between the formal and informal sectors might admit 'small-scale' firms featuring a range of technological levels and capital intensities, assets and market shares. Thereby important information about the urban productive structure with a significant bearing upon the urban labour market and rural-to-urban migration is, quite possibly, masked.

An ideal information set for sorting between rival hypotheses would go beyond the standard sectoral characterizations that are available in the present data, and present quantitative data (output, profit, factor-mix, substitution elasticities, etc.) on the industry category and establishment type of the migrants' firms of employment, including data on the structure of production and the infrastructural and price environment facing various classes of urban employers at the level of the city region. The ways in which such information might lend itself to the construction of a more comprehensive picture of wage formation in Third World urban labour markets and carry valuable insights for what is the objective here, viz., study of the decision to migrate to cities, are numerous. For example, recognizing the presence of agglomeration economies[12] in certain kinds of production may account for the strength of the urban 'pull' exerted on migrants. The exploration of input–output linkages between urban subsectors might help explain firm motivations to maintain a wage differential. Informal sector job attribute studies may highlight any learning, information-gathering or contact-building experience offered by tenure there. Examining urban product-mixes and industry fluctuations may illuminate possible insurance considerations in decisions of risk-averse labour to commit itself to an urban subsector or, indeed, to a particular urban destination. Appropriate elaboration of data on urban productive structure can thus prove rich in potential insights that may find their way into empirically testable hypotheses about the microfoundations of rural-to-urban migration.

The ultimate challenge to the conception of a formal–informal sectoral dichotomy must contend with whether the urban economy is polarized along conventionally delineated lines, or features, instead, a continuum of types of economic organization and a spectrum of labour market interactions.[13] To discard the Harris–Todaro paradigm, it is incumbent (1) to put criticisms of the productive characterization on a more comprehensive empirical footing along the lines suggested above, and (2) to demonstrate an alternative theory (or theories) of migration and urban labour markets that exhibit a greater degree of realism and utility. Banerjee's work has earned an important place in the literature that is now examining these critical regions of inquiry. Only the outcome of further such investigations, perhaps in a wider variety of case-contexts, will decide the fate of the dual labour market formulations — either confirm their having brought valuable insights to the explanation of Third World urbanization with great economy of abstraction, or forcing them to yield ground to a fresh set of refinements or an entirely new typology of urban labour market interactions in the developing country context.

IV

As stated earlier, the normative implications of such an empirical study of the rural-to-urban migration phenomenon are far-reaching. While the present work does not definitively resolve all questions about the desirability — or otherwise — of cityward migration in the developing country context, it very substantially indicates certain directions that rationally based sets of policies towards migration and urbanization must take.

Most importantly, it vindicates urban growth through migration as being privately welfare augmenting and not merely the result of mass miscalculation. It amply demonstrates that rural migrants, by and large, know what they do when they make the move. The degree of *ex post* error in terms of the reality not being in accordance with expectations is nowhere near as acute as envisaged in the Harris–Todaro framework. Such compelling evidence of migrant rationality and unambiguous real and perceived material improvement must call into question prescriptions premised on a view of rural-to-urban migration as a social cost and a private mistake.[14] If migration imposes external costs in terms of putting pressure on the cities' infrastructure and social amenities, then this must properly be treated as an issue by itself, to be resolved innovatively either by more efficient service provision technologies or by imaginative financing options ensuring that urban services are paid for. The answer to reducing pressure on urban services does not lie in stifling urban expansion *per se*, much less artificially curbing migration.

Accounts of the earning activities of urban migrants attest to the fact that they are generative, not parasitic. Persistent rural-to-urban migration reflects higher returns to the migrants' labour in cities than in the rural areas. That higher wages are paid and responded to by mobile migrant labour bespeaks the fact that the urban activities they engage in are profitable and that increasing labour allocation to them commands value in terms of the social product. The denial of this revealed that productivity advantage of cities — whether due to agglomeration economies inherent in urban-based production, or even to the superior stocks of productive infrastructure that cities carry — may lead to output and efficiency losses most LDCs can ill-afford.[15]

That this value-creation is by no means limited to the formal sector is another inescapable conclusion this investigation reinforces. The informal sector, typically looked upon as a derivative or secondary sector, absorbing migrant spillover from the primary, formal sector, but not much more than a subsistence-wage pool of underemployed surplus labour emerges in a fresh light. Banerjee's findings support a re-evaluation of official attitudes towards the informal sector that is only now beginning to occur. This sector, until recently viewed as not contributing seriously either to output or to the provision of employment relief, has been routinely neglected and sometimes even actively discouraged as a nuisance by policies of several LDC governments. Through studies such as this, the informal sector is revealed to hold promise not only for labour absorption and employment generation, but also for value production and entrepreneurship development. More positive attitudes, if not policies, towards the informal sector, can meaningfully tap innate developmental impulses in the decentralized private sector — to the extent this sector is indeed a competitively self-supporting segment of the economy which, far from being parasitic or marginal, both generates productivity and pays for itself, its benign acceptance is consistent not only with recent liberalizing and privatization moves, but also with imperatives to conserve public resources for more essential interventions.

In this study, Banerjee does find evidence to support the Harris–Todaro proposition that segmentation of the urban labour market exists, with measurably differentiated wage structures between its subsectors. Whether the segmentation is due to the still-unexplained 'structural' characteristics or attributable to asymmetries in access to information reinforced by operation of kinship search networks or, indeed, to systematic nepotism in hiring is, however, a topic that awaits further investigation. Prescriptions for interventions in the labour market sphere are thus not entirely clear from the analysis, but the range of possible policy options becomes more evident. The stipulated sources of the segmentation hold the key to the design of appropriate legal or social actions. Accordingly, the resolution of competing hypotheses may recommend either human capital formation through formal or vocational education, or institutional intervention in the form of the enforcement of anti-discriminatory practices or equal opportunity/affirmative action labour laws as policy instruments that can be brought to bear upon the problem of narrowing the earnings gap between the two sectors. Alternatively, elimination of informational deficiencies or asymmetries in search and hiring may be called for to smooth out inefficiencies or inequities in the functioning of the urban labour market — for instance, spatial information policy may entail the setting up of employment exchanges in the rural as well as in the urban areas, and making them suitably responsive to the need for achievement of better employee–employer matchings.

Without doubt, the origin-end ramifications of rural-to-urban labour flows are of enormous importance in a predominantly agricultural country such as India. While, understandably, due to previously cited data constraints following from the researcher's choice of sectoral emphasis, the study cannot be altogether direct and unequivocal in its rural policy implications,[16] some light is shed on the rural-end consequences of cityward migration through the findings on rural–urban family linkages. There is some evidence that private remittance flows are partially used to aid agriculture. That close bonds are maintained, more often than not, between the rural and urban (migrant) components of Indian households, has generally positive economic and sociological implications for the rural areas. Several potentially meaningful relationships between the urban and rural sectors in markets other than the labour market may be facilitated as a result of migration — such as spatial consumption or production linkages, agricultural innovation and technology transfer, or, indeed, intersectoral flows of financial, human or social capital — and await further study. Nothing emerging from the present analysis gives reason to assume, *a priori*, that the net effects of migration to cities upon the rural economy are necessarily deleterious.

From the finding that it is not exclusively the poorest that show a high propensity to migrate, it would appear that raising rural incomes is not the panacea for stemming the tide of migration that it is often thought to be, and it is likely that distributional consequences of rural development efforts may have to be factored in to obtain realistic predictions of migrant streams. However, rural development as a place-oriented development strategy has self-evident benefits independent of its migration consequences. On the other hand, to the extent that the members of rural households, wherever they may be, are benefited as a result of access to urban opportunities, migration as a people-oriented welfare strategy is surely an economy-wide desirable phenomenon. Furthermore, in a long-term perspective, the Indian economy's structural transformation will demand increasing industrialization and urbanization. Migration to urban areas, and particularly the growth and development of small towns and medium-sized cities, will be the mechanisms whereby many of these changes will be effected. Thus it is important to look upon the migration process as a concomitant of the country's development effort, and one that contributes to spatial integration and the efficient functioning of its economy.

Banerjee's analysis is valuable in opening up discussion that facilitates a re-evaluation of policy conclusions in the areas of sectoral emphasis, urban-to-rural flows, urban labour markets and city growth. These are key issues, affecting growth and welfare, not only in the Indian context but for developing countries in general. One hopes that the book will serve both as an eye-opener for policy-makers and as a catalyst for further scholarship in this crucial area of economic development.

NOTES

Reproduced from *Indian Journal of Agricultural Economics*, Bombay, Vol 43, No 4, October–December 1988.

1 An example of a study of the social valuation of labour in the context of intersectoral migration is Lal (1973).
2 A recommendation explicit in Harris and Todaro (1970).
3 Yap (1977) cites results from early empirical work.
4 See Greenwood (1985) for a review covering both the developed country (DC) and less developed country (LDC) contexts.
5 All quotes in this paper pertain to the book under review.
6 The author is grateful to Professor M. L. Dantwala for drawing her attention to this point.
7 Joshi and Joshi (1976); Papola (1977, 1978); Papola and Subrahmanian (1975); Kashyap et al. (1980, 1981); Government of India (1981).
8 One such study is Mazumdar (1983).
9 The decision to conduct a rural search or an urban one (with or without accepting interim employment) may also be modelled in discrete terms through logistic regressions using rural-end data.
10 Likewise, it is possible to formulate a conditional logit model of differential participation in the formal versus informal sector, given suitable data, to explicitly test competing hypotheses of information-based denial of access, discrimination or differential occupational preferences on the supply side.
11 Analysis of a self-employed sample, of course, circumvents this problem by collapsing the firm and the worker into one observational unit, and is amenable to application of household production models of the type recently used in agriculture.
12 Shukla and Stark (1988) explores the connection between agglomeration economies and urban labour market dualism in a Harris–Todaro framework.
13 Kannappan (1985) reviews empirical studies of the informal sector to argue this point.
14 The literature on 'urban bias' in LDCs originates in Lipton (1977).
15 Shukla (1988) measures the productivity advantage of large Indian cities.
16 See Dhar (1980) for a rural-area oriented migration study and potential policy implications.

REFERENCES

Bhagwati, Jagdish and T.N. Srinivasan (1974), 'On Reanalysing the Harris–Todaro Model: Policy Rankings in the Case of Sector-specific Sticky Wages', *The American Economic Review*, LXIV, No. 3.

Da Vanzo, Julie (1978), 'Does Unemployment Affect Migration? — Evidence from Micro Data', *The Review of Economics and Statistics*, Vol. LX.

Dhar, Sanjay (1980), 'An Analysis of Internal Migration in India', Doctoral Dissertation, Yale University, New Haven, USA.

Fields, Gary S. (1975), 'Rural–Urban Migration, Urban Unemployment and Underemployment, and Job-search Activity in LDCs', *Journal of Development Economics*, Vol. 2.

Government of India (1981), 'Informal Sector in a Metropolis — Case Study of Delhi Informal Industrial Cluster: Anand Parbat', Town and Country Planning Organization, Ministry of Works and Housing, mimeo.

Greenwood, Michael J. (1971a), 'An Analysis of the Determinants of Internal Labour Mobility in India', *Annals of Regional Science*.

———(1971b), 'A Regression Analysis of Migration to Urban Areas of a Less-Developed Country: The Case of India', *Journal of Regional Science*.

———(1985), 'Human Migration: Theory, Models and Empirical Studies', *Journal of Regional Science,* Vol. 25, No. 4.

Harris, John R. and Michael P. Todaro (1970), 'Migration, Unemployment and Development: A Two-Sector Analysis', *The American Economic Review,* Vol. LX, No. 1.

Joshi, Vijay and Heather Joshi (1976), *Surplus Labour and the City: A Study of Bombay*, Oxford University Press, Delhi.

Kannappan, Subbiah, ed., (1977), *Studies of Urban Labour Market Behaviour in Developing Areas,* International Institute for Labour Studies, Geneva.

———(1985), 'Urban Employment and the Labour Market in Developing Nations', *Economic Development and Cultural Change,* Vol. 33, No. 4.

Kashyap, S.P., R.S. Tiwari and D.R. Veena (1980), *Facets of an Urban Economy (Economic Case Study of Ahmedabad),* Sardar Patel Institute of Economic and Social Research, Ahmedabad.

Lal, Deepak (1983), 'Disutility of Effort, Migration, and the Shadow Wage Rate', *Oxford Economic Papers,* Vol. 25 (New Series), No. 1.

Lipton, Michael (1977), *Why Poor Stay Poor: Urban Bias in World Development,* Harvard University Press, Cambridge, Massachusetts.

Lucas, Robert E.B. and Oded Stark (1985), 'Motivations to Remit', *Journal of Political Economy*, Vol. 93, No. 5.

Mazumdar, Dipak (1983), 'The Rural–Urban Wage Gap, Migration and the Working of the Urban Labour Market: An Interpretation Based on a Study of the Workers of Bombay City', *Indian Economic Review,* Vol. XVIII, No. 2.

Papola, T.S. (1977), 'Mobility and Wage Structure in an Urban Labour Market: A Study in Ahmedabad', in S. Kannappan, ed., *Studies of Urban Labour Market Behaviour in Developing Areas*, International Institute for Labour Studies, Geneva.

———(1978), *Informal Sector in an Urban Economy: A Study in Ahmedabad,* Giri Institute of Development Studies, Lucknow.

Papola, T.S. and K.K. Subrahmanian (1975), *Wage Structure and Labour Mobility in a Local Labour Market: A Study in Ahmedabad,* Sardar Patel Institute of Economic and Social Research, Ahmedabad.

Shukla, Vibhooti (1988), *Urban Development and Regional Policy in India: An Econometric Analysis,* Himalaya Publishing House, Bombay.

Shukla, Vibhooti and Oded Stark (1988), 'Why are Urban Formal Sector Wages in LDCs above the Market-Clearing Level', University of Texas at Dallas, Richardson, Texas, USA, mimeo.

Stark, Oded and Robert E.B. Lucas (1988), 'Migration, Remittances and the Family', *Economic Development and Cultural Changes,* Vol. 36, No. 3.

Todaro, Michael P. (1976), 'Urban Job Expansion, Induced Migration and Rising Unemployment — A Formulation and Simplified Empirical Test for LDCs', *Journal of Development Economics,* Vol. 3, No. 3.

Yap, Lorene Y. L. (1977), 'The Attraction of Cities: A Review of the Migration Literature', *Journal of Development Economics,* Vol. 4, No. 3.

III / Sectoral Versus Spatial Considerations

9 / The Pace of Indian Urbanization

VIBHOOTI SHUKLA
BRIAN J.L. BERRY

I. Introduction: The Tolley Model

In 1984, George S. Tolley proposed a simple supply-driven urban growth model for the two-sector economy of a country closed to foreign immigration or emigration (Tolley and Thomas 1987)[1] but open to trade in commodities. Contrary to the 'traditional' income-elasticity-driven view of economic development and urban growth that emphasizes domestic demand factors and makes prices endogenous, Tolley set out to enunciate a more 'general' explanation, one applicable in an international trade setting where countries could be considered to be price takers.

A crucial prediction of the conventional model[2] of urbanization has growth in urban productivity leading to less, and that in non-urban productivity to more, urbanization. As rural labour necessary to satisfy a given level of demand for agricultural goods falls, its release to the secondary goods sector becomes possible. Based on the idea that world economic development involves a rapid transfer of the more mobile urban technologies, Tolley's alternative model predicts greater urban productivity leading to more urbanization in response to the incentives of international specialization. Given that rising productivity in urban areas 'enhances cities' ability to compete in international markets and to compete with production in rural areas' (Tolley and Thomas, p. 21), Tolley claims that 'the idea that urbanization is primarily explained by massive changes in relative prices of urban goods is not appealing' (Tolley and Thomas, p. 22).

The growth rates of urban and rural output or income (Y_u, Y_r)[3] were postulated to be the sum of the growth rates attributable to non-labour (A_u,A_r) and labour (eN_u, eN_r) sources, where e is the labour elasticity of output and N_u, N_r are the growth rates of the urban and rural populations, respectively:

$$Y_u = A_u + eN_u \tag{1}$$

$$Y_r = A_r + eN_r \tag{2}$$

The growth rates of wages (W_u, W_r) were postulated to be a function of the growth rates of prices (P_u, P_r), and output/income (Y_u, Y_r) and population (N_u, N_r):

$$W_u = P_u + Y_u - N_u \tag{3}$$

$$W_r = P_r + Y_r - N_r \tag{4}$$

If real wage growth at the margin is equated between sectors, then:[4]

$$Y_u - N_u = Y_r - N_r \tag{5}$$

Letting N be the population growth rate of the country as a whole (equals natural increase due to the closure assumption), when F_u and F_r are the urban and rural fractions of the total population,

$$N = F_u N_u + F_r N_r \tag{6}$$

By substituting equations (1) and (2) into equation (5), we get

$$N_r = (A_r - A_u)/(1 - e) + N_u \tag{7}$$

Finally, substituting equation (7) into equation (6) and solving for the variable of interest, N_u, we obtain

$$N_u = N + F_r A_u /(1 - e) - F_r A_r/(1 - e) \tag{8}$$

The urban growth rate is decomposed into the rate of growth of the population due to natural increase (N), a contributory urban productivity factor $F_r A_u/(1 - e)$. Both of the latter factors are more potent when F_r is large (that is, when the country is least urbanized) and when the elasticity of output with respect to labour e is the greatest. Since N is that part of the urban growth rate attributable to natural increase, the productivity difference $F_r/(1 - e)[A_u - A_r]$ is the complementary portion of the urban growth rate due to rural-to-urban migration.

Various tests of this model have been undertaken. Pribadi and Berry (1986) showed reasonably good fits for Indonesia as a whole, but poor performance for that country's principal islands because the closure assumption was violated. The model was reformulated to yield estimates of the main inter-island migration streams. Kilbourne and Berry (1989) showed poor fits for the individual countries of West Africa, where markets are poor fits for the individual countries of West Africa, where markets are poorly developed and where national boundaries are weak, but a better fit for the region as a whole, where the closure assumption is more nearly satisfied. Yet even at this scale other non-market factors were believed to be important sources of urbanward migration. Among these sources are governmental policies, explored by Ran and Berry (1989) in the case of China. Deviations of actual from computed Chinese urbanization rates in the period 1949–86 were found to coincide in direction and magnitude with that country's principal policy objectives. Shifts in deviations were consistent with shifts in the overarching policy regime.

The purpose of this study is to extend these explorations of Tolley's formulation, using the Indian experience as a case. Tolley's own preliminary application of the model to a set of countries revealed variations from the general pattern for India, and he suggested that more detailed analysis was needed if we are to have a more refined identification of the factors affecting urbanization. In Section II we therefore attempt to explain the model's mixed performance in tracking the progress of urbanization in India over 1951–81, both in terms of failure to satisfy the model's assumptions and in terms of India's changing policy environment over that time-span. A modified version of the model, adjusted for inter-regional migration, is then simulated for individual Indian states in Section III for the 1971–81 period. As regional units within a national economy, the price-taking scenario of Tolley's model might be expected to apply more realistically to the states.

The model's assumptions then are tested in Section IV through a cross-sectional econometric examination of the relationship between urban growth rates and intertemporal translog productivity growth indices for the two sectors, again using the states as observations. Section V follows with a more causal exploration of reasons for the model's poor performance, focusing upon the possible effects of structural differences between the states. The paper concludes with a brief examination of the insights provided by the simulation, econometric and exploratory exercises for policies and modelling relating to urban growth in less-developed countries.

II. Tolley's Model Applied to India as a Whole

Tables 1 and 2 and Figure 1 provide background information on Indian urbanization in the twentieth century. Urban growth has been driven both by the rising tide of natural increase and the cyclical upswings and downswings of urbanward migration. In the interwar period, and especially during partition, internal migration streams were joined by substantial urbanward in-migration. By contrast, in the twenty years

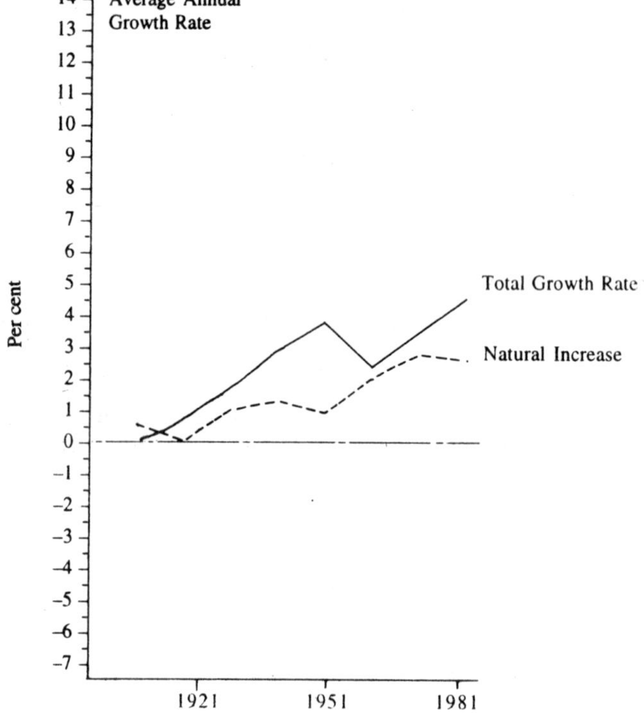

Figure 1a: Components of India's urban population growth rate, 1901–81. The average annual growth rate for each decade is plotted at the end-point year of the decade. The graph shows the total growth rate and the portion of that growth rate due to natural increase. The area between the lines is the portion due to migration.

1951–71, not all of the net rural emigration was destined for India's cities: India's net emigration was 2.35 million during that period. Since 1971, these aggregate foreign flows have reversed again, however; in the 1971–81 decade, 21.4 million rural-to-urban migrants were joined by an additional 1.57 million urbanward in-migrants, owing largely to the impact of refugee flows into India's eastern border states associated with the secession of Bangladesh from Pakistan.

The Tolley-model results are presented in Table 3 and Figure 2. Columns C1 and C2 present the model's estimates of average annual growth rates in urban and rural non-labour income sources. These are combined with observed demographic changes to produce the estimated urban growth rates in C4, according to equation (8). C5 reports the

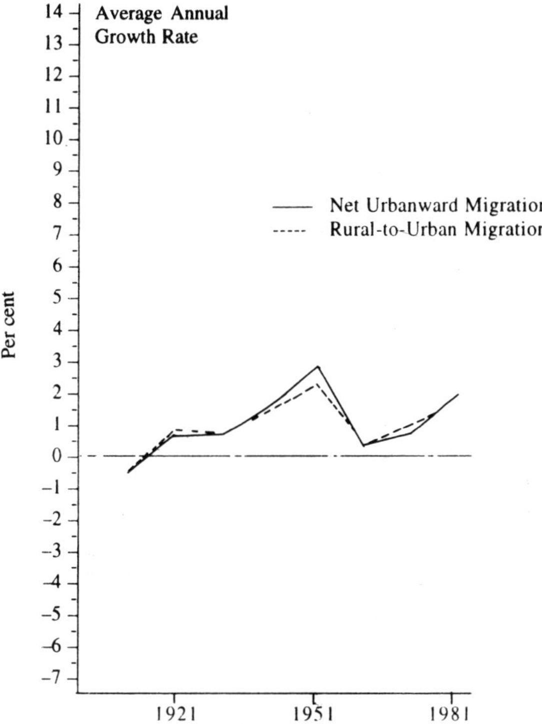

Figure 1b: Components of India's urban growth rate due to migration, 1901–81. The share of urban growth rate due to urbanward migration is compared with what the rate would have been if all rural emigrants had moved to the cities. Net immigration is revealed especially during partition, whereas there was net emigration during the 1970s.

discrepancy between actual and predicted rates. The model significantly underpredicts India's urbanization in the 1951–61 and 1961–71 decades, and overpredicts it in 1971–81, despite the fact that the urban growth rate was reduced in the first two decades by emigration and enhanced in the third decade by immigration. One thus cannot invoke lack of closure as the reason for the model's failure.

Column C6 tests for consistency of the observed data with the stipulation of the condition implicit in equation (5), viz., that average labour productivity changes by the same proportion in both sectors. It is seen that average labour productivity growth in urban activities fell below that in non-urban activities during 1951–71, but exceeded the latter in the 1971–81 decade.

Table 1: Key Urban Population and National Income Statistics: India, 1901–81

Year	A1	A2	A3	A4	A5	A6	A7	A8	A9
1911	25.58	10.4	–	–	26.200	1.64	–0.29	–1.39	–1.68
1921	27.69	11.3	–	–	26.700	0.25	–0.44	2.30	1.86
1931	32.98	12.2	–	–	27.700	3.17	0.06	2.06	2.12
1941	43.56	14.1	–	–	30.500	4.74	0.65	5.19	5.84
1951	61.63	17.6	9.136	52	17.469	4.38	2.81	10.89	13.69
1961	77.56	18.3	13.999	55	25.424	13.79	–0.10	2.23	2.14
1971	106.97	20.2	36.452	100	36.452	23.29	–2.25	8.36	6.11
1981	159.73	24.3	113.846	224	50.711	29.79	1.57	21.40	22.97

The variables are as follows:
A1: Urban population, as defined in the national census, in millions.
A2: Urban population as per cent of total population.
A3: Nominal national income, in billions of the national currency.
A4: Price index for national income.
A5: Real national income, in billions of the national currency.
A6: Intercensal change in urban population due to natural increase, in millions.
A7: Intercensal change in urban population due to foreign migration, in millions.
A8: Intercensal change in urban population due to rural migration, in millions.
A9: Intercensal change in urban population due to all migration, in millions.
Note: Definition of Urban areas includes all places having 5,000 or more inhabitants, a density of not less than 1,000 persons per square mile or 390 per square kilometre, pronounced urban characteristics and at least three-fourths of the adult male population employed in pursuits other than agriculture. All data after 1941 are for post-partition India.

Table 2: Population and National Income Growth Rates: India, 1901–81

Period	B1	B2	B3	B4	B5	B6	B7	B8
1901–11	0.56	–0.01	1.54	0.93	0.64	–0.11	–0.54	–0.66
1911–21	–0.07	0.83	0.19	0.26	0.10	–0.17	0.90	0.73
1921–31	1.08	1.91	0.37	–0.64	1.14	0.02	0.74	0.76
1931–41	1.41	3.21	1.01	–0.35	1.44	0.20	1.57	1.77
1941–51	1.32	4.15	–	–	1.01	0.64	2.50	3.14
1951–61	2.14	2.59	4.55	1.98	2.24	–0.02	0.36	0.35
1961–71	2.45	3.79	4.34	1.52	3.00	–0.29	1.08	0.79
1971–81	2.44	4.93	3.91	1.18	2.79	0.15	2.00	2.15

The variables are as follows:
B1: Average annual percentage change in total population.
B2: Average annual percentage change in urban population.
B3: Average annual percentage change in real national income.
B4: Average annual percentage change in real national income per capita.
B5: Average annual percentage change in urban population due to natural increase.
B6: Average annual percentage change in urban population due to foreign migration.
B7: Average annual percentage change in urban population due to rural migration.
B8: Average annual percentage change in urban population due to all migration.
Note: National income data are reported in million rupees up to 1941, and in crores (10 m) thereafter. Urban outputs include the outputs of manufacturing and services, except for 1944-59, when they also include construction and transport/communication.

Yet if this discrepancy is small relative to total income and population changes, the prediction error attributable to the non-equivalence of average productivity growth rates will be minimized. Column C7 reports an error-of-fit measure for the model, calculated as the ratio of the intersectoral difference in average labour productivity growth to the mean of

Table 3: Components of the Tolley Model for India, 1951–81

Period	C1	C2	C3	C4	C5	C6	C7
1951–61	–0.46	1.66	2.59	–3.63	–6.22	–2.28	–0.91
1961–71	1.68	1.88	3.79	1.94	–1.85	–0.68	–0.06
1971–81	3.31	–0.67	4.93	12.49	7.56	3.05	1.18

The variables are as follows:
C1: Average annual percentage change in urban non-labour income (A_u).
C2: Average annual percentage change in rural non-labour income. (A_a).
C3: Actual average annual percentage change in urban population.
C4: Predicted average annual percentage change in urban population (N_u).
C5: Difference between predicted and actual change in urban population.
C6: Consistency check for the Tolley model.
C7: Tolley-model error of fit.

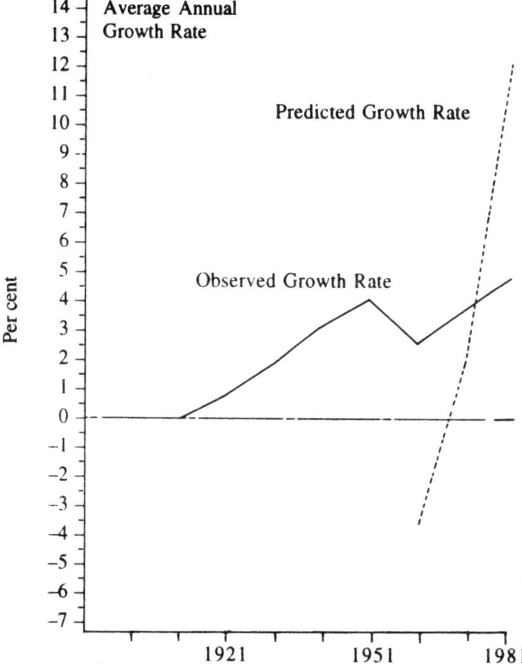

Figure 2: Predicted and actual urban growth rates compared. Data availability on sources of productivity growth limits the predictions to the period past Independence.

urban and rural population growth,[5] viz., $[A_u - A_r]/[(N_u + N_r)/2]$. The smaller its value in absolute terms, the lower is the proportion of the observed variation in employment and output that is explained by violations of the assumptions of the model or factors which it ignores. Rather substantial departures from zero of the measure suggest this may not have been the case for 1951–61 or 1971–81.

Other than a breakdown of the more obvious of the model's maintained hypotheses, what else may have been at work? One possible explanation is the important development policy shift that occurred between the period of the fifties and sixties and that of the seventies in India. The former were decades of strong government intervention and foreign-aid-driven investment in heavy industry, and an import substitution trade regime which may have favoured urbanization in ways not captured by the model. The seventies, following the successive disastrous droughts of the late sixties, featured, by contrast, a renewed emphasis on agriculture. Policies aimed at realizing and extending the gains of the Green Revolution fostered a reverse bias towards private and public rural employment creation.[6]

III. Tolley's Model Applied to the Indian States

Clearly, it is necessary to take a closer look at the Tolley model's assumptions and omissions. To do this, we now isolate the 1971–81 period in a cross-sectional analysis of the Indian states. The single time span holds the broad aspects of the national policy environment constant across states, while inclusion of their regional diversity should permit insightful comparisons of the model's performance in each instance.

The use of subnational units of regional analysis necessitates accounting for inter-regional labour flows. Pribadi and Berry (1986) modified the Tolley model in their study of urban growth in Indonesia to incorporate inter-island migration. Basically, this involves the recognition that population growth in any regional unit comprises natural increase, I, as well as inter-regional net population inflows, M, in both its urban as well as rural components, so that:

$$N = \{F_u(I_u)\} + F_a(I_r)\} + \{F_u(M_u) + F_a(M_r)\} \qquad (9)$$

where F_u and F_a are the region's urban and rural population shares. M_u is the rate of net in-migration to urban areas of the region and M_r that to its rural areas, so that intra-regional movements cancel out, leaving only inter-regional net inflows in the second term of equation (9). Substituting (9) into equation (8), we get

$$\dot{N}_u = [\{F_u(I_u) + F_a(I_r)\} + \{F_u(M_u) + F_a(M_r)\}] + [F_u A_u/(1-e) - F_a A_a/(1-e)] \quad (10)$$

where the first and second terms, respectively, summarize the contributions of demographic and productivity factors in regional urban growth. Although linguistic barriers in India prevent interstate migration from attaining quite the same quantitative importance as inter-island movements do in Indonesia,[7] we also make the correction implicit in the first term of equation (10) for the simulations in this section.

Our analysis in the present section differs from the application in Section II in two other ways. The simulations in that section used population in lieu of employment for the computation of the urban and rural productivity factors. This was necessitated by the non-comparability of the broader 1961 and more restrictive 1971 Census definitions of employment. The 1971 and 1981 definitions are compatible, however, and we are able to use the more appropriate employment variable in the sectoral productivity measures for the states.[8] For the computation of these measures, we make an explicit identification of rural activities with agriculture and urban activities with manufacturing. Thus, wherever appropriate, subscripts *u* and *r* are replaced by *m* and *a*, respectively; for example, F_r becomes F_a in (9) and (10). We do this for two reasons. First, it is impossible to allocate the not inconsiderable Indian service sector unambiguously to either urban or rural areas. Second, it is the agriculture/manufacturing sectoral division that has been assumed in most conventional two-sector discussions of urbanization and structural change. The degree of success or failure of the model's application would enable us to speculate counterfactually upon the consequences of our omission of the service sector as well as the Tolley model's disregard for the substantial levels of rural non-farm employment documented in India, and thus evaluate the strict thesis that urbanization is the outcome of relative productivity shifts in the two major 'export good' sectors of a developing economy.[9]

Sources for our state-level demographic and production data appear in the notes.[10] Net interstate in-migration flows were calculated from a matrix of gross flows between the fourteen major Indian states for which the complete set of data is available. Background information on variables relevant as ingredients to the Tolley model is presented in Columns A1 to A5 of Table 4. Columns A8 and A9 of the table contain

Table 4: Population and Productivity Growth Rates for Indian States, 1971–81

States	A1	A2	A3	A4	A5	A6	A7	A8	A9
Andhra Pradesh	2.11	2.12	0.17	–0.03	23.32	2.15	3.15	2.81	–0.07
Bihar	1.87	2.25	0.20	–0.04	12.47	–4.05	–4.44	–1.38	0.76
Gujarat	2.15	2.64	0.19	–0.07	31.10	–0.31	0.38	1.79	0.03
Haryana	1.90	2.74	0.29	–0.00	21.88	4.42	4.49	4.71	0.72
Karnataka	1.82	2.66	0.13	–0.05	28.89	7.94	11.24	6.77	–1.60
Kerala	1.96	1.75	–0.09	–0.01	18.74	2.98	1.94	3.01	0.89
Madhya Pradesh	2.22	2.32	0.21	–0.03	20.29	2.09	3.60	3.00	–0.43
Maharashtra	1.87	2.44	0.27	–0.07	35.03	3.25	0.55	3.49	2.92
Orissa	2.00	1.85	0.29	–0.03	11.79	0.79	0.05	2.01	1.26
Punjab	1.90	2.10	0.20	–0.01	27.68	6.60	4.17	5.90	2.53
Rajasthan	2.26	3.10	0.11	–0.03	21.04	–6.41	–3.47	–1.30	–1.88
Tamil Nadu	1.70	1.61	0.09	–0.05	32.95	1.49	5.54	2.41	–2.42
Uttar Pradesh	2.03	2.38	0.09	–0.04	17.95	1.63	0.79	2.53	1.15
West Bengal	1.42	2.37	0.25	0.03	26.46	–2.61	–4.40	–0.38	2.06

The variables are as follows:
A1: I_u A2: I A3: M_u A4: M_r A5: $F_u = 1 - F_a$ A6: $Y_m - N_m$
A7: Consistency check for the Tolley model
A8: A_m A9: A_a

Table 5: Components of Tolley Model of Urban Growth for Indian States, 1971–81

States	B1	B2	B3	B4	B5	B6	B7	B8	B9
Andhra Pradesh	0.0221	0.0717	0.0019	0.0736	0.0957	0.8449	0.0500	0.0722	0.9576
Bihar	0.0214	–0.0403	–0.0220	–0.0623	–0.0409	–0.7089	–0.0261	–0.0047	–0.4943
Gujarat	0.0252	0.0412	–0.0006	0.0405	0.0658	0.4099	0.0370	0.0622	0.6234
Haryana	0.0285	0.1226	–0.0188	0.1038	0.1323	0.8288	0.0762	0.1047	1.0137
Karnataka	0.0244	0.1604	0.0380	0.1984	0.2228	1.9225	0.1263	0.1507	2.0399
Kerala	0.0166	0.0815	–0.0242	0.0573	0.0739	14.6064	0.0403	0.0569	17.1150
Madhya Pradesh	0.0238	0.0797	0.0115	0.0911	0.1149	0.8485	0.0640	0.0878	0.9935
Maharahstra	0.0248	0.0757	–0.0632	0.0125	0.0373	0.1811	0.0107	0.0355	0.2586
Orissa	0.0191	0.0591	–0.0370	0.0222	0.0413	0.2128	0.0231	0.0423	0.3700
Punjab	0.0226	0.1423	–0.0611	0.0812	0.1038	1.0425	0.0602	0.0828	1.2883
Rajasthan	0.0293	–0.0341	0.0494	0.0153	0.0445	0.1199	0.0274	0.0567	0.3594
Tamil Nadu	0.0163	0.0539	0.0540	0.1079	0.1243	1.3234	0.0702	0.0865	1.4340
Uttar Pradesh	0.0225	0.0691	–0.0314	0.0377	0.0602	0.4514	0.0336	0.0561	0.6713
West Bengal	0.0252	–0.0093	–0.0504	–0.0597	–0.0344	–0.7532	–0.0273	–0.0021	–0.5747

The variables are as follows:
B1: N B2: $[F_a(A_m)]/[1 - 0.7]$ B3: $[F_a(A_a)]/[1 - 0.7]$
B4: $[F_a(A_m - A_a)]/[1 - 0.7]$ B5: Pred. N_u $(e = 0.7)$
B6: Tolley-model error of fit (e = 0.7)
B7: $[F_a(A_m - A_a)]/[1 - 0.5]$ B8: Pred. N_u $(e = 0.5)$
B9: Tolley-model error of fit $(e = 0.5)$

rates of non-labour productivity increase in manufacturing and agriculture, respectively, as estimated under the Tolley model's stipulation that rates of labour productivity growth are equalized between sectors.[11] Column A6 presents actual rates of growth of the average productivity of labour in manufacturing, and Column A7 subtracts from these the analogous rates for agriculture. Substantial departures from consistency with assumption (5) are in evidence and will be commented upon shortly.

Table 5, reports the magnitudes of the components of equation (10) under two alternative values of the labour elasticity, *e*. Columns B1 through B6 pertain to simulations with $e = 0.7$ which was the assumed value in the all-India application of Section II. B1 summarizes the demographic component and B4 the productivity component of urban growth for the various states; these two are summed to obtain the predicted average annual rates in Column B5. The relative importance of the productivity factor ranges from a low of 34 per cent for Rajasthan to a high of 89 per cent of the model's predicted average annual rate of urban growth for the state of Karnataka. Column B6 reports the error-of-fit

Table 6: Deviations of Tolley-Model Predictions from Actual Urban Growth Rates, Indian States, 1971–81

States	C1	C2	C3	C4	C5
		$e = 0.7$		$e = 0.5$	
Andhra Pradesh	4.90	9.57	4.67	7.22	2.32
Bihar (BH)	5.52	–4.09	-9.61	–0.47	-5.99
Gujarat (GJ)	4.18	6.58	2.40	6.22	2.04
Haryana (HY)	6.00	13.23	7.23	10.47	4.47
Karnataka (KT)	5.11	22.28	17.17	15.07	9.96
Kerala (KL)	3.80	7.39	3.59	5.69	1.89
Madhya Pradesh (MP)	5.65	11.49	5.84	8.78	3.13
Maharashtra	4.03	3.73	–0.30	3.55	–0.48
Orissa (OR)	6.91	4.13	–2.78	4.23	–2.68
Punjab (PJ)	4.49	10.38	5.89	8.28	3.79
Rajasthan (RJ)	5.92	4.45	–1.47	5.67	–0.25
Tamil Nadu (TN)	2.82	12.43	9.61	8.65	5.83
Uttar Pradesh(UP)	6.11	6.02	–0.09	5.61	–0.50
West Bengal (WB)	3.20	–3.44	–6.64	–0.21	–3.41
Value of Loss Function			7.05		4.19

The variables are as follows:
C1: Act. N_u C2: Pred. N_u ($e = 0.7$) C3. [Pred. N_u – Act. N_u] ($e = 0.7$)
C4: Pred. N_u($e = 0.5$) C5: [Pred. N_u – Act. N_u] ($e = 0.5$)
Loss Function $[\Sigma \text{ Pred. } N_u - \text{Act. } N_u)^2/14]^{1/2}$

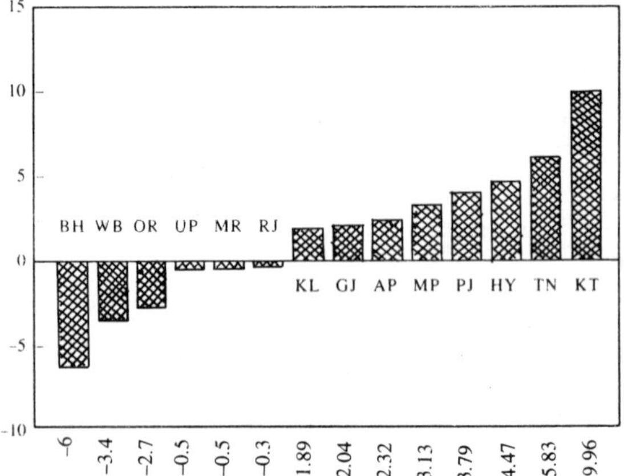

Figure 3: Tolley-Model Prediction Deviations. X-axis: predicted minus actual average annual urban growth rate, 1971–81

statistic, with varying degrees of departures from zero for the various states. Columns B7 through B9 parallel Columns B4 through B6 for the case where $e = 0.5$.

Finally, Table 6 compares predicted with actual urban growth rates for the states. Columns C2 and C4 express predicted values obtained from Table 5 in terms of per cent per annum over the inter-census period for simulations with $e = 0.7$ and $e = 0.5$, respectively. Columns C3 and C5 report discrepancies between the predicted and actual growth rates in each case. The C5 deviations are arrayed along the bar graph in Figure 3.

As in the national exercise, urban growth is overestimated for the bulk of the states between 1971 and 1981. As the loss function[12] values indicate, overestimation is reduced when the assumed labour elasticity of output goes from 0.7 to 0.5, where the translation of productivity differentials into sectoral employment effects is dampened. The magnitude of overprediction is highest for the states of Karnataka, Tamil Nadu, and Haryana, and somewhat lower for Punjab, Madhya Pradesh, Andhra Pradesh, and Gujarat. Reference to Tables 4 and 5 reveals that this overshooting is foreshadowed in failures of the consistency condition and radical departures from zero of the error of fit. All appear to be states (Punjab included) where non-labour manufacturing productivity growth is in considerable excess of that in agriculture. Urban growth in Kerala, where the error of fit is spectacular, would no doubt exhibit a much higher degree of overprediction, were it not for its negative net urban in-migration rate, an outcome of the large-scale exodus of its workers to the Gulf countries during the years of the oil price boom.

At the other end of the spectrum are the handful of states where urban growth has been underpredicted. The principal cases, Bihar, West Bengal, and Orissa, are precisely those states that witnessed foreign influxes as a result of the Bangladesh war. The refugee count is very likely understated by documented migration flows, although it is hinted at in the positive rural in-migration rate recorded for West Bengal; Assam, the state that arguably hosted the largest permanent influx, is omitted from the analysis due to the inability of census-takers to conduct a 1981 headcount that would have been controversial precisely due to it.

For three states only, Maharashtra, Rajasthan, and Uttar Pradesh, do predictions conform closely to reality. The thrust of the results of the state-level simulations — widespread overprediction — is consistent with those obtained in the national-level exercise.

IV. An Econometric Test of the Tolley Model

With accumulating information on the Tolley model's performance, we now attempt to test more rigorously its central premise that intersectoral non-labour productivity differentials motivate urban growth. This section presents a cross-sectional econometric exercise for the period 1971–81 using the Indian state as observations. While such an investigation is more feasible than a time series formulation, the number of observations for which both demographic and production data are available is restricted. We therefore fit a regression model omitting the demographic influences to conserve degrees of freedom. Our aim is to test the hypothesis that the principal Tolley-model productivity constructs display the expected sign and significance.

Estimation proceeds in a different way from the computations, resulting in Columns A8 and A9 in Table 4. For the measurement of the productivity influence, we employ intertemporal translog indices of labour, non-labour, and total factor productivity change for the two sectors, manufacturing and agriculture.[13] Assuming an underlying production framework of the translog form, the total factor productivity (TFP) change over 1971–81 is given, in manufacturing, by

$$MPROD = [\ln V_m - \ln V'_m] - [\{Sl_m + Sl_m)/2\}\ \{\ln L_m - \ln L'_m\}] \\ -[\{Sk_m + S'k_m)/2\}\ \{\ln K_m - \ln K'_m\}] \qquad (11)$$

and in agriculture, by

$$APROD = [\ln V_a - \ln V'_a] - [\{(Sl_a + S'l_a)/2\}\ \{\ln L_a - \ln L'_a\}] - [\{(Sk_a + S'k_a)/2\}\{\ln K_a - \ln K'_a\}] \quad (12)$$

where V represents value added in each sector, L and K the quantities of labour and capital employed, and Sl and Sk their respective factor shares. The primed (′) symbols refer to 1971 values of these variables. Intertemporal non-labour productivity changes (NLTP) are obtained, *a fortiori*, by deleting the third terms on the right-hand sides of (11) and (12); labour productivity changes (LTP) by deleting the second.

The average annual urban growth rate for 1971–81 is then regressed against both the manufacturing and agricultural productivity change measures to permit each of the two sectoral influences to contribute separately to observed values of the dependent variable. The exercise is repeated for each of the intertemporal indexes, NLTP, LTP, and TFP, Results appear in Table 7.[14]

As may be expected, standard errors (in parentheses) are all quite high relative to the magnitudes of parameter estimates, due to the small sample. Nevertheless, some tentative observations may be made. The contributions of sectoral productivity to urban growth are lower for the non-labour productivity change index (NLTP) than for either the labour or total factor productivity indexes (LTP, TFP). Regressions using the latter two also exhibit superior explanatory power. Agricultural productivity enters in all cases with a positive sign, suggesting that a productive agriculture may not necessarily discourage urban growth. The interactions between agriculture and the urban sector are many, and go

Table 7: Productivity Determinants of Average Annual Urban Growth Rate, 1971–81

(n = 14)	NLTP	LTP	TFP
INTERCEPT	1.82	3.62	3.79
	(2.25)	(0.81)	(0.73)
MPROD	1.11	2.52	2.42
	(1.29)	(1.63)	(1.69)
APROD	1.23	1.31	1.50
	(1.33)	(1.48)	(1.55)
R^2	0.1679	0.2195	0.2083

Notes: Figures in parentheses are standard errors of estimates.
NLTP = Intertemporal non-labour productivity index, 1971-1981.
LTP = Intertemporal labour productivity index, 1971-1981.
TFP = Intertemporal total factor productivity index, 1971-1981.

beyond intersectoral labour flows. In a predominantly rural country such as India, the consumption effects and backward input linkages of agriculture with urban areas, which the model omits, are bound to be sizeable.

It might be worthwhile to observe the effects of disaggregating total urban growth in the states to rates specific to its constituent city size classes. Table 8 reports the results of regressing disaggregated urban growth indexes[15] on the states' indexes of intertemporal non-labour productivity change. Manufacturing productivity attains significance at the 10 per cent level for large cities, while non-labour productivity in agriculture, though not significant, registers a negative sign. This suggests that the largest cities do indeed perform specialized export functions as Tolley's model implies. On the other hand, these influences are reversed for small cities and medium-sized towns, which are likely to be more hinterland-oriented with significant rural market functions.

While these results do not constitute a conclusive indictment of the applicability of the Tolley model to the Indian states, the econometric support for his model is quite weak. Yet if state-specific non-uniformities in rates of sectoral productivity advance in manufacturing and agriculture cannot satisfactorily explain variations in urban growth rates in India, what can? We take up this question in the following section, looking for possible roles of factors outside the scope of the Tolley model. To accomplish this, we abandon the econometric approach in favour of a more causal one.

Table 8: Sector-Sepcific Intertemporal Non-Labour Productivity Growth Indexes and Average Annual Urban Growth Rates by Size Class, 1971–81

(n = 14)	LC	SC	LT	MT	ST
INTERCEPT	–20.46	69.24	25.01	13.67	1.32
	(21.45)	(25.91)	(26.81)	(12.81)	(9.19)
MPROD	23.82	–40.94	–2.08	–9.04	1.07
	(12.13)	(14.85)	(15.37)	(7.34)	(5.25)
APROD	–2.91	8.60	–9.02	10.60	0.44
	(12.28)	(15.32)	(15.85)	(7.57)	(5.43)
R^2	0.3925	0.4096	0.0363	0.2003	0.0055

Notes: Figures in parentheses are standard errors of estimates.
LC = Large cities (population 500,000 and above)
SC = Small cities (population 100,000 – 499,999)
LT = Large towns (population 50,000 – 99,999)
MT = Medium towns (population 20,000–49,999)
ST = Small towns (population 20,000 and under)

V. Toward Explanations of Tolley-Model Prediction Deviations

Our approach is to study correlates of the deviations of actual growth rates from those predicted by the model, inasmuch as these deviations represent variations in the model's performance across the Indian states. Instead of doing this analytically, we array the deviations of Figure 3 in order of the ranking of a series of pertinent variables. These variables are chosen to reflect a set of candidate explanations for the deviations. The natural place to look for possible sources of failure is in the model's simplifications and omissions. We consider three broad categories of such sources: (1) structural economic factors not considered in the model; (2) sectoral complexity not accounted for by it, and (3) public policy interventions as they impinge differently on the states.

(1) The wage-equalizing labour-force transfer mechanism of the model might not be realistic for intersectoral migration in India. Several structural reasons may exist for non-uniformities in mobility propensities among the states. General economic backwardness, institutional dualism, or rigidities in asset and labour markets can render a rural population inoptimally mobile from a strict productivity viewpoint, resulting in either excessive or deficient flows.

We first examine the states' developmental levels as reflected in their per capita incomes for any systematic association with the pattern of Tolley-model deviations by arraying the latter, sorted ordinally by the former, along the X-axis of the bar graph in Figure 4. Lower values of an index of per capita state income at 1975–76 prices (all-India = 100) at the left appear to be associated predominantly with states where 'overurbanization' in the Tolley sense seems to have occurred, while the more highly developed states, towards the right, are those where predicted urban growth rates exceeded the actuals. West Bengal is an exception, an industry-significant state with a relatively impoverished rural population but a large primary city, Calcutta. Punjab and Haryana are agriculturally rich states with high overall incomes. The use of an alternative development indicator in Figure 5, per cent population below the poverty line (1977–78),[16] confirms that it is the more economically advanced states that have registered less than the predicted rates of urban growth. Mobility is 'excessive' in *poor* states. Thus, lack of development cannot be held responsible for barriers to movement from rural to urban areas.

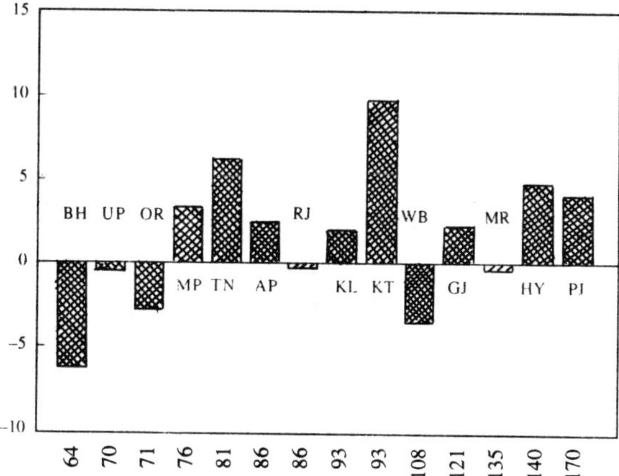

Figure 4: Tolley-Model Prediction Deviations. X-axis: index of per capita state income at current prices, 1975–76 (all India = 100)

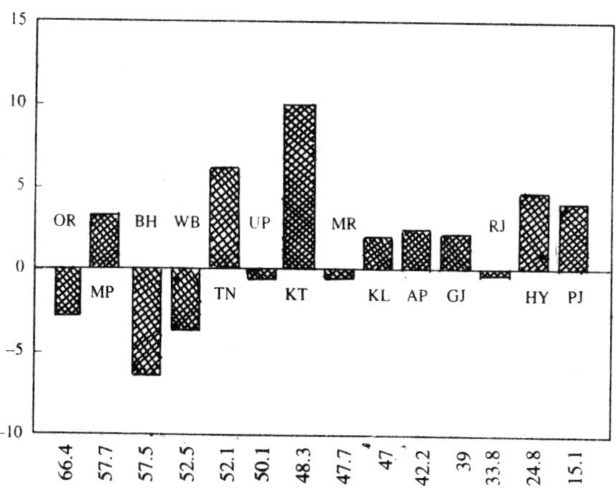

Figure 5: Tolley-Model Prediction Deviations. X-axis: per cent population below poverty line, 1977–78

In Figures 6 and 7, we focus upon rural-end circumstances that might explain 'push' migration above that warranted by productivity differentials. In India, due to the predominance of the rural population, states that are poor, by and large, are those that are agriculturally poor. In Figure 6, an index of rural land pressure, agricultural employment per hectare, is seen to be positively associated with abnormally high urban growth

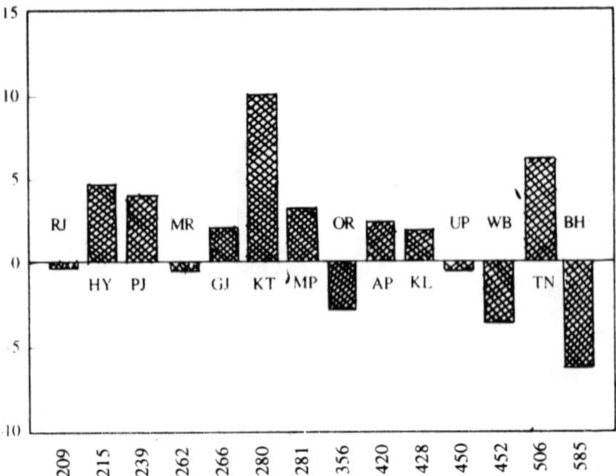

Figure 6: Tolley-Model Prediction Deviations. X-axis: agricultural employment per hectare of cultivable land

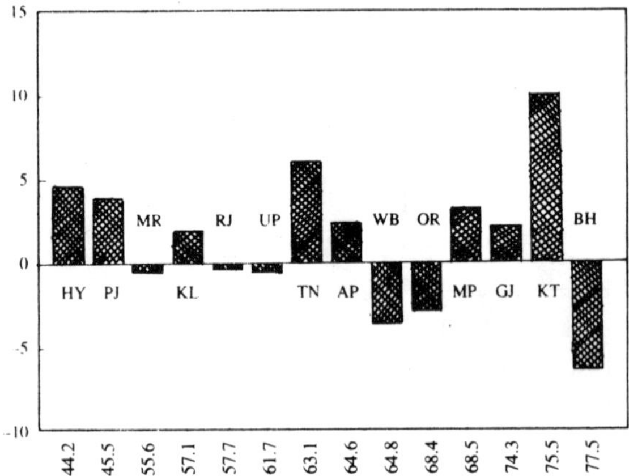

Figure 7: Tolley-Model Prediction Deviations. X-axis: casual workers as percentage of male wage labourers in agriculture, 1977–78

rates, while Figure 7 portrays a somewhat weaker but similar link with the share of casual labourers in agricultural wage workers.

(2) While it appears that rural poverty and landlessness contribute to unproductive urbanward migration, agriculture is not the sole employer in rural areas. Indeed, manufacturing (and the large-scale factory sector in particular) and agriculture do not exhaust the sum of employment opportunities available either in urban or rural areas. This sectoral dichotomy

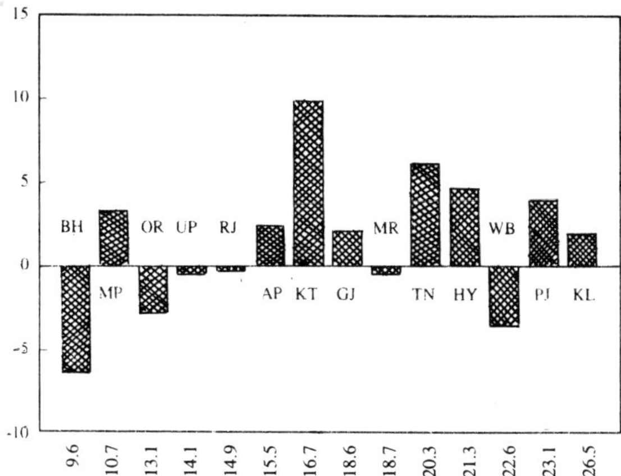

Figure 8: Tolley-Model Prediction Deviations. X-axis: workers in service industries (trade and commerce, transport, etc., and other services) as percentage of total workforce, 1971

and its spatial overlay were adopted in Section III to focus the argument upon the conventionally agreed-upon components of structural economic change. Not only is this particular sectoral assignment inexact, but the idea of such a dichotomy is itself limited by the presence of the urban informal sector, the service sector, and significant rural non-agricultural activity.

Figure 8 sets the share of the service sector in total state employment (by 1971 main activity) against the deviations. One might speculate that a high proportion of employment in the comparatively low productivity-growth service sector may well go hand in hand with a perceived overurbanization from a two-sector viewpoint, if the 'overurbanized' states' service sector shares were relatively high. The pattern observed is, in fact at variance with this conjecture. It is the 'underurbanized' states (again, with the exception of West Bengal) that register the highest shares of service employment. Figure 9, which repeats this exercise using the share of services in state income for 1970–71, replicates this pattern, more or less, suggesting that the omission of the service sector cannot be blamed for 'excessive' urban growth. Rather, the exercise confirms what regional economic theory tells us: that the service sector is a non-basic, derivative sector flourishing where basic activities prosper. A related possibility is that the exclusion of the more traditional forms of manufacturing activity from the model may lead to systematic underprediction by the two-sector framework where such activities are overrepresented. We proxy for the presence of informal sector activities

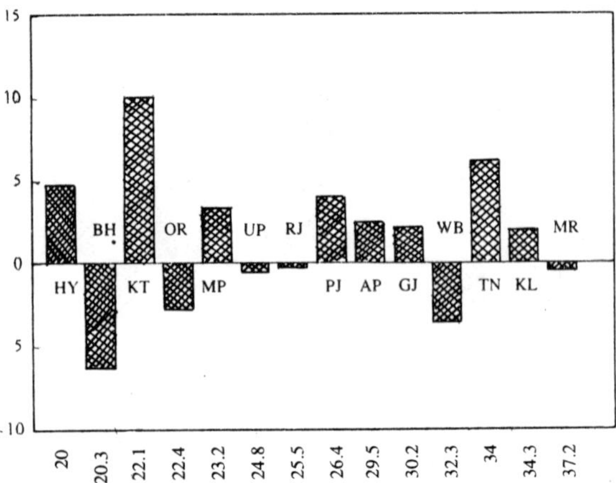

Figure 9: Tolley-Model Prediction Deviations. X-axis: percentage share of services in total state income, 1970–71

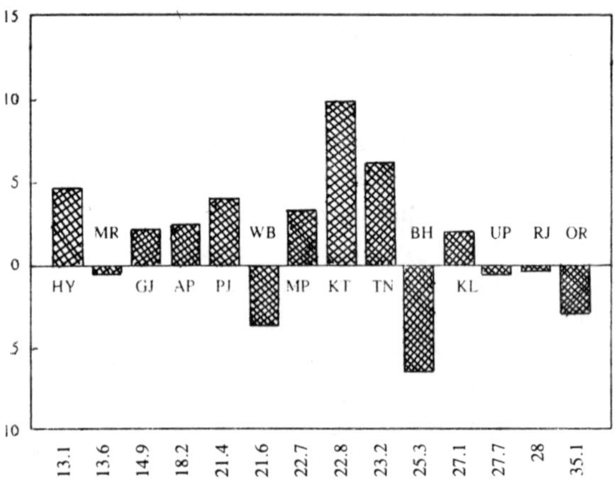

Figure 10: Tolley-Model Prediction Deviations. X-axis: per cent share of 1980 employment of manufacturing and repair industries in establishments with one to five workers

through the use of the percentage share of the 1–5 employment size class in state manufacturing employment. Figure 10 plots the Tolley-model deviations against this variable and indicates that states with higher than predicted rates of urban growth do exhibit larger shares of small firms in manufacturing employment, pointing to a contributory role for the omitted urban informal sector.

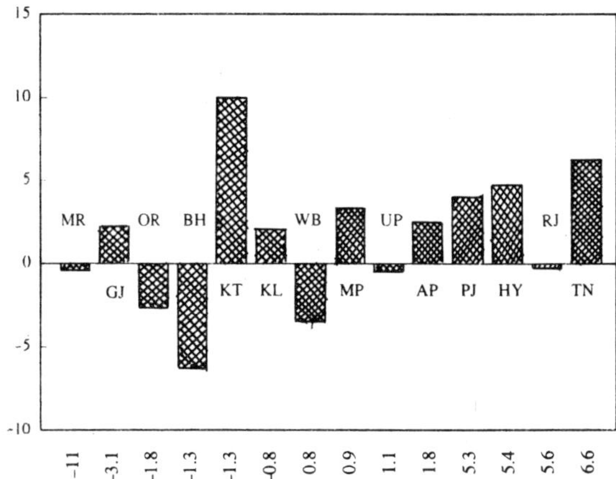

Figure 11: Tolley-Model Prediction Deviations. X-axis: change in percentage of rural male workers engaged in non-farm activities, 1972–78

Of course, not all of the employment of Figure 10 can be assumed to occur in urban areas. Figure 11 arrays the percentage growth in *rural* non-farm employment (not all of which, admittedly, occurs in manufacturing) to show a distinct coincidence of 'overurbanization' in the Tolley sense with sharp declines in rural non-agricultural employmnent. The inference seems to be that states with high poverty incidence and land pressure are experiencing urbanward migration accompanied by the release of labour from rural non-agricultural occupations. By contrast, the share of the latter is rising in some of the very states that are underurbanized as per the Tolley-model criteria. This suggests a role for the rural non-agricultural sector as a possible rural out-migration deterrent.

(3) The above considerations lead one to ask: what is the part played by government policy in all of this? A reasonable course for policy might be to encourage rural non-farm activities in the 'overurbanized' states, while letting the natural forces of urbanization respond to warranted intersectoral productivity growth differentials in those that are not. We might fruitfully look for a government intervention explanation in the latter instances, where urban growth is obviously being checked by forces beyond the model's scope.

Figure 12 attempts to track gross variations in states' development efforts through their 1975–76 per capita state expenditure on developmental activities. When this variable is arrayed against the Tolly-model deviations, it becomes clear that the states deficient in such spending are

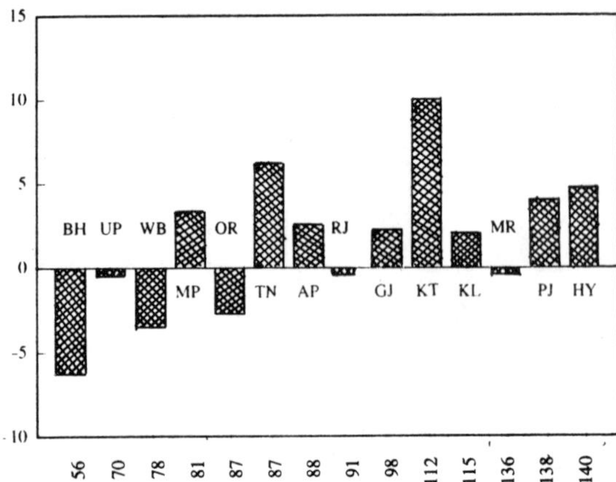

Figure 12: Tolley-Model Prediction Deviations. X-axis: per capita development expenditure (revenue + capital accounts) in rupees, 1975–76

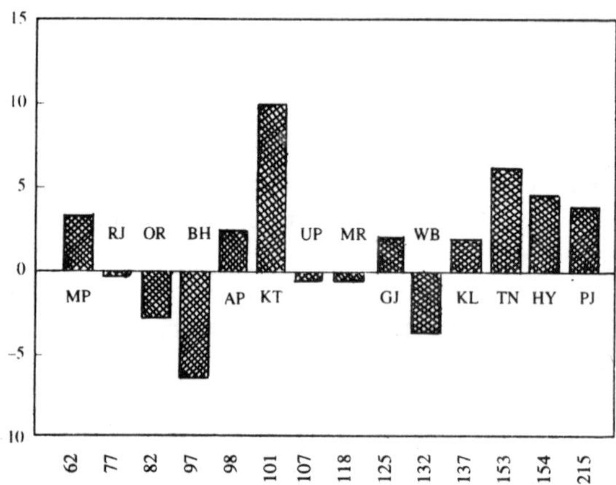

Figure 13: Tolley-Model Prediction Deviations. X-axis: CMIE index of relative development of state infrastructure, 1981 (all India = 100)

the ones experiencing the most 'excessive' rates of growth. To ensure that this observation is not a fluke resulting from the use of a budgetary flow over a single year, we repeat the exercise using a comprehensive index of relative state-wide physical infrastructure development[17] in Figure 13. The pattern is similar, except for the usual anomaly of West Bengal.

To result in checks to urban growth, the nature of this development spending and infrastructural effort must be such as to impact rural

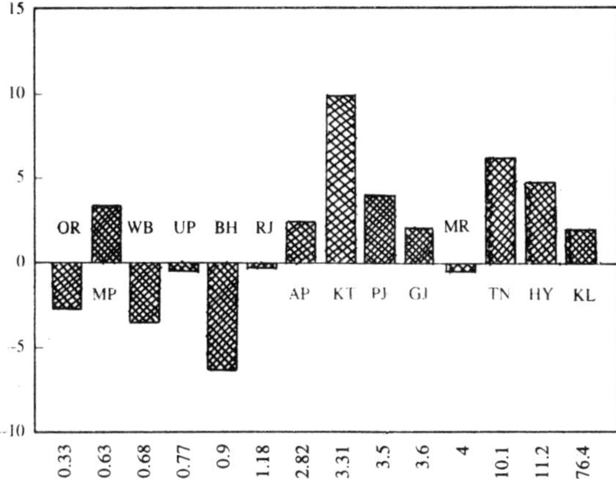

Figure 14: Tolley-Model Prediction Deviations. X-axis: percentage of villages served by six basic amenities, 1971

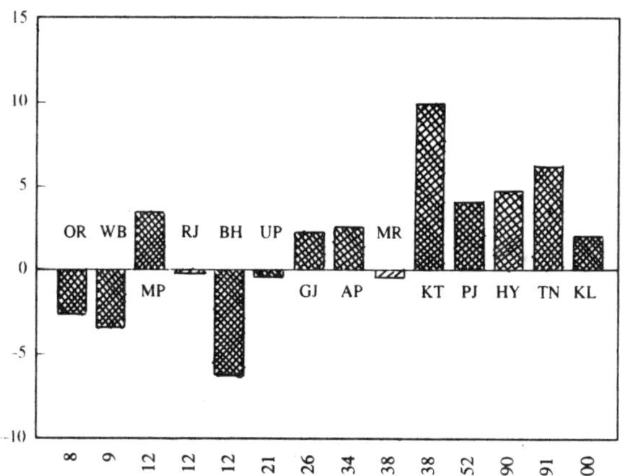

Figure 15: Tolley-Model Prediction Deviations. X-axis: percentage of villages electrified, 1971

areas specifically. We find in Figures 14 and 15 that more narrowly defined measures of rural infrastructure and amenities for the different states confirm this to be the case. Figure 14 plots the percentage of villages served by a group of six amenities[18] against the deviations. It shows that high levels of rural service provision may have discouraged out-migration through rural welfare improvement. Figure 15 focuses on village electrification to verify the same role for 'productive' infrastructure investment. We comment upon the policy implications of these findings below.

VI. Conclusions and Policy Implications

Two different and not altogether inconsistent perspectives may be employed to extract conclusions and policy implications from the foregoing. One entails a positive evaluation of the empirical validity of the model, relating its departures from reality to a need for further modelling refinements. The second involves the application of a normative standard to actual deviations from what can be viewed as a model-specified 'optimality' criterion for urban growth. This requires that we assume the model reflects efficiency-inducing specialization and spatial labour allocation commensurate with differences in rates of intersectoral non-labour productivity advance.

In evaluating the realism of the Tolley model and its ability to account for the important influences at work, it is instructive to compare the states' actual urban growth rates against the predictions of alternative explanations that Tolley explicitly rejected in favour of his view of urbanization. According to the competing demand-driven hypothesis, at low incomes a relatively high income elasticity of demand for food might retard urbanization, as initial increments to incomes are allocated largely to expenditure on agricultural commodities. While it is possible that India's consumption patterns might fit these circumstances, by the same reasoning, comparatively prosperous states with a presumably greater elasticity of demand for urban commodities should have, other things being equal, a higher rate of urbanization. Yet Table 6 reveals that states such as Bihar, Orissa, and UP, at the low end of Figure 4's development scale, registered greater growth than Gujarat and Maharashtra, at the higher end. Again, a purely demand-side view would have land scarcity decrease output per worker in agriculture to keep more workers on the farm to produce a given agricultural output, but once more, as evidenced by the cases of Orissa and Bihar in Figure 6, one sees that urbanward mobility is greater, not less, in the face of severe population pressures on land. Thus, simple demand-side explanations alone are unlikely to be able to accurately account for Indian urban growth any more than Tolley's can.

The more traditional supply-side explanations have gains from agricultural research and innovation leading to rapid urbanization, especially if they involve the substitution of capital for labour. If, instead, as is arguably the case with the Green Revolution, the innovations are land-augmenting rather than labour-saving, this need not happen, as evidenced by the states of Punjab and Haryana. (In an unreported exercise we found that states with high incidence of fertilizer consumption — an index of new technology adoption — as well as tractor use were also underurbanized by Tolley-model standards.) Urbanization will be retarded, however, if the substitution of capital for labour is higher in urban than in non-urban production, and this does seem to have been the case, at least in the factory sector in India.[19]

Tolley also rejected as unappealing the sluggish mobility hypothesis, which seeks to explain underurbanization as a result of 'permanent nonpecuniary attachments' to a rural way of life. Although we do see higher urbanization rates for Bihar, Karnataka, Madhya Pradesh, and Orissa, states with large shares of casual workers unattached to land (see Figure 7), differential migration propensities more likely have to do with land tenure systems, access to physical and human capital, and to publicly sponsored improvements in rural welfare opportunities. Intersectoral wage equalization does not tell the entire story.

From a positive viewpoint, then, we can summarize our overall assessment of the adequacy of a simple two-sector framework for explaining LDC urban growth as follows. The rather weak support for the Tolley model in the Indian case shows the need for realistic analytic extensions. Given the country's large size and low income level, an approach that simultaneously brings in demand as well as supply factors and, in the light of its less-than-perfect openness to international trade, recognizes some measure of price endogeneity for its imperfectly substitutable domestic goods is perhaps inevitable.[20] The greatest pay-offs to a more detailed sectoral treatment of the determinants of urban growth might lie in the inclusion of both the urban informal sector and the rural non-farm sector, in a more elaborate delineation of urban–rural linkages (preferably with urban classes disaggregated by sizes and functions), and in a more explicit modelling of land and human capital factors in the rural–urban migration mechanism. Additionally, the seemingly strong impact of development interventions suggests modelling the government sector with realistic sectoral public expenditure allocation mechanisms.

Adopting the second, or normative, viewpoint allows one to assess the role of policy in the Indian urbanization experience. First, it is well to reiterate that both national- and state-level simulations concurred in their finding of widespread 'underurbanization' by the model's norms. If the Tolley model's central premise, namely, that the undeniable efficiency benefits from specialization will result in a larger urban sector than dictated by domestic demand elasticities, is accepted, then one may attribute the failure of the Indian economy as a whole, and the majority of its states, to fulfil, over the 1971–81 period, the urban growth potential of their inter-sectoral productivity differentials, to a serious lapse from optimality. In motivating his explanation of urbanization in the light of several countries recent export-driven development successes, Tolley states: 'It is not surprising that developing countries are increasingly getting out of the agricultural business and into urban-based production' (Tolley and Thomas 1987, p. 21), and that 'Changes in the degree (and nature) of international specialization may accelerate the rate of urbanization during development' (Tolley and Thomas 1987, p. 18). It is conceivable that India's pursuit of agricultural self-sufficiency has led to the missing of gainful opportunities of international specialization in urban-based industrial activities.

Section V, which looked at the effects of government spending and infrastructural investment across the states, uncovered the association of rural impoverishment with 'excessive' urbanization where it had occurred, and of rural development interventions with cases where urban growth was 'deficient' over the 1971–81 decade. But while the apparent success of such policies, whether directed at direct welfare improvement, infrastructure investment or employment generation, offers hope for stemming urbanward migration in areas where unproductive urban growth is taking place, a vigorous espousal of 'rural bias' in industrialized states with a productive urban sector will result in efficiency losses due to governmentally induced distortions. Forcing industry to disperse to small towns and industrially backward rural areas which deny it valuable urban agglomeration benefits will do so likewise.[21]

As Tolley mentions, 'one of the effects of economic development is the gradual elimination of so-called traditional production in both urban and non-urban areas. Urbanization will be speeded if there is more of this traditional production to be eliminated in non-urban than in urban areas... This phenomenon is merely part of the increased specialization that has been mentioned' (Tolley and Thomas 1987, p. 19). While highly industrialized states such as Maharashtra have experienced steep declines in the non-farm shares of rural employment (Figure 11), their rates of urbanization are not as high as one would expect. On the other hand, during economic development, as Tolley adds, 'if people are released from traditional employment in agricultural areas where there are no expanding employment opportunities, they will seek employment in urban areas, and urbanization will increase' (Tolley and Thomas 1987, p. 19). The impoverished states of Orissa and Bihar exemplify this point.

Non-farm employment in Punjab and Haryana is probably of a very different nature than that in Tamil Nadu, but one can ask why non-agricultural rural production in these states has not been out-competed by other forms of production.[22] Haryana is only now industrializing, while Punjab faces political discontent from lack of urban opportunities quite evident in the extent of its underurbanization. Such interstate variations in the spatial opportunity structures of jobs may arise in part from government intervention itself, which can either accentuate or neutralize them, depending upon the processes and objectives of regional policy-making within a national framework.

Thus, we see that the uniform application of national sectoral policy to the states can be inefficient due to its differential incidence, given their existing structures, when the latter themselves may be the outcomes of patterns of past intervention. Any government policy applied indiscriminately results in an inability to benefit from comparative advantages; however, normative judgment becomes even more complicated by issues of equity between the states. Have states such as Punjab and Haryana specialized in response to their natural advantage in agriculture?[23] What are the distributional aspects of public intervention's role there? More systematic research on the urban growth impacts of implicit or explicit spatial policy biases, both between nations and subnational regions, is needed.

Appendix 1: Data Used in Calculation of Productivity Indexes

1971	MVAL71	MLAB71	MCAP71	MSL71	AINC71	ALAB71	ACAP71	ASL71
AP	1076	411	5603	0.08	13274.1	3208.90	54060	0.42
BH	1668	442	8753	0.07	16270.8	3528.47	110701	0.40
GJ	2399	867	6762	0.06	8793.2	1368.84	48588	0.37
HY	602	169	2681	0.07	5138.4	426.01	28710	0.34
KT	1671	349	5508	0.09	10140.9	1753.82	41870	0.50
KL	800	267	2565	0.09	4505.5	811.74	30245	0.54
MP	1002	319	6580	0.07	12126.1	3001.22	61223	0.37
MR	7716	1604	19911	0.06	10406.5	2945.85	70024	0.52
OR	567	162	4846	0.08	6503.3	1321.46	22118	0.32
PJ	503	142	2906	0.06	6805.6	597.83	49364	0.45
RJ	539	169	3204	0.09	8330.4	1457.71	39851	0.36
TN	2926	861	10782	0.08	11115.7	2291.20	43917	0.42
UP	1879	636	11282	0.08	20539.8	5118.94	185499	0.55
WB	3957	1621	15046	0.10	12846.7	1867.15	44851	0.32

(*Contd.*)

Appendix 1: (*Contd.*)

1981	MVAL81	MLAB81	MCAP81	MSL81	AINC81	ALAB81	ACAP81	ASL81
AP	6956.9	941.69	25689.3	0.09	42200	3994.27	222517	0.64
BH	9223.8	680.79	50061.4	0.09	31750	4021.20	361332	0.83
GJ	12590.2	942.43	41578.5	0.05	24270	1643.74	107875	0.62
HY	4476.4	285.34	12704.7	0.05	16700	536.19	134348	0.44
KT	6734.8	510.25	19207.4	0.08	25580	2293.38	152860	0.42
KL	4393.7	326.43	12816.9	0.07	13300	749.78	264526	0.63
MP	7909.0	515.66	35709.7	0.09	29870	3774.65	201145	0.77
MR	33857.3	1752.08	84432.2	0.07	42420	3702.84	257802	0.63
OR	2310.3	167.84	14302.0	0.08	20030	1605.51	72089	0.44
PJ	4295.5	331.30	21820.6	0.05	23500	672.28	204437	0.37
RJ	3702.2	389.62	19173.2	0.07	25680	1740.76	182665	0.51
TN	14301.3	1252.88	44194.8	0.07	18520	2896.01	137269	0.90
UP	14849.0	893.19	51703.4	0.09	63760	5822.69	720288	0.66
WB	14419.6	1529.46	42848.0	0.13	27360	2201.17	160352	0.52

Variable definitions are as follows.
MVAL = Manufacturing – Value added (m Rs)
MLAB = Manufacturing – Man hours worked (m)
MCAP = Manufacturing – Total productive capital (m Rs)
MSL = Manufacturing – Share of labour in total cost (%)
AINC = Agriculture – Income originating from agriculture (m Rs)
ACAP = Agriculture – Aggregate value of capital assets (m Rs)
ALAB = Agriculture – Man years worked (m)
ASL = Agriculture – Share of labour in total agricultural income (%)

1971 Data were obained from S. Verma, 'Urbanization and Productivity in Indian States', in *Studies in Indian Urban Development*, edited by E.S. Mills and C. M. Beker, The World Bank, Washington, D.C., 1986.

1981 Data were developed by the authors using comparable computations with data drawn from Central Statistical Organization, *Annual Survey of Industries 1981–82 — Summary Results for the Factory Sector*; Reserve Bank of India, *All-India Debt and Investment Survey*, 1981–82; Census Commissioner for India, *Census of India 1981*; Centre for Monitoring Indian Economy, *Basic Statistics Relating to the Indian Economy: States*, 1987; Government of India, Ministry of Agriculture, *Agricultural Wages in India*, 1984–85.

Appendix 2: Data on Urban Growth by City Size Class

Table A: Average Annual Change in Index of Growth of Urban Population, 1971–81, Computed by the Instantaneous method, that is, not accounting for Reclassification of Urban Places Between Censuses

States	LCITY	SCITY	LTOWN	MTOWN	STOWN
AP	12.9	16.8	12.2	10.2	–0.9
BH	–	11.1	20.3	11.2	–1.7
GJ	25.1	–2.0	21.8	4.9	1.7
HY	–	–21.4	–6.0	1.8	4.2
KT	18.8	8.7	6.1	14.6	2.3

(*Contd.*)

Table A (*Contd.*)

KL	–	–3.7	1.3	25.5	–0.1
MP	37.3	–4.0	26.5	0.7	9.8
MR	12.3	15.4	–0.2	6.5	–0.1
OR	–	50.3	47.0	12.1	9.9
PJ	–	–6.7	16.1	4.7	2.7
RJ	14.1	7.4	6.5	13.1	2.3
TN	12.6	4.9	12.8	0.9	–0.3
UP	19.8	5.3	11.3	4.6	10.5
WB	0.7	17.0	6.9	1.4	9.5

Size class definitions are as follows:

	Urban places with pop
LCITY	500,000 and above
SCITY	100,000 – 499,999
LTOWN	50,000 – 99,999
MTOWN	20,000 – 49,999
STOWN	below 20,000

Table B: Average Annual Growth Rate of Urban Population, 1971–81, computed by the continuous method, that is, for cohorts of towns and cities formed on the basis of initial size class of urban places

States	I	II	III	IV	V	VI
AP	4.2	4.5	4.8	4.9	4.4	4.7
BH	5.0	5.6	4.8	4.2	6.3	5.6
GJ	4.3	2.9	3.5	3.2	3.0	2.2
HY	5.4	4.9	3.9	3.4	3.0	7.2
KT	5.5	3.7	3.7	3.3	4.1	3.4
KL	2.2	1.3	2.3	12.1	19.8	–0.5
MP	4.9	4.3	4.7	3.6	3.8	3.1
MR	4.0	4.3	3.3	2.7	3.0	2.4
OR	6.1	4.5	5.4	4.3	5.6	2.2
PJ	3.9	4.3	3.3	3.4	3.9	5.1
RJ	5.3	4.0	4.7	4.1	3.5	9.3
TN	2.6	3.1	2.4	2.2	2.7	5.4
UP	3.0	3.6	4.2	4.0	4.2	4.0
WB	1.5	3.1	3.2	3.6	5.2	9.0

Size class definitions are as follows:

	Urban places with pop.
I	100,00 and above
II	50,000 – 99,999
III	20,000 – 49,999
IV	10,000 – 19,999
V	5,000 – 9,999
VI	below 5,000

Data sources are Office of the Registrar General, India, *Urban Growth in India 1951–81* (A Statistical Analysis) 1984, and *Study on Levels and Trends of Urbanization,* Occasional Paper 1 of 1986.

NOTES

Versions of this paper were presented at the Annual Meetings of the Regional Science Association, 9–11 November 1990, and the Allied Social Sciences Associations, 28–30 December 1990.
Reproduced with permission from Geographical Analysis, Vol. 23, No. 3 (July 1991) © 1991 Ohio State University Press, revised version accepted 1/11/91.

1 Originally proposed as Tolley (1984); subsequently published in Tolley and Thomas (1987).
2 Implied by $N_u = [\{(E_u/E_a)T_a - T_u\}/\{(E_u/E_a)(P_u/P_a) + 1\} + N]$, where N_u and N are the rates of growth of urban and total population, respectively; P_u and P_a are urban and rural population levels; E_u and E_a are the income elasticities of demand for urban and rural products; and T_u and T_a are rates of growth of output per person in urban and rural activities.
3 Time derivatives of production relations of the type $Y = AN^e$.
4 If wages are paid according to marginal product in each sector, e should equal the share of product paid to labour, that is, $e = wn/py$ or $w = epy/n$, the lower case denoting levels.

Assuming e is a stable parameter in each sector, applying rates of change to w for the two sectors yields (3) and (4). If labour adjusts to keep relative earnings of urban and rural employment the same over time, then condition (5) results — average labour productivities change by the same proportion.
5 Tolley defines as an error-of-fit measure the proportionate change in average labour productivity as a fraction of the mean of proportional urban and rural population growth. Thus, a value of substantially less than unity indicates that relatively little of the observed variation in output and employment is associated with departures from his hypotheses.
6 Public sector expenditures on agriculture, irrigation, and flood control increased steadily from the 20 per cent of actual plan outlays during the period of the Second Plan (1956–61) to 20.5 per cent during the Third Plan (1961–66) to 21.7 per cent during the Annual Plans (1966–69) and 23.3 per cent during the Fourth Plan (1969–74). The combined share of rural development categories in planned outlays stood at 37.4 per cent in the Fifth Plan (1974–79) and rose to 43.1 per cent in the Sixth Plan (1978–83).

Much the same trend toward diminished rural out-migration rates due to rising rural welfare has been documented, albeit more journalistically, by Critchfield (1984), for other agrarian Asian economies although he tends to attribute this to lowered rates of rural fertility as well as rising agricultural productivity.
7 Only about 14 per cent of all migration within India recorded in 1971 represented interstate moves.
8 The 1971 Census used a narrower definition of 'main worker', which resulted in unlikely declines in measured employment and labour force participation rates over 1961–71.
9 Economic base models in regional science make the distinction between 'export' or basic and non-basic production activity.

10 Data sources for the national-level exercise include: Tata Services Ltd. (1989); Mitchell (1982); Padmanabha (1981); Rinn-Sup Shinn et al. (1970); United Nations Department of Social and Economic Affairs (various years). Data for the states came from CMIE (1987); Social Studies Division (1986); and Census Commissioner for India (various years).

11 Practically, the simple average annual growth of labour productivity is first calculated for each sector, and then added to the population (or employment) growth rates for the respective sectors to 'purge' the estimated growth rates of sectoral incomes to conform to the requirement of (5).

12 A crude measure of fit, the square root of the mean of the squares of the deviation of the predicted from observed values is employed to compare the two scenarios.

13 Expressions (11) and (12) follow the indexes of technical change derived from the transcendental logarithmic production function in Jorgenson and Nishimizu (1978).

14 Data used in the computation of the sectoral productivity change indexes are reported in Appendix 1.

15 Data on urban population growth by size class are reported in Appendix 2. Two size classification systems were available, one for the change in an urban population growth index (A), and the other for urban growth rates (B) for the states. In Table 8, we report results obtained using (A), as this classification permits the isolation of the very large cities, upon which we wish to focus attention. Results using (B) were substantially similar in providing poor support for the model, but with the broader first size class I now registering positive coefficients for both sectoral productivity change indexes.

16 The estimates are derived using the all-India minimum daily calorie requirement of 2400 per person in rural areas and 2100 per person in urban areas (Rs 65 and Rs 75 per capita per month, respectively in 1977–78 prices).

17 This index covers sixteen different state-wide indicators under the following categories, with the weight of each of the categories in parentheses: Power (20%); Irrigation, Roads (15%); Railways (20%); Post Offices (5%); Education (10%); Health (4%); and Banking (6%).

18 The six groups of rural amenities are Educational Facility, Medical Facility, Electricity, Drinking Water, All-Weather Road, Post and Telegraph Office.

19 The factory sector in India includes registered enterprises which use power and employ ten or more workers, and those that do not use power and employ twenty or more workers. The ratio of total labour emoluments to value added in this sector was 0.54 in 1973–74.

20 Interestingly, the ten-sector dynamic computable general equilibrium (CGE) formulation in Becker, Mills, and Williamson (1986), the most ambitious among simulation models of Indian urbanization, also concludes that 'the central engine of city growth is not the demand side through Engels' effects but rather the supply side through unbalanced productivity advance' (p. 30). Their counterfactual exercises attribute the city growth slowdown of the seventies to the poor productivity performance of manufacturing and the

decline in net foreign capital inflows. The study also found that growth in agricultural productivity does release labour to the cities, but its impact on urban growth is quite modest, and that push factors such as arable land scarcity are not important to urbanization. By contrast, Pandey (1977) found the thesis of overurbanization due to rural land pressure also unsupported but the level of agricultural development negatively related to urbanization in a state-level cross-sectional econometric exercise for 1971.

21 Shukla (1988) finds compelling evidence of agglomeration economies of large city size for India, and presents a critique of industrial dispersal policies in this light.

22 Vaidyanathan (1986) reports that about 20 per cent of male employment in rural areas of India in 1977–78 occurred in non-agricultural occupations, based on usual employment status. Shukla (1990a) and (1990b) explore the structural and policy determinants of the size of this sector.

23 The extent of deliberate rural bias in the states of Punjab and Haryana is documented in the discussion by Westley (1986).

REFERENCES

Becker, Charles M., Edwin S. Mills and Jeffrey G. Williamson (1986), 'Modelling Indian Migration and City Growth, 1960–2000', *Economic Development and Cultural Change,* Vol. 35.

Census Commissioner for India (various years), *Census of India*, Migration Tables.

———(1984), *Urban Growth in India, 1951–81* (A Statistical Analysis), Census of India, New Delhi.

Centre for Monitoring Indian Economy (CMIE) (1987), Economic Intelligence Service, *Basic Statistics Relating to the Indian Economy, Vol. 2: States,* Bombay.

Critchfield, R. (1984), 'Reassessing Asian Villagers' Return from the City', *Asian Wall Street Journal,* May 5.

Department of Economics and Statistics (1989), *Statistical Outline of India, 1989-90,* Tata Services Ltd, Bombay.

Jorgenson, D.W. and M. Nishimizu (1978), 'U.S. and Japanese Economic Growth, 1952–74: An International Comparison', *Economic Journal*, Vol. 88.

Kilbourne, Barbara and Brian J.L. Berry (1989), 'West African Urbanization: Where Tolley's Model Fails', *Urban Geography*, Vol. 10.

Mitchell, B.R. (1982), *International Historical Statistics:* Africa and Asia, New York University Press, New York.

Padmanabha, P. (1981), *Census of India 1981,* Series-1: India, Paper 2 of 1981, Registrar General's Office, New Delhi.

Pandey, S.M. (1977), 'Nature and Determinants of Urbanization in a Developing Economy: The Case of India', *Economic Development and Cultural Change,* Vol. 25.

Pribadi, Krishna Nur and Brian J.L. Berry (1986), 'Urbanization in Indonesia: Application and Extension of a Model Suggested by Tolley', *Urban Geography*, Vol. 7.

Ran, Maoxing, and Brian J.L. Berry (1989), 'Underurbanization Policies Assessed: China, 1949–1986', *Urban Geography,* Vol. 10.

Shinn, Rinn-Sup, et al. (1970), *Area Handbook for India,* American University Press, Washington, D.C.

Shukla, Vibhooti (1988), *Urban Development and Regional Policy in India,* Himalaya Publishing House, Bombay.

———(1990a), 'An Empirical Model of Rural Non-Farm Activity', The University of Texas at Dallas, mimeo, June. A version of this paper was submitted at a seminar sponsored by the Indian Society of Agricultural Economics and Gujarat Institute of Development Research on 29-31 March 1989 at Ahmedabad, India. Revised version entitled, 'Rural Non-Farm Activity — A Regional Model and Its Empirical Application to Maharashtra' published in *Economic and Political Weekly* (1991), Vol XXVI, No. 45, Nov. 9. Also in Pravin Visaria and Rakesh Basant (eds) (1994). *Non-Agricultural Employment in Inda: Trends and Prospects,* Sage Publications, New Delhi.

———(1990b), 'Rural Non-Farm Employment in India: Issues and Policy', The University of Texas at Dallas: mimeo, July. Revised version 'Rural Non-Farm Employment in India: Issues and Policy', *Economic and Political Weekly* (1992), Vol. XXVII, No. 28, July 11.

Social Studies Division (1986), *Study on Distribution of Infrastructural Facilities in Different Regions and Levels and Trends of Urbanization,* Census of India, New Delhi.

Tata Services Ltd. (1989), *Statistical Outline of India, 1989–90,* Department of Economics and Statistics, Bombay.

Tolley, George S. (1984), 'Urbanization and Economic Development', unpublished manuscript, University of Chicago.

Tolley, George S. and Vinod Thomas, eds, (1987), *The Economics of Urbanization and Urban Policies in Developing Countries,* The World Bank, Washington, D.C.

United Nations Department of Social and Economic Affairs (various years) *Demographic Yearbook,* United Nations, New York.

———(1985), Statistical Yearbook, United Nations, New York.

Vaidyanathan, A. (1986), 'Labour Use in Rural India — A Study of Spatial and Temporal Variations', *Economic and Political Weekly*, Vol. XXI, No. 52, December 27.

Westley, J.R. (1986), *Agriculture and Equitable Growth: The Case of Punjab and Haryana*, Westview Press, Boulder, Colo.

10 / Rural Non-farm Activity: A Regional Model and its Empirical Application to Maharashtra

VIBHOOTI SHUKLA

I. Introduction

The rural non-farm sector in India has been growing in aggregate size and appears to perform an increasingly significant rural income augmentation function. Lately, considerable attention has been focused on this sector's role and potential for employment generation in India, but much of it has been rather partial and sector-specific. A comprehensive picture of the rural non-farm economy cannot be confined to consumption and welfare alone, or even to the labour market alone, but rather must be viewed in the context of changes taking place in both agriculture and industry, and set against events in rural as well as in urban areas.

The focus on employment highlights, naturally, the labour market connections that govern individual choices between employment in the rural non-farm and the rural farm subsectors. However, deeper structural factors underlie these labour market manifestations in framing the opportunities for such choices. The most commonly recognized are links between the output and factor markets within the rural economy. One conceptualization focuses upon the food and labour markets as two separate but interacting rural entities. It suggests that technological change in agriculture, depending upon its bias, may increase or decrease labour's relative share in foodgrains output, raising or lowering labour's supply price to non-agricultural activities.

A related perspective is offered by formulations recognizing consumption linkages between the agricultural and non-agricultural outputs of the rural economy.[1] They give consideration to the stimulus that a prospering agricultural economy can give to consumption demand for the products of local non-farm activity. This last possibility highlights an important intra-rural spatial connection between the two rural subsectors. Similar intersectoral spatial linkages may be articulated, in the labour market, through the possibility of migratory flows between rural and urban areas, and in the output market, through the urban demand for the products of rural non-farm industry, or the urban supply of competing substitutes for them. While the geographical mobility of labour and goods in India is far from costless, such flows must necessarily assume increasing importance as development and spatial integration take place.

Unfortunately, most conventional dual-economy formulations, be they guided by growth or by equity concerns, oversimplify the spatial dimension of economic development by locating the non-agricultural sector largely in urban areas. A spatial perspective on rural non-farm activities is fruitfully augmented by considerations pertaining to the locational aspects of rural enterprises. Their input–output linkages with the products of agriculture, and the factor intensities with which they operate will influence the magnitude of employment in rural non-farm activity, and indicate the potential for, say, agroprocessing or ancillary activities. Investigation of the nature of rural entrepreneurship, and the role of (site-specific) rural infrastructure, or of the locational impact of explicitly or implicitly spatial government action can potentially identify bottlenecks to rural industrial growth and facilitate realistic policy towards engendering local environments conducive to generating rural industrialization indigenous to these areas through natural incentive structures or the appropriate investments in socio-economic infrastructure.

A few empirical studies focusing separately upon some of the individual links mentioned above have been undertaken, mainly for other countries, and need to be attempted in the case of India.[2] Most of these are on the micro level — and should be, if the detailed technological, labour supply and consumption relationships are to be rigorously investigated. However, an integrative synthesis of the relationships outlined above and the exploration and measurement of their cumulative effects, working through the gamut of direct and indirect channels, on the level and growth of the rural non-farm sector can only be done within the context of an aggregative regional framework.

Are industrialization and urbanization in the regional economy complementary with or substitutes for high shares and growth of rural non-farm activity? Is a thriving non-farm sector related to a prosperous regional agriculture or to the lack of on-farm work opportunities? What types of labour market flows give rise to observed regional non-farm employment patterns?

Clearly, such questions cannot be answered through casual inspection or simple two-way associations. Complexity in the regional phenomena under study requires that the influence of each of the many contributory factors be controlled to isolate the importance of any one. Systematic statistical analysis is necessary to probe the sources of regional variations in the non-farm sector, and to determine whether the growth of this sector represents inevitable structural changes accompanying economic development, or a greater pauperization of the rural economy. We address ourselves to formulating a model which can be equal to this task.

Our endeavour at this stage is modest. We delineate the outlines of a unifying framework which is capable of taking a comprehensive account of the influences mentioned above and of exploring alternative hypotheses and addressing relevant policy issues in an empirically organized fashion. We do so only as a first approximation to a multi-sectoral specification that can more fully and exactly model the rural non-farm sector in terms of all its economic linkages with the rest of the economy. At best, we can hope this exercise may inform such a future enterprise.

From a modelling viewpoint, our principal handicap is that data available on the sector itself are largely restricted to employment patterns, and we are able to bring few output or price variables to bear on the analysis. Accordingly, we analyse the magnitude, composition and growth of the rural non-agricultural sector through an investigation formulated in employment terms.

We perform a series of exploratory empirical exercises, using spatial and sectoral aggregates, on employment in various types of rural non-agricultural activity in a region, with a view to discovering its spatial determinants. The analysis is cross-sectional, with a district in Maharashtra state envisaged as the regional economic unit. With 26 districts for which comparable comprehensive and reliable data are available, Maharashtra provides, in our opinion, a good setting for a regional study. There is sufficient variability as to levels and patterns of industrial and agricultural development, urbanization and migration patterns, social and productive infrastructure.

The formal modelling framework is developed and outlined in Section II, and is implemented through the regression exercises of Sections III, IV and V, where we respectively attempt to explain 1971 *levels* of district non-farm employment — in the aggregate and by industry — as well as *growth* therein over the 1971–81 decade. Section VI concludes with future modelling and research directions.

II. Regional Modelling Framework for Rural Non-farm Employment

The model presented below is envisaged as a rough framework within which some of the questions raised above can be analytically set and empirically explored. It is unabashedly tailored to suit a data availability situation that as yet provides neither critical information on regional price variables nor comprehensive production data such as value of inputs or outputs for the sector under study.[3]

The framework is cast in supply and demand terms, yet with no explicit claims made as to equilibrium within or between components of the relevant markets. Basically, the rural non-farm sector is perceived as a regional labour market competing for labour with the spatially coterminous agricultural sector, and the physically removed urban sector that is nevertheless connected to the rural through labour migration flows. While supply of labour to the rural non-farm sector is thus determined by regional population characteristics and in-migration or out-migration, the demand for workers in this sector depends upon the nature of local consumption and production linkages, regional factors such as the extent of urban demand for and agglomeration benefits accruing to the product of the activity, and on the availability of location- (and sector-) specific capital, credit, infrastructural or government policy support.

No doubt emphasizing the distinction between 'supply' and 'demand' sides may not be entirely appropriate here, as when dealing with self-employment or household industry activities and, indeed, many variables used in actual implementation may capture elements of both influences at once. However, it is felt necessary to make the formal division to bring into the discussion several regional determinants of non-farm activity that have hitherto been neglected. And, in the course of applying the model to distinct subcomponents of aggregate non-farm employment, we hope to be able to admit hypotheses about the relative importance of each set of factors. (See box below for the Model.)

The level of rural non-farm employment, N, is determined jointly by N^D, the demand for and N^S, the supply of such labour to that sector. On the supply side, labour availability characteristics such as rates of overall labour force participation, age and educational distribution of the rural population, or rates of in-migration to and out-migration from the rural area will serve to determine the size of the labour pool available for employment in the non-farm sector. For instance, in-migration may be expected to augment, and out-migration, deplete, this pool.

Demand for labour in non-farm activities comes from enterprises (own-account or establishment) and is both derived from the demand, Y^D (local and urban), for the output of this sector, as well as conditioned by factors (inputs, costs, the productive environment) governing its production and supply, Y^S. Local demand for the output of non-farm activity is articulated through rural consumption linkages, depending largely upon agricultural income and its distribution; regional urban areas may provide either markets or competition for this output, depending, in many

THE MODEL

Rural non-farm employment	$N^S = f\,[N^S(.), N^D(.)]$	(1)
Labour supply to non-farm sector	$N^D = g(L, M)$	(2)
Demand for rural non-farm labour	$N^D = h\,[Y^D(.), Y^S(.)]$	(3)
Demand for rural industry output	$Y^D = j\,(C, U)$	(4)
Supply of rural industry output	$Y^S = k\,[(R\,(.), S\,(.), A]$	(5)
Raw material input in rural industry	$R = I\,(P)$	(6)
Other inputs in non-farm enterprise	$S = m(I, K. B, G)$	(7)

EXOGENOUS VARIABLES:

C : rural consumption of output of non-farm activity
P : agricultural product used as input in non-farm activity
L : regional labour availability level
M : labour flows into and out of rural areas
U : urbanization characteristics of the region
A : regional agglomeration characteristics
I : level of rural infrastructure
K : measure of physical capital used in rural non-farm activity
B : credit availability to rural non-agricultural enterprise
G : incidence of government policy affecting non-farm employment

cases, on the nature of the product. Non-farm production processes utilize purchased and non-purchased inputs: use of agricultural raw material will reflect the strength of production linkages with that sector, as use of physical or financial capital may point to complementarity or substitutability with labour in non-farm technologies. Availability of non-purchased or subsidized inputs in the form of infrastructure or government developmental assistance might also presumably constitute a positive (labour) demand-side influence on rural non-farm employment, as might the operation of productivity-enhancing external economies of scale due to the spatial agglomeration of population or economic activity within regions.

The seven-equation structural model may be reduced in linear form to yield a single equation (8), amenable to least squares regression estimation:

$$N = b_0 + b_1 C + b_2 P + b_3 L + b_4 M + b_5 U + b_6 A + b_7 I + b_8 K + b_9 B + b_{10} G \quad (8)$$

We propose to employ this broad estimation framework to investigate the regional correlates of rural non-farm activity, in its aggregate, as well as in the sector's various subcomponents. Within this framework, we shall experiment with several alternative measures of the independent variables, depending upon the hypothesis we wish to specify for any particular exercise. Sometimes, due to restrictions posed by the exigencies of data available, variable selection may be such as to compromise the 'purity' of an empirical proxy in acting as an unambiguous channel of influence. We shall endeavour to note explicitly where this might be the case. Likewise, we shall attempt to minimize other statistical problems endemic to using regional aggregates, such as heteroscedasticity or multicollinearity between independent variables, by appropriate variable choice and normalization.

A more serious problem, of course, is the potential for simultaneity bias introduced by the prospect that some of the 'independent' variables should properly be endogenous to the system. At this time, however, the data just do not support simultaneous estimation. We shall return later to this issue.

District-level data on main workers[4] by industry at the one-digit National Industrial Classification (*NIC*) level, as available from the 1971 and the 1981 Population Censuses of Maharashtra, are used as dependent variables for the regression exercises. The limitations of the population census data in respect of measuring employment status on the basis of single-point-of-time-administered questionnaire are well perceived. The incidence of these limitations, however, is likely to be less on data relating to employment in rural non-agricultural industrial categories, where the identification of main activity of persons enumerated will not be beset with as much ambiguity as may be the case with the agricultural sector. The usual status and daily status of employment particularly in the non-seasonal of these industries should be roughly coterminous. Ambiguity may admittedly arise in the case of household and some seasonal industries, such as construction. The population census does, however, report secondary activities of main workers engaged in different non-farm industries. The information on these might yield a picture of any discrepancies, and will be utilized.

A district-level study is also beset with availability of less than ideal spatially disaggregated economic data on the several explanatory variables that go into the estimating equations. Ideally, the consumption-led demand parameters should be estimated from more direct evidence on expenditure patterns and income distribution than we have been able to utilize. As no precise data on input and production linkages with a technologically dynamic agricultural sector are available, we have had to evaluate the incidence of such effects through indirect indicators. Due to non-existent data, no direct estimations could be attempted using private capital stock/investment in rural non-agricultural industries at the district level. A rough approximation used for self-employment activities is the incidence of houses used as places of business. Similarly, data on various infrastructural facilities and government assistance are typically available for rural areas at large — and rarely focused exclusively on the non-farm sector. We have used, accordingly, several alternative indicators for these in our exercise to infer relationships with rural non-agricultural employment specifically.

Inevitably, the data situation has forced us to select independent variables that relate to different years between 1971 and 1981, with some 'stock'-type variables not exactly cotemporal. Insofar as variations in accretions to these variables are not very wide across districts, the regression results should not, we feel, be substantially affected. A list of data sources appears in the references, and definitions of specific variables used in a particular exercise are appended to the table reporting relevant results. The next section discusses the regressions and presents their outcomes.

III. Results from Static Aggregate Estimations

In this section we describe the various OLS (ordinary least squares) regression exercises conducted with the full specification of equation (8) of Section II. We first take up for investigation the aggregate non-farm sector, and, in the next section, several of its industrial subcomponents. In each case, the choice of the dependent variable focuses on the rural non-farm activity being investigated, and selection of particular explanatory variables from among the generic categories of independent variables presumed to operate in the manner specified by the model is usually indicative of the hypothesis being tested. Occasionally, estimation is performed in a more exploratory spirit, as when several different indicators or proxies within the same class of independent variables are experimented with to study their differential effects on non-agricultural employment in any given subsector. A static investigation of the relative magnitude of non-farm employment will precede the dynamic examination of the growth in this sector.

We regress employment measures of non-agricultural rural activity in the economy, with a view to discovering its broad determinants. Results appear in Table 1. Three different measures of the dependent variables are used: column one reports coefficients for the regression of *N*1, the share of non-farm in total rural employment, on various explanatory variables; column two for *N*2, or rural non-agricultural employment per capita; and lastly, column *N*3 for rural non-farm employment density.[5] We may comment upon the choice and performance of hypothesized explanatory variables as follows.

Consumption

This variable, in principle, is presumed to capture the effects of local consumption linkages on the demand for the product of non-farm activity, and thence upon aggregate employment in that sector. The rationale behind the choice of 'net sown area per agricultural worker (ha)' is that this consumption demand comes largely from incomes in agriculture, the still dominant rural activity. The selected independent variable — an observation on the ratio of a critical income-earning asset to some factor of the population that must consume from its proceeds — is thus a proxy for average rural farm income for a district.[6] The coefficient for the variable is positive and significant — and of consistently high magnitude — for each of the three regressions reported in

Table 1: Regional Correlates of Aggregate Rural Non-farm Activity

n=25 *Independent Variables*	*Dependent Variables Means* N1 14.26	N2 5.56	N3 6.87	Sample Means
C (Consumption)	2.1827*	0.5294†	1.1976*	3.61
	(4.074)	(2.393)	(3.585)	
P (Production)	0.0020	0.0002	0.0019†	974.64
	(1.395)	(0.395)	(2.153)	
L (Labour)	0.3353	0.1792	0.2836‡	36.80
	(1.275)	(1.650)	(1.729)	
M (Migration)	0.5007*	0.1876†	0.1388	9.62
	(2.984)	(2.708)	(1.326)	
U (Urbanization)	0.0518‡	0.0187	0.0561*	25.76
	(1.852)	(1.621)	(3.216)	
A (Agglomeration)	0.0024*	0.0010*	0.0018*	862.76
	(4.524)	(4.612)	(5.614)	
I (Infrastructure)	–0.0199	–0.0137	0.0676‡	36.05
	(–0.335)	(–0.556)	(1.824)	
K (Physical capital)	1.4308*	0.7699*	1.1004*	2.92
	(4.769)	(6.216)	(5.882)	
B (Credit)	–0.0034	–0.0030	0.0026	114.14
	(–0.494)	(–1.059)	(0.594)	
G (Govt. policy)	0.0217	0.0076	0.0266	7.36
	(0.546)	(0.460)	(1.071)	
Constant	–19.3024	–7.7769	–20.2398†	1.00
	(–1.586)	(–1.548)	(–2.667)	
R-squared	0.9139	0.9180	0.9392	

Notes: Figures in parentheses are t-values; * = 1 per cent; † = 5 per cent; ‡ = 10 per cent significance levels in a two-tailed test.

*N*1 Share of non-farm (workers in other than cultivation) in total rural employment by main activity, 1971 (per cent).

*N*2 Workers with main activity other than cultivation per 100—1971 district rural population.

*N*3 Workers with main activity other than cultivation per sq km district rural geographical area.

C Net sown area per agricultural worker, hectares.

P Value of output of major crops per hectare of net sown area (Rs).

L Rate of labour force participation for district (per cent).

M Share of in-migrants (males not born in place of enumeration) in rural male population (per cent).

U Share of district urban population in small towns—with population, 5000 to 19,999 (per cent).

A Average daily employment in factories per 1,00,000 district population.

I Percentage of district villages with electricity (per cent).

K Houses used as shops/workshops of total rural residences (per cent).

B Average borrowing per member, non-agricultural credit societies (Rs).

G Government expenditure on community, tribal and multipurpose development blocks per village covered ('000 Rs).

Table 1, implying strong spatial consumption linkages between the agricultural and non-agricultural rural subsectors.

Production

By contrast, the local input linkages of agriculture with non-farm employment are sought to be investigated with this variable. What is being tested is the hypothesized importance of agroprocessing in manufacturing, or of trade in agricultural commodities in generating employment off the farm. In the aggregate, the performance of the measure, output value of major crops per hectare net sown area seems mixed, with the effects showing up significantly in increased non-farm employment density, but not in share. This would seem to suggest that regions with high average land productivity (or those featuring improved agricultural technologies) do not necessarily feature a large relative size of the non-farm sector once the consumption effect has been controlled for. Further attempts will be made to separately trace the effects of such hypothesized regional agricultural production linkages on various non-farm subsectors such as manufacturing, trade, transport, etc., through the analysis reported in Table 2.

Labour

The purpose of this conceptual category is to capture the effects of labour supply or availability, and ultimately shed light on the validity of the 'labour push' argument in explaining regional non-farm employment. At this stage, only a comprehensive[7] measure, labour force participation rate — for the district at large — is used to measure general labour availability and its influence on the share, incidence and density of rural non-farm employment. The expectation is that if the coefficient on this variable proves positive and strongly significant, a net increase in the proportion of persons working full time must take place to accommodate an increased share in employment in non-farm activities, rather than merely a labour transfer out of the agricultural and into the non-agricultural sector. While the implications of this are ambiguous without additional knowledge about leisure preferences or wage rates, the case for a tight labour market and welfare improvement rather than 'immiserization' is then supported. Since the coefficient of this variable in the share or incidence regressions is not significant, the conjecture is unresolved at this stage, but we shall return to the issue.

Table 2: Regional Determinants of Rural Non-farm Activity by Industry

n=25	*Dependent Variables Means*					
Independent Variables	N2, 3	N5	N6	N7	N8	N9
	4.90	0.84	1.67	0.60	01.17	3.96
C (Consumption)	0.2984†	0.2004*	–0.0268	0.1733†	–0.0329†	0.2477†
	(2.522)	(3.037)	(–0.546)	(2.296)	(–2.310)	(2.394)
P (Production)	–0.0145	0.0002	0.0175*	0.0001	0.0002†	0.0001
	(–1.276)	(0.416)	(3.629)	(0.558)	(2.225)	(0.691)
L (Labour)	–0.0752	0.0723†	0.0146	0.0508	0.0099‡	–0.1185†
	(–1.265)	(2.427)	(0.489)	(1.433)	(–1.781)	(–2.652)
M (Migration)	–0.0420	0.0725*	0.0454†	0.1160*	–0.0038	0.1120*
	(–0.906)	(2.530)	(2.406)	(4.554)	(–0.874)	(3.092)
U (Urbanization)	–0.0763*	0.0038	0.0025	0.0007	0.0003	0.0071‡
	(–5.182)	(0.955)	(0.755)	(0.146)	(0.427)	(1.924)
A (Agglomeration)	0.0017*	0.0038	0.0059	0.0097†	0.0049‡	0.0259*
	(13.003)	(1.076)	(0.456)	(2.263)	(2.007)	(3.407)
I (Infrastructure)	0.0755*	–0.1371*	0.0682‡	–0.1003‡	0.0138‡	0.0028
	(3.437)	(–3.224)	(1.840)	(–2.065)	(1.769)	(0.037)
K (Physical capital)	1.3115*	0.3851‡	–0.1150*	–0.0310	–0.0055	0.1192†
	(18.124)	(1.904)	(–3.004)	(–0.743)	(–0.832)	(2.723)
B (Credit)	–0.005	–0.0011	–0.0016†	–0.0003	–0.0001	0.0004
	(–0.373)	(–1.401)	(–2.310)	(–0.339)	(–0.672)	(0.312)
G (Govt. policy)	–0.0880	–0.1563	0.2679	0.0211	0.0322	0.0185*
	(–0.242)	(–0.864)	(1.647)	(0.101)	(0.992)	(2.928)
Constant	1.8636	–3.5635†	–0.6647	–3.7718†	0.4995†	4.4680†
	(0.742)	(–2.177)	(–0.519)	(–2.296)	(2.420)	(2.272)
R-squared	0.9864	0.6916	0.8289	0.7991	0.8651	0.8935

Notes: Figures in parentheses are t-values; * = 1 per cent; † = 5 per cent; ‡ = 10 per cent significance levels in a two-tailed test.

Dependent Variables

*N*2, 3 Percentage of rural employment in NIC 2 and 3: manufacturing, processing, servicing and repairs.

*N*5 Percentage of rural employment in NIC 5: construction.

*N*6 Percentage of rural employment in NIC 6: wholesale and retail trade, restaurants and hotels.

*N*7 Percentage of rural employment in NIC 7: transport, storage and communication.

*N*8 Percentage of rural employment in NIC 8: financing, insurance, real estate and business services.

*N*9 Percentage of rural employment in NIC 9: community, social and personal services.

Independent variables common to all regressions unless otherwise stated:

C Net sown areas per agricultural worker (hectares)

P Value of output of major crops per hectare of net sown area (Rs)

L Rate of district labour force participation (main workers) (per cent)

M Share of males born outside place of enumeration in district rural male population (in-migration rate) (per cent)

K Houses used as shops/workshops (including household industries) as percentage of total rural residences.*

(Contd.)

Table 2: (*Contd.*)

B	Average borrowing per member, non-agricultural credit societies (Rs).
G	Dummy variable indicating 1 = 'Backward' district; O = otherwise
Independent variables that are industry-specific:	
NIC 2,3:	(manufacturing, processing, servicing and repairs).
P	Ratio of area under all non-food crops to total area under crops (per cent).
U	Percentage of district population living in urban areas.
A	Average daily employment in factories per 1,00,000 district population.
I	Percentage of district villages with 'pucca' road approach.
NIC 5:	(construction).
U	Share of small (population 5000–19,999) towns in district urban population (per cent).
A	Rural population density (persons per sq km).
I	Per cent of district villages with power, 'pucca' roads, post and telegraph, education, medical and drinking water facilities.
K	Percentage of census houses used as shops (excluding eating houses).
NIC 6:	(wholesale and retail trade, restaurants and hotels).
P	Ratio of area under food crops to net sown area (per cent).
U	Share of small (population 5000–19,999) towns in district urban population (percentage).
A	Rural population share of large (population 5,000+) villages (percentage).
I	Percentage of district villages with power, 'pucca' roads, post and telegraph, education, medical and drinking water facilities.
NIC 7:	(transport, storage and communication).
U	Share of small (population 5,000–19,999) towns in district urban population (percentage).
A	Rural population density (persons per sq km).
I	Percentage of district villages with power, 'pucca' roads, post and telegraph, education, medical and drinking water facilities.
NIC 8:	(financing, insurance, real estate and business services).
C	Average size of operational holdings (hectares).
P	Average borrowing per member, agricultural credit and multipurpose society.
U	Share of medium (population 20,000–99,999) towns in district urban population (percentage).
I	Percentage of district villages with power, 'pucca' roads, post and telegraph, education, medical and drinking water facilities.
NIC 9:	(community, social and personal services)
U	Share of medium (population 20,000–99,999) towns in district urban population (percentage).
A	Rural population share of small (population 0–999) villages (percentage).
I	Per capita expenditure by village panchayats (Rs).
* *Alternative physical capital proxies*:	
K1 =	Houses used as shops/workshops (including household industries) as percentage of total rural residences.
K2 =	Houses used as shops (excluding eating houses) as percentage of total census houses.
K3 =	Houses used as business houses/offices as percentage of total census houses.
K4 =	Houses used as factories, workshops and worksheds as percentage of total census houses.
K5 =	Houses used as shops, business houses, factories, workshops and worksheds as percentage of total census houses.

Migration

It was desired to focus, in addition, on another component of labour supply to a region, viz., in-migration, and investigate the extent to which out-migration and non-farm employment were competing options for the (male) rural population. If out-migration were positively associated with the share of non-farm in total rural employment, the inference might be of a 'push' out of agricultural employment, jointly manifested in both spatial movement and the occupational migration inherent in a shift from farm to non-farm employment within the rural sector. A negative association would imply, on the other hand, that (spatial) out-migration and local occupational transition were competing but ranked alternatives, perhaps with different opportunities facing different segments of the rural workforce.

To our surprise, we found instead that it was the in-migration variable that showed consistently positive and highly significant effects on the share of non-farm in total rural employment. The success of the variable employed — percentage of rural population not born locally — leads one to speculate that labour inflows to a rural area are directly or indirectly involved in non-agricultural activity.

Urbanization

The influence of urbanization may enter in two ways: firstly, through the non-farm 'supply side', in providing location and productive support to rural employment off the farm. In a few cases, non-farm employees enumerated in rural areas may physically commute to workplaces in nearby towns. We see from Table 1 that the share of small towns in district urban population acts favourably upon the magnitude and share of rural non-farm employment, suggesting at least a limited rural–urban complementarity. Another avenue of the urban sector's influence on the non-farm subsector is through the demand for the product of non-farm activity: depending upon the nature of the urban place hierarchy and extent of the spatial integration of markets, small towns or large cities may provide either marketing opportunities or price/product competition for rural non-agricultural 'exports'. We will pursue this question further in Section IV.

Agglomeration

This influence, seeking to capture external scale economies, is hypothesized as operating largely on the production side in manufacturing activities. It is hypothesized that benefits from regional industrialization at large confer broad localization benefits on similar activity in rural areas, as greater ease of technology transfer, input availability, and business sophistication make all employed resources more productive, thus creating a derived demand for labour in non-farm activity. The hypothesis is strongly and consistently borne out, as can be seen in Table 1, where the agglomeration proxy used is the incidence of overall district employment in factories. Analogous coefficients may, however, be differently interpreted in their effects on the levels and shares of employment for rural activities such as trade, transport and services, where they are likely to reflect scale economies or diseconomies in distribution as well as in production. Appropriately different proxies will be utilized, to that end, for studying the influence on these subsectors in the disaggregated analysis that follows shortly.

Infrastructure

Like agglomeration effects, rural infrastructure is a hypothesized regional influence upon the magnitude of non-farm employment that is presumed to be operating through the production or product supply side. Our first choice as a proxy for this variable was the village electrification rate, as an instance of a productive infrastructural input. Somewhat unexpectedly, this variable was observed to impinge negatively upon non-farm employment share and incidence, leading to the speculation that infrastructural investment in rural areas often serves to enhance agriculture's position vis-à-vis the former. That it shows up with a positive — and significant — coefficient in respect of the density regression, demonstrates, however, that it is far from counterproductive to the rural non-farm component.

Physical Capital

As noted earlier, this category was not altogether satisfactory in terms of data availability, as data on private capital employed in rural non-farm activity are virtually non-existent. Census data on physical buildings were therefore used as regional proxies, but even so, information on worksite area or structural quality are lacking. In the regressions of Table 1, the hypothesis that the share of rural census residences that doubled as shops or workshops would be an indicator of the capacity of the household sector in particular to generate aggregate non-agricultural employment was strongly supported in all cases. It should be interesting to note how this variable behaves when we disaggregate combined non-farm employment into its industry components in Table 2.

Credit

This is a potentially powerful explanatory variable, that should, in principle, permit discussion of the development and employment effects of credit. Unfortunately, most of the commercial bank interventions in rural credit took place during the decade of the Seventies, and are therefore not coterminous with the period of the dependent variable. Thus, only co-operative credit for non-agricultural purposes is utilized here as a proxy, although there is some question as to whether it is not ultimately farm-related. The coefficient turns out to be negative—though insignificant — for share and incidence, and mildly positive —and insignificant — for density, somewhat corroborating this contention.

Government Policy

The purpose of this category is to enable investigation of the effects of government policy, whether through broad developmental expenditure, selection for subsidization or other preferential treatment. To the extent that district community development expenditure represents a measurement of the government's commitment in assisting the rural region, a positive sign is expected on its coefficient; if instead it reflects a greater overall developmental need (or indeed, for the share regression, a bias in favour of agriculture) a negative sign will be observed. As it happens, the coefficient is consistently positive but non-significant in the regressions of Table 1. We will return to the effects of government expenditure on the *growth* of rural non-farm employment in the dynamic analysis reported in Table 3.

IV. Industry-wise Regressions

Next, we perform industry-wise regressions on the one-digit industrial subcomponents of the non-farm sector. The non-farm sector is far from homogeneous, and inferences from the aggregate may well obscure some important intersectoral differences. The disaggregation of this section will enable tests of industry-specific hypotheses, by using different explanatory variables when deemed necessary. For this reason, we interpret Table 2 — which presents the results of regressions for the rural employment shares of six separate non-farm *NIC* categories — industry by industry.

Manufacturing, Processing, Servicing and Repairs (NIC 2, 3)

The strong consumption linkage suggests vigorous rural demand for the product of non-farm industry. The employment effect on rural industry through agricultural processing activities was sought to be traced via the share of area under non-food crops in total district area under crops, but evidence of production linkages appears poor, with a coefficient on the variable that is actually negative. Thus, either rural agroprocessing opportunities have been underutilized, or have negligible employment effects. Overall employment in this industry does not seem to be drawing on a net addition to the labour force (for either 'push' or 'pull' reasons), nor are in-migrants important to its broad share. As expected, a high overall level of district urbanization is inimical to rural manufacturing, presumably due to the comparative advantages of urban manufacture, but positive localization effects appear to confer employment benefits to rural areas situated in highly industrialized districts. The infrastructure component heavily favouring rural manufacturing seems to be village access roads, and of various physical capital proxies experimented with (see bottom of Table 2), the one suggesting a preponderance of household industry is most significant. It will be interesting to compare these effects with those found in Section V, where we further decompose total employment in *NIC* 2 and 3 into household/non-household and fuel-usage categories, as well as employment classes by establishment size.

Construction (NIC 5)

Again, consumption linkages are strong, suggesting an income-elastic demand for residential housing. The agglomeration proxy suggests that high population density by itself does not seem to contribute significantly to such building activity. (It is likely that construction of houses for the rural poor is largely undertaken by the households themselves or through community effort.) Again, direct linkages with agricultural production appear weak. The influence of the physical capital variable denoting the percentage of rural census houses used as shops is, however, strong, pointing to significant business demand for construction from those quarters. We believed there might be high construction demand associated with building infrastructural facilities, but apparently it does not lead to sustained local employment in this industry. The coefficients on the labour and migration variables confirm the suspicion that workers

Table 3: Urban and Rural Non-farm Employment by Industry

n = 25 *Independent Variables*	*Dependent Variables* *Means*	Δ*N*1 55.69	Δ*N*2, 3 53.72	Δ*N*2, 3*H* 9.27	Δ*N*2, 3*NH* 273.82	Δ*N*5 137.08	Δ*N*6 73.37	Δ*N*7 107.11
Δ*LFPR*	4.0347	1.2722	0.8964	–0.5453	–89.6998‡	–32.2601*	3.6768†	4.2764
		(0.816)	(0.423)	(–0.184)	(–1.718)	(–2.790)	(2.147)	(1.193)
Δ*LAB/AGR*	–3.0022	–2.9845†	–4.973*	–1.4739	–99.3156†	–2.3674	–0.3839	–7.9202†
		(–2.542)	(–3.114)	(–0.625)	(–2.275)	(–0.258)	(–0.285)	(–2.719)
Δ*RURPOP*	9.6180	1.6219	2.802‡	4.1907†	39.3657*	0.1632	0.0115	0.4531
		(1.517)	(1.926)	(2.132)	(3.041)	(0.023)	(0.010)	(0.181)
Δ*URB*	2.8920	1.9312	1.0617	1.0665*	31.7446*	2.9726‡	–0.5494‡	1.6503†
		(1.659)	(0.670)	(3.118)	(3.080)	(1.800)	(–2.020)	(2.440)
Δ*INFRA*	852.6168	0.0440†	0.0579†	0.8353‡	1.8827†	0.3940†	–0.0426†	1.0475†
		(2.319)	(2.242)	(1.699)	(2.553)	(2.685)	(–2.362)	(2.092)
Δ*GPOL*	25.8804	0.1801	0.1369	0.4451	–18.8405*	–1.6490	–0.0002	0.0273
		(0.967)	(0.540)	(1.288)	(–2.853)	(–1.391)	(–0.001)	(0.067)
Constant	1.0000	–21.7526	–47.7179	–88.8481*	–229.4878	178.7747	104.6885*	8.8763
		(–1.031)	(–1.663)	(–2.838)	(–0.853)	(0.119)	(0.119)	(0.211)
R-squared		0.5785	0.5734	0.7127	0.5869	0.4854	0.4185	0.6756

Notes: Figures in parentheses are t-values.
* = 1 per cent; † = 5 per cent; ‡ = 10 per cent significance levels in a two-tailed test.

Dependent variables:

$\Delta N1$	Growth rate of aggregate rural employment in activities other than cultivation, 1971–81 (per cent).
$\Delta N2, 3$	Growth rate of employment in total *NIC* 2 and 3 (process, servicing and repairs), 1971–81 (per cent).
$\Delta N2, 3H$	Growth rate of employment in household *NIC* 2 and 3, 1971–81 (per cent).
$\Delta N2, 3NH$	Growth rate of employment in non-household *NIC* 2 and 3, 1971–81 (per cent).
$\Delta N5$	Growth rate of employment in *NIC* 5 (construction), 1971–81 (per cent).
$\Delta N6$	Growth rate of employment in *NIC* 6 (wholesale and retail trade, restaurants and hotels), 1971–81 (per cent).
$\Delta N7$	Growth rate of employment in *NIC* 7 (transport, communication and storage), 1971–81 (per cent).

Independent variables:

$\Delta LFPR$	Change in rural labour force participation (by main activity) rate, 1971–81.
$\Delta LAB/AGR$	Change in share of labourers in total agricultural workers, 1971–81.
$\Delta RURPOP$	Rate of male in-migration to rural district (percentage) (rate of net male out-migration from district for non-household 2 and 3 industry).
$\Delta GPOL$	Percentage change in level of per capita district government (zilla parishad) expenditures, 1967–74 to 1974–80.
ΔURB	Change in district per cent urban, 1971–81, for aggregate non-farm and total *NIC* 2 and 3 industry; for *NIC* 2 and 3 (household). growth rate of population in Class III towns; for *NIC* 5 and 6, growth rate of population in Class IV towns; for *NIC* 2 and 3 (non-household) and *NIC* 7, growth rate of population of small (Classes IV, V and VI) towns (per cent).
$\Delta INFRA$	Change in infrastructure, proxied by state government development expenditure, per (rural) capita, 1974–75 to 1982–83: for aggregate non-farm, total *NIC* 2 and 3 and *NIC* 6, plan and non-plan expenditure per capita (Rs); for *NIC* 7, non-plan expenditure per capita on agriculture and allied activities (Rs); for *NIC* 2 and 3 (household), expenditure per capita on incentive packages for industry (Rs); for *NIC* 2 and 3 (non-household) and *NIC* 5, expenditure per capita on major irrigation projects (Rs).

in this industry are drawn either from migrant streams, or may be casually supplied to the activity (and enumerated at the time) through increased workforce participation, particularly by women.

Wholesale and Retail Trade, Restaurants and Hotels (NIC 6)

The trade component of this category is expected to be dominated by marketing functions related to agricultural activity. Accordingly, the production linkages with the latter are positive and strong, particularly with respect to the importance of food crops. Somewhat to our surprise, none of the rural physical capital proxies were very successful in establishing complementarity with this activity, the proportion of houses used as shops/workshops actually exhibiting a significantly negative association, suggesting that a large part of this activity may be in the 'non-household' sector. Hypothesizing that such operations might be associated with small towns or large villages in particular, we examined employment variations with the respective shares of these in urban and rural district population, but with no great success. Very likely, since economies of scale differ as between wholesale and retail trade — which are clubbed together under this category — their separate effects may be cancelling out. Not surprisingly, the share of in-migrants in rural population raises the share of traders (and restaurateurs) in rural employment. General infrastructure investments seem to boost employment in trade activities, as one might suspect that road building or market site construction would. Unexpectedly, credit extended by non-agricultural societies is negatively associated with the incidence of trade. Possibly, activities of co-operatives undermine local private trading; we shall pursue this later.

Transport, Storage and Communication (NIC 7)

Like the category above, this too is a mixed aggregate. We expect the transport and storage components to be closely agriculture-related; however, production linkages are empirically weak, possibly because we work with value, and not tonnage, or because of large traders (public or private) maintaining their own means of transport. The consumption linkage is strong, however, and one inference is that we are seeing in this employment category a reflection of the income-elastic demand for travel by people. A rural density variable significantly adds to the employment share of this industrial category, and the negative and significant coefficient on composite village infrastructure indicates that the lower the percentage of villages served, more travel to avail of public services such as post and telegraph, education and medical facilities will be necessitated. Likewise, in-migration appears to be important to this sector, perhaps adding long distance to local travel needs.

Financing, Insurance, Real Estate and Business Services (NIC 8)

Here again, strong agricultural sector linkages are hypothesized. The proxies selected to capture these are land and credit usage in agriculture.[8] Notably, the smaller the average size of holdings — or the greater their number — the greater the demand for real estate or financial services. Presumably, these functions – especially credit — are internalized to a greater degree with large landholdings. We classified the average borrowing per member of the local agricultural credit and multipurpose societies as a production proxy because of the possible forward linkage with agriculture. The more heavy the borrowing, the more the employment created in this sector. This choice of variable, however, probably neutralizes any effect our credit proxy — average borrowing per non-agricultural credit society — may have, reflecting the ultimate fungibility between rural credit types. Infrastructure and agglomeration are other factors that tend to boost this category's employment share, the latter presumably through the business services component allied with its urban counterparts.

Community, Social and Personal Services (NIC 9)

As expected, the demand for personal services, which is almost wholly local, is reflected in strong rural income or consumption linkages with employment in this category. A large part of this demand must be serviced by household establishments, as evidenced by the positive coefficient on the physical capital measure thought to capture the incidence of household activity. There are two recognizable components to this category, however, viz., private and public, and the latter probably dominates many of the regional explanatory variables. For example, the government policy variable chosen, viz., the 'backward' district dummy is positively associated with employment in this category, as presumably such districts command a greater commitment of public resources. We believe the greater the dispersal of the rural population, the more the social and community workers that are needed due to absence of scale economies in rural service delivery. This is borne out by a significantly positive coefficient on the share of small villages in rural population. We attempt to measure the influence of government expenditure at the village level, but this seems not to make any appreciable contribution to the overall category's employment share.

Lastly, we may summarize in brief the behaviour of the 'backward district' dummy across the various industrial classes. Industrial backwardness is associated with lower employment shares for manufacturing and construction, but higher shares for trade, transport, and business services, which we believe to have stronger overall linkages with agriculture. This is consistent with the criteria used in the industrial backwardness definition.

V. Dynamic Estimations

The foregoing exercises were aimed at investigating influences bearing upon the level or share of non-agricultural employment (and its industrial components) in total rural employment. We now turn to the task of attempting to explain the changes that occurred in such employment over the 1971–81 decade for the districts of Maharashtra.

The regression exercise on determinants of rural non-farm employment levels is in two parts for the following reason: The estimations just reported, based on 1971 data, sought to capture reasons behind 'spontaneous' inter-regional variations in shares and levels of non-farm in total rural activity before many of the major policy interventions of the seventies targeting (to some degree) this subsector went into effect. We complement this with an investigation of the changes between 1971 and 1981 in order to measure the impact of such interventions, as also to impart a measure of dynamism to the empirical analysis.

The method used for the dynamic exercise is also that of linear regression on cross-sectional variations in data with the district as the regional unit, the chief difference being that the relevant variables, both dependent and independent, appear in the form of decadal growth rates. Also, some explanatory variables are dropped to sharpen the focus on key labour market and public policy questions.

The static equation (8) of Section II is accordingly modified to the specification of equation (9) below:

$$\mathrm{gr}N = b_0 + b_1(\mathrm{gr}L_w) + b_2(\mathrm{gr}L_c) + b_3 M + b_4(\mathrm{gr}U) + b_5(\mathrm{gr}I) + b_6(\mathrm{gr}G). \quad (9)$$

The first three explanatory variables all pertain to the regional labour market. (grL_w) denotes growth in overall rural labour force participation and (grL_c) proxies changes in the composition of the agricultural workforce as between labourers and cultivators. *M*, as before, is expected to capture changes in aggregate rural district population due to (male) in-migration or out-migration (gr*U*) attempts to trace the influence of changes either in overall per cent urban district population or growth rates of towns in its constituent size classes, where care has been taken to preserve the members of each size class as classified in 1971. The change in rural infrastructure has been proxied by per capita rates of state government (developmental) investment expenditures incurred during the period, while changes in rates of zilla parishad spending approximate public assistance at that level.

There has been change in the concept of 'worker' resulting from the change in reference period between the 1971 and 1981 Population Censuses. In the case of the 1981 Population Census a uniform reference period was prescribed for both seasonal and non-seasonal work. It was the period of one year preceding the date of enumeration of the individual. If a worker had put in work for six months or more, i.e. for 183 days or more prior to that date, he was classified as 'main worker', and if for less than 183 days, as 'marginal worker'. The concept of marginal worker (1981) is comparable with that of non-worker having secondary work (1971), but is not coterminous. This statistical blurring may not, however, be systematically different across districts, and should, hopefully, not seriously affect a comparative change analysis confined to main workers in the non-agricultural sector.

Again, estimations are in respect of aggregate growth rates, as well as those in the component industrial categories. Employment in *NIC* 2 and 3 has been split up into its household and non-household components. By contrast with the static exercise, *NIC* 8 and *NIC* 9 have been omitted from consideration because of data incompatibility.

The categorization of single-digit industrial divisions followed in the 1971 Population Census was slightly altered in the 1981 Population Census. Divisions 4, 8 and 9 relating to the non-agricultural categories — electricity, gas and water; financial, insurance, real estate and business services; and community, social and personal services — are clubbed together as 'other services', in Category IX. An additional category of 'marginal workers' appears, as described above. For the purpose of the dynamic exercise, we have, therefore, used only comparable categories at the single-digit industry levels.

Results of the regression estimations of equation (9) are presented in Table 3. We discuss the performance of the labour market variables first, and then take up the urbanization, infrastructure and government expenditure variables.

Labour

Labour force participation in rural areas of districts grew by an average of 4.03 per cent over 1971–81. This growth was positively associated with growth in the trade and the transport, storage, etc., industries. By contrast, such growth was negatively (and significantly) associated with growth in non-household manufacturing and construction. This suggests that manufacturing and construction grew most in those districts where rates of participation were already high and could not rise much further. Another implication is that additional employment in these industries comes from transfers out of agriculture rather than net increases in rural employment rates. Employment growth also appears, in overall manufacturing — and in its household component — to be positively associated with changes in rural population due to in-migration.

There seems to have been an average decline in the share of labourers (by main activity) in total agricultural workers over the 1971–81 decade. The greater the decline, the lower, on average, the algebraic value of this variable, and the correspondingly higher the increase in non-farm employment. This seems true for the aggregate non-farm category, non-household manufacturing and transport, with the relationship not significant for household manufacturing, construction or trade.

Inferences about the labour market are difficult from the above results. A caveat may be in order regarding possible multicollinearity between the labour proxies. In general, though, it appears that agricultural labourers may have moved significantly into non-farm activity, their place possibly taken by rural in-migrants. Remarkably, non-household manufacturing seems to have received a much stronger boost than household, suggesting perhaps, that such a move represents a step up rather than the pauperization alleged. Non-household manufacturing enterprises, whether public or private, presumably constitute a 'formal' non-farm sector, which one would expect to provide job opportunities evaluated as superior to full-time farm labour. The positive and significant association of employment increases in non-household manufacturing with the net rate of male out-migration is in contrast to the positive association with in-migration of growth in the household manufacturing category; in other words, non-household industry grew in rural areas where out-migration rates were also high. Possibly, out-migration to urban areas is preferred over local non-farm employment in non-household manufacturing, which in turn is preferred over household manufacturing, which is preferred to wage work in agriculture, but wage data and micro level studies of occupational choice are needed to confirm or revise popular perceptions of labour market segmentation and the rural employment hierarchy.

Urbanization

Growth of aggregate non-farm and total employment in *NIC* 2 and 3 is positively associated with the change in district per cent urban over the decade, suggesting that the process of transition of the rural workforce to non-farm activities is part and parcel of the structural transformation of which urbanization is a manifestation. Regarding effects on the sector of growth in particular urban size classes, it is seen that employment growth in household manufacturing is affected favourably by the growth of Class III towns (population 20,000–49,999); that in construction by the growth of Class IV towns (population 10,000–19,999), and employment in non-household manufacturing and transport, etc., by the growth of small towns (population 10,000 and below), which may include locations at the fringes of more major urban areas. While the latter connection is presumably one of actual location, the former probably reflect demand-driven market relationships. If so, only trade and commerce appear to be threatened by the growth of Class IV towns, which are likely to supplant village-based operations for similar activities on a more efficient scale.

Government Expenditures

Per capita state government development expenditure, presumed to partially reflect increments to public infrastructure, is responsible for growth in aggregate non-farm, manufacturing and trade employment. Of the expenditure categories, growth in household manufacturing appears related to expenditures per capita on incentive packages for industry, that in transport, expectedly, to expenditures on agriculture and allied activities, and that in construction to spending on major irrigation projects. Remarkably, non-household manufacturing appears to be particularly benefited by such projects also, probably reflecting the results of consumption-driven demand multipliers.

The negative response of trade, etc., to overall developmental expenditures is interesting. Our belief is that while the 1971 levels (and shares) of employment in various non-farm categories reflect the result of natural market forces, the increase over the 1971–81 decade in at least some of the categories is due to a variety of government development policy interventions in both industry as well as agriculture. It is interesting to speculate that the latter may have contributed to the slowdown in private trading that is apparent here.

Lastly, growth in zilla parishad or district government expenditure has a generally non-significant effect on overall non-farm employment growth or that in most of its categories, with the exception of a strong negative association with growth in non-household manufacturing. The latter may reflect the concentration of such expenditures on districts having the greatest need, that is, where the least spontaneous industrial expansion tends to take place. While this is consistent, again, with the industrially backward classification, it is no great testimony to the success of industrial development incentives.

VI. Conclusions

The contribution envisaged for this paper to the study of the non-farm sector has been primarily one of offering a paradigm to examine the substantive issues relating to rural non-farm employment in a regional framework that explicitly recognizes the role of sectoral and spatial dimensions in affecting rural labour market flows. We feel the exercise to have been fairly successful in delineating the broad strokes of that framework, and in documenting the roles of the hypothesized influences in a manner usually consistent with theoretical predictions. Where theory was ambiguous or absent, several substantive insights have been gained, we feel, for future, more specific, theorizing.

We recognize the limitations of the recursive estimation. The true utility of an aggregative regional formulation lies in accounting for the full range of endogenous and interdependent economic influences that constitute the macro framework. Lack of data has forced us to accept as exogenous several influences that are manifestly endogenous to the level and growth of employment in the non-farm sector — specifically, agricultural output and incomes, rural labour force rates and occupational structure, in-migration and out-migration. Implementation of a simultaneous estimation of the structural rather than reduced form version of the model on a dataset capable of supporting it is the next logical step to verifying the causal nature of the relationships and validating them as beyond mere empirical associations.

At the aggregate level, formulating dynamic price-endogenous, general equilibrium models might take one even further. Analytically complex, such models may be 'solved' computationally, combining econometric estimation with simulation techniques, to overcome sparse data availability. A few such exercises have been attempted for India,[9] but there is need for one that makes the rural non-farm sector the centrepiece of its design. Such aggregative approaches are best complemented by behaviourally based microeconomic studies, e.g., of non-farm production structures and spatial consumption patterns, and of occupational choice and migration, preferably with household- and establishment-level data. A challenging research agenda awaits.

NOTES

Reproduced from *Economic and Political Weekly*, 9 November 1991. The original version of this paper was submitted at Seminar sponsored by the Indian Society of Agricultural Economics and Gujarat Institute of Development Research on 29-31March 1989 at Ahmedabad, India. A revised version was published in Pravin Visaria and Rakesh Basant (eds) (1994), *Non-Agricultural Employment in India: Trends and Prospects*, Sage Publications India Pvt Ltd., New Delhi.

Research on this paper was done as part of a larger study, 'Rural Non-Farm Activity in Economic Development—Spatial Determinants, Issues and Policy'. The author is indebted to Tara Shukla for the motivation to think about the problem, to the participants of the March 1989 ISAE–GIAP workshop, where a preliminary version was presented, and to the helpful comments of Pravin Visaria and an anonymous reviewer, which led to many improvements in its present form.

1 Theoretical perspectives on aggregative interrelationships in a dynamic two-sector framework include Uma Lele and John Mellor, 'Technological Change, Distributive Bias and Labour Transfer in a Two-Sector Economy', *Oxford Economic Papers,* Vol. 33(3), November 1981. An estimation-simulation model of the Japanese economy appears in Yair Mundlak, *Intersectoral Factor Mobility and Agricultural Growth*, Research Report 6, International Food Policy Research Institute, Washington, D.C., February 1979. As examples of studies exploring the spatial microfoundations of these macro sectoral linkages, see Robert P. King and Derek Byerlee, 'Factor Intensities and Locational Linkages of Rural Consumption Patterns in Sierra Leone', *American Journal of Agricultural Economics*, Vol. 60, May 1978, and C.S. Ahammed and R.W. Herdt, 'Measuring the Impact of Consumption

Linkages on the Employment Effects of Mechanisation in Philippine Rice Production', *Journal of Development Studies*, January 1984.

2 The terms 'non-farm' and 'non-agricultural' have been used interchangeably in the text. They include workers involved in rural economic pursuits other than agriculture and allied agricultural activities. In other words, the terms relate to National Industrial Classification Categories 2 and 3, and 5–9.

3 Data sources used include: Government of India, *Population Census of India*, 1971, 1981; Government of Maharashtra, *Statistical Abstract of Maharashtra State*, various years; Government of Maharashtra, *Report of the Fact-finding Committee on Regional Imbalances in Maharashtra*, 1984; Centre for Monitoring Indian Economy, *District Level Data*, various years, and tables. Detailed information on sources of specific variables used in the econometric exercises has been suppressed in the interests of brevity, but is available upon request from the author.

4 We acknowledge the potential problems of strict comparability between the 1971 and 1981 census data on workers, which should be borne in mind while interpreting the results. For example, main workers in the rural population stood at 38.59 per cent in 1971 and 42.69 per cent in 1981 for Maharashtra. Non-workers having secondary work constituted 0.86 per cent of the rural population in 1971, whereas marginal workers formed 5.46 per cent of the rural population in 1981. Against this, non-workers constituted 59 per cent and 52 per cent of the rural population in 1971 and 1981, respectively. The increase in main workers between 1971 and 1981 has been 32 per cent, whereas that in secondary non-workers/marginal workers was 183 per cent. This suggests that possibly some of the categories of workers enumerated as main workers in 1971 were reclassified as marginal workers in 1981, as were some of the non-workers having secondary work in 1971.

The cross-sectional exercises are, of course, unaffected by these definitional problems. In the 1971–81 comparative change exercise, we feel their impact on the magnitudes of the estimated coefficients is likely to be minimized by virtue of our use of main workers only in the major non-agricultural categories. Alternatively, it has been suggested that comparisons confined to male workers only would largely mitigate these problems.

5 These three different measurement concepts, while each serves an econometric normalization function, lend themselves to distinct interpretations: the first focuses on the importance of non-agricultural relative to agricultural employment, the second on the general population's sustainability of non-farm activity, and the third relates to the spatial intensity of such pursuits.

6 The value of crop output per agricultural worker could, alternatively, have been used as a consumption proxy. However, agricultural production in Maharashtra has been characterized by considerable instability over the seventies (see, for example, S. Mahendra Dev, 'Growth and Instability in Foodgrains Production: An Interstate Analysis', *Economic and Political Weekly*, 26 September 1987). By contrast, the proxy we select, though imperfect, contains fewer distortions.

7 This is not to deny that we recognize the substantial heterogeneity and segmentation which characterize labour supply and market outcomes in rural

India. That, however, is a topic for a much more data-intensive formulation than this, and best addressed in micro studies of occupational choice.

8 The proxy used for capital involves a stock concept. The flows of financial capital from agricultural to non-agricultural activities are captured therein, inasmuch as they are capitalized and get reflected in physical assets.

9 Computable general equilibrium models with spatial and sectoral focus for India include Charles M. Becker, Edwin S. Mills, and Jeffrey G. Williamson, 'Dynamics of Rural–Urban Migration in India: 1960–81', *Indian Journal of Quantitative Economics*, Vol. 11, No 1, 1986.

11 / Rural Non-farm Employment in India: Issues and Policy

VIBHOOTI SHUKLA

I. Introduction

The rural non-farm sector in India has attracted attention[1] in recent years as performing an increasingly significant rural income augmentation function. A popular view, focusing upon the expansion of employment in non-farm activities, sees it as a residual or 'sponge' sector fed by a secular pauperization of the rural population, and would target it as the focus for rural anti-poverty programmes. Although such measures may well turn out to be warranted, it seems that a broader perspective than is usually appealed to in this context might be brought to bear upon a component of the economy having undeniable functional links with its other counterparts. These links ensure that not one but several different development policies are likely to impact it.

The rural non-farm sector is expected to feature accordingly in sectoral policy debates regarding 'immiserizing' agricultural growth and calls for the rapid diversification of rural economic activities away from agriculture, as well as in those relating to the consequences of the alleged 'urban bias', and the perceived need for industrial dispersal. More broadly, however, the sector can play a critical role in matters of economy-wide growth and distribution. It is now generally recognized that increased labour absorption in agricultural and allied pursuits cannot be expected to contribute significantly to providing employment for the rapidly growing rural labour force. Equally, it is physically impossible that the structural transformation which accompanies economic development will be articulated through massive movement to the cities. Whereas eventually the widespread urbanization of portions of presently rural areas is inevitable, the process is likely to take the intermediate form of substantial local labour absorption within the small urban and rural non-agricultural sectors. Clearly, in view of the nature of its ties, the study of the rural non-farm sector is best undertaken in a multisectoral (rather than sector-specific) setting with an explicitly recognized spatial (rather than aspatial) dimension.

We attempted, in an earlier paper,[2] to formulate an estimable model of rural non-farm employment that took account of these various intersectoral and interspatial relationships. With the help of this we performed a series of exploratory regression analyses, using spatial and sectoral aggregates, of employment in various types of rural non-agricultural activity in the districts of Maharashtra, with a view to discovering its regional determinants. With 26 districts for which comparable comprehensive and reliable data are available, Maharashtra provides, in our opinion, a good setting for a regional study. There is sufficient variability as to levels and patterns of industrial and agricultural development, urbanization and migration patterns, and the distribution of social and productive infrastructure. In many ways this reflects variability in economic conditions throughout India, making the Maharashtra case, we hope, somewhat of a representative one, with transferable implications to regions in the rest of the country.

The model and empirical methodology used are briefly sketched in Section II. Section III presents the main hypotheses and summarizes the preliminary results. Section IV conducts more detailed investigation of selected issues within the same framework, and Section V derives public policy implications from the exercise. Section VI recapitulates and concludes.

II. Empirical Model of Rural Non-farm Employment

The model presented below is envisaged as a rough framework within which some of the questions raised above can be analytically set and empirically explored. While implemented in a positive spirit in the earlier paper, its application in this one is somewhat more normatively oriented towards policy issues.

The level of rural non-farm employment, N, is determined jointly by N^D, the demand for and N^S, the supply of such labour to that sector. On the supply side, labour availability characteristics such as rates of overall labour force participation, age and educational distribution of the rural population, or rates of in-migration to and out-migration from the rural area will serve to determine the size of the labour pool available for employment in the non-farm sector. For instance, in-migration may augment, and out-migration, deplete, this pool.

Demand for labour in non-farm activities comes from enterprises (own-account or establishment) and is both derived from the demand, Y^D, (local and urban) for the output of this sector, as well as conditioned by factors (inputs, costs, the productive environment) governing its production and supply, Y^S. Local demand for the output of non-farm activity is articulated through rural consumption linkages, depending largely upon agricultural income and its distribution; regional urban areas may provide either markets or competition for this output, depending in many cases, on the nature of the product.

Non-farm production processes utilize purchased and non-purchased inputs: local availability and use of agricultural raw material will reflect the strength of production linkages with that sector. Supply of the product of non-farm industry will also depend upon physical or financial capital available to that sector, which, given the capital's substitutability or complementarity with labour will likewise affect labour demand. Availability of non-purchased or subsidized inputs in the form of infrastructure or government developmental assistance might also presumably constitute a positive (labour) demand-side influence on rural non-farm employment, as might the operation of productivity-enhancing external economies of scale due to the spatial agglomeration of population or economic activity within regions.

The Model

Rural non-farm employment:

$$N = f(N^S(\cdot), N^D(\cdot)) \tag{1}$$

Labour supply to non-farm sector:

$$N^S = g(L, M) \tag{2}$$

Demand for rural non-farm labour:

$$N^D = h(Y^D(\cdot), Y^S(\cdot)) \tag{3}$$

Demand for rural industry output:

$$Y^D = j(C, U) \tag{4}$$

Supply of rural industry output:

$$Y^S = k(R(\cdot), S(\cdot), A) \tag{5}$$

Raw material input in rural industry:

$$R = l(P) \tag{6}$$

Other inputs in non-farm enterprise:

$$S = m(I, K, B, G) \tag{7}$$

Exogenous Variables

C : rural consumption of output of non-farm activity

P : agricultural product used as input in non-farm activity
L : regional labour availability level
M : labour flows into and out of rural areas
U : urbanization characteristics of the region
A : regional agglomeration characteristics
I : level of rural infrastructure
K : measure of physical capital used in rural non-farm activity
B : credit availability to rural non-agricultural enterprise
G : incidence of government policy affecting non-farm employment

Estimating Equations

Dependent Variable: 1971 Rural Share, Incidence or Density of N:

$$N = b_0 + b_1 C + b_2 P + b_3 L + b_4 M + b_5 U + b_6 A + b_7 I + b_8 K + b_9 B + b_{10} G \quad (8)$$

Dependent Variable: Growth Rate of N, 1971–81:

$$\mathrm{gr}N = b_0 + b_1 (\mathrm{gr}L_w) + b_2 (\mathrm{gr}L_c) + b_3 M + b_4 (\mathrm{gr}U) + b_5 (\mathrm{gr}I) + b6 (\mathrm{gr}G) \quad (9)$$

The seven-equation structural model above may be reduced in linear form to yield the single equation (8), amenable to estimation by ordinary least squares.[3] Similarly, a 'dynamic' exercise can be performed with the help of linear regression on cross-sectional variations in data with the relevant dependent and independent variables cast in the form of decadal growth rates.[4] The static equation (8) is accordingly modified to (9). Also, some explanatory variables are dropped to sharpen the focus on key labour market and policy questions.

The first three explanatory variables in equation (9) all pertain to the regional labour market; ($\mathrm{gr}L_w$) denotes growth in overall rural labour force participation; and ($\mathrm{gr}L_c$) proxies changes in the composition of the agricultural workforce as between labourers and cultivators. M, as before, is expected to capture changes in aggregate rural district population due to (male) in-migration or out-migration; ($\mathrm{gr}U$) attempts to trace the influence of changes either in overall per cent urban district population or growth rates of towns in its constituent size classes, where care has been taken to preserve the members of each size class as classified in 1971. The change in rural infrastructure has been proxied by per capita rates of state government (developmental) investment expenditures incurred during the period, while changes in rates of zilla parishad spending approximate public assistance at that level.[5]

III. Summary of Results of Earlier Estimations

As a point of departure for the more detailed investigations proposed in this paper, we summarize — variable by variable — the broad hypotheses and principal results from the preliminary results of the exercises reported in our earlier paper.

Consumption: This variable, in principle, is presumed to capture the effects of local consumption linkages on the demand for the product of non-farm activity, and thence upon aggregate employment in that sector. With net sown area per agricultural worker (ha) as the proxy for average rural farm income — and consumption — the coefficient for the variable is positive and significant — and of consistently high magnitude, implying strong spatial consumption linkages between the agricultural and non-agricultural rural subsectors.

Production: By contrast, the local input linkages of agriculture with non-farm employment are sought to be investigated with this variable. What is being tested is the hypothesized importance of agroprocessing in manufacturing, or of trade in agricultural commodities in generating employment off the farm. In the aggregate, the performance of the measure, output value of major crops per hectare of net sown area, seems mixed, with the effects showing up significantly in increased non-farm employment density, but not in share.

Labour: The purpose of this conceptual category is to capture the effects of labour supply or availability, and ultimately shed light on the validity of the 'labour push' argument in explaining regional non-farm employment. At first, only a comprehensive measure, the labour force participation rate — for the district at large — is used to measure general labour availability and its influence on the share, incidence and density of rural non-farm employment. Since the coefficient of this variable in the share or incidence regressions is not significant, the conjecture is unresolved at this stage, but we shall return to the issue.

Migration: It was desired to focus, in addition, on another component of labour supply to a region, viz., in-migration, and investigate the extent to which out-migration and non-farm employment were competing options for the (male) rural population. Somewhat to our surprise, we found that the in-migration variable showed consistently positive and highly significant effects on the share of non-farm in total rural employment. The success of this variable — percentage of rural population not born locally — leads one to speculate that labour inflows to a rural area are directly or indirectly involved in non-agricultural activity.

Urbanization: The influence of urbanization may enter in two ways: first, through the non-farm 'supply side', in providing location and productive support to rural employment off the farm. In a few cases, non-farm employees enumerated in rural areas may physically commute to workplaces in nearby towns. We found that the share of small towns in district urban population acts favourably upon the magnitude and share of rural non-farm employment, suggesting at least a limited rural–urban complementarity. Another avenue of the urban sector's influence on the non-farm subsector is through the demand for the product of non-farm activity: depending upon the nature of the urban place hierarchy and extent of the spatial integration of markets, small towns or large cities may provide either marketing opportunities or price/product competition for rural non-agricultural 'exports'. We will pursue this question further in Section IV.

Agglomeration: This spatial influence, seeking to capture external scale economies, is hypothesized as operating largely on the production side in manufacturing activities. It is hypothesized that benefits from regional industrialization at large confer broad localization benefits on similar activity in rural areas, as greater ease of technology transfer, input availability, and business sophistication make all employed resources more productive, thus creating a derived demand for labour in non-farm activity. The hypothesis is strongly and consistently borne out, where the agglomeration proxy used is the incidence of overall district employment in factories. Appropriately different proxies will be utilized for studying the influence on the manufacturing subsectors in the analysis that follows shortly.

Infrastructure: Like agglomeration effects, rural infrastructure is a hypothesized regional influence upon the magnitude of non-farm employment that is presumed to operate through the production or product supply side. Our first choice as a proxy for this variable was the village electrification rate, as an instance of a productive infrastructural input. Somewhat unexpectedly, this variable was observed to impinge negatively upon non-farm employment share and incidence, leading to the speculation that infrastructural investment in rural areas often serves to enhance agriculture's position vis-a-vis the former. That it shows up with a positive — and significant — coefficient in respect of the non-farm employment density regression, demonstrates, however, that it is far from counterproductive to the rural non-farm component.

Physical Capital: This category was not altogether satisfactory in terms of data availability, as data on private capital employed in rural non-farm activity are virtually non-existent. Census data on physical buildings were therefore used as regional proxies, but even so, information on worksite area or structural quality are lacking. In the earlier regressions, the hypothesis that the share of rural census residences that doubled as shops or workshops would be an indicator of the capacity of the household sector in particular to generate aggregate non-agricultural employment was strongly supported in all cases.

Credit: This is a potentially powerful explanatory variable, that should, in principle, permit discussion of the development and employment effects of credit. Unfortunately, most of the commercial bank interventions in rural credit took place during the seventies, and were therefore not coterminous with the period of the dependent variable. Thus, only co-operative credit for non-agricultural purposes is utilized here as a proxy, although there is some question as to whether it is not ultimately farm-related. The coefficient turns out to be negative — though insignificant — for share and incidence, and mildly positive — and insignificant — for density, somewhat corroborating this contention. We will elaborate on this below.

Government Policy: The purpose of this category is to enable investigation of the effects of government policy, whether through broad developmental expenditure, selection for subsidization or other preferential treatment. District community development expenditure, as it happens, representing a measurement of the government's commitment in assisting the rural region, featured a consistently positive but non-significant coefficient in the earlier regressions. We will return to the effects of government expenditure on the *growth* of rural non-farm employment in the dynamic analysis reported in Section IV.

In the present paper also, regressions (8) and (9) will be used to further explore some of the questions that the previous analysis has raised. However, we attempt to be more specific here in experimenting with variants of the explanatory variables which relate explicitly to issues that have bearing on policy. The next section reports the outcomes of these new regressions. Section V will then summarize their broad policy implications.

IV. Exploration of Selected Non-farm Issues

In this section, we further pursue explorations in respect of specific hypotheses and issues using limited regressions more tailor-made to addressing specific questions. While the paradigmatic framework of the earlier sections is maintained, the discussion is sought to be made more directly policy-related. Often, due to multicollinearity between independent variables, or to focus detailed attention on particular determinants, we will attempt modified specifications with only a subset of the former. A list of data sources appears in the note, and definitions of specific variables used in a particular exercise are appended to each table reporting the relevant results.

Four broad questions are taken up for discussion in this section: (i) How strong are the linkages of the non-farm sector with agriculture and what is their predominant nature? (2) What is the character of the rural labour market insofar as it relates to non-farm employment? (3) What are the salient features of the structure of non-farm industry? (4) What forms of governmental interventions, if any, have had an impact on the size and share of this sector in the rural economy?

Agricultural Linkages

We first investigate the agricultural and labour market linkages of the rural non-farm sector, using only consumption, production, migration and labour force variables. The truncated specification emphasizes the four explanatory variables of importance in the present instance, while minimizing the possibility of multicollinearity as far as possibile. The hypothesis, stated earlier and partially borne out by the full regressions, is that local agricultural linkages matter in explaining and fostering rural non-farm employment, presumably acting through spatial interactions. To focus on their precise nature and relative importance, we explore the effects of alternative consumption and agricultural production proxies on aggregate rural non-farm employment in Tables 1a and 1b. It is sought to infer from the overall relative contributions of the hypothesized consumption and production effects from the income and output variables respectively.

Table 1a presents the results controlling for the effects of regional labour force participation and changes in the rural population (the latter suspected to play a role in agricultural production in a manner to be discussed below) through alternative specifications for the migration variable. Net sown area per agricultural worker (hectares) is the

Table 1: Agricultural Income, Output and Factor Linkages of Rural Non-farm Employment
1a: *Effects of Alternative Migration Specification*

n = 25 *Independent Variable*	*Means*	Ma (14.25)	Mb (14.26)	Mc (14.26)	Md (14.26)	Me (14.26)	Mf (14.26)
C = CI (Consumption)	3.61	3.3106*	2.5757*	3.7496*	2.8856*	2.5390†	2.9072*
		(4.500)	(2.908)	(5.008)	(3.471)	(2.607)	(3.109)
P = PI (Production)	974.64	0.0064*	0.0071*	0.0050*	0.0040†	0.0068*	0.0069*
		(4.585)	(4.061)	(3.553)	(2.087)	(3.5937)	(3.875)
L (Labour)	36.80	1.0174*	0.7417†	0.9626*	0.5375‡	0.5283	0.5695
		(3.511)	(2.126)	(3.484)	(1.736)	(1.436)	(1.677)
M (Migration) § a,b,c,d,e,f	(§§)	0.8486*	0.6293‡	1.6082*	0.1791*	–0.0803	–0.1851‡
		(4.108)	(1.873)	(4.351)	(2.747)	(–0.460)	(–1.700)
Constant	1.00	–49.5306*	–34.0539‡	–42.9077*	–23.3456	–20.1182	–23.5208
		(–13.492)	(–2.010)	(–3.282)	(–1.617)	(–1.170)	(–1.483)
R – squared		0.6853	0.5064	0.7019	0.5787	0.4259	0.4931

Notes: Figures in parentheses are t-values. § Migration variables and §§ (means): Ma = Rate of in-migration (9.6 per cent): Mb = Within-state ‡ in-migration rate (7.5 per cent); Mc = Out-of-state* rate (2.1 per cent); Md = Nonstate/total in-migrants (19.9 per cent); Me = Rate of out-migration (11.5 per cent): Mf = Rate of net out-migration (1.9 per cent).

* = 1 per cent; † = 5 per cent; ‡ = 10 per cent significance levels in a two-tailed test.

Dependent variable: *N* = Share of non-farm in total rural employment (per cent); *L* = Rate of labour force participation for district (per cent).

1b: *Effects of Alternative Consumption and Agricultural Production Proxies*

	Proxies	*Co-efficient Sign*	* = *Significance at (0–10) per cent*
Consumption			
*C*1	Net sown area per agricultural worker, (hectares)	+	*
*C*2	Average size of operational holdings, (hectares)	–	*
*C*3	Share of size group 5–20 ha in total operational holdings (per cent)	–	*
*C*4	Share in size group 20+ ha in total operational holdings (per cent)	+	
*C*5	Share of size group 5–20 ha in total operated area (per cent)	–	*
*C*6	Share of size group 20+ ha in total operated area (per cent)	+	
*C*7	Commercial bank deposit per capita for district (Rs)	+	*
*C*8	Average deposit per member, agricultural credit and multipurpose societies ('000 Rs)	+	
*C*9	Average deposit per member, non-agricultural credit and multipurpose societies ('000 Rs)	+	*
Production			
*P*1	Value of output of major crops per hectare of net sown area (Rs)	+	*
*P*2	Value of output of major crops per capita (Rs)	–	
*P*3	Ratio of area under total food crops to net sown area (per cent)	+	*
*P*4	Ratio of area under sugar crops to total net sown area (per cent)	–	
*P*5	Ratio of area under total oilseeds to total area under crops (per cent)	+	*
*P*6	Ratio of area under total fibre crops to total net sown area (per cent)	–	
*P*7	Ratio of area under all non-food crops to total area under crops (per cent)	–	
*P*8	Average yield of all cereals (kg/ha)	+	
*P*9	Average yield of all cereals and pulses (kg/ha)	+	*
*P*10	Average yield of sugarcane (kg/ha)	–	*
*P*11	Average yield of cotton (kg/ha)	+	
*P*12	Gross irrigated area as percentage of gross cropped area (per cent)	+	*
*P*13	No. of irrigation pumpsets and tubewells energized per 1000 ha net sown area ('000)	–	*
*P*14	Number of tractors per 100 hectares of net sown area (No.)	–	
*P*15	Consumption of NPK fertilizers per hectare of gross cropped area (kg/ha)	+	
*P*16	Per hectare commercial bank credit for agriculture (Rs)	+	
*P*17	Per capita commercial bank credit for agriculture (Rs)	+	
*P*18	Average borrowing per member, agricultural credit societies ('000 Rs)	–	*

consumption variable, $C1$, serving as a rough measure of the average rural purchasing power generated by regional agriculture. Aggregate agricultural output is represented by $P1$, the value of output of the region's major crops per hectare of net sown area. Statistically significant agricultural consumption and production linkages are in evidence, quite consistent across migration specifications. Across all six specifications, the average value of the estimated coefficient on $C1$ is 2.992, that on $P1$ being 0.006. Multiplied by their respective sample means, this implies for consumption an effect on rural non-farm employment share that is almost twice in magnitude than that of production.

Further, we are interested in substituting specific for overall consumption and production proxies to analyse their compositional effects. Accordingly, Table 1b reports the signs and significance of coefficients on selected appropriate indicators. It appears that the smaller the average size of operational farm holdings, the greater the non-farm employment effects. Distributional consumption effects are also sought to be captured through land size group shares. A *U*-shaped relationship is in evidence with regard to the distribution of landholdings: the greater the share of the smallest and largest of the size classes in total number of and area under operational holdings, the more the proportion of rural employment in non-agricultural activities, pointing to heterogeneous rural consumption patterns. A dominance of food crops in the agricultural output of a district (as inferred from the region's cropping pattern) boosts the share of non-farm employment, with cereals, pulses and oilseeds contributing to it, but sugar crops detracting from it. High food crops yields, similarly, augment non-farm employment, whereas areas with high sugarcane yields feature less of it. With regard to inputs, utilization of fertilizers and agricultural credit in general help non-farm employment, while the usage of tractors seems to inhibit it. Non-farm employment's share is high where gross irrigated area as percentage of cropped area is high, but intensity of pumpsets and tubewells is negatively related to it.

The general impression is that the backward — or input — linkages of agriculture with the non-farm sector are weak, and that networks servicing agricultural production tend to bypass, by and large, the local labour force.

We note in Table 1a the differential results arrived at through using alternative migration specifications to motivate a picture of the role of inter-regional labour flows in rural labour markets. This experimentation was based upon the premise that migration and occupational choice are part and parcel of the same household labour supply decision, and that agricultural prosperity, input usage or crop patterns all had possible bearing upon migration's role in substituting for or contributing to labour allocation to the rural non-farm sector.

Somewhat to our surprise, rates of rural in-migration, not out-migration, showed the greatest affinity with non-farm employment share. Coefficients on the rates of rural in-migration (total, from within state and out of state) are found to be positive and significant, with a strong additional indication that non-farm employment is associated with a higher share of out-of-state in total (male) in-migrants. The negative sign on net out-migration rates is attributable to the dominant — and positive — influence of in-migration. The results would seem to argue either that migrant agricultural workers are replacing locals who have gone over to more remunerative work in the non-farm sector, or that non-farm employees are themselves migrants. The argument points to the possibility of segmented markets, which is explicitly investigated below.

Rural Labour Markets

Our method in addressing the question of possible segmentation is to hypothesize different effects of the same set of variables as used in equation (1) above on identifiably different segments of the rural workforce. Table 2 investigates first male–female differences in labour supply to three components of the rural non-farm sector, viz., household manufacturing and non-household manufacturing and trade. The dependent variables are shares of non-household industry employment (in *NIC*s 2 and 3, 6 and 8) in total rural employment by main workers and the share of household industry workers in total *NIC* 2 and 3 workers. In addition, non-household industry employment is decomposed into shares of its four constituent categories, viz., employers, employees, single and family workers. The regressions for the proportion of rural workers in aggregate non-household industry omit the share of cultivators in total rural workers as an explanatory variable for econometric reasons, and the 'female' regressions omit male in-migration rates.

Rural labour force participation variables, for total persons and by gender, are used to examine whether non-farm activity draws additional workers into the labour force, or merely reallocates them from other

Table 2: Male-Female Labour Supply Differences in Household and Non-household Industry by Employment Category

Persons	*Means*	$N23H_p$ (59.49)	$NNHW_p$ (11.33)	$NoNH_p$ (3.60)	$NeNH_p$ (59.69)	$NsNH_p$ (28.22)	$NfNH_p$ (8.39)
$LFPR_p$	39.06	1.2303	−0.0124	−0.1298	0.2544	−0.0550	−0.1558
Per cent $CULT_p$	46.45	0.9911		0.0838	−0.3586	0.3034	−0.0086
LAB/AGR_p	45.28	1.0006	−0.1272*	0.0810	−0.5232‡	0.4726	−0.0245‡
$MIGR_p$	9.62	−3.1337*	0.6970*	0.0403	1.2512*	−0.9847*	−0.2188
Constant		−49.7638	10.8622*	1.4981	78.0667‡	0.0481*	18.0865
R-squared		0.6034	0.7991	0.2282	0.7544	0.7245	0.3237
Males	*Means*	$N23H_m$ (57.68)	$NNHW_m$ (14.93)	$NoNH_m$ (3.80)	$NeNH_m$ (60.27)	$NsNH_m$ (28.28)	$NfNH_m$ (7.69)
$LFPR^m$	52.66	1.9579	−0.0147	−0.1529	−0.1972	0.0913	0.2560‡
Per cent $CULT^m$	50.80	1.0051		0.0768	−0.5103	0.2008	0.2312‡
LAB/AGR^m	37.28	0.9676	−0.1905*	0.0701	-0.5751*	0.4311‡	0.0755
$MIGR^m$	9.62	−2.8321†	0.9323*	−0.0599	1.1465*	−1.0152*	−0.0755
Constant		−105.3053	13.8364	5.9051	106.9861*	6.9703	−19.6259
R-squared		0.5930	0.7872	0.1732	0.7642	0.7225	0.4093
Females	*Means*	$N23H_f$ (77.27)	$NNHW_f$ (3.54)	$NoNH_f$ (2.06)	$NeNH_f$ (52.90)	$NsNH_f$ (29.22)	$NfNH_f$ (15.82)
$LFPR^f$	24.91	−0.6040	−0.0211	−0.0941†	0.5336	−0.1324	−0.3155‡
Per cent $CULT^f$	35.95	−1.2481		0.0489	−1.4710	0.9692	0.4493
LAB/AGR^f	61.61	−1.0327	−0.0386*	0.0490	−1.4228	1.0055	0.3688
Constant		200.8139	6.4458*	−0.2750	180.1498	−64.277	15.1911
R-squared		0.0777	0.3004	0.2452	0.2664	0.1646	0.2370

Notes: Subscript p = persons; m = males; f = females; * = 1 per cent; † = 5 per cent; ‡ = 10 per cent significance levels in a two-tailed test.
Per cent of non-household industry workers who are: employers–*NoNH*; employees—*NeNH*, single workers—*NsNH*; family workers—*NfNH*.

N23H — Per cent share of household industry workers in total *NIC* 2 and 3 workers.
NNHW — Per cent share of non-household industry (*NICs* 2 and 3, 6 and 8) workers in total rural main workers.
LFPR — Rate of (rural) labour force participation (per cent); Per cent *CULT* — Cultivators as percentage of total rural workers by main activity.
LAB/AGR — Agricultural labourers as percentage of total agricultural workers; *MIGR* — Rate of (male) in-migration to rural district (per cent).

labour market activities. It is seen that the share of household in manufacturing industry employment is positively associated with increases in labour force participation for males, but negatively for females. By contrast, work as employees in non-household manufacturing industry for females rises with increases in their rate of workforce participation, whereas, for males, it falls. Whether the increased labour force participation is due to high remuneration or to low reservation wages for these workers is moot, and can be verified only in the presence of wage data, but it is clear that male-female work preferences and/or opportunities differ as between segments of the non-farm sector.

The positive association of a high share of farm labourers in total agricultural workers with rural household non-farm manufacturing shares may mean it is likely that farm labourers and non-farm workers share the same labour pool for this segment. This also seems to be the case for single workers, especially males, in non-household industry; for employees, however, the relationship is negative. By the same token, the positive relationship observed between the share of cultivators in the rural workforce and the share of the family worker group in non-household industry employment might suggest that those labour markets are interconnected. In consonance with earlier results, (male) in-migration is seen to be strongly and positively associated with overall non-household and employee categories, and conversely, negatively with household or single-worker jobs.

In additional (unreported) regression exercises bearing upon the labour market aspects of rural non-farm activity, we also investigated the effect of the age and educational composition of the rural labour pool on regional occupational profiles, and the characteristics of secondary workers employed in non-household manufacturing. The main points of the results obtained are as under: Rural professional, technical, administrative and executive workers appear to draw from a pool of middle-aged college graduates; clerical and sales workers tend to be younger, with education up to the secondary school level. Production workers are even younger, and are drawn from among the general pool of literates, while service workers span diverse educational levels.

The incidence of secondary employment in non-household manufacturing among main workers in other categories is quite low, and tends to occur among cultivators and agricultural labourers where labour force participation rates are high. The share of non-workers in total rural population is naturally in inverse relation to labour force participation rates, but also negatively associated with the share of labourers in agricultural workers and in-migration; it varies positively — as expected — with the share of the very young, old and women in the population.

Structure of Rural Industry

Labour market segmentation, if a valid picture of reality, must have a counterpart in structural differentiation among firms within rural industry. Table 3 probes a possible rural manufacturing hierarchy through an exploration of regional influences upon the distribution of manufacturing employment between its household and non-household subsectors, and between establishments using and not using fuel or power. For the purpose at hand, we choose to focus upon regional influences comprehended in the *U, A, I* and *K* variable classes. In particular, the effects of urbanization, industrial agglomeration and, to an extent, rural infrastructure, are experimented with using alternative proxies. More detailed analysis of the effects of infrastructure is taken up later.

Dependent variables are shares of household in total *NIC* 2 and 3 employment, and the shares of workers in establishments using fuel/power in household and non-household manufacturing, respectively. Coefficients in the regression having as dependent variable the share of household workers in total *NIC* 2 and 3 employment (reported) are exactly equal in magnitude and opposite in sign to (unreported) coefficients for the share of non-household workers in that category. The same is the case with the coefficients for the regressions reporting employment shares of fuel/power-using units versus non-using units in household and non-household manufacturing and repair.

Overall urbanization is positively (negatively) associated with household (non-household) manufacturing employment shares, and strongly so with the employment share of non-fuel/power-using establishments within household industry. Broad localization economies, on the other hand, tend to favour non-household industry, and employment in household units using fuel/power. Likewise, composite infrastructure differentially favours non-household industry, especially in its fuel-using component. Not surprisingly, joint workshop–residences are inversely related to jobs in both household and non-household units with fuel or power but positively associated with overall household employment.

Table 3: Regional Influences on Employment in Household and Non-household *NIC* 2 and 3 Units Using Fuel/Power

n = 25 *Independent Variable*	*Means*	*N23H* (59.59)	*N2HFP* (19.25)	*N2MFP* (70.92)
U (Urbanization)	20.23	0.2885 (0.924)	−0.1843† (−2.506)	0.3103 (0.893)
A (Agglomeration)	862.76	−0.0117* (−3.601)	0.0027* (3.549)	−0.0003 (−0.088)
I (Infrastructure)	4.33	−2.6806† (−2.061)	−0.2884 (−0.942)	2.9362‡ (2.029)
K (Physical capital)	2.92	1.9350 (1.488)	−1.4184* (−4.633)	−6.0172* (−4.158)
Constant		69.6794* (8.224)	26.0358* (13.054)	69.7663* (7.402)
R-squared		0.6005	0.6786	0.5380
Alternative urbanization proxies (used with A, I, K as above)				
*U*1 = District urban population density		0.0017	−0.00005	−0.0002
*U*3 = Average urban population per town		0.0002	−0.0001‡	0.00009
*U*4 = Growth rate of urban population, 1961–71		1.1039†	−0.0607	0.2706
*U*5 = Urban population share of large(*f*) cities (per cent)		0.0194	−0.0461‡	0.0172
*U*6 = Urban population share of medium(*ff*) towns (per cent)		0.1642	0.0127	0.0350
*U*7 = Urban population share of small(*fff*) towns (per cent)		−0.3393†	0.0860†	−0.1036
Alternative infrastructure proxies (used with U, A, K as above)				
I1 = Per cent of villages with electricity		−0.5523†	0.0753	0.6686†
I2 = Per cent of villages with 'pucca' road approach		−0.8883†	0.1111	−0.0723
I3 = Per cent of villages with post and telegraph facility		0.4892†	−0.0869	0.2626
I6 = Composite (productive and social) amenity index		−0.1920*	−0.0170	0.1334
I7 = Composite 'socially' weighted amenity index		−0.2050†	−0.0215	0.1545
I8 = per capita village panchayat expenditure (Rs)		−4.3645*	0.3153	2.9041

Notes: Figure in parentheses are t-values.
∗ = 1 per cent; † = 5 per cent; ‡ = 10 per cent significance levels in a two-tailed test.
N23H — Per cent share of household industry workers in *NIC* 2 and 3 (manufacturing, processing, servicing, repairs) workers.
N2HFP — Per cent share of *NIC* 2 and 3 household workers employed in establishments using fuel/power.
N2MFP — Per cent share of *NIC* 2 and 3 non-household workers employed in establishments using fuel/power.
U = *U*2 = Percentage of district population living in urban areas.
A = *A*1 = Average daily employment in factories per 1,00,000 district population.
I = *I*4 = Per cent of villages *w*/6 amenities: power, road, post–telegraph, education, institution, medical facility, drinking water.
K = *K*1 = Houses used as shops/workshops as per cent of rural residences.
f Large = Class I cities (1,00,000 and above).
ff Medium = Class II and III towns (20,000–99,999)
fff Small = Class IV, V and VI towns (5000–19,999).

Effects on regressions run with alternative urbanization and infrastructure proxies are presented in the lower panel. Higher urban growth rates boosted the employment share of the household component of rural industry and, conversely, seem to have diminished the importance of its non-household component. Urban population concentrated in large cities favours the non-fuel using household subsector, while a high share of small towns in urban population is associated with non-household manufacturing and the fuel-using component household industry. As expected, electricity and roads favour the non-household component of manufacturing industry, with electricity in particular clearly favouring the power-using subcomponent of the latter. Composite infrastructure investments — both productive and social — (and village panchayat expenditure) seemingly bias employment creation in favour of a greater non-household share in manufacturing jobs.

Table 4 looks more closely at the question of whether regional urbanization and/or industrial agglomeration help or hinder the incidence of non-farm industry in rural areas. We attempt to investigate the effects of urbanization and agglomeration on size shares of employment in registered and unregistered non-household *NIC* 2 and 3 units, as well as in establishments in the trade, etc., and business services categories. Again, truncated regressions featuring only the urbanization, agglomeration, infrastructure and physical capital variables are estimated, with only coefficient signs and indications of significance reported. The *U*+ and *A*+ specifications exhibit the urbanization or agglomeration variable that showed a positive relationship with the independent variable when that variable was used in place of *U*2 or *A*7 (in Table 4(B and C)) with the others.

Results may be interpreted as follows: Employment in *registered* non-household *NIC* 2 and 3 (manufacturing, etc.,) units is negatively associated with overall regional urbanization levels in its smallest and two largest size classes, but positively for establishments of employment size 20–99 workers. A high share of district urban population in medium-sized towns favours the smaller of such units, while a high share of urban population in small towns favours the larger of such units. Presumably, genuine demand linkages (and/or the absence of competition to rural units from small towns) may be reflected in the former circumstance, and physical location and/or government dispersal policy efforts in the latter. Localization benefits, as captured by the effect of district factory employment, are, expectedly, in evidence for the largest of the registered units, but, interestingly, also for the larger unregistered ones.

Table 4: Differential Effects of Agglomeration and Urbanization of Rural Industry by Employment Size Classes

Independent Variables	*(A) Size Shares of Employment in NIC 2 and 3 Non-household Registered*[@]					*and*	*Unregistered Units*[@@]	
	Class 1	*Class 2*	*Class 3*	*Class 4*	*Class 5*	*Class 1*	*Class 2*	*Class 3*
*U*2	–	+	+	–	–	–	–	+
U+	*U*6*f*	*U*6	*U*5	*U*6,*U*7	*U*5, *U*7	*U*6*f*	*U*5, *U*7	*U*5, *U*7
*A*1	–	–	–	+	+	–*f*	+*f*	+*f*
I	–	–	+	+	+	+	+	–
K	–	–	+*f*	+	–	–*f*	+	+*f*

Independent Variables	*(B) Establishment Size Shares in NIC 6 Employment**				*(C) Establishment Size Shares in NIC 8 Employment***			
	Class 1	*Class 2*	*Class 3*	*Class 4*	*Class 1*	*Class 2*	*Class 3*	*Class 4*
*U*2	–	+	–	–	–	+	+	–
U+	*U*6, *U*7	*U*6, *U*7	*U*6	*U*5	*U*6, *U*7	*U*6, *U*7	*U*5, *U*6	*U*5
*A*7	–	+	+	+	+	–	–	+
A+	*A*3	*A*4, *A*5	*A*4, *A*5	*A*3, *A*4	*A*3	*A*5	*A*5*f*	*A*3, *A*4*f*
I	+	+	+	–	–	–	+	+
K	+	+	–	–	–*f*	–	+	+*f*

Notes: *I* = Infrastructure and *K* = Physical capital proxies; *U*2 and *A*7 as defined below:
f = significant at 1–10 per cent levels.
U+ and *A*+ represent alternative urbanization and agglomeration variables positively associated with each size class.
*U*2 = Per cent district population in urban areas.
*U*5 = Urban population share of large (1,00,000 +) cities.
*U*6 = Urban population share of medium (20,000–99,999) towns.
*U*7 = Urban population share of small (5000–9999) towns.
*A*1 = Average daily factory employment per 1,00,000 district population.
*A*3 = Rural population share of small (0–999) villages.
*A*4 = Rural population share of medium (1,000–4,999) villages.
*A*5 = Rural population share of large (5000 +) villages.
*A*7 = Rural population density (persons per sq km).

@ *NIC* 2 and 3 (*R*) Units		**NIC* 6 Units:	
Class 1	10–19	Class 1	1–4
Class 2	20–49	Class 2	5–19
Class 3	50–99	Class 3	20–49
Class 4	100–299	Class 4	50+
Class 5	300+		

@@ *NIC* 2 and 3 (*U*) Units		***NIC* 8 Units:	
Class 1	1–4	Class 1	1–4
Class 2	5–9	Class 2	5–19
Class 3	10–19	Class 3	20–49
		Class 4	50+

In respect of *NIC* 6 (trade, etc.), the more concentrated the urban population in large and medium towns (or the weaker the small towns), the greater the share of industry employment held by the relatively larger firms. Perhaps the absence of trading activity based in small towns may engender and sustain larger rural private trading operations. Also, the higher the rural population density, the more robust the employment share of these larger units. As the size share effects from rural population dispersion are mixed, there seems no consistent evidence pointing to scale economies in the conduct of such activities, although the concentration of population in large and medium villages does tend to be associated with more large trading firms.

Employment in *NIC* 8 (business services, etc.), like that of *NIC* 2 and 3, features the positive association of the share of its medium-size groups with overall urbanization. The implications of urban distribution are less clear. Unlike trade, a high rural population density does not by itself favour the dominance of the larger firms in this industry, while the concentration of this population in large and medium villages unambiguously does. Dominance of small villages makes for small firms in this activity, and that of medium and large villages, of medium and large units, suggesting market-size effects of spatial demand. On the cost side, infrastructure is seen to mildly favour large registered but small unregistered units in manufacturing, the smaller units in trading firms, and the larger business service establishments. We further explore infrastructure effects below.

Government Assistance and Rural Non-farm Sector

We approach the subject of government intervention as operationalized via three channels: through the siting of village infrastructure, through credit assistance, and through direct government expenditures under various heads. The coefficients presented in each exercise refer to intervention measures alternatively used in truncated forms exclusively featuring the locational and policy variables, viz., *U*, *A*, *I*, *K*, *B* and *G*. Coefficients of control variables other than the one under focus are not reported, but are mostly of expected sign.

Table 5 presents the contribution of rural infrastructure to employment in the aggregate non-farm, manufacturing and trade categories. The dependent variables for the first two are in terms of shares in total rural employment, and that for trade in terms of density, given its market-area dependence. The relative contributions of the infrastructure

Table 5: Rural Infrastructure and Employment in Total Non-farm Activity, Manufacturing and Trade

n = 25 *Infrastructure Variable*	*Means*	*MMF* (6.87)	*e*1	*M*2,3 (4.90)	*e*2	*M*6 (78.36)	*e*3
I1 (Electricity)	36.05	0.0676‡ (1.824)	36	0.0111 (0.576)	8	1.0151‡ (1.905)	47
I2 ('Pucca' roads)	25.09	0.1461* (3.534)	53	0.0407 (1.586)	21	1.8046† (2.605)	58
I3 (Post and telegraph)	24.21	0.0472 (1.291)	17	0.0424* (3.392)	21	0.1543 (0.233)	5
I4 (All amenities)	4.33	0.3881† (2.205)	24	0.1529‡ (1.911)	14	6.7591† (2.671)	37
I5 (All-India rank)		–0.0046* (–3.056)		–0.0028† (–3.524)		–0.8881† (–2.219)	
I6 (Unweighted index)	151.24	0.0199‡ (2.039)	44	0.0124* (2.755)	38	0.2792 (1.531)	54
I7 (Weighted index)	149.8	0.0192‡ (1.814)	42	0.0121† (2.376)	37	0.2922 (1.514)	56
I8 (Panchayat exp. per capita)	5.95	0.2560 (0.716)	22	–0.0178 (–0.169)	–2	7.2134† (2.652)	55
I9 (Exp. per village)	6102.38	0.0001 (1.182)	12	0.0001† (2.076)	13	0.0030‡ (2.001)	23
I10 (Exp. per panchayat)	8996.56	0.0001 (0.936)	17	0.0001 (1.3555)	18	0.0040* (3.186)	46

Notes: t - values in parentheses;

* = 1 per cent; † = 5 per cent; ‡ = 10 per cent significance levels in a two-tailed test.

MMF Workers with main activity other than cultivation per sq km district rural geographical area.

*M*2, 3 Per cent of rural employees in *NIC* 2 and 3: manufacturing, processing, servicing and repairs.

*M*6 Workers in *NIC* 6: wholesale and retail trade, restaurants and hotels per sq km rural geographical area.

el = (Δ*MMF*/ΔI) x (I/*MMF*) = elasticity (at sample means) of rural non-farm employment density with reference to infrastructure.

e2 = (Δ*M*2, 3/ΔI) x (I/*M*2, 3) = elasticity (at sample means) of rural employment share of *NIC* 2 and 3 with reference to infrastructure.

e3 = (Δ*M*6, 3/ΔI) x (I/*M*6) = elasticity (at sample means) of *NIC*6 rural employment density with reference to infrastructure.

Rural infrastructural proxies

I1 = Percentage of villages with electricity.

I2 = Percentage of villages with 'pucca' road approach.

I3 = Percentage of villages with post and telegraph facilities.

I4 = Per cent of villages with above 3 and additional 3 social amenities: educational institution, medical facility and drinking water.

I5 = Composite all-India rural amenity availability rank of district.

I6 = Composite (with above 6) rural amenity index—unweighted.

I7 = Composite rural amenity index weighted in favour of 3 'social' components above.

I8 = Per capita expenditure by village panchayats (Rs).

I9 = Per village expenditure by village panchayats (Rs '000).

I10 = Average expenditure per panchayat for district (Rs '000).

components (save rank) to each employment category may be compared within each industry group through 'elasticities' calculated at sample means.

For non-farm employment density at large, village roads are relatively the most important component of infrastructure, with electricity in second place. Density of employment in trade follows more or less the same pattern as that for aggregate non-farm employment, but with social and panchayat expenditures for some reason more strongly associated with the former.

For increasing the employment share of manufacturing industry in total rural employment, post and telegraph facilities prove most important, with the joint effects of the composite proxies higher than that of any one component. Expectedly, 'productive' infrastructure, proxied by the unweighted index is marginally more effective than the socially biased weighted index. Effects of the all-India 'rank' variable are, naturally, negative—the stronger a district's position with regard to infrastructure, the higher its rank or lower its numerical value, and correspondingly greater the impact on rural employment.

We turn next to the influence of credit availability in serving as a possible 'engine of growth' for the non-farm sector. Table 6 explores the effect of various types of credit proxies on various industrial categories of non-farm employment. We have classified credit sources into three groups and, within them, sought to use explanatory variables approximating credit assistance to the non-farm sector. In a few cases, the separation of rural or non-agricultural credit has not been possible, and some of the proxies include data much beyond 1971. Therefore, caution is advised while interpreting the results. It is likely that the negative signs on the co-operative credit variables arise from the possibility that they might indirectly measure assistance to agriculture, raising its rural employment share disproportionally at the expense of the non-farm sector. Again, interestingly, co-operative activity is revealed as 'displacing' employment in trade, and perhaps adding personnel directly to the financial services category rather than via second-round effects.

The informal credit component is probably the most purely 'private' measure of the lot, presumably reflecting spontaneous credit availability, but its performance, too, while not uniformly negative, is not satisfactory, with only the construction industry being slightly benefited. It is also somewhat interesting to find employment in trading and transport negatively associated with loans to non-traders. It is possible that lending activity by moneylenders may be high only where traders are unable to self-finance. The generally

Table 6: Credit and Rural Non-farm Employment by Industry

n =25 *Credit Variable*	*Dependent Variable Means: Sample Means*	*M*2, 3 (4.90)	*M*5 (0.84)	*M*6 (1.67)	*M*7 (0.60)	*M*8 (0.17)	*M*9 (3.96)
I Co-operative credit	3.601	–0.14090	0.02125	–0.07204	–0.05150	0.03673‡	0.00809
*B*1		(–1.236)	(0.277)	(–0.966)	(–0.612)	(2.048)	(0.075)
*B*2	114.14	–0.0054	–0.00111	–0.00162†	–0.00031	0.00012	0.00038
		(–0.373)	(–1.401)	(2.310)	(–0.339)	(0.672)	(0.312)
II Informal credit							
*B*3	9.03	0.01445	–0.00345	–0.01365	–0.026230†	–0.00366	–0.01583
		(0.565)	(–0.392)	(–1.164)	(–2.708)	(–1.685)	(–0.942)
*B*4	69.76	0.00080	0.00064‡	–0.00002	0.00056	–0.00004	–0.00043
		(0.964)	(1.757)	(–0.063)	(1.280)	(–0.431)	(–0.863)
*B*5	359.40	0.00015	–0.00011	–0.00031†	0.00035†	0.00004	–1.72807
		(0.497)	(–1.067)	(–2.526)	(–4.006)	(–1.319)	(–0.001)
III Commercial credit							
*B*6	3.78	–0.13053	–0.00938	0.05829	–0.00376	0.00766	–0.0365
		(–0.980)	(–0.113)	(1.035)	(–0.041)	(0.628)	(3.407)
*B*7	49.32	0.00131	–0.00143	0.00144	–0.00320	–0.0007	–0.0046
		(0.154)	(–0.532)	(0.617)	(–1.149)	(–0.147)	(0.037)

Notes: Figures in parentheses are t-values; * = 1 per cent, † = 5 per cent, ‡ = 10 per cent significance in a two-tailed test.
*M*2,3 = Per cent of rural employment in *NIC* 2 and 3 (manufacturing, processing, servicing and repairs).
*M*5 = Per cent of rural employment in *NIC* 5 (construction).
*M*6 = Per cent of rural employment in *NIC* 6 (wholesale and retail trade, restaurants and hotels).
*M*7 = Per cent of rural employment in *NIC* 7 (transport, storage and communication).
*M*8 = Per cent of rural employment in *NIC* 8 (financing, insurance, real estate and business services).
*M*9 = Per cent of rural employment in *NIC* 9 (community, social and personal services).
*B*1 = Number of co-operative bank branches per 1,00,000 district population.
*B*2 = Average borrowings per member of non-agricultural credit society (Rs).
*B*3 = Number of licensed moneylenders per 1,00,000 district rural population.
*B*4 = Loans advanced to traders by licensed moneylenders (Rs '000).
*B*5 = Loans advanced to non-traders by licensed moneylenders (Rs '000).
*B*6 = Number of commercial bank branches per 1,00,000 population.
*B*7 = Commercial banks' advances to service sector for district.

lacklustre performance of commercial bank credit may be attributed partially to data deficiencies; in part, it is possible that the generally negative signs reflect a higher degree of involvement by this sector in the least 'developed' districts as a matter of corrective policy.

Lastly, Table 7 seeks to examine the impact of government policy expenditures upon *growth* in rural non-farm employment by detailed expenditure sources and category. The coefficients presented are for alternative specifications of the variable, representing growth in regional infrastructure of different types. The last column presents the mean contribution, to aggregate non-farm employment growth, of each proxy.

Separately, the effect of various categories of state government expenditures on growth in rural non-farm employment is not impressive across the board, but some instructive lessons are to be learned. Expectedly, expenditure on incentive packages for industry, roads and bridges, and urban development contribute positively to this growth. (It would be interesting to be able to break down the last into expenditures by size class.) The strongest positive contributory influences flow from major irrigation projects and, to a lesser extent, from expenditures in the power sector.

Aggregated subgroups allow the joint effect of these separate interventions to be examined. For example, we see that the sum of expenditures toward agriculture and allied activities with the major irrigation works has a positive impact, which becomes mildly negative once the latter component is removed. The cumulative effect of what we have dubbed 'pro-industry' expenditures on non-farm employment growth is, by contrast, positive. Planned expenditures are more effective than non-plan, and the last column shows the contribution of aggregate direct state-level spending (36.66) to go further than either that of zilla parishad (3.47) or village panchayat (1.64) expenditures.

In the next section, we take a much broader view of policies toward non-farm employment, but insights obtained above can usefully instruct the design and implementation of specific measures, once a rationally based and coherent policy stance toward the sector as a whole has been characterized. To this task we now turn, drawing upon the major findings of the study.

V. Policy Implications of the Study

We may now recapitulate our overall findings about the determinants of non-farm employment, and summarize the broad policy implications that emerge from the results of our analysis:

Table 7: Impact of Government Policy Expenditures upon Growth in Rural Non-farm Employment

n = 25 Dependent Variable: *A N f* Means 6.07 per cent

Category of Government Expenditure (Independent Variables)	*Means*	*Regression[f] Coefficient*	*t-value*	*Contribution to Growth Rate[ff]*
State government: planned development expenditure (Rs) per capita, 1976–81, on				
*j*1 District level schemes	472.18	–0.0328	–0.659	–15.49
*j*2 Major irrigation projects	155.41	0.0522†	2.096	8.11
*j*3 Power sector *fff*	145.26	0.0478	1.371	6.94
*j*4 Incentive packages for industry	11.65	0.2432	0.882	2.83
State government: non-plan development expenditures (Rs) per capita, 1976–81, on				
*j*5 Agriculture	1.97	–2.0842	–0.675	–4.10
*j*6 Animal husbandry	1.44	–5.9484	–0.827	–8.57
*j*7 Dairy development	14.17	0.0055	0.024	0.08
*j*8 Primary education	25.83	0.3568	0.522	9.21
*j*9 Secondary education	16.68	–1.1840	–1.182	–19.75
*j*10 Roads and bridges	3.66	0.5380	0.215	1.97
*j*11 Urban development	4.37	0.3459	0.515	1.51
Zilla parishad expenditures per capita (Rs)				
*j*12 1974–80	271.55	0.0366	0.306	9.94
*j*13 1976–77 (1 year only)	130.89	0.0265	1.238	3.47
Village-level expenditure per capita (Rs)				
*j*14 1976–77 (1 year only)	5.95	0.2751	0.111	1.64
Aggregate expenditure per capita (Rs) under				
$J1 = j1 + j2 + j3 + j4$ = planned category	784.50	0.0418†	2.231	32.79
$J2 = j5 + j6 + j7 + j8 + j9 + j10 + j11$ = non-plan	68.17	0.0131	0.060	0.89
$J3 = j2 + j5 + j6 + j7$ = agriculture and allied	172.98	0.0547†	2.153	9.46
$J4 = j5 + j6 + + j7 = J3$ above without *j*2	17.57	–0.0120	–0.051	–0.21
$J5 = j3 + j4 + j10 + j11$ = 'pro-industry'	164.94	0.0444	1.394	7.32
$J6 = J5$ above without *j*11	160.56	0.0436	1.365	7.00
$J7 = J1 + J2$ = (all state-level exp.)	852.62	0.0430†	2.276	36.66
$J8 = J7$ above *w/o j*8 and *j*9 (productive)	810.11	0.0422†	2.254	34.19
$J9 = j8 + j9$ = 'social' category	42.51	–0.1610	–0.236	–6.84

Notes: † = significant at 5 per cent level.

f Dependent variable ΔN = growth rate of rural non-farm employment, 1971–81 (per cent).

ff Coefficient $\times \Delta N$ (evaluated at sample mean).

fff Represents assistance through SIICOM (State Industrial and Investment Corporation of Maharashtra).

Strong spatial consumption linkages are observed between the agricultural and non-agricultural subsectors in the rural economy, both at the aggregate level as well as for individual industrial categories. Agricultural households presumably generate demand for locally manufactured consumption goods, as well as those 'imported' from the urban sector. In the absence of detailed information on the allocation of rural consumption expenditures between 'non-traded' (i.e. locally produced goods and services that are entirely consumed within the region), and 'imported' components in food and non-food groups, our results suggest that greater agricultural prosperity seems to be generally accompanied by vigorous rural demand for products/services of the non-farm sector within a region.

The high, positive and significant correlation of rural non-farm employment shares with average sizes of operational holdings indicates that the consumption linkage is quite broad-based, and that, despite possible leakages on account of urban bias in rural consumption patterns (either due to demand for goods with a comparative cost advantage or a preference on the part of high-income groups for specific prestige or 'status' items), the net multiplier effect seems to be working favourably in affecting the proportion of rural employment in non-agricultural activities. This finding generally corroborates the results of studies with more detailed data available from other developing countries that have quantified consumption linkages in rural areas. One such study for the Philippines[6] reveals that each 1 per cent increase in agricultural incomes generated a 1.2 per cent increase in most sectors of the local non-farm economy. Our results also suggest that the broader the income base in the agricultural sector, the higher will be the consumption demand for locally available goods and services leading to commensurably greater employment in non-agricultural activity.

It is true that to some extent poorly developed infrastructure and communication links between villages and towns impede farm households' access to urban non-food goods and services and, in forcing them to buy high-cost and possibly inferior local substitutes, may worsen their terms of trade as food producers. But the beneficial effects of agricultural growth through consumption linkages on the growth of the rural non-farm sector can be especially reinforced where the goods and services produced in the latter have elastic supplies and comparative cost advantages over similar goods and services available from the urban sector. Variations in consumption patterns amongst the different farm size classes can to a large extent be minimized, except those on account of the status factor.

Production linkages forging the agricultural and non-agricultural components of the rural economy are expected to show up through the non-farm sector's forward linkages with agriculture in areas such as input distribution, and through backward linkages with the farm economy in the form of processing, marketing, etc., of agricultural produce. Overall production linkages with aggregate non-farm employment are significant only in respect of employment density. However, in the industry-by-industry analysis, various general agricultural output measures are found to increase shares of rural employment in the trade, transport, financial and business service sectors.

With the increased use of purchased farm inputs, the forward agricultural linkages of the non-farm sector might be expected to undergo tremendous and fast changes. The share of five inputs — chemical fertilizers,[7] irrigation charges, electricity, pesticides and insecticides, diesel oil — in the value of all material inputs in agriculture has increased from 15 per cent in 1973–74 to 37 per cent in 1980–81 and 43 per cent in 1984–85. These changes, admittedly, are not adequately covered in our static equations, but our independent variables reflecting purchased input usage do not perform as well as expected in indicating non-farm jobs.

There may be several reasons for this. It is likely, for instance, that the primary multiplier effects of four out of the five inputs mentioned above (*sans* irrigation, whose rural impact is dramatically demonstrated as will be summarized later) will be felt in the urban sector, although their secondary effect in the rural non-farm sector through trade and commerce by way of delivery or distribution systems should also be significant. Again, notwithstanding the increase in purchased non-traditional inputs, the share of labour and traditional inputs in total inputs remains quite sizeable and has only marginally decreased over time. Regarding fertilizer, which is by far the most important amongst purchased inputs, it is observed that only about two-thirds of the total irrigated area in India was fertilized by 1976–77 and that application rates varied greatly amongst crops. The number of villages per fertilizer outlet was more than ten in the majority of the states (Maharashtra being one of them) and most of them were concentrated at railheads within the districts. Besides, the system or vehicle of distribution can play an important institutional role as rural change agent. The fertilizer distribution system in Maharashtra has been basically conceptualized and implemented as a credit-linked one, with a view to ensuring the end use of the latter. The low coverage of the credit system has resulted in circumscribing the coverage of the fertilizer distribution system, to which fertilizer pricing policy has added another shackle. With the result, it may be argued that a potential village entrepreneur has not emerged on a large scale who, diversifying from fertilizer sales and extending to related goods, might ultimately assume the role of a producer of goods and services. Such potential production linkages thus remain unrealized.

The potentials for both agricultural input and output linkage vary from crop to crop, which should hence create varied multiplier effects on the share, incidence and density of non-farm employment in the rural sector. Our analysis does show that the base of agricultural output linkages with non-farm employment that have emerged is, as in the case of consumption linkages, quite wide. Our general comment is that marketing of agricultural output has proved more successful than input distribution in creating off-farm jobs in rural areas. The main thrust seems to be coming from food crops (except sugarcane). Cereals, pulses and oilseed crops have proved more robust compared to commercial crops in generating impact on the size of rural non-farm employment by way of forward agricultural linkages. The lack of commercial crops' impact on the rural non-agricultural sector is due in part to the poor agroprocessing linkages discussed below.

One would have expected rural non-farm activity to reflect stronger backward linkages with agriculture via processing activities, which tend to locate near-raw material sources due to their weight-losing nature. This linkage, however, does not manifest itself in increased non-farm employment share (although it does raise the density). Many of the processing units are located, rather, in consumption centres away from production centres, perhaps for historical reasons (such as wheat processing capacity having gotten concentrated in port cities due to freight policies followed by the colonial regime), or because of infrastructural bottlenecks (roads, power, etc.) preventing these activities from realizing scale or transport cost advantages, etc. The industrial dispersal policy pursued by the government[8] has concentrated more on dispersing urban sector industries to rural areas through various kinds of inefficient subsidies rather than on engendering local environments conducive to generating rural industrialization indigenous to these areas through natural incentive structures or appropriate investments in socio-economic infrastructure. Agroprocessing is a prime case in point.

It may be mentioned, incidentally, that our study is not alone in finding stronger consumption than production linkages of agriculture with the non-farm sector. A study of the Muda[9] irrigation project in Malaysia also found that only one-third of the 80 per cent income multiplier was due to agriculture's increased demand for inputs and processing, transport and marketing services, against two-thirds on account of increased household demand for consumption goods. The secondary effects of production linkages are likely to be more powerful and sustainable than those of consumption linkages, however, and it is necessary that any road blocks rendering the primary effects weak be removed to facilitate a healthy rural productive base.

The possibility that rural workers who cannot get adequate work in agriculture spill over into rural non-farm activity and that, as a consequence, the latter acts as a 'sponge' — a residual sector — was very much kept in mind while analysing the determinants of labour supply to the non-farm sector. It has not, however, been conclusively borne out by this study that non-farm employment occurs, other things being equal, where rural labour is relatively more demand-constrained due to limited opportunities in agriculture.

By and large, the share or size of non-farm employment is high where workforce participation is high, but the latter is a natural concomitant of modernization and structural economic change. Our static results do seem to suggest a greater proportion of non-farm in rural employment where labourers' share in agricultural workers is lower, and the decadal change data corroborate that, for the districts of Maharashtra, the proportion of labourers in total agricultural workers declined as growth in rural, non-farm employment took place. The dynamic regressions revealed that, on average, the larger this decline, the greater the positive effect — across the board — on growth in rural non-farm categories. Further research needs to determine whether the decline is real or statistical, and whether the occupational transition was to better- or worse-paying jobs.

While some amount of agricultural labour displacement may occur into certain types of low-productivity household employment, that there are segments of the market for rural non-farm employees which may even be supply-constrained is suggested by the consistently positive and highly significant coefficients on the rural in-migration variable, indicating that labour inflows to a rural region may be directly or indirectly involved in non-agricultural activity. The age and educational composition of the non-farm labour pool, as also the characteristics of secondary workers employed in non-household manufacturing, indicate that many non-farm jobs no doubt represent a move upwards. Our indirect evidence of segmentation in access to different types of non-farm activity conjures up a more realistic picture of the rural labour market as some mix of competitiveness and segmentation, rather than the spectre of a progressively pauperized homogeneous labour force. Such a recognition might be more constructively employed, from a policy viewpoint, in buttressing arguments for selective labour market interventions targeted more sharply on groups identified as being at a disadvantage in their access to productive employment.

The shares of non-farm activity in the period before any substantial interventions in the form of explicit policies toward industrial location went into effect are an interesting study in rural–urban balance and its relationship to the development process. Where the level of overall urbanization was high, the incidence of non-farm employment in rural areas was lower, reflecting the spontaneous polarization between agriculture-related and manufacturing activities in rural and urban areas, respectively. Whether such 'specialization' is the result of natural advantage or of rural bottlenecks to the establishment of industry is an important issue that policy must address. The share of non-farm in rural employment, moreover, proves sensitive to the way the region's overall urban population is distributed among towns of different size classes. For example, the relative importance of small towns in total urban population seems to be positively associated with greater rural shares of all non-farm activity, presumably either through direct, locational effects, or possibly due to the absence of regional competition from products and services of large and medium cities.

Of manufacturing, in particular, the following is suggested: Generally, the more sophisticated the manufacturing activity (such as non-household, or fuel/electricity-using household units), a high level of district urbanization tends to pre-empt rural employment opportunities in that industry. In addition, the share of non-household in total rural manufacturing employment seemed hurt by rapid regional urban growth. In fact, a higher share of the non-household component in rural manufacturing employment is associated positively with the urban preponderance of small towns — i.e. in those regions where sizeable medium and large towns are present, very little such activity takes place in rural areas. By contrast, higher levels of overall urbanization favour a higher share of household industry, conceivably because the products of such activity are not in direct competition as substitutes. The share of the largest employment size classes in rural registered non-household manufacturing or trade units, or rural business service establishments also tend to be lower in districts with high urbanization levels, presumably reflecting the superior scale advantages afforded by urban locations.

Despite this emerging picture of specialization, however, the overall presence of industry in a region — irrespective of urban or rural location — is generally favourable for rural non-farm employment shares in that region due to diffusion of benefits through the agglomeration influence. This influence is seen to be uniformly robust and significant in magnitude. And despite their negative association with overall district per cent urban levels, the employment shares of the larger of the rural non-household manufacturing establishments tended to be positively associated with a concentration of that urban population in large cities.

To summarize, then, substantial rural employment in manufacturing does not spontaneously take place in rural areas in the presence of more competitive urban locations. This is not necessarily a bad thing if it reflects natural productivity advantages, but the relative disadvantages of rural locations for industry should be the focus of corrective policy to the extent that this can be attributed to infrastructural bottlenecks or policy-induced urban bias. At the same time, those activities in which rural areas have an inherent competitive advantage should be supported — agro-based processing, whose natural rural locational advantages have been underutilized due to colonial distortions, is one such area. Additionally, as the measured agglomeration influence demonstrates, highly industrialized regions do create tendencies towards greater non-farm employment shares in their hinterlands. This suggests that emphasis on efforts to support industrialization in rural areas of already industrialized regions may lead to greater pay-offs than otherwise. These are some of the study's implications for the successful and efficient design of industrial dispersal and rural industrialization policies.

The interaction of the natural forces of structural transformation with policy interventions is brought into sharper focus by the study of rural non-farm employment *growth* over the decade of the seventies.

Here it is found that the increase in a region's overall per cent urban is *positively* associated with *growth* both in its rural aggregate non-farm and manufacturing industry employment, showing that urbanization has indeed been accompanied by a conversion of a portion of the agricultural workforce to non-farm activity. Thus, urbanization — a result in large part of spatial migration — appears to go hand in hand with rural occupational transition. This establishes rural industrialization as being at least partially attributable to the same structural change process as is responsible for urbanization.

For the household component of rural manufacturing, this employment growth appeared to be accompanied by the growth of population in medium-sized towns, and for transport, by the growth of small towns. We believe these to reflect natural polarizing outcomes. The revealed positive association between the particularly strong growth of non-household manufacturing employment with that of small towns, on the other hand, may be interpreted as indicating to some extent the direct locational consequences of government industrial policy incentives.

Since a major policy instrument for generating rural non-farm employment, as warranted, where it does not spontaneously occur is investment in rural infrastructure, it is worthwhile to summarize the role of existing stock and accretions to it, as revealed by our study. Most rural infrastructure, we found, is understandably partial to agricultural activity, though not detrimental in absolute terms to non-farm activity. Of the latter, trading activity seems especially benefited by rural roads. The contact with other regions facilitated thus may, if the regional history of developed nations is a guide, initially polarize non-agricultural activity in favour of urban areas in a sort of 'backwash' effect, but would increasingly, as a rural productive base came to be developed through complementary infrastructure, improve the competitive position of its products. To a promising extent, it is seen, rural infrastructure already benefits manufacturing — especially of the non-household, electricity/fuel-using variety. Household activity, on the other hand, does not appear to be favoured by infrastructural support, and actually seems relatively disadvantaged in its presence.

Per capita village panchayat expenditures positively influence the overall share of manufacturing in total and of non-household in manufacturing employment, but the direction of causality between industrial activity and high local spending is not clear. These presumably operating expenditures are positively associated with growth in rural non-farm employment, but less strongly so than are combined state-level planned development expenditures. The spending categories at the state level with the greatest impact by far are major irrigation projects and roads. Whether the employment increase brought on by these reflect merely the first-round effect of construction jobs (as public works) or the more enduring indirect effects of income augmentation in agriculture and improved productive environment for rural industry through the removal of bottlenecks (such as lack of communication access or power availability) upon rural incomes and welfare needs to be explored. It is not amiss to observe here that the Malaysian Muda irrigation project study cited earlier found that for each dollar of income created directly in agriculture by the project, an additional 80 cents of value added was created indirectly in the local economy.

VI. Conclusion

To reiterate: By and large, levels and shares of rural employment off the farm are strongly linked to agricultural output and incomes — most intimately, it appears, through consumption linkages. A strong agricultural policy is perhaps the single best means of engendering appropriate types of non-farm employment in rural areas in a manner which most efficiently engages the forces of naturally competitive spatial advantage. The promotion of agroprocessing enterprises as part of such a strategy is a promising but underutilized policy option. Government policy incentives aimed at securing large increases of employment in rural non-household manufacturing need to be more judicious in choice of location and industry, and should focus on strengthening such natural comparative advantages rather than forcing or subsidizing investments which may have realized higher returns in urban areas. In respect of infrastructure provision, one of the most efficacious instruments for generating overall non-farm employment growth appears to be capital expenditures on major irrigation projects and roads.

In recent times, increased urbanization has resulted concomitantly in rural non-farm employment growth, a development at least partially reflecting the forces of structural economic change. Rural areas in regions with already high levels of industrial development are the best placed to secure the greatest *growth* in non-farm activity. While some rural labour may be 'pushed' into certain low-wage segments of the rural non-farm economy (e.g. the household sector), the perception of the non-farm as a homogeneous residual rural subsector seems generally unrealistic. In view of the high degree of differentiation in non-farm jobs and in the access of the rural labour pool to them, efforts to overcome market segmentation and to ease the occupational transition of disadvantaged groups should facilitate the eventual structural transformation of the Indian economy.

This paper has been an attempt to enunciate issues and questions relating to rural non-farm employment in India, and pose them in a policy-relevant framework. The investigation was conducted with the help of a simple but analytically based regression model. The principal findings of the study point towards a need for future micro-level analyses of consumption linkages, labour market behaviour, the technology of agroprocessing industries, and the rural roles of small urban areas.

The utility of econometric techniques for the investigation of such issues as the design of credit and other government incentives lies principally in laying out the bases of action, and pointing out potential inconsistencies of various measures proposed. This may be usefully combined with more qualitative and institutionally sensitive analyses for insights into the implementation aspects of a policy once it has been adjudged appropriate. The policy areas of credit, agricultural marketing, industrial incentives, entrepreneurship development, public employment and integrated rural programmes are all deserving of evaluation in the non-farm context. It is hoped that the present investigator and others can take on some of these tasks in the near future.

NOTES

Reproduced from *Economic and Political Weekly*, 11 July 1992.

1 The current spurt of interest in the Indian non-farm sector is owed in large measure to A. Vaidyanathan's seminal article, 'Labour Use in Rural India: A Study of Spatial and Temporal Variations', *Economic and Political Weekly*, 27 December 1986.

2 The earlier analysis appears in Vibhooti Shukla, 'Rural Non-farm Activity: A Regional Model and Its Empirical Application in Maharashtra State', *Economic and Political Weekly*, 9 November 1991. [The earlier paper has also been reproduced in this volume on pp. 2587—95. Sections II and III of this paper briefly sketched the model and methodology, and summarized the preliminary results of the earlier paper for ready reference in view of the gap of some months that had occurred between the publication of the two papers.]

3 A more serious problem, of course, is the potential for simultaneity bias introduced by the prospect that some of the 'independent' variables should

properly be endogenous to the system. At this time, however, the data just do not support simultaneous estimation.

4 While the 1971 *levels* or shares analysis captures variations in shares and levels of non-farm in total rural activity before many of the major policy interventions of the seventies targeting (to some degree) this subsector went into effect, an investigation of the *changes* between 1971 and 1981 is in order so as to measure the impact of such interventions, as also to impart a measure of dynamism to the empirical analysis.

5 Data sources used include: Government of India, *Population Census of India*, 1971, 1981; Government of Maharashtra, *Economic Census*, 1977, 1980; Government of Maharashtra, *Statistical Abstract of Maharashtra State*, various years; Government of Maharashtra, *Report of the Fact Finding Committee on Regional Imbalances in Maharashtra*, 1984; Centre for Monitoring Indian Economy, *District Level Data*, various years, various tables.

6 See Arthur Gibb, Jr, 'Agricultural Modernization, Non-Farm Employment and Low-Level Urbanization: A Case Study of a Central Luzon Sub-Region', Ph.D thesis, University of Michigan, 1974.

7 Trends in fertilizer use are discussed in Gunvant Desai, 'Sustaining Rapid Growth in India's Fertilizer Consumption', International Food Policy Research Institute, Washington, D.C., 1982.

8 For an empirically based critique of some aspects of this policy, see Vibhooti Shukla, *Urban Development and Regional Policy in India: An Econometric Analysis*, Bombay, Himalaya Publishing House, 1988.

9 Results of this study and others are reported in Peter Hazell and Alisa Roell, *Rural Growth Linkages: Household Expenditure Patterns in Malaysia and Nigeria*, Research Report 41, International Food Policy Research Institute, Washington, D.C., 1983.

VI

IV / City Structure and Employment Dynamics

12 / Firm Location and Land Use in Discrete Urban Space: A Study of the Spatial Structure of Dallas–Fort Worth

VIBHOOTI SHUKLA
PAUL WADDELL

I. Introduction

What implications do intra-metropolitan firm location choices have for contemporary urban form? This paper is motivated by the desire to pose the above question empirically through a behavioural model of intra-urban firm location that can yield insights into urban land use patterns and structure. With employment decentralization a fact of growing importance and concern for urban policy, and the validity of the monocentricity paradigm increasingly called into question, we hope that answers might be able to inform both positive and normative urban issues.

The context we seek to describe is the Dallas–Fort Worth area, one that has seen rather dramatic changes in growth and structure during the past decade and a half.[1] The impact of such a significant growth spurt in relatively recent times makes the area (futuristically called the 'Metroplex' by its promoters) somewhat of a prototype of modern polycentric urban areas that should be quite instructive to study. An idea of the spatial structure of the Dallas–Fort Worth metropolitan area and the degree of dispersion of employment that exists in various types of jobs may be made by reference to Figures 1(a) and 1(b). The two urban centres, the Dallas and the Fort Worth CBDs (Central Business Districts), are superimposed along with the major transportation arteries upon a map of the zip code zones that are to be our units of spatial analysis. The graphical exposition reveals rather substantial departures from strong monocentricity, with rather marked asymmetries between the north and southern parts of Dallas, and interesting contrasts between the zones around Dallas and those around Forth Worth.

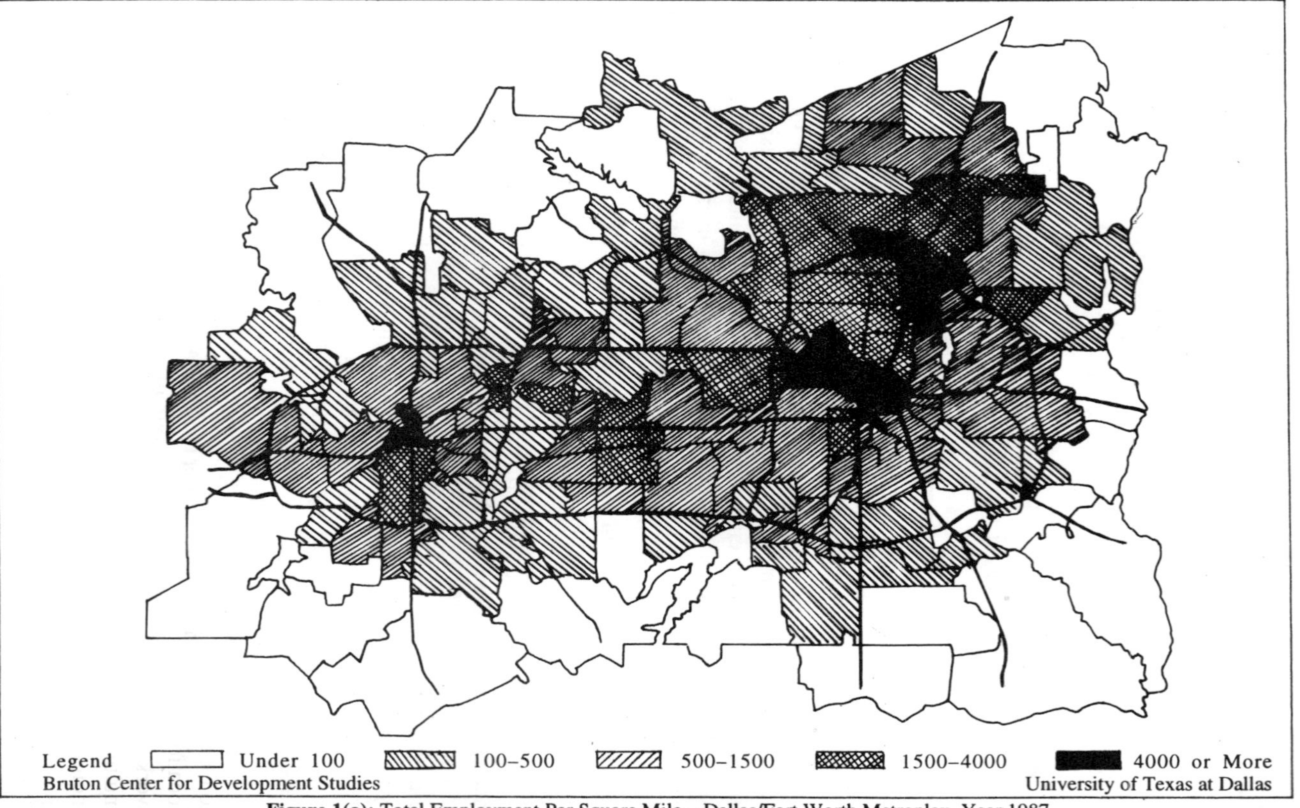

Figure 1(a): Total Employment Per Square Mile—Dallas/Fort Worth Metroplex, Year 1987

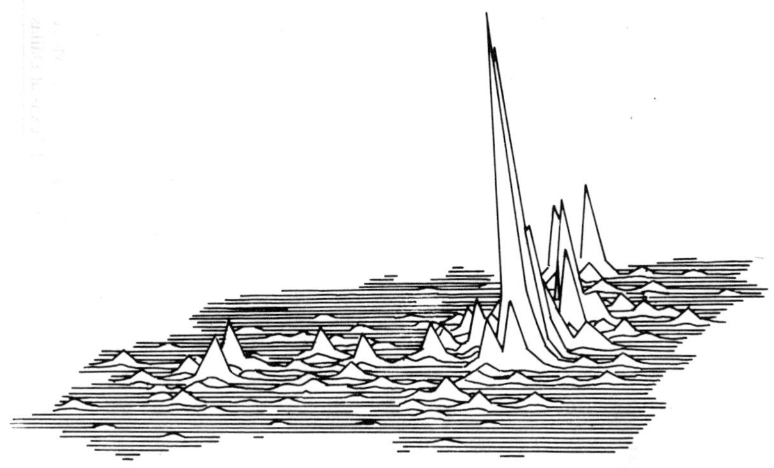

Figure 1(b)

An understanding of employment decentralization is central to the study of the 'new urban structure'. Our aim is to probe some of the underlying causes of this spatial employment spread by examining the intra-metropolitan location decisions of area firms in the major industrial categories. Particularly, we model the location decisions of establishments through a discrete choice model suggested by various theoretical perspectives and appropriately sensitive in its specifications to the polycentric nature of the context. The probabilities of location of a particular type of activity in a zip are approximated by the zips' establishment shares of particular industries or industry groups. The nature of the explained variable enables us to interpret it as a spatial choice variable, which we assume to be the outcome of a business location decision.[2]

We use discrete space to characterize the set of spatial alternatives available to profit-maximizing firms. The universe of choice is assumed to be sites in zip code zones within the Metroplex area, and the decision to locate and operate in any particular zip bearing a specified set of locational attributes is cast and estimated in a multinomial logit framework. An innovative feature of our study is that it seeks to account for multidimensional spatial interactions in a way not possible in purely monocentric approaches to the problem. Wheaton (1979), in an evaluative review of monocentric models of urban land use, pointed out the desirability of approximating space by discrete parcels or cells for a realistic treatment of complex accessibility notions and multiple employment centres. A major aim of our study is to test the resilience of the simple monocentric access concept in the presence of more general hypothesized spatial interactions. We are also interested in the extent to which these hypothesized interactions can simulate an empirical identification of nodes of high establishment and employment density. We hope that any success in thus 'explaining' the observed urban spatial structure might illuminate efforts at modelling departures from the traditional monocentricity assumptions and their implications.

The plan of the paper is as follows: Section II reviews some of the theoretical and empirical considerations bearing on the formulation of our methodology. Section III sets forth the specification of the location model and estimation procedure. Section IV presents and discusses the results. Finally, Section V illustrates some of their implications for urban structure.

II. Review of General Methodological Issues

In this section, we review some general considerations relevant to a model of urban employment location. The survey is claimed to be neither exhaustive nor representative: our limited purpose here is to identify broad implications, such as can be derived from the theory of urban structure and prior empirical work on firm location, for the choice of model formulation. More specific hypotheses will be discussed in Section III.

Urban Economic Theory and Urban Structure

We first attempt to summarize the salient aspects of the recent theoretical literature on urban structure, especially as it relates to departures from the monocentricity assumption of the traditional Alonso–Mills–Muth formulations. In general, two types of approaches are identifiable in equilibrium models of urban structure: those which take this structure as given, and those that model it as arising endogenously out of the behaviour of individual agents in the urban economy. The early monocentric models, of course, fall into the former category, as do those non-monocentric equilibrium models where the existence of employment subcentres, or some exogenous transportation feature, is assumed.

White (1976) considers location choice under an assumed suburban export node rendered attractive by freight transportation cost savings (due to, say, the presence of a circumferential highway) to derive a non-monotonic bid-rent function for manufacturing firms. White's (1988) model of residence and job choice in a monocentric city with decentralized employment, featuring the idea of firm suburbanization motivated by their having to pay workers lower wages when commuting journeys are shortened, implies non-monotonic wage gradients in certain cases. Sivitanidou and Wheaton (1990) simulate a linear city with two pre-specified centres to demonstrate that commercial rents do not fully capitalize firm locational advantages between employment centres in the presence of commuting flows—wages may capture a large part of spatial amenity variations within metropolitan areas.

While the strand of literature inspired by concerns with intra-urban commuting patterns promises to be one where the modelling of departures from monocentricity should yield potentially testable empirical implications in future, its development at this stage features much exogenous structure and rather limited forms of spatial interaction. Thus, any rent or wage relationships these imply cannot be guaranteed to characterize equilibrium under any but a very restrictive set of circumstances. Consequently, most studies of multicentric urban structure wishing to admit more general forms of commuting, input and information flows involving non-monocentric space have tended to recourse to tests of the *assumptions* rather than of the city-wide equilibrium implications of theoretical models.[3]

Equilibrium models that endogenize important aspects of urban structure, such as employment centres, model them as results of the interplay between the attractive forces of spatial agglomeration and the repelling ones of travel friction and congestion. Agglomeration economies are at the heart of urban processes, yet, its explicit recognition in models of urban structure (as opposed to urban growth or in location theory) is quite recent. Tauchen and Witte (1984) model agglomeration as the outcome of an endogenous contact pattern arising out of economies from the transactions externalities of proximity in an explicitly spatial context,[4] and Pascal and McCall (1980) motivate a search-theoretic rationale for agglomeration. Ogawa and Fujita (1980) derive implications for urban land use structure in a model where the productivity of each firm depends (uniformly) upon accessibility to all other firms under the assumption of a linear interaction cost function.[5] Tests of the behavioural underpinnings of these models tend to require quite elaborate data on firms' transactions and their costs.

The other class of models concerned with urban land use trace their lineage to the Beckmann-type discrete programming models. They treat space in discrete parcels, to which activities are optimally assigned. While these may not always be as soundly based on behavioural underpinnings, such models can, and increasingly have been made to incorporate behavioural insights and reconciled with equilibrium. Given the analytical complexity of the first class of models under the requirements of realistically detailed spatial characterizations, this strand of modelling is regarded by many as the more promising for further developments in the study of non-monocentric urban structure.[6] They are, in several ways, easier to relate to operationalization than the more abstract former class.

Empirical Directions in the Study of Firm Location

Next, we summarize some of the pertinent trends in empirical work on land use and urban structure. The considerable work on density gradient estimation, or the parametric characterization of wage-or rent-distance functions represent the empirical legacy of the monocentric model. Empirical work on intra-urban residential location informed by the distinct implications of urban land use theory was pioneered by Ellickson (1981). An analogous firm location model formulated by Lee (1982) appeals to spatial profit equalization among firms in a context of competing urban land uses.[7] Its equilibrium bid-rent approach reflects the urban economic perspective of allocating uses to sites as opposed to the location-theoretic one of assigning sites to uses.

Briefly, Lee predicts the probability that a given site will be occupied by a firm of a particular type which can outbid those of other types for it. Thus if k indexes firm types and Z, a vector of site characteristics, then this probability is given by

$$p(k{:}Z) = p[h(Z)]. \qquad (1)$$

The function h is defined as a consequence of spatial profit equalization among similar firms and the existence of an equilibrium rent profile that is derived with explicit reference to distance from the city centre. The monocentricity property ensures the existence and well-behavedness of $h(\cdot)$.

With urban subcentres or employment decentralization, such tractability is no longer guaranteed, as we have observed. Empirical work involving firm location in non-monocentric urban space has, in the absence of clear operationalizable theoretical direction, drawn upon the location-theoretic paradigm. Of course, location theory itself, mainly in the inter-regional domain of choice, has had a long tradition of empirical implementation. Despite its dominant emphasis on factors relating to transportation, and its somewhat cavalier treatment of land prices, its spatial cost minimization or profit maximization perspective has come to be applied in empirical work involving choices over shorter distances.[8]

Recent developments in statistical applications to discrete choice have enabled the rationalization of urban selection models in terms of sound behavioural foundations. McFadden (1973, 1974) and others have pioneered the application of discrete choice models to a variety of urban problems, most notably in the field of travel mode choice among a finite number of discrete alternatives. The statistical model of random utility maximization over a set of discrete spatial alternatives has a natural applicability in the context of urban site selection of profit maximizing firms.

By contrast with Lee's multinomial logit model, using this approach to model employment location leads to the specification of a discrete choice model in which the probability that a firm of a particular type k will choose a site with a specified set of characteristics Z is[9]

$$p(Z{:}k) = p\,[g(Z)]. \tag{2}$$

This, as we shall see, basically entails a hedonic type of stock-adjustment approach to employment location, which, while maintaining the hypothesis of optimizing agents, is less restrictive as to reliance on the assumptions of monocentric urban structure or market-clearing spatial profit equalization among firms. A possible difficulty in estimation, however, may arise in dealing with a large number of spatial alternatives, which can prove computationally burdensome. In fact, Lee rejected this approach on the ground that it would force the specifying of only a limited number of subareas with a resulting restriction of variations in site characteristics.

Faced with the need to orient our empirical work to any implications and demands of departures from monocentricity, we adopt the less restrictive discrete choice framework in our proposed investigation of observed employment location patterns. We avoid an arbitrary restriction upon the number of alternatives by resorting to the method of random sub-sampling. Finally, we account as fully as we can for the role of spatial association between the alternatives by introducing a rather comprehensive set of spatial interaction variables in the logit specification.

To articulate the role of space, we invoke the basic concepts of access and interaction that underlie the agglomerative tendencies which make for employment concentration. In keeping with the suggestions of the literature, we recognize several sources of agglomeration benefits, all of which share the characteristic of conferring upon firms technological economies arising from interaction and transaction opportunities facilitated by the advantages of spatial proximity. These productive benefits may follow from access to information and public infrastructure services produced under scale economies, or the flexibility afforded by the ready availability of a variety of qualitatively differentiated inputs. We incorporate the spatially variant and multidimensional nature of this beneficial interaction by applying various degrees of distance decay to variables proxying for the quantum of each type of hypothesized interaction (relating to output, labour, or intermediate inputs, etc.). The distance between any point i to all points j represents an approximation to the frictional barriers to interaction with the entities of interest located in them, and pre-multiplying a vector of the latter by the matrix of these distances yields a measure of generalized access. That the negative exponential distance decay formulation is a special case of the more general class of additive-interaction access functions has been demonstrated by Fujita and Smith (1990).[10]

Implementation of the approach should permit an empirical recognition of both monocentricity as well as the more complex forms of spatial interaction that may exist within an urban area. In particular, we would like to explore the extent to which unidimensional access to a CBD may be attractive, whether in and of itself, or a summarizing of the influences of factors important to a locating firm, in the presence of variables explicitly accounting for generalized access in the manner described above. This procedure should permit a broad test of monocentricity.

III. A Model of Firm Location in Discrete Space

The Model

We seek to estimate a model of establishment location in six major employment categories for the Dallas–Fort Worth area. In the interest of comprehensiveness, we work with broad industrial categories at roughly the one-digit SIC (Standard Industrial Classification) level. This will enable us to make the appropriate connections with the aggregate patterns of land use that determine urban form.

A firm's location decision is motivated as an outcome of the following profit maximization problem over possible locations i:

$$\text{Max } PF\,(X_i, L_i, Z_i) - P_x\, X_i - R_i L_i,$$

where X_i, L_i, Z_i are respectively the purchased non-land and land inputs and a vector of non-purchased inputs having to do primarily with various types of access opportunities, as spatial agglomeration attributes. The f.o.b. output price, P, and P_x, the prices of variable inputs such as labour and capital are assumed invariant with location within a metropolitan area, while land price, R_i, varies spatially. The firm chooses the optimal quantities of X_i, L_i and Z_i, so that an indirect profit function in factor prices and the non-price attributes of location i can be specified.

$$V_i = V_i\,(P, P_x, R_i, Z_i). \quad (3)$$

If one further assumes that firms of any given type face the same non-land prices within the urban area, and that input employment is governed by technological considerations, then the above function can be summarized as the industry-specific formulation of the maximum profit attainable by a firm in industry k at location i:

$$V_{ik} = V_{ik}\,(R_i, Z_i) + e_{ik}. \quad (4)$$

A type-k firm locates in i^* provided that profits are highest there, i.e. $V_{i^*} = \max V_i$ over all i. This profit maximizing selection can be cast as a random utility process subject to a stochastic error which, if assumed to have a generalized extreme value distribution, results, as McFadden has demonstrated,[11] in the following logit specification, with the probability of a firm in each industry k (subscript dropped) locating at i as:

$$P_i = \text{pr}(i) = \exp\,[V_i]/\Sigma_i \exp\,[V_i]. \quad (5)$$

The Data

Our data include information on the number of establishments, total employment and the distribution of establishments by employment size class by zip code zone. Hence, the dependent variable pr(i) will be approximated by each zip's share of total establishments in the sample. Our demographic data is likewise available by zip. Coverage is over 141 zips in the Metroplex area, which constitute the firms' domain of choice.

The real geography of the region was taken into account by entering zip code area boundaries into a Geographical Information System, calculating the area of each zip through polygonal approximation, and computing the bilateral distances between any given zip's centroid and those of all others. This yielded a matrix of straight line distances used in all decay specifications of the pertinent variables. Radial and circumferential highways, the D/FW airport, and the Dallas and Fort Worth CBDs were superimposed upon this digital map. Data sources are listed in a note to Table 1.

Table 1: List of Zip Characteristics used in Estimation

I. *Structural variables*		
DISDCBD	=	Distance (mi.) to Dallas CBD, if zip in Dallas MSA
DISDCBDsq	=	(DISDCBD) squared
DISFCBD	=	Distance (mi.) to Fort Worth CBD, if zip in Fort Worth MSA
DISFCBDsq	=	(DISFCBD) squared
DISDFW	=	Distance (mi.) to Dallas–Fort Worth International Airport
FRWY	=	Dummy = 1 if zip contains/borders major radical, circumferential or mid-city highways; 0 otherwise
II. *Control variables*		
SHRDEVL	=	Zip's share of region's total usable (non-flood plain) area
PCTDEVL	=	Percentage of zip's area that is developed
III. *Agglomeration variables*		
TOTPOP87d1	=	1987 total population within decay radius 1 of zip
MDHINC87d2	=	1987 median household income, subj. to distance-decay 2
PCTBLK87d2	=	1987 per cent black, subj. to distance-decay 2
EMPLCMW85d2	=	1985 empl. in Construction, Manufacturing and Wholesale Trade within decay radius 2 of zip
EMPLMTF85d2	=	1985 empl. in Mining, Transport, Comm. and Utilities and FIRE within decay radius 2 of zip
EMPLRSR85d2	=	1985 employment in Retail Trade and Services within decay radius 2 of zip

Note on data sources: Establishment and employment data: County Business Patterns, 1983–87; Demographic data: CACI, Demographic Data Files, 1985, 1987; Land Use Data: North Central Texas Council of Govts., 1988 Data File.

Zip code boundaries were digitized and mapped using MAPSCO base maps by the Bruton Center for Development Studies, University of Texas at Dallas. Features of the transportation network were extracted from data files prepared by ETAK, Incorporated.

A few words in defence of aggregation to the level of zip code zones when the elemental alternatives are sites within such zones may not be out of place here. Although some researchers take the extreme view that any sort of spatial aggregation compromises results in studies of business location, others such as Anas (1981) have demonstrated and defended the behavioural validity of estimates drawn from zonal aggregate data in the context of intra-urban residential choice.[12] A distinct disadvantage of *dis*aggregated data, moreover, is that predictions generated from estimates based thereon are not readily projected to the population, a requirement for inferring aggregate land use patterns.

Sampling Strategy and Estimation Procedure

Intra-metropolitan location between 141 zip code zones represents choice over a relatively large number of alternatives. To compress this set by the use of a dimension such as distance from city centre by, for example, grouping them into a small number of successive concentric rings, would defeat our purpose of testing the monocentricity assumption and impose an unrealistic assumption of symmetry. On the other hand, admitting all the alternatives at once would impose a prohibitive computational burden for multinomial logit estimation. Fortunately, the discrete choice-based multinomial logit model may be efficiently estimated with only a subset of the alternatives. As regards the method of sub-sampling of the alternatives, several possibilities exist, of which we shall adopt the strategy of simple random sampling, where we draw randomly and without replacement, groups of five alternatives from the set of available ones. This procedure of drawing alternative sub-samples utilizes the independence from irrelevant alternatives (IIA) property to ensure that the logit model yields consistent estimates.[13] We plan to conduct the estimations for three models, each incorporating within it the preceding model, in order to observe the effects of adding successive variables. For comparability, identical models are specified for establishments with under 50 workers for Manufacturing, Construction, Wholesale Trade, Retail Trade, FIRE (Finance, Insurance, and Real Estate) and Services.[14] Maximum likelihood estimates are obtained using the LIMDEP (Limited Dependent Variables) statistical package on an IBM mainframe.[15]

Specific Hypotheses to be Tested: Explanatory Variables

The linear-in-parameters function V is specified for each industry as conditioned by the variables listed in Table 1. The full set of variables comprises three groups: the first, 'structural' group incorporates the basic monocentricity hypothesis, adapted to the special urban form of the Metroplex. In explicit recognition of the duocentric nature of the area, we first assign each zip code zone to one of either the 'Dallas' or the 'Fort Worth' sphere of influence, and then interact the dummies for the latter with the straight line (or 'airline') distance from its centroid to the appropriate CBD. This allows for a 'tighter' measurement of the centralizing influences. These monocentricity variables enter through a quadratic specification. In addition, we include distance to the D/FW airport, and account for existing transportation networks through a freeway dummy for the presence of a major highway in any given zip.

The second group of variables indexes zonal characteristics intended to capture the land supply aspects of each zip. The first of these is a size control variable—the zip's percentage share of usable land, i.e., area adjusted for land in the flood plain, to yield a measure of its developable land relative to the total. The other variable in this group represents the per cent of a zip's area that has actually been developed, which in practice tends to act as a proxy for the relative importance of residential use of a zip's usable land. Together, these might be expected to reflect both topographic considerations and zoning interventions that may restrict land or permit employment of land uses near residential activity.[16]

The third group of variables is the most important one for our objectives: it is intended to measure the spatial interaction opportunities that agglomeration benefits are attributed to and address the question, 'What other factors besides CBD distance matter to firms?' In so doing, it may be expected to convey a sense of which assumptions are behaviourally realistic for purposes of future modelling of employment location in non-monocentric theories of urban structure. Hypothesized sources of urbanization and localization influences emanating from all zones in the area are distance-decayed with respect to each zip to yield 'spatial interaction proxies' of the form

$$A_{iq} = \sum_j A_{ijq}^{-aDij} \tag{6}$$

which summarizes the effects of an agglomerative influence q impinging upon any zip i from all zips j at a distance, D_{ij} with respect to it, where 'a' is a pre-specified coverage parameter.[17] For the A_q's, we recognize possible urbanization, broad localization and interindustry linkages. We decay total population over a fairly wide spatial extent ($a = 0.25$), to represent the comprehensive urbanization benefits of large residential concentration, ranging from command over a commuting labour shed to the direct and indirect infrastructural and amenity advantages of pure urban size. The choice of these explanatory variables incorporates the well-known suggestions of theory that spatial agglomeration has its basis in transaction benefits of information and input quality and in scale economies of size and density in the production and delivery of local public services.

Median household income and per cent black in the zip are the two other demographic variables used, with smaller decay radius ($a = 0.75$). Conceptually, it is possible to make a distinction between advantages of customer access for non-basic sectors such as retail trade (and some activities within the construction and services categories), and labour-market access of firms seeking proximity to specialized labour pools. Our original intent was to capture the former through the use of an index of purchasing power and proxy access to white-collar labour through median education levels for the zones, but these proved to be severely correlated with household income. Likewise, we had sought to hypothesize access to unemployed labour as a location attraction for certain types of firms, but here again, the proposed proxy displayed a high degree of correlation with per cent black. We selected the two socio-economic attributes we use for their policy and distributional relevance, realizing, however, that they confound the influences of several factors, including the amorphous one of high vs. low 'prestige' locations. Note that the income variable does not enter with an unambiguous sign *a priori*: by the pure agglomeration interpretation, a positive sign is expected when the variable reflects buying power or the character of the broader area's labour force, but a zone's income might have a negative sign if low rents—and incomes—compensate for proximity to incompatible or fiscally onerous non-residential uses.[18]

Lastly, we employ distance-decayed aggregations of employment in three categories to account for the effects of own-industry and inter-industry spatial linkage opportunities. The three combinations, viz., Construction-Manufacturing-Wholesale, Mining-Transport/Communications-FIRE, and Retail-Services are so grouped to reflect presumed commonalities in land and labour use. These broad aggregations and the use of employment data to denote levels of industrial activity is to minimize any built-in affinity with the dependent variables in any given case. Also, the proxies for the localization and interindustry effects are invested with a dynamic dimension, in that they refer to industry concentrations of an earlier period, 1985, by contrast with the other variables which are at their current 1987 values.

IV. Results and Discussion

Results appear in Tables 2 to 7. For each industry, coefficient estimates and their associated asymptotic t-values are reported for the three consecutive runs, as are goodness-of-fit measures, in the form of the Likelihood Ratio Index, both unadjusted and adjusted for degrees of freedom. We discuss these industry by industry. Table 8 presents the direct aggregate probability elasticities computed at sample means using the predicted values and coefficients from the last run, so that relative magnitudes of the various influences may be compared.

For Manufacturing, the 'structural' group of variables is found to explain less than a third of the variation explained by the full set of variables, but the Dallas CBD distance influence retains its significance throughout. It exhibits a convex shape that features an upturn, implying a rapid exhaustion of the attractiveness of CBD access in favour of a decentralized locational preference. The probability elasticity for the CBD distance variable computed at the sample mean is positive, reflecting the overwhelmingly decentralized nature of the industry. The Fort Worth CBD fails to exert a strong centralizing influence, while access to the D/FW airport is found to sustain a significant pull. Freeway access, likewise, is valued, and remains so in the presence of the agglomeration variables. Of the latter, both urbanization and localization benefits to location are evident.

Construction establishment location is the most poorly explained of all the industrial categories considered here, the first group of variables explaining only a small fraction of the low total explained variation. Elasticity computations reveal this category to be substantially decentralized with respect to both CBDs. Airport and freeway access are valued, but far less than manufacturing, as befits a widely dispersed but largely local form of activity. Both urbanization and localization economies are significantly present, and somewhat less so, a positive effect of high median household income. The latter, along with affinity to areas with a high percentage of developed land probably reflects the propensity of such activity to locate in predominantly residential areas. The avoidance of zips with high proportions of minority residents suggests the avoidance of areas where little new construction is occurring or anticipated.

Wholesale firms, as may be expected, value freeway access considerably, engaged as they are in the storage and regional and local distribution of goods. Establishments in this category tend to locate in proximity to manufacturing and other warehousing firms, as evidenced by the significant coefficients and high elasticity for the *EMPCMW* variable, but also display strong interindustry linkage with retail firms. This dual spatial attraction is likely to be a consequence of their functions as intermediaries between manufacturing and retail outlets, in an activity with rather high transport costs. Notably, access to D/FW airport is also at a premium, given the Dallas area's geographical role as a regional and national distribution centre.

While Wholesale activities are divided between export and local functions, Retail may be said to be almost exclusively locally oriented. It is also, quite expectedly, the most decentralized for that reason. Retail establishments display a natural propensity to locate in the more developed zones. The results show the effect of pure urbanization economies to be significant and quite substantial, but the median household income variable, representing, among other things, spatial purchasing power, has an unexpected negative sign. This could be because our consideration of firms with under 50 employees omits relatively large retail establishments such as department stores, which tend to locate disproportionately in the shopping malls of affluent suburbs. Notably, firms in our sample exhibit relatively little aversion to location in the lower income predominantly black neighbourhoods. Finally, own-industry employment linkages are significant and large, indicating a clustering to capture advantages of shopping trip economies.

The Finance, Insurance and Real Estate industry is a major presence in the economy of Dallas–Fort Worth. It is the most centralized around the Dallas CBD, appears to enjoy substantial urbanization economies, and otherwise tends to locate in proximity to perceived high prestige, high-income zones with low per cent black resident populations. Firms in this industry bear higher locational affinity with retail and service concentrations than with manufacturing and warehousing, but the negative sign on the own-industry grouping of *EMPMTF*—employment in mining, transport/communication/utilities and FIRE is puzzling.[19] We speculate that this might be partly the result of heterogeneity in this group, and partly due to the measurement of the localization proxy at its 1985 value. One must

Table 2: Location of Manufacturing Establishments in the Metroplex

Dep. var.: Probability of location in zone *i*

Indep. var.	COEFF	ASYMP.-T	COEFF	ASYMP.-T	COEFF	ASYMP.-T	COEFF	ASYMP.-T
DISDCBD	0.006	0.60	–0.038	–3.37	–0.073	–3.45	0LD	0LD
DISDCBDsq	–0.002	–4.37	–0.002	–3.01	0.004	5.41	0.001	1.87
DISFCBD	–0.088	–5.46	–0.162	–9.19	–0.037	–1.07	0.018	2.58
DISFCBDsq	0.003	2.73	0.005	4.24	0.002	1.21	0.000	0.12
DISDFW	–0.034	–13.08	–0.050	–17.34	–0.007	–2.18	–0.100	–6.65
FRWY	0.525	8.19	0.414	6.44	0.401	5.90	0.484	7.23
SHRDEVL			0.876	15.50	0.613	9.74	38.964	6.90
PCTDEVL			–0.002	–2.04	0.003	1.96	0.005	3.30
TOTPOP87d1					4.0E-06	6.78	1.0E-05	11.76
MDHINC87d2					–1.0E-05	–2.33	5.5E-05	9.11
PCTBLK87d2					–3.3E-03	–1.60	–9.2E-03	–3.87
EMPCMW85d2					8.8E-05	26.03	7.1E-05	20.12
EMPMTF85d2					–1.7E-05	–4.38	–3.2E-06	–0.74
EMPRSR85d2					–1.4E-05	–2.89	1.2E-04	11.19
							–0.130	–7.59
RHO-SQ	0.0496		0.0668		0.1483			
ADJ.RHO-SQ	0.0488		0.0657		0.1463			

Table 3: Location of Construction Establishments in the Metroplex

Dep. var.: Probability of location in zone *i*

Indep. var.	COEFF	ASYMP.-T	COEFF	ASYMP.-T	COEFF	ASYMP.-T	COEFF	ASYMP.-T
DISDCBD	0.130	13.49	0.052	4.98	–0.079	–4.59	0LD	0LD
DISDCBDsq	–0.005	–12.16	–0.002	–4.45	0.003	5.95	0.001	1.87
DISFCBD	0.128	9.20	0.006	0.36	–0.095	–3.47	0.018	2.58
DISFCBDsq	–0.006	–7.26	0.000	0.15	0.005	3.96	0.000	0.12
DISDFW	–0.015	–7.49	–0.017	–7.58	0.007	2.68	–0.100	–6.65
FRWY	0.400	8.32	0.178	3.74	0.182	3.58	0.484	7.23
SHRDEVL			0.940	22.22	0.794	17.44	38.964	6.90
PCTDEVL			0.018	18.18	0.015	12.68	0.005	3.30
TOTPOP87d1					2.6E-06	5.54	1.0E-05	11.76
MDHINC87d2					5.2E-06	1.59	5.5E-05	9.11
PCTBLK87d2					–1.5E-02	–9.14	–9.2E-03	–3.87
EMPCMW85d2					4.2E-05	14.96	7.1E-05	20.12
EMPMTF85d2					–1.9E-05	–4.41	–3.2E-06	–0.74
EMPRSR85d2					–6.5E-06	–1.54	1.2E-04	11.19
							–0.130	–7.59
RHO-SQ	0.0153		0.0685		0.0938			
ADJ.RHO-SQ	0.0147		0.0677		0.0926			

Table 4: Location of Wholesale Trading Establishments in the Metroplex

Dep. var.: Probability of location in zone *i*								
Indep. var.	COEFF	ASYMP.-T	COEFF	ASYMP.-T	COEFF	ASYMP.-T	COEFF	ASYMP.-T
DISDCBD	0.033	4.10	–0.007	–0.85	–0.027	–1.51	0LD	0LD
DISDCBDsq	–0.004	–9.57	–0.003	–8.01	0.002	3.15	0.001	1.87
DISFCBD	–0.119	–9.30	–0.190	–13.56	0.071	2.42	0.018	2.58
DISFCBDsq	0.003	3.80	0.005	5.84	–0.006	–3.77	0.000	0.12
DISDFW	–0.062	–30.92	–0.075	–34.21	–0.025	–9.47	–0.100	–6.65
FRWY	0.994	16.59	0.886	14.84	0.759	11.94	0.484	7.23
SHRDEVL			0.816	18.65	0.628	12.12	38.964	6.90
PCTDEVL			–0.000	–0.18	0.000	0.19	0.005	3.30
TOTPOP87d1					3.3E-06	7.09	1.0E-05	11.76
MDHINC87d2					–1.8E-05	5.18	5.5E-05	9.11
PCTBLK87d2					1.1E-03	0.66	–9.2E-03	–3.87
EMPCMW85d2					8.4E-05	33.39	7.1E-05	20.12
EMPMTF85d2					4.0E-05	–13.18	–3.2E-06	–0.74
EMPRSR85d2					–4.2E-05	11.75	1.2E-04	11.19
							–0.130	7.59
RHO-SQ	0.1179		0.1319		0.2877			
ADJ.RHO-SQ	0.1174		0.1313		0.2866			

Table 5: Location of Retail Trading Establishments in the Metroplex

Dep. var.: Probability of location in zone *i*								
Indep. var.	COEFF	ASYMP.-T	COEFF	ASYMP.-T	COEFF	ASYMP.-T	COEFF	ASYMP.-T
DISDCBD	0.050	9.16	–0.040	–6.72	0.025	2.45	0LD	0LD
DISDCBDsq	–0.003	–11.99	0.001	2.11	0.000	0.74	0.001	1.87
DISFCBD	0.080	10.04	–0.055	–6.27	0.144	8.35	0.018	2.58
DISFCBDsq	–0.007	–14.53	–0.000	–0.75	–0.009	–10.47	0.000	0.12
DISDFW	–0.027	–21.66	–0.031	–23.34	–0.010	–5.55	–0.100	–6.65
FRWY	0.806	23.95	0.641	19.27	0.462	12.95	0.484	7.23
SHRDEVL			0.817	30.08	1.128	35.87	38.964	6.90
PCTDEVL			0.017	27.08	0.008	10.29	0.005	3.30
TOTPOP87d1					1.7E-06	5.94	1.0E-05	11.76
MDHINC87d2					–1.5E-05	–7.09	5.5E-05	9.11
PCTBLK87d2					–1.3E-03	–1.41	–9.2E-03	–3.87
EMPCMW85d2					6.7E-06	3.96	7.1E-05	20.12
EMPMTF85d2					–4.9E-05	–24.61	–3.2E-06	–0.74
EMPRSR85d2					8.8E-05	39.54	1.2E-04	11.19
							–0.130	–7.59
RHO-SQ	0.0397		0.0768		0.1473			
ADJ.RHO-SQ	0.0395		0.0765		0.1469			

Table 6: Location of FIRE Establishments in the Metroplex

Dep. var: Probability of location in zone *i*

Indep. var.	COEFF	ASYMP.-T	COEFF	ASYMP.-T	COEFF	ASYMP.-T	COEFF	ASYMP.-T
DISDCBD	–0.072	–9.05	–0.140	–16.63	–0.112	–6.37	0LD	0LD
DISDCBDsq	0.001	2.19	0.004	9.87	0.004	6.22	0.001	1.87
DISFCBD	–0.160	–13.02	–0.284	–20.81	–0.008	–0.28	0.018	2.58
DISFCBDsq	0.004	5.16	0.011	13.69	–0.002	–1.65	0.000	0.12
DISDFW	–0.045	–22.57	–0.044	–20.50	–0.006	–2.26	–0.100	–6.65
FRWY	0.832	14.03	0.663	11.35	0.293	4.68	0.484	7.23
SHRDEVL			0.394	8.97	0.831	15.55	38.964	6.90
PCTDEVL			0.020	21.54	0.003	2.38	0.005	3.30
TOTPOP87dl					2.2E-06	4.90	1.0E-05	11.76
MDHINC87d2					2.5E-05	6.96	5.5E-05	9.11
PCTBLK87d2					–7.1E-03	–4.10	–9.2E-03	–3.87
EMPCMW85d2					–8.4E-07	–0.32	7.1E-05	20.12
EMPMTF85d2					–5.5E-05	–19.02	–3.2E-06	–0.74
EMPRSR85d2					1.2E-04	34.80	1.2E-04	11.19
							–0.130	–7.59
RHO-SQ	0.0837		0.1111		0.2846			
ADJ.RHO-SQ	0.0832		0.1106		0.2836			

Table 7: Location of Service Establishments in the Metroplex

Dep. var: Probability of location in zone *i*

Indep. var.	COEFF	ASYMP.-T	COEFF	ASYMP.-T	COEFF	ASYMP.-T	COEFF	ASYMP.-T
DISDCBD	–0.020	–4.88	–0.098	–21.80	–0.090	–10.59	0LD	0LD
DISDCBDsq	–0.001	–4.57	0.002	11.70	0.004	13.71	0.001	1.87
DISFCBD	–0.071	–11.01	–0.201	–28.11	–0.013	–0.93	0.018	2.58
DISFCBDsq	0.000	0.215	0.007	16.73	–0.001	–1.32	0.000	0.12
DISDFW	–0.038	–35.32	–0.040	–33.66	–0.009	–6.44	–0.100	–6.65
FRWY	0.561	21.41	0.434	16.74	0.202	7.26	0.484	7.23
SHRDEVL			0.554	24.22	0.828	31.46	38.964	6.90
PCTDEVL			0.018	36.45	0.008	14.29	0.005	3.30
TOTPOP87dl					2.7E-06	12.02	1.0E-05	11.76
MDHINC87d2					3.2E-06	1.80	5.5E-05	9.11
PCTBLK87d2					–4.4E-03	–5.52	–9.2E-03	–3.87
EMPCMW85d2					'1.9E-05	14.52	7.1E-05	20.12
EMPMTF85d2					–4.5E-05	–31.44	–3.2E-06	–0.74
EMPRSR85d2					7.9E-05	43.98	1.2E-04	11.19
							–0.130	–7.59
RHO-SQ	0.0564		0.0856		0.1709			
ADJ.RHO-SQ	0.0563		0.0854		0.1706			

remember that between 1985 and 1987, this industry group lost quite heavily as a consequence of the oil slump, the greatest absolute losses occurring, naturally, in areas of its maximum concentration.

Services represent a rather diverse group of activities, incorporating both personal and business components. The personal component appears to respond to residential concentrations in their location patterns, as evidenced by relatively large urbanization effects. Like in the retail category, there is a marked tendency to locate in already built-up areas, and a significant proximity to high-income zones, but by contrast with it, a somewhat stronger centralizing influence. There appear to be strong spatial linkages between service firm locations and employment in service and retail industries and a milder but significant affinity with the manufacturing, construction and wholesale categories. The latter probably reflects the growing business component of firms in this group.

V. Summary and Conclusion

We have attempted to model the outcomes of firm location decisions in a discrete choice framework where spatial alternatives are zip code zones in the Dallas–Fort Worth area. These alternative locations are

Table 8: Direct Aggregate Probability Elasticities[a]

Variable	MANUF	CONSTR	WHOLES	RETAIL	F.I.R.E.	SERVICES
DISDCBD	0.1092	0.0503	0.0729	0.1396	–3.7153	0.0414
DISFCBD	0.0197	0.0599	–0.0902	–0.1170	–0.1189	–0.0696
DISDFW	–0.0878	0.0888	–0.2537	–0.1148	–0.0633	–0.1059
FRWY	0.2566	0.1215	0.4347	0.3024	0.1642	0.1261
SHRDEVL	0.2814	0.4257	0.2496	0.5508	0.3322	0.3742
PCTDEVL	0.1465	0.8701	0.0099	0.4117	0.1235	0.4324
TOTPOP87dl	0.5418	0.3581	0.4129	0.2345	0.2706	0.3786
MDHINC87d2	–0.2294	0.1270	0.3559	–0.3435	0.4960	0.0705
PCTBLK87d2	–0.0323	–0.1276	–0.0094	–0.0120	–0.0558	–0.0412
EMPCMW85d2	0.6143	0.2622	0.5488	0.0454	–0.0053	0.1347
EMPMTF85d2	–0.0834	–0.0725	–0.1986	–0.2430	–0.2730	–0.2417
EMPRSR85d2	–0.1213	–0.0507	0.3638	0.8089	1.0928	0.7496

a Direct aggregate elasticity definition

$$EiK = \frac{Bk}{N\ \bar{Pi}} \sum_{n=1}^{N} Pn(i)[1 - Pn(i)]Zik$$

where $Pn(i)$ =Predicted location probability for sample n. Zik = Sample mean value of attribute variable k, N = Number of sub-samples in population, $\bar{Pi}$ = Population means of zips' establishment shares, Bk = Estimated coefficient of kth attribute.

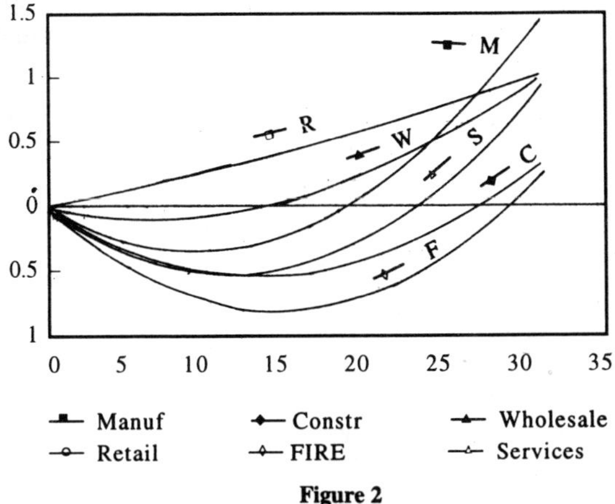

Figure 2

indexed by a set of structural, land supply and agglomeration-interaction attributes, and we have sought in particular to investigate differences in spatial response to these among units in broad industry groups. Almost all hypothesized effects are found to impact location in an expected manner, though with important similarities and contrasts across industries.

The results confirm a considerable degree of decentralization in all industries other than FIRE with respect to the Dallas CBD, though a somewhat more monocentric pattern remains with respect to the Fort Worth CBD, owing to the relatively lower degree of development in the western half of the Metroplex. The D/FW airport appears to have exerted a striking influence on firm location in most industries since its inception less than two decades ago, particularly for wholesale trade firms. Access to freeways further conditions firm location, with wholesale trade, retail, and manufacturing showing the highest responsiveness. These considerations lend support to the emphasis on the role of transportation-induced decentralization in theoretical formulations of firm suburbanization such as White (1976).

Our proxies for urbanization and localization economies perform quite well, with general population and related-industry accessibility exerting the hypothesized positive effect for all industries. Related-industry proximity is found important not only for manufacturing and wholesale, but also for retail and services. Moreover, we have found that the addition of explicit spatial agglomeration measures substantially

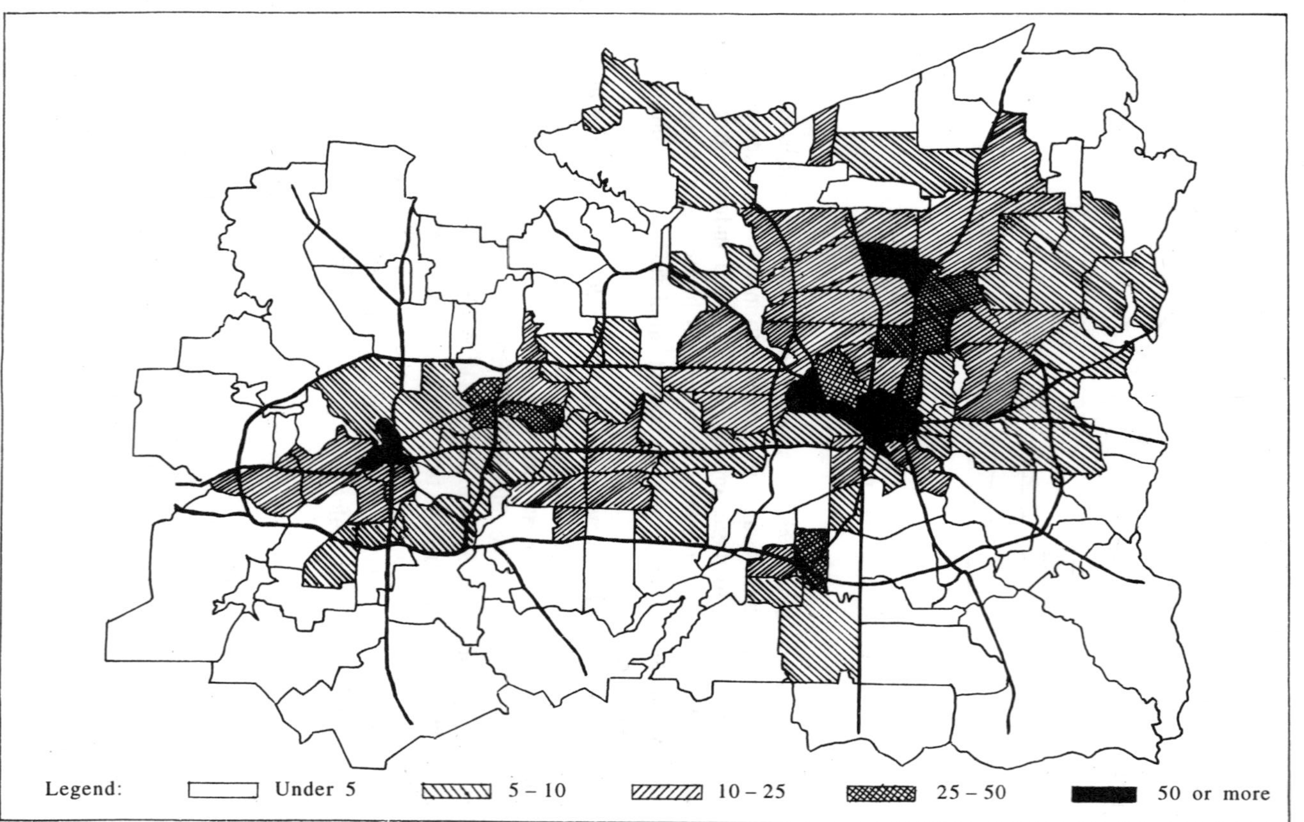

Figure 3(a): Total Observed Establishments Per Square Mile

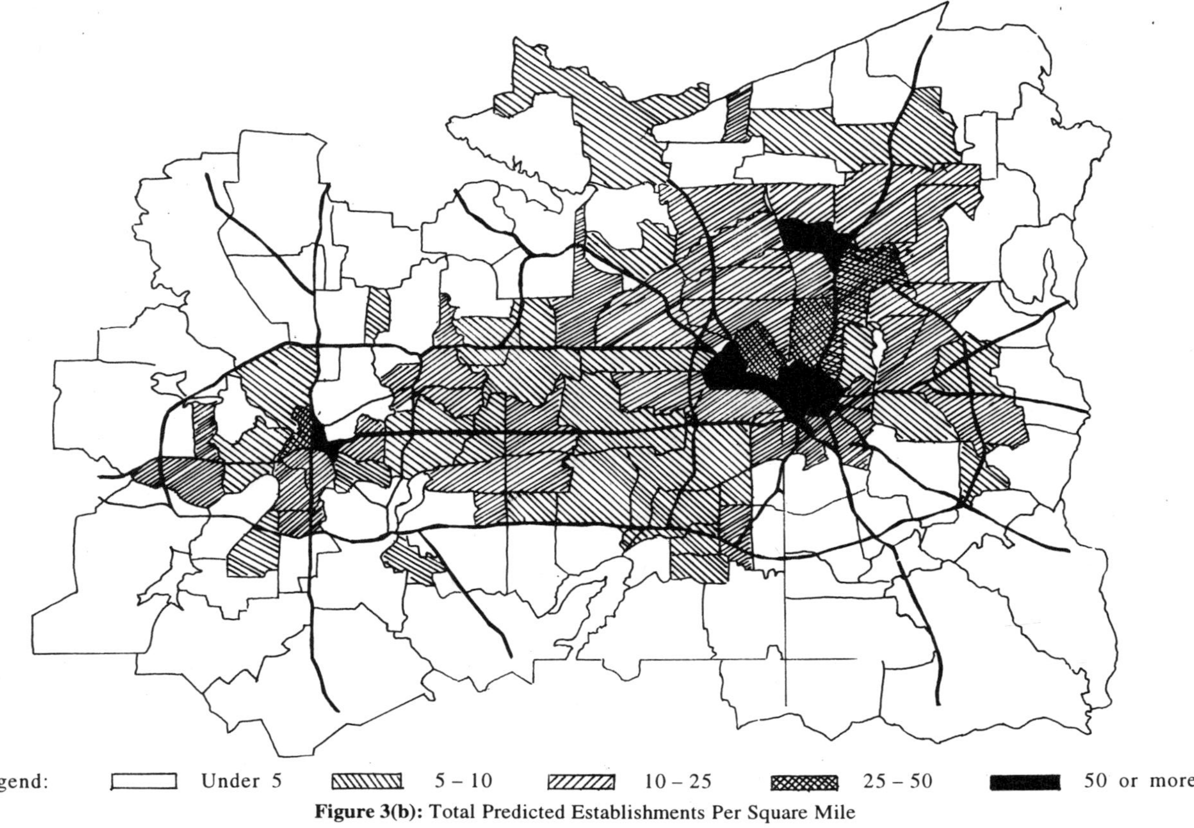

Figure 3(b): Total Predicted Establishments Per Square Mile

improves the explanatory power of the specifications. Of course, in a cross-sectional study it is impossible to discount the historical impact that structural attributes such as the two CBDs or the transport interventions may have had on the existing spatial employment and population distributions. However, once the latter have been controlled for, the residual attraction of CBD access *per se* vanishes in most cases (with the important exception of FIRE) at the mean values of the elasticities.

Figure 2 is based on the coefficients of the Dallas CBD and CBD-squared terms in the final runs of the model for the various industries. The relative partial predicted probability is evaluated in each case with distance from the Dallas city centre. While the *y*-values have no direct interpretation, the *x*-values of the turning points are instructive, representing the gradual (or not-so-gradual) attenuation of the residual influence of the Dallas CBD once other factors have been controlled for. Most 'upturns' occur within 10 to 15 miles of the CBD, approximately the distance of the first major beltway (LBJ Freeway), and close enough to reflect the CBD as being simply one among several 'centres'. This confirms the polycentricity of urban structure as motivated from the basics of firm location. A comparison of the results in Figure 2 by industry reveals the degree of CBD orientation within each industry, confirming expectations that financial industries maintain the strongest attraction to the CBD, with manufacturing and wholesale trade showing substantially less CBD orientation. Significantly, though perhaps not surprisingly, retail trade exhibits the least CBD orientation.

Due to our use of zonal aggregates, the land use of a particular site or elemental alternative within a zip code is, of course, not possible to predict—each zone will be shared by several activities, albeit in a unique industrial mix. Nevertheless, we can examine the implications of revealed location behaviour for aggregate land use by mapping predicted probabilities for each industry and, comparing these with observed densities, reveal the extent to which locational preference translates into land use. In Figure 3, the predicted graph compares remarkably well with the actual. Major employment subcentres such as the North-Dallas/Richardson node, the Stemmons industrial corridor, and the Las Colinas complex are replicated nicely, attesting to the power of our approach.

While the use of broad spatial and industrial aggregates, as we have employed them in this paper, lends itself to motivating choice-based non-monocentric employment land use in a feasible and intuitive manner, further research might aim at the rigorous pursuit of more finely tuned hypotheses to address some of the limitations of an operationalization such as ours. For instance, a finer industrial classification may reduce the degree of heterogeneity reflected in the low overall explanatory power obtained with our broad one-digit SIC groups as dependent variables. The use of 2-3-and 4-digit industrial groups would facilitate better targeting and customizing of hypotheses about the nature of agglomeration and localization effects, as would more elaborate firm-level data. For instance, a more detailed analysis of certain retail sectors might permit the recognition of market area discontinuities not capturable with our uniform continuous measure of 'general accessibility'. Tracking the spatial mobility of individual establishments might provide quite different insights about factors important in location dynamics and equilibrium than evident from a stock approach such as the present one, as might an explicit modelling of bidirectional causality between business location and residential development.[20]

NOTES

This paper was prepared for presentation at the 1990 TRED Conference on *Causes and Consequences of the Changing Urban Form* held in Boston, 12–13 October. Financial support in the form of a grant from the State of Texas Advanced Research Program and the technical support of the Bruton Center for Development Studies, The University of Texas at Dallas, are gratefully acknowledged. We have benefited from the comments and encouragement of Brian J.L. Berry and Irv Hoch and are indebted to Bill Wheaton, Jerry Rothenberg and other participants of the conference for suggestions leading to many improvements.
Reproduced from *Regional Science and Urban Economics* 21 (1991) 225–53, North-Holland.

1 According to preliminary results from the 1990 Census, reported in the 16 Sept. 1990 issue of the *Dallas Morning News*, the Dallas–Fort Worth area, with an enumerated 1990 population of 4,246,576, led Texas urban area growth at 29.7 per cent over the last decade. The City of Dallas grew at 9.6 per cent, Dallas County about twice that rate, while Dallas' northern suburbs grew the fastest, with the northerly Collin and Denton Counties registering 81.3 per cent and 88.8 per cent growth, respectively. With virtually unlimited land supplies available for expansion, the forces of oil-driven Texas prosperity and those of the more general sunbelt shift converged during that period to 'remake' the face of much of the urban area, visibly changing the urban landscape and the extent of its reach.

2 Note that we are trying to infer spatial behaviour from the observed current aggregate spatial distribution of establishments. Locational decision-making has also been studied in the literature by looking at flows over time rather than static activity levels, and with firm-level observations rather than zonal aggregates. While the micro approach is clearly preferable for behavioural inferences where data are available, the aggregative estimation methodology has some advantage in facilitating prediction of aggregate land use patterns.

3 One study which attempts to do some of both is by Clapp (1980) who motivates an office location model by hypothesizing the need for face-to-face contact, develops an empirical subcentre construct that proxies the opportunities for such contact, and proceeds to estimate a hedonic bid-rent function conditioned on various office demand-and-supply characteristics. He justifies this by ascertaining that the labour-scarcity driven wage gradient implied in White (1976) is not a strong restraining influence for office location in Los Angeles.

4 Tauchen and Witte (1984). Also, for a square-grid model of the CBD featuring the attractiveness of agglomeration, see O'Hara (1977).

5 Ogawa and Fujita (1980) prove the existence of non-monocentric equilibrium in a one-dimensional city. Fujita and Ogawa (1982) show that with concave cost functions, many types of subcentres and multiple equilibria are possible.

6 Richardson (1988) makes this argument.

7 See Lee (1982). The discussion below draws from Lee (1989).

8 See Hansen (1987) for an application to intra-regional choice and Erickson and Wasylenko (1980) for an implementation in the intra-metropolitan context. In an exercise permitted by his firm-level data, Carlton (1983) estimates a discrete-continuous model of inter-SMSA (Standard Metropolitan Statistical Area) location.

9 Maddala (1983) demonstrates the algebraic identity of the discrete choice and standard multinomial logit models.

10 See Fujita and Smith (1990). The many sources of urban agglomeration economies are well documented in standard works such as Mills and Hamilton (1984). Henderson (1985) treats agglomeration economies in the urban business sector as an external size-shift factor in a firm's production function. His formulation assumes that firms within a CBD receive the same amount of external economies regardless of location. Kanemoto (1987) discusses the need for explicit modelling of the spatial nature of externalities between firms when considering intra-urban spatial firm distribution. Kanemoto states that when accompanied by production indivisibilities, inter-firm interaction costs may be interpreted as externalities between firms under the assumption that each firm (within an industry) interacts with other firms (at a given distance) uniformly. However, endogenous contact models such as Tauchen and Witte (1984) can more properly handle cases of firm interaction with only some of the other firms in a sector. Empirical implementation of such 'specialized' (compared with our 'generalized') access requires, of course, detailed information at the establishment level.

11 The logit expression is operationally very similar to Lee's, which is derived from an assumption of Weibull-distributed error terms in the bid-rent function. The practical difference is that with the latter, the discrete alternatives have different coefficient vectors, while in McFadden's Gumbel-derived logit, the estimated coefficients on explanatory variables are common among alternatives, and represent implicit prices for their characteristics. To the extent that land rents capitalized site advantages, a hedonic price regression might provide information similar to that which the estimation of our stock-adjustment model implies. However, Sivitanidou and Wheaton (1990) suggest significant capitalization only if land supply is constrained or regulated, an unlikely Dallas scenario.

12 Anas (1981). See Schmenner (1977) for the contrary view.

13 Ben-Akiva and Lerman (1985) discuss aggregation and strategies for the sampling of alternatives in discrete choice analysis, and the justifiability of the IIA assumption. Ben-Akiva and Lerman suggest that IIA may be more or less believable depending on whether heterogeneities in the population are accounted for in the model. In our case, its use is defended on grounds of the industrial grouping of firms and the attempt to account as fully as possible for spatial interdependencies through the agglomeration terms.

14 These industries account for more than 90 per cent of Metroplex employment, while establishments with under 50 employees constituting over 94 per cent of total area firms. The use of smaller firms, while eliminating only a small fraction of the establishments from the sample, focuses on more highly mobile establishments, which is an important consideration in a study of locational choice within a stock framework. By industry, the percentages of large firms (with over 50 employees) for Construction, Manufacturing, Wholesale Trade, Retail, FIRE, and Services are, respectively, 4.1, 15.7, 5.2, 5.8, 6.0, and 4.4 per cent.

15 Regression of the log establishment ratio for each pair of zones on their attributes by ordinary least squares will also yield unbiased and efficient estimates. Our choice of the maximum likelihood estimation methodology was dictated by a desire to perform tests of alternative nested decision structures in future. Also, Schultz (1982), which compares 'log odds' OLS with ML results for a model of place-to-place migration reports superior goodness-of-fit for the latter.

16 About 75 per cent of developed land in the zip code zones, on average, represents that committed to residential uses. While the residual 25 per cent would include land in industrial and commercial uses, the risk of tautology with the dependent variables is small, given that the latter are more disaggregated. Another qualifier that pertains to the 'control' variables is that we cannot directly account for zoning interventions in the absence of contemporaneous data. In a land-abundant environment where zoning changes are easy and frequent, however, it is unlikely that any firm desiring to locate in a zip code zone will be seriously constrained in finding a site within its boundaries.

17 When spatial zones are relatively small, an argument can be made for

excluding zone $j=i$ from a gravity summation proxy, particularly for measures of the own- and interindustry localization effects. With zip code zones of our considerable size, so doing would lose much of the intra-zonal interaction that we feel to be important, and introduce an artificial threshold for what are continuous spatial effects. Nevertheless, several precautions have been taken to minimize direct simultaneity: the dependent variable represents a zone's current share of small establishments in a given one-digit industry, while the proxy measures index contiguous lagged total employment in all enterprises for a composite industrial aggregate. A quantitative summary of the small degree of influence of the $j=i$ component of the distance-decayed variables is given by the median ratios of the localization proxies to the employment total in each of the component industries in zone i. For Construction, this ratio is 9.7, 3.9 for Manufacturing, 12.1 for Wholesale Trade, 6.0 for Retail, 4.3 for FIRE, and 5.1 for Services.

18 Our spatial population measure is a general catch-all, hypothesized to capture technological as well as public service economies of large size, all of which presumably exert a positive influence on business location. Nevertheless, both for population and income, negative predicted associations may follow for other reasons: See, for example, Fischel (1975). Jurisdictions may enact zoning restrictions in areas of high population and incomes, responding to homeowner pressure reflected in the willingness to pay to avoid the externalities associated with industrial and commercial development, hence *reducing* the probability of establishment location. Here too, however, the comment at the end of note 16 applies.

19 Note that FIRE is clubbed with the highly centralized TCU sector, in the belief that these share a greater affinity in land use. It might alternatively have been aggregated with Services, although the tremendous heterogeneity of the latter category may have diluted responsiveness to its business component alone. This may, however, partially explain the unexpected result.

20 With disaggregated industries or at the individual establishment level, one can point out quite different forms of interdependence within the same industry. General accessibility may not necessarily be a good proxy for expected interaction costs where duplicate input or customer locations are available to establishments in any given industry class and firms make all-or-nothing transaction decisions. Past development may have one kind of influence on the probability of additional development now; but a quite different meaning with respect to development already there, distinguishing an incremental from a stock approach. We are indebted to Jerry Rothenberg for pointing out these considerations.

REFERENCES

Anas, A. (1981), 'The Estimation of Multinomial Logit Models of Joint Location and Travel Mode Choice from Aggregated Data', *Journal of Regional Science,* Vol. 21.

Ben-Akiva, M. and S.R. Lerman (1985), *Discrete Choice Analysis: Theory and Application to Travel Demand* (MIT Press, Cambridge, MA).

Carlton, D.W. (1983), 'The Location and Employment Choices of New Firms: An Economic Model with Discrete and Continuous Endogenous Variables', *Review of Economics and Statistics,* Vol. 65.

Clapp, J.M. (1980), 'The Intrametropolitan Location of Office Activities', *Journal of Regional Science,* Vol. 20, No. 3.

Ellickson, B. (1981), 'An Alternative Test of the Hedonic Theory of Housing Markets', *Journal of Urban Economics*, Vol. 9.

Erickson, R.A. and M. Wasylenko (1980), 'Firm Relocation and Site Selection in Suburban Municipalities', *Journal of Urban Economics* 8.

Fischel, W. (1975), 'Fiscal and Environmental Considerations in the Location of Firms in Suburban Communities' in E.S. Mills and W.E. Oates, eds., *Fiscal Zoning and Land Use Controls* (Lexington Books, Lexington, MA).

Fujita, M. and H. Ogawa (1982), 'Multiple Equilibria and Structural Transition of Nonmonocentric Configurations', *Regional Science and Urban Economics,* Vol. 12, No. 2.

———— and T.E. Smith (1990), 'Additive-interaction Models of Spatial Agglomeration, *Journal of Regional Science,* Vol. 30, No. 1.

Hansen, E.R. (1987), 'Industrial Location Choice in Sao Paulo, Brazil, *Regional Science and Urban Economics,* Vol. 17, No. 1,

Henderson, J. V. (1985), *Economic Theory and the Cities*, 2nd edition (Academic Press, New York).

Kanemoto, Y. (1987), 'Externalities in Space', in T. Miyao and Y. Kanemoto, *Urban Dynamics and Urban Externalities* (Harwood Academic Publishers, London).

Lee, K.S. (1982), 'A Model of Intra-urban Employment Location: An Application to Bogota, Colombia', *Journal of Urban Economics,* Vol. 12.

————(1989), 'The Location of Jobs in a Developing Metropolis: Patterns of Growth in Bogota and Cali', Colombia (The World Bank, published by Oxford University Press, New York).

Maddala, G.S. (1983), '*Limited-dependent and Qualitative Variables in Econometrics* Cambridge University Press, Cambridge.

McFadden, D. (1973), 'Conditional Logit Analysis of Qualitative Choice Behaviour' in Paul Zarembka, *Frontiers in Econometrics,* Academic Press, New York.

————(1974), 'The Measurement of Urban Travel Demand', *Journal of Public Economics,* Vol. 3.

Mills, E.S. and B.W. Hamilton (1984), *Urban Economics*, 3rd edition (Scott Foresman, Glenview, IL).

Ogawa, H. and M. Fujita (1980), 'Equilibrium Land Use Patterns in a Nonmonocentric City', *Journal of Regional Science,* Vol. 20.

O'Hara, D.J. (1977), 'Locations of Firms Within a Square Central Business District', *Journal of Political Economy,* Vol. 85.

Pascal, A.H. and J.J. McCall (1980), 'Agglomeration Economies, Search Costs and Industrial Location', *Journal of Urban Economics,* Vol. 8.

Richardson, H.W. (1988), 'Monocentric vs. Polycentric Models: The Future of Urban Economics in Regional Science', *The Annals of Regional Science,* Vol. 22.

Schmenner, R.W. (1977), 'Urban Industrial Location: An Evolutionary Mode', *Journal of Regional Science,* Vol. 17.

Schultz, T.P. (1982), 'Lifetime Migration within Educational Strata in Venezuela: Estimates of Logistic Model, *Economic Development and Cultural Change,* Vol. 30.

Sivitanidou, R. and W.C. Wheaton (1990), 'Wage and Rent Capitalization in the Commercial Real Estate Market', Working Paper (Department of Economics, MIT, Cambridge, MA).

Tauchen, H. and A.D. Witte (1984), 'Socially Optimal and Equilibrium Distributions of Office Activity: Models with Exogenous and Endogenous Contacts', *Journal of Urban Economics,* Vol. 15.

Wheaton, W.C. (1979), 'Monocentric Models of Urban Land Use: Contributions and Criticisms' in P. Mieszkowski and M. Straszheim, eds, *Current Issues in Urban Economics* (Johns Hopkins University Press, Baltimore, MD).

White, M. (1976), 'Firm Suburbanization and Urban Subcenters', *Journal of Urban Economics,* Vol. 3.

———(1988), 'Location Choice and Commuting Behavior in Cities with Decentralized Employment', *Journal of Urban Economics,* Vol. 24.

13 / Employment Dynamics, Spatial Restructuring, and the Business Cycle

PAUL WADDELL
VIBHOOTI SHUKLA

Urban areas are being transformed by a combination of long-term economic restructuring, cyclical economic volatility, and the emergence of new metropolitan forms. The interactions between these forces in reshaping urban geography are, however, poorly understood. To address this problem, what we explore in this paper are their relationships, as evidenced by differential patterns of employment gain or loss in the Dallas–Forth Worth metroplex.

There is a literature that relates the business cycle to the process of suburbanization, but it is contradictory and inconclusive. Some researchers (Kain 1975; Noll 1970) have made the case that central city employment is likely to be more volatile than suburban employment in response to the business cycle, while others (Manson 1983; Nelson and Patrick 1975; Howland and Peterson 1988) have argued that suburbs face higher volatility.[1] Both groups seem to agree that suburbs are likely to capture a disproportionate share of economic growth during an expansion period; the difference focuses on the relative impact of recessions on central city and suburban employment.

While this question of how the business cycle differentially impacts central city and suburb is a pressing public policy question affecting the fiscal outlook for municipalities, we suggest that the framing of the question in suburban–central city language has impeded our understanding of the nature and pace of spatial restructuring under way in modern metropolitan areas. A more realistic spatial perspective is required.

The dispersion of employment into multiple centres of regional significance rivalling the central business district has led numerous researchers to begin describing urban areas as 'polycentric', 'multicentric', or 'multinodal' (the terms are used synonymously), and to question urban economic theory founded on the concept of monocentricity. A substantial literature has emerged on the empirical identification of these emerging employment centres (McDonald 1987; Cervero 1989; and Dunphy 1982). Results of our analysis of Dallas–Fort Worth suggest that even the language of polycentricity may be too confining to adequately conceptualize the degree to which the dispersion of employment and population has already occurred, however. The bulk of employment growth may now lie outside the major regional employment centres generally identified by those appealing to the notion of polycentricity. It may be distributed instead across widely dispersed concentrations and corridors, and in myriad lesser clusters throughout the urban landscape. In Section I of this paper we use a new dataset[2] to characterize this evolving spatial pattern. Section II then discusses the upswings and downswings of the Dallas–Fort Worth business cycle, and Section III explores the influence of this cycle on relative job gain and loss by sector and location, and thus on the evolving spatial form. Finally, in Section IV, we develop and estimate for selected industries a model of spatial employment change that appeals to quite general characterizations of intra-metropolitan spatial interactions appropriate to the decentralized Dallas–Fort Worth context.

I. Location of Employment: The Evolving Spatial Pattern

The organization of economic activities in urban space has changed dramatically since the development of the monocentric model of urban structure by Alonso (1964), Mills (1967), and Muth (1969). No longer are cities in the United States characterized by a dominant central business district, around which land uses and economic activities are distributed in a classical distance decay gradient. Rather, the pattern of land use and economic activity in modern metropolitan areas is characterized by rapid dispersion, by the presence of multiple nodes of economic influence, and by widely dispersed economic activity throughout zones of predominant residential land use.

Much of the now substantial literature on the identification of employment centres seems to presume that as urban areas evolve away from monocentric patterns, suburban employment centres will develop to become comparable in regional significance to the CBD in a pattern of polycentricity. Underlying most of this literature is the *a priori* expectation that the future of the American metropolis involves multiple employment centres scattered across the urban landscape, each with its area of economic influence. The presumption seems to be that employment centres will continue to capture a large share of regional employment. How valid is this expectation? We are fortunate to have at our disposal sectorally disaggregated employment data at the five-digit zip code level of spatial detail that tell a very different story when combined with land-use data interpreted from low-level aerial photography.

In perhaps the most comprehensive review on the literature of subcentre identification to date, Giuliano and Small (1990) identify a broad variety of approaches ranging from the use of centres defined by regional planning agencies to the use of municipal boundaries. Few researchers, they conclude, have attempted to develop systematic identification criteria using small-area data. The methods they describe include examination of gross employment density, employment–population ratio, density relative to adjacent zones, the quantity of commercial floor space, commuting flows, aerial photography, and land uses. As Giuliano and Small note, the lack of standard methods has led to substantial differences in the number of centres identified by different researchers for the same metropolitan areas.

Most researchers fail to take adequate note of the sensitivity of their identification methods to the size and configuration of the spatial units chosen for the analysis. Zones that are defined for different purposes, that is, census tracts for census enumeration, traffic analysis zones for transportation planning, or, in our case, zip codes for postal delivery, will fail to bound employment centres neatly. Instead, most zonal systems are likely to include a mixture of land uses, and the particular size and configuration of a zone will affect its gross employment density, its ratio of employment to population, its land use mix, and many of the other candidate component measures of employment centres. Therefore, if several zones that are predominantly residential each capture a portion of an employment centre that sits at their intersection, the employment density and employment-to-population ratio might fall below an often arbitrary threshold identifying it as a centre.

If we were to rely on zip code zones as the unit of analysis in this study, our results, too, would be subject to this 'modifiable aerial unit problem'. Perhaps the most direct way to overcome it is to begin with a sufficiently small unit of geography to completely segregate employment-related land uses from residential, vacant, and other land uses. This is accomplished with land-use polygons identified from aerial photography as homogeneous land-use zones, using a detailed four-digit land-use classification. Manually interpreted low-level aerial photography (1:1200 scale) was captured in a detailed digital map of the metropolitan area by the regional planning agency in Dallas–Fort Worth (North Central Texas Council of Governments 1988), and was obtained as a GIS database for this analysis.

To combine the small-area employment data from the zip code country business patterns tabulations with the digitized land-use map to make it possible to allocate employment to the employment-related land uses within each zip code, we implemented the following methodology: By polygonal intersection using the GIS, we added zip codes to the land-use database, and obtained measurements of the total employment-related land uses.[3] By assuming that the land uses identified as employment uses within each zip code are of homogeneous density within the zip code, we assigned the employment of each zip code to the employment land-use polygons within the zone, based on the proportion that each employment land-use polygon represents the total employment land area in that zone.[4] Although some fraction of employment is likely to occur outside of land uses identified as employment-related, it would seem reasonable to use land-use zones defined by close visual inspection of aerial photography as exhausting the potential set of firm locations. This allocation procedure is constrained by both the total employment of the zip code, and the locations identified as employment-related land uses.

While measures employed in earlier studies such as the ratio of employment to population are highly sensitive to the spatial configuration of the zonal boundaries, the use of land areas identified as employment-related eliminates this problem by segregating these land uses. Gross employment density, like the employment-to-population ratio, is an appropriate measure for arbitrary zonal systems which do not segregate employment-related land uses, but this measure again is sensitive to the configuration of the zonal boundaries. The use of other proposed measures such as total employment, total area, or (net) employment density are consolidated, using our methodology, into one measure, total employment, since the assignment procedure calculates the total employment within each polygon using its land area, the zip code employment land area, and total employment (each polygon within a given zip code having the same density, by assumption).

We can now examine the spatial distribution of these land-use polygons and their employment levels in our effort to identify major

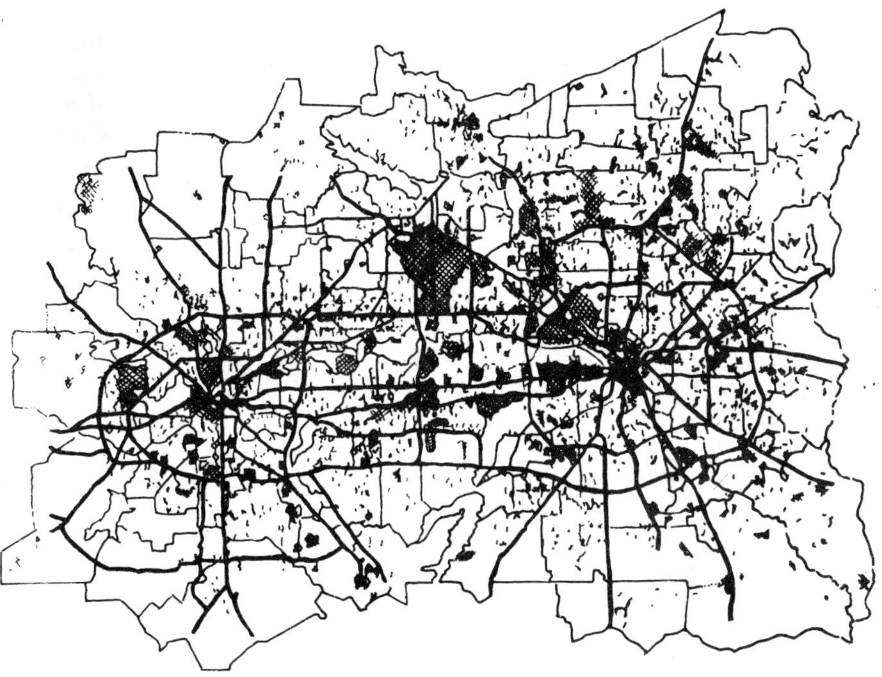

Figure 1: Employment-related Land-use Polygons, 1988

regional employment centres and other components of the spatial pattern. In Figure 1, we present a map of employment-related land uses in the metropolitan area, with an overlay of the zip code boundaries and the freeway system. The distribution appears widely dispersed, fragmented

Table 1: Cumulative Distribution of Employment and Employment-related Land Use

Percentile (Per cent)	Polygons	Cum Empl	SQMI Area
100	8410	1,556,000	245
95	7935	1,555,000	244
90	7622	1,554,000	243
75	6310	1,543,000	238
50	4219	1,493,000	222
25	2103	1,354,000	191
10	841	1,117,000	148
5	420	922,000	117
1	84	526,000	66

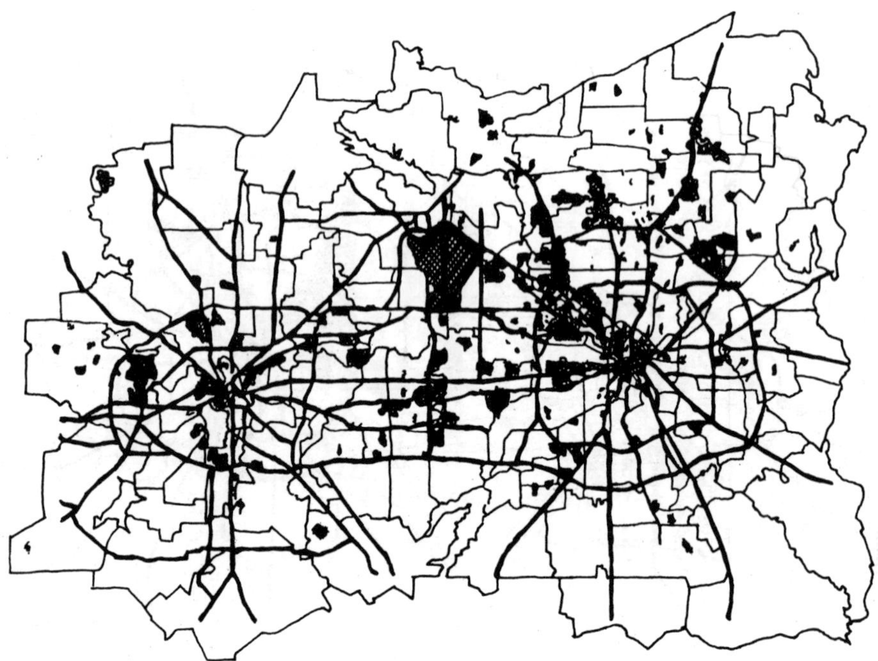

Figure 2: Employment-related Land-use Polygons: Top 5 Per cent in Employment

among a large number of small polygons scattered through the metropolitan area. Employment centres of regional significance are difficult to distinguish. The assignment of zip code employment totals to employment land-use polygons within zip codes does, however, enable us to examine the spatial distribution of employment at a finer resolution than the zip code. The total employment within each land-use polygon serves as a reasonable and parsimonious measure with which to develop a criterion for the identification of major employment centres, and a measure to assess their relative significance.

If we examine the frequency distribution of the employment land-use polygons once the employment allocation is completed (Table 1), we find that the top 5 per cent of the land-use polygons (420 out of 7935) account for almost 60 per cent of the metropolitan employment (922 out of 1555 thousand jobs), while the top 1 per cent of the land-use polygons (84 out of 7935) account for just over 33 per cent of the total metropolitan employment, or some 5,26,000 jobs. Figure 2 maps the

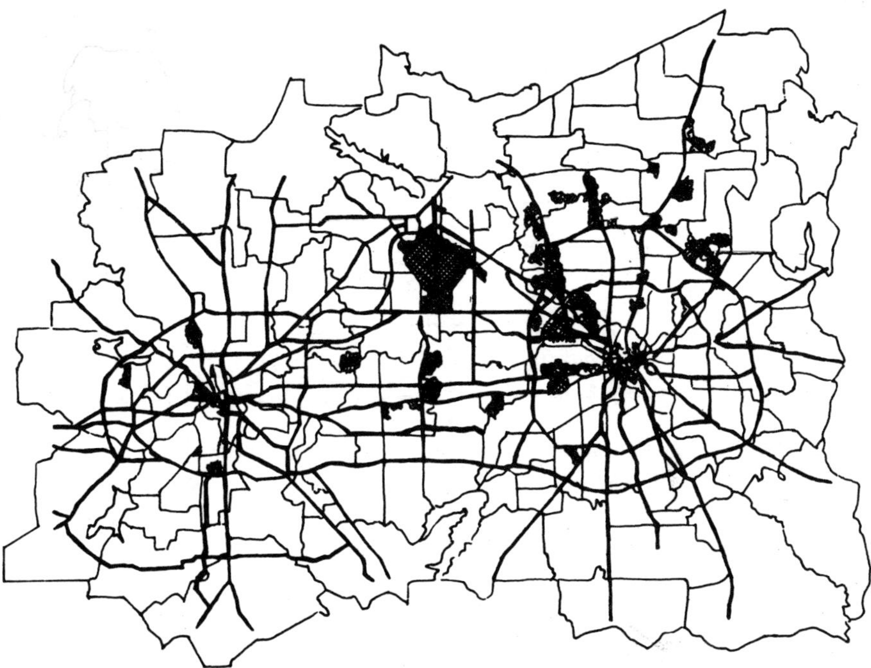

Figure 3: Employment-related Land-use Polygons: Top 1 Per cent in Employment

top 5 per cent of land-use polygons by employment, and Figure 3 the top 1 per cent of land-use polygons identified by this procedure. The top 1 per cent, representing 84 land-use polygons, correspond rather well to expected major employment centres.[5] To the extent that the Dallas–Fort Worth region is polycentric, Figure 3 provides a narrower and Figure 2 a broader definition of the polycentres.

While the concentration of one-third of the employment in 1 per cent of the employment land area indicates that these large employment centres are a significant dimension of the spatial economy, the fact that they account for only one-third of the total employment suggests that more attention needs to be paid to the remainder. An additional third of employment is accounted for by the clusters added in Figure 2, as the remaining one-third of the employment is dispersed throughout the remaining 95 per cent of the land-use polygons. Cumulative employment is plotted against cumulative employment land area in Figure 4, showing an almost linear relationship, which indicates a fairly flat

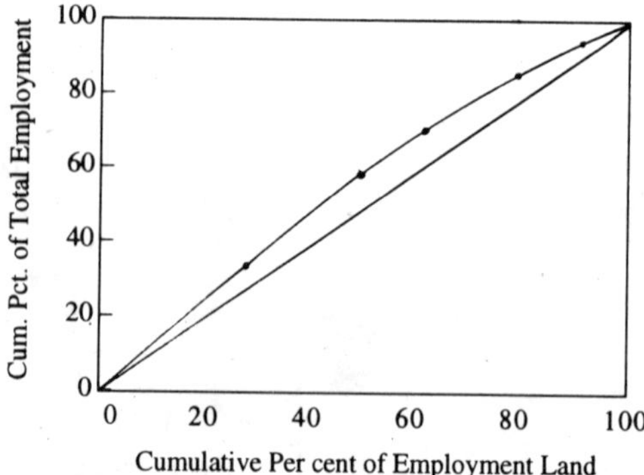

Figure 4: Cumulative Employment versus Cumulative Employment-related Land Use

density distribution across the metropolitan area. These results confirm an advanced state of employment dispersion that suggests the need to consider more general frameworks to describe the emerging urban structure than are provided by even the concept of polycentricity.

II. Pulsations of Restructuring: Relationship to the Regional Business Cycle

We now turn to the argument put forward by Howland (1984) and Howland and Peterson (1988) that employment in smaller firms is likely to be the most sensitive to recession, thus making outer developing areas, where new capital tends to locate, more volatile than already developed core areas in their response to business cycle. Dallas–Fort Worth remains the case that is studied. Figures 5–7 portray annual employment change by industry in Dallas–Fort Worth from 1970 to 1987, revealing that three full business cycles have unfolded. The figures also reveal a long-term shift towards retail; finance, insurance, and real estate (FIRE); transport, communications and public utilities (TCPU) and service sectors, which are likely to have substantially different locational requirements than the slower-growing or declining sectors. As is clear from these figures, the 1983–87 period covers a much more volatile business cycle than the two prior to it, including a boom fuelled by investment-driven development as a result of tax-law changes, falling interest rates, and savings and loan deregulation in the early 1980s, followed by a bust driven by the collapse of oil prices and of the finance and real estate industries. The Dallas area was at the centre of the real

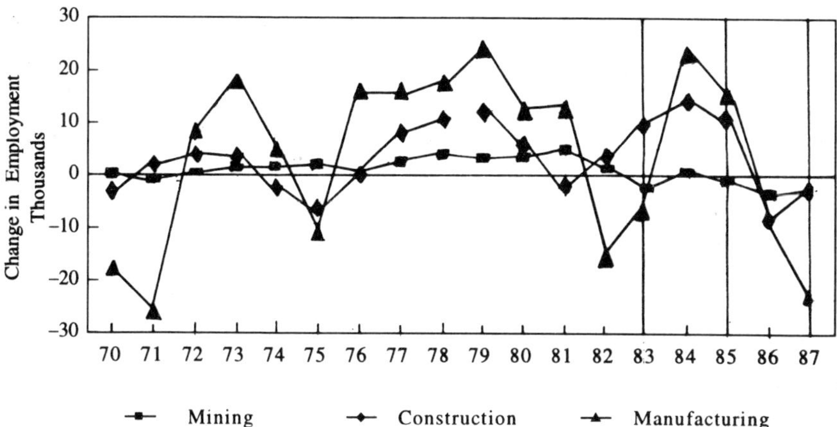

Figure 5: Employment in Mining, Construction, and Manufacturing in Dallas–Fort Worth

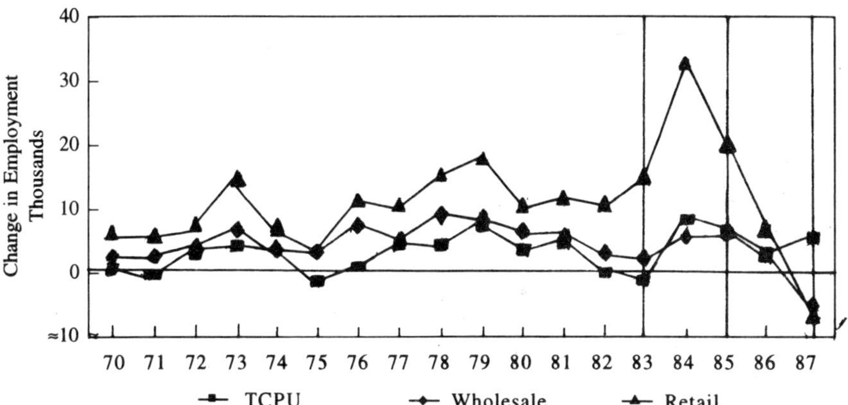

Figure 6: Employment in TCPU, Wholesale Trade, and Retail Trade in Dallas–Fort Worth

estate and savings and loan collapse, and may provide something of a preview of events in other urban areas. The Dallas economy was widely called 'recession-proof' as it weathered the 1981–82 national recession almost unscathed, but discovered that it was not after 1985. Employment in retail; finance, insurance and real estate; and service sectors showed high growth throughout the 1970–87 period, accounting for most of the boom in the early 1980s. These sectors experienced their first major recessionary downturn in the 1985–87 period.

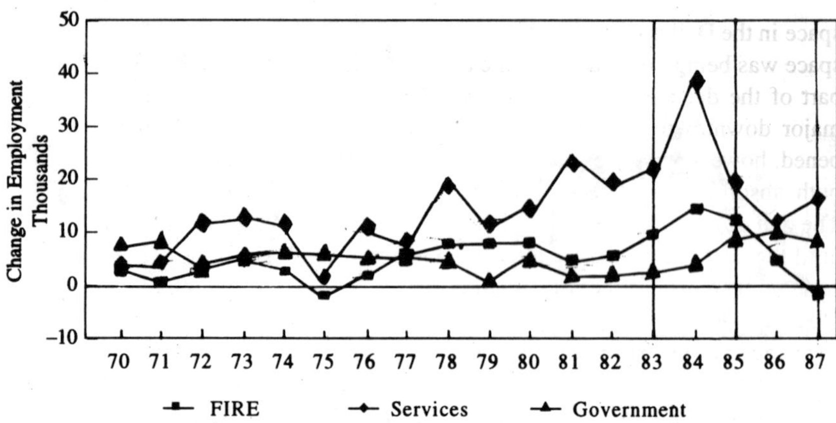

Figure 7: Employment in FIRE, Services, and Government in Dallas–Fort Worth

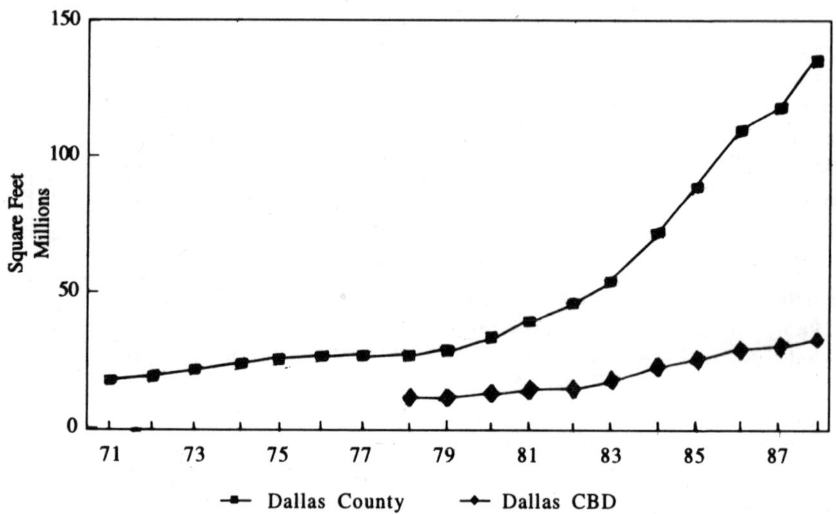

Figure 8: Dallas CBD and Dallas County Office Space

The boom of the early 1980s also fuelled an unprecedented degree of construction in the office, retail, and multifamily sectors. The surge in availability of funding and an abundance of speculative optimism led to a period of investment-driven development relatively unconstrained by demand concerns. Figure 8 reveals the dramatic increases in office space in the Dallas CBD and the remainder of Dallas County. As office space was being constructed in the central business district in the early part of the decade, many observers assumed they were witnessing a major downtown revitalization. What appears to have actually happened, however, is a serious erosion of the CBD employment base in both absolute and relative terms, after a small surge in the early 1980s. The glut of office space in the CBD, in spite of healthy absorption rates until the economic collapse broadened in 1985–86, masked the movement of businesses out of older buildings into new buildings both in the CBD and to more suburban locations where an even larger glut of space had been constructed.

Over the 1983–87 portion of the most recent business cycle, which captures the turning point from boom to bust in Dallas–Fort Worth, small establishments appear to have fared worse than large firms in the expansion period 1983–85, but actually fared better than large firms in the economic contraction of 1985–87. Hicks (1988) documents that fully 87.1 per cent of continuing businesses or 'survivors' over the January 1983–July 1987 period were small establishments employing fewer than twenty workers. Characterizing the 'job-churn' in the area's economy, he also reports that 78.6 per cent of all jobs entering the Metroplex economy during this interval were attributable to new business startups, typically small firms. This pattern is in direct contrast to that proposed by Howland.

Table 2 summarizes the number of small and large establishments (under and over fifty employees, respectively), by major sector, for 1983, 1985, and 1987. It is apparent from this table that the share of large establishments increased from 6.5 per cent of total establishments in

Table 2: Distribution of Establishments by Size

Major Sectors	1983			1985			1987		
	< 50	> 50	%>50	< 50	> 50	%>50	<50	> 50	%>50
Mining	904	74	7.6	991	76	7.1	824	43	5.0
Construction	5979	340	5.4	7380	435	5.6	6776	291	4.1
Manufacturing	4089	913	18.3	4460	998	18.3	4545	847	15.7
TCPU	1760	292	16.6	2105	328	13.5	2356	323	12.1
Wholesale Trade	7571	429	5.4	8001	504	5.9	8329	457	5.2
Retail Trade	16,412	987	5.7	17,450	1213	6.5	18,602	1152	5.8
FIRE	6563	456	6.5	8048	526	6.1	8354	530	6.0
Services	21,344	1004	4.5	24,195	1233	4.8	28,151	1284	4.4
Total	64,622	4495	6.5	72,630	5313	6.8	77,937	4927	5.9

1983 to 6.8 per cent in 1985, during the boom. On the downswing, however, large firms declined from 6.8 per cent to 5.9 per cent in 1987. While some firms might have dropped from just over fifty employees to just under during the recession, the overall pattern suggests a deconcentration from larger to smaller firms. It is of note that the industries with the highest initial concentration of large firms (manufacturing and transportation, communications, and public utilities) are sectors that are being far outstripped in their growth by industries dominated by smaller firms. In addition, these industries downsized significantly over the short span of four years of this study. It is likely that the pattern of economic restructuring leading to this downsizing trend among most industries has begun to have significant implications for urban spatial structure, and that it favours more rapid spatial employment dispersion than would a pattern of increasing firm size. This is the question to which we now turn.

III. Spatial Restructuring: Upswing and Downswing Variations

The classical measure of urban structure is the density gradient from the CBD (Muth 1969). Although the density gradient is related to the monocentric conception of urban form, it nevertheless gives us an index of the degree of decentralization of an urban area. We present in the Appendix results from a set of regressions of the gross employment density gradients for zip codes in Dallas–Fort Worth in 1983, 1985, and 1987, in order to evaluate how the degree of employment decentralization responded to the business cycle.[6] Since the metropolitan area contains two large central cities, regressions were run separately for zip codes nearer the Dallas CBD and those nearer the Fort Worth CBD. An additional set were run pooling all zip codes and using the distance to the closest CBD. The models were run separately by industry, as well as for total employment. It is noteworthy that in all cases, except the finance, insurance, and real estate industry, the density gradients flattened both in boom and in bust. This would tend to corroborate the aggregate findings in the prior section, which showed that larger firms fared worse than smaller firms during a recession. The trend towards decentralization appears to have continued unabated through the course of the business cycle, with outlying gains in employment outpacing those of the central core

Table 3: Employment by Geographic Sector

Geographic Sector	*Total Employment*			*Employment Change*		*Per Cent of Metro Employment*			*Ratio to Metro Per cent Change*	
	1983	1985	1987	83–85	85–87	Per cent 83	Per cent 85	Per cent 87	83–85	85–87
Dallas CBD	135251	139763	117352	4512	–22411	8.87	8.52	7.54	0.44	3.11
Stemmons Corridor	88646	87528	71773	–1118	–15755	5.81	5.34	4.61	–0.17	3.49
Central Corridor	64670	60476	55268	–4194	–5208	4.24	3.69	3.55	–0.85	1.67
Central Dallas Total	288567	287767	244393	–800	–43374	18.93	17.54	15.71	–0.04	2.92
LBJ Corridor	81867	100685	95072	18818	–5613	5.37	6.14	6.11	3.02	1.08
Rem Dallas City	352442	372826	347181	20384	–25645	23.12	22.73	22.31	0.76	1.33
Outer Dallas Total	434309	473511	442253	39202	–31258	28.49	28.86	28.42	1.19	1.28
Dallas City Total	722876	761278	686646	38402	–74632	47,42	46.40	44.13	0.70	1.90
Fort Worth CBD	43133	39225	32537	–3908	–6688	2.83	2.39	2.09	–1.19	3.31
Rem Fort Worth	156477	158101	155270	1624	–2831	10.26	9.64	9.98	0.14	0.35
Fort Worth Total	199610	197326	187807	–2284	–9519	13.09	12.03	12.07	–0.15	0.94
Las Colinas	38489	46571	40810	8082	–5761	2.52	2.84	2.62	2.76	2.40
Rem Dallas County	331499	365730	360194	34231	–5536	21.75	22.29	23.15	1.36	0.29
Rem Tarrant County	183587	199350	206004	15763	6654	12.04	12.15	13.24	1.13	–0.65
Dallas County Total	1092864	1173579	1087650	80715	–85929	71.69	71.54	69.90	0.07	1.42
Tarrant County Total	383197	396676	393811	13479	–2865	25.14	24.18	25.31	0.46	0.14
Collin County	26168	42302	47405	16134	5103	1.72	2.58	3.05	8.10	–2.34
Denton County	17010	22341	21399	5331	–942	1.12	1.36	1.38	4.12	0.82
Ellis County	571	1062	1127	491	65	0.04	0.06	0.07	11.30	–1.19
Johnson County	4653	4554	4583	–99	29	0.31	0.28	0.29	–0.28	–0.12
Metropolitan Total	1524463	1640514	1555975	116051	–84539					

during expansion, and above-average losses in central employment during contraction.

Aside from providing a summary measure of continued decentralization, however, these density gradients shed little light on the evolving spatial structure of the metropolitan area. In the balance of this section, we therefore examine the nature of the spatial economy in greater geographic detail, in an attempt to gain a descriptive understanding of the patterns of change. To accomplish this we assign zones to traditional employment centres such as the CBDs of Dallas and Fort Worth, and as well to other prominent employment centres or corridors such as the Central Expressway corridor, the Stemmons Freeway corridor, the LBJ Freeway corridor, and the Las Colinas centre. Each of these emerged empirically from the elemental land use methodology of Section I, and specific zip codes are identified with these centres, bearing in mind the limitation that these zones may include substantial residential area in addition to the employment centre or corridor. The remaining zip codes are allocated to the remainder of the cities of Dallas and Fort Worth, the remainder of the central counties of Dallas and Tarrant, and to the portions of the adjacent counties of Collin, Denton, Ellis, and Johnson that fall inside our study area. This allocation of zip codes to employment centres and to broader geographic sectors allows us to examine in greater geographical detail the nature of the spatial restructuring that took place over the course of the business cycle.

In Table 3 we present tabulations of the employment and the change in employment by geographic sector between 1983 and 1987. The total employment and employment changes are shown in the first section of the table, followed by the per cent of metropolitan employment and by the ratio of the per cent change in sector employment to the per cent change in metropolitan employment for each time period. The latter allows us to examine the share of the geographic sector's employment gain or loss relative to the metro area's. Total employment in the study area grew by 1,16,000 between 1983 and 1985, then declined by 85,000 in the following two years. The relative shares of the increase and the decline are the focal point of this table, and provide a clearer view of the changing spatial patterns than do the density gradients.

The Dallas and Fort Worth CBDs accounted respectively for a paltry 8.9 per cent and 2.9 per cent of metropolitan employment in 1983, and this share dwindled by 1987 to 7.5 per cent and 2.1 per cent. Though the

Dallas CBD enjoyed a growth spurt between 1983 and 1985, its ratio to metropolitan growth was .44, or less than half the metropolitan rate of growth. In the downside of the cycle, however, the Dallas CBD rate of decline was more than three times higher than average rate of decline from 1985 to 1987. The Fort Worth CBD declined both in the boom and bust phases of the cycle, also over three times faster than the average decline. The older employment corridors along radial freeways emanating from the Dallas CBD also fared quite poorly during the business cycle, showing employment losses in both boom and bust phases of the cycle. Their rates of decline were 3.5 and 1.7 times higher, respectively, than the average rate of decline between 1985 and 1987. The total central Dallas area lost employment during the boom, and lost employment at a rate almost three times faster than the metropolitan average during the bust.

The LBJ Freeway corridor, which represents one of the newer office corridors along the major beltway in the northern part of Dallas County, crosses numerous municipal boundaries, but is assigned in our tabulations to the city of Dallas since the majority of the employment is located within the Dallas City limits. This corridor captured more than three times the average rate of growth during the boom, and suffered only slightly greater than average losses during the bust. The remainder of the city of Dallas fared approximately 33 per cent worse than average during the gain, and 33 per cent worse than average during decline. A similar pattern existed in the balance of the city of Fort Worth. It is not until we reach the outer portions of the Dallas and Tarrant counties that we find sectors that gained more than average employment during the boom, and lost less than average employment during the bust. The balance of Tarrant County, subtracting Fort Worth, showed slightly higher growth than average during the boom, and experienced moderate employment growth during the contraction of the metropolitan economy. Collin and Denton counties on the northern edge of development, and Ellis County to the south, however, had the highest ratios during the growth period, and continued to grow even in the bust period (except for Denton County, which lost less than average).

These results present a clear and unmistakable pattern of the fastest growth occurring along beltway employment corridors and newer peripheral areas during the boom, while the older core areas experienced minor employment losses. When the business cycle turned downward, on the other hand, some of the peripheral areas continued to grow, while the core areas faced major erosion in their employment base. This evidence, though rooted in one urban area and one distinct time period, indicates that the pattern of volatility suggested by Howland (1984) was not experienced in Dallas–Fort Worth during this cycle. On the contrary, these results conform to the patterns suggested by Kain (1975) and Noll (1970). To the degree that the overbuilding in the commercial real estate sectors during the boom precipitated an acceleration of the process of suburbanization, these results may have a bearing on other metropolitan areas which have experienced similar overbuilding in the past decade.

IV. A Model of Employment Change in a Non-Monocentric Urban Area

What explains these changes in the patterns of employment location over the 1983–87 business cycle? We now formulate a model appropriately sensitive to a complex urban structure, recognizing multiple nodes of attraction and multidimensional spatial interactions. In a separate paper, Shukla and Waddell (1991) developed a cross-sectional discrete choice model of firm location within the Dallas–Fort Worth metropolitan area. That model attempted to measure the relationship between business location and spatial agglomeration economies, urbanization economies, infrastructure, and accessibility using a multinomial logit framework. In doing so, it was possible to simulate observed employment location patterns from the fundamentals of firm location choice. Here, we apply a similar model to the change in employment by industry over 1983–85, and again over 1985–87. Since the explained variable is a continuous one, our method is ordinary least squares regression analysis.

The dependent variable is the change in regional share of employment in a given industry (identified at a two-digit SIC level) captured by a given zip code.[7] The lagged regional share of employment in the industry (*LAGSHREM*) is included to capture hypothesized intra-industry localization effects. Distances to the two central business districts (*DISDALCBD, DISFWCBD*) measure the influence of monocentricity. A central city dummy (*CENCITY*) tests for a central city–suburb differential. A freeway dummy variable (*FRWY*) estimates the impact of freeway access within a zip code. The zip's share of regional developed land area (*SHRDEVL*) is used as a control for zone size.

Table 4: Regresssion Results

Variable	Fabricated Metals		Trucking And Warehousing		Communications		Real Estate		Business Services	
N = 141	1983-85	1985-87	1983-85	1985-87	1983-85	1985-87	1983-85	1985-87	1983-85	1985-87
Intercept	−1.950E − 3	2.436E − 3	4.339E − 4	1.688E − 3	−8.974E − 3	−8.076E − 5	−5.717E − 3	−1.716E − 4	−3.594E − 3	−3.160E − 3
	(−1.236)	(1.081)	(.189)	(.733)	(−2.428)†	(−.033)	(−3.071)†	(−.093)	(−2.419)†	(−2.150)†
Lagshrem	−.1196	−.1626	−.4869	−.3103	−.5849	−.2581	−3.090E − 2	−8.807E − 2	−1.089E − 1	−1.281E − 1
	(−3.611)*	(−3.40)*	(−18.60)†	(−7.29)†	(−9.187)*	(−5.202)*	(−.932)	(−2.778)†	(−3.033)†	(−3.367)†
Disdalcbd	7.751E − 5	−3.354E − 5	1.095E − 4	−1.607E − 7	2.925E − 4	−1.540E − 4	8.711E − 5	−2.034E − 4	6.104E − 5	2.569E − 5
	(.944)	(−.293)	(.893)	(−.001)	(1.494)	(−1.214)	(.917)	(−2.221)†	(.847)	(.359)
Disfwcbd	1.090E − 4	−4.840E − 5	1.484E − 4	6.112E − 5	3.289E − 4	−2.697E − 4	9.233E − 5	−2.063E − 4	5.827E − 5	4.380E − 5
	(1.031)	(−.336)	(.940)	(.413)	(1.307)	(−1.697)‡	(.756)	(−1.794)	(.630)	(.488)
Cencity	−4.315E − 4	−9.434E − 4	−5.16E − 4	−9.43E − 4	1.582E − 3	2.813E − 4	−3.084E − 4	−1.818E − 3	−4.353E − 4	−6.393E − 4
	(−.770)	(−1.215)	(−.614)	(−1.174)	(1.186)	(.330)	(−.473)	(−2.936)†	(−.865)	(−1.312)
Frwy	3.418E − 4	−6.461E − 4	7.192E − 4	5.667E − 4	2.887E − 3	9.758E − 4	1.113E − 3	8.957E − 5	6.638E − 4	4.528E − 4
	(.552)	(−.750)	(.780)	(.641)	(1.961)†	(1.025)	(1.546)	(.129)	(1.176)	(.844)
Shrdevl	−1.399E − 4	3.125E − 5	9.871E − 4	−1.561E − 4	−4.988E − 4	−1.968E − 4	−3.456E − 4	2.641E − 4	1.414E − 4	6.703E − 5
	(−.253)	(.041)	(1.249)	(−.205)	(−.396)	(−.244)	(−.561)	(.447)	(.304)	(.145)
Popdecay	1.129E − 8	5.198E − 9	3.281E − 9	1.909E − 9	2.034E − 8	−1.856E − 8	1.500E − 8	8.123E − 9	1.146E − 8	9.985E − 9
	(2.355)†	(.803)	(.459)	(.285)	(1.794)‡	(−2.619)*	(2.721)†	(1.574)	(2.755)†	(2.491)†
Incdecay	4.30E − 10	−2.359E − 8	−7.140E − 8	−3.573E − 8	2.909E − 8	1.178E − 7	8.785E − 8	7.895E − 8	5.140E − 8	6.366E − 8
	(.011)	(−.482)	(−1.251)	(−.716)	(.319)	(2.242)†	(1.919)‡	(2.014)†	(1.464)	(2.079)†
Cmwdecay	8.384E − 8	1.039E − 7	5.351E − 7	2.301E − 7	9.865E − 8	1.635E − 7	−1.185E − 7	−1.032E − 7	1.688E − 8	−4.216E − 8
	(1.205)	(1.196)	(6.437)†	(2.838)†	(.777)	(2.228)†	(−1.958)‡	(−1.951)‡	(.320)	(−.882)
Mtfdecay	8.132E − 9	5.288E − 8	−3.208E − 7	−1.198E − 7	9.564E − 8	2.187E − 8	1.567E − 7	1.567E − 7	8.189E − 9	1.800E − 7
	(.120)	(.559)	(−3.472)†	(−1.247)	(.648)	(.226)	(2.205)†	(2.192)†	(.140)	(2.932)†
Rsdecay	−8.774E − 8	−1.460E − 7	4.325E − 8	−9.024E −9	7.696E − 8	8.235E − 8	−1.174E − 7	−8.928 − 8	−3.954 − 8	−1.349E − 7
	(−1.794)‡	(−2.068)†	(.594)	(−.123)	(.610)	(1.030)	(−1.773)‡	(−1.365)	(−.732)	(−2.361)†
R^2	.197	.147	.742	.328	.450	.269	.183	.216	.278	.355

*; †; ‡ : Significant at 1 per cent, 5 per cent, 10 per cent confidence levels, respectively.

A measure of urbanization economies (*POPDECAY*) is included as the distance-weighted sum of population within a broad decay radius of the zip code, whereas interindustry linkages between a two-digit industry and firms within broad industrial aggregations are introduced by more localized weighted totals of employment (*CMWDECAY, MTFDECAY, RSDECAY*) by industry sector.[8] The three sectoral aggregations used for these interindustry agglomeration economies are construction, manufacturing, and wholesale trade; mining, TCPU, and FIRE; and retail and services. A distance-weighted average income variable (*INCDECAY*) measures the sensitivity of firm location to the socio-economic status of the labour force and market within the area.

The results of these regressions for fabricated metals manufacturing, trucking, and warehousing, communications, real estate, and business services are presented in Table 4. In these results the urbanization economies represented by the distance-decayed population totals, the intra-industry agglomeration variable, and the interindustry linkages, specified as distance-decayed total employment by broad industry aggregations, completely overshadow the monocentricity, central city, freeway, and size variables, which are insignificant in almost all cases. A solitary exception is communications, which is mildly responsive to the Fort Worth CBD variable during the downturn, and to the freeway dummy during the upturn.

We take this result to indicate that the economic determinants which explained the monocentric city of the past now measure the extent to which the locus of population and economic activity has decentralized from the CBD. Even fabricated metals, an industry in which one might expect the more conventional behaviour associated with manufacturing location, is strongly responsive to broad urbanization economies represented by the distance-weighted population measure during the upswing. Indeed the population centre of gravity of the Dallas–Fort Worth metropolitan area now lies decidedly north of the CBD, and growth continues in that direction.

The coefficients on distance-weighted income were negative but insignificant for trucking and warehousing firms, not a surprising result considering their relatively low occupational demands, and also insignificant for fabricated metals, with its lack of orientation to the residential market. Both real estate and business services had positive coefficients on distance-weighted income, with higher significance in the 1985–87 decline period than in 1983–85, not surprising considering their market orientation and high occupational demands, respectively. Communications, too, had a significant positive coefficient on this variable during the downswing period.

The variable *LAGSHREM* denotes a zip's lagged share of the area's employment in the given industry and, as such, may be considered to capture intra-industry localization effects. A negative sign on its coefficient might represent general tendencies for new employment to locate away from old employment centres, or for closing and cutbacks to be most severe in the more esablished areas of an industry's presence. The intra-industry localization variables were largely significant, the strong negative signs for trucking and warehousing, real estate, and business services indicating aversion of firms to areas already saturated by competing establishments, and underlining dispersion trends quite consistently across the local market-oriented industries.

The pattern of coefficients on the interindustry linkage variables varies by industry, and conforms to expectations regarding the likely economic ties with firms in each of the three industry aggregations. Trucking and warehousing, for example, shows an affinity for locations close to firms in construction, manufacturing, and wholesale trade industries, while averse to locations high in office dwelling firms in mining, TCPU, and FIRE industries. Real estate firms, on the other hand, favoured locations close to the office-related industries, and away from construction, manufacturing, and wholesale trade, as well as retail and services. Business services were attracted to locations high in access to office firms, and low in access to retail and service firms. Firms in the fabricated metals and communications industries, notably, exhibited affinity with locations having significant retail and services sector employment.

In examining these results for differences in the determinants of firm location in boom and bust phases of the business cycle, several observations can be made. In the trucking and warehousing results, there was a decrease in the magnitude of the negative coefficient on the intra-industry agglomeration measure, and a decline in the magnitude of the interindustry linkage coefficients, which suggests that the effects of the recession were more spatially random than the locational choices made by these firms during expansion. An increase in the absolute value of the coefficient of *LAGSHREM* during the downswing compared with the upswing denotes a relatively large loss of employment, or, more likely, a failure to gain new employment during the bust phase of the business cycle. This occurred for all other industries (with

Appendix: CBD Distance Decay Gradients

		Dallas Area zips with respect to distance from Dallas CBD			Fort Worth Area zips with respect to distance from Fort Worth CBD			All zips with respect to distance from nearest CBD		
		1983	1985	1987	1983	1985	1987	1983	1985	1987
Wholesale	R-square	0.3437	0.2907	0.2601	0.2679	0.2447	0.2049	0.2771	0.2394	0.2125
	Intercept	4.397	4.245	4.026	2.75	2.83	2.69	3.76	3.69	3.51
	In/Discbd	–0.198	–0.176	–0.161	–0.156	–0.146	–0.129	–0.18	–0.161	–0.146
	T-Intercept	–12.19	11.71	11.26	6.77	7.02	6.73	12.84	12.73	12.35
	T-Discbd	–6.83	–6.04	–5.593	–4.19	–3.94	–3.51	–7.3	–6.61	–6.12
Retail	R-square	0.4454	0.4002	0.301	0.2335	0.1805	0.1466	0.3441	0.291	0.2712
	Intercept	5.37	5.37	5.08	4.1	3.96	3.86	4.89	4.84	4.69
	InDiscbd	–0.205	–0.183	–0.158	–0.169	–0.14	–0.11	–0.19	–0.166	–0.148
	T-Intercept	17.85	18.15	16.11	8.5	8.43	8.69	18.47	18.49	19.16
	T-Discbd	–8.45	–7.7	–6.12	–3.82	–3.25	–2.87	–8.5	–7.55	–7.19
Service	R-square	0.4686	0.4223	0.3222	0.2464	0.254	0.2412	0.3548	0.3263	0.2645
	Intercept	6.01	5.89	5.77	4.3	4.32	4.38	5.36	5.29	5.23
	InDiscbd	–0.24	–0.219	–0.192	–0.191	–0.181	–0.159	–0.22	–0.202	–0.177
	T-Intercept	17.85	17.43	15.72	8.17	8.82	9.86	17.91	18.03	17.58
	T-Discbd	–8.85	–8.06	–6.5	–3.96	–4.04	–3.9	–8.74	–8.2	–7.07
Manufacturing	R-square	0.2741	0.2101	0.2216	0.1563	0.15	0.1397	0.2259	0.1806	0.187
	Intercept	4.88	4.73	4.56	4	4.01	3.95	4.55	4.44	4.32
	InDiscbd	–0.018	–0.152	–0.149	–0.154	–0.145	–0.136	–0.171	–0.147	0.143
	T-Intercept	12.58	12.14	12.42	7.11	7.36	7.41	14.29	14.04	14.4
	T-Discbd	–5.79	–4.86	–5.03	–2.98	–2.91	–2.79	–6.36	–5.35	–5.65

FIRE	R-square	0.3128	0.2616	0.2768	0.1808	0.1208	0.1513	0.2407	0.1887	0.2116
	Intercept	4.32	4.32	4.35	2.3	2.19	2.45	3.6	3.55	3.67
	InDiscbd	−0.201	−0.185	−0.188	−0.12	−0.1	−0.114	−0.174	−0.157	−0.163
	T-Intercept	11	10.53	10.83	5.72	5.07	5.78	11.56	10.8	11.56
Construct	R-square	0.3413	0.2317	0.255	0.0867	0.07	0.0805	0.2457	0.1647	0.1821
	Intercept	3.93	3.79	3.59	2.39	2.52	2.33	3.42	3.35	3.15
	InDiscbd	−0.156	−0.126	−0.121	−0.069	−0.065	−0.061	−0.13	−0.101	−0.102
	T-Intercept	13.79	12.54	13.14	6.81	6.7	7.14	14.84	13.81	14.42
	T-Discbd	−6.79	−5.18	−5.51	−2.13	−1.9	−2.05	−6.72	−5.23	−5.56
Total Emp	R-square	0.4422	0.3815	0.3563	0.2604	0.2461	0.2351	0.3567	0.3097	0.2895
	Intercept	7.37	7.26	7.14	5.83	5.82	5.81	6.81	6.73	6.64
	InDiscbd	−0.22	−0.2	−0.18	−0.17	−0.161	−0.15	−0.209	−0.188	−0.173
	T-Intercept	21.79	21.14	21.41	12.59	13.11	13.67	24.02	23.76	24.31
	T-Discbd	−8.4	−7.7	−7.019	−4.11	−3.95	−3.84	−8.78	7.89	−7.52

the exception of communications), highlighting the vulnerability of older, more established locations, irrespective of centrality.

In the real estate industry, the strongest declines appear to have occurred in areas most saturated with competing firms, since the negative coefficient on lagged share of same-industry employment increased in magnitude and significance in the recession phase. Similarly, the urbanization variable lost significance while the income variable gained, from boom to recession, highlighting a shift to more upscale markets as the economy soured. Interindustry linkage coefficients remained stable in boom and bust. The business services sector experienced a similar increase in the magnitude of the negative coefficient on the lagged share of same-industry employment, and a shift significance from the population variable to income. There were shifts in the interindustry linkages in this sector as well, favouring locations high in office-related firms, and avoiding locations high in retail and service establishments.

While these results are characterized by relatively low overall explanatory power, they are suggestive of the changing locational strategies and conditions faced by firms in different industries as the local economy expands and contracts. They are also indicative of the diverse and spatially diffused nature of economic influences that are played out within the complex structure of the contemporary urban landscape. We summarize some of the implications of these findings in the concluding section below.

V. Conclusions

The results of our analysis of the spatial restructuring of the Dallas–Fort Worth economy during the course of the last business cycle have three major ramifications:

- The evolving patterns of intra-metropolitan employment dispersion point to a need for revamping monocentric urban economic theory beyond the consideration of polycentricity concepts in favour of even more general spatial frameworks;
- Distinct effects of the business cycle upon these spatial patterns over its upswing and downswing phases are in evidence, but they work to reinforce secular dispersion trends;
- Staple urban economic concepts such as agglomeration are of value in explaining observed employment location patterns, but, increasingly,

these forces operate so as to lead to new rather than traditional spatial configuration of economic activity in modern metropolitan areas.

NOTES

1 Kain (1975) and Noll (1970) have argued that central city employment is more sensitive to the business cycle, since the obsolete and inefficient capital stock, older infrastructure, and less educated labour force of central cities would be likely to place these economies at a competitive disadvantage in an economic downturn, while suburbs would be in a better position with their advantages to capitalize on an economic upswing. Manson (1983), Manson, Howland, and Peterson (1984), and Nelson and Patrick (1975), on the other hand, have suggested that suburbs will experience higher volatility in the business cycle. Howland (1984) and Howland and Peterson (1988) have supported this view, suggesting that sensitivity to recession is higher for newer capital, and that smaller firms are less able than large firms to downsize in response to economic contraction. The failure rates of small, new firms, then, would place newer suburban employment centres at a disadvantage in a recession.

2 We appeal to an urban geographic framework to capture this evolving spatial pattern. Much prior study of intra-metropolitan change in employment has been restricted to a suburb–central city dichotomy because of a paucity of reliable spatially disaggregated data. A new data set has become available recently which may lend itself to some of the needs of spatially detailed urban research. The data are zip code tabulations of the county business patterns, and contain total employment and an establishment size distribution by zip code and by four-digit standard industrial classification (SIC). The data are prepared by the Bureau of Labour Statistics, and distributed by private firms such as Markets Statistics (1989). In addition to the employment data, demographic profiles of zip codes were obtained from CACI (1990). A digital map of existing land uses was obtained from the North Texas Council of Governments (1988), and overlaid on zip code boundaries using a geographic information system (GIS) to measure the land mix within each zip code.

Zip codes are admittedly a problematic geographic unit for longitudinal analysis, since the boundaries can, and do, change. This is particularly true in fast-growing areas such as Dallas–Fort Worth. Most of the boundary changes involve simple splits of zip codes to create smaller delivery areas where growth has begun to overload the postal delivery system. Using a GIS, we were able to reconcile the boundary changes in zip codes over the span of our study. A zonal structure based on aggregations of zip codes to the smallest comparable unit was developed using this approach. Zip codes for the contiguous urbanized area were selected as the focus of the study, so as to minimize problems of scarce data in peripheral rural areas.

3 Using the US Geological Survey land-use classification system, we selected the following two-digit categories: (12) commercial and services, (13) industrial, (14) transportation, communications, and utilities, (15) industrial and commercial complexes. The following three-digit categories were subtracted from these: (141) transportation, including railways and truck terminals, (142) roadway, and (143) utilities, including sewage treatment plants and water treatment plants. The omitted categories were excluded on the basis of the relatively large quantities of land in these uses with little or no accompanying employment.

4 A refinement of this allocation method would be to allocate employment by major industry to the appropriate subclassifications of employment-related land uses. The cross-classification of industrial and land-use categories is somewhat problematic itself, however, and goes beyond the scope of this paper.

5 It is worth noting that the centres identified by Giuliano and Small (1990) using a totally distinct method also accounted for one-third of the total Los Angeles metropolitan employment. The identification solution proposed by Giuliano and Small, perhaps the most rigorous and systematic approach to date, uses traffic analysis zones for the Los Angeles metropolitan area to apply a combination of contiguity, threshold density, and cumulative employment criteria for the identification of multiple zone centres.

6 The simple formulation of the model is the standard distance decay gradient:

$$D(u) = D_0^{-\gamma u}$$

where D is gross employment density at distance u. In linear form, the model becomes

$$\ln D(u) = \ln D_0 - \gamma u.$$

There has been some work on more complex density characterization, such as Anderson's (1982) cubic spline urban density functional form or Gordon, Richardson, and Wong's (1986) polycentric density gradients, much of it involving the prior identification of employment nodes in one way or another. Our main purpose, however, being explanation rather than characterization, we prefer to pursue the problem through a model of spatial employment change from a firm location perspective in Section IV.

7 The five two-digit industries for which we implement the model are as follows: fabricated metals (SIC:34); trucking and warehousing (SIC 42); communications (SIC 48); real estate (SIC 65); and business services (SIC 73). They are chosen to sample an industrial spectrum covering basic to locally oriented firms, as well as to reflect sectors of economic pre-eminence in the Dallas–Fort Worth context.

8 The form of the distance decay weight applied to the population variable is $e^{-\delta d}$ where d is distance from centroid to centroid in miles and δ is the decay gradient coefficient, set to 0.25 for the population variable, and to 0.75 for the interindustry agglomeration variables. The larger coefficient implies a steeper gradient, and serves to localize the influence of the variable. Since we attempt to measure broad urbanization economies with the population variable, a smaller gradient is appropriate compared to spatial agglomeration economies, which measure localized influences.

REFERENCES

Alonso, W. (1964), *Location and Land Use*, Harvard University Press, Cambridge, Mass.

Anderson, J. (1982), 'Cubic-Spline Urban Density Functions', *Journal of Urban Economics,* Vol. 12, pp. 155–67.

Cervero, R. (1989), *America's Suburban Centres: The Land Use Transportation Link*, Unwin Hyman, Boston, Mass.

Dunphy, R.T. (1982), 'Defining Regional Employment Centres in an Urban Area', *Transportation Research Record,* Vol. 861, pp. 13–15.

Giuliano, G. and K.A. Small (1990), 'Subcentres in the Los Angeles Region', Paper presented at the TRED Conference (12–13 October 1990), Lincoln Institute of Land Policy, Cambridge, Mass., pp. 1–33.

Gordon, P., H.W. Richardson and H.L. Wong (1986), 'The Distribution of Population and Employment in a Polycentric City: The Case of Los Angeles, *Environment and Planning,* Vol. A 18, pp. 161–73.

Hicks, D.A. (1988), 'The Regenerating Economy: Job Creation and Destruction in Texas and the D/FW Metroplex', D/FW Airport, Texas, Paper, Regional Research and Technology Program, North Texas Commission.

Howland, M. (1984), 'Age of Capital and Regional Business Cycles', *Growth and Change,* Vol. 15, pp. 29–37.

Howland, M. and G.E. Peterson (1988), 'The Response of City Economies to National Business Cycles', *Journal of Urban Economics,* Vol. 23, pp. 71–85.

Kain, J. (1975), 'The Distribution and Movement of Jobs and Industry', in *Essays on Urban Spatial Structure*, edited by J.F. Kain, Ballinger, Cambridge, Mass.

Manson, D. (1983), 'The Sensitivity of Income in Cities and Suburbs to National Business Cycle Fluctuations', The Urban Institute, Washington, D.C.

Manson, D., M. Howland and G. Peterson (1984), 'The Effects of Business Cycles on Metropolitan Suburbanization', *Economic Geography,* Vol. 60, pp. 71–80.

McDonald, J. F. (1987), 'The Identification of Urban Employment Subcentres', *Journal of Urban Economics*, Vol. 21, pp. 242–58.

Mills, E.S. (1967), 'An Aggregative Model of Resource Allocation in a Metropolitan Area', *American Economic Review,* Vol. 57, pp. 197–210.

Muth, R.F. (1969), *Cities and Housing,* University of Chicago Press, Chicago, Ill.

Nelson, K.P. and C. Patrick (1975), 'Decentralization of Employment during the 1969–1972 Business Cycle: The National Regional Record', ORNL–UR 123, Oak Ridge National Laboratory, Oak Ridge. Tenn.

Noll, R. (1970), 'Metropolitan Employment and Population Distribution and the Conditions of the Urban Poor', in *Financing the Metropolis,* edited by J.P. Crecine, Sage Press, Beverley Hills, Cal.

North Central Texas Council of Governments (1988), *1988 Land Use Data*.

Shukla, V. and P. Waddell (1991), 'Firm Location and Land Use in Discrete Urban Space: A Study of the Spatial Structure of Dallas–Fort Worth', *Regional Science and Urban Economics,* Vol. 21 [reprinted in this volume].

14 / Manufacturing Location in a Polycentric Urban Area: A Study in the Composition and Attractiveness of Employment Subcentres

PAUL WADDELL
VIBHOOTI SHUKLA[1]

I.

The tale of centre-city decline and employment decentralization in favour of the suburbs has been told several times, and describes a process that had its origin several decades ago. Several attempts are under way to modify conventional monocentric urban structure theories to take cognizance of what seems to be now the dominant pattern of urban development.[2] Manufacturing decentralization has received much scholarly analysis, both in the context of intra-metropolitan moves and, more commonly, as part of the study of long-distance industrial location decisions (e.g., see Schmenner 1982).

There has arisen, in recent times, an increasingly sophisticated empirical literature on urban employment subcentres. Works in this genre have tended to focus on issues of subcentre identification and characterization. The study by Giuliano and Small (1991) of the Los Angeles region, for example, represents one such careful exercise. Their finding of the existence of a coherent set of subcentres in what is perceived to be perhaps the region with the most dispersed settlement pattern in the US metropolitan spectrum suggests there is discernible order even within the seeming chaos of low-density 'sprawl'.

Our hoped-for contribution is to link these themes of manufacturing employment dispersion and subcentre formation in a behaviourally motivated model. To what extent do manufacturing firms respond to differences in subcentre characteristics within a metropolitan area? To what degree do employment subcentres systematically reflect differences in their industrial attributes? Can the spatial coincidence of certain employment-centre characteristics and industry-mix attributes be explained by a model that involves locational decision-making by rational firms? Results of our exercise should enable judgment on the utility of the employment-centre concept and on industrial location behaviour in a modern urban context.

The paper is organized as follows: the first section describes a methodology for the empirical identification of our units of study, viz., employment-centres in the Dallas–Fort Worth area, via the 'mapping' of employment-related land uses onto zip code geographic units, and compares the emergent centres in terms of their spatial characteristics. The second section characterizes the data on manufacturing employment, and, in particular, profiles the dispersion patterns of establishments by various industrial attributes. The third section delineates the firms' location decision model and its econometric implementation. The general attractiveness to manufacturing firms of various locational characteristics of these centres is studied by using a discrete choice framework. The industrial attributes of firms choosing employment centres are next investigated through multinomial logit formulation. Then, a 'mixed' conditional logit model is specified and estimated to identify special affinities between types of firm and kinds of locations. The next section presents the results of these exercises, and the final section concludes.

II. The Identification of Employment Centres in the Metroplex

Empirical subcentre identification approaches vary from the arbitrary to the methodologically sophisticated (see Giuliano and Small 1991).[3] Many studies rely on designations based on subjective or locality-specific knowledge of historical growth poles or transportation nodes. Several use existing jurisdictional boundaries, such as a planning region or municipality, to classify postulated subcentres and demarcate their boundaries. Relatively few attempt to apply systematic identification criteria using small-area data that are less limiting than geographies intended for other functional uses. These criteria have included employment–population ratios, local gross employment, population density peaks, commuting patterns, land-use patterns, and many others.

Even for researchers working at a relatively fine level of geographical detail, identification methods are likely to be sensitive to the size and configuration of the spatial units chosen for the analysis. In a recent paper,

Waddell and Shukla (1991) attempted to overcome this modifiable areal unit problem by beginning with a unit of geography sufficiently small to completely segregate employment-related land uses from residential, vacant, and other uses. This was accomplished for the Dallas–Fort Worth area with land-use polygons identified from manually interpreted low-level aerial photography and digitally mapped into a Geographical Information System (GIS). By using polygonal intersection procedures, zip codes were added to the land-use database to allocate employment data from zip code-level county business patterns tabulations to the employment-related land-use polygons. With employment thus allocated among a large number of polygons scattered throughout the metropolitan area, employment clusters of regional significance were identified on the basis of total employment within each polygon. The top 1 per cent of the polygons (ranked by cumulative employment) account for just over 33 per cent of total Metroplex employment. The proportion of the region's employment accounted for by these large centres, and their dispersion (Figure 1), confirms the polycentricity of this metropolitan area.

Superimposing the employment clusters recovered in this way from elemental land-use data on zip code boundaries permits their geographic association, and provides a link to other employment and demographic data available by zip code. Zip codes are identified with an employment cluster polygon if the latter happens to lie fully or partially within them. These, then, constitute our employment 'centres'. Nineteen such centres were identified. Although the use of zip code boundaries to construct these employment centres is dictated by data exigencies, the fact that each centre contains within its limits non-employment land uses corresponds well with the idea of multinucleated communities around employment cores.

Data on selected variables for each of the 19 centres thus defined are summarized in Table 1. Centre-specific values are derived through a weighted average over all zip codes constituting any particular centre. The first three variables measure a centre's total area, the percentage of it that is developed, and the percentage of such land given over to employment-related uses. The next three variables reflect a centre's total employment, net employment density, and manufacturing employment. The following six report the percentage shares of selected broad one-digit industry groups in the total employment of the centre. The next two variables relate to rent and occupancy rates for industrial sites within each centre; the final set of variables are total population within a specified decay radius of a centre, its gross population density, median household income, and per cent black.

A brief qualitative description highlights the rather diverse nature[4] of the identified centres: 1,2,15,16 and 18 are geographically self-explanatory; 4 through 8 are related to major transportation arteries; 9 and 10 are suburban jurisdictions; 3, 11 and 13 are airport zones; 12 and 19 are planned industrial or commercial developments; 14 and 17 are dominated by large, single employers.

III. Spatial Profile of Manufacturing Industry Location Choices

The employment data available to us originated from County Business Patterns tabulations by zip code. Our tabulations identify a number of establishments by employment size class in each of 141 zip codes for 145 manufacturing industries at the three-digit SIC level. Precise location within a zip code is not identified, nor are firm-specific characteristics other than size and industrial classification, since these are not establishment-level data. Our research design, therefore, will be one partly shaped by these limitations. Fortunately, the industrial classification itself carries some relevant information worthwhile in our investigations, namely the industry averages for a number of indicators such as wages, fuel intensity, building requirements, etc. from national data sources such as the Census of Manufactures.[5] In this section, we utilize this information for a preliminary characterization of the spatial dispersion of industries in the Metroplex.

To gauge the general degree of dispersion among firms in the three-digit manufacturing industries of our sample of Dallas–Fort Worth zip codes, we characterize their location patterns through two industry-specific summary measures: (*a*) the Standard Distance; and (*b*) the Contiguity Index (see Lee 1989). The first is a measure of firms' spatial concentration, computed not with respect to an arbitrarily designated business centre but, rather, with reference to the centroid for an industry. Thus, the Standard Distance, D, for an industry j is defined as:

$$D_j = \sqrt{\frac{\sum_i E_{ij}(x_i - x_j)^2 + \sum_i E_{ij}(y_i - y_j)^2}{\sum_i E_{ij}}}$$

where $$y_i = \frac{\sum_i E_{ij} y_i}{\sum_i E_{ij}} \qquad \text{and} \qquad x_j = \frac{\sum_i E_{ij} x_i}{\sum_i E_{ij}}$$

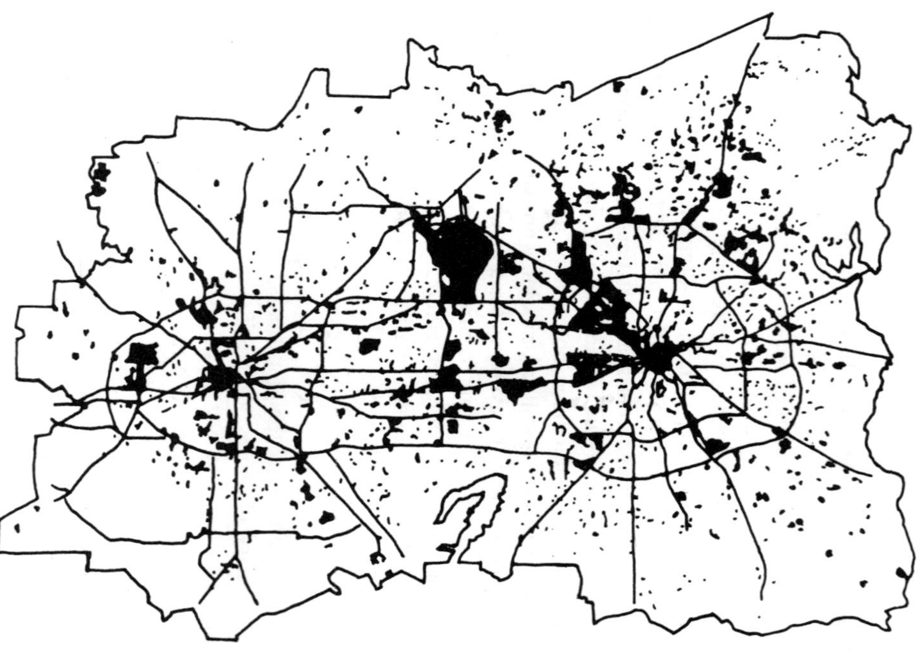

Figure 1a: Employment-related Land Use in Dallas–Fort Worth, 1988

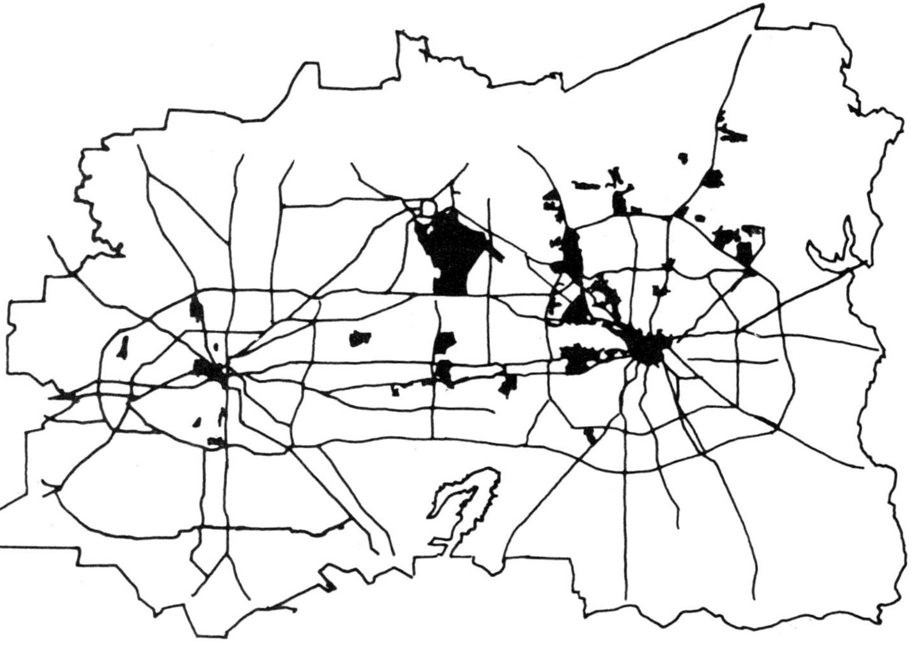

Figure 1b: Major Employment Centre in Dallas–Fort Worth, 1988

Table 1: Spatial Characteristics of Identified Employment Centres

Location	LANDSQ	PCTDEV	PCLEMP	TOTEMP (thous.)	NEMPDN (thous.)	MANEMP (thous.)	PCTMAN	PCTTCU
1 Dallas Central	64	85	16	164	16.3	14	8	18
2 West Dallas	203	80	15	54	1.8	20	37	22
3 Love Field/S. IH35	97	66	19	134	7.5	27	20	12
4 LBJ FWY/N. IH35	224	88	13	103	3.6	22	21	8
5 LBJ FWY-N	97	87	7	69	9.6	3	4	2
6 Central Expressway	117	81	5	65	10.9	4	6	2
7 LBJ/Central Exp S.	36	75	17	46	7.9	12	27	2
8 LBJ/Central Exp E.	286	84	8	59	2.7	14	24	4
9 Richardson	167	87	13	55	2.6	15	28	4
10 Plano	66	69	11	13	1.9	3	19	3
11 Redbird	14	67	14	10	4.1	2	16	0
12 GSW-Arlington	180	78	18	79	2.4	22	27	7
13 DFW Airport	116	58	22	23	0.9	1	4	46
14 Bell Helicopter	25	77	12	20	6.1	9	43	1
15 Central Fort Worth	146	73	8	73	6.8	10	14	8
16 South Fort Worth	81	89	9	20	2.7	7	36	4
17 General Dynamics	127	40	7	25	2.9	22	88	0
18 North Fort Worth	77	81	14	15	1.3	6	40	7
19 Las Colinas	134	72	13	64	3.7	11	17	11
20 Rem. Dallas City	906	84	8	104	1.5	19	19	7
21 Rem. Dallas County	1213	76	9	123	1.1	23	19	5
22 Rem. Fort Worth	656	85	11	59	0.8	11	19	3
23 Rem. Tarrant County	1794	77	10	117	0.7	26	22	6
24 Rem. Collin County	423	69	5	34	1.7	2	6	1
25 Rem. Denton County	420	59	7	21	0.7	5	21	5
26 Rem. CMSA	295	54	5	6	0.4	1	16	2

Location	PCTWST	PCTRET	PCTFIR	PCTSER	POPDEC (thous.)	GPOPDN (thous.)	MEDINC (thous.)	PCTBLK
1 Dallas Central	4	9	26	30	279	1.1	18	31
2 West Dallas	5	9	2	19	165	0.7	21	29
3 Love Field/S. IH35	14	7	9	29	145	0.6	26	23
4 LBJ FWY/N. IH35	16	14	5	25	168	0.6	40	10
5 LBJ FWY-N	12	27	18	30	113	0.9	43	8
6 Central Expressway	2	27	24	35	276	1.4	29	18
7 LBJ/Central Exp S.	10	10	14	32	107	1.1	34	11
8 LBJ/Central Exp E.	9	24	4	27	315	0.7	34	13
9 Richardson	9	16	14	25	124	0.6	46	8
10 Plano	9	24	7	27	36	0.6	41	6
11 Redbird	5	49	4	25	24	0.3	33	32
12 GSW-Arlington	11	18	5	27	131	0.6	29	10
13 DFW Airport	1	17	5	25	22	0.2	37	6
14 Bell Helicopter	5	25	2	17	46	1.4	34	10
15 Central Fort Worth	7	10	12	44	125	0.6	17	22
16 South Fort Worth	4	15	6	29	86	0.7	23	20
17 General Dynamics	1	5	0	5	21	0.2	27	7
18 North Fort Worth	17	17	3	12	51	0.7	20	14
19 Las Colinas	25	17	6	16	109	0.7	33	13
20 Rem. Dallas City	4	24	11	31	847	0.6	26	28
21 Rem. Dallas County	8	26	6	28	560	0.4	35	15
22 Rem. Fort Worth	5	38	6	23	404	0.4	27	16
23 Rem. Tarrant County	7	24	6	25	588	0.3	35	8
24 Rem. Collin County	5	30	5	43	119	0.2	52	5
25 Rem. Denton County	5	27	3	27	77	0.2	48	4
26 Rem. CMSA	5	37	4	21	47	0.2	35	13

E_{ij} is the employment in the *j*th industry in the *i*th zip; (x_i, y_i) is the centre of the *i* th zip, and (x_j, y_j) is the centroid of industry *j* in (x,y) coordinates.

As Lee (1989) observed, the Standard Distance as a measure of an industry's degree of concentration does not allow for the possibility of multiple centres of employment. To take account of such a possibility, an index of general contiguity, CONTIG, was constructed in two steps. First, a measure of proximity (M) of an industry *j*'s employment to the *s*th zip is defined in terms of its employment, E, and distance, d, between zip s and other zips, t:

$$M_{js} = \sum_{t,t=s} \frac{E_{lt}}{d_{st}^2}$$

For any given industry, the value of M of a zip, s, will be high when a large amount of employment in the industry is located in zips close to s. Then, the contiguity index for that industry is defined as the correlation coefficient between M and E across all zips, viz., $\text{CONTIG}_j = \text{corr.}(M_{js}, E_{js})$.

Firms in an industry with a high contiguity index, indicating a great deal of spatial 'lumpiness' or clustering, can exhibit either a small standard distance or a large one; in the former case, it is a single-centred industry, and in the latter, a multicentred one. A low value for the contiguity index, by contrast, can come about if an industry is either present only in a small subarea to the exclusion of others, or characterized by rather far-flung firms. Coupled with a low value for standard distance, this implies relative concentration for the industry; a high standard distance between firms, on the other hand, implies a spatially dispersed location pattern.

In the Dallas–Fort Worth area most industries are either multicentred or dispersed. A fair number of 'high-technology' industries are observed to follow a multicentric pattern, suggesting a preference for clustering.[6] High standard distances underscore a propensity for the area's manu–facturing firms to value a variety of spatially distinct alternatives—the most labour-intensive industries, notably, display somewhat more dis-persed locational tendencies than capital-intensive ones.

IV. Modelling Intra-urban Business Location

Early models of intra-urban land use recognized the possibility of business location only in central part of a city, around a single exogenously specified export node for urban output (Mills 1967). Subsequently, in deference to more contemporary stylized patterns of urban development, some (e.g., White 1976) have allowed for nonmonocentric location of business through the establishment of a suburban export node, and in a few models (e.g., Fujita and Ogawa 1982) business locations are modelled within a multicentric framework. In recent models (such as Tauchen and Witte 1984), business (office) centres are formed not on the basis of an arbitrary export shipment point, but arise from agglomeration economies modelled explicitly as interactions between firms. In models such as White (1976), partially segregated land-use patterns in competitive spatial producer equilibrium within an urban area are motivated as firms' locational reactions to cheaper suburban labour. Urban centre formation due to agglomeration economies may be generally derived from firm location response to cost reductions in the exchange of local intermediate inputs.

Characterization of firm location in manufacturing, an export activity for any given area, has traditionally drawn on the Weberian paradigm (see Stahl 1987), which focuses on input-market oriented cost-minimizing decisions over a many-region choice set. As Stahl observes,[7] within the context of intra-urban firm location, a useful adaptation of this approach is one that incorporates local inputs, thereby establishing more explicit links with the land-use paradigm: 'In view of a better understanding of intraurban location decisions, single firm location models could also account for additional features; for instance, for the phenomenon that labour is spatially distributed in non-uniform densities, implying that the cost of drawing it to the plant varies in space; or that manufacturing processes of different sorts demand floor space for production that can be supplied only in specific proportions of building capital or land; or that the performance of different functions within a firm makes attractive the choice of different intra-urban locations for the different functions.'

Previous empirical studies of firms' intra-urban location decisions have focused either upon the choice between specific sites (e.g., Lee 1989; Blackley 1984) or between jurisdictions (e.g., Erickson and Wasylenko 1980), typically concentrating on either firm variations or location variations, but not both.[8] Our objective in this study is to attempt an empirical implementation of firms' spatial decision-making between alternative employment-centre locations in a way that is both well suited to our purpose as well as sensitive to the theoretical considerations mentioned above. While the rational producer's decision is still based on minimizing costs, we explicitly incorporate both access to local agglomeration economies afforded by each spatial alternative, as well as industry characteristics that may realize benefits from such access. The general form of the cost function of a firm of type i locating at a site j, then, is $C_{ij}(x_{ij}, y_i)$, where the arguments x and y represent vectors of centre characteristics and industry attributes, respectively.

The discrete choice model of McFadden (1974) postulates a random utility formulation (which may here be taken as the negative of the cost function) that the rational decision-making firm maximizes over a set of m qualitative alternatives. Assuming this objective function to be linear in the alternative characteristics x, and the errors to be independently identically distributed with the Weibull distribution, the model yields the following probability that a manufacturing firm i chooses employment centre j:

$$P_{ij} = \frac{e^{\beta' x_{ij}}}{\sum_{k=1}^{m} e^{\beta' x_{ik}}}$$

The problem analysed here is akin to that dealt with in a hedonic price index formulation, as the estimated parameter vector provides a decomposition of the locational probability based on the implicit preferences for the centre characteristics (see Maddala 1983).

By contrast, the usual multinomial logit model specifies probabilities that a firm i will choose the jth location as functions of its own attributes:

$$P_{ij} = \frac{e^{\alpha'_j y_i}}{\sum_{k=1}^{m} e^{\alpha'_k y_i}}$$

With some normalization as alpha = 0, the number of parameters to be estimated here is equal to the number of firm (or industry) attributes multiplied by m–1, where m is the number of locational alternatives, in our case, employment centres.

The difference between the McFadden discrete choice model and the multinomial logit model is that the former considers the effects of the characteristics of the alternatives on the determinants of choice probabilities, whereas the latter makes these probabilities dependent on chooser characteristics. The questions answered by the two models are somewhat different: the discrete choice model takes the perspective of a firm of fixed characteristics making bids on alternative locations whose characteristics vary, whereas the multinomial logit model takes the perspective of a location of fixed characteristics upon which alternative firms with varying characteristics are making bids. The two models may be viewed as special cases of a general model where choice probabilities depend on both alternative characteristics (x) and on chooser characteristics (y):

$$P_{ij} = \frac{e^{\beta' x_{ij} + \alpha'_j y_i}}{\sum_{k=1}^{m} e^{\beta' x_{ik} + \alpha'_k y_i}}$$

In our implementation of the cost-minimizing manufacturing firm's location decision between employment centres in the Dallas–Fort Worth area, we shall first estimate the discrete choice model, then the multinomial logit model, and finally the more general 'mixed' model. We turn now to these exercises.

V. Empirical Findings on Centre Attractiveness and Composition

In this section, we examine manufacturing firms' choices between the employment centres we have empirically identified in the Dallas area. The broad hypotheses to be tested are that such firms' location reflects systematic selection conditioned upon centre characteristics and/or industry attributes. The centre alternatives modelled correspond to 1 through 13, and 19 in Table 1, and represent the major employment centres in the Dallas Primary Metropolitan Statistical Area.

We first test the responsiveness of manufacturing firms to locational characteristics 'packaged' in the various employment centres. To do this, we implement the discrete choice model. The list of variables (described in Table 2) hypothesized to influence centre choice includes size controls (LANDSQ and PCTDEV), general employment characteristics of the centre (TOTEMP and NEMPDN), industrial linkage proxies (PCTWST and PCTFIR), and, importantly, variables capturing urban spatial agglomeration economies associated with each centre. Of the latter, PCTMAN is a localization proxy, while POPDEC is assumed to reflect broader urbanization advantages in the form of access to labour and markets.[9] The estimations test for the attractiveness of each of these factors in the choice between the fourteen centre alternatives considered, and coefficients can be interpreted as the values attached to these features by the sample of firms.

Results, reported in Table 3, reveal that manufacturing firms prefer to locate in relatively built-up or infrastructurally endowed employment centres, responding to centres with greater shares of developed land, rather than merely those with large land area. Manufacturing establishments' choices are also found to display affinity to centres with high proportions of manufacturing employment, but exhibit aversion to high

Table 2: Explanatory Variables Used in Multinomial Logit Model

		FIRM ATTRIBUTES
BIG	=	Dummy for employment size [100–500]
VBIG	=	Dummy for employment [>500]
		INDUSTRY ATTRIBUTES
WAGE	=	Average hourly wages for production workers in industry
FUEL	=	Share of fuel in material and factory overhead
RAWMAT	=	Share of raw material cost in value of shipments
BLDG	=	Share of structure assets and building rent payments
HTECH2	=	Dummy for industries with a proportion of technology-oriented workers and a ratio of R&D expenditures to net sales greater than the average for manufacturing industries
		SPATIAL ATTRIBUTES
D	=	Standard distance of regional firms in industry
CONTIG	=	Contiguity index of regional firms in industry
D_j	=	$\frac{E_{ij}(x_i - x_j) + E_{ij}(y_i - y_j)}{E_{ij}}$, where (x_j, y_j) is the location of the centroid of the jth industry
CONTIG	=	$C_j = C(P_{js}, E_{js})$, where $P_{js} = \frac{E_{jt}}{d^2_{st}}$; $j = 1,2, .. J; s, t = 1,2, —T$
		DISCRETE CHOICE MODEL Centre Characteristics
LANDSQ	=	Centre land area in square miles
PCTDEV	=	Percentage of centre area that is developed (1988)
TOTEMP	=	Total non-agricultural/non-government employment in centre
NEMPDN	=	Net employment density in centre
PCTMAN	=	Percentage of centre employment in Manufacturing
PCTWST	=	Percentage of centre employment in Wholesale Trade
PCTFIR	=	Percentage of centre employment in FIRE
POPDEC	=	Population distance-decayed around centre *i*
POPDEC	=	$N_i = N_{ij}^{-adij}$ where *dij* is the distance between zips comprising the centre to all others.

net total employment density, suggesting the presence of localization economies that confer specific advantages of proximity to other manufacturing employment. The results show positive interindustry linkages between manufacturing and wholesale trade, and a tendency to segregate spatially from office-based activities. These interindustry linkage results may reflect a combination of true preferences rooted in economic interactions between firms in related industries, as well as zoning constraints on the location of such firms. Strong urbanization economies are also found, confirming the importance of general workforce accessibility in the choice between the employment centres.

While the foregoing helps to explain the relative importance of certain features of employment centres to manufacturing firms regardless of size or industry, it is likely that such preferences will vary depending on the characteristics of the firm. The next set of estimations examines the nature of the sorting of manufacturing firms of different types between the various employment centres. The differences among firms as to employment size class and nature of activity are now explicitly recognized through the specification of attributes enumerated in Table 2. The first two are establishment-specific size attributes, while the rest relate to industry averages for firms in particular SIC groups. WAGE and FUEL attempt to gauge the importance of labour and capital, respectively, in firms' internal technologies; RAWMAT attempts to capture the possible role of input access, and BLDG, to proxy for space requirements associated with a particular production process. The HTECH2 dummy for high technology is intended to capture any locational proclivities of industries so defined.

Table 3: Locational Choice Between Employment Centres

Discrete Choice Model: Choice of Spatial Attributes
Dependent Variable: Centre Chosen
Log of Likelihood FN = –6100.99
Number of Cases = 2584

	B	*t*
PCTMAN	0.061829	30.8684
PCTWST	0.041243	5.09933
PCTFIR	–0.10309	–18.4909
PCTDEV	0.011064	2.79129
POPDEC	0.145231	16.6844
TOTEMP	–0.00262	–2.48197
LANDSQ	–0.01799	–22.237
NEMPDN	–0.06703	–14.3351

The multinomial logit procedure tracks the effect of these attributes on the probabilities of locating in each of the centres relative to location in the Dallas central zone (used here as a referent that is also meaningful from a policy viewpoint). One might turn our perspective of testing for the influence of industry attributes on choice between centres around to interpret results from the exercise as enabling a systematic identification of tendencies towards their functional specialization. In so doing, we will then have motivated the employment centres' compositional differences, or industry-mix, from the behavioural foundations of firm location decisions.

The centre-wise coefficients are to be interpreted as the location probability associated with each centre relative to the Dallas CBD that are exhibited by firms with the specified industrial attributes (Table 4). We find that large and medium firms prefer the Love Field/S.I-35 area compared to the CBD, although they do not appear to disperse farther north on the freeway and along the circumferential LBJ Expressway. Firms in industries with lower wages almost uniformly choose locations other than the Dallas CBD, confirming one of the most often-cited reasons for manufacturing decentralization. The Dallas CBD tends to attract a preponderance of establishments in fuel-intensive industries (most likely due to the presence of the headquarters of the major utility companies in the CBD: Lone Star Gas, Texas Utilities, and Dallas Power & Light), while many suburban centres, particularly those along the major transportation arteries, feature the location of raw material-oriented and building-intensive firms, pointing to the advantages of truck access and space availability at such sites. Firms in the high-technology industries avoid the CBD, generally preferring employment centres to the north, where access to a technically skilled labour pool is high. Industries characterized by high standard distances are over-represented in suburban centres, while relatively highly concentrated industries (low contiguity measures) appear in specialized centres such as the Dallas–Fort Worth Airport area (DFW) and the Greater South-west Industrial Park (GSW).

Finally, we implement the 'mixed' model, which explores the propensities of firms to sort themselves into centres by attribute when the attraction of other, more generally quantifiable, centre characteristics has been separately controlled for. This model, then, tests for the residual distinctiveness of our employment entres in attracting a given kind of manufacturing firm (Table 5). Comparing the first part with the pure discrete choice results of Table 3, we find that the signs on centre characteristics are generally unchanged, although their magnitudes and significance levels decline. When choice between specific centres is incorporated into the model, many general characteristics lose their appeal, showing up instead in centre-specific affinities. This, to some extent, validates the idea of analysing choices between specialized employment centres, as opposed to general spatial attributes. However, the agglomeration variables PCTMAN and POPDEC, reflecting localization and urbanization variables, respectively, retain their significance, attesting to the value to firms of general agglomeration economies offered by employment centres.

Many of the coefficients of industry attributes, likewise, diminish relative to those in Table 4, when previously explained centre-specific advantages are now better captured by general characteristics. For example, the relative wage advantage of the non-central Dallas centres yields to the agglomeration economies proxied by centre characteristics, to the extent both reflect the locational pull of labour availability. Yet significant industry-specific affiliations with particular centres that transcend general attractions for all manufacturing firms should be retained by this procedure and would remain in evidence. Interestingly, the distinctiveness of some centres' specific advantages is accentuated. The North Dallas suburban centres maintain or improve their high-tech orientation *vis-a-vis* central Dallas, while for other centres, coefficients turn negative or insignificant. Similarly, the Dallas CBD's unique position with respect to fuel-intensive firms (major utility companies) appears sharpened. Richardson's compositional character as it emerges from these findings, for example, confirms a strong high-technology presence and a predisposition to be a location favoured by relatively dispersed industries. Below, we broadly summarize and evaluate the import of our exercise.

VI. Conclusion

Polycentric urban development is now a well-established phenomenon recognized as worthy of systematic study. As Stanback noted, 'Older, simplistic views of the suburbs as largely residential extensions of the city must give way to a view of these areas as economies in the process of becoming increasingly complex and mature'. Nevertheless, he added: 'The importance of agglomeration economies to suburban development

Table 4: Locational Choice Among Employment Centres in the Dallas Area: Multinomial Logit Model

Multinomial Logit Model-Industry Attributes

Dependent variable: Centre chosen
(normalized W.R.T. Dallas Central Area)

Log of Likelihood Function = –5818.75

Number of cases = 2584

2. W. DALLAS	*b*	*t*
BIG2	–0.982	–1.320
VBIG2	–1.153	–1.364
WAGE2	–0.028	–0.490
FUEL2	2.246	0.444
BLDG2	3.776	0.690
HTECH22	0.104	0.270
D2	0.061	1.511
CONTIG2	–1.590	–2.088

3. LOVE/S.I-35	*b*	*t*	4. LBJ/N.I-35	*b*	*t*	5. LBJ/NORTH	*b*	*t*	6. CEN.EXPWY	*b*	*t*
BIG3	1.338	2.023	BIG4	–1.016	–1.575	BIG5	–0.887	–1.095	BIG6	–0.889	–0.994
VBIG3	1.447	1.984	VBIG4	–0.757	–1.055	VBIG5	–1.702	–1.723	VBIG6	–1.699	–1.545
WAGE3	–0.137	–2.957	WAGE4	–0.136	–2.748	WAGES	–0.056	–0.849	WAGE6	–0.118	–1.482
FUEL3	–10.236	–2.174	FUEL4	–8.345	–1.732	FUEL5	–11.957	–1.815	FUEL6	–11.955	–1.259
RAWMAT3	1.299	1.680	RAWMAT4	2.447	2.996	RAWMAT5	0.906	0.839	RAWMAT6	–0.967	–0.795
BLDG3	10.600	2.423	BLDG4	16.512	3.662	BLDG5	18.603	3.288	BLDG6	9.788	1.501
HTECH23	0.596	2.024	HTECH24	0.888	2.903	HTECH25	0.277	0.684	HTECH26	1.199	2.860
D3	–0.041	–1.269	D4	0.026	0.749	D5	–0.092	–2.041	D6	0.053	0.940
CONTIG3	0.231	0.398	CONTIG4	-0.441	-0.689	CONTIG5	0.010	0.012	CONTIG6	0.759	0.819

7. LBJ/CENEXPY	*b*	*t*	8. LBJ EXPWY/E	*b*	*t*	9. RICHARDSON	*b*	*t*	10. PLANO	*b*	*t*
BIG7	0.186	0.197	BIG8	0.564	0.793	BIG9	–0.560	–0.742	BIG10	–1.088	–1.174
VBIG7	–0.453	–0.419	VBIG8	0.519	0.661	VBIG9	–1.376	–1.548	VBIG10	–1.053	–1.002
WAGE7	–0.188	–2.473	WAGE8	–0.175	–3.388	WAGE9	–0.160	–2.329	WAGE10	–0.206	–2.460
FUEL7	–31.981	–2.459	FUEL8	–11.913	–2.234	FUEL9	–59.862	–3.768	FUEL10	–9.696	–1.124
RAWMAT7	0.219	0.182	RAWMAT8	1.289	1.511	RAWMAT9	0.799	–0.741	RAWMAT10	0.015	0.012
BLDG7	12.874	2.200	BLDG8	13.367	2.920	BLDG9	22.115	4.385	BLDG10	14.348	2.213
HTECH27	1.572	4.089	HTECH28	1.246	4.100	HTECH29	1.887	5.422	HTECH210	1.046	2.337
D7	–0.023	–0.441	D8	-0.010	–0.299	D9	0.026	0.537	D10	0.066	1.169
CONTIG7	1.350	1.523	CONTIG8	-0.223	–0.346	CONTIG9	2.090	2.623	CONTIG10	–0.862	–0.818
11. REDBIRD	*b*	*t*	12. GSW/ARL	*b*	*t*	13. D/FWAIRPT	*b*	*t*	19. LASCOLINAS	*b*	*t*
BIG11	–1.742	1.668	BIG12	–0.791	–1.168	BIG13	–1.166	–1.048	BIG19	0.251	0.170
VBIG11	–1.263	–1.065	VBIG12	–0.869	–1.145	VBIG13	–1.699	–1.257	VBIG19	–0.085	–0.050
WAGE11	–0.203	–1.831	WAGE12	–0.093	–1.800	WAGE13	0.218	–2.128	WAGE19	–0.392	–3.077
FUEL11	–23.924	–1.281	FUEL12	–7.374	–1.481	FUEL13	–2.936	–0.382	FUEL19	–36.780	–1.256
RAWMAT11	1.745	1.044	RAWMAT12	1.564	1.820	RAWMAT13	1.831	1.139	RAWMAT19	4.188	2.035
BLDG11	13.416	1.500	BLDG12	13.629	2.903	BLDG13	13.702	1.617	BLDG19	3.468	0.275
HTECH211	0.688	1.084	HTECH212	0.951	3.023	HTECH213	–0.025	–0.036	HTECH219	–17.235	–0.004
D11	0.005	0.066	D12	0.011	0.305	D13	0.016	–0.259	D19	–0.029	–0.407
CONTIG11	–0.730	–0.496	CONTIG12	–1.301	–1.891	CONTIG13	–5.527	–3.035	CONTIG19	–2.095	–1.183

Table 5: Locational Choice Among Employment Centres in the Dallas Area: Mixed Conditional Logit Model—Industry and Centre Attributes

						Centre Attributes			Industry Attributes		
									2. W.DALLAS	*b*	*t*
							b	*t*	BIG2	3.011	1.440
Dependent variable: Centre chosen						PCTMAN	0.101	3.037	VBIG2	2.765	1.301
(normalized W.R.T Dallas Central Area)						PCTWST	0.309	1.589	WAGE2	0.050	0.823
						PCTFIR	–0.164	–1.461	FUEL2	–0.790	–0.155
Log of Likelihood Function = –5802.62						PCTDEV	0.064	0.845	RAWMAT2	1.813	1.731
						POPDEC	0.343	1.744	BLDG2	10.551	1.823
Number of Cases = 2584						TOTEMP	–0.053	–2.151	HTECH22	0.042	0.108
						LANDSQ	–0.031	–1.558	D2	0.090	2.173
						NEMPDN	–0.133	–1.379	CONTIG2	–0.930	–1.185
INDUSTRY/CENTER INTERACTIONS											
3.LOVE/S.I-35	*b*	*t*	4.LBJ/N.I-35	*b*	*t*	5. LBJ/NORTH	*b*	*t*	6. CEN. EXPWY	*b*	*t*
BIG3	0.997	1.396	BIG4	0.798	1.065	BIG5	0.110	0.314	BIG6	1.016	0.087
VBIG3	1.083	1.425	VBIG4	1.002	1.257	VBIG5	–0.732	–0.744	VBIG6	0.148	0.112
WAGE3	–0.115	–2.389	WAGE4	–0.076	–1.434	WAGE5	–0.033	–0.466	WAGE6	–0.045	–0.519
FUEL3	–11.119	–2.352	FUEL4	–10.790	–2.216	FUEL5	–12.910	–1.939	FUEL6	–14.639	–1.528
RAWMAT3	1.689	2.079	RAWMAT4	3.852	4.208	RAWMAT5	1.369	1.138	RAWMAT6	0.458	0.337
BLDG3	12.482	2.773	BLDG4	21.655	4.536	BLDG5	20.589	3.454	BLDG6	14.831	2.171
HTECH23	0.579	1.960	HTECH24	0.838	2.727	HTECH25	0.258	0.635	HTECH26	1.136	2.706
D3	–0.032	–1.001	D4	0.046	1.330	D5	–0.085	–1.864	D6	0.075	1.313
CONTIG3	0.385	0.659	CONTIG4	0.040	0.061	CONTIG5	0.172	0.193	CONTIG6	1.198	1.274

7. LBJ/CENEXPY	b	t	8. LBJ EXPWY/E	b	t	9. RICHARDSON	b	t	10. PLANO	b	t
BIG7	1.437	1.208	BIG8	1.816	1.870	BIG9	0.848	1.049	BIG10	1.576	1.031
VBIG7	0.762	0.591	VBIG8	1.733	1.710	VBIG9	–0.010	–0.010	VBIG10	1.536	0.960
WAGE7	–0.150	–1.861	WAGE8	–0.135	–2.495	WAGE9	–0.111	–1.434	WAGE10	–0.116	–1.291
FUEL7	–33.637	–2.573	FUEL8	–13.639	–2.543	FUEL9	–61.849	–3.885	FUEL10	–12.866	–1.474
RAWMAT7	1.054	0.793	RAWMAT8	2.167	2.376	RAWMAT9	0.235	0.187	RAWMAT10	1.899	1.288
BLDG7	16.101	2.656	BLDG8	16.699	3.520	BLDG9	25.878	4.811	BLDG10	20.907	3.039
HTECH27	1.538	3.984	HTECH28	1.210	3.963	HTECH29	1.844	5.273	HTECH210	0.969	2.161
D7	–0.011	–0.204	D8	0.003	0.073	D9	0.041	0.830	D10	0.092	1.604
CONTIG7	1.624	1.814	CONTIG8	0.055	0.084	CONTIG9	2.403	2.974	CONTIG10	–0.252	–0.235
11. REDBIRD	b	t	12. GSW/ARL	b	t	13. D/FWAIRPT	b	t	19. LASCOLINAS	b	t
BIG11	–0.107	–0.094	BIG12	0.687	0.921	BIG13	2.942	1.210	BIG19	5.702	1.858
VBIG11	0.309	0.245	VBIG12	0.565	0.700	VBIG13	2.314	0.903	VBIG19	5.313	1.662
WAGE11	–0.138	–1.225	WAGE12	–0.046	–0.838	WAGE13	–0.132	–1.252	WAGE19	–0.345	–2.701
FUEL11	–26.892	–1.429	FUEL12	–9.341	–1.861	FUEL13	–6.590	–0.846	FUEL19	–40.127	–1.347
RAWMAT11	3.321	1.823	RAWMAT12	2.619	2.779	RAWMAT13	4.118	2.141	RAWMAT19	5.461	2.408
BLDG11	18.765	2.052	BLDG12	17.593	3.565	BLDG13	22.152	2.414	BLDG19	7.986	0.616
HTECH211	0.627	0.989	HTECH212	0.908	2.876	HTECH213	–0.125	–0.178	HTECH219	–17.261	–0.004
D11	0.023	0.308	D12	0.027	0.739	D13	0.012	0.200	D19	–0.018	–0.251
CONTIG11	–0.243	–0.165	CONTIG12	–0.956	–1.361	CONTIG13	–4.626	–2.503	CONTIG19	–1.696	–0.949

is not as readily recognized as in the case of the central cities. Yet there is considerable evidence that economic growth in the suburbs is increasingly focused on a restricted number of magnet areas in which locational advantages associated with agglomeration play a key role.'[10]

This paper has elicited empirical support for the existence of multiple employment centres and factors that make them attractive as location prospects for manufacturing firms. To summarize some of the unique features of the exercise, we (*a*) recovered these employment centres from an elemental land-use identification procedure, (*b*) motivated an explanation of their manufacturing industry mix from the behavioural underpinnings of firms' optimization decisions, and (*c*) tested for the locational pull of their cost-minimizing agglomeration influences through the specification of intra-urban spatial linkage variables. The substantive results reinforce the validity of the idea of employment centres and confirm their relevance to the phenomenon of manufacturing decentralization.

There are two major sorts of policy implications for metropolitan development that might follow from our methodology. One, the exercise can identify what kinds of firms are likely to prefer central or suburban employment locations with certain characteristics. These affinities provide insight into the nature of competing employment centres (indeed, it is possible to 'rank' them along each dimension), and can guide attempts by associated jurisdictions to target promotional activities at the most likely prospects. However, the utility of the exercise transcends interjurisdictional competition (as, say, between central city and suburbs) for business activity in revealing information about centres' comparative strengths. Manufacturing activity tends to be a basic or 'export' activity from the viewpoint of the metropolitan economy at large, and its location (or retention) anywhere within the latter's sphere of influence, given the close spatial and sectoral interactions characterizing any such economy, is likely to benefit the whole. A polycentric metropolitan area that can exhibit a rich diversity of functional specialization in its major employment centres to 'match' firms with location possibilities has an unequivocal advantage over one that does not.

There are two extensions of the analysis we think might be particularly promising, both from the standpoint of furthering our knowledge about intra-urban location decisions as well as from a policy perspective. First, a more detailed study of a high-profile segment of manufacturing, viz., high-technology industry, which has in this context demonstrated rather clear-cut spatial preferences, may be worthwhile. Second, an explicit investigation of the hierarchical decision-making structure between jurisdictions, employment centres and subzones within the latter (probably by using a nested logit formulation) might better illuminate the role of specific fiscal or infrastructural incentives local governments can (and often do) bring to bear upon business location. These are being pursued in concurrent and future work on the Dallas–Fort Worth metropolitan area.

NOTES

Reproduced with permission from *Urban Geography*, 1993, 14, 3, pp. 277–96.

1 This paper is dedicated to the memory of Vibhooti Shukla, who was lost in a tragic accident in 1992. We wish to acknowledge Royce Hanson, Brian J.L. Berry, and John Kain for their valuable insights and suggestions in the course of the research. We also thank Santiya Eag-Ark and Pornpong Sumanan for their able research assistance. This study was funded by the Texas Advanced Research Program.

2 Overviews of two recent concerted efforts to address the challenge to the monocentric model from the 'new' urban forms, and its consequences for urban economics research, may be found in Ladd and Wheaton (1991) and Berry and Kim (1993, forthcoming).

3 Giuliano and Small (1991) provide the most comprehensive and up-to-date review of this literature that we know of. Their own subcentre identification methodology relies upon a definition of an employment centre as a contiguous set of zones fulfilling a minimum relative (in spatial terms) density and an absolute total employment criterion.

4 Cervero (1989), examining 57 (primarily office-based) suburban centres throughout the US, classified them as office parks, office and convention centres, large-scale mixed-use developments, moderate-scale mixed-use developments, subcities, and large-scale office growth corridors. Giuliano and Small (1991), through cluster analysis, identified five centre types for the Los Angeles area: specialized manufacturing, mixed industrial, mixed service, specialized entertainment, and specialized service centres. Others, such as Hartshorn and Muller (1986), have studied the growth processes of suburban centres to identify four stages in the development of 'suburban downtowns': bedroom community, independence, catalytic growth, and high rise/high technology. Our centre descriptions here are merely indicative, as we do not wish to prejudge the issue by classifying centres formally. Rather, it is hoped that a behaviourally meaningful taxonomy might emerge from the location analysis to follow.

5 Our 1985–87 employment data from *County Business Patterns* includes information on the number of establishments, total employment, and the

distribution of establishments by employment size class by zip and employment centre. Statistics on industry attributes (defined in Table 2) come from the US Dept. of Commerce, 1985, *Annual Survey of Manufactures*, Washington, D. C.: Bureau of the Census.

6 Contiguity Index scores are plotted against Standard Distances using our employment data for industries in the top decile of values for each industrial attribute shown, with the exception of the 'hi-tech' category. In the case of the latter, all industries satisfying the definition for high technology industries in Table 2 are depicted. This definition is adapted from R. Riche, D. Hecker, and J. Burgan, 'High Technology Today and Tomorrow', *Monthly Labour Review*, November 1983.

7 Stahl (1987, p. 769). See Stahl for a thorough review of models of business location. See Shukla and Waddell (1991) for a fuller discussion of the empirical implementation of urban land use theory in the context of firm location issues.

8 Blackley's (1984) methodology involves implementation of a manufacturing location model of site allocation outcomes based on a bid-rent hedonic price approach identical to that used by Lee (1989). Not surprisingly, given the study's orientation, he finds a dominance of structural or site characteristics over locational attributes. While he also estimates a set of attribute demand equations through a binary logit model, his method deals with firm (industry) and site (centre) attributes in a step-wise fashion, rather than simultaneously. See Shukla and Waddell (1991) for a comparison of Lee-type approaches with our approach, as one more suited to choice between centres rather than sites.

9 POPDEC = N_i, for each centre, i, is constructed as follows:

$$N_i = \sum_j N_j^{-ad_{ij}}$$

where d_{ij} is the distance between the zips comprising centre i and all others, j; N_j is the population residing in zip j. Data for the demographic variables come from CACI, *Demographic Data Files*, 1985, 1987.

10 Stanback (1991, pp. 8, 60).

REFERENCES

Berry, B.J.L. and H.M. Kim (1993), 'Challenges to the Monocentric Model', *Geographical Analysis*, Vol. 25, No. 1, pp. 1-4.

Blackley, P. (1984), 'A Hedonic Approach to the Decentralization of Manufacturing Activity', *Journal of Regional Science*, Vol. 24, pp. 541–57.

Cervero, R. (1989), *America's Suburban Centers: The Land Use–Transportation Link,* Unwin Hyman, Boston, MA.

Erickson, R. and M. Wasylenko (1980), 'Firm Relocation and Site Selection in Suburban Municipalities', *Journal of Urban Economics*, Vol. 8, pp. 69–85.

Fujita, M. and H. Ogawa (1982), 'Multiple Equilibria and Structural Transition of Non-Monocentric Urban Configurations', *Regional Science and Urban Economics*, Vol. 12, pp. 161–96.

Giuliano, G. and K. Small (1991), 'Subcenters in the Los Angeles Region', *Regional Science and Urban Economics*, Vol. 21, pp. 163–82.

Hartshorn, T. and P. Muller (1986), *Suburban Business Centres: Employment Expectations*, Final Report for US Dept. of Commerce, EDA Washington, D.C.: US Dept. of Commerce.

Ladd, H. and W. Wheaton (1991), 'Causes and Consequences of the Changing Urban Form', *Regional Science and Urban Economics*, Vol. 21, pp. 157–62.

Lee, K.S. (1989), *The Location of Jobs in a Developing Metropolis*, World Bank/Oxford University Press, New York.

Maddala, G.S. (1983), *Limited-dependent and Qualitative Variables in Econometrics*, Cambridge University Press, Cambridge.

McFadden, D. (1974), 'The Measurement of Urban Travel Demand', *Journal of Public Economics*, Vol. 3, pp. 303–28.

Mills, E.S. (1967), 'An Aggregative Model of Resource Allocation in a Metropolitan Area', *American Economic Review*, Vol. 57, pp. 197–210.

Schmenner, R. (1982), *Making Business Location Decisions*, Prentice-Hall, Englewood Cliffs, NJ.

Shukla, V. and P. Waddell (1991), Firm Location and Land Use in Discrete Urban Space, *Regional Science and Urban Economics*, Vol. 21, pp. 225-53. [Reproduced in this volume, pp. 277–308].

Stahl, K. (1987), 'Theories of Urban Business Location' in E.S. Mills, ed., *Handbook of Regional and Urban Economics*, Vol. 2, North-Holland, New York, pp. 759–820.

Stanback, T. (1991), *The New Suburbanization—Challenge to the Central City*, Westview Press, Boulder, CO.

Tauchen, H. and A. Witte (1984), 'Socially Optimal and Equilibrium Distributions of Office Activity: Models with Exogenous and Endogenous Contacts', *Journal of Urban Economics*, Vol. 15, pp. 66–86.

Waddell, P. and V. Shukla (1993), 'Employment Dynamics, Spatial Restructuring, and the Business Cycle, *Geographical Analysis*, Vol. 25, No. 1, pp. 35–52.

White, M. (1976), 'Firm Suburbanization and Urban Subcenters, *Journal of Urban Economics*, Vol. 5, pp. 219–40.

V / Consequences of Urban Growth

15 / The Environmental Consequences of Urban Growth: Cross-national Perspectives on Economic Development, Air Pollution, and City Size[1]

VIBHOOTI SHUKLA
KIRIT PARIKH

I.

There has been a strong revival of interest in environmental matters in developed countries and a long-overdue recognition of environmental problems in countries that have come late to the development game. The less developed countries (LDCs) are now thought to hold potential for much greater pollution than is anticipated for developed economies, given that they have far to go along the path of industrialization, and have fewer means to avoid or correct for the environmentally detrimental concomitants of this process. However, much of the discussion that has taken place is quite speculative in terms of how much pollution is involved, what its character might be, and costs of measures that may be taken to ameliorate its impact. In this paper, we seek to take an initial step toward assessing the magnitude of one aspect of the problem — air pollution — facing cities of developing countries. Since it cannot be assumed that developing country strategies for combating pollution can or should closely follow those pursued by developed nations, we feel an empirical examination of differences and similarities between the two contexts to be of value.

Some noteworthy points of difference have been cited between the development experiences of today's advanced economies and the present-day developing nations. These differences include greater population pressures, more rapid rates of urbanization, the unbalanced growth of certain large 'megacities', and an elevated degree of overall resource use predicated by technologies more appropriate to higher development levels. Such technologies are often employed in response to pressures (fuelled by the 'revolution of rising expectations') to catch up with the living standards and lifestyles of the rich. Researchers such as Berry (1990) foresee a pattern of counter-urbanization for the economically advanced countries, where a 'transformation is unfolding that is resulting in dispersed and relatively low-density urban networks ...[whereas] it is from the Third World's economic growth and urban concentration that the most serious regional threats to the global environment will come'. The 1988–89 report of the World Resources Institute (1989) characterized six urban trends as significant 'for understanding the problems, challenges, and opportunities of human settlements'.[2]

1. The percentage of population living in urban areas is increasing.
2. Urban population is increasing at high rates in less developed countries and at declining rates in more developed countries.
3. Large increases are expected in the absolute numbers of urban residents over the next two decades, especially in less developed countries.
4. The number of cities in all size categories is growing in less developed countries.
5. The number and size of megacities is growing in less developed countries while the growth rate in major metropolitan areas in more developed countries is declining.
6. The distribution of people living in absolute poverty is shifting from rural to urban settlements at an increasing rate.

Alarms about the potential for environmental damage from urbanization in developing countries take the form, then, (1) of concerns with the total magnitude, share, and rates of increase of their urban populations and (2) of fears about the large sizes and rapid growth of their individual cities. How realistic are these fears, and how should policy address them? We do not question here the desirability of economic growth and industrialization in these countries' quest for higher living standards. But one can legitimately ask if the attendant changes in settlement patterns are inevitable or costless.

Urbanization comes about because technologies used to make non-agricultural commodities needed to fulfil consumption demands at higher incomes thrive on spatial concentration because of economies of scale. The benefits of large city size for industrial production have been empirically documented and measured for developed as well as for developing countries.[3] These 'agglomeration economies' are advantages of spatial concentration and urban scale that make certain economic activities relatively efficient in large urban areas. If anything, these economies are more important in less developed countries where high transaction costs resulting from paucity of transport and communication facilities make the gains from proximity more salient. Agglomeration economies may be viewed as generating positive externalities from urban growth. Firms locating in an urban area and contributing to its expansion confer economic benefits to its productive environment at large. Set against these are social costs resulting from urban expansion. Among the most widely cited of such costs are adverse environmental impacts from urban growth, i.e., negative externalities of urban growth. However, these environmental 'costs' of urbanization or urban bigness must be weighed carefully against gains from urbanization and the advantages of large city size.

We attempt in this study a quantitative assessment of the environmental consequences of urbanization in general and city bigness in particular, with specific reference to the process of economic development. Such an assessment cannot, of course, be comprehensive enough to consider all the social costs, or even the total environmental costs, of urban growth.[4] Discussion rather is limited to the problem of air pollution and characterization of its 'behaviour' with respect to the urbanization experiences of a cross-section of developed and developing countries. We hope that the insights obtained might provide a guide to better policy for economic development and a safer living environment.

The next section of this paper views the air pollution problem in the context of the various countries' development processes. Since it is localized atmospheric concentrations rather than aspatial aggregate emissions that constitute the chief danger from air pollution, concerns about the detrimental effects of air pollution should properly be focused upon the concentration of economic activity and population in large urban areas with high densities, rather than on the magnitude of urbanization *per se*. Accordingly, the pollution literature insofar as it relates to city size and form is reviewed. The next section explores the local impact of urban pollution by comparing ambient air quality over various zone types across urban areas of different sizes in developed and developing countries. Then, the paper re-examines the relationship between pollution and city size using a fuller range of contextual variables that explicitly control for a country's level of economic development. We then discuss environmental implications for policies toward city size and spatial structure, based on trends discernible in the spectrum of international experiences with pollution emissions and control. A final section presents some conclusions.

II. Economic Development, Air Pollution, and City Size

The close relationship between industrialization, economic development, and urban growth is widely recognized. As Chenery, Robinson, and Syrquin (1986) state in their structural comparisons of country growth experiences, 'Historically, the rise in the share of manufacturing in output and employment as per capita income increases, and the corresponding decline of agriculture, are among the best documented generalities about development.' Since income elasticities for agricultural goods are smaller than those for industrial products, with development, increasing amounts of economic resources are committed to the production of industrial goods. Mills and Becker (1986) presented an analysis of the relationship between urbanization and economic development using data from most of the countries in the world. In addition to GNP per capita, their regressions on the cross-sectional determinants of urbanization utilized a variety of measures of structural change as indicators of economic development, including labour force share in agriculture, which resulted in a strongly negative relationship. Thus, empirically, the expansion of non-agricultural production goes hand in hand with urbanization. Such production, we have seen, is technologically most suited to — and hence profitably located in urban areas. This describes the channels through which rising overall incomes may translate into the process of urbanization.[5]

Often empirically associated in the development processes of countries, economic growth, industrialization, and urbanization are, however, distinct though interdependent phenomena. Sources of pollution are many and one may try to distinguish in principle between the aggregate pollution effects resulting from industrialization and high consumption levels on the one hand, and those attributable to density and resource use patterns associated with a peculiarly urban lifestyle on the other. This conceptual distinction helps clarify the course of policy action, although the different channels of influence may be somewhat difficult to separate. In Parikh, Parikh, Gokarn, Painuly, Saha, and

Shukla (1991), multiple regression analysis using proxy variables to capture the various structural features of the development process was used to explain estimated pollutant emissions at the country level. These revealed weak or no association between countrywide emission rates and urbanization as distinct from the effects of incomes, population, and shares of manufacturing activity.[6] Thus we have found only inconclusive evidence that urbanization imposes higher environmental costs in terms of aggregate discharges of the air pollutants studied.

Why, then, the prevailing fears about urbanization's high potential for environmental damage? The answer lies in recognizing that most ill-effects associated with urban air pollution arise from inordinately high localized concentrations of pollutants after they have been emitted over a relatively small but densely settled area. As Mills and Hamilton explained:

> The first 'urban' observation is that many environmental problems are not problems at all when population densities are small. High density creates a problem by increasing the number of victims of any environmental degradation. If air quality reduction imposes a cost of $100 per year per exposed resident, it is of much more quantitative importance in a city of two million than in a town of 5000. Second, in addition to increasing the number of pollution victims, and therefore the social costs of pollution, a concentration of people and economic activity generally increases the density of pollutants as well. This is important, because damage generally rises more than proportionately with the volume of discharges... many effluents are innocuous at low densities.[7]

By focusing upon a country's volume of polluting discharges, regardless of location, we miss some of the essential concerns about their deleterious effects. A more suitable unit of analysis for examination, therefore, may be the individual urban area rather than the country at large, and a more appropriate index of the harmful effects of the negative aspects of urban growth captured by measured ambient air pollution rather than estimated emissions or discharges.

Tolley (1979) noted that pollutant concentrations tend to increase with city size for all three major sources of air pollution: industrial establishments, which emit gases because of fuel use and because of chemical reactions connected with particular manufacturing processes; household fuel consumption because of heating and cooking; and motor vehicles. He stated, 'The growth of a city brings more and more emissions relative to air available for dilution in a vicinity... If there is enough city growth to have an effect on residential and industrial density, sources of pollution will also tend to crowd together. Because there will then be less opportunity for dilution between emitting sources, pollution concentration in the city will further increase' (Tolley 1979, p. 66). We now wish to summarize theoretical perspectives on pollution, city size, and urban density, which leads in particular to a consideration of the environmental impact of the growth of individual cities and a consequent concern with policies toward city size and structure.

A class of models known as equilibrium city size models (e.g., Henderson 1987), although static in formulation, is useful in framing the arguments for intervention in urban growth. Such models view an urban area as a large spatial labour market for the specialized production of goods for export to the rest of the world. The equilibrium city size results from the derived demand for labour by industry located within the area. In Figure 1, the demand curve, N^d, slopes downward as profit maximization by firms would imply; the supply curve, N^s, is upsloping, since spatial utility maximization by households entails in-migration only at wages high enough to compensate for increasing costs of living and rising disamenities as the urban area grows. Equilibrium city size is at N^e.

It is easy to see that there may be externalities in the process of urban growth that cause the optimal size of the urban area to diverge from the equilibrium. Firms factor the economies of urban scale into their employment decisions, but may fail to perceive that each hiring action will enhance them. Thus, industrial agglomeration economies might cause the marginal benefit curve of increasing city size to lie above private labour demands, so that N^* exceeds N^e, warranting regional development-type incentives to sustain the optimum as an equilibrium. Similarly, the marginal resident, in deciding to migrate to the city, may take account of the pollution there, but ignores the fact that his entry adds to it, imposing additional costs on others. Thus, external diseconomies due to negative spillovers from urban growth, such as pollution or congestion, may be characterized as placing the marginal social cost from continued in-migration above private costs, yielding an optimal size such as N^{**}, below equilibrium size, N^e.

The net magnitude of these effects determines, for any particular city, the desirability of policies encouraging or curbing further urban

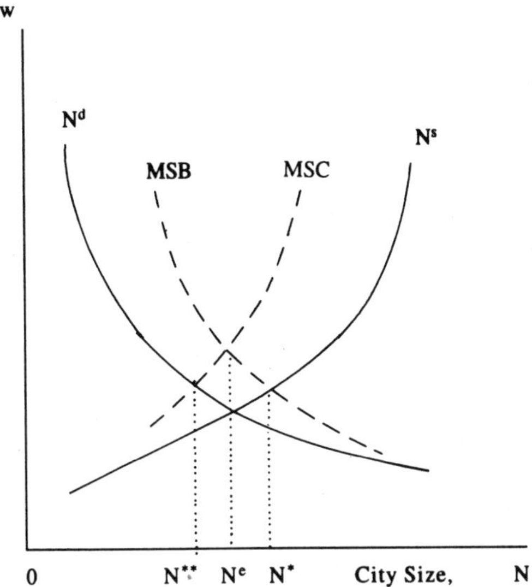

Figure 1: Externalities in Urban Growth

expansion. Thus, it is of some importance to be able to assess the relative strengths of the positive agglomeration influences, and the negative pollution damages resulting from increasing city size. Several measurements of the benefits to factor productivity of urban scale have yielded 'agglomeration elasticity' estimates of about .04 to .06 for developed country and about .10 for developing country contexts, implying for the latter about a 10 per cent gain in resource efficiency for every 100 per cent increase in city size.[8] This suggests there might be a relatively greater income loss in poorer economies if urban growth there were restricted as a measure to control pollution.

Damage to human life as a deleterious health effect from pollution may also be measured directly. Lave and Seskin (1977) suggested that a microgram of suspended particulates may increase the death rate by four persons per million. They also estimated that halving ambient concentrations of sulphur oxides and particulates over a typical US metropolitan area from their 1960 levels would add about one year to life expectancy in the metropolitan area. Thomas (1986), in an empirical study of the spatial variations in air-pollution-related health damages within 37 municipalities of the Greater Sao Paulo (GSP) area in Brazil, found population density to be an important determinant of the incremental damages from a given amount of pollution. According to Thomas's calculations, a 50 per cent reduction in industrial particulates alone (a 33 per cent reduction in total particulate emissions, of which industries contributed 65 per cent in GSP) would be associated with a 1.2 per cent fall in the mortality rate. Both studies imply significant gains from pollution control.

Tolley (1979) has attempted to translate such health damage effects of pollution into the pecuniary costs of urban growth, representing potential gains from the restriction of city size. He used Lave and Seskin's (1977) estimate to reckon that the addition of a worker would result in an increase of yearly deaths of 0.0024 for a city of six million persons. He further made a 'liberal allowance' of $225,000 per life lost due to the unknown consequences of loss of life and sickness from diseases caused by air pollution to arrive at a $540 cost of adding one worker to a city of six million persons. His estimates imply that eliminating a 10 per cent growth in such a city's population would entail a saving in air pollution costs equalling about $81 million. A similar calculation for cities in developing countries is not available, nor do we have a pecuniary estimate for productivity losses due to size restriction. However, it may be reasonable to speculate that higher urban densities in developing countries and peoples' failure to treat or avoid health damages due to pollution would tend to nudge these gains from curbing city growth upwards, whereas their lower life expectancies and earnings potentials would depress them.

Tolley conceded that his estimates of pollution-induced costs of urban growth ignored spatial adaptation to pollution—the idea that urban residents will try to avoid pollution and other disamenities by locating away from areas of heavy industrial pollution. He observed that because of land availability, economies of association, and zoning regulations, industries tend to locate near one another, confining their main pollution effects to worksites. Thus costs from industrial pollution in market economies are significantly lowered by spatial adaptation. However, cities in developing countries are likely to show a lower degree of pollution damage perception among residents, and private avoidance measures like spatial adaptation (and public ones, such as zoning) may be less widespread there.[9]

This suggests that in addition to the aggregate sizes of cities, the nature of their spatial structures also has implications for the effects of

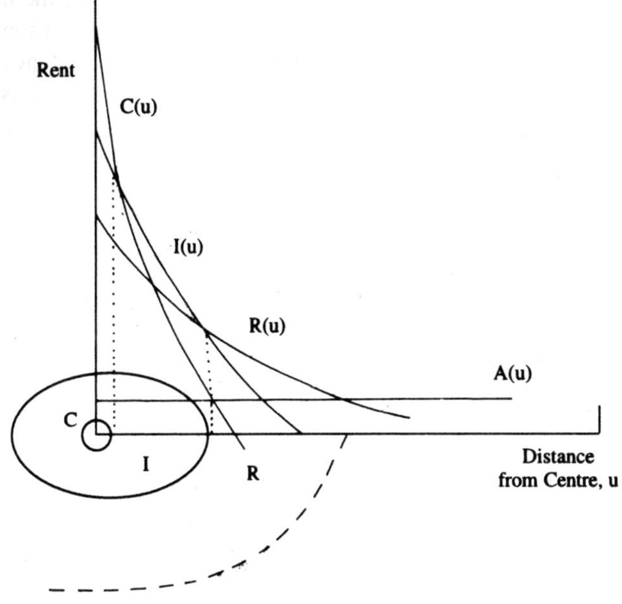

Figure 2: Urban Spatial Structure

air pollution in urban areas. The standard monocentric model of land use within an urban area, which posits an attractive central node (such as a port or railway terminal) around which economic activities will symmetrically cluster, is shown in Figure 2.[10] Activities locating close to the node enjoy economies of goods transportation or commuting, but will bid up the price of land closer into the city's centre until profits are spatially equalized with their counterparts farther out. The higher the attractiveness of proximity to the node for a sector, the greater is the rent for sites around it. The figure shows the 'bid-rent' curves of four sectors, commercial [C(u)], industrial [I(u)], urban residential [R(u)], and agricultural [A(u)] for land at various distances from the centre. Not surprisingly, office activities are in the closest concentric circle around the node, and agricultural activities locate beyond the urban fringe marked by the broken line.

This model will approximate urban form or layout with a single city centre. Some differences between urban areas of developed and developing countries may be illustrated by this model. The greater the importance and attractiveness of a single centre and the greater the cost of transportation, the steeper will be the density gradient, and the closer will be the intersection with A(u) that defines the limits of the urban area. In developed countries, industry has been 'decentralizing' for some time, following the suburbanization of population driven by income increases, demand for better housing, and steady transportation improvements that reduce commuting costs.

This is not the case in most developing country cities, where scarce transportation and housing resources, coupled with the continued importance of spatial agglomeration economies, keep proximity to the city centre overwhelmingly attractive. As a result, cities in developing countries tend to be more compact, packing economic activities far more densely than those in developed countries. These high densities would place a much greater burden on the environment for the same level of aggregate polluting discharge. Moreover, while flattening density gradients characterize cities in developed countries, high population growth rates in cities in developing countries imply higher urban densities at each radial distance from the centre. We now turn to an empirical examination of some of these ideas.

III. Air Pollution in Developed and Developing Countries

Any policy prescriptions for modifying urban growth patterns to avoid the social costs of pollution must be informed by a quantitative assessment of the problem. Although not a strictly 'physical' one, the relationship between measured pollution concentrations and city size is critical to the argument for curbing urban growth on environmental grounds.[11]

We seek, in this section, to examine this relationship empirically, using data on ambient air quality for sulphur dioxide (SO_2) and particulates (SPM) monitored in different urban zones across an international sample of cities. An important purpose of the analysis is to probe the existence of any verifiable differences in these relationships between cities in developed and developing countries.[12]

The World Resources Institute (1989) reported air quality in most large cities of developing countries to be far below that of the cities of Western Europe and North America, and well below internationally accepted standards for good health. The report noted particularly poor air quality in cities of India that are industrializing and depend upon coal and wood for fuel. High carbon monoxide and sulphur dioxide

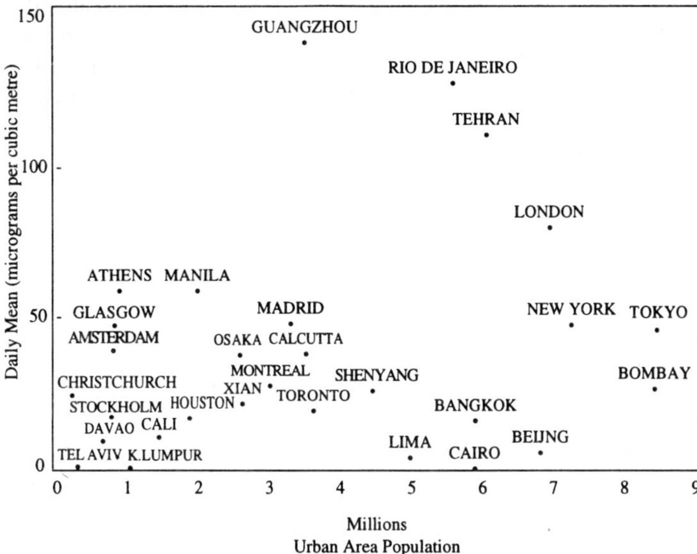

Figure 3: SO_2 Concentrations and City size — Residential Zones, 1979–81

levels from automobile exhaust are widely prevalent; Mexico City, because of the concentration of industries (foundries, metal processing, paint manufacturing, cement production, and smelting operations) and its peculiar topography, is reported to have one of the highest levels of suspended particulates of any Latin American city. Vehicle emissions and stationary fuel combustion, in addition to industrial processes, are the primary sources of air pollution in Latin American cities, such as Sao Paulo.

While the data appear to corroborate the popular perception of relatively highly polluted developing and former Eastern-Bloc country cities, preliminary impressions of the relationship between ambient air quality and city size reveal no readily discernible pattern.[13] Figure 3, which plots mean residential sulphur dioxide levels against city size, suggests that residential areas in the cities of developing countries are subject to greater pollutant concentrations than in their developed counterparts. But notably, polluted small cities as well as relatively clean large ones are in evidence, and it is interesting to ask why this might be the case. Accordingly, we proceed to a more systematic analysis of our data.

The first six rows of Table 1 present average pollution levels by location and zone type, when the sample of cities is segmented into urban areas in LDCs and those in DCs. Particulate levels for a representative LDC city are many times higher than for a typical DC city in the sample, across both central city and suburban locations. Sulphur dioxide levels in commercial and suburban residential zones are also higher in LDC urban areas. Comparisons of pollution levels across monitoring zones

Table 1: Average Pollution Levels[a] by Zone Type in DC and LDC Cities

Levels	*Sulphur dioxide*			*Particulates*		
	DC	LDC		DC	LDC	
CCC	46.20	60.00		75.10	187.80	
CCI	51.00	44.20		80.00	184.70	
CCR	63.10	55.10		58.80	247.50	
SC	24.00	36.00		28.50	245.00	
SI	42.80	37.10		65.50	282.10	
SR	34.40	37.70		67.10	183.50	
Ratios	DC	LDC	Differential means test *t*	DC	LDC	Differential means test *t*
CCC/CCI	N=5	N=9		N=5	N=4	
	1.3856	2.3719	–0.9627	0.9636	1.1351	–1.3497‡
	(0.72)	(2.71)		(0.14)	(0.18)	
CCI/CCR	N=3	N=6		N=3	N=7	
	0.8787	1.6860	–1.1397	0.9756	1.0732	–0.2991
	(0.18)	(1.56)		(0.40)	(0.40)	
CCC/CCR	N=4	N=13		N=2	N=6	
	0.7931	1.8303	–2.6168†	1.1695	1.4955	0.2576
	(0.27)	(1.27)		(0.17)	(1.69)	
SI/SR	N=8	N=10		N=6	N=10	
	1.3042	3.9281	–1.5498#	1.0814	1.4652	–1.5501‡
	(0.70)	(3.74)		(0.41)	(0.50)	
CCR/SR	N=2	N=6		N=2	N=3	
	1.7900	4.4313	–1.0662	1.5650	1.7803	–0.2519
	(0.03)	(5.54)		(0.31)	(1.13)	

[a] Pollution levels are measured in micrograms per cubic metre.
Monitoring Zones:
CCC = Central City Commercial SC = Suburban Commercial
CCI = Central City Industrial SI = Suburban Industry
CCR = Central City Residential SR = Suburban Residential
* = 1%; † = 5%; ‡ = 10%; # = 20% levels of significance in two-tailed tests.
Figures in parentheses are standard errors.
Source: *World Resources, 1990*, World Resources Institute.

are not entirely valid, since readings in each category are not reported for every city, but generally lower average values are recorded (with a few exceptions for particulates) in suburban than in central zones for both developed and developing country cities.

The second part of Table 1 compares the average ratios of zone-specific pollution for cities when the sample has been held constant in each case. Pollution in central city commercial zones exceeds that in central industrial and residential zones for both sulphur dioxide and particulates in developing country urban areas. Pollution in central city industrial zones exceeds that in central residential zones. Surprisingly, central city residential zones seem to fare worse than central industrial zones in cities of developed countries, but this may be a quirk of the small samples in each case. Suburban industrial and central city residential pollution problems are worse than those in suburban residential zones for cities in both contexts.

More rigorous comparisons of the ratios between developed and developing city readings are performed through difference of means tests.[14] Relative to residential pollution, commercial pollution is significantly worse in the central cities of developing country urban areas for sulphur dioxide, as is commercial pollution relative to industrial pollution for particulates. Similarly, suburban industrial pollution relative to residential pollution is significantly higher in LDC than in DC urban areas for both types of pollutant. Central residential areas feature worse air quality relative to suburban areas in LDCs.

In general, the results accord with expectations. Higher overall LDC urban densities are associated in most cases with lower ambient air quality measured over cities. Densities decline with distance from the centre, and so should measured pollution levels. Assuming the spatial layout of activities approximately follows patterns of land allocation implied by the monocentric model — commercial, then industrial, then residential — such an attenuation may be inferred from comparisons of readings across the various zonal types. Moreover, interzonal variation within both central city and suburban areas is sharper in LDC than in DC urban areas, and so also is the central city–suburban residential differential. Given that a much greater proportion of urban area residents is to be found in central cities in developing countries compared to developed countries, this last result means that larger numbers of residents are nevertheless at higher risk.

Turning to the relationship between air quality and city size, Table 2 reports the results of regressions of measured concentrations of sulphur

Table 2: Pollution and City Size by Monitoring Zones

ALL COUNTRIES	CCC	CCI	CCR	SR	SI	CCC	CCI	CCR	SR	SI
	Sulphur dioxide					Particulates				
N	46	17	23	36	26	23	12	15	25	21
Constant	40.1488	23.7978	58.5985	19.3698	26.7206	28.9589	−22.2120	−65.1540	58.9432	22.1996
CSIZE	8.43E-06	1.67E-05	−9.09E-06	1.03E-05‡	9.48E-06	5.32E-05#	9.31E-05#	1.80E-04*	3.39E-05	1.05E-04‡
	(0.88)	(1.31)	(−0.60)	(1.19)	(1.03)	(137)	(1.79)	(3.61)	(1.10)	(1.75)
CSIZESQ	−9.08E-13	−1.71E-12	1.41E-12	−9.86E-13	−1.15E-12	−4.24E-12	−8.17E-12	−1.98E-11*	−3.00E-12	−1.12E-11#
	(−0.75)	(−1.17)	(0.92)	(−0.92)	(−0.92)	(-0.87)	(−1.23)	(−3.19)	(−0.79)	(−1.40)
R^2	0.0203	0.1212	0.0865	0.06282	0.0490	0.2122	0.4440	0.5618	1.1045	0.2304
DEVELOPED COUNTRIES										
N	23	8	8	18	14	14	6	7	14	10
Constant	45.9474	19.4191	−70.3895	36.6813	36.8603	43.4802	−24.4406	72.3427	69.2326	41.7730
CSIZE	9.06E-07	2.86E-05#	1.78E-04#	−3.22E-06	−1.59E-06	3.49E-05	8.66E-05*	−1.68E-05	4.61E-06	2.87E-05
	(0.06)	(1.57)	(1.68)	(−0.51)	(−0.17)	(1.06)	(5.80)	(−0.19)	(0.17)	(0.70)
CSIZESQ	1.38E-14	−3.10E-12#	−2.15E-11#	6.60E-13	8.25E-13	−5.68E-12	−1.01E-11*	2.13E-12	−1.26E-12	−4.20E-12
	(0.01)	(−1.47)	(−1.65)	(0.87)	(0.57)	(−1.17)	(−5.38)	(0.20)	(−0.36)	(−0.72)
R^2	0.0029	0.3416	0.3622	0.1329	0.1620	0.1139	0.9196	0.0100	0.0462	0.0689

DEVELOPING COUNTRIES										
N	23	9	15	18	12	9	6	8	11	11
Constant	37.9209	19.3588	43.7497	−3.0916	7.1977	−10.7952	12.1008	−96.3032	56.9488	52.4562
CSIZE	1.24E-05	1.44E-05	−8.68E-06	2.63E-05#	2.21E-05	1.17E-04#	6.77E-05	1.95E-04‡	7.63E-05#	1.54E-04#
	(0.81)	(0.67)	(−0.75)	(1.58)	(1.16)	(1.53)	(0.72)	(2.14)	(1.78)	(1.82)
CSIZESQ	−147E-12	−1.39E-12	1.57E-12#	−2.98E-12	−2.76E-12	−1.13E-11	−2.44E-12	−2.03E-11‡	−7.80E-12#	−1.84E-11#
	(−0.79)	(−0.57)	(1.47)	(−1.42)	(−1.16)	(−1.27)	(−0.20)	(−1.95)	(−1.53)	(−1.68)
R^2	0.0316	0.0826	0.3945	0.1506	0.1319	0.3636	0.6158	0.4965	0.3336	0.3082

Explanatory Variables:
CSIZE = City Population.
CSIZESQ = City Population Squared, circa 1985.
* = 1%; † = 5%; ‡ = 10%; # = 20% levels of significance in two-tailed tests.
Figures in parentheses are *t*-statistics.
Source: *World Resources*, 1990, World Resources Institute.

dioxide and particulates by monitoring zone on urban population and population squared. Regressions were run for cities in developed and developing countries separately, as well as for the combined sample. The quadratic specification was chosen to permit a downturn in pollution levels as city size grew large (as the scatter of data points suggested) and proved to perform better than alternatives such as the double-logarithmic form.

Most signs on the coefficients of the city size term are positive, whereas most on the coefficients of the squared term are negative, confirming that the hypothesized downturn does occur. Due (though only in part) to the small number of observations in each category, many of them are not significant. Figure 4 plots actual values in juxtaposition with predicted values based on the estimated relationship for particulates in central city residential zones, one of which performs relatively well with respect to significance for the combined sample. The smooth line in the graph is derived using the estimated coefficients (and constant) in conjunction with hypothetical values of city population within a range analogous to that of actual observations in the sample. Such a graph helps identify outliers, i.e., cases where actuals depart drastically from

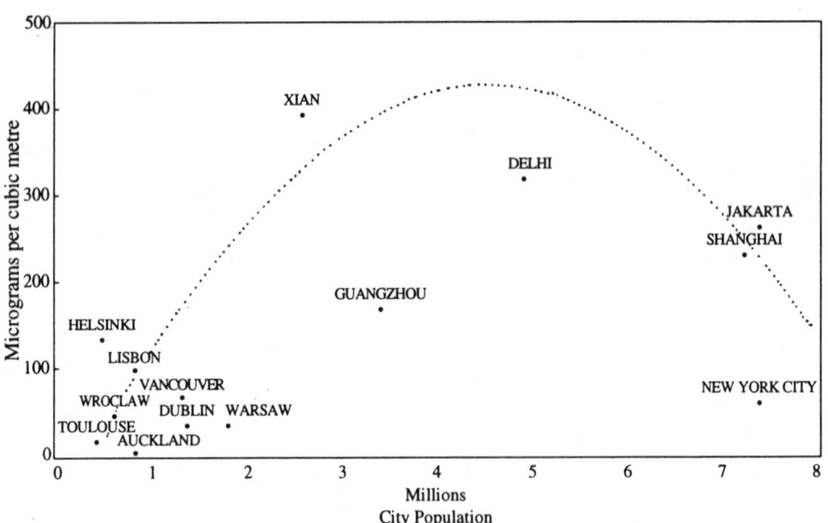

Figure 4: Actual vs. Predicted Pollution Levels, Particulates – Central City Residential Zone

estimates, but also points to possibly distinct developed vs. developing country relationships.

Examining the results from the separate regressions, we note that segmentation of the sample into LDC and DC cities appears to have been justified — both significance and explanatory power for the separate sets are generally higher than for the combined dataset. To illustrate the differences between the two samples, Figures 5 and 6 graph the relationship between pollution and city size for those cases where reasonable significance levels are observed with the separate samples. In these figures, predicted pollution levels are calculated at actual data points for urban population, using the relevant parameter estimates, to provide an idea of the city size ranges involved. In all cases, the relationship exhibits a non-monotonic, inverted-U shape, somewhat better articulated for developing countries than developed.

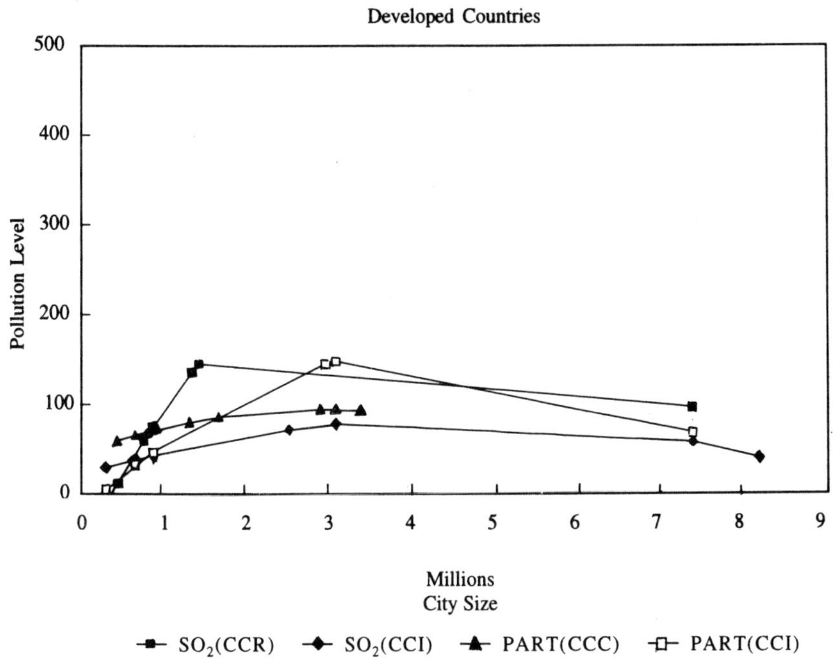

Figure 5: Ambient Air Quality and City Size

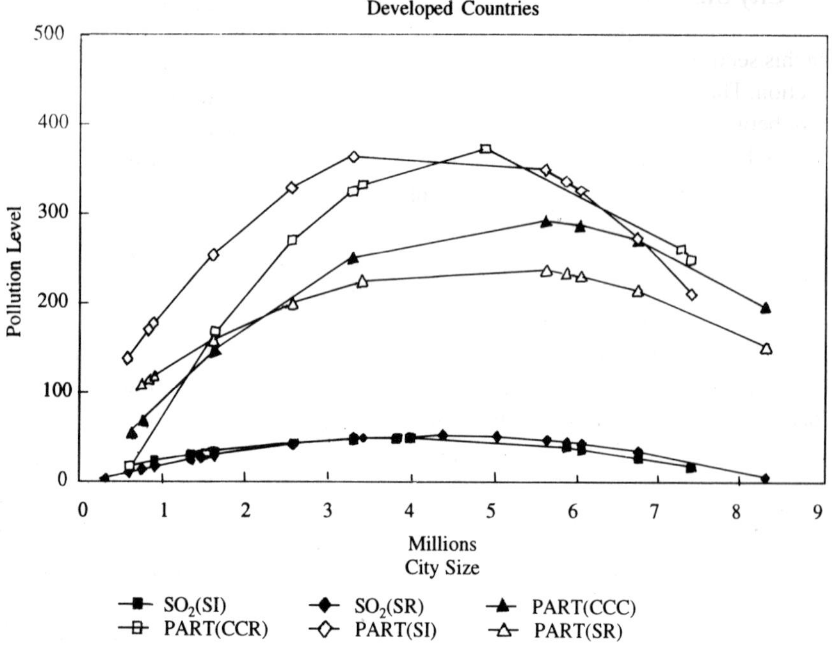

Figure 6: Ambient Air Quality and City Size

Comparing the two sets of curves, the higher levels of particulate pollution in almost all zones of LDC cities are apparent, but it is also observed that the 'downturn' tends to take place earlier (in the 1–3 million range) for the cities of developed countries than for those of developing (in the 4–6 million range). For example, particulate levels over central city commercial zones 'fall' at a city size of 6 million in developing countries, compared with about 3 million in developed countries.[15] Although the results are stronger for particulates than for sulphur dioxide, SO_2 levels appear to peak at similar population levels in each context. For developing country cities, central city residential particulate pollution starts declining at lower city sizes than in central commercial zones. Also, suburban particulate pollution in industrial zones rises faster and declines earlier than for residential zones. Below, we hypothesize that the relative affluence of the developed countries prompts early awareness of pollution and timely abatement interventions as urban growth proceeds.

City Size and Ambient Air Quality in Economic Context

In this section, we try to extend the investigation initiated in the previous section. The cross-national empirical evidence showed us that the association between pollution and urban growth is not typically monotonic in city size. What interpretation, then, may be attached to the observed slowdown and decline in pollution concentration at very large city sizes?

Before we attempt to deal with this question, it should be noted that cities of a given population size vary in amount of pollution for a number of reasons, including kinds of industry, types of fuel used, degree of reliance on automobile transportation, and weather differences. 'These reasons for variation in amount of pollution other than city population complicate the task of interpreting empirical evidence on pollution and city size ... ' (Tolley 1979).[16] We now examine the empirical relationship between measured ambient air quality levels and city size in the presence of other relevant contextual variables.

We regress measures of the incidence of poor air quality, indexed by the average and maximum number of days on which measured levels of sulphur dioxide, particulate and smoke emissions exceeded specified thresholds over a given monitoring period, for some 45 urban areas internationally.[17] The regressions are performed on contextual control variables such as a country's GNP per capita and its square. The inclusion of this index of development level enables a test of the hypothesis that the declines in pollution levels at smaller city sizes in developed countries come about as a consequence of higher average incomes. The absolute size of population (and its square) are, as before, specific to the urban area. The square term is used to capture any acceleration/deceleration/downturn that may occur in ambient air quality with increasing city size. In the hypothesized specification, we accord separate recognition to the roles of absolute size and urban density. We experimented with two measures of urban density, one a city-specific measure, persons per room, and the other a country-wide measure of total population density, with the presumption that high overall national densities make for higher densities in individual urban areas, diminishing the potential for diffusion or dilution of large concentrations of gases emitted into the air.

The results are presented in Table 3. There is a monotonically declining relationship with GNP per capita for all three types of pollutants, indicating that, for the countries in the sample at least, higher

Table 3: Sulphur Dioxide, Particulates, Smoke Emissions and City Size

	Sulphur dioxide				Particulates				Smoke			
N	48	48	48	48	30	30	30	17	13	13	13	13
Dependent Variable Mean	15.20	15.20	36.50	36.50	70.30	70.30	115.90	47.88	20.20	20.20	49.90	49.90
Dependent Variable	SO_2 AVG (1)	SO_2 AVG (2)	SO_2 MAX (3)	SO_2 MAX (4)	PART AVG (1)	PART AVG (2)	PART MAX (3)	PART MAX (4)	SMOK AVG (1)	SMOK AVG (2)	SMOK MAX (3)	SMOK MAX (4)
GNPCAP	–0.0041	–0.0051	–0.0066	–0.0073	–0.0278*	–0.0258†	–0.0423*	–0.0317†	0.0149	–0.0191‡	–0.0436	–0.0518‡
	(–1.49)	(–1.63)	(–1.32)	(–1.26)	(–2.65)	(–2.18)	(–3.65)	(–2.47)	(–1.40)	(–2.17)	(–1.46)	(–1.96)
GNPCAPSQ	1.47E–07	1.85E–07	1.87E–07	1.86E–07	1.27E–06‡	1.04E–06	1.87E–06†	1.30E–06‡	7.35E–07	8.66E–07	2.28E–06	0.0000025
	(0.87)	(1.06)	(0.60)	(0.57)	(1.87)	(1.48)	(2.50)	(1.70)	(0.91)	(1.31)	(1.00)	(1.27)
CITPOP	3.21E–06	4.05E–06	1.06E–05	1.34E–05	4.57E–05†	4.38E–05‡	4.92E–05‡	4.64E–05‡	1.24E–05	1.78E–05	3.87E–05	4.93E–05
	(0.60)	(0.77)	(1.07)	(1.36)	(2.06)	(1.89)	(2.00)	(1.85)	(1.27)	(1.90)	(1.41)	(1.75)
CITPOPSQ	–1.93E–13	–2.78E–13	–9.32E–13	–1.20E–12	–4.95E–12‡	4.42E–12‡	–5.18E–12‡	4.59E–12	–1.26E–12	–1.9E–12‡	–4.1E–12	–5.3E–12‡
	(–0.35)	(–0.51)	(–0.91)	(–1.18)	(–1.96)	(–1.70)	(–1.85)	(–1.63)	(–1.32)	(–1.98)	(–1.54)	(–1.87)
POPDENS	0.0009		0.0078		0.2158		0.2554		–0.0034		–0.0064	
	(0.18)		(0.82)		(1.46)		(1.56)		(–0.56)		(–0.38)	
PERSROOM		–3.5633		–5.3190		–4.3333		19.5236		–37.8705		–74.0500
		(–0.69)		(–0.55)		(–0.28)		(1.17)		(–1.56)		(–1.02)
Constant	24.8485‡	32.7698‡	48.6767†	57.9415‡	55.6803	87.7742	134.3362‡	106.3231	56.0517	98.2578	147.6042	229.8489
R^2	0.2245	0.2325	0.2640	0.2577	0.6291	0.5975	0.7529	0.7426	0.5571	0.6562	0.5416	0.5920
Adjusted R^2	0.1321	0.1412	0.1763	0.1693	0.5518	0.5136	0.7014	0.6890	0.2408	0.4107	0.2142	0.3007

Explanatory Variables:

CITPOP=Population of urban area circa 1985.

PERSROOM = Living space (person per room).

Dependent Variables:

SO_2AVG=Average no. of days per year SO_2 conc. exceeds 150 micrograms/cu.mt.

PARTAVG=Average no. of days per year SPM conc. exceeds 230 micrograms/cu.mt

SMOKAVG=Average no. of days per year smoke conc. exceeds 150 micrograms/cu.mt.

SO_2MAX=Maximum no. of days per year SO_2 conc. exceeds 230 micrograms/cu.mt.

PARTMAX=Maximum no. of days per year SPM conc. exceeds 230 micrograms/cu.mt.

SMOKMAX=Maximum no. of days per year smoke conc. exceeds 150 micrograms/cu.mt.

* =1%; † =5%; ‡ =10% levels of significance in two–tailed tests. Figures in parentheses are t-statistics.

Sources: *World Resources* 1990–91, World Resources Institute; LIFE: THE WORLD'S 100 LARGEST CITIES, Population Crisis Council.

income levels are associated with lower measured incidence of poor air quality. The decline occurs at a decreasing rate, however, suggesting both the increased difficulty and lower urgency of securing successive reductions in pollution levels. The signs on city size and city size squared are, by and large, as hypothesized, revealing an inverted U-shaped relationship as pollution incidence first rises and then falls with increasing city size. However, except for particulates, these variables all but lose significance after the development variables are controlled for. Population density is found to be almost uniformly positive but insignificant in increasing the incidence of poor urban air quality (recall, the variable comprises overall country-wide densities, and is only an imperfect gauge of actual urban densities). The persons-per-room variable (which is urban-area specific and, therefore, a conceptually purer potential proxy for the influence of residential density) is also generally not significant, its unexpected negative sign possibly owing to its correlation with GNP per capita, a strong determinant of housing consumption, and thus, of living space per household.

To summarize, the results confirm, by and large, a positive impact of city size upon urban pollutant concentrations, but this association becomes considerably less significant once other variables are controlled for. The empirical associations remain reasonably strong in respect of particulate pollution, and somewhat so in the case of smoke. By contrast, sulphur dioxide concentrations have fewer consistent associations with city size. The positive coefficients on particulates and smoke are consistent with the hypothesized consequences of heightened transportation and construction activity in large urban areas. Higher R^2 figures point to a superior explanatory power for the extended model relative to the earlier one, although the two are not strictly comparable.

On the basis of estimated coefficients of the various regression specifications, it was once again possible to compute a 'turnaround' city size, up to which pollution levels rise and beyond which they are observed to decline. Figure 7 depicts the new implied relationships.[18] It is interesting to note that for particulates, the turnaround in pollution incidence takes place in the 4–6 million city size range, a result consistent with the developing country case noted earlier. The fact that a pattern similar to the developing country case is recovered from the combined sample where the effects of any pollution control intervention have been controlled for suggests that this range may represent a 'natural' turning point in the pollution–city-size relationship.

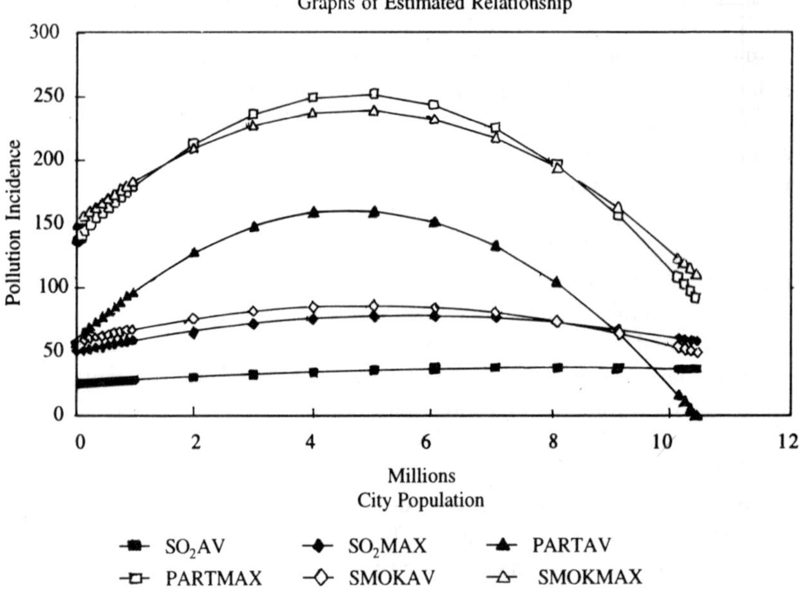

Figure 7: Air Pollution and City Size

It is fair to speculate whether this decline reflects compositional changes accompanying city growth, or because large concentrations generated by urban growth might prompt pollution control and abatement measures beyond a sufficiently high urban size threshold, regardless of a country's development level. Several perspectives on how the industrial mix of cities should vary with their size exist, such as the market-area driven association of large cities with a variety of higher-order functions derived from central place theory, or the supply-side agglomeration externality-driven technological association between urban/industrial specialization and city size. If, for any reason, industries entering a large urban area are either of a non-polluting character, or can employ less polluting technologies, the results we observe may be explained. Given our limited data, we can only infer the influence of urban industry-mix on pollution from the 'behaviour' of its residual relationship with city size. We cannot test for it. The next section, however, attempts to discover insights for policy from the GNP–pollution relationship evidenced by our findings.

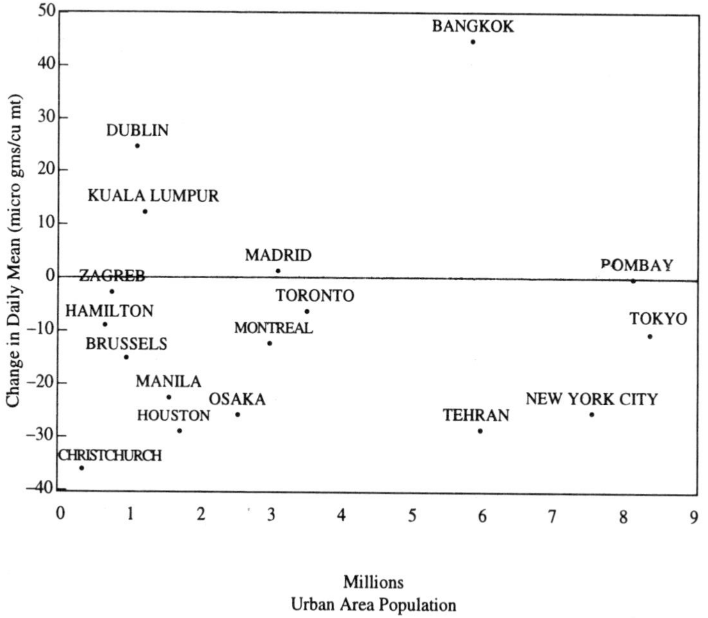

Figure 8: Change in SPM Concentrations and City Size—Residential Zones, 1976–85

IV. Pollution Trends and Policy Implications

While the present analysis is somewhat limited by less-than-optimal data availability and restricted samples, the qualitative thrust of the results seems clear. Even as a crude empirical summary of international experience, we must conclude that there is no strict inevitability about large city sizes and higher pollution concentrations. The GNP–pollution relationship suggests that significant pollution reductions possibly come about as a result of intensive and effective abatement efforts in cities of affluent countries. One implication is that restricting urban growth or curbing city size is by no means the only, or even the best, instrument to secure a better urban environment.

To offer an intuitive feel for where the most sizeable reductions in urban pollution have occurred, Figure 8 plots changes in particulate concentrations in the residential areas of various cities over the 1976–85 period. Several of the larger cities appear to have experienced declines in pollution levels, while some of the smaller urban areas featured

Table 4: Changes in Pollution Levels of Cities, 1976–85

Zone	Trend	Sulphur dioxide All	DC	LDC	Particulates All	DC	LDC
		(Average percentage shares)					
		N=12	*N*=2	*N*=10	*N*=11	*N*=6	*N*=5
CCC	Rise	75.50	15.00	87.60	24.20	21.40	27.50
		N=19	*N*=15	*N*=4	*N*=15	*N*=10	*N*=5
	Fall	–91.30	–39.00	–27.30	–24.40	–29.20	–14.80
		N=4	*N*=1	*N*=3	*N*=3	*N*=1	*N*=2
CCI	Rise	16.90	4.60	20.90	10.20	10.00	10.30
		N=6	*N*=5	*N*=1	*N*=7	*N*=5	*N*=2
	Fall	–51.6	–45.00	–84.60	–27.20	–33.70	–10.80
		N=4	*N*=0	*N*=4	*N*=7	*N*=3	*N*=4
CCR	Rise	123.10	0.00	123.10	23.80	23.70	23.90
		N=7	*N*=6	*N*=1	*N*=5	*N*=2	*N*=3
	Fall	–26.90	–25.70	–33.90	–15.80	–20.70	–12.50
		N=5	*N*=2	*N*=3	*N*=5	*N*=3	*N*=2
SI	Rise	52.90	39.40	72.40	24.10	34.30	8.70
		N=12	*N*=9	*N*=3	*N*=12	*N*=7	*N*=5
	Fall	–39.00	–35.70	–49.00	–31.20	–27.30	–36.50
		N=9	*N*=3	*N*=6	*N*=5	*N*=2	*N*=3
SR	Rise	23.50	9.90	30.20	16.50	13.00	18.90
		N=13	*N*=9	*N*=4	*N*=13	*N*=9	*N*=4
	Fall	–38.70	–42.80	–29.50	–22.50	–20.00	–28.20

	Correlation Coefficients: For city size SO_2av	Part.av	For density SO_2av	Part.av
	N=31	*N*=26	*N*=31	*N*=26
CCC	0.0532	0.0953	0.2570#	0.1762
	(0.78)	(0.64)	(0.16)	(0.39)
	N=10	*N*=10	*N*=10	*N*=10
CCI	–0.1973	0.0002	0.2075	0.5020#
	(0.59)	(1.00)	(0.57)	(0.14)
	N=11	*N*=12	*N*=11	*N*=12
CCR	0.1430	–0.2777	0.9497*	0.0645
	(0.67)	(0.38)	(0.00)	(0.84)
	N=17	*N*=17	*N*=17	*N*=17
SI	0.0951	–0.5949*	0.0851	-0.1950
	(0.72)	(0.01)	(0.75)	(0.45)
	N=22	*N*=18	*N*=22	*N*=18
SR	–0.0941	0.0647	0.3919‡	0.3678#
	(0.68)	(0.80)	(0.07)	(0.13)

Monitoring Zones:

CCC = Central City Commercial SC = Suburban Commercial
CCI = Central City Industrial SI = Suburban Industrial
CCR = Central City Residential SR = Suburban Residential

* = 1%; † = 5%; ‡ = 10%; # = 20% levels of significance in two-tailed tests
Figures in parentheses are Prob>/*R*/ under H_0: Rho = 0.
Source: *World Resources,* 1990, World Resources Institute.

deteriorating air quality over the same period. In large cities such as New York and Tokyo, part of the reason for air quality improvement no doubt lay in the implementation of pollution control and abatement measures, and part of it in the decentralization of manufacturing and structural change in favour of non-polluting services. These pollution changes may be examined more systematically.

Table 4 reports movements in pollution concentrations of sulphur dioxide and particulates over 1976–85 in various monitoring zones of urban areas of developed and developing countries, averaged separately over those cities recording rising and falling or unchanged pollution levels in each category. More LDC cities registered rising than falling pollution levels over this period, while, in almost all cases, the majority of DC cities had decreasing pollution. With few exceptions, rises were higher in developing countries than in developed; decreases, where they occurred, were generally smaller. Particularly noteworthy are the large percentage increases of sulphur dioxide concentrations in most zones of LDC cities, compared with particulates. Overall, declines dominate rises.

The bottom part of Table 4 presents correlations between city size and density (as approximated by persons per room) and algebraic values of the changes in pollutant concentrations. A positive sign would connote the exacerbation of environmental degradation with increasing size or concentration: the greater an urban area's population (or density), the greater the increase or lower the fall in its pollution levels over the 1976–85 period. In no case is a statistically significant positive association with city size apparent. In fact, suburban industrial air quality for particulates seems to have improved in the larger cities. High densities, on the other hand, have a much more discernible impact on the deterioration of air quality over time. Partly, this reflects their inverse correlation with development levels.

Is there, then, a compelling argument for pollution control through city size restriction in developing countries? Our characterization of the international development experience, which indicates that pollution has fallen without regard to city size, but rather in conjunction with high incomes, suggests not. This is not to minimize the gravity of the pollution problem facing cities of developing countries, but to question the sagacity of policies that would seek to 'solve' it without appreciation of the large implicit costs involved in this particular choice of instrument. For, as we have seen, curbing urban growth is fraught with productivity losses, which are higher both in magnitude and relative importance in the

LDCs. On the other hand, facilitating higher urban incomes is likely to result in spontaneous dispersal, a stronger public 'demand' for abatement and greater societal wherewithal to undertake it as a matter of policy.

Nor is it necessarily true that restricting city size would, by itself, guarantee lower pollution levels. Where it does not take place spontaneously, as Mills and Graves (1986) state,

> the disadvantages of dispersal of manufacturing activities away from urban areas may be great. They often require a large labour force which may be loath to relocate or commute to rural or small-town workplaces. Likewise, manufacturing plants are dependent upon urban suppliers of inputs and buyers of outputs. Large-scale dispersal of manufacturing from urban areas would be costly, both in production and relocation costs. In addition, dispersal would increase the total transportation of people and goods that would be necessary. Thus, to some extent, dispersal of discharges would result in increases in total discharges because of increased transportation.

This is not to deny that the results achieved in the affluent countries have entailed considerable costs. Pollution abatement draws upon valuable social resources. But the costs of rational abatement measures are likely to be lower and produce far less distortion than a policy of outright restrictions on city growth or the ad hoc mandating of manufacturing location away from major metropolitan areas. The air quality improvements that have taken place in the urban areas of developed countries largely came about (apart from spontaneous industrial dispersion) through technology and market incentives for abatement, focused directly upon the pollution-generating activities rather than their employment by-product. Economic theory holds that externalities are best addressed within the market where they arise; compensating for them elsewhere is always an inefficient second-best. There are, for example, cost-effective innovative technological solutions to environmental problems such as requiring emitters to pollute only at certain times of the day, locating them downwind from residential areas within a metropolitan region, or even diverting particularly large polluters (e. g., power plants) to other locations where they are clearly not at a productivity disadvantage. We only caution against the advisability of blanket policies to influence industrial location and urban development on environmental grounds alone.

As Mills and Hamilton (1984) expressed it, 'external diseconomies are by no means technologically linked to urban population [and] ... urban size distortions are no more than symptoms of resource misallocation....[If] an activity distorts urban sizes, the activity should be controlled directly. Population redistribution is about as costly a pollution control program as could be imagined.'[19] This investigation does not purport to be conclusive on whether Third World cities are 'too large' or, indeed, 'too small'. To deny that there is a compelling environmental argument for restricting city size is scarcely tantamount to ruling on other allegations of urban distortions in less developed countries. Many, for example, feel that developing country cities are too large as a result of policy-induced distortions resulting from 'excessive' government infrastructural investments. Similarly, others cite labour market distortions that create an 'excessive' migrant influx to the unregulated urban informal sector. Such arguments must be evaluated on their own merits in enabling judgment on the optimality of city size in developing countries.[20]

V. Conclusions

In the light of past development patterns (and given current technology), urbanization is an inevitable concomitant of industrialization and economic growth. While aggregate emission increases result from these activities, localized effects attributable to discharges into the air over specific urban areas are of greater concern. High urban densities do result in considerably higher concentrations of ambient air pollution in the cities of developing than developed countries, putting large numbers of residents at risk of health damage. However, the positive association between poor air quality and city size is not inevitable, as several cities, large and small, have achieved significant pollution abatement, the capacity for which seems to increase with economic affluence.

Given overall developmental goals and the necessary role of industrialization in securing and sustaining higher incomes and consumption levels, policies to curb urban growth in less developed countries may not be the best or even necessarily effective strategies to reduce the effects of environmental pollution. Such reduction is best undertaken with a variety of economic instruments designed to deal with specific polluting sources in a technologically appropriate and economically non-distorting manner. Within urban areas, judicious land-use zoning can be brought to bear on facilitating spatial structures that avoid excessive exposure to industrial pollution for urban residents. Higher incomes and better knowledge of environmental management promise that there will be less additional pollution with future city growth than historically, enabling larger (and more productive) cities to be sustained at much lower cost than in the past.

Appendix A: Estimated Annual Pollutant Emissions at the National Level[a]

	Nitrogen oxide emissions			Sulphur dioxide emissions			Particulate emissions			Carbon monoxide emissions		
N	16	16	16	16	16	16	11	11	11	10	10	10
Dependent Variable Mean	3.71	3.71	3.71	4.48	4.48	4.48	0.88	0.88	0.88	13.84	13.84	13.84
	(1)	(2)	(3)	(1)	(2)	(3)	(1)	(2)	(3)	(1)	(2)	(3)
GNPCAP	0.0002	0.0002	0.0002	–0.0009†	–0.0008‡	–0.0008‡	–0.00007	–0.00003	0.00002	0.0001	0.0001	0.0006‡
	(0.63)	(0.66)	(0.63)	(–2.26)	(–1.81)	(–1.92)	(–0.78)	(–0.24)	(0.18)	(0.29)	(0.38)	(2.17)
MFGGDP	0.0430	0.0463	0.0423	0.2246	0.2298	0.2237	0.0656	0.0637	0.0682†	0.6706*	0.7236*	0.6549*
	(0.38)	(0.39)	(0.36)	(1.47)	(1.43)	(1.40)	(1.79)	(1.64)	(2.10)	(4.52)	(6.12)	(8.15)
POPDENS	0.0262*	0.0266*	0.0266*	0.0085	0.0092	0.0090	0.0018	0.0021	0.0042	0.0657*	0.0643*	0.0775*
	(4.09)	(3.88)	(3.78)	(0.98)	(0.99)	(0.95)	(0.79)	(0.86)	(1.68)	(7.19)	(8.99)	(13.09)
URBAN	0.0225	0.0273	0.0200	0.2333*	0.2411†	0.2301†	0.0127	0.0196	0.0037	0.0360	–0.0151	–0.0115
	(0.38)	(0.43)	(0.31)	(2.90)	(2.76)	(2.67)	(0.67)	(0.85)	(0.21)	(0.37)	(–0.19)	(–0.21)
PRIMECITY		0.0182			0.0293			0.0169			–0.1638	
		(0.28)			(0.33)			(0.61)			(–2.06)	
URBCON			0.0079			0.0100			0.0250			0.1201†
			(0.20)			(0.18)			(1.62)			(3.62)
Constant	–3.8882	–5.2427	–4.3468	–9.7701	–11.9477	–10.3476	–1.2555	–2.5744	–3.1175	–16.9033	–10.8232	–24.9249
R^2	0.7847	0.7864	0.7855	0.6950	0.6982	0.6960	0.5521	0.5833	0.7062	0.9674	0.9842	0.9924
Adjusted R^2	0.7064	0.6795	0.6783	0.5841	0.5473	0.5440	0.2535	0.1665	0.4123	0.9414	0.9645	0.9829

[a]Thousands of tons per km^2.

Explanatory Variables:

GNPCAP = Gross National Product per capita (US$)
URBAN= Urban Population as per cent of total population (%)
MFGDP= Share of manufacturing in gross domestic product (%)
PRIMECITY = Per cent of urban population in largest city (%)
POPDENS = Total population density (persons per sq km)
URBCON = Per cent of urban population in cities exceeding 500,000 (%)

* = 1%; † = 5%; ‡ = 10% levels of significance in two-tailed tests. Figures in parentheses are *t*-statistics.

Sources: *World Tables and Social Indicators of Development,* World Bank, 1985; *World Resources, 1990-91*, World Resources Institute.

Appendix B: Master List of Cities in the Sample

	City		City
North America		**Asia**	
Canada	Hamilton	Israel	Tel Aviv
	Montreal	Japan	Osaka
	Toronto		Tokyo
	Vancouver	Malaysia	Kuala Lumpur
United States	Birmingham	Philippines	Manila
	Chattanooga	Korea, Rep	Seoul
	Chicago	Thailand	Bangkok
	Fairfield	**Europe**	
	Houston	Belgium	Brussels
	New York	Denmark	Copenhagen
	St. Louis	Finland	Helsinki
South America		France	Gourdon
Brazil	Rio de Janeiro	German, Fed Rep	Frankfurt
	Sao Paulo		Munich
Chile	Santiago	Greece	Athens
Colombia	Cali	Ireland	Dublin
	Medellin	Italy	Milan
Venezuela	Caracas	Netherlands	Amsterdam
Asia		Poland	Warsaw
China	Beijing		Wroclaw
	Guangzhou	Portugal	Lisbon
	Shanghai	Spain	Madrid
	Shenyang	United Kingdom	Glasgow
	Xian		London
Hong Kong	Hong Kong	Yugoslavia	Zagreb
India	Bombay	**Oceania**	
	Calcutta	Australia	Melbourne
	Delhi		Sydney
Indonesia	Jakarta	New Zealand	Auckland
Iran	Tehran		Christchurch

Sources: Global Environment Monitoring System (GEMS), as reported in *World Resources, 1990-91*, World Resources Institute.

NOTES

1. Research for this paper was performed as part of a project culminating in a report to the United Nations Conference on Environment and Development, over February–May 1991, while Vibhooti Shukla was visiting the Indira Gandhi Institute of Development Research (IGIDR) in Bombay, India. The authors would like to thank Brian J.L. Berry and two anonymous referees for useful comments and suggestions on an earlier version of the draft. The authors are also grateful to Madhukar Nagare and Annabella Pronesti for research assistance and help with the preparation of the manuscript.

2. See Berry (1990); World Resources Institute (1989). For statements of productivity—and environmentally-oriented urban policy agendas for the cities of developing countries, see World Bank (1991) and United Nations (1991) respectively.
3. For an excellent survey of the developed and developing country estimates, and a discussion of the chief empirical issues involved, see Montgomery (1988). Kelley and Williamson (1984) provide by far the most comprehensive modelling framework for the causes of Third World city growth.
4. Other environmental problems cited in the context of urbanization in developing countries include water pollution and solid waste disposal. To a large extent, there are direct trade-offs between releasing pollutants to the environment in the form of gases, liquids and solids. For an investigation into the relationship between per capita waste generation and a country's level of urbanization, see Parikh et al. (1991). A companion paper to this one, Shukla and Parikh (1991), explores the connections between urbanization, energy use and global greenhouse effects. The latter is printed in this volume.
5. Engels' Law states that income elasticity of the demand for food being low, a falling proportion of consumer expenditures goes to food items as incomes rise. Economic base theories distinguish between export-oriented or 'basic' (typically manufacturing) and 'non-basic' (typically service) urban functions.
6. We examined cross-national variations in estimated discharges of sulphur dioxide (largely originating from the combustion of fossil fuels in electric power plants, factories and homes), carbon monoxide (from automobile exhaust), suspended particulate matter (from industrial processes), and nitrogen oxides (from combustion in vehicles and stationary combustion systems). Coefficients revealed that emissions per sq km were affected more by manufacturing's share in GDP than by income. The performance of a country's urban percentage — the urbanization proxy — was generally poor, except in the case of sulphur dioxide. Of the indexes of urban concentration (e.g., the importance of cities of over one million in a country's urban population), the only pollutant to be affected significantly was carbon monoxide, possibly due to the role of automobile use in highly urbanized contexts requiring extensive commuting.
7. See Mills and Hamilton (1984), p. 358.
8. Most of the estimates of the urban productivity advantage cited in note 2 use a production function approach, with city size or some measure of urban concentration specified as causing Hicks-neutral scale shifts representing agglomeration effects. The elasticity is then empirically recovered from their estimation using cross-section or time-series data on firms, industries, and cities. For a theoretical discussion of population relocation between cities of different size in response to positive agglomeration externalities, see Shukla and Stark (1986). For analogous discussion of reassignment in the presence of negative environmental externalities, see Mills and Hamilton (1984).

9. There is an alternative pollution abatement benefits measurement literature that relies upon rational equilibrating spatial adjustments by mobile residents to locational variations in environmental amenities. For long-distance (interurban) moves, their effects are assumed to be manifested in labour markets; shorter-distance (intra-urban) adjustments are assumed to be capitalized in the market for land. For example, Hoch and Drake (1974) estimate the disamenities of city size through compensatory wage premia associated with large cities. Polinsky and Rubinfeld (1977) study variations in property values within the St. Louis Standard Metropolitan Statistical Area (SMSA) to put the present value of a 50 per cent reduction in suspended particulates at about $900 per capita. Anderson and Crocker (1971) have estimated for Chicago that an additional microgram per cubic metre detracts about $48 from the sale price of a residential house and lot, working out to a yearly equivalent of $2.40 to $4.80 per property. While these techniques are valuable for providing alternatives to direct health-damage assessments, their reliance on perfect perception and response would limit their accuracy in developing country contexts.
10. Alonso (1964), Mills (1967), and Muth (1969) pioneered the early monocentric model of urban form. Its realism has been increasingly challenged by the emergence of a more complex network of urban 'polycentres' in the cities of developed countries through recent times. Its continued relevance in the developing country context, however, is likely. Mills and Tan (1980) survey both developed and developing country estimates of density gradients implied by the monocentric model. They find that urban areas in developed countries have flatter density functions than do those for developing countries. This is attributed by them to the higher incomes, larger urban areas, and better transportation systems in the developed economies.
11. The effect of urban scale on variations in pollution concentrations across US cities was estimated by Hoch (1972). Subsequently, Berry et al. (1974), in a comprehensive study of the effects of urban form on environmental quality, examined variations resulting from different patterns of land use across a sample of US cities. Comparable data on urban characteristics across an international cross-section of cities, are, however, difficult to compile, and for many developing country urban areas, non-existent — hence the rarity of analyses of this type.
12. Data on SO_2 and particulates measured by the World Health Organization and the United Nations Environment Programme over the 1976–85 period for various zones of a cross-section of developing and developed country cities are reported in World Resources Institute (1989). For the purposes of categorization, we have classified cities of Eastern Bloc countries and China with those of developing countries, to reflect certain structural and behavioural similarities in their economies. High levels of sulphur dioxide and suspended particulate matter (SPM) are reported to cause respiratory problems among adults and children, and may also result in illnesses of the lower respiratory tract. SPM concentrations measured by the high-volume gravimetric sampling method were used for the analysis.

13. In this and other representations and all statistical procedures throughout the paper, the sample of cities in the analysis is dictated strictly by data availability. Further, sample sizes and observations may differ between components of the analysis because of the differential availability of data on covariates. We recognize, of course, the possibility of non-randomness in the monitoring and reporting of ambient air quality, but have no reason to suspect any systematic biases that influence results in predictable directions. To the extent that air quality measurement takes place largely in cities with non-trivial discharges, the available sample may be taken as representative from the viewpoint of inferences about significant urban pollution problems. The Appendix to this paper provides a comprehensive list of cities included in the analyses, from which all sub-samples result. The city size data, it may be noted, span diverse years in the early 1980s, and rely upon self-reporting by countries, presumably on the basis of administrative boundaries. It would be interesting to verify the relationships characterized here using future pollution data analysed in conjunction with internationally standardized population figures for urban agglomerations, as these become available. To the extent that air quality monitoring stations are also within legal city limits, the potential distortion from reliance upon the latter for population totals may, in effect, be small.
14. In each case, the value of a *t*-statistic for the difference in mean ratios for the developed and developing countries is computed under the assumption that the two populations of cities have different standard deviations. See Blalock (1979) for details of the procedure.
15. Because of the use of actual city populations, the plotted relationship looks less 'smooth' than if hypothetical *x*-coordinate values with uniform increments were used to generate the graph. For this reason, depicted 'turnaround' points may be somewhat approximate. However, exact city sizes where pollution 'stops increasing and starts to fall' may be calculated by setting the first derivatives of the estimated regression equations to zero in order to satisfy the first-order (necessary) condition for the maximum.
16. See Tolley (1979), p. 66. Also, although we do not take account of temperature variations directly here, it may be mentioned that there have been some attempts at calculating the 'heat island' effect of city size. Berry et al. (1974) reports that in large cities of over 10 million, the mean annual minimum temperature may be as much as 4° Fahrenheit higher than that of the surrounding periphery. The urban heat island serves as a trap for atmospheric pollutants.
17. Air quality data used for this set of estimation are reported in World Resources Institute (1990), measured over a time period (circa 1985) comparable with the time period of supporting explanatory variables. Air quality in selected cities is given for the number of site years of observation for SO_2, SPM, and smoke. These data are presented for the minimum, average, and the maximum number of days that the pollutant exceeded WHO guidelines for all years of observation. The size of the available sample is somewhat larger here in the absence of a detailed breakdown by urban zone. Because both SO_2 and SPM levels can be affected by

seasonal patterns in emissions and meteorological conditions, the use of average as well as maximum readings over multiple monitoring periods are more reliable in providing a more comprehensive, seasonality-adjusted idea of exposures. See Appendix B for a master list of all cities in the sample.

18. The graph uses regression coefficients from specifications (1) and (3) for various pollutants in Table 4. The curves were generated for hypothetical values of city size and city size squared, holding values of other covariates at zero. Alternatively, the latter could be held at the values of sample means, or any other specified values. While y-values are sensitive to this choice (and should not be interpreted to reflect predicted incidence here), either procedure would leave the x-value 'turnaround' points unaffected.
19. For a comprehensive discussion of optimal policies to control environmental pollution, see Baumol and Oates (1975). Henderson (1987) models the problem of industrial air pollutant emissions that disperse into the residential sector of a city in an explicitly spatial manner in the context of an urban area of monocentric form. He shows that optimal environmental policy in a spatial setting will involve not just Pigouvian taxes on pollution, but also some form of land use regulation. Henderson also explores the implications of optimally taxing pollution for city sizes in a system of urban areas. He notes that such taxation will raise the cost of 'polluting' relative to 'non-polluting' goods, so while the size of any city producing a polluting good may actually increase because of the sizeable air quality improvements, the number of cities specialized in the manufacture of such goods may decline.
20. The counter-arguments in this debate are: (1) urban infrastructural investments are essential complements for sustaining the economic viability of existing industry and (2) the urban informal sector augments urban productivity by providing firms with flexibility in hiring, in addition to serving as a subsistence 'safety net' for unskilled labour. See Lipton (1976) for a seminal discussion of alleged 'urban bias' in the development process. Kannappan (1985) has an excellent survey of developing country urban labour markets, and the so-called 'informal sector'.

REFERENCES

Alonso, W. (1964), *Location and Land Use,* Harvard University Press, Cambridge, MA.

Anderson, R. and T. Crocker (1971), 'Air Pollution and Residential Property Values', *Urban Studies*, Vol. 7.

Baumol, W.J. and W.E. Oates (1975), *The Theory of Environmental Policy*, Prentice-Hall, Englewood Cliffs.

Berry, B.J.L. (1990), 'Urbanization', in B.L. Turner II et al., eds, *The Earth as Transformed by Human Action: Global and Regional Changes in the Biosphere over the Past 300 Years*, Cambridge University Press, New York.

Berry, B.J.L. et al. (1974), *Land Use, Urban Form and Environmental Quality* (A Report to the Office of Research and Development, Environmental

Protection Agency), Chicago, IL: The Department of Geography, University of Chicago.

Blalock, H.M. (1979), *Social Statistics*, revised second edition, McGraw-Hill Publishing Company, New York.

Chenery, H., S. Robinson and M. Syrquin (1986), *Industrialization and Growth — A Comparative Study*, Oxford University Press/The World Bank, Washington, D.C.

Henderson, V.J. (1987), *Economic Theory and the Cities*, second edition, Academic Press, New York.

Hoch, I.B. (1972), 'Urban Scale and Environmental Quality, *Population, Resources, and Environment*, Vol. III.

Hoch, I. and J. Drake (1974), 'Wages, Climate, and Quality of Life', *Journal of Environmental Economics and Management*, Vol. 1, pp. 268–95.

Kannappan, S. (1985), 'Urban Employment and the Labour Market in Developing Nations', *Economic Development and Cultural Change*, Vol. 33, pp. 669–730.

Kelley, A.C. and J.G. Williamson (1984), *What Drives Third World City Growth*? Princeton University Press, Princeton, NJ.

Lave, L. and E. Seskin (1977), *Air Pollution and Human Health*, Johns Hopkins Press, Baltimore, MD.

Lipton, M. (1976), *Why Poor People Stay Poor: Urban Bias in World Development*, Harvard University Press, Cambridge, MA.

Mills, E.S. (1967), 'An Aggregative Model of Resource Allocation in a Metropolitan Area', *American Economic Review*, Vol. 57, pp. 197–210.

Mills, E.S. and C. M. Becker (1986), *Studies in Indian Urban Development*, Oxford University Press, The World Bank, Washington, D.C.

Mills, E.S. and J.P. Tan (1980), 'A Comparison of Urban Population Density Functions in Developed and Developing Countries', *Urban Studies*, Vol. 17, pp. 303–21.

Mills, E.S. and B.W. Hamilton (1984), *Urban Economics*, Scott, Foresman and Company, Glenview, IL, pp. 371–3.

Mills, E.S. and P.E. Graves (1986), 'Resources, Production, Consumption, and Pollution', in *The Economics of Environmental Quality*, W.W. Norton & Company, New York.

Montgomery, M. (1988), 'How Large is too Large? Implications of the City Size Literature for Population Policy and Research', *Economic Development and Cultural Change*, Vol. 36, pp. 691–720.

Muth, R.F. (1969), *Cities and Housing*, University of Chicago Press, Chicago, IL.

Parikh, J., K.Parikh, S. Gokarn, J.P. Painuly, B. Saha and V. Shukla (1991), *Consumption Patterns: The Driving Force of Environmental Stress*. A Report prepared for the United Nations Conference on Environment and Economic Development, mimeo, Indira Gandhi Institute of Development Research, Bombay, India.

Polinsky, A.M. and D. Rubinfeld (1977), 'Property Values and the Benefits of Environmental Improvements: Theory and Measurement', in Lowdon Wingo and Alan Evans, eds, *Public Economics and the Quality of Life*, Johns Hopkins Press, Baltimore, MD.

Shukla, V. and J. Parikh (1991), 'Urbanization, Energy Use and Greenhouse Effects in Economic Development: Results from a Cross-national Study of Developing Countries' published in this volume; an abridged version accepted for publication in *Global Environmental Change*, Butterworth Publishers, UK.

Shukla, V. and O. Stark (1986), 'Urban External Economies and Optimal Migration', in *Research in Human Capital and Development*, Vol. 4. JAI Press Inc, Greenwich, CT.

Thomas, Vinod (1986), 'Evaluating Pollution Control: The Case of Sao Paulo', in George S. Tolley and Vinod Thomas, eds, *Economics of Urbanization and Urban Policies in Developing Countries*, The World Bank, Washington, D.C.

Tolley, George S. (1979), 'The Environment and City Size', in George S. Tolley, Philip E. Graves and John L. Gardner, eds, *Urban Growth Policy in a Market Economy*, Academic Press, New York.

United Nations (1991), *Sustainable Cities Demonstrations*, United Nations Centre for Human Settlements, Nairobi, Kenya.

World Bank (1991), *Urban Policy and Economic Development: An Agenda for the 1990s*, The World Bank, Washington, D.C.

World Resources Institute (in collaboration with the United Nations Environmental Programme and the United Nations Development Programme), 1989, *World Resources 1988–89*, Oxford University Press, New York.

———(1990) *World Resources 1989–1990*, Oxford University Press, New York.

16 / Determinants of Country Participation in Global Environmental Agreements

KURT J. BERON
JAMES C. MURDOCH
VIBHOOTI SHUKLA

I. Introduction

Early global environmental research focused on the scientific basis for linking emissions to global environmental quality. Only recently has there been a growing recognition of the human dimensions of the subject and the critical role social scientists may play in evaluating environmental change and public policy. According to Miller (1991), while continued research in the natural sciences may be expected to contribute to a reduction of uncertainty in key areas, the human dimension actually increases the complexity of the research: 'Because of social and cultural diversity, interacting political and institutional structures, and competing economic, military, and religious imperatives that influence human social behaviour — in short, because of the analytically messy essence of human behavior that is the subject of social science—socioeconomic research on global change will inevitably introduce an exponential increase in the complexity of research on global change ...'

The primary purpose of this paper is to develop and test models for understanding the political economy of behaviour regarding the global environment. Our unit of analysis is the individual nation; hence, we desire to investigate theoretical and empirical models of country behaviour. Specifically, we examine the determinants of voting for the Montreal Protocol on chlorofluorocarbons (CFC) emissions. In the next section, we develop a simple model of country behaviour in the absence of cooperation on environmental problems. The model is characterized by a Nash equilibrium. Then, we investigate how nations could improve themselves by cooperating; i.e., by signing an international agreement. This exercise generates an empirical model of behaviour which is presented in the third section. The parameters of the empirical model are estimated using a Probit estimator. The results are summarized and some implications for future research are presented in the final section.

II. Theoretical Model

To highlight the theoretical determinants of a country's decision to participate or not participate in a global environmental treaty, we first consider a model of individual country behaviour in the presence of a global externality. This model was developed by Cornes and Sandler (1986). Recently, Sandler (1992) illustrated the wide applicability of the model and its connection to the collective action paradigm of Olson (1965). Hoel (1991) used a similar model to analyse the logic of unilateral actions to improve the global environment.

We begin by denoting Q^0 as the initial environmental quality and Q as the environmental quality at the end of the current period. A particular country (i) can contribute to Q by reducing emissions. Let X_i denote the amount of emissions reduced by country i in the current period. If there are n countries, then the aggregate emissions reduction (X) is simply the sum over all X_i's; i.e.,

$$X = \sum_{i=1}^{n} X_i = \tilde{X}_i + X_i \tag{1}$$

In (1), the aggregate emission reduction is divided into i's contribution (X_i) and everybody else's contribution ($\tilde{X}_i$). The change in the environmental quality in the current period is a function of the magnitude of the aggregate emission reduced. Thus,

$$\Delta Q = Q - Q^0 = f\left(\sum_{i=1}^{n} X_i\right) \tag{2}$$

The first derivative of f (f') is positive, meaning that as global emission reductions increase, Q increases. Solving equation (2) for Q yields

$$Q = f\left(\sum_{i=1}^{n} X_i\right) + Q^0 \tag{3}$$

Each country must decide how much emission reduction to undertake. This choice problem is modelled as a utility maximization problem. Let Y denote a composite commodity ('all other goods'). Then,

$$U_i = U_i\,(Y_i, Q) \tag{4}$$

is a twice continuously differentiable, strictly concave function, where U_i is used to denote the preferences of the ith country. The utility (or welfare) of country i depends on the amount of Y_i and Q that it 'consumes'. The partial derivatives of U_i are both positive. More of Y_i and Q is preferred to less. Note that in (4), Q is not subscripted. Since Q denotes the global environmental quality, the amount available to i is identical to the amount available to the other countries; i.e., Q is a pure public good.

The country is constrained in its choice of Y_i and X_i by its national income. This constraint is given as

$$M_i = Y_i + P_i X_i \tag{5}$$

where M_i denotes national income and P_i is the relative cost of a unit of X. Equation (5) shows that a country can allocate its resources to consumption of 'all other goods' and/or emission reductions. P_i gives the marginal cost of emission reductions in terms of forgone other goods. Thus, we see that the total cost of emission reduction is the forgone national income that could have been consumed without the effort to reduce emissions.

The first-order necessary conditions for a maximum of (4) subject to (1), (3) and (5) imply

$$f' MRS^i_{QY} = P_i \tag{6}$$

where MRS^i_{QY} is i's marginal rate of substitution for Q in terms of Y. Condition (6) shows that a country contributes to emission reduction up to the point where the marginal valuation of Q (the left hand side) is just equal to the marginal cost (the right hand side). In the maximization problem, the individual countries take as given the contributions to Q by the other nations; hence, $\widetilde{X}_i$ is exogenous. This is an assumption about behaviour (the Nash assumption). Given that all nations solve the same type of choice problem, a Nash equilibrium is obtained when a level of Q is provided such that all countries are in equilibrium.

The first-order conditions implicitly define X_i as a function of the exogenous variables. Thus,

$$X_i = X_i (M_i, P_i, \widetilde{X}_i) \tag{7}$$

Equation (7) is like a demand function (see Murdoch and Sandler 1984). Holding P_i and M_i constant, equation (7) is also called a reaction path. The reaction path interpretation is especially common when developing two-country examples (Cornes and Sandler 1986). The two-country example is instructive since it facilitates a picture of the Nash equilibrium.

To see this, consider Figure 1 which shows the indifference curves for country 1, assuming just two countries in the world. The indifference curves are in the X_1, X_2 space and are generated by substituting (3) and (5) into (4) and fixing M_i and P_i:

$$U_i = U_i\,(M_i - P_i\,X_i, f\,(X_1 + X_2) + Q^0) \tag{8}$$

Since by definition the utility does not change along an indifference curve, the slope of the curve is found by setting the total differential of (8) to zero and solving for the slope. This is

$$\frac{dX_2}{dX_1} = \frac{P_1}{f'\,MRS^1_{QY}} - 1 \tag{9}$$

Looking at (9), we see that the slope is zero when equation (6), the utility maximization condition, is satisfied. Thus, for any given level of X_2, say X_2^0, country 1 maximizes U_1 by reducing emissions until the horizontal line beginning at X_2^0 is just tangent to the indifference curve. Two utility maximizing points are illustrated in Figure 1 (E_1 and E_2). However, an entire locus of equilibrium points can be generated by choosing alternative values for X_2.

Only when country 1 and country 2 are simultaneously satisfied do we have a Nash equilibrium. Thus, a Nash equilibrium is characterized by zero slopes of both countries' indifference curves. For country 1, the zero slope appears in the X_1, X_2 space, while for country 2, the zero slope appears in the X_2, X_1 space. This situation is illustrated in Figure 2. The indifference curve U_1^* looks just like those shown in Figure 1. What about U_2^*? By turning the diagram 90 to the left we can see that U_2^* is the indifference curve for country 2 in the X_2, X_1 space. Moreover, both countries are maximizing utility at point E. Thus, $X^* = X_1^* + X_2^*$ is a Nash equilibrium.

In the next section, we are interested in estimating the determinants of a favourable vote for an international treaty aimed at controlling ozone-depleting emissions. Before cooperation, we expect that country behaviour will be characterized by Nash-type behaviour. Thus, Figure 2 helps to highlight the nature of the determinants of an international agreement. Starting from the Nash equilibrium point (E), country 1 will vote for any treaty that offers an allocation into the horizontally shaded area. Similarly, country 2 will vote for any

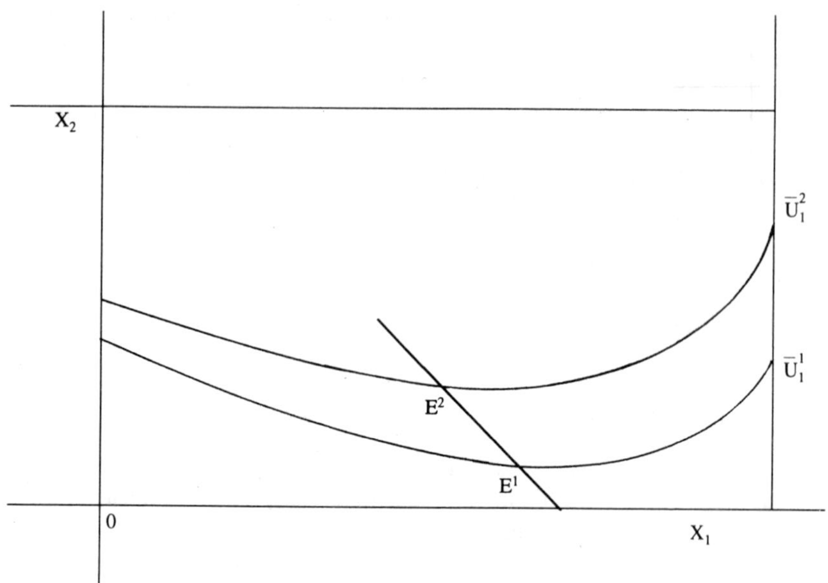

Figure 1: Two Utility Maximization Points for Nation 1

allocation that moves them into the vertically shaded region. Note that both are made better off by an allocation into the cross-shaded region.

The existence of the cross-shaded region implies that the Nash equilibrium is not Pareto optimal; i.e., both can gain from cooperative, rather than Nash-type, behaviour. However, specific instances of international cooperation on global environmental issues are rare. One of the reasons for this lies in the nature of how cooperation is established when there is a public good. To see this, compare the Nash-type behaviour just developed with what we see with respect to private goods, with clearly defined property rights.

With private goods, the benefits and costs from providing the goods accrue within the country of origin. Because there are no spillovers, international exchange of goods is (relatively) easily accommodated through markets. Exchange takes place as long as each country sees a net benefit (benefits minus costs) from making the exchange. There exists a 'self-interest' incentive for each country to continuously, or at least incrementally, adapt to changing market conditions by pursuing

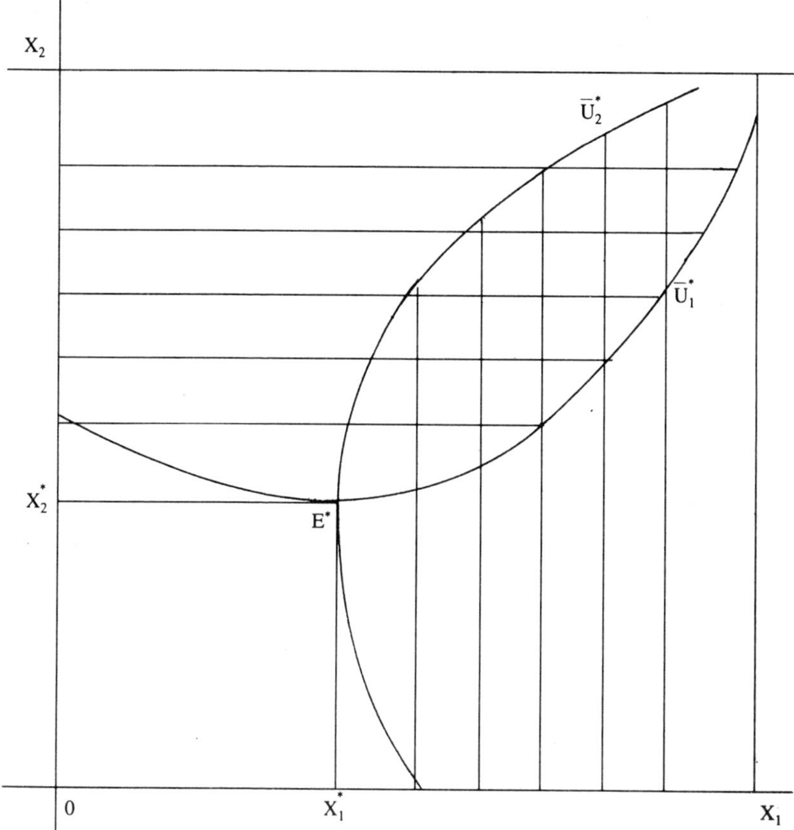

Figure 2: A Nash Equilibrium Point and the Pareto-Superior Region

additional exchanges. Moreover, mutually beneficial exchanges, by definition, are Pareto-superior and lead towards a Pareto optimum. Therefore, we can say that the welfare of the international community is enhanced without explicit institutions to foster cooperation.

With a public good, like the global environment, we do not expect this type of continuous exchange. Two reasons for this are the presence of spillovers and the imperfect information surrounding the benefits and costs of the good. Spillovers provide a self-interest motive for free riding — consuming a good without paying for it. Imperfect information reduces the ability of a country to assess the benefit of providing the good and determining its ultimate costs, thereby limiting the value of undertaking any exchange. Both of these factors serve to reduce the volume of 'trades' involving public goods. In contrast to the private goods case, with public goods self-interest does not necessarily complement international welfare.

This is not to say that exchange of environmental goods cannot occur. After all, Figure 2 makes clear that all parties stand to gain from cooperation. Rather, it points to exchanges being rather infrequent. Because markets fail to exist, the terms of trade must be negotiated and the institutions for enforcement must be agreed upon. Unfortunately, we cannot study markets to learn how to make predictions about behaviour. One way to proceed, however, is to study their votes on environmental treaties.

III. Empirical Model and Results

Each potential treaty affects the welfare of a country. We measure this as utility in equation (4). The utility from any given treaty, holding all other arguments in the function constant, could range from being strongly negative to strongly positive. Obviously, if a treaty increases the level of utility that can be obtained, then a country will favour the treaty. When all countries benefit from a treaty, we observe all countries voting in favour of the treaty. The fact that we observe some voting in favour and some against means that some countries perceive a positive utility gain from the treaty and others a utility loss. It is these observations that facilitate inferences about the determinants of international co-operation on the environment.

Formally, let U_i^p be the utility for country i if a treaty passes and U_i^f be utility if it fails. Also, let Z_i denote the 1 by k vector of goods that determine utility. The Z_i vector contains the determinants of Y_i and Q as shown in equations (5) and (3). Assuming a linear form for the utility function and using matrix notation, we have:

$$U_i^p = Z_i\beta + \varepsilon_i^p$$
$$U_i^f = Z_i\alpha + \varepsilon_i^f$$

as the value of utility if the treaty passes or fails, respectively. The k by 1 vectors β and α are unknown parameters, while the ε's represent random error terms.

The probability that a country would vote in favour of an agreement can be expressed as

$$P(U_i^p > U_i^f) = P(Z_i\beta + \varepsilon_i^p > Z_i\alpha + \varepsilon_i^f) = P[\varepsilon_i^f - \varepsilon_i^p < Z_i(\beta - \alpha)] \quad (10)$$

Since the choice of whether or not a country votes for an agreement (V) is observed, the unknown parameters in the model above can be estimated by assuming some distribution for the difference in the error terms. We assume a normal distribution which gives the Probit estimator. Thus,

$$P(V_i) = P(U_i^p > U_i^f) = \Phi[Z_i(\beta - \alpha)] \quad (11)$$

where Φ is the standard normal distribution function. Equation (11) represents a statistical model with unknown parameters α and β. The unknown parameters can be estimated with cross-sectional data by assuming that each country's utility function is the same, except for measurable influences. Thus, the Z_i vector must include 'utility function shifters' when the model is estimated. Note that what is estimated is the difference in each set of coefficients, $(\beta - \alpha)$, not the separate coefficients. Thus the interpretation of a variable's parameter estimate is how it effects the difference in the utility from the agreement passing or not passing.

The international environmental agreement we use to test our theory deals with the reduction of chlorofluorocarbons (CFCs). CFCs have been widely used in coolants in air conditioning and refrigeration, aerosol sprays, and as a cleaning agent for electrical components. A scientific link between the use of CFCs and damage to the stratospheric ozone layer was hypothesized in the early 1970s and has been increasingly accepted. Degradation of the ozone layer has been connected to a variety of health problems and ecosystem damage.

The Montreal Protocol, signed in 1987 and amended in 1990, was an outgrowth of the Vienna Convention for the Protection of the Ozone Layer that was signed in 1985. Briefly, the Convention laid out a non-binding framework of cooperation between participants on matters related to the Ozone Layer while the Montreal Protocol specified specific reduction targets for CFCs and other ozone-depleting substances. Incentives to participate in the agreement were included such as provisions to restrict trading in controlled substances with non-participants and through the establishment of a fund to aid developing countries in complying with the Protocol. The World Resources Institute reports that by 1990, 58 countries had either signed and/or ratified the protocol. Due to missing data in some of the other variables, the countries signing or ratifying the Protocol in our sample is 51. On the other hand,

Table 1: Descriptive Statistics, Variable Descriptions and Data Sources

Variable	Mean	Std. Dev.	Minimum	Maximum	Notes	Source
VOTE	0.490	0.502	0	1	VOTE = 1 for nations who signed or ratified the Protocol; 0 otherwise	WRI (1991)
OTHEMTPC	0.143	0.0069	0.100	0.180	Sum of the emissions of all other countries divided by the sum of all other countries population (000)	WRI (1991)
RGDPCH86	0.394	0.452	0.0	1.725	Real per capita GDP in 1986 (0000)	Summers and Heston (1990)
LATIABS	24.383	17.299	1.0	65.0	Absolute value of latitude	Cleveland (1990)
G6086	0.022	0.024	–0.081	0.104	Growth rate in RGDPCH from 1960–86	Summers and Heston (1990)
EMITPC	0.204	0.300	0	0.900	CFCs emissions ÷ population (000)	WRI (1990)
HEALEXP	2.798	2.751	0.200	11.2	Per cent of GNP in public health expenditures (developing nations) or per cent of GDP in total health expenditures (industrial nations).	UN (1991)
POLRIT	4.029	2.205	1.0	7.0	Political rights (1 for greatest, 7 for least)	Gastil (1985)
CIVLIB	4.192	2.029	1.0	7.0	Civil liberties (1 for greatest, 7 for least)	Gastil (1985)

our dataset contains 53 countries that have not signed or ratified the protocol. The countries included in the analysis are listed in the Appendix. The variables, descriptive statistics, and sources of data are listed in Table 1.

The model implies that the likelihood of voting for an environmental agreement depends on the national income, the emissions of other countries, the cost of compliance and tastes and preferences. Our income variable is the 1986 per capita gross domestic product (GDP) for each country in purchasing power parities (RGDPCH86). We hypothesize that per capita GDP will be positively related to the probability of voting for the Montreal Protocol. This hypothesis follows from the assumption that environmental quality is a normal good. The measure of other countries' emissions is the sum of all other countries' emissions in the sample divided by all other countries' populations (OTHEMTPC). A direct relationship between OTHEMTPC and how a country votes on the CFC agreement is expected. Holding a country's own emissions constant, we expect that increases in other countries' emissions will lead a country to support an agreement requiring future reductions by other countries.

The cost of compliance (P_i) is more difficult to measure. We use three variables, the growth rate in per capita income over the period 1960 to 1986 (G6086), the per capita emissions of a country (EMITPC), and the absolute value of the country's latitude (LATIABS). We expect the growth rate of per capita income to be directly related to the vote. This is due to the conventional argument that industrialized countries are more prone to vote for the CFC agreement due to their already having achieved a certain level of development, a consequence of CFC use. Developing countries, on the other hand, are less likely to vote for the agreement since they aspire to the same type of standard that industrialized countries have achieved that is, in part, a consequence of CFC use. Thus, countries experiencing low rates of growth see this reduction in their potential standard of living as a cost and are likely to support restrictions on their acquisition of CFCs.

The use of per capita emissions as a cost variable is based on a major provision of the Montreal Protocol. The Protocol imposes sanctions on non-participants to the agreement by requiring participants to stop importing ozone-depleting products from non-participants. In addition, the Protocol seeks to deter participants from exporting technologies to non-participants that contribute to ozone depletion. Therefore, we expect countries that emit greater CFCs to be more likely to sign the agreement than those emitting fewer CFCs due to the inducement effect of the treaty.

The absolute value of the country's latitude is included to account for the perception of the cost of not reducing CFC emissions. Since countries closer to the equator are predicted to suffer less from the consequences of increased CFC emissions than those further away, we expect a direct relationship between latitude and the likelihood of voting for the treaty.

Finally, to control for individual country preferences (utility function shifters) we include measures of a country's health expenditures (HEALEXP), political climate (POLRIT), and civil liberties climate (CIVLIB). The per cent of a country's income devoted to health care is included due to increased CFC exposure being associated with increases in skin cancer, cataracts, and a general reduction in a body's ability to fend off disease. A greater portion of current income devoted to health care could signal a country's preference to prevent disease and so lead to a better chance of their voting for the agreement. Alternatively, health care might be viewed as a substitute for the effect of CFC exposure. In this case, a country devoting more of their income to health care might vote against the agreement since they anticipate being able to compensate for increased exposure with increased health care.

The two variables indicating the degree of political freedom and of civil liberty in a country are based on a scale from one to seven, with one being the greatest degree of political freedom and civil liberty (Gastil 1986). The political rights variable is a measure of the ability 'to participate meaningfully in the political process' while the civil liberties variable indicates 'rights to free expression, to organize or demonstrate, as well as rights to a degree of autonomy such as is provided by freedom of religion, education, travel, and other personal rights' (Gastil 1986, p. 8). They suggest the type of political constraints that can affect the formation of a consensus in a country around an environmental agreement. Increases in political freedom are associated with more viewpoints that must be accommodated in any agreement. This need to satisfy the desires of multiple parties would be expected to decrease the likelihood of achieving an acceptable accord and so reduce the probability of voting for the Protocol. A country where citizens enjoy a variety of civil liberties, on the other hand, would be more likely to vote in favour of the pact. This is due to their being accustomed to having, and gaining, rights and protections covering an array of issues. A new environmental right, then, would be expected to be seen favourably. In a country where civil rights are the exception, however, there is less likelihood of (outspoken) citizen support for a new right.

The empirical results, shown in Table 2, generally support the stated hypotheses. In particular, an increase in income, an increase in the growth of income, and an increase in a country's own emissions, all are positively related to voting for the Montreal Protocol and all are significant. The per cent of a country's income going to health expenditures is negatively related to voting for the agreement, suggesting that health care may be considered a substitute for reductions in CFCs. The variables measuring the degree of civil liberty and of political freedom within a country also support the theory and are statistically significant. Countries with fewer political freedoms and with more civil liberties tended to have voted for the Montreal Protocol. Neither the variable for other countries' emissions or for the latitude of a country is significant.

The parameter estimates show the direction of the relationship. To help interpret the results, we computed the effect of a one unit increase in an independent variable on the probability of signing the Montreal Protocol evaluated at the means of the independent variables, i.e.,

$$\frac{f P (V_i = 1)}{f Z_k} = \phi (Z' \beta)\beta_k, \tag{12}$$

where ϕ is the standard normal density function. The model predicts a probability of 0.55 at the mean value of all variables. The marginal

Table 2: Coefficient Estimates for the Probit Model

Variable	Coefficient	T-Value
RGDCH86	0.021	2.474
G6086	21.233	2.921
OTHEMTPC	–46.750	–0.738
LATIABS	–0.006	–0.479
EMITPC	2.959	2.417
HEALEXP	–0.281	–1.877
POLRIT	0.393	2.093
CIVLIB	–0.484	–2.142
CONSTANT	6.301	0.688

probabilities can be used to show how this changes when one of the independent variables changes and all others are held constant. For example, we find that a one per cent increase in a country's per capita GDP is expected to lead to an increase of 0.334 in this probability of voting for the agreement. A one per cent increase in the growth rate is expected to lead to a 0.182 increase in the probability.[1]

It is interesting to look at the marginal effects of the political and civil liberties variables. To help in assessing these variables consider how the countries are ranked. As an illustration, Egypt, in the 1985/86 rankings, is ranked four on both scales, about the average for the sample. Brazil has a political rights rank of three and a civil rights rank of two, while Hungary has a rank of five on both scales. The marginal probabilities for these variables, since they are on an ordinal rather than a cardinal scale, show the expected effect for a one unit rise in a country's standing on the scale. We find that the marginal probability for the political rights variable, which shows the changes in the probability of voting yes given one unit higher (having fewer political rights) rank, is 0.155. On the other hand, an increase in the civil rights variable by one unit (having more civil rights) leads to an increase in the probability of 0.19.

IV. Conclusions

Our paper has constructed a theory of environmental agreements and found empirical support for most of its predictions. This approach is likely to be quite useful in future environmental negotiations since it can help focus the bargaining on incentives designed to increase support for an agreement.

Consider, for example, an environmental treaty that is up for consideration that pits developing countries against industrialized countries. The type of quantitative conclusions found here might first help in predicting who is likely to vote for the treaty. By entering the variables for each country into the equation the probability of their voting for the treaty can be estimated.

Given the public good nature of many environmental problems, it may well be necessary to increase support for the treaty beyond those predisposed to vote for it. The model can then aid in determining, for example, the type of financial assistance that may be necessary to increase the probability of voting for the agreement. In the CFC case we

Appendix: Countries in the Dataset

Country	Vote	Country	Vote
Angola	0	Kuwait	0
United Arab Emirates	1	Liberia	0
Argentina	1	Sri Lanka	1
Australia	1	Lesotho	0
Austria	1	Luxembourg	1
Burundi	0	Morocco	1
Belgium	1	Madagascar	0
Benin	0	Mexico	1
Bangladesh	0	Mali	0
Bolivia	0	Mozambique	0
Brazil	0	Malawi	0
Botswana	0	Malaysia	1
Central African Republic	0	Niger	0
Canada	1	Nigeria	1
Switzerland	1	Nicaragua	0
Chile	1	Netherlands	1
China	0	Norway	1
Cote d'Ivoire	0	Nepal	0
Cameroon	1	New Zealand	1
Congo, People's Republic	1	Oman	0
Colombia	0	Pakistan	0
Costa Rica	0	Peru	0
Germany, Federal Republic	1	Philippines	1
Denmark	1	Poland	0
Ecuador	0	Portugal	1
Egypt, Arab Republic of	1	Paraguay	0
Spain	1	Rwanda	0
Ethiopia	0	Saudi Arabia	0
Finland	1	Sudan	0
France	1	Senegal	1
Gabon	0	Singapore	1
United Kingdom	1	Sierra Leone	0
Ghana	1	El Salvador	0
Greece	1	Somalia	0
Guatemala	1	Sweden	1
Honduras	0	Syrian Arab Republic	1
Haiti	0	Chad	0
Hungary	1	Togo	1
Burkina Faso	1	Thailand	1
Indonesia	1	Tunisia	1
India	0	Turkey	0
Ireland	1	Tanzania	0
Iran, Islamic Republic of	0	Uganda	1
Iraq	0	Uruguay	0
Iceland	1	United States	1
Israel	1	Venezuela	1
Italy	1	Yemen Arab Republic	0
Jamaica	0	Yugoslavia	0
Jordan	1	South Africa	1
Japan	1	Zaire	0
Kenya	1	Zambia	0
Korea, Republic of	0	Zimbabwe	0

found that increasing a country's real GDP by one per cent led to a substantial increase in the probability of voting for the Montreal Protocol. While this particular magnitude of assistance is perhaps unrealistic, it does provide a bound that can be used in determining a viable assistance programme.

The use of our results in the ways suggested above rest on the assumption that our model is generalizable. Clearly, this assumption is yet to be tested. We hope to address this in future research where we plan on extending our model to other treaties. An additional extension is to explore the robustness of our results to other specifications. One model extension that seems worthwhile is to link the votes on one treaty with the votes on other treaties, for example by correlating the error terms in equations separately specified for different treaties.

NOTES

Presented at the Association for Policy Analysis and Management Fourteenth Annual Conference, October 1992.

1 The value of .334 is found by multiplying the marginal probability of per capita GDP by the average value of per capita GDP, while .182 equals the marginal probability of growth times the average value for growth.

REFERENCES

Breslin, W. (1990), *Nine Case Studies in International Environmental Negotiation*, Cambridge: Program on Negotiation at Harvard Law School.

Cleveland, William A. (1990), *Britannica Atlas*, Encyclopaedia Britannica, Inc, Chicago.

Cornes, Richard and Todd Sandler (1986), *The Theory of Externalities, Public Goods, and Club Goods*, Cambridge University Press, Cambridge.

Gastil, Raymond D. (1986), *Freedom in the World: Political Rights and Civil Liberties, 1985/6*, Greenwood Press, New York.

Hoel, Michael (1991), 'Global Environmental Problems: The Effects of Unilateral Actions Taken by One Country', *Journal of Environmental Economics and Management*, Vol. 20, pp. 55–70.

Miller, Roberta B. (1991), 'Social Science and the Challenge of Global Environmental Change', *International Social Sciences Journal*, Vol. 130, pp. 609–17.

Murdoch, James C. and Todd Sandler (1984), 'Complementarity, Free Riding, and the Military Expenditure of NATO Allies', *Journal of Public Economics*, Vol. 25, pp. 83–101.

Olson Mancur (1965), *The Logic of Collective Action*, Harvard University Press, Cambridge, Massachusetts.

Sandler, Todd (1992), *Collective Action*, University of Michigan Press, Ann Arbor.

United Nations (1991), *Social Indicators of Development*, United Nations, New York.

World Resources Institute (1990), *World Resources 1990–91*, Oxford University Press, New York.

17 / Urbanization, Energy Use, and Greenhouse Effects in Economic Development: Results from a Cross-national Study of Developing Countries

VIBHOOTI SHUKLA
JYOTI PARIKH

I. Introduction

Urbanization is thought to be a major human intervention in natural ecosystems responsible for the exponential rise in the degree of environmental stress as economic development proceeds. Admittedly, urbanization alone does not bear the full brunt of criticism for environmental degradation. Rural areas have their own problems, such as: deforestation due to the encroachment of farming activity upon marginal lands, large-scale irrigation projects, discharge of chemical fertilizers and pesticides into water resources. These arise, however, from the intensification of agriculture, which is the rural counterfoil to increasing urbanization.

In fact, agricultural intensification, industrialization and urbanization are all consequences of the process of economic development, and are driven ultimately by rising consumption standards. Historically, significant rises in incomes have been generally achieved with a large-scale withdrawal of labour force from primary agricultural pursuits to urban-based industrial ones. Identification between industry and urban production is not accidental. A variety of secondary activities are best and most profitably undertaken under conditions of density and large economic size that characterize urban areas.

Urban economic activities and settlement patterns may have two distinct environmental consequences quite apart from those generally dictated by higher incomes, consumption levels, and industrialization per se. First, higher urban densities might place an excessive burden on the absorptive capacities of the local environment. Secondly, urbanization and high urban densities might influence economy-wide patterns of resource use, and global environmental quality. In particular, the indirect and direct energy requirements of urban living (quite apart from the content of urban production and the consumption patterns facilitated by high incomes) are thought to contribute significantly to the adverse environmental impacts from urbanization.

The current world debate on global greenhouse warming is increasingly focused on the economic development process. Countries undergoing the development transition today are viewed as having the greatest potential for incremental degradation, and are consequently thought to offer the greatest promise, through appropriate measures, for realizing globally significant environmental gains. These rapidly urbanizing countries are likely to be under severe pressure from the international community to make the required trade-offs between economic growth and environmental quality. Among other policy options, the debate will involve discussion of alternative urbanization scenarios and ways to modify them. Before such choices can be made, however, it is necessary to empirically confirm the real sources of environmental problems as development proceeds, and quantitatively assess the nature of trade-offs if environmental degradation is to be arrested or reversed.

This paper seeks an exploratory assessment of the global greenhouse consequences of development in general and urbanization in particular, especially insofar as they relate to changing patterns of energy use. Section II elaborates upon the nature of the relationship between increased resource use and urbanization. Section III empirically analyses the impact of the development transition upon levels of resource consumption, using cross-national variations in urbanization and other development indicators to estimate a fixed-effects model of the determinants of total energy usage. Section IV uses the same set of hypothesized determinants to measure their contribution to estimated country-wise greenhouse gas emissions. Section V focuses upon developing countries exclusively to study the effects of urbanization upon their evolving profiles of energy use, disaggregated by final use sector and fuel type, and subsequently traces the greenhouse effects attributable to each of these component fuel uses. Finally, Section VI discusses some implications of the results for policies toward urbanization and energy strategies for developing countries in the context of global environmental management imperatives.

II. The Development Transition, Resources, and the Environment

Figure 1 summarizes the chain of phenomena necessitated by sustaining the consumption patterns entailed by high living standards, leading to the concentration of industrial production in highly urbanized areas. A country's level of urbanization does impose certain resource usages distinct from those that would be incurred with a completely rural settlement pattern, and these may have a variety of local environmental consequences, spanning the degradation of air, water or land quality. The focus of our inquiry, however, is on the possible global environmental consequences of urbanization, with reference to their source in specific types of urban activities.[1] The schema does not claim to be comprehensive in tracking all possible interactions in the development–greenhouse equation. Specifically, we are interested in investigating the relationship between urbanization patterns and energy use as an intermediary in contributing to greenhouse gas emissions and their attributed global warming.

Energy use in stationary and mobile activities is a major contributor to atmospheric emissions of pollutants, such as sulphur dioxide and particulate matter, which largely have effects ranging from the local to the regional scale. But it is also the single most important factor in greenhouse gas (GHG) emissions. Various activities within an urbanizing economy involve fuel combustion to a large or small degree, with high concomitant emissions. Urban growth and lifestyles impose three identifiable types of energy usage which can ultimately result in GHG emissions: (a) energy conversion from one form to another; (b) indirect energy consumption in goods-producing activities; and (c) direct energy consumption in final uses such as transportation.

The development transition leads to increase in energy usage for several reasons. Industrialization itself involves the substitution of human power by mechanical energy, converted by one means or another. In addition, industrialization entails the shift of workers from primary economic pursuits (agriculture and extractive activities) to secondary ones which are more energy intensive. To sustain consumption patterns demanded at higher levels of income, various resources, including land and labour, are increasingly committed to non-agricultural activity. This leads to more intensive cultivation (with higher intensity of fertilizer, pesticide and power-using irrigation pumpsets) to produce a given or

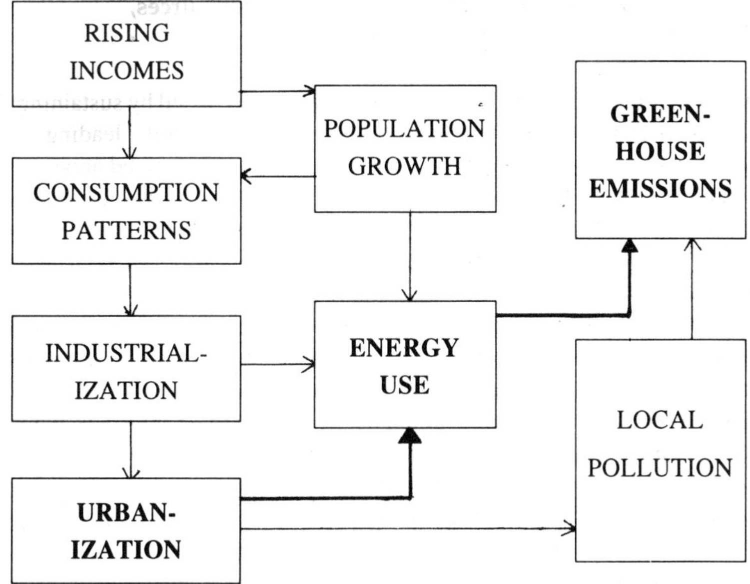

Figure 1: Urbanization—Energy Use Greenhouse Linkages

augmented level of food with fewer workers and finite land supplies. Agriculture becomes more mechanized, requiring more fuel as labour is reallocated to the more productive and remunerative secondary and tertiary sectors. With progressive technological sophistication, the structure of manufacturing itself has moved historically from simple production to highly energy-intensive metal products, and thence to the even more fuel-resource-using synthetic materials industry.

This large-scale shift of workers from agriculture to industry is accompanied by significant movements of population from rural to urban areas, for reasons having to do with the natural affinity of industry with urban locations that was mentioned earlier. The locational division of labour entails movement of goods from places where they are produced to where they are consumed, resulting in cross rural–urban freight transportation requirements. Specialization in general, as development proceeds, and increased market size permit the concentration of industry due to economies of scale, both internal and external, again increasing the need for energy-intensive transport. As more and more stages are added to industrial processing of primary raw materials with increasing commercialization, higher transportation costs — and energy usage — are incurred.

The rapid urban growth which accompanies economic development and industrialization is actualized partly through natural increase (as the demographic transition concurrently works its way through the population), but overwhelmingly through rural-to-urban migration. This increased rural–urban mobility leads to higher person transport; but, more importantly, the size and nature of productive urban areas leads to recurrent intra-urban movements of people from residences to their places of work. Thus, urbanization facilitates non-agricultural activities, but involves expenditure of large amounts of energy resources. Of course, resources expended in commuting are sensitive to urban spatial structure; but generally, they may be expected to be far larger per capita in urban than in rural areas, and tend to involve more polluting types of fuel consumption than commuting resource use accompanying the more interspersed rural settlement patterns.

Urban areas may be expected to be energy intensive in other ways too, owing to their physical layout. Importance of accessibility to a transport node or agglomeration of economic activities (such as a central business district) implies that activities would have tendency to cluster in close proximity with the centre of attraction. This drives up values of scarce land in the vicinity of the nodes, resulting in the substitution of capital for land in building structures — hence making economically necessary the high-rise buildings that have come to be the distinguishing characteristic of the modern urban landscape. (We see the most dramatic examples of such substitution in activities where production technologies permit it most — commercial and office-type activities are a case in point — hence their observed propensity to locate in the highest land rent districts, closest to the central attracting node.) Building technologies that go with such structures tend to be intensive in cement and other materials, the manufacture of which involves large proportions of indirect energy usages. Cement manufacture, incidentally, also involves carbon dioxide emissions thought to contribute directly to the so-called global greenhouse effects.

More than rural areas, a city is a spatial environment with a high proportion of space committed to public uses. The functioning of urban areas necessitates the provision of public infrastructure, much of which is in the form of constructed facilities. Indirect demand for energy from such sources would add to increased aggregate demand for energy during the process of urbanization. Many urban public infrastructure investments are mandated by the needs of living and conducting business under conditions of high density — e.g., road networks, water supply, sewage disposal, sanitation and drainage systems that are qualitatively different from technologies used to perform analogous functions in rural areas, where settlement is sparse. In such cases, infrastructure provision may impose additional resource costs of urbanization. Of course, on the other hand, certain site-specific public services must be provided to urban and rural areas equally — e.g., health, education, etc., and there is a case to be made that there are significant economies of scale (and energy-cost savings) in both production and delivery with a more concentrated population than otherwise.

Does urbanization impose a distinctive and empirically verifiable pattern of energy consumption, as suggested above? Do the concomitants of economic development bear a systematic and measurable relationship with the potential for global warming? How important is the role of energy in the economic-development–greenhouse equation? The following sections will attempt to confirm and measure any relationships that may exist between urbanization and energy usage on the one hand, and urbanization and greenhouse gas emissions on the other, in the context of the broader process of economic development. Our methodology is multiple regression analysis using aggregate data from a cross-section of the world's countries. This paper is essentially proposed as a first thrust at the problem, an exploratory exercise, aimed largely at uncovering correlates, rather than demonstrating causality. As Figure 1 indicates, a more elaborate and rigorous modelling of the complex processes at work would properly demand simultaneous equation estimation procedures or a computable general equilibrium formulation. At present, however, data are inadequate to support such efforts, and we leave them to future research.

III. Economic Development, Urbanization, and Energy Consumption

In this section, we examine the variation of the aggregate energy requirements of economies with the development process in general and urbanization in particular. To this end, we regress the total energy consumption per capita (in oil equivalents) over the period 1965–87 of a sample of developed and developing countries on various national indicators relevant to the development transition. The time-series and the cross-national dimensions of the data should help us track trends in energy resource use as economic development proceeds.[2] We distinguish conceptually between aggregate energy usage due to industrialization and high consumption levels, on the one hand, and that attributable to density and resource-use patterns associated with a peculiarly urban lifestyle, on the other. This distinction is sought to be maintained, in empirical implementation, with the determinants of national energy use per capita hypothesized to include these separate influences through appropriate proxies in the regression analysis.

As a measure of average levels of income and consumption, as well as a broad, albeit imperfect proxy for general development levels, we shall use GNP per capita in US dollars. As an index of structural change, we use the share of agriculture in a country's GDP. The expectation is that both higher aggregate consumption levels and larger shares of industrial activity in the economy create a propensity for greater energy use. The effect of sheer population pressure on a country's energy resource usage is sought to be captured through the population density variable (land area being, roughly, an indicator of its 'supply' of environmental quality or basic capacity to absorb environmental stress). Special consequences of urbanization (including the resource consumption patterns dictated specifically by urban density as opposed to overall density) are expected to be reflected through the per cent urban variable, indicating the extent to which a country's population resides in areas fulfilling national urbanization criteria.[3]

A double-logarithmic regression model is accordingly specified and estimated. Table 1 reports results from an ordinary least squares estimation run on the pooled time-series and cross-section data with the four explanatory variables reflecting income, economic structure, population pressures and urbanization. The signs and significance levels of the income and structural change coefficients are as expected, increases in GNP per capita and the degree of industrialization are associated with substantially higher levels of per capita energy usage. While a country's overall population density appears to be statistically unrelated to energy use, the high and highly significant coefficient on urbanization suggests an urbanization elasticity with respect to per capita (commercial) energy consumption in oil equivalents of 0.47.[4]

This estimation procedure may not, however, yield the best possible coefficient estimates with the time-series–cross-section data at hand, treating as it does each country and time period equivalently, devoid of any specific differences in per capita energy demands. To address the latter possibility, we repeat the estimation with a fixed-effects model.[5] This estimation methodology recognizes variations in rates of energy use due to country- and time-specific constancies that are not accounted for by the set of independent variables in our specification. These may be due either to uncontrolled-for structural demand characteristics of these countries (such as their policy orientation), or to supply-side factors such as their oil-resource endowments, and to any temporal fluctuations in the international price and availability of oil.

With such 'fixed effects' accounted for, all coefficients for explanatory variables tend to fall, while retaining their significance. In particular, the energy use elasticity of urbanization falls to 0.28, indicating that other influences held constant, a doubling of a country's urban population would increase its per capita fuel consumption by 28 per cent. The fixed-effects estimation methodology makes it possible to retrieve the country-specific shifters of the hypothesized relationship, which appear arranged in descending order of magnitude in Appendix I. Examining the list, it is evident that the top fuel-using countries are either

Table 1: Aggregate Energy Consumption Per Capita, 1965–87

Model	*Pooled OLS*	*Fixed Effects*
N	78 countries × 23 years	
LN (GNPCAP)	0.4722*	0.2504*
	(17.62)	(9.32)
LN (AGRGDP)	–0.6822*	–0.1761*
	(19.79)	(5.23)
LN (POPDENS)	–0.0131	0.0935
	(–1.25)	(0.85)
LN (URBAN)	0.4734*	0.2813*
	(14.48)	(5.09)
Constant	3.1386	
R-squared	0.8049	0.7600

Dependent Variable: Logarithm of energy consumption per capita (oil equivalents).
Explanatory Variables:
GNPCAP = Gross National Product per capita (US$)
AGRGDP = Share of agriculture in gross domestic product (per cent)
POPDENS = Total population density (persons per sq km)
URBAN = Urban population as per cent of total population (per cent)
* = 1%; † = 5%; ‡ = 10% levels of significance in two-tailed tests (*t*-statistics in parentheses).
Data Source: *Social Indicators of Development,* World Bank, 1987.

those with policies in place which heavily favour energy use, such as the United States, or those that are significant oil producers themselves, such as Saudi Arabia or Venezuela, suggesting a relative price effect resulting in the substitution of oil for more traditional fuel energy sources. Near the bottom of the list are the impoverished countries of Sub-Saharan Africa, and Nepal, where biofuels use, not accounted for by commercial energy sources, is likely to be predominant.

IV. Urbanization and Greenhouse Effects

In recent times, global greenhouse effect has generated considerable interest. The four most important greenhouse gases are carbon dioxide (CO_2), methane (CH_4), nitrous oxide (N_2O), and the chlorofluorocarbons (CFC 11 and 12). The main anthropogenic sources of current greenhouse gas additions to the carbon dioxide flux are cement, liquid fuel, solid fuel, gas and gas flaring. In addition, land use changes due to deforestation result in the flux of carbon to the atmosphere; however, reservations regarding data are expressed by J. Parikh et al. (1991). Methane emissions come from municipal solid waste along with methane from livestock, hard-coal mining, gas pipeline leakages and the practice of wet-rice agriculture.

In this section, we seek to correlate country-level greenhouse gas emissions to levels of economic development, using the same set of explanatory variables as used in Section III. We concentrate here on CO_2, CH_4, the CFCs, and, lastly, on the net total increases in atmospheric emissions of all greenhouse gases (in carbon equivalents) in terms of metric tonnes per capita. The data are for a world-wide sample of 83 countries, for the year 1985/86. Carbon dioxide emissions from the manufacture of cement and burning of fossil fuels have been estimated for these countries.[6] Methane emissions from municipal solid waste were calculated by multiplying the 1986 population by per capita emission coefficients developed for each country.

The use of fossil fuels and cement in estimated CO_2 emissions could be related to the transportation and construction requirements of urbanization, and may be expected to have a positive association with the percentage share of urban population in total, referred to as 'per cent urban'. Similarly, the municipal solid waste component of methane emissions is likely to be associated with measures of the magnitude of the urban population, whereas discharges of chlorofluorocarbons are more likely to vary with particular types of consumption associated with high income levels. Accordingly, we regress the estimated per capita emissions of these gases on this measure of urbanization, as well as other development indicators employed in the previous section.

Results are presented in Table 2. As expected, per cent urban is uniformly significant in the per capita fluxes of all greenhouse gases (with the exception of CFC) and average incomes for all cases except carbon dioxide. The stronger association of urbanization relative to general consumption with CO_2 emissions is notable, an association that is maintained in the regression for the net per capita total atmospheric increase due to aggregate emissions. About 50 per cent of the variation in the latter is explained by our set of explanatory variables, a not insubstantial proportion considering the inevitable unevenness in data reporting and emission estimation across countries.

Estimates obtained hitherto may be to project the energy use and global warming consequences of alternative developing country future

Table 2: Estimated Annual Additions to Greenhouse Gas Emissions

	CO_2 *Discharge*	CH_4 *Discharge*	CFC *Discharge*	*Net Total Additions*
N	83	83	83	83
	PCAPCO$_2$	PCAPCH$_4$	PCNETCFC	PCNETINC
GNPCAP	0.00003	0.00007†	0.00004*	0.0012*
	(0.52)	(3.07)	(8.12)	(3.94)
AGRGDP	0.0025	0.0108	–0.0011	0.0212
	(0.14)	(1.59)	(–0.73)	(0.24)
POPDENS	–0.0002	–0.0004*	0.0003*	–0.0009
	(–0.59)	(–2.48)	(7.56)	(–0.42)
URBAN	0.0306†	0.0140*	0.0007	0.1869*
	(2.14)	(2.55)	(0.54)	(2.64)
Constant	0.2017	–0.4230	0.0155	0.5135
R-squared	0.1780	0.3281	0.7681	0.5048

Dependent Variables:
PCAPCO$_2$ = Anthropogenic additions to carbon dioxide flux (metric tonnes carbon per capita)
PCAPCH$_4$ = Anthropogenic additions to methane flux (metric tonnes methane per capita)
PCAPCFC = Net atmospheric increase in chlorofluorocarbons (metric tonnes per capita)
PCNETINC = Net total increase in atmospheric concentrations of greenhouse gas emissions (metric tonnes carbon per capita)
Explanatory Variables: See Table 1.
* = 1%; † = 5%; ‡ = 10% levels of significance in two-tailed tests (t-statistics in parentheses).
Data Source: *World Resources, 1990–91*, World Resources Institute.

income and urban growth scenarios, based upon the past and present spectrum of international experiences at different levels of development. However, such an extrapolation would presume that developing country consumption, energy use and urbanization patterns are identical with those in developed countries. Yet, there are reasons to believe that such an assumption may not be realistic. Thus, potential variations in rates of fuel usage and their greenhouse consequences call for a more disaggregated analysis focused specifically upon the group of developing countries. Section V addresses itself to this task.

V. Disaggregated Patterns of Fuel Use in Developing Countries

Understanding energy consumption patterns of countries at a disaggregated level helps us better locate the sources of energy-related environmental problems. Below, we investigate relationships between urban development, patterns of energy use and their attendant greenhouse emissions by fuel type and final uses for the restricted sub-sample of developing countries.[7] This separate empirical treatment of less developed economies both enables sharper focus on the energy use and emission behaviour of the group of countries whose emissions are likely to increase and should facilitate a more realistic discussion of their energy policy options, and choices that may be feasibly anticipated with development.

Studies of energy issues in developing countries have ranged from empirical cross-national exercises such as this one, to single-country energy-sector policy simulation models.[8] Approaches to the study of the relationship between energy use and economic development include analysis of historical data on energy use by countries that are developed today over the period they were industrializing, or explorations of energy-use patterns in present-day developing contexts. These kinds of study depend largely on detailed case comparisons, but have potential insights for the cross-country statistical exercise undertaken here to draw more general inferences about the process.

Jones (1988) documents historical sector-shifts in energy use for the UK and the US, pointing out that '[a] major difference between the experiences of the industrialized and developing countries is that in the former, the mechanization and energization of transportation paralleled or followed the mechanization and energization of industry, while the reverse generally is the case in today's developing coutries'. Similarly, he notes that residential, relative to industrial, electrification has proceeded more rapidly in today's developing countries than it historically did in the industrialized economies, tending to create exaggerated demands for electricity. Jones also observes that by contrast with the developed countries, developing countries, while possessing larger indigenous reserves of coal than oil, have come to development at a time dominated by oil-using technologies in both industry and transport, and anticipates an accelerated switching to fossil fuels in the latter.

A review of studies of urban energy use in less developed countries by Sathaye and Meyers (1985) generally supports these observations. Income rise has led to fuel substitution from firewood to charcoal to kerosene, and from kerosene to liquified petroleum gas or electricity in several Asian cities. Urban growth has entailed the replacement of traditional human- and animal-powered transport modes typical of developing country rural areas by motor-powered vehicles. Finally, Sathaye and Meyers document large and growing electricity demands in urban office activities. As developing economies and their cities increase their shares of the commercial and institutional sector, it is reasonable to expect high final demands for electricity consumption, often met by power generation through the environmentally harmful burning of fossil fuels.

To what extent are the above patterns indicated in our cross-sectional analysis of disaggregated energy use profiles? Table 3(A) examines the determinants of the shares of individual fuel types in developing countries, using the set of explanatory variables used in the previous section. Industrialization is more definitely associated with a shift towards heavy petroleum and electricity, and away from derived biomass energy. Per cent urban unambiguously contributes to a rising share of light petroleum products and a fall in the share of biomass energy use. The rise in the share of these transportation fuels in total energy use as urbanization proceeds is a finding with important ramifications for greenhouse effects due to CO and CO_2 emissions, as is the positive association of electricity's share with urbanization. We shall return to both in our later discussion of policy.

Table 3(B) disaggregates fuel usage by final use sector, and regresses sectoral shares in total fuel use against the same set of independent variables. The share of construction in fuel use rises, as expected, with income, but surprisingly, falls with per cent urban, possibly due to the

Table 3(A): Determinants of Shares of Fuel Type in Developing Country Energy Consumption, All Sectors

Fuels	N	GNPCAP	AGRGDP	POPDENS	*Urban*	*Constant*	*R-squared*
Light Petroleum	43	0.00002	–0.1032	–0.0023	0.2000†	9.5460	0.3550
		(0.04)	(–0.67)	(–1.64)	(2.28)		
Heavy Petroleum	43	–0.0002	–0.8303*	0.0016	–0.0085	41.6713	0.4426
		(–0.22)	(–3.28)	(0.73)	(–0.06)		
Electricity	43	–0.0004	–0.2064*	0.0027*	0.0629	10.6073	0.6170
		(–1.33)	(–2.60)	(3.86)	(1.39)		
Biomass Energy	42	–0.0013	1.1200*	0.0019	–0.3831†	34.2667	0.6743
		(–0.65)	(3.11)	(0.58)	(–1.98)		

Table 3(B): Determinants of Shares of Final Use Sectors in Developing Country Energy Consumption, All Fuels

Sectors	N	GNPCAP	AGRGDP	POPDENS	*Urban*	*Constant*	*R-squared*
Ind & Constr	43	0.0011	–0.7796†	0.0006	0.1084	49.1482	0.3429
		(1.00)	(–2.56)	(0.22)	(0.62)		
Construction	42	0.0017‡	–0.8383*	–0.0014	–0.4641*	51.7498	0.3434
		(1.70)	(–3.44)	(–0.64)	(–3.32)		
Transport	43	–0.0004	–0.4099†	–0.0039†	0.1550	24.5798	0.4269
		(–0.57)	(–2.27)	(–2.44)	(1.50)		
Roads	40	0.0002	–0.1751	–0.0040†	0.1718‾	12.9520	0.3762
		(0.33)	(–1.08)	(–2.67)	(1.68)		
Hhold & Other	43	0.0029	2.2040	0.0098	–1.1549	66.9471	0.1327
		(0.32)	(0.90)	(0.45)	(–0.83)		
Household	43	0.0005	1.4181*	0.0027	–0.1956	19.1630	0.6802
		(0.46)	(4.78)	(1.04)	(–1.15)		
Agriculture	34	–0.0009	–0.0533	–0.0003	0.0457	3.0778	0.1991
		(–1.29)	(–0.85)	(–0.43)	(1.28)		

Note: Regression results should be read left to right.

All dependent variables are proportions of total fuel use (in terajoules per capita).

Explanatory Variables:

GNPCAP = Gross National Product per capita (US$)

AGRGDP = Share of agriculture in gross domestic product (per cent)

POPDENS = Total population density (persons per sq km)

URBAN = Urban population as per cent of total population (per cent)

* = 1%; † = 5%; ‡ = 10% levels of significance in two-tailed tests (figures in parentheses are t-statistics).

Data Source: *Energy Balances,* 1985, United Nations.

need for a proliferation of public facilities in a more dispersed settlement pattern. The share of the household sector in total fuel use is high where agriculture is predominant, and tends to fall unambiguously with industrialization, in favour of the shares of the industry and transportation sectors. Notably, the share of energy use in road transport rises significantly with a country's per cent urban, pointing once more to increased fuel requirements for transportation as urban development proceeds.[9]

How do disaggregated energy use patterns contribute to greenhouse gas emissions in developing countries? Tables 4(A) and 4(B) present results from the regressions of anthropogenic additions to the carbon dioxide flux and net additions to all greenhouse gas emissions on sets of variables reflecting the fuel-mix and sector-mix, respectively, of these countries' total energy consumption. Explanatory variables in the specifications are as follows: (1) per capita fuel consumption and (2) logarithm of the latter. The significant contribution of high levels and shares of light petroleum product usage to both carbon dioxide and total greenhouse gas emissions is noteworthy. Fuel consumption by the transport sector, likewise, is shown to add significantly to net annual greenhouse emissions for some specifications (and positively for all). Since both petroleum energy and transportation use have been found to be strongly associated with a country's share of urban population, they are major sources of greenhouse emissions in urbanizing economies. The contribution of the use of biomass fuels and household energy consumption (in the logarithmic specification) to greenhouse emissions, on the other hand, suggests that this source should diminish in relative importance as urbanization proceeds, although the household sector's large share in developing country fuel consumption, and its high propensity for electricity usage with development are likely to slow this decline.

The comprehensiveness of the foregoing set of regressions in covering all combinations of energy usage has been limited by the small sample sizes that result when disaggregated types of fuel use are crossed with final use sectors. Several gaps exist in the developing country dataset, with many deficiencies in detailed fuel-use breakdowns for any given country, leading to changing and often less than viable numbers of observations for each case. Appendixes II and III attempt to fill some of the gaps in characterization of these countries' disaggregative energy use patterns by reducing the number of independent variables to

Table 4(A): Energy Use Patterns by Fuel Type and Greenhouse Effects in Developing Countries

Fuels	*Anthropogenic Additions to CO_2 Flux*		*Net Additions to Greenhouse Gas Emissions*	
N	35	35	35	35
	(1)	(2)	(1)	(2)
Light Petroleum	0.1481	0.9324†	0.1085	0.7612*
	(0.89)	(2.47)	(1.37)	(2.76)
Heavy Petroleum	–0.0296	–0.2993	0.0035	–0.2676
	(–0.42)	(–0.70)	(0.10)	(–0.86)
Electricity	0.0820	0.0377	–0.0068	0.0422
	(0.22)	(0.10)	(–0.04)	(0.16)
Biomass Energy	0.1787†	0.0614	0.1015†	0.0256
	(2.07)	(0.95)	(2.46)	(0.54)
Constant	0.1557	–0.5132	0.0315	–0.6415
R-squared	0.1890	0.3394	0.3462	0.3983

Table 4(B): Energy Use Patterns by Sector and Greenhouse Effects in Developing Countries

Sectors	*Anthropogenic Additions to CO_2 Flux*		*Net Additions to Greenhouse Gas Emissions*	
N	35	35	35	35
	(1)	(2)	(1)	(2)
Ind & Constr	–0.0936	–0.1367	–0.0310	–0.1200
	(–1.21)	(–0.47)	(–0.83)	(–0.58)
Transport	0.1759‡	0.5481	0.1032	0.4714‡
	(1.17)	(1.49)	(1.42)	(1.81)
Household	0.1080	0.3911‡	0.0586	0.3614‡
	(1.23)	(1.75)	1.36)	(2.29)
Other	0.1821	0.1216	0.0846	0.0986
	(0.22)	(0.39)	(0.22)	(0.45)
Constant	0.6895	-1.1247	0.2994	-1.2777
R-squared	0.1716	0.3578	0.3517	0.4578

Note: Specifications (1) are in linear and (2) in double-logarithmic form.

Dependent variables are in metric tonnes carbon per capita.

Explanatory variables are energy consumption by fuel types and final use sectors in terajoules per capita.

* = 1%; † = 5%; ‡ = 10% levels of significance in two-tailed tests (figures in parentheses are t-statistics).

Data Sources: *Energy Balances*, 1985, United Nations and *World Resources, 1990–91*, World Resources Institute.

economize on degrees of freedom. Appendixes II and III, using double-logarithmic specifications, report elasticities of fuel use by type with respect to GNP per capita and per cent urban, respectively, in each sector for which adequate data exist.[10] These detailed results are quite interesting: they suggest, for example, that for every 1 per cent increase in GNP per capita, developing countries may be expected to increase their consumption of light petroleum in road transportation by nearly 1.2 per cent. A 1 per cent increase in per cent urban, on the other hand, increases such usage by as much as 1.8 per cent, *ceteris paribus*.

Appendixes IV and V report CO_2 and total greenhouse gas emission elasticities with respect to fuel use by type and sector for developing countries. The CO_2 emission elasticity[11] due to light petroleum product use in transportation is quite high (0.46), as is that for electricity use in the household and other consumption sector (0.48). The elasticities of net additions to greenhouse gas emissions for total LPP and HPP consumption across sectors are 0.53 and 0.40, respectively; the analogous elasticity attributable to total electricity use is 0.43. Doubling the total energy use (over all fuel types) in the transportation sector could potentially raise carbon dioxide emissions by 58 per cent and total emissions by 51 per cent; doubling total energy use in the household and other consumption sector would augment CO_2 flux by 91 per cent and net additions to total greenhouse effects by 74 per cent. A 100 per cent increase in total energy consumption, aggregated over all fuel types and sectors, will increase CO_2 emissions by 95 per cent and total greenhouse effects by 85 per cent. These figures indicate strong linkages between energy use and greenhouse emissions in developing countries.

Following the estimates of Appendixes II–V, we can perform the following simple simulations: (1) A 1 per cent increase in developing country per capita incomes would increase total energy consumption by 0.70 per cent; if a 1 per cent increase in total energy consumption increases net greenhouse emissions by 0.85 per cent, this implies that a 1 per cent increase in per capita incomes in these countries should increase their net annual greenhouse emissions to the global atmosphere by approximately 0.60 per cent. (2) A 1 per cent increase in urban population would increase total energy consumption by 0.85 per cent, and given that a 1 per cent increase in total energy consumption increases net greenhouse emissions also by 0.85 per cent annually, a

1 per cent growth in developing countries' urban population would augment their contribution to the atmospheric greenhouse effect to the tune of 0.72 per cent.[12] It is easy to extrapolate these simulation results to a variety of economic growth and urban growth scenarios for any developing country, or groups of such countries, to arrive at rough quantitative approximations of their future GHG emission potentials.

As incomes rise and urbanization proceeds, there will be fuel-switching and sectoral shifts in today's developing countries. Developing country group energy use from both GNP and urban growth could increase substantially, and this increase could translate into substantial increments in their GHG contributions. However, judicious policies can influence outcomes in desired directions. With this in mind, we turn to exploring policy alternatives that might be feasibly deployed to transcend any implied grim global warming scenarios.

VI. Policy Implications of Urban Energy Use—GHG Emissions Results

In this section, we evaluate the arguments for policy imperatives to reduce greenhouse gas emissions of developing countries, based upon our findings about urbanization and energy use in the course of economic development. Briefly, our conclusions from the foregoing empirical exercises may be summarized as follows: (*a*) Estimated greenhouse effects do appear to be positively correlated with countries' urbanization levels; (*b*) Aggregate energy use rises with urbanization, confirming the strong link between energy consumption and greenhouse emissions with development; (*c*) Disaggregate energy-use profiles suggest that the sectoral and fuel-use shifts accompanying urbanization have greenhouse-augmenting potential, particularly from the rising electricity and transportation needs of development.

Given past development patterns and the constraints of currently available technology, urbanization is an inevitable concomitant of industrialization and economic growth. Given an acceptance of the desirability of basic developmental goals and the necessary role of industrialization in securing and sustaining higher incomes and consumption levels, policies to restrict urban growth in less developed countries are not the best strategies to reduce the concomitant global environmental pollution.

Economic theory holds that any such negative externality is best addressed directly with reference to the specific pollution-causing activity or activities.[13] We have attempted to demonstrate that, at least as far as energy use is concerned, we can more or less pinpoint where and to what extent the problems occur. Our disaggregative analysis brought out the pre-eminent role of petroleum-based fuel use in transportation in contributing to high levels of per capita energy consumption. This heightened transportation energy use may not all be due to the overall magnitude of urbanization, but is attributed by some to commuting activities that occur disproportionately within *large* metropolitan areas. Our results also anticipate a dominant role for electricity use in final demands for energy by significant sectors of developing economies. Accordingly, we take up for discussion four areas of intervention: (1) policies toward city sizes; (2) urban transportation policies; (3) options for power-generation; and (4) policies relating to energy conservation.

It is easy to extend some of the arguments of Section II to formulate hypotheses about the additional impact of large cities in augmenting a country's energy requirements, over and above energy use associated with the magnitude of urbanization, as represented by a country's per cent urban. Energy consumption in transportation may be high in large agglomerations due to the considerably higher demand for intra-urban commuting, and energy-wasteful urban congestion when it occurs during peak traffic periods. Thus, the dominance of large urban areas in a country's city size distribution may well cause higher rates of per capita commercial energy consumption. On the other hand, having the bulk of the urban population and economic activity concentrated in large cities might save on goods transportation costs, due to economies in the transportation of tradeables across large distances, compared with a more dispersed urban network. Likewise, it might be possible to economize on some of the energy-intensive infrastructure of public service provision with a more concentrated than dispersed urban system. The net effect is thus unclear, on *a priori* grounds.

To ascertain the net effects of the pattern of urbanization on aggregate energy use, as distinct from the total magnitude of the phenomenon accounted for by the standard explanatory variables of Table 1, we utilize the residual country-specific influences captured through the fixed-effects intercepts reported in Appendix I. In addition to the possible effects of urban concentration, the magnitudes of these intercepts, as we have observed, are also likely to reflect policy or fuel-availability-induced energy choices. Accordingly, we regress these country-specific intercepts on cross-sectional variables relating to (*a*) a country's urbanization structure, and (*b*) its vulnerability to international oil prices. The variables representing the hypothesized influences of city size in a country's urban population distribution are PRIMACY (the largest city's share of a country's urban population), URBCON (the percentage of its urban population residing in cities with population in excess of 500,000), NUMCIT (the number of cities with population in excess of 500,000), and, finally, PARETO (a parameter estimate of the exponent of the Pareto distribution fitted to the country's rank-size structure), a rather more broad-based distribution parameter.[14]

Results are presented in Table 5 of various combinations of these explanatory variables. Coefficients of the oil price vulnerability index, OPRINDX,[15] representing the 'price effect' on national energy demand,

Table 5: Fixed Effects Intercepts, Oil Price Sensitivity and Urban Structure

N	66	69	69	24	24	24	24	24	22
	(1)	(2)	(3)	(4)	(5)	(6)	(7)	(8)	(9)
PRIMACY	–0.0036					–0.0068			
	(–0.56)					(–0.64)			
URBCON		0.0189*					0.0207*		
		(4.38)					(2.83)		
NUMCIT			0.0228†					0.0483†	
			(2.35)					(2.54)	
PARETO				0.6801					2.3779†
				(0.75)					(2.16)
OPRINDX					–0.0821†	–0.0912†	–0.0457	–0.1209*	–0.0419
					(–2.12)	(–2.19)	(–1.27)	(–3.20)	(–0.99)
Constant	3.3874	2.5447	3.1546	2.9202	3.1320	3.3859	2.1882	3.0538	0.6141
R-squared	0.0048	0.0229	0.0761	0.0250	0.1702	0.1863	0.3997	0.3652	0.2002

Dependent Variable: Intercepts from fixed effects regression reported in Table 1.
Explanatory Variables:
PRIMACY = Per cent of urban population in largest city (per cent)
URBCON = Per cent of urban population in cities exceeding 500,000 (per cent)
NUMCIT = Number of cities with population exceeding 500,000
PARETO = Estimated parameter from Pareto distribution of city sizes (see text)
OPRINDX = Oil price sensitivity index (see text)
* = 1%; † = 5%; ‡ = 10% levels of significance in two-tailed tests (figures in parentheses are t-statistics).
Data Sources: *Social Indicators of Development,* World Bank; Appendix I.

are expectedly negative. Most specifications reveal our measures of urban concentration (with the striking exception of PARETO) to contribute to high per capita levels of energy usage, suggesting the fuel-intensive nature of urban networks dominated by large cities. This exercise would thus indicate a potential impact of policies toward urbanization on energy-use-related greenhouse gas discharges. But, how reasonable is it to use the city-size distribution as an instrument for reducing energy use on greenhouse effect grounds? To the extent that the high energy usages incurred as a concomitant of urban growth may be considered the legitimate costs of production in large cities, warranted by the productivity advantages of agglomeration,[16] it is moot whether the distant and somewhat questionable benefits of reducing additions to greenhouse emissions outweigh the unquestionable gains from concentration. It may not be justifiable to force upon poor countries (where extreme urban concentration occurs precisely to realize such benefits) a course of action that would deny them the urban agglomeration economies so essential to the process of productive industrialization and economic growth.

If large-city energy use is attributable, as has been suggested, to 'excessive' commuting, congestion, and motorized vehicle use, a better targeting of emission-control efforts seems warranted. Rather than comprehensive policies towards city size, selective urban transportation options should be exercised to reduce global warming potential. The quantum and type of energy consumed in transportation will be sensitive to the kind of urban transit modes used in any context — these vary from the high per capita gasoline-using private automobile to the relatively low per capita energy-using electric rail mass transit.[17] It is appropriate to factor the global warming implications of alternative systems into any consideration of urban transportation choices. Actions to reduce greenhouse discharges associated with urban living might include more emphasis on mass transit in large cities of developing countries than many developed countries have seen fit to accord. So too, is a focus on facilitating urban spatial structures that avoid excessive energy-intensive commuting. We shall see below that the choice of electric energy as opposed to gasoline and diesel for transportation and stationary fuel uses seems favoured in view of *indirect* emissions as well.

The disaggregated analysis of the last section highlighted the prospect of increased final use demands for electricity with urbanization and economic development. Electricity consumption increases entail, of course, more power generation. While some developing countries, such as Brazil, depend on hydroelectric power generation, many burn fossil fuels to produce electricity. Hence a move from petroleum-based fuel use to electricity in many final demand sectors (including transportation) may not necessarily mitigate the problem of greenhouse discharges, but merely shift it to an earlier 'stage' in the economy-wide production chain. How might energy choices between petroleum and electricity in developing countries be made sensitive to the global warming question? To examine the implications of greenhouse effects of energy sector policy, we focus on the examination of CO_2 emissions stemming from the relatively narrow category of fossil fuel use in a cross-section of the world's countries. This category includes both fossil fuel largely committed to transportation uses, as well as that used in thermal power generation. Thermal power generation—a CO_2-emitting activity—goes

Table 6: Greenhouse Emissions — Transportation vs. Power Generation

LN (CO_2) due to	*Solid, Gas and Liquid Fuel Use*			*Liquid Fuel Use Only*		
N	68 (1)	68 (2)	68 (3)	68 (1)	68 (2)	68 (3)
LN(MOTGAS)	0.3693* (5.60)			0.4999* (7.68)		
LN(GASDIE)		0.4868* (5.12)			0.6903* (7.47)	
LN(TRNGAS)			0.4780* (5.62)			0.6642* (8.13)
LN(THMPWR)	0.4405* (8.55)	0.3694* (5.57)	0.3878* (6.59)	0.2281* (4.48)	0.1132‡ (1.75)	0.1470* (2.60)
Constant	–0.4856	–0.1358	–0.3405	–1.4636	–0.8495	–1.1959
R-squared	0.8677	0.8603	0.8680	0.8295	0.8250	0.8388

Dependent Variable: Log of anthropogenic additions to carbon dioxide flux (metric tonnes carbon per capita)

Explanatory Variables:

MOTGAS = Motor gas consumption (metric tonnes per capita)

GASDIE = Gas-Diesel oil consumption (metric tonnes per capita)

TRNGAS = Sum of MOTGAS and GASDIE (metric tonnes per capita)

THMPWR = Thermal power generation (million kilowatt hours)

* = 1%; † = 5%; ‡ = 10% levels of significance in two-tailed tests (figures in parentheses are t-statistics).

Data Sources: *Energy Statistics Yearbook, 1985,* United Nations; *World Resources, 1990–91*, World Resources Institute.

together with, as we have remarked, final use of electricity in various sectors of the economy.

To assess the relative contributions of transportation and non-transportation uses to per capita emissions from the burning of fossil fuels, we regress the latter against actual per capita consumption levels of motor gasoline, gasoline and diesel, the sum of the two, and against thermal power generation activity across the sample of countries.[18] Results appear in Table 6. Greenhouse flux elasticities are by and large significantly smaller with respect to electricity generation compared with those of gasoline or diesel or total transport fuel consumption. The superiority of thermal power over combined gasoline and diesel consumption is implied, for example, by equation (3), which confirms that electricity generation (usage is relatively emission-free) is generally less damaging to the global environment than is the direct combustion of fossil fuels, an advantage, (not surprisingly) further accentuated when only liquid fuels are considered. The implied social preference for electricity use in the entire range of final use sectors—industry and transportation in particular—subsumes favouring electric mass transit over automobile-based urban transportation options.

Finally, we return to the issue raised at the end of Section V. How realistic are extrapolations based on existing fuel uses in both developed and developing countries as accurate predictors of the contribution of development-related energy use by the latter to the alleged global warming? Just as developing countries are different from developed countries as to sector-mix and fuel endowment, today's developing countries are likely to experience very different energy-efficient technological options in future—new technologies arising in response to more stringent norms will be available in the latters' course of development, which were absent when today's industrialized countries developed. Even the recent experience of developed countries in this regard gives cause for optimism. Over the past decade, per capita energy consumption in Organization for Economic Co-operation and Development (OECD) countries has either declined or remained constant while their economies continued to grow; increased automotive fuel efficiency, more efficient cooking and heating devices and major energy efficiency improvements in the commercial sector, especially in building and lighting, have substantially aided energy performance in developed countries. Such innovations and others hold promise for developed and developing countries alike, the latters' development potential itself often providing special opportunities for their application. Modernizing agriculture, for example, offers scope for much potential gain in fuel efficiency from design improvements in say, irrigation pumpsets. Energy conservation in the course of industrialization may be achievable by reducing energy-intensity coefficients, both by lowering fuel consumption norms through appropriate technological design, as well as by realizing productivity gains through enlarging the scale of production due to the expansion of trade or with urban growth.[19]

According to World Resources Institute (1989), the World Bank, in 1983, expected electricity production in developing countries to triple by 1995, implying an annual growth rate of 7.7 per cent. Additional power sources necessary for this increase could exact a heavy toll on the environment. However, the report noted, increasing the efficiency of electricity use in developing countries instead of expanding capacity offers the unambiguous advantage of avoiding the negative environmental effects of increasing supply. According to the report, '[p]roblems of acidic deposition, climate change, stratospheric ozone depletion, Third World debt, global economic development, and national security are all exacerbated by wasteful energy use. Finding more efficient ways of using energy must, therefore, be a part of any comprehensive approach to dealing with the issue ... The environmental consequences of burning fossil fuels make energy conservation an attractive means of addressing a variety of critical problems ranging from local air pollution to global climatic change.'[20] Cities of developing countries face more serious immediate consequences as a result of local rather than global pollution; it is likely that priority efforts will be directed at the former rather than the latter. However, energy conservation, as a consensus goal, is more likely to be embraced by developing country policy-makers due to the other significant benefits it can confer on these countries. International organizations concerned with short-term financial stability, long-term world development, and with monitoring and policing the global environment would do well to heed this essential message in crafting any broadly acceptable greenhouse agreement.

Appendix I: Ranking of Intercepts From Fixed Effects Estimation

Fourth Quartile		Third Quartile	
Norway	5.513	Botswana	4.108
United States	5.357	Jamaica	4.034
Panama	5.287	Mexico	4.013
Trinidad	5.239	China	3.894
Surinam	5.054	Colombia	3.878
Saudi Arabia	4.931	Zambia	3.844
South Africa	4.843	Uruguay	3.824
Oman	4.749	Korea, Rep. of	3.809
Venezuela	4.621	Fiji	3.748
Germany, Fed. Rep.	4.545	Syrian Arab Rep.	3.736
Yugoslavia	4.482	Turkey	3.679
Gabon	4.382	Swaziland	3.666
Japan	4.358	Brazil	3.659
Argentina	4.333	Algeria	3.648
Singapore	4.289	Peru	3.594
Barbados	4.252	Costa Rica	3.571
Greece	4.245	Malta	3.556
Australia	4.237	Liberia	3.553
Zimbabwe	4.186	Egypt	3.549
		Papua New Guinea	3.361
Second Quartile		**First Quartile**	
Bolivia	3.356	Paraguay	2.724
Senegal	3.351	Sudan	2.696
Tunisia	3.302	Cameroon	2.516
Thailand	3.215	Zaire	2.425
Nicaragua	3.174	Tanzania	2.286
Kenya	3.146	Malawi	2.248
Philippines	3.092	Myanmar	2.231
Honduras	3.043	Somalia	2.104
Hong Kong	3.037	Togo	2.101
Indonesia	3.008	Uganda	2.042
Pakistan	2.981	Nigeria	2.032
Ghana	2.978	Benin	1.854
Mauritania	2.977	Niger	1.708
Mauritius	2.951	Rwanda	1.659
India	2.946	Central African Rep.	1.657
Morocco	2.939	Ethiopia	1.509
Congo, People's Rep.	2.922	Chad	1.415
Cote d'Ivoire	2.892	Burkina Faso	1.169
Sri Lanka	2.763	Nepal	1.078
El Salvador	2.734		

Appendix II: Fuel Use Elasticities With Respect to GNP Per Capita, Developing Countries

	INDUSTRY & CONSTRUCTION				TRANSPORTATION					OTHER CONSUMPTION				
Fuel Type	*Ind & Con Subtotal*	*Iron & Steel*	*Chemical*	*Other*	*Trans Subtotal*	*Road*	*Rail*	*Air*	*Water-ways*	*Oth Con Subtotal*	*House-hold*	*Agri-culture*	*Other*	*Final Consump*
HLP	N=29			N=19	N=12		N=12			N=15			N=13	N=31
	0.1174			0.2403	−1.9682		−1.9682			0.1174			−2.2134	0.0273
	(0.14)			(0.26)	(.096)		(−0.96)			(0.07)			(−1.20)	(0.04)
	Rsq			Rsq	Rsq		Rsq			Rsq			Rsq	Rsq
	0.0007			0.0038	0.0844		0.0844			0.0004			0.1155	0.0000
LPP	N=15			N=16	N=48	N=46		N=46		N=48	N=40	N=14	N=21	N=48
	2.2086^{-}			2.2236‡	1.0383*	1.1685*		−0.1447		0.5742*	0.5495*	−1.9861	−0.1708	0.9985*
	(1.99)			(1.92)	(11.94)	(12.17)		(−0.32)		(4.62)	(3.80)	(−1.10)	(−0.19)	(15.22)
	Rsq			Rsq	Rsq	Rsq		Rsq		Rsq	Rsq	Rsq	Rsq	Rsq
	0.1467			0.2090	0.7557	0.7709		0.0023		0.3165	0.2747	0.0920	0.0020	0.8342
HPP	N=46			N=29	N=48	N=34	N=15		N=15	N=38	N=14	N=28	N=27	N=48
	1.4443*			1.4038*	0.9152*	0.8142*	0.5406		1.3311*	0.7955*	2.2128	1.1293*	0.7901*	1.0352*
	(10.95)			(7.71)	(9.35)	(5.20)	(1.76)		(3.14)	(4.75)	(0.85)	(4.40)	(3.92)	(13.68)
	Rsq			Rsq	Rsq	Rsq	Rsq		Rsq	Rsq	Rsq	Rsq	Rsq	Rsq
	0.7316			0.6879	0.6554	0.4580	0.1926		0.4313	0.3848	0.0569	0.4265	0.3805	0.8027
GAS	N=24			N=13						N=15	N=11		N=9	N=24
	1.3291*			1.1729*						0.9281*	0.9617*		0.8099	1.2755*
	(5.22)			(3.10)						(3.39)	(2.84)		(1.57)	(5.94)
	Rsq			Rsq						Rsq	Rsq		Rsq	Rsq
	0.5530			0.4661						0.4696	0.4729		0.2599	0.6159

(*Contd.*)

Appendix II: *(Contd.)*

Fuel Type	INDUSTRY & CONSTRUCTION				TRANSPORTATION					OTHER CONSUMPTION				
	Ind & Con Subtotal	*Iron & Steel*	*Chemical*	*Other*	*Trans Subtotal*	*Road*	*Rail*	*Air*	*Water-ways*	*Oth Con Subtotal*	*House-hold*	*Agri-culture*	*Other*	*Final Consump*
ELE	N=48	N=14	N=16	N=36	N=12					N=48	N=47	N=26	N=47	N=48
	0.9317*	1.6498	1.3230	0.8235*	1.5078					1.1372*	1.1794*	–0.3697	1.1881*	1.0661*
	(8.99)	(1.52)	(1.64)	(5.38)	(1.03)					(17.20)	(17.74)	(–0.59)	(11.50)	(14.99)
	Rsq	Rsq	Rsq	Rsq	Rsq					Rsq	Rsq	Rsq	Rsq	Rsq
	0.6371	0.1614	0.1610	0.4593	0.0965					0.8656	0.8750	0.0141	0.7462	0.8301
BIO	N=34			N=35						N=46	N=44			N=47
	0.5914†			0.6000†						–1.5968	–1.6438*			–1.4395*
	(2.61)			(2.62)						(–4.09)	(–4.14)			(–3.70)
	Rsq			Rsq						Rsq	Rsq			Rsq
	0.1757			0.1726						0.2753	0.2895			0.2337
TOTAL	N=48	N=25	N=22	N=46	N=48	N=45	N=20	N=48	N=17	N=48	N=48	N=37	N=47	N=48
	1.0903*	0.8967	2.3086†	0.8345*	0.9851*	1.0002*	0.5275	–0.5605	1.3762	0.2600*	0.1948‡	–0.0449	1.0180*	0.6996*
	(12.33)	(1.27)	(2.74)	(5.24)	(14.66)	(13.87)	(1.26)	(–1.22)	(1.18)	(3.20)	(1.88)	(–0.08)	(12.05)	(14.61)
	Rsq	Rsq	Rsq	Rsq	Rsq	Rsq	Rsq	Rsq	Rsq	Rsq	Rsq	Rsq	Rsq	Rsq
	0.7678	0.0658	0.2730	0.3845	0.8235	0.8174	0.0804	0.0313	0.0848	0.1821	0.0712	0.0002	0.7633	0.8225

Appendix III: Fuel Use Elasticities With Respect to Urbanization, Developing Countries

	INDUSTRY & CONSTRUCTION				TRANSPORTATION					OTHER CONSUMPTION				
Fuel Type	*Ind & Con Subtotal*	*Iron & Steel*	*Chemical*	*Other*	*Trans Subtotal*	*Road*	*Rail*	*Air*	*Water-ways*	*Oth Con Subtotal*	*House-hold*	*Agri-culture*	*Other*	*Final Consump*
HLP	N=29			N=19	N=12		N=12			N=15			N=13	N=31
	–0.7456			–0.0657	–2.7247		–2.7247			1.0220			–2.8406	–0.7256
	(–0.62)			(–0.05)	(–1.16)		(–1.16)			(0.42)			(–0.98)	(–0.65)
	Rsq			Rsq	Rsq		Rsq			Rsq			Rsq	Rsq
	0.0136			0.0001	0.1190		0.1190			0.0135			0.0800	0.0144
LPP	N=25			N=16	N=48	N=46		N=47		N=48	N=40	N=14	N=22	N=48
	3.8117[†]			3.6222[†]	1.5570[*]	1.7821[*]		–0.4759		1.0270[*]	1.0137[*]	–2.9987	–0.5322	1.4752[*]
	(2.08)			(2.20)	(7.85)	(7.85)		(–0.56)		(4.88)	(4.10)	(–1.21)	(–0.42)	(8.54)
	Rsq			Rsq	Rsq	Rsq		Rsq		Rsq	Rsq	Rsq	Rsq	Rsq
	0.1582			0.2565	0.5722	0.5837		0.0070		0.3409	0.3065	0.1083	0.0089	0.6131
HPP	N=46			N=29	N=48	N=34	N=15		N=15	N=38	N=14	N=28	N=27	N=48
	2.1103[*]			2.2790[*]	1.2518[*]	1.1813[*]	0.9449		1.2249[‡]	1.1931[*]	0.9533	1.3018[*]	0.9698[*]	1.5122[*]
	(7.71)			(5.91)	(5.69)	(4.38)	(2.20)		(1.71)	(4.64)	(0.20)	(3.83)	(2.88)	(7.92)
	Rsq			Rsq	Rsq	Rsq	Rsq		Rsq	Rsq	Rsq	Rsq	Rsq	Rsq
	0.5746			0.5637	0.4129	0.3752	0.2712		0.1839	0.3740	0.0034	0.3606	0.2490	0.5766

(Contd.)

Appendix III: (*Contd.*)

	INDUSTRY & CONSTRUCTION				TRANSPORTATION					OTHER CONSUMPTION				
Fuel Type	*Ind & Con Subtotal*	*Iron & Steel*	*Chemical*	*Other*	*Trans Subtotal*	*Road*	*Rail*	*Air*	*Water-ways*	*Oth Con Subtotal*	*House-hold*	*Agri-culture*	*Other*	*Final Consump*
GAS	N=24			N=13						N=15	N=11		N=9	N=24
	1.7312†			1.2902						1.4738‡	1.4557‡		1.8717	1.9219*
	(2.29)			(1.15)						(2.11)	(1.86)		(2.07)	(2.98)
	Rsq			Rsq						Rsq	Rsq		Rsq	Rsq
	0.1927			0.1072						0.2556	0.2767		0.3797	0.2871
ELE	N=48	N=14	N=16	N=36	N=12					N=48	N=47	N=26	N=47	N=48
	1.5920*	3.1750‡	2.8787‡	1.3331*	3.5261‡					1.7466*	1.7705*	0.1114	1.7889*	1.6961*
	(8.78)	(1.97)	(1.96)	(4.43)	(2.15)					(10.06)	(10.19)	(0.12)	(8.19)	(10.55)
	Rsq	Rsq	Rsq	Rsq	Rsq					Rsq	Rsq	Rsq	Rsq	Rsq
	0.6263	0.2441	0.2096	0.3658	0.3167					0.6875	0.6975	0.0006	0.5985	0.7075
BIO	N=34			N=35						N=46	N=44			N=47
	0.8368†			0.8446†						–1.8641*	–1.9111*			–1.7022†
	(2.56)			(2.56)						(–2.69)	(–2.71)			(–2.46)
	Rsq			Rsq						Rsq	Rsq			Rsq
	0.1703			0.1660						0.1410	0.1487			0.1184
TOTAL	N=48	N=25	N=22	N=46	N=48	N=45	N=20	N=48	N=17	N=48	N=48	N=37	N=47	N=48
	1.5846*	1.5104	4.6534†	1.1922*	1.4290*	1.5003*	1.1784†	–0.3539	2.2131	0.1741	0.0232	0.2511	1.5202*	0.8496
	(7.44)	(1.13)	(2.70)	(3.87)	(8.03)	(7.98)	(2.25)	(–0.44)	(1.39)	(1.14)	(0.13)	(0.33)	(8.25)	(5.63)
	Rsq	Rsq	Rsq	Rsq	Rsq	Rsq	Rsq	Rsq	Rsq	Rsq	Rsq	Rsq	Rsq	Rsq
	0.5460	0.0525	0.2663	0.2537	0.5835	0.5969	0.2188	0.0042	0.1140	0.0275	0.0003	0.0030	0.6021	0.4084

Appendix IV: CO_2 Emission Elasticities With Respect to Fuel Use, Developing Countries

	INDUSTRY & CONSTRUCTION				TRANSPORTATION					OTHER CONSUMPTION				
Fuel Type	*Ind & Con Subtotal*	*Iron & Steel*	*Chemical*	*Other*	*Trans Subtotal*	*Road*	*Rail*	*Air*	*Water-ways*	*Oth Con Subtotal*	*House-hold*	*Agri-culture*	*Other*	*Final Consump*
HLP	N=23			N=11	N=11		N=11			N=12			N=10	N=24
	0.0647			0.0236	–0.0417		–0.0417			–0.0117			–0.0336	0.0608
	(1.17)			(0.29)	(–0.62)		(–0.62)			(–0.19)			(–0.52)	(1.12)
	Rsq			Rsq	Rsq		Rsq			Rsq			Rsq	Rsq
	0.0614			0.0060	0.0404		0.0404			0.0034			0.0328	0.0537
LPP	N=20			N=13	N=36	N=34		N=35		N=36	N=30	N=13	N=18	N=36
	0.1441*			0.1222	0.5345*	0.4630*		0.1298		0.3245	0.2656	–0.0642	0.0126	0.5964*
	(2.92)			(1.53)	(3.83)	(3.43)		(1.65)		(1.86)	(1.37)	(–1.20)	(0.17)	(4.04)
	Rsq			Rsq	Rsq	Rsq		Rsq		Rsq	Rsq	Rsq	Rsq	Rsq
	0.3218			0.1746	0.3016	0.2390		0.0760		0.0925	0.0632	0.1164	0.0019	0.3243
HPP	N=35			N=22	N=36	N=25	N=12		N=10	N=31	N=12	N=25	N=21	N=36
	0.2414†			0.2054	0.4607*	0.4280†	0.0029		0.5136†	0.4116†	–0.0248	0.3570†	0.4815‡	0.4496
	(2.17)			(1.27)	(2.99)	(2.43)	(0.01)		(3.10)	(2.31)	(–0.57)	(2.21)	(1.89)	(2.96)
	Rsq			Rsq	Rsq	Rsq	Rsq		Rsq	Rsq	Rsq	Rsq	Rsq	Rsq
	0.1244			0.0744	0.2079	0.2043	0.0000		0.5454	0.1553	0.0315	0.1755	0.1575	0.2053
GAS	N=16									N=11				N=16
	0.2649									0.2770				0.2501
	(1.45)									(1.13)				(1.30)
	Rsq									Rsq				Rsq
	0.1297									0.1233				0.1073

(Contd.)

Appendix IV: (*Contd.*)

	INDUSTRY & CONSTRUCTION				TRANSPORTATION					OTHER CONSUMPTION				
Fuel Type	*Ind & Con Subtotal*	*Iron & Steel*	*Chemical*	*Other*	*Trans Subtotal*	*Road*	*Rail*	*Air*	*Water-ways*	*Oth Con Subtotal*	*House-hold*	*Agri-culture*	*Other*	*Final Consump*
ELE	N=36 0.3842† (2.42) Rsq 0.1471	N=12 0.8692* (10.63) Rsq 0.1014	N=13 0.0715 (0.80) Rsq 0.0552	N=28 0.3791‡ (2.04) Rsq 0.1375	N=9 0.0199 (0.22) Rsq 0.0069					N=36 0.4826* (3.22) Rsq 0.2336	N=35 0.4820* (3.22) Rsq 0.2394	N=21 0.1304 (0.67) Rsq 0.0233	N=35 0.3591† (2.41) Rsq 0.1500	N=36 0.4848* (3.15) Rsq 0.2254
BIO	N=27 0.3340 (1.59) Rsq 0.0923			N=28 0.3814‡ (1.92) Rsq 0.1238						N=35 –0.0410 (–0.65) Rsq 0.0128	N=33 –0.0542 (–0.86) Rsq 0.0235			N=35 –0.0397 (–0.63) Rsq 0.0118
TOTAL	N=36 0.4232* (2.80) Rsq 0.1876	N=20 0.0639 (0.88) Rsq 0.0416	N=17 0.0820 (1.41) Rsq 0.1171	N=35 0.4005† (2.65) Rsq 0.1759	N=36 0.5823* (3.82) Rsq 0.3005	N=33 0.5706* (3.57) Rsq 0.2915	N=17 –0.1133 (–0.62) Rsq 0.0247	N=36 0.1186 (1.53) Rsq 0.0646	N=12 0.0048 0.06) Rsq 0.0004	N=36 0.9060* (3.25) Rsq 0.2367	N=36 0.5411† (2.26) Rsq 0.1306	N=30 0.2182 (1.67) Rsq 0.0907	N=35 0.5473* (3.04) Rsq 0.2184	N=36 0.9468* (4.00) Rsq 0.3203

Appendix V: Total Greenhouse Gas Emission Elasticities With Respect to Fuel Use, Developing Countries

	INDUSTRY & CONSTRUCTION				TRANSPORTATION					OTHER CONSUMPTION				
Fuel Type	*Ind & Con Subtotal*	*Iron & Steel*	*Chemical*	*Other*	*Trans Subtotal*	*Road*	*Rail*	*Air*	*Water-ways*	*Oth Con Subtotal*	*House-hold*	*Agri-culture*	*Other*	*Final Consump*
HLP	N=23			N=16	N=11		N=11			N=12			N=10	N=24
	0.0135			0.0056	0.0074		0.0074			–0.0353			–0.0576	0.0103
	(0.33)			(0.10)	(0.15)		(0.15)			(–0.79)			(–1.36)	(0.25)
	Rsq			Rsq	Rsq		Rsq			Rsq			Rsq	Rsq
	0.0051			0.0006	0.0024		0.0024			0.0584			0.1866	0.0029
LPP	N=20			N=13	N=36	N=34		N=35		N=36	N=30	N=13	N=18	N=36
	0.0900†			0.0608	0.4770*	0.4162*		0.0973		0.2917†	0.2515	–0.0540	–0.0194	0.5273*
	(2.49)			(1.12)	(4.68)	(4.13)		(1.56)		(2.17)	(1.69)	(-1.44)	(-0.37)	(4.90)
	Rsq			Rsq	Rsq	Rsq		Rsq		Rsq	Rsq	Rsq	Rsq	Rsq
	0.2561			0.1020	0.3919	0.3475		0.0691		0.1220	0.0929	0.1585	0.0085	0.4137
HPP	N=35			N=22	N=36	N=25	N=12		N=10	N=31	N=12	N=25	N=21	N=36
	0.2276†			0.1799	0.4103*	0.3582*	–0.0054		0.3287†	0.3071†	–0.0290	0.2931*	0.3129	0.4038*
	(2.70)			(1.51)	(3.54)	(2.75)	(–0.03)		(2.48)	(2.35)	(–0.93)	(2.69)	(1.68)	(3.55)
	Rsq			Rsq	Rsq	Rsq	Rsq		Rsq	Rsq	Rsq	Rsq	Rsq	Rsq
	0.1810			0.1028	0.2690	0.2472	0.0001		0.4353	0.1598	0.0792	0.2498	0.1300	0.2703
GAS	N=16									N=11				N=16
	0.2919									0.2885				0.2878
	(2.11)									(1.57)				(1.97)
	Rsq									Rsq				Rsq
	0.2416									0.2152				0.2177

(*Contd.*)

Appendix V: (*Contd.*)

Fuel Type	INDUSTRY & CONSTRUCTION: Ind & Con Subtotal	Iron & Steel	Chemical	Other	TRANSPORTATION: Trans Subtotal	Road	Rail	Air	Water-ways	OTHER CONSUMPTION: Oth Con Subtotal	House-hold	Agri-culture	Other	Final Consump
ELE	N=36	N=12	N=13	N=28	N=9					N=36	N=35	N=21	N=35	N=36
	0.3207†	0.0551	0.0500	0.2555	0.0172					0.4506*	0.4459*	0.0606	0.3295*	0.4311*
	(2.61)	(0.84)	(0.65)	(1.73)	(0.25)					(4.12)	(4.19)	(0.43)	(3.00)	(3.74)
	Rsq	Rsq	Rsq	Rsq	Rsq					Rsq	Rsq	Rsq	Rsq	Rsq
	0.1673	0.0666	0.0373	0.1029	0.0088					0.3325	0.3472	0.0010	0.2140	0.2909
BIO	N=27			N=28						N=35	N=33			N=35
	0.2821‡			0.2731‡						–0.0550	–0.0651			–0.0542
	(1.92)			(1.91)						(–1.16)	(–1.40)			(–1.13)
	Rsq			Rsq						Rsq	Rsq			Rsq
	0.1285			0.1231						0.0391	0.0598			0.0374
TOTAL	N=36	N=20	N=17	N=35	N=36	N=33	N=17	N=36	N=12	N=36	N=36	N=30	N=35	N=36
	0.3772*	0.0421	0.0654	0.3032†	0.5156*	0.5106*	–0.0100	0.0917	–0.0074	0.7364*	0.4832†	0.1841‡	0.4666*	0.8482*
	(3.31)	(0.77)	(1.35)	(2.61)	(4.61)	(4.28)	(0.07)	(1.51)	(–0.13)	(3.41)	(2.64)	(1.98)	(3.49)	(4.96)
	Rsq	Rsq	Rsq	Rsq	Rsq	Rsq	Rsq	Rsq	Rsq	Rsq	Rsq	Rsq	Rsq	Rsq
	0.2432	0.0321	0.1078	0.1707	0.3845	0.3712	0.0345	0.0630	0.0017	0.2551	0.1699	0.1230	0.2689	0.4196

NOTES

Research for this paper was performed while Vibhooti Shukla was visiting the Indira Gandhi Institute of Development Research in February–May 1991. The authors are grateful to Shantanu Deshpande, Ravindra Rao, Mahesh Mohan, Andrew Ewoh and Annabella Pronesti for research assistance and help with the preparation of the manuscript. An abridged version of this paper has been accepted for publication in *Global Environmental Change*, Butterworth Publishers, UK.

1 See Shukla and Parikh (1992) for a cross-national discussion of local air pollution issues in the context of urbanization.
2 The 1965–87 data series used is from World Bank (1989), and covers most of the world's countries, both developing and developed.
3 Ideally, an econometric investigation of energy consumption would include expenditure shares and prices of various types of fuél. Since these are not available for all countries in our sample over a comparable period of any length, we omit energy prices from our list of independent variables for the time-series-cross-sectional analysis. To some extent, these omitted influences are captured through the fixed-effects specification described in Note 5 below. In Section VI, we more systematically investigate the role of cross-national variation in fuel prices (through an 'oil price sensitivity index') in explaining countries' energy consumption differences. See Berndt and Wood (1975) for an example of a rigorous empirical implementation of a production-based energy demand system for the US economy.
4 If ECpc = a country's per capita energy consumption, and URB = the percentage of its population that is urban, the elasticity of energy demand with respect to urbanization is defined as [dECpc/dURB] × [URB/ECpc], and may also be expressed in natural logarithms as [dlnECpc/dlnURB]. The elasticity estimate of 0.47 is to be interpreted as follows: A 1 per cent increase in a country's urban population leads to a 0.47 per cent rise in its per capita total energy consumption. For a comparable cross-sectional exercise with a 1980 sample of developing countries only, see Jones (1989).
5 The proposed structure for treating pooled cross-sectional and time-series data is to decompose the disturbance term (e_{it}) in the hypothesized relationship into a time-invariant, country-specific effect and remaining random effects representing the net influence of omitted variables which vary over both countries and time, as follows: $e_{it} = u_i + v_{it}$. The fixed-effects model estimated here treats u_i as a fixed but unobserved constant differing across countries, responsible for an intercept shift in their energy consumption rates. Such a model may be implemented by introducing country-specific dummies in an ordinary least squares regression. Values for dummies are reported by country in Appendix I. See Dielman (1989) for a general econometric discussion of error components models.
6 Additions to the carbon dioxide flux from various activities are estimated annually for a group of the world's countries by the Carbon Dioxide

Information Analysis Center (CDIAC), Environmental Sciences Division, Oak Ridge National Laboratory. WRI (1989) compiles and presents published and unpublished data on global greenhouse gas emissions from this and other sources.

7 Data for fuel use by type and final use sector are from United Nations (1988a), a recurrent publication which presents energy data for developing countries in the format of overall energy balances and electricity profiles.

8 See, for example, Parikh (1980) for a cross-national study of energy demand and supply in developing countries, and Parikh (1981) for a policy simulation model of energy demand for India.

9 In other, unreported, regressions, we document the sensitivity of fuel-switching within selected sectors to the hypothesized set of development indicators. In the industry and transportation sector, energy from heavy petroleum production, and significantly, electricity, appears to replace that from hard coal, lignite and peat with urbanization. The transportation sector, likewise, features shifts from hard coal, etc., to petroleum products with increasing incomes. In the household sector, the transition from biomass to light petroleum energy (including kerosene used for cooking fuel and lighting) and thence a progression to electricity are in evidence. Finally, as agricultural intensification associated with urbanization proceeds, electricity also replaces light petroleum use (through electric irrigation pumps replacing gasoline-powered ones, for example) in that sector.

10 The elasticities estimated are, respectively, [dlnFUpc/dlnGNP] and [dln FUpc/dlnURB], where FUpc = fuel use per capita (for a given fuel type and final use sector), GNPpc = a country's Gross National Product per capita, and URB = the percentage of its population living in urban areas. The elasticities for total energy consumption (bottom right cell in Appendixes II and III) in each case are higher than those reported in Table 1. This is partly due to structurally higher rates of energy use in developing countries, and partly because of the non-inclusion of other contextual variables and the absence of control for fixed effects due to the smaller sample sizes in the present case. The latter should not, however, compromise the utility of these estimates for order-of-magnitude prediction exercises.

11 Definitions of the elasticities reported in Appendixes IV and V are [dln CO_2pc/dlnFUpc], and [dlnGGpc/dlnFUpc], where CO_2pc = per capita annual discharges of carbon dioxide, GGpc = per capita net additions to total greenhouse gas emissions, and FUpc = per capita energy use by fuel type and final demand sector.

12 These simple calculations are based on the formula: [dlnGGpc/dlnGNPpc] = [dlnFUpc/dlnGNPpc] × [dlnGGpc/dlnFUpc] for GNP per capita, and analogously, for per cent urban. Such 'greenhouse emission elasticities' may be computed for each disaggregated fuel-type–final-demand category.

13 The idea is that departures from such a 'first best' policy cause distortions in the form of resource misallocations in other markets. See

Baumol and Oates (1975) for a theoretical discussion of the economic consequences and relative merits of various types of environmental intervention.

14 As an alternative measure of primacy, or the dominance of large cities in a country's urban hierarchy, Rosen and Resnick (1980) estimated the exponent 'a' in the Pareto city size distribution, $R = AS^{-2}$, for 44 countries. R = the number of cities in a country with population greater than or equal to S = city population; A is a constant. A high value of this index would imply that a country's urban population is relatively evenly distributed between its cities; the lower its value of PARETO, the more 'primate' a country's city size distribution. Thus PARETO is inversely related to the other measures of urban concentration used in this analysis.

15 Parikh (1980) proposed (and computed for 35 of the world's countries) the following indicator to measure the vulnerability of a country to oil prices: {[7.5 Poil] / [X/N] × 100}, where Poil was the 1973 international price of oil in Dollars/litre, N the country's population and X, its export earnings in 1973 dollars. The indicator measures the percentage of a country's export earnings required to increase its oil consumption by 10 kgce (7.5 litres of oil) per person per year in 1973, the peak of the first oil crisis. Here, as OPRINDX, it stands as a summary proxy for the effective price premium faced by a country relative to the world price of oil in any given time period.

16 See Sveikauskas (1975) and Segal (1976) for empirical documentation of the productivity advantages of large urban agglomerations for US cities. For econometric studies of agglomeration economies in developing countries, see Shukla (1988) and Henderson (1988) for India and Brazil, respectively. Reported estimates of the 'agglomeration elasticity' or the total factor efficiency advantages of urban growth are in the vicinity of 0.06 per cent for developed, and 0.10 per cent for developing countries, for every one per cent rise in city size over observable ranges of the latter.

17 Sathaye and Meyers (1985) report studies which esitmate that for three Latin American cities, automobile use is responsible for 65–75 per cent of energy use in passenger transportation, but carries only 25–35 per cent of the total volume of traffic in terms of passenger miles. Further, energy efficiencies calculated for Hong Kong show the automobile as being some 10–15 times more energy intensive than buses. For several Latin American countries, buses are estimated to be 5–10 times more energy efficient than the automobile. The authors make the general observation that energy efficiency in transportation depends in part on the load factor of the vehicles, i.e., how well its capacity is utilized, as well as upon traffic conditions: congestion, which is often severe in many Third World cities, leads to less efficient operation of motorized vehicles. Such factors argue well for the superiority of rapid train systems in these cities, where high densities and monocentric structure would ensure ridership rates that make rail economically viable as well as congestion-reducing and energy-saving.

18 Greenhouse gas emission data are from WRI (1989). Electricity generation

and motor fuel consumption data are from United Nations (1988b), which presents information on production, trade, apparent consumption, etc. for individual energy commodities for approximately 200 countries and areas of the world.

19 Energy intensity in an activity is defined as [Energy Use/Value Added] in that industry. It may be reduced either by lowering consumption norms or raising overall productivity in an activity. For example, Rao et al. (1981) estimate energy intensities for Indian manufacturing, ranking them by industry. Among the high-intensity industries are cement, iron and steel, and fertilizers, all basic to a developing economy. Parikh (1981) reports results of international comparisons of electricity and thermal energy use per dollar of value added which show much higher figures for Indian industry than in the developed countries. This relatively inefficient use of energy is attributed to old technology, poor maintenance, and the inferior quality and wide use of coal as an energy source.

20 WRI (1989), pp. 109, 141.

REFERENCES

Baumol, W.J. and W.E. Oates (1975), *The Theory of Environmental Policy,* Prentice Hall, Englewood Cliffs.

Berndt, E.R. and D.O. Wood (1975), 'Technology, Prices and the Derived Demand for Energy', *The Review of Economics and Statistics,* Vol. 57, pp. 259–68.

Dielman, T.E. (1989), *Pooled Cross-Sectional and Time Series Data Analysis,* Marcel Dekker, Inc, New York.

Henderson, J.V. (1988), 'Evidence on the Nature of Agglomeration Effects' in *Urban Development: Theory, Fact, and Illusion,* Oxford University Press, New York.

Jones, D.W. (1988), *Energy Use and Fuel Substitution in Economic Development: What Happened in Developed Countries and What Might Be Expected in Developing Countries?* ORNL-6433, Prepared by the Oak Ridge National Laboratory, Oak Ridge, Tennessee, p 9.

————(1989), 'Energy Implications of Urbanization in the Third World', in *Spatial Policy Analysis,* ed. L. Lundqvist, L-G. Mattson and E. Erickson. Gower Publishing Company Ltd, Brookfield, VT.

Parikh, J.K. (1980), *Energy Systems and Development: Constraints, Demand and Supply of Energy for Developing Regions,* Oxford University Press, New Delhi.

————(1981), *Modelling Energy Demand for Policy Analysis.* New Delhi: Planning Commission, Government of India.

Parikh, J., K. Parikh, S. Gokarn, J. Painuly, B. Saha and V. Shukla (1991), *Consumption Patterns: The Driving Force of Environmental Stress,* a report prepared for the United Nations Conference on Environment and Development by the Indira Gandhi Institute of Development Research, Bombay.

Rao, S.S., M. Raizada, S. Iyer and A. Ramanathan (1981), 'Determinants of Energy Costs and Intensities of Goods and Services in the Indian Economy—An Input–Output Approach', in M. Chatterji, ed., *Energy and Environment in the Developing Countries,* Wiley, New York, N.Y.

Rosen, K.T. and M. Resnick (1980), 'The Size Distribution of Cities: An Examination of the Pareto Law and Primacy', *Journal of Urban Economics,* Vol. 8, pp. 165–86.

Sathaye, J. and S. Meyers (1985), 'Energy Use in Cities of the Developing Countries', *Ann. Rev. Energy,* Vol. 10, pp. 109–33.

Segal, D. (1976), 'Are There Returns to Scale in City Size?', *The Review of Economics and Statistics,* Vol. 58.

Shukla, V. (1988), *Urban Development and Regional Policy in India: An Econometric Analysis,* Himalaya Publishing House, Bombay.

Shukla, V. and K. Parikh (1992), 'The Environmental Consequences of Urban Concentration: Cross-national Perspectives on Economic Development, Air Pollution and City Size', *Urban Geography,* Vol. 13, September–October 1992.

Sveikauskas, L. (1975), 'The Productivity of Cities', *Quarterly Journal of Economics,* Vol. 89.

DATA SOURCES

United Nations, Statistical Office of the Secretariat (1988a) *Energy Balances and Electricity Profiles,* and (1988b) *Energy Statistics Yearbook;* World Bank (1989) *Social Indicators of Development;* World Resources Institute (1989); *World Resources, 1989–90.*

VI / Research Agenda

18 / Rethinking Development

VIBHOOTI SHUKLA

Book Review of *The Political Economy of Development and Underdevelopment* edited by Charles K. Wilber and Kenneth P. Jameson, Fifth Edition, McGraw-Hill, New York, 1992; pp. xvi + 656.

The book under review is the fifth edition of a compendium of readings on economic development, many of them previously published or otherwise presented in a multidisciplinary variety of fora. Prior editions span several 'epochs', from the period of early optimism of the pioneers of development thought through the recent resurgence of free market ideas and the concurrent attack on 'development' economics. This edition, as the editors put it, '... is published at the beginning of the last decade of the twentieth century, a time when the old verities are collapsing. The cold war is ending, the eastern European countries are moving from centrally planned economies of the second world to market-oriented underdeveloped countries of the third world'.

The selections in the current edition are ideologically eclectic, and provide a balanced retrospective and contemporary representation of principal forces in the thought-development of the field. While, by and large, of high scholarly quality, they are also quite accessible to the lay reader and to policy-makers. The editors' agenda is summarized thus: In the wake of a somewhat painful realization on the part of the development community that '(t)here are no easy answers'... if progress is to be made against the poverty that afflicts the majority of humankind the "bias for hope" must be rekindled and combined with serious analysis of problems and solutions. We hope this book is a contribution to that rekindling and analysis'.

This review attempts neither to trace the chronological evolution of the volume's successive editions, nor to inventory the entire set of readings presented in this one. Rather, we choose to evaluate the current set of selections for their relevance and comprehensiveness with respect to two trends in the theory and practice of development that seem pertinent in the present context: One, the calling into question of orthodox policy prescriptions in the practice of development;

secondly, and more fundamentally, the questioning of the validity and distinctiveness of the body of theory that has come to be known as development economics.

On the one hand, absolute declines in living standards in many parts of the developing world have called into question the once mainstream tenets of capital fundamentalism, import-substituting industrialization and strategic sectoral emphasis in the pursuit of rapid economic growth. The more spectacular economic and political breakdown of the planned economies of the former Eastern Bloc, on the other, has put doctrinaire socialism on the defensive. Both have contributed to significant disillusionment with proactive development efforts in general, and, in particular, have led to a reappraisal of widespread involvement in such affairs by that traditional instrument of development, the state.

Arguably, the disenchantment with current development approaches has more to do with pragmatic concerns than with pure ideological shifts. In development economics (as in general economics, and, indeed, most social sciences), the history of thought was shaped by the prevailing circumstances. So too, much of the recent questioning of the adequacy of development models in addressing the problems of development is rooted in immediate past experience. But there is an inescapable implication for development theorizing. A recognition of the failure of received paradigms to anticipate or respond to problems creates the imperative for (*a*) a positive analysis of this failure, and (*b*) an agenda for revised methods of addressing perceived deficiencies.

Thus far, expectedly, critiques have been more forthcoming than theoretical reconstructions. The epistemological challenge facing development economics today is to seize the offensive to participate in this needed reconstruction of development theory. In a sense, the deference to market institutions signalled by the current World Bank stance[1] might be construed as a triumph (of sorts) for neoclassical economics; however, it is one that leaves the status of development economics unresolved. Does the separateness of the development economics subdiscipline have an intellectual legitimacy, apart from a 'particularistic' rather than universal application of neoclassical economics? Do development contexts have a specialness distinct enough to require new themes and paradigms? What accommodations must neoclassical economics make, if any, in recognition of these special circumstances?

One can reasonably ask if the literature in general has responded to these questions, and, in particular, whether the selections in the present book of readings reflect any movement in such a direction. In his requiem for development economics, Albert Hirschman,[2] one of its early pioneers, states: '... our sub-discipline had achieved its considerable lustre and excitement through the implicit idea that it could slay the dragon of backwardness virtually by itself, or at least, that its contribution to this task was central. We now know that this is not so.' Hirschman cites a lack of sensitivity to indigenous institutions and aspirations on the part of development economists, accusing them of condescendingly imposing an essentially simplistic growth path.

The editors of the present volume reiterate that its readings emphasize the *political economy* rather than the narrowly *economic* approach and issues. 'Many of the readings are excellent examples of radical political economy ... radical in the sense that they are willing to question and evaluate the most basic institutions and values of society.' This is encouraging, because a large part of the justification for the need for a separate economics for developing countries is predicated on institutional differences. The near-exclusive focus of conventional economics on the institution of the market naturally raises questions about the promises (and pitfalls) of borrowing from disciplines where primacy is accorded to the study of other institutions. What are some of the new directions that are indicated by economists and non-economists in this regard?

In the section entitled Theory and Method in Economic Development, Amartya Sen's article, 'Development: Which Way Now?' marshals evidence to defend the thematic congruence of the earlier corpus of beliefs and argues against a summary debunking of traditional development theory, concluding that average experiences are not at variance with them, notwithstanding particular successes and failures. He contends that the real thematic deficiency of traditional development economics was its inadequate recognition that economic growth is no more than a means to some other objectives, and goes on to offer his characterization of economic development in terms of the expansion of broader entitlements generating ultimate human capabilities, with the further implication that entitlements may not operate only through market forces, but through a variety of social and political mechanisms.

The role of one such institution, the state, is subject to scrutiny and critique in the same section by Deepak Lal in the article 'The Misconceptions of "Development Economics" '. He assails what he labels the '*dirigiste* dogma', rooted in the justification that neoclassical economics was '... unrealistic because of its behavioural, technological, and institutional assumptions'. Echoing the approach of the 'new or neoclassical political economy', Lal asserts that even intellectually valid arguments against *laissez-faire* based on market failure were insufficient grounds for assuming the state's bureaucratic capacity to redress failures of efficient resource allocation. Imperfections in political and administrative institutions, he asserts, are endemic to the Third World, and may well surpass any market imperfections considered peculiar to these contexts. In a rejoinder to this approach, G. K. Helleiner, in his 'Conventional Foolishness and Overall Ignorance: Current Approaches to Global Transformation and Development', reciprocally challenges the general deduction that compels Lal's choice of market over state imperfections.

It would seem the question of market failure versus government failure might be amenable to empirical resolution in particular instances. As Helleiner cautions: 'The only weapon with which we can fight effectively is hard evidence that challenges the simplistic nostrums of the fundamentalists of economic, political, and other doctrines.' Whether development economics offers appropriate positive frameworks under which the issue of state versus market efficiency may be rigorously put to the test is moot. In the section entitled Industry in Development, Helen Shapiro and Lance Taylor's article 'The State and Industrial Strategy' reviews some of the formal models of interaction between state and economy directed at showing how government intervention may produce inefficiencies, from Mancur Olson's collective action framework, to Buchanan's public choice approach and its application to trade and development as presented in the literature on rent-seeking and directly unproductive profit-seeking activities, to Douglas North's property rights-based characterization of the trade-off between economic efficiency and state power in a historical context.

Shapiro and Taylor concede that the early development theorists committed a fundamental flaw in accepting the neoclassical separation of the economic and political spheres, '... since they relied upon the state as an agent of change and presumed that it had the requisite political autonomy and administrative tools to carry out the task'. However, they also fault the neomarket literature, both on grounds of the tenuousness of demonstrated empirical connections between microeconomic price reform and significantly improved aggregate economic performance, and for its proponents' positive theories of the state.[3] 'More fundamentally, the neoclassical isomorphisms between absence of distortions, efficiency and growth are ahistorical and timeless ... As they reify the market, the neoclassical political economists elude an explicit discussion of the state, despite their claim to making public action an endogenous variable ... A more sophisticated political economy is required, to *explain* and not just postulate the relationship between state and society.

What new insights do claimants to the legacy of the classical political economists have to offer? Current thinking on political economy in the Marxian tradition is represented in the readings under the rubric of the section Economic Development and Underdevelopment in Historical Perspective by 'Perspectives on Underdevelopment: Frank, the Modes of Production School, and Amin'. The authors, David F. Riccio and Lawrence H. Simon, analyse and attempt to reconcile three of the theories that have emerged as contending positions on the left. The authors comment that these radical alternatives to 'bourgeois' development theory 'see' a different reality in the currently less-developed or underdeveloped countries because neoclassical and neo-Marxian theorists have different conceptual entry points — 'Orthodox theorists tend to focus on individual decision-making ... [while] the radicals start with either the circulation of commodities, modes of production, or the relations of exchange'. The difficulty with both traditions, the authors conclude, is that each attempts 'to reduce the explanation of a complex and diffuse phenomenon — world development in the past four hundred years — to an ultimately determining factor ... One can be justifiably wary of whether any theory of this sort can provide an entirely convincing account'. Political ideology aside, this calls for a development theory not blind to historical insight and which reconciles the logic of social action with that of microbehaviour is one that neoclassicists might heed.

Interestingly, considerable scepticism about the robustness and relevance of the Marxist paradigm itself is in evidence in the aftermath of socialism's apparent demise. In his article, 'Revolution in Eastern Europe: Lessons for Democratic Social Movements (and Socialists)' in the section of the volume entitled, Development, Democracy, and Contemporary International Institutions, Andre Gunder Frank characterizes a context where the economics versus politics dichotomy disregards the former at its peril: Where nationalism and ethnicity have helped mobilize people into social movements in former Eastern Bloc countries, he says, '...(I)ndeed the most urgent political problem after "liberation" is widely presented as what to do about the state'. He notes, however, that 'the euphoria of democratic success has relegated problems of economic structure and process that are hardly transformable by political euphoria alone'. In the final analysis, Frank lays out little hope for a resurgence of socialist ideology that would be 'obliged by the hard facts of life to rethink socialism [and] take account of competition'. In 'Beyond Capitalism and Socialism in Africa', Richard Sklar speaks for many developing contexts when he observes that 'African socialists today have no useful socialist models of high economic achievement for third world countries in the late twentieth century ... In Africa, outside of South Africa, the premise of competition between capitalism and socialism has very little significance outside intellectual circles, where it does impair the ability of the theorists to contribute new ideas to the campaign for development ... this conception of ideological conflict no longer serves as a guide to policy or statecraft in African countries.

In 'Toward a Non-Ethnocentric Theory of Development: Alternative Conceptions from the Third World', Howard Wiarda, a political sociologist, dismissing the western development model as parochial and Eurocentric, calls for an assertion of indigenous Third World development models. Traditional institutions, such as patronage networks, clan groups, religious institutions and movements, extended families and the like, 'have been woefully understudied and represent some immense gaps in our knowledge concerning these societies...'; studying them, Wiarda says, '... should seem to represent the next great frontier in the social sciences'. Optimistic about prospects for new indigenous intellectual constructs, his argument is then taken to a disturbing extreme: 'Not only must we re-examine a host of essentially western social science assumptions but we must also be prepared to accept an Islamic social science of development, an African social science of development, a Latin American social science of development, and so on ...' Indeed, employing Wiarda's own distinction between a theory of development that comes from many sources and different theories of development for different regions, one may wish to sound a caveat about the epistemological pitfalls inherent in confusing the latter with the former.

Another potential roadblock to any objective discussion or purposeful action is fatuous questioning of the fundamental premise that development is desirable. The issue of development as a value-laden concept recurs in critique of conventional economic theory, and must be dealt with pragmatically in any reconstruction of the subject — legitimate as the quest for positive explanations of attitude and value formation might be for broader social science, a new development economics can ill-afford to stray far afield from the normative implications of its mandate that its central concern is economic betterment. In their article 'The Human Dilemma of Development' in part six of the collection, The Human Dimension of Development, Denis Goulet's and Charles Wilber's eminently apt rejoinder to those who would cite the social costs of development is that there are more onerous costs in remaining underdeveloped. As a useful middle ground, they propose agreeing upon standards for evaluating the acceptability of these costs relative to the benefits of the process. (One example is the possible incorporation of an explicit criterion such as environmental sustainability into economic growth prescriptions.) And while it might not always be possible to keep development value-free, a broadening of the concept may be entirely in order. Accordingly, Keith Griffin and John Knight's article, 'Human Development: The Case for Renewed Emphasis' in the book's final section, What Is to Be Done? invokes Sen's conception of development as a process of the expansion of human capabilities to support protection of education, health and nutrition objectives against the fiscal squeeze often accompanying structural adjustment imperatives.

The article, 'The New Development Economics' by Joseph Stiglitz in the Agriculture in Development section develops a basis for a continued justification of the subject's claim to a separate identity. His case rests on the rationality of individuals but the costliness of information, the argument in this instance applied to an explanation of features of rural organization — in particular, market interlinkages — frequently found in developing countries. More broadly, Stiglitz distinguishes his emphasis on imperfect information from irrationality assumptions, departures from competitiveness, or exploitation hypotheses, and lays out a set of internal and external criteria under which alternative theories may be evaluated. Interestingly, despite the affinity of his information cost/incentive approach to the transactions cost approach, he faults the latter on the ground that theories based on it fail the test of falsifiability: transactions costs are often unobservable. Nevertheless, he recognizes a more general need to explain rather than assume institutional frameworks: 'Institutions adapt to reflect these information (and other transaction) costs. Thus institutions are not to be taken as exogenous, but are endogenous, and changes in the environment may lead, with a lag, to changes in institutional structure'.

To base a reconstruction of development economics on the foundation of the information or even a transactions cost approach is admittedly too narrow and restrictive; it would surely be a pale 'new' development economics that would emerge from exclusive reliance on such a justification. A broader institutional emphasis holds significantly more promise. Yet one might do well to heed Stiglitz's insistence on methodological rigour. As he asserts, 'important instances of currently dysfunctional institutions and customs can clearly be identified ... Yet, as social scientists, our objective is to identify the systematical components, the regularities of social behaviour, to look for general principles underlying a variety of phenomena. It is useful to describe the institutions found in the rural sector of LDCs, but description is not enough.' We agree. With Shapiro and Taylor, we also reject as unfruitful more purist approaches from other narrow disciplinary frameworks that would seek to 'reduce economic development to a problem of domestic institution building ...' A multiplicity of isolated discipline-specific approaches to development would only foster splintering of the subject into an amorphous and fragmented field, and ultimately erode its policy relevance. Nevertheless, contributions from endeavours of inquiry which have specialized in the study of institutions other than the market can no longer be naively disregarded by mainstream development economists, as they have been.

There is much to be said for the attractiveness of a transdisciplinary dialogue that can evolve new mutually comprehensible frameworks by selectively synthesizing useful insights afforded by the various social sciences in a way that does not compromise adherence to scientific rigour. The strength of economics, and the comparative advantage of its analytical tool kit over its fellow social sciences in the development area has always lain in the high degree of consensus about its central paradigm. In the wake of the breakdown of the old wisdom, a new consensus will need to be forged in the field of development. Development economics has a fresh opportunity for assuming a leading role in the current rethinking about and framing of a proactive agenda for development. Within general economics, approaches such as the 'new institutional economics' (which endogenize institutional change) and public choice or the 'new political economy' (which explain political decision-making) offer promising applications to development, if sensitive to multidisciplinary perspectives. An interdisciplinary revitalization of development economics through an eclectic borrowing from other disciplines such as political science, anthropology, or social psychology while retaining its own disciplinary strengths should serve to extend the frontier of economics itself, not hegemonistically, but in ways benefiting all social science.[4] Certainly, the selections (including several not cited in this review) in a volume such as this show the scope for, if not the actualization of such an integrative synthesis.

NOTES

Reproduced from *Economic and Political Weekly*, 22 August 1992.

1 The call for more 'market-friendly' development is articulated in World Bank, *World Development Report, 1991,* OUP, New York, 1991.
2 In Albert Hirschman [1981], 'The Rise and Decline of Development Economics' in *Essays in Trespassing: Economics to Politics and Beyond,* Cambridge University Press, Cambridge.
3 This theme is echoed by Albert Fishlow [1991], 'Review of Handbook of Development Economics', *Journal of Economic Literature,* December. Fishlow argues that what development economics lacks is an adequate theory of government policy.
4 The beginning of an interdisciplinary dialogue (limited albeit to measurement issues in economic development) may be found in Pranab Bardhan (ed.) [1989], *Conversations between Economists and Anthropologists: Methodological Issues in Measuring Economic Change in Rural India,* OUP, Delhi.

19 / The Unfinished Statement

VIBHOOTI SHUKLA

I. Research and Related Activity

Briefly, my motivation for undertaking graduate study stems from an interest in development policy. It is inescapable, growing up in the development decades of the Sixties and Seventies in India, to appreciate problems of development and the imperative to develop and this has served as fountainhead and guided my incursion into my scholarly endeavour. I mention these considerations as they have, to a large extent, shaped my research agenda, as it has evolved through the years, and conditions my approach to its future directions as well.

My fields of graduate study were Urban Economics, and Development Economics and Labour Economics. Urban development, as a microcosm of economy-wide development, offered scope and comprehensiveness, in addition to having developed sufficiently powerful and rigorous tools of analysis. Dissertation research urbanization policies, given the concomitancy of urbanization with economic development processes. Attendant debates. Training in Urban Economics offered a development-relevant subject, as well as one which had sufficiently developed tools to do rigorous analysis, and I came to it at a time when their application to developing countries was relatively new, and therefore challenging.

How much urbanization explored from fundamentals of the nature of cities and reasons for their existence ... fortunate in guidance from Mills at Princeton. My dissertation work was on urban agglomeration economies ... Thesis ... 1 ... (Abstract attached), econometric exercise in a production function framework drawing upon the equilibrium city size paradigm, followed by prescriptions for industrial dispersion policies motivated both by regional development and urban size restrictions. Found evidence of such economies, and a measure of efficiency losses if dispersal policies were pursued. Defined conditions under which dispersion might be justified. At Harvard, extended these ideas to formulate optimal rural–urban migration policies, with

2 ... *Econ Letters* ... provided a further analysis of instruments for optimal dispersal. Whereas these analyses are in a partial regional framework, in 3. *Human Capital* ..., I was able, subsequently to use an agglomeration economies augmented general equilibrium formulation, to demonstrate economy-wide welfare effects of taking cognizance of urban agglomeration economies in simulations with a developing country dual-economy model in ... 4 ... *Journal of Urban Econ* ...

Through my interest in migration, came to appreciate the need for research on urban labour markets in LDCs. In a survey article ... 5 ... *Indian Journal of Agric. Economics* ... the case is made for an intensified study of urban labour markets along the lines rural markets and labour supply to urban areas have been analysed from the point of view of the demand for labour by urban firms. The work on rural–urban wage dichotomy led to a theoretical investigation on some causal mechanisms of urban labour market segmentation rooted in agglomeration economies, and their possible internalization through a seemingly "disequilibrium" institutional urban formal sector wage. Through my graduate training came to appreciate both the power and limitations of neoclassical economics, but interdisciplinary social sciences in ... What Drives ... 6

I consider my work on urban agglomeration economies to be a recognized contribution to the profession. In an article ... 7 ... Mark Montgomery ... commended my research work as pioneering of a class of studies that have looked at the empirical underpinnings of the question of city size in the context of developing countries. My work on optimal inter-regional population flows has been cited in a survey of studies on migration in 8 ... Jeff Williamson's article in the *Handbook of Development Economics*. Finally, 9 ... Oded Stark's book on the *Economics of Labour Migration* contains excerpts from our joint work, including the JUE article in its entirety. Citations in SSCI ...

I have continued to complement my scholarly interest in urban efficiency and growth with a desire to inform policy-making toward urbanization in developing countries, and India in particular. The publication of my book in India *Urban Development And Regional Policy in India: An Econometric Analysis* ... was motivated by a perceived need for the dissemination of ideas regarding the inadvisability of artificial urban growth restraints and accompanying loss of productivity, loss that a developing country can ill-afford. The book has been well-received, with reviews in scholarly journals ... *Journal of*

Regional Science and Regional Studies ... but its review in daily newspaper in India was particularly gratifying from the point of view of one trying to reach opinion and policy-making audiences in the country. (Attach) Sales of the book have been above the average for academic books, according to the Publisher, who deals both with general purpose and academic-use books.

In an article applying Tolley's model of urban growth driven by non-labour productivity change to India and its constituent states, we find systematic underurbanization in the country, below levels that might be suggested by manufacturing-agricultural productivity differentials in ...10 Tolley model....This is believed to be partly a result of a pro-rural development strategy which has arguably resulted in neglect and restraint of urban development in this country. The viability of a popular sentiment in favour of rural industrialization as an alternative to urbanization and overcrowding in large cities in India is explored through a two-part series of articles on rural non-farm employment in India 11 and 12 ... *Economic and Political Weekly* ... an influential journalistic forum, which, through its Special Articles section constitutes one of the most prestigious and effective foremost avenues of publication for research in the Social Sciences in India. The first article, 11 ... attempts to implement an exploratory model of determinants of the magnitude and composition of non-farm activity, and the second 12 ... traces the potential of policy impact on that sector to derive implications for the success of rural industrialization attempts. The overall message suggested by the research is that such attempts are costly/inefficient if pursued indiscriminately.

In the research on developed country urbanization, the treatment of agglomeration effects tended to be at the level of a city/sector/or region, but I remained interested in its spatial underpinnings at the intra-urban level. Models of city structure are premised on these economies, and their role in the changing state of urban economic theory from models that take cognizance of the evolution of contemporary city structure in monocentric to multicentric forms. This interest was actualized in a second, parallel strand of research through an opportunity offered by a $65,000 three-year grant from the Texas Advanced Research Program for the study of firm location within contemporary developed country metropolitan areas. Competition for the grant was intense (surpassing NSF rejection ratios), our proposal was ranked 14th among 440 awardees out of a total of 3280 applications. The study of business location in the context of these new evolving form was both methodologically and substantively in keeping with my developing-country interests on long-distance industrial movements. An excellent data source was provided in the Dallas–Fort Worth area, a metropolitan area particularly representative of the new urban landscape.

Both subject and context have proven rich in yielding empirical insights which, one hopes, may inform the next stage of model formulation that seems imminent in the Urban Economics field at this juncture. The first of the articles to emerge from this line of inquiry 13 ... *Journal of Regional Science and Urban Economics* ... motivated the spatial employment structure of the Dallas–Fort Worth area from the behavioural underpinnings of the firm location choices over discrete urban space. The second, 14 '... *Geographical Analysis*, forthcoming, explored the dynamics of employment decentralization through the regional economic upswing and downswing. While the latter studies focused on broad industrial groups (at the one-digit SIC level), two subsequent works focus upon important industrial subgroups: 15 ... *Employment Center* ... uses a multinomial logit model to explore the attractiveness of systematically identified employment centres within the metropolitan area to establishments in Manufacturing, while ... *Technology* ... explore spatial determinants of location of firms in a high-technology group of industries. A final work-in-progress ... *Jurisdiction* ... investigates the decision-making process is influenced by jurisdiction-specific as opposed to purely spatial or employment-nodal attributes. Taken severally, these papers each investigate particular hypotheses; together they will provide a rather comprehensive picture of various facets of decision-making and relevant domains of choice for intra-metropolitan employment in urban areas of the future.

The University of Texas at Dallas being an urban institution with responsibilities to the local community, the foregoing research has inescapable policy applications, which have been disseminated as part of the ... *State of the Region Report, 1992* ... published by the Bruton Center for Development Studies, a UTD think-tank on regional matters. More globally, I have had an opportunity to participate in the preparation of a report for the United Nations Conference for Environment and Development while visiting the Indira Gandhi Institute of Development Research in Bombay, a policy research institute set up by India's central bank. My contribution to the team report ... Consumption

Patterns ... was motivated by an attempt to trace the implications for local and global environmental degradation of third world urbanization. My involvement in this spawned two articles, 16 ... Pollution and City Size, in ... Urban Geography ... dealing with the question of whether developing country city size restrictions are justified on environmental grounds, and 17 ... Global Environmental Change ... tracing the possible greenhouse implications of the energy-use requirements of urbanization in the course of the process of development. Thus, my participation in the writing of these Technical Reports has enabled a mutual reciprocity between scholarship and policy formulation quite gratifying to my enduring interests.

These dual interests, and the inevitably close relationships inherent in policy-oriented research, and the interdisciplinary nature of my work environment have guided my choice of publication vehicles over the span of my career. My two principal criteria for the choice of journals have been quality and substantive relevance. For example, *JUE* and *JRSUE* are the top economics journals in these range from the top journals in the field. In addition, I have chosen to publish in quality journals in fields (GA and UG) other than economics where a more interdisciplinary audience might be reached. My publications in *Human Capital Journal* and the *Indian Journal of Agricultural Economics* reflect both methodological appropriateness and a good substantive 'fit' between the medium and the message. Further, I have sought publication in outlets most likely to reach practitioners of urban and regional development or urban/regional policy, in contexts where so doing has been my intent. In the short term, I have drafts of articles out to the *Journal of Regional Science, Regional Studies, Urban Studies, Southern Economic Journal,* and *Global Environmental Change*.

From the point of departure of my initial research, and within the parameters of my broad interests, my intellectual development has drawn constructively from new opportunities, institutional milieu, and from interaction with my professional colleagues. The advance of knowledge, especially is a collective activity, and collaborative ventures often tend to provide the checks and balances that ensure one's contribution remains within a mainstream and does not get lost or isolated. I am firm in my belief that research, particularly applied research, should not take place in an intellectual vacuum, and I have, accordingly, sought out and enjoyed collaboration with those with shared substantive interests wherever possible. However, these collaborative contacts have been forged at my initiative, and in a way through which the overall integrity of my research agenda was not compromised. My contribution to various co-authored articles has typically been at least one-half, and often greater, especially in cases where I have provided a collaborative project with the seed of the research idea. (See attached for a formal documentation of my estimated share and nature of my contribution to any given research effort.)

Equally, I have enjoyed and derived intellectual sustenance from interchanges with co-researchers in my fields of interest through professional conferences. I firmly believe in the utility of seminar presentations, especially of research-in-progress, and have been a frequent and enthusiastic participant at various conferences, both of disciplinary and substantive relevance. A sample of fora where I have presented competitively accepted papers include the meetings of the American Social Science Association (ASSA-AEA), the Southern Economic Association, the Regional Science Association of North America, the Population Association of America, and the TRED meetings of the Lincoln Land Policy Institute in Cambridge Massachusetts. Forthcoming conferences at which ongoing research is scheduled to be presented include the APPAM (Association of Public Policy and Management) and the South and Southeast Asian meetings of the Econometric Society (see attached). University seminars I have participated include those at Harvard University, the University of North Carolina and the University of Southern California.

Over the years, I have been able to serve the research community of my area of specialization by organizing a session, ... '... at the Western Economic Association International meetings (where I have also been invited to host a session), serving as session chair for the urban studies group at the Western Social Science Association meetings, and as session discussant for ...' ... the 1992 meetings of the Population Association of America, as well as on several other occasions. Through my research and related activities, I have carved out a professional niche for myself ... a position that is reflected in my being called upon to write book reviews in my principal chosen areas of interest. My review of an edited volume on Asian urbanization for the *Journal of Regional Science*, of a book on migration for *Regional Studies* and on firm location in a developing country metropolis also for the *Journal of Regional Science* (see footnote; attached in publications packet), fall quite closely within my field of expertise,and I have been able to bring to bear both critical and synthetic perspectives on them in a way that seeks not just to comment upon, but to influence the direction of research in these fields. In addition, I have served as referee for several development journals, including *World Development.*

Another avenue available to me for both learning from and disseminating research ideas to the practitioner community has been through the vehicle of consulting. I have been very fortunate in the consulting opportunities that have come my way in that they have all been in areas where I could fruitfully contribute by virtue of my specialized interests. For example, I have consulted for the World Bank's Population, Health and Nutri-tion Division on 18.1 ...', as background for their focus on development in Sub-Saharan Africa. Likewise, I was able to participate in a project on industrial dispersal policies in the Philippines funded by the Asian Development Bank, culminating in my report, 18.2 '... which was subsequently adopted for use as a teaching manual by officials in that country charged with the implementation of that country's industrial estates program. Finally, I had the interesting opportunity to study an important case in the process of policy formulation through my archival study of the history of Ford Foundation assistance to Indian agriculture, in 18.3...' My selection of consultancy assignments has been guided by the presence of opportunities for insights into the practice of development, relevance to my field of expertise, the prospect of a role in informing active policy-making. (Although detailed project output not attached see report summaries.)

While, in my subjective assessment, several research objectives set for this stage of my academic career have been met, I would hope in future to further consolidate these accomplishments, especially in areas where I am likely to have the maximum impact. In the medium term (2–3 years), several other research projects that I am currently involved with should culminate in further journal articles — in particular, a CGE model of rural non-farm activity and a logit model of occupational/locational choice by rural workers. As well, I expect to have several sets of related researches that may best find expression in book-length works having the advantage of association and comprehensiveness. For example, I am close to completing a manuscript on a book extending my preliminary work on ... Rural Non-farm Employment in India ... (see attached table of contents), which my Indian publisher has expressed an interest in publishing. In addition, I have substantial portions of another compilation ... Issues in Indian urbanization ... which focuses, among other things, upon the role of infrastructure in urban development completed (see attached table of contents) ... I plan to seek a US publisher once the manuscript is complete. Finally, the heretofore piecemeal work on Dallas–Fort Worth spatial economy will likely be attempted to be presented in its entirety as a monograph.

In addition, it is appropriate, at this juncture, to define the broad directions in which I expect to be headed professionally in the coming years. In the longer term (4–5 years), I hope to bring successfully to completion at least three new lines of research, which I am planning to initiate, or have already done so. One relates to my continuing interest in urban spatial structure, encompassing both the theoretical frontiers of Urban Economics, and their applied implications, particularly (but not exclusively) to the cities of developing countries. Likewise, I hope to extend my current interests in global environmental issues in what bears a natural methodological affinity to some of the externality situations of urban/regional contexts, and an almost certainly critical substantive significance for development. With two of my UTD colleagues, I am currently in the process of preparing a research proposal for submission to the National Science Foundation on behavioural aspects of country co-operation in global environmental efforts.

Both above behavioural motivation, cost-benefit terms, public goods decision-making in the presence of public goods. Market externalities, and the intertwined role of different institutions, social, political and economic. The purely economic approach to policy-making segregates the economic process from the political one; study the state as one such institution as an instrument of economic development. In the near future, in collaboration with two other colleagues, I plan to submit a research proposal for the study of the role of the state in development, using formalized Political Economy perspectives.

An agent of pluralistic interests. I see here an opportunity for a unique and enduring theoretical contribution.

In a forthcoming book review, 19. '... I argue for a formal integration of interdisciplinary perspectives within mainstream Development Economics, if the latter is to maintain a dynamism and relevance to many of the still-intractable problems of economic growth, and the perceived failure of conventional received theory to address them. Areas of coincidence of my professional trajectory with UTD's institutional objectives are highlighted in the following two sections.

II. Teaching and Related Activity

It is my firm conviction that teaching and research are, to a large extent, complementary. One of the primary set of factors influencing my decision to join the University of Texas at Dallas was the nature of teaching opportunities afforded there at each level. The closely integrated multidisciplinary environment that draws our graduate students from diverse disciplinary backgrounds, the small size of the more mature urban non-traditional student body at the undergraduate level, and the clear commitment to interdisciplinarity at the levels of both the School and the University combine to make teaching at UTD a unique and rewarding experience. My teaching involvement over the past five years, which has spanned all these levels, has proven both intellectually stimulating and personally gratifying. My teaching assignments have been divided between graduate and undergraduate courses in almost equal parts (List attached). In each instance, I have enjoyed time spent with students, both in the classroom and in the office. My rapport and effectiveness with students may be gauged by formal teaching evaluations, as well as their informal comments and letters (summaries).

My tenure at UTD has seen an expansion as well as a restructuring of the graduate programme at the Masters' and Doctoral levels. My graduate teaching has been in my broad fields of interests, viz., ... Urban, Regional and Development Analysis ... as well as in specialized areas more closely allied with my current research programmes. Through the years, my teaching at the graduate level has encompassed courses taught in various formats, ranging from standard topics courses, to special topics courses, to more advanced research workshops and proseminars. New course development opportunities through which I could bring my own perspective and interests to bear directly on our graduate curriculum have included ... Urban and Regional Policies in Developing Countries ... which enabled my designing a course around my own particular sub-speciality, a Workshop in '... Economic Development and Spatial Change ... which enabled me to operationalize several components of the research carried forth under the TARP-funded metropolitan firm location project, and which sought to expose graduate students to both conceptual and practical aspects of research design and implementation, and the ... Introduction to Computable General Equilibrium Models for Development Policy ... Workshop, which exposes students to aspects of economy-wide multi-sector model formulation, implementation and simulation.

I have sought to utilize these workshops as vehicles to acquaint our graduate students with both the substance and techniques of high-quality research in the Social Sciences. An interesting feature of the courses taught in the Workshop is the opportunity they provide to involve our graduate students earning degrees in Public Policy. Exposure to research methodologies and application would enable those who plan to terminate their graduate study with the Masters degree to analyse and digest information that comes to them in the form of technical reports, and upon the basis of which they may engage in informed decision-making. To the extent our Masters' pool often serves as a source for future Doctoral candidates in our Political Economy program, such research experiences may be important in providing motivation needed for further study. In-depth substantive area coursework and hands-on research workshops provide our doctoral students with exposure to a range of techniques valuable in subsequent dissertation research. It is hoped that by bringing to their attention analytical tools such as applied general equilibrium modelling and its programming counterpart, quantitative techniques such as log linear and logit models, and latent variables methods, as has been my objective, our students may be facilitated in writing cutting-edge interdisciplinary dissertations comparable with those generated by the top-rung disciplinary graduate programmes in the country.

Some time ago, our Ph.D. programme was restructured to better reflect our collective comparative advantage as a faculty through the identification of certain areas of concentration and the flexible 'bundling' of multidisciplinary graduate courses around these substantive fields. I was heavily involved in helping design the slate of requirements and options for students wishing to study and do dissertation research within the 'Development' concentration, an area that has traditionally generated substantial interest on the part of our graduate student body, and one in which I believe we have the potential for cultivating national recognition. As part of an effort to strengthen this area and give it definition, I developed a 'Foundations' course for this concentration, which sought to synthesize disciplinary perspectives on and distil commonalities in development processes and experiences at local, regional and national levels; next semester, I hope to teach a state-of-the-subject literature review 'proseminar' in the field. As an outgrowth of the nature of my involvement in graduate teaching, I have been privileged to serve on numerous dissertation committees (see attached list), and provided opportunities for directly shaping their research (e.g. attachments). It is truly a pleasure for me to work with these students; often, my involvement with their research has transcended scholarly guidance to include collaborative work or sponsorship of student research presentations in academic conferences. Invariably, my investment of time in dissertation-level graduate students has been repaid manifold by the satisfaction of seeing them develop into mature and independent researchers with growing self-confidence in their putative areas of expertise.

At the undergraduate level, my primary involvement has been with teaching in the Economics and Finance major within the School of Social Sciences. The courses I have taught range from staple 'core' courses such as Microeconomic Theory and Mathematical Economics to topics-oriented courses such as Urban and Development Economics. The former stress techniques and rigor that is part and parcel of any economist's toolkit; the latter aim to generate substantive interest through an application of the same. I have tried to introduce innovations with these courses from time to time, through structuring them to include active student participation, formal presentations, as well as writing and research components. As I have endeavoured to nurture research skills in my Research Assistants, so also, I have tried to inculcate teaching skills in my Teaching Assistants by involving them in various aspects of course preparation, class management and grading to our mutual advantage. Last spring, I team-taught a course with one of our graduate students, engaging her in a sort of apprenticeship situation prior to her taking full responsibility for that course. I am also one of the few instructors involved in implementing teaching curricula for the initial cohorts of freshmen and sophomores admitted under the recent transition of UTD to a four-year undergraduate institution. Finally, I have contributed enthusiastically to our menu of undergraduate Interdisciplinary Studies requirements by developing a course ... The City: Form, Function and Design ..., which attempts to use audio-visual presentation techniques to integrate economic, social, political and architectural perspectives on the modern urban area, with the Dallas–Fort Worth Metroplex as a context for the study of cases.

My proposed teaching plans for the future would include, at the graduate level, an attempt at formal synthesis of economic and political perspectives on policy formulation to secure a stronger pedagogical foundation for the study of Political Economy. As mentioned in connection with my future research, the subject's theoretical underpinnings are an area of considerable interest to me. Our graduate programme is a natural 'consumer' of relevant new paradigms; I am convinced we have the potential, given our faculty, students, and their interests, to pioneer the 'production' of a truly interdisciplinary corpus of theory. As an Economist within the School, I feel I can usefully bring to this multidisciplinary endeavour and transmit to our students the particular strengths and rigor of my disciplinary training. Our undergraduate programs can stand to gain, likewise, from such an interdisciplinary orientation. To this end, I plan to develop and teach an undergraduate course on Political Economy within our Economics major, often a fertile recruiting ground for good graduate students. Within the major itself, emphasis must be on the continual upgrading of academic standards for disciplinary coursework as well. The introduction of the four-year undergraduate curriculum at UTD, with its enhanced admissions standards affords us a unique opportunity to move, over time, towards the goal of bringing the quality of training our Economics and Finance graduates receive on a par with that of their Ivy League counterparts. My specific contribution to this effort might take the form of upgrading the content and rigor of the intermediate Microeconomics course and extending the reach of Mathematical Economics to students working towards either the B.A. or the B.S. degree, rather than exclusively the latter. Finally, I propose to develop another interdisciplinary undergraduate course, 'The Political Economy of Globalization' to help fulfil the University's responsibility of preparing our student body at large for the educational imperatives of the growing internationalization of economic activity and political life.

III. Service to the Institution

I look upon service to the institution both as an instrument for enabling a better working environment for myself and my colleagues, and as an opportunity to develop the necessary management skills for effective academic administration. My formal committee assignments have, fortunately, closely paralleled and complemented my research and teaching interests. Within the School of Social Sciences, I have served on the Theory Exam Committee ( ), Ad Hoc Curriculum Committee for the Development Concentration ( ), and the Committee for Graduate Studies. More or less in line with my substantive interests, as previously mentioned, I have served on several Dissertation Committees and an Options Exam Committee. This year, I serve on the newly formed Working Papers Committee charged with establishing procedures for dissemination to institutions with programs similar to ours of the research output of our students and faculty. My service on University-wide committees has included a two-year stint on the Commencement Committee, a period during which a change of venue for the exercises to the Plano Convention Centre was discussed, voted on and successfully implemented. This forthcoming academic year, I have been invited to serve on the Committee on Undergraduate Requirements. Last year, I was elected to the Academic Senate by the Social Sciences faculty as one of their representatives, and I look forward to participating in the democratic processes of academic governance at UTD with the interest and involvement of one who desires a long-term stake in the institution.

My informal institutional contributions have, likewise, been of a piece with my substantive research and teaching interests. In —, I participated in the Dallas 2000 Conference organized by the School of Social Sciences as part of an urban campus's mandate to forge better understanding between various groups in the Dallas economy. Along with a group of colleagues in the School of Social Sciences, I was involved in the formulation of the initial set of ideas that culminated in the establishment of the Bruton Center of Development Studies through a three-year seed grant from a local foundation, with the purpose of studying the Dallas–Fort Worth region as an urban development laboratory. The securing of the TARP grant to study business location in the Metroplex has since contributed to its activity base, both through student and software support. I follow with interest the use and extension of the Geographical Information System (GIS) maintained by the Center as having potential applicability to comparative urban developing country research. Over the longer term, I anticipate my research on the socio-political aspects of global environmental decision-making as relevant to and benefiting from the envisaged scholarly activities of the Green Center for Science and Society. Finally, I anticipate forging a future relationship between the School of Social Sciences and an institution sharing its Development emphasis, such as IGIDR in India that could systematize a mutual exchange of students and faculty visitors. As a tenured member of the faculty, I would generally expect both my formal as well as institutional involvement to both increase and diversify. As Social Scientists, we have more than a practical interest in effective institution-building; our very paradigms impress upon us the importance of academic institutions as essential vehicles for carrying forward societal education goals, and indeed, in the transmission of human culture.

APPENDIX

In this appendix to the 'Unfinished Statement', details are provided for the blanks kept by Dr Vibhooti Shukla in her draft.

1 'The Productivity of Indian Cities and Some Implications for Development Policy' (Ph.D. Diss., Princeton University, Department of Economics, 1984), published as *Urban Development and Regional Policy in India: An Econometric Analysis*, Himalaya Publishing House, Bombay, 1988.
2 On Agglomeration Economies and Optimal Migration, Economic Letters, Greenwich, 1985.
3 'Urban External Economics and Optimal Migration', in Oded Stark (ed.) *Research in Human Capital and Development*, Vol. 4, Migration, Human Capital and Development, CT: JAI Press, Greenwich, 1986.
4 Policy Comparisons with an Agglomeration Effects-Augmented Dual Economy Model, *Journal of Urban Economics* 27, 1–15 (1990).
5 'Rural Migration to an Indian Metropolis: Examining the Micro Foundations of the Harris–Todaro Paradigm' (A Review and Further Research Agenda), *Indian Journal of Agricultural Economics*, Vol 43, No 4, Oct.–Dec. 1988.
6 Why Are Urban Formal Sector Wages in LDCs Above The Market-Clearing Level? Discussion Paper Number 44, June 1989 prepared by Vibhooti Shukla and Oded Stark at Migration and Development Program, Harvard University in 1989. (Article based on this research included in this volume entitled 'High Wages and Unemployment in the Urban Labour Markets of LDCs'.)
7 Mark R. Montgomery, 'How Large Is Too Large? Implications of the City Size Literature for Population Policy and Research', *Economic Development and Cultural Change*, 1988.
8 Jeffrey Williamson, 'Migration and Urbanization', Chapter II, *Handbook of Development Economics*, Vol. I, ed. H. Chenerey and T. N. Srinivasan, 1988.
9 Oded Stark, *The Migration of Labor*, Blackwell Publishers, 1991.
10 'The Pace of Indian Urbanization', *Geographical Analysis*, Vol. 23, No. 3 (July 1991), Ohio State University Press.
11 'Rural Non-Farm Activity — A Regional Model and Its Empirical Application in Maharashtra', *Economic and Political Weekly*, Vol. XXVI, No. 45, 9 Novemebr 1991, pp. 2587-2595.

12 Rural Non-Farm Employment in India: Issues and Policy, *Economic and Political Weekly*, Vol. XXVII, No. 28, 11 July 1992.
13 Firm Location and Land Use in Discrete Urban Space: A Study of the Spatial Structure of Dallas–Fort Worth, *Journal of Regional Science and Urban Economics* 21 (1991), pp. 225–53, Elsevier Science Publishers B.V. (North Holland).
14 'Employment Dynamics in a Multinodal Urban Area: Spatial Restructuring and the Business Cycle', *Geographical Analysis* (1993).
15 'Manufacturing Location in a Policentric Urban Area: A Study in the Composition and Attractiveness of Employment Sub-Centers', *Urban Geography*, March 1992.
16 'The Environmental Consequences of Urban Growth: Cross-National Perspectives on Economic Development, Air Pollution and City Size', *Urban Geography*, February 1992.
17 Urbanization, Energy Use and Greenhouse Effects in Economic Development: Results from a Cross-national Study of Developing Countries. Abridged Version accepted for publication in 'Global Environmental Change', The Butterworth Publishers, UK, March 1992.
18 *Consultation Reports*
  18.1 *Optimal Population Distribution for Economic Development in Sub-Saharan Africa*, Health and Nutrition Division, World Bank.
  18.2 A Theoretical Framework for the Analysis of Urban Growth and Formulation of Regional Policy—prepared for the NIEP/ADB Consultant Team Assisting NEDA in the *Analysis of Industrial Dispersal Policies in the Philippines*.
  18.3 The Ford Foundation and Rural Development in India 1950–70; A Study in the Effectiveness of Institutional Assistance in Developing Agriculture, Economic Policy Division, World Bank.
19 Rethinking Development, *Economic and Political Weekly*, 22 August 1992.

Editors' Note: This is the incomplete text of what was to be a summary of Vibhooti's past, present and planned work, as supporting documentation for her tenure requirements at the University of Texas at Dallas. Vibhooti was working on this statement on the afternoon of 8th August 1992. Hours later she was no more.

No attempt has been made to edit this draft, which is actually no more than the framework of a first draft. It has been included because, despite these limitations, it does position Vibhooti Shukla in the totality of her discipline and indicates her view of the current state of the art and the directions in which she planned to proceed and which others in her field might consider for pursuit. A researcher's work is never complete, however long a lifetime allowed her, but it is to be hoped that in the hands of those now active in the field some of Vibhooti's projects and plans will reach fulfilment.

Index